The TeXbook

The T_EXbook

DONALD E. KNUTH *Stanford University*

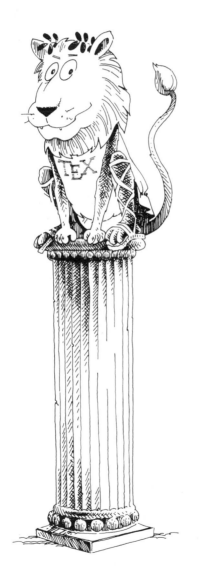

Illustrations by
DUANE BIBBY

**ADDISON–WESLEY
PUBLISHING COMPANY**

Reading, Massachusetts
Menlo Park, California
New York
Don Mills, Ontario
Wokingham, England
Amsterdam · Bonn
Sydney · Singapore · Tokyo
Madrid · San Juan

This manual describes TeX Version 3.0. Some of the advanced features mentioned here are absent from earlier versions.

The quotation on page 61 is copyright © 1970 by Sesame Street, Inc., and used by permission of the Children's Television Workshop.

TeX is a trademark of the American Mathematical Society.

METAFONT is a trademark of Addison–Wesley Publishing Company.

Library of Congress cataloging in publication data

Knuth, Donald Ervin, 1938-
    The TeXbook.

    (Computers & Typesetting ; A)
    Includes index.
    1. TeX (Computer system). 2. Computerized
typesetting. 3. Mathematics printing. I. Title.
II. Series: Knuth, Donald Ervin, 1938-   .
Computers & typesetting ; A.
Z253.4.T47K58 1986   686.2'2544   85-30845
ISBN 0-201-13447-0
ISBN 0-201-13448-9 (soft)

Nineteenth printing, revised, October 1990

ISBN 0-201-13448-9
2021222324-DO-9594939291

To Jill:
For your books and brochures

Preface

G ENTLE READER: This is a handbook about TeX, a new typesetting system intended for the creation of beautiful books—and especially for books that contain a lot of mathematics. By preparing a manuscript in TeX format, you will be telling a computer exactly how the manuscript is to be transformed into pages whose typographic quality is comparable to that of the world's finest printers; yet you won't need to do much more work than would be involved if you were simply typing the manuscript on an ordinary typewriter. In fact, your total work will probably be significantly less, if you consider the time it ordinarily takes to revise a typewritten manuscript, since computer text files are so easy to change and to reprocess. (If such claims sound too good to be true, keep in mind that they were made by TeX's designer, on a day when TeX happened to be working, so the statements may be biased; but read on anyway.)

This manual is intended for people who have never used TeX before, as well as for experienced TeX hackers. In other words, it's supposed to be a panacea that satisfies everybody, at the risk of satisfying nobody. Everything you need to know about TeX is explained here somewhere, and so are a lot of things that most users don't care about. If you are preparing a simple manuscript, you won't need to learn much about TeX at all; on the other hand, some things that go into the printing of technical books are inherently difficult, and if you wish to achieve more complex effects you will want to penetrate some of TeX's darker corners. In order to make it possible for many types of users to read this manual effectively, a special sign is used to designate material that is for wizards only: When the symbol

appears at the beginning of a paragraph, it warns of a "dangerous bend" in the train of thought; don't read the paragraph unless you need to. Brave and experienced drivers at the controls of TeX will gradually enter more and more of these hazardous areas, but for most applications the details won't matter.

All that you really ought to know, before reading on, is how to get a file of text into your computer using a standard editing program. This manual explains what that file ought to look like so that TeX will understand it, but basic computer usage is not explained here. Some previous experience with technical typing will be quite helpful if you plan to do heavily mathematical work with TeX, although it is not absolutely necessary. TeX will do most of the necessary formatting of equations automatically; but users with more experience will be able to obtain better results, since there are so many ways to deal with formulas.

Some of the paragraphs in this manual are so esoteric that they are rated

$$\text{\small⚠⚠} \; ;$$

everything that was said about single dangerous-bend signs goes double for these. You should probably have at least a month's experience with TEX before you attempt to fathom such doubly dangerous depths of the system; in fact, most people will never need to know TEX in this much detail, even if they use it every day. After all, it's possible to drive a car without knowing how the engine works. Yet the whole story is here in case you're curious. (About TEX, not cars.)

The reason for such different levels of complexity is that people change as they grow accustomed to any powerful tool. When you first try to use TEX, you'll find that some parts of it are very easy, while other things will take some getting used to. A day or so later, after you have successfully typeset a few pages, you'll be a different person; the concepts that used to bother you will now seem natural, and you'll be able to picture the final result in your mind before it comes out of the machine. But you'll probably run into challenges of a different kind. After another week your perspective will change again, and you'll grow in yet another way; and so on. As years go by, you might become involved with many different kinds of typesetting; and you'll find that your usage of TEX will keep changing as your experience builds. That's the way it is with any powerful tool: There's always more to learn, and there are always better ways to do what you've done before. At every stage in the development you'll want a slightly different sort of manual. You may even want to write one yourself. By paying attention to the dangerous bend signs in this book you'll be better able to focus on the level that interests you at a particular time.

Computer system manuals usually make dull reading, but take heart: This one contains JOKES every once in a while, so you might actually enjoy reading it. (However, most of the jokes can only be appreciated properly if you understand a technical point that is being made—so read *carefully*.)

Another noteworthy characteristic of this manual is that it doesn't always tell the truth. When certain concepts of TEX are introduced informally, general rules will be stated; afterwards you will find that the rules aren't strictly true. In general, the later chapters contain more reliable information than the earlier ones do. The author feels that this technique of deliberate lying will actually make it easier for you to learn the ideas. Once you understand a simple but false rule, it will not be hard to supplement that rule with its exceptions.

In order to help you internalize what you're reading, EXERCISES are sprinkled through this manual. It is generally intended that every reader should try every exercise, except for questions that appear in the "dangerous bend" areas. If you can't solve a problem, you can always look up the answer. But please, try first to solve it by yourself; then you'll learn more and you'll learn faster. Furthermore, if you think you do know the solution, you should turn to Appendix A and check it out, just to make sure.

The TEX language described in this book is similar to the author's first attempt at a document formatting language, but the new system differs from the old one in literally thousands of details. Both languages have been called TEX; but henceforth the old language should be called TEX78, and its use should rapidly fade away. Let's keep the name TEX for the language described here, since it is so much better, and since it is not going to change any more.

I wish to thank the hundreds of people who have helped me to formulate this "definitive edition" of the TEX language, based on their experiences with preliminary versions of the system. My work at Stanford has been generously supported by the National Science Foundation, the Office of Naval Research, the IBM Corporation, and the System Development Foundation. I also wish to thank the American Mathematical Society for its encouragement, for establishing the TEX Users Group, and for publishing the *TUGboat* newsletter (see Appendix J).

Stanford, California   — D. E. K.
June 1983

> *'Tis pleasant, sure, to see one's name in print;*
> *A book's a book, although there's nothing in 't.*
> — BYRON, *English Bards and Scotch Reviewers* (1809)

> *A question arose as to whether we were covering the field*
> *that it was intended we should fill with this manual.*
> — RICHARD R. DONNELLEY, *Proceedings, United Typothetæ of America* (1897)

Contents

1   The Name of the Game   1

2   Book Printing versus Ordinary Typing   3

3   Controlling TEX   7

4   Fonts of Type   13

5   Grouping   19

6   Running TEX   23

7   How TEX Reads What You Type   37

8   The Characters You Type   43

9   TEX's Roman Fonts   51

10   Dimensions   57

11   Boxes   63

12   Glue   69

13   Modes   85

14   How TEX Breaks Paragraphs into Lines . . .   91

15   How TEX Makes Lines into Pages   109

16   Typing Math Formulas   127

17   More about Math   139

18   Fine Points of Mathematics Typing . . .   161

19   Displayed Equations   185

20   Definitions (also called Macros)   199

21   Making Boxes   221

22   Alignment   231

23   Output Routines   251

24   Summary of Vertical Mode   267

25   Summary of Horizontal Mode   285

26   Summary of Math Mode   289

27   Recovery from Errors   295

Appendices

A   Answers to All the Exercises   305

B   Basic Control Sequences   339

C   Character Codes   367

D   Dirty Tricks   373

E   Example Formats   403

F   Font Tables   427

G   Generating Boxes from Formulas   441

H   Hyphenation   449

I   Index   457

J   Joining the TEX Community   483

1

The Name of
the Game

English words like 'technology' stem from a Greek root beginning with the letters $\tau\epsilon\chi\ldots$; and this same Greek word means *art* as well as technology. Hence the name TₑX, which is an uppercase form of $\tau\epsilon\chi$.

Insiders pronounce the χ of TₑX as a Greek chi, not as an 'x', so that TₑX rhymes with the word blecchhh. It's the 'ch' sound in Scottish words like *loch* or German words like *ach*; it's a Spanish 'j' and a Russian 'kh'. When you say it correctly to your computer, the terminal may become slightly moist.

The purpose of this pronunciation exercise is to remind you that TₑX is primarily concerned with high-quality technical manuscripts: Its emphasis is on art and technology, as in the underlying Greek word. If you merely want to produce a passably good document—something acceptable and basically readable but not really beautiful—a simpler system will usually suffice. With TₑX the goal is to produce the *finest* quality; this requires more attention to detail, but you will not find it much harder to go the extra distance, and you'll be able to take special pride in the finished product.

On the other hand, it's important to notice another thing about TₑX's name: The 'E' is out of kilter. This displaced 'E' is a reminder that TₑX is about typesetting, and it distinguishes TₑX from other system names. In fact, TEX (pronounced *tecks*) is the admirable *Text EXecutive* processor developed by Honeywell Information Systems. Since these two system names are pronounced quite differently, they should also be spelled differently. The correct way to refer to TₑX in a computer file, or when using some other medium that doesn't allow lowering of the 'E', is to type '`TeX`'. Then there will be no confusion with similar names, and people will be primed to pronounce everything properly.

▶ **EXERCISE 1.1**
After you have mastered the material in this book, what will you be: A TₑXpert, or a TₑXnician?

*They do certainly give
very strange and new-fangled names to diseases.*
— PLATO, *The Republic*, Book 3 (c. 375 B.C.)

*Technique! The very word is like the shriek
Of outraged Art. It is the idiot name
Given to effort by those who are too weak,
Too weary, or too dull to play the game.*
— LEONARD BACON, *Sophia Trenton* (1920)

2
Book Printing versus Ordinary Typing

When you first started using a computer terminal, you probably had to adjust to the difference between the digit '1' and the lowercase letter 'l'. When you take the next step to the level of typography that is common in book publishing, a few more adjustments of the same kind need to be made; your eyes and your fingers need to learn to make a few more distinctions.

In the first place, there are two kinds of quotation marks in books, but only one kind on the typewriter. Even your computer terminal, which has more characters than an ordinary typewriter, probably has only a non-oriented double-quote mark ("), because the standard ASCII code for computers was not invented with book publishing in mind. However, your terminal probably does have two flavors of single-quote marks, namely ' and '; the second of these is useful also as an apostrophe. American keyboards usually contain a left-quote character that shows up as something like `, and an apostrophe or right-quote that looks like ' or ´.

To produce double-quote marks with TeX, you simply type two single-quote marks of the appropriate kind. For example, to get the phrase

"I understand."

(including the quotation marks) you should type

`''I understand.''`

to your computer.

A typewriter-like style of type will be used throughout this manual to indicate TeX constructions that you might type on your terminal, so that the symbols actually typed are readily distinguishable from the output TeX would produce and from the comments in the manual itself. Here are the symbols to be used in the examples:

```
ABCDEFGHIJKLMNOPQRSTUVWXYZ
abcdefghijklmnopqrstuvwxyz
0123456789"#$%&@*+-=,.:;?!
()<>[]{}''\|/_^~
```

If your computer terminal doesn't happen to have all of these, don't despair; TeX can make do with the ones you have. An additional symbol

␣

is used to stand for a *blank space*, in case it is important to emphasize that a blank space is being typed; thus, what you *really* type in the example above is

`''I␣understand.''`

Without such a symbol you would have difficulty seeing the invisible parts of certain constructions. But we won't be using '␣' very often, because spaces are usually visible enough.

Book printing differs significantly from ordinary typing with respect to dashes, hyphens, and minus signs. In good math books, these symbols are all different; in fact there usually are at least four different symbols:

> a hyphen (-);
> an en-dash (–);
> an em-dash (—);
> a minus sign (−).

Hyphens are used for compound words like 'daughter-in-law' and 'X-rated'. En-dashes are used for number ranges like 'pages 13–34', and also in contexts like 'exercise 1.2.6–52'. Em-dashes are used for punctuation in sentences—they are what we often call simply dashes. And minus signs are used in formulas. A conscientious user of TEX will be careful to distinguish these four usages, and here is how to do it:

> for a hyphen, type a hyphen (-);
> for an en-dash, type two hyphens (--);
> for an em-dash, type three hyphens (---);
> for a minus sign, type a hyphen in mathematics mode ($-$).

(Mathematics mode occurs between dollar signs; it is discussed later, so you needn't worry about it now.)

▶ **EXERCISE 2.1**
Explain how to type the following sentence to TEX: Alice said, "I always use an en-dash instead of a hyphen when specifying page numbers like '480–491' in a bibliography."

▶ **EXERCISE 2.2**
What do you think happens when you type four hyphens in a row?

If you look closely at most well-printed books, you will find that certain combinations of letters are treated as a unit. For example, this is true of the 'f' and the 'i' of 'find'. Such combinations are called *ligatures*, and professional typesetters have traditionally been trained to watch for letter combinations such as `ff`, `fi`, `fl`, `ffi`, and `ffl`. (The reason is that words like 'find' don't look very good in most styles of type unless a ligature is substituted for the letters that clash. It's somewhat surprising how often the traditional ligatures appear in English; other combinations are important in other languages.)

▶ **EXERCISE 2.3**
Think of an English word that contains two ligatures.

The good news is that you do *not* have to concern yourself with ligatures: TEX is perfectly capable of handling such things by itself, using the same mechanism that converts '--' into '–'. In fact, TEX will also look for combinations of adjacent letters (like 'A' next to 'V') that ought to be moved closer together for better appearance; this is called *kerning*.

To summarize this chapter: When using TEX for straight copy, you type the copy as on an ordinary typewriter, except that you need to be careful about quotation marks, the number 1, and various kinds of hyphens/dashes. TEX will automatically take care of other niceties like ligatures and kerning.

(Are you sure you should be reading this paragraph? The "dangerous bend" sign here is meant to warn you about material that ought to be skipped on first reading. And maybe also on second reading. The reader-beware paragraphs sometimes refer to concepts that aren't explained until later chapters.)

If your keyboard does not contain a left-quote symbol, you can type `\lq`, followed by a space if the next character is a letter, or followed by a `\` if the next character is a space. Similarly, `\rq` yields a right-quote character. Is that clear?

`\lq\lq␣I␣understand.\rq\rq\␣`

In case you need to type quotes within quotes, for example a single quote followed by a double quote, you can't simply type `'''` because TEX will interpret this as "' (namely, double quote followed by single quote). If you have already read Chapter 5, you might expect that the solution will be to use grouping—namely, to type something like `{'}''`. But it turns out that this doesn't produce the desired result, because there is usually less space following a single right quote than there is following a double right quote: What you get is "', which is indeed a single quote followed by a double quote (if you look at it closely enough), but it looks almost like three equally spaced single quotes. On the other hand, you certainly won't want to type `'␣''`, because that space is much too large—it's just as large as the space between words—and TEX might even start a new line at such a space when making up a paragraph! The solution is to type `'\thinspace''`, which produces '" as desired.

▶ **EXERCISE 2.4**
OK, now you know how to produce "' and '"; how do you get "' and '"?

▶ **EXERCISE 2.5**
Why do you think the author introduced the control sequence `\thinspace` to solve the adjacent-quotes problem, instead of recommending the trickier construction `'$\,$''` (which also works)?

> *In modern Wit all printed Trash, is*
> *Set off with num'rous Breaks——and Dashes—*
> — JONATHAN SWIFT, *On Poetry: A Rapsody* (1733)

> *Some compositors still object to work*
> *in offices where type-composing machines are introduced.*
> — WILLIAM STANLEY JEVONS, *Political Economy* (1878)

3

Controlling TEX

Your keyboard has very few keys compared to the large number of symbols that you may want to specify. In order to make a limited keyboard sufficiently versatile, one of the characters that you can type is reserved for special use, and it is called the *escape character*. Whenever you want to type something that controls the format of your manuscript, or something that doesn't use the keyboard in the ordinary way, you should type the escape character followed by an indication of what you want to do.

Note: Some computer terminals have a key marked 'ESC', but that is *not* your escape character! It is a key that sends a special message to the operating system, so don't confuse it with what this manual calls "escape."

TEX allows any character to be used for escapes, but the "backslash" character '\' is usually adopted for this purpose, since backslashes are reasonably convenient to type and they are rarely needed in ordinary text. Things work out best when different TEX users do things consistently, so we shall escape via backslashes in all the examples of this manual.

Immediately after typing '\' (i.e., immediately after an escape character) you type a coded command telling TEX what you have in mind. Such commands are called *control sequences*. For example, you might type

    \input MS

which (as we will see later) causes TEX to begin reading a file called 'MS.tex'; the string of characters '\input' is a control sequence. Here's another example:

    George P\'olya and Gabor Szeg\"o.

TEX converts this to 'George Pólya and Gabor Szegö.' There are two control sequences, \' and \", here; these control sequences have been used to place accents over some of the letters.

Control sequences come in two flavors. The first kind, like \input, is called a *control word*; it consists of an escape character followed by one or more *letters*, followed by a space or by something besides a letter. (TEX has to know where the control sequence ends, so you must put a space after a control word if the next character is a letter. For example, if you type '\inputMS', TEX will naturally interpret this as a control word with seven letters.) In case you're wondering what a "letter" is, the answer is that TEX normally regards the 52 symbols A...Z and a...z as letters. The digits 0...9 are *not* considered to be letters, so they don't appear in control sequences of the first kind.

A control sequence of the other kind, like \', is called a *control symbol*; it consists of the escape character followed by a single *nonletter*. In this case you don't need a space to separate the control sequence from a letter that follows, since control sequences of the second kind always have exactly one symbol after the escape character.

▶**EXERCISE 3.1**
What are the control sequences in '\I'm \exercise3.1\\!'?

▶**EXERCISE 3.2**
We've seen that the input `P\'olya` yields 'Pólya'. Can you guess how the French words 'mathématique' and 'centimètre' should be specified?

When a space comes after a control word (an all-letter control sequence), it is ignored by TₑX; i.e., it is not considered to be a "real" space belonging to the manuscript that is being typeset. But when a space comes after a control symbol, it's truly a space.

Now the question arises, what do you do if you actually *want* a space to appear after a control word? We will see later that TₑX treats two or more consecutive spaces as a single space, so the answer is *not* going to be "type two spaces." The correct answer is to type "control space," namely

    `\␣`

(the escape character followed by a blank space); TₑX will treat this as a space that is not to be ignored. Notice that control-space is a control sequence of the second kind, i.e., a control symbol, since there is a single nonletter (␣) following the escape character. Two consecutive spaces are considered to be equivalent to a single space, so further spaces immediately following `\␣` will be ignored. But if you want to enter, say, three consecutive spaces into a manuscript you can type '`\␣\␣\␣`'. Incidentally, typists are often taught to put two spaces at the ends of sentences; but we will see later that TₑX has its own way to produce extra space in such cases. Thus you needn't be consistent in the number of spaces you type.

Nonprinting control characters like ⟨return⟩ might follow an escape character, and these lead to distinct control sequences according to the rules. TₑX is initially set up to treat `\⟨return⟩` and `\⟨tab⟩` the same as `\␣` (control space); these special control sequences should probably not be redefined, because you can't see the difference between them when you look at them in a file.

It is usually unnecessary for you to use "control space," since control sequences aren't often needed at the ends of words. But here's an example that might shed some light on the matter: This manual itself has been typeset by TₑX, and one of the things that occurs fairly often is the tricky logo 'TₑX', which requires backspacing and lowering the E. There's a special control word

    `\TeX`

that produces the half-dozen or so instructions necessary to typeset 'TₑX'. When a phrase like 'TₑX ignores spaces after control words.' is desired, the manuscript renders it as follows:

    `\TeX\ ignores spaces after control words.`

Notice the extra `\` following `\TeX`; this produces the control space that is necessary because TₑX ignores spaces after control words. Without this extra `\`, the result would have been

    TₑXignores spaces after control words.

On the other hand, you can't simply put \ after \TeX in all contexts. For
example, consider the phrase

    `the logo '\TeX'.`

In this case an extra backslash doesn't work at all; in fact, you get a curious
result if you type

    `the logo '\TeX\'.`

Can you guess what happens? Answer: The \' is a control sequence denoting
an acute accent, as in our P\'olya example above; the effect is therefore to put
an accent over the next nonblank character, which happens to be a period. In
other words, you get an accented period, and the result is

    the logo 'TEX́

Computers are good at following instructions, but not at reading your mind.

TEX understands about 900 control sequences as part of its built-in
vocabulary, and all of them are explained in this manual somewhere. But you
needn't worry about learning so many different things, because you won't really
be needing very many of them unless you are faced with unusually complicated
copy. Furthermore, the ones you do need to learn actually fall into relatively
few categories, so they can be assimilated without great difficulty. For example,
many of the control sequences are simply the names of special characters used
in math formulas; you type '\pi' to get 'π', '\Pi' to get 'Π', '\aleph' to get '$\aleph$',
'\infty' to get '∞', '\le' to get '$\le$', '\ge' to get '$\ge$', '\ne' to get '$\ne$', '\oplus' to
get '$\oplus$', '\otimes' to get '$\otimes$'. Appendix F contains several tables of such symbols.

> There's no built-in relationship between uppercase and lowercase letters in
> control sequence names. For example, '\pi' and '\Pi' and '\PI' and '\pI' are
four different control words.

The 900 or so control sequences that were just mentioned actually aren't
the whole story, because it's easy to define more. For example, if you want to
substitute your own favorite names for math symbols, so that you can remember
them better, you're free to go right ahead and do it; Chapter 20 explains how.

About 300 of TEX's control sequences are called *primitive*; these are the
low-level atomic operations that are not decomposable into simpler functions.
All other control sequences are defined, ultimately, in terms of the primitive
ones. For example, \input is a primitive operation, but \' and \" are not; the
latter are defined in terms of an \accent primitive.

People hardly ever use TEX's primitive control sequences in their manuscripts, because the primitives are ... well ... so *primitive*. You have to type
a lot of instructions when you are trying to make TEX do low-level things; this
takes time and invites mistakes. It is generally better to make use of higher-level
control sequences that state what functions are desired, instead of typing out
the way to achieve each function each time. The higher-level control sequences

need to be defined only once in terms of primitives. For example, `\TeX` is a control sequence that means "typeset the TEX logo"; `\'` is a control sequence that means "put an acute accent over the next character"; and both of these control sequences might require different combinations of primitives when the style of type changes. If TEX's logo were to change, the author would simply have to change one definition, and the changes would appear automatically wherever they were needed. By contrast, an enormous amount of work would be necessary to change the logo if it were specified as a sequence of primitives each time.

At a still higher level, there are control sequences that govern the overall format of a document. For example, in the present book the author typed '`\exercise`' just before stating each exercise; this `\exercise` command was programmed to make TEX do all of the following things:

- compute the exercise number (e.g., '3.2' for the second exercise in Chapter 3);
- typeset ' ▸ **EXERCISE 3.2**' with the appropriate typefaces, on a line by itself, and with the triangle sticking out in the left margin;
- leave a little extra space just before that line, or begin a new page at that line if appropriate;
- prohibit beginning a new page just after that line;
- suppress indentation on the following line.

It is obviously advantageous to avoid typing all of these individual instructions each time. And since the manual is entirely described in terms of high-level control sequences, it could be printed in a radically different format simply by changing a dozen or so definitions.

How can a person distinguish a TEX primitive from a control sequence that has been defined at a higher level? There are two ways: (1) The index to this manual lists all of the control sequences that are discussed, and each primitive is marked with an asterisk. (2) You can display the meaning of a control sequence while running TEX. If you type '`\show\cs`' where `\cs` is any control sequence, TEX will respond with its current meaning. For example, '`\show\input`' results in '`> \input=\input.`', because `\input` is primitive. On the other hand, '`\show\thinspace`' yields

```
> \thinspace=macro:
->\kern .16667em .
```

This means that `\thinspace` has been defined as an abbreviation for '`\kern .16667em `'. By typing '`\show\kern`' you can verify that `\kern` is primitive. The results of `\show` appear on your terminal and in the log file that you get after running TEX.

▸ **EXERCISE 3.3**
Which of the control sequences `\␣` and `\⟨return⟩` is primitive?

In the following chapters we shall frequently discuss "plain TEX" format, which is a set of about 600 basic control sequences that are defined in Appendix B. These control sequences, together with the 300 or so primitives, are usually present when TEX begins to process a manuscript; that is why TEX claims to know roughly 900 control sequences when it starts. We shall see how plain TEX can be used to create documents in a flexible format that meets many people's needs, using some typefaces that come with the TEX system. However, you should keep in mind that plain TEX is only one of countless formats that can be designed on top of TEX's primitives; if you want some other format, it will usually be possible to adapt TEX so that it will handle whatever you have in mind. The best way to learn is probably to start with plain TEX and to change its definitions, little by little, as you gain more experience.

Appendix E contains examples of formats that can be added to Appendix B for special applications; for example, there is a set of definitions suitable for business correspondence. A complete specification of the format used to typeset this manual also appears in Appendix E. Thus, if your goal is to learn how to design TEX formats, you will probably want to study Appendix E while mastering Appendix B. After you have become skilled in the lore of control-sequence definition, you will probably have developed some formats that other people will want to use; you should then write a supplement to this manual, explaining your style rules.

The main point of these remarks, as far as novice TEX users are concerned, is that it is indeed possible to define nonstandard TEX control sequences. When this manual says that something is part of "plain TEX," it means that TEX doesn't insist on doing things exactly that way; a person could change the rules by changing one or more of the definitions in Appendix B. But you can safely rely on the control sequences of plain TEX until you become an experienced TEXnical typist.

▶ **EXERCISE 3.4**
How many different control sequences of length 2 (including the escape character) are possible? How many of length 3?

Syllables govern the world.
— JOHN SELDEN, *Table Talk* (1689)

I claim not to have controlled events,
but confess plainly that events have controlled me.
— ABRAHAM LINCOLN (1864)

4
Fonts
of Type

Occasionally you will want to change from one typeface to another, for example if you wish to be **bold** or to *emphasize* something. TEX deals with sets of up to 256 characters called "fonts" of type, and control sequences are used to select a particular font. For example, you could specify the last few words of the first sentence above in the following way, using the plain TEX format of Appendix B:

> `to be \bf bold \rm or to \sl emphasize \rm something.`

Plain TEX provides the following control sequences for changing fonts:

> `\rm` switches to the normal "roman" typeface: Roman
> `\sl` switches to a slanted roman typeface: *Slanted*
> `\it` switches to italic style: *Italic*
> `\tt` switches to a typewriter-like face: `Typewriter`
> `\bf` switches to an extended boldface style: **Bold**

At the beginning of a run you get roman type (`\rm`) unless you specify otherwise.

Notice that two of these faces have an "oblique" slope for emphasis: *Slanted type is essentially the same as roman, but the letters are slightly skewed, while the letters in italic type are drawn in a different style.* (You can perhaps best appreciate the difference between the roman and italic styles by contemplating *letters that are in an unslanted italic face.*) Typographic conventions are presently in a state of transition, because new technology has made it possible to do things that used to be prohibitively expensive; people are wrestling with the question of how much to use their new-found typographic freedom. Slanted roman type was introduced in the 1930s, but it first became widely used as an alternative to the conventional italic during the late 1970s. It can be beneficial in mathematical texts, since slanted letters are distinguishable from the italic letters in math formulas. The double use of italic type for two different purposes—for example, when statements of theorems are italicized as well as the names of variables in those theorems—has led to some confusion, which can now be avoided with slanted type. People are not generally agreed about the relative merits of slanted versus italic, but slanted type is rapidly becoming a favorite for the titles of books and journals in bibliographies.

Special fonts are effective for emphasis, but not for sustained reading; your eyes would tire if long portions of this manual were entirely set in a bold or slanted or italic face. Therefore roman type accounts for the bulk of most typeset material. But it's a nuisance to say '`\rm`' every time you want to go back to the roman style, so TEX provides an easier way to do it, using "curly brace" symbols: You can switch fonts inside the special symbols { and }, without affecting the fonts outside. For example, the displayed phrase at the beginning of this chapter is usually rendered

> `to be {\bf bold} or to {\sl emphasize} something.`

This is a special case of the general idea of "grouping" that we shall discuss in the next chapter. It's best to forget about the first way of changing fonts, and to use grouping instead; then your TEX manuscripts will look more natural, and you'll probably never* have to type '\rm'.

▶ **EXERCISE 4.1**
Explain how to type the bibliographic reference 'Ulrich Dieter, *Journal für die reine und angewandte Mathematik* **201** (1959), 37–70.' [Use grouping.]

We have glossed over an important aspect of quality in the preceding discussion. Look, for example, at the *italicized* and *slanted* words in this sentence. Since italic and slanted styles slope to the right, the d's stick into the spaces that separate these words from the roman type that follows; as a result, the spaces appear to be too skimpy, although they are correct at the base of the letters. To equalize the effective white space, TEX allows you to put the special control sequence '\/' just before switching back to unslanted letters. When you type

> {\it italicized\/} and {\sl slanted\/} words

you get *italicized* and *slanted* words that look better. The '\/' tells TEX to add an "*italic correction*" to the previous letter, depending on that letter; this correction is about four times as much for an '*f*' as for a '*c*', in a typical italic font.

Sometimes the italic correction is not desirable, because other factors take up the visual slack. The standard rule of thumb is to use \/ just before switching from slanted or italic to roman or bold, unless the next character is a period or comma. For example, type

> {\it italics\/} for {\it emphasis}.

Old manuals of style say that the punctuation after a word should be in the *same* font as that *word;* but an italic semicolon often looks wrong, so this convention is changing. When an italicized word occurs just before a semicolon, the author recommends typing '{\it word\/};'.

▶ **EXERCISE 4.2**
Explain how to typeset a roman *word in the midst of an italicized sentence.*

Every letter of every font has an italic correction, which you can bring to life by typing \/. The correction is usually zero in unslanted styles, but there are exceptions: To typeset a bold '**f**' in quotes, you should say a bold '{\bf f\/}', lest you get a bold '**f**'.

▶ **EXERCISE 4.3**
Define a control sequence \ic such that '\ic c' puts the italic correction of character *c* into TEX's register \dimen0.

The primitive control sequence \nullfont stands for a font that has no characters. This font is always present, in case you haven't specified any others.

---

* Well ..., hardly ever.

Fonts vary in size as well as in shape. For example, the font you are now reading is called a "10-point" font, because certain features of its design are 10 points apart, when measured in printers' units. (We will study the point system later; for now, it should suffice to point out that the parentheses around this sentence are exactly 10 points tall—and the em-dash is just 10 points wide.) The "dangerous bend" sections of this manual are set in 9-point type, the footnotes in 8-point, subscripts in 7-point or 6-point, sub-subscripts in 5-point.

Each font used in a TeX manuscript is associated with a control sequence; for example, the 10-point font in this paragraph is called `\tenrm`, and the corresponding 9-point font is called `\ninerm`. The slanted fonts that match `\tenrm` and `\ninerm` are called `\tensl` and `\ninesl`. These control sequences are not built into TeX, nor are they the actual names of the fonts; TeX users are just supposed to make up convenient names, whenever new fonts are introduced into a manuscript. Such control sequences are used to change typefaces.

When fonts of different sizes are used simultaneously, TeX will line the letters up according to their "baselines." For example, if you type

```
\tenrm smaller \ninerm and smaller
\eightrm and smaller \sevenrm and smaller
\sixrm and smaller \fiverm and smaller \tenrm
```

the result is smaller and smaller and smaller and smaller and smaller and smaller. Of course this is something that authors and readers aren't accustomed to, because printers couldn't do such things with traditional lead types. Perhaps poets who wish to speak in a still small voice will cause future books to make use of frequent font variations, but nowadays it's only an occasional font freak (like the author of this manual) who likes such experiments. One should not get too carried away by the prospect of font switching unless there is good reason.

An alert reader might well be confused at this point because we started out this chapter by saying that '`\rm`' is the command that switches to roman type, but later on we said that '`\tenrm`' is the way to do it. The truth is that both ways work. But it has become customary to set things up so that `\rm` means "switch to roman type in the current size" while `\tenrm` means "switch to roman type in the 10-point size." In plain TeX format, nothing but 10-point fonts are provided, so `\rm` will always get you `\tenrm`; but in more complicated formats the meaning of `\rm` will change in different parts of the manuscript. For example, in the format used by the author to typeset this manual, there's a control sequence '`\tenpoint`' that causes `\rm` to mean `\tenrm`, `\sl` to mean `\tensl`, and so on, while '`\ninepoint`' changes the definitions so that `\rm` means `\ninerm`, etc. There's another control sequence used to introduce the quotations at the end of each chapter; when the quotations are typed, `\rm` and `\sl` temporarily stand for 8-point unslanted sans-serif type and *8-point slanted sans-serif type*, respectively. This device of constantly redefining the abbreviations `\rm` and `\sl`, behind the scenes, frees the typist from the need to remember what size or style of type is currently being used.

▶**EXERCISE 4.4**
Why do you think the author chose the names '\tenpoint' and '\tenrm', etc.,
instead of '\10point' and '\10rm'?

▶**EXERCISE 4.5**
Suppose that you have typed a manuscript using slanted type for emphasis,
but your editor suddenly tells you to change all the slanted to italic. What's an easy
way to do this?

Each font has an external name that identifies it with respect to all other fonts
in a particular library. For example, the font in this sentence is called '**cmr9**',
which is an abbreviation for "Computer Modern Roman 9 point." In order to prepare
TeX for using this font, the command

    \font\ninerm=cmr9

appears in Appendix E. In general you say '\font\cs=⟨external font name⟩' to load
the information about a particular font into TeX's memory; afterwards the control
sequence \cs will select that font for typesetting. Plain TeX makes only sixteen fonts
available initially (see Appendix B and Appendix F), but you can use \font to access
anything that exists in your system's font library.

It is often possible to use a font at several different sizes, by magnifying or
shrinking the character images. Each font has a so-called design size, which
reflects the size it normally has by default; for example, the design size of **cmr9** is
9 points. But on many systems there is also a range of sizes at which you can use
a particular font, by scaling its dimensions up or down. To load a scaled font into
TeX's memory, you simply say '\font\cs=⟨external font name⟩ **at** ⟨desired size⟩'. For
example, the command

    \font\magnifiedfiverm=cmr5 at 10pt

brings in 5-point Computer Modern Roman at twice its normal size. (Caution: Before
using this '**at**' feature, you should check to make sure that your typesetter supports
the font at the size in question; TeX will accept any ⟨desired size⟩ that is positive and
less than 2048 points, but the final output will not be right unless the scaled font really
is available on your printing device.)

What's the difference between **cmr5 at 10pt** and the normal 10-point font,
cmr10? Plenty; a well-designed font will be drawn differently at different point
sizes, and the letters will often have different relative heights and widths, in order to
enhance readability.

Ten point type is different from magnified five-point type.

It is usually best to scale fonts only slightly with respect to their design size, unless
the final product is going to be photographically reduced after TeX has finished with
it, or unless you are trying for an unusual effect.

Another way to magnify a font is to specify a scale factor that is relative to
the design size. For example, the command

    \font\magnifiedfiverm=cmr5 scaled 2000

is another way to bring in the font `cmr5` at double size. The scale factor is specified as an integer that represents a magnification ratio times 1000. Thus, a scale factor of 1200 specifies magnification by 1.2, etc.

▶ **EXERCISE 4.6**
State two ways to load font `cmr10` into TeX's memory at half its normal size.

At many computer centers it has proved convenient to supply fonts at magnifications that grow in geometric ratios—something like well-tempered tuning on a piano. The idea is to have all fonts available at their true size as well as at magnifications 1.2 and 1.44 (which is 1.2×1.2); perhaps also at magnification 1.728 ($= 1.2 \times 1.2 \times 1.2$) and even higher. Then you can magnify an entire document by 1.2 or 1.44 and still stay within the set of available fonts. Plain TeX provides the abbreviations `\magstep0` for a scale factor of 1000, `\magstep1` for a scaled factor of 1200, `\magstep2` for 1440, and so on up to `\magstep5`. You say, for example,

> `\font\bigtenrm=cmr10 scaled\magstep2`

to load font `cmr10` at 1.2×1.2 times its normal size.

"This is cmr10 at normal size (\magstep0)."

"This is cmr10 scaled once by 1.2 (\magstep1)."

"This is cmr10 scaled twice by 1.2 (\magstep2)."

(Notice that a little magnification goes a long way.) There's also `\magstephalf`, which magnifies by $\sqrt{1.2}$, i.e., halfway between steps 0 and 1.

Chapter 10 explains how to apply magnification to an entire document, over and above any magnification that has been specified when fonts are loaded. For example, if you have loaded a font that is scaled by `\magstep1` and if you also specify `\magnification=\magstep2`, the actual font used for printing will be scaled by `\magstep3`. Similarly, if you load a font scaled by `\magstephalf` and if you also say `\magnification=\magstephalf`, the printed results will be scaled by `\magstep1`.

Type faces—like people's faces—have distinctive features
indicating aspects of character.
— MARSHALL LEE, *Bookmaking* (1965)

This was the Noblest Roman of them all.
— WILLIAM SHAKESPEARE, *The Tragedie of Julius Cæsar* (1599)

5

Grouping

Every once in a while it is necessary to treat part of a manuscript as a unit, so you need to indicate somehow where that part begins and where it ends. For this purpose TEX gives special interpretation to two "grouping characters," which (like the escape character) are treated differently from the normal symbols that you type. We assume in this manual that { and } are the grouping characters, since they are the ones used in plain TEX.

We saw examples of grouping in the previous chapter, where it was mentioned that font changes inside a group do not affect the fonts in force outside. The same principle applies to almost anything else that is defined inside a group, as we will see later; for example, if you define a control sequence within some group, that definition will disappear when the group ends. In this way you can conveniently instruct TEX to do something unusual, by changing its normal conventions temporarily inside of a group; since the changes are invisible from outside the group, there is no need to worry about messing up the rest of a manuscript by forgetting to restore the normal conventions when the unusual construction has been finished. Computer scientists have a name for this aspect of grouping, because it's an important aspect of programming languages in general; they call it "block structure," and definitions that are in force only within a group are said to be "local" to that group.

You might want to use grouping even when you don't care about block structure, just to have better control over spacing. For example, let's consider once more the control sequence \TeX that produces the logo 'TEX' in this manual: We observed in Chapter 3 that a blank space after this control sequence will be gobbled up unless one types '\TeX\ ', yet it is a mistake to say '\TeX\' when the following character is not a blank space. Well, in *all* cases it would be correct to specify the simple group

> {\TeX}

whether or not the following character is a space, because the } stops TEX from absorbing an optional space into \TeX. This might come in handy when you're using a text editor (e.g., when replacing all occurrences of a particular word by a control sequence). Another thing you could do is type

> \TeX{}

using an *empty* group for the same purpose: The '{}' here is a group of no characters, so it produces no output, but it does have the effect of stopping TEX from skipping blanks.

▶ **EXERCISE 5.1**
Sometimes you run into a rare word like 'shelfful' that looks better as 'shelfful' without the 'ff' ligature. How can you fool TEX into thinking that there aren't two consecutive f's in such a word?

▶ **EXERCISE 5.2**
Explain how to get three blank spaces in a row without using '\␣'.

But TeX also uses grouping for another, quite different, purpose, namely to determine how much of your text is to be governed by certain control sequences. For example, if you want to center something on a line you can type

```
\centerline{This information should be centered.}
```

using the control sequence \centerline defined in plain TeX format.

Grouping is used in quite a few of TeX's more intricate instructions; and it's possible to have groups within groups within groups, as you can see by glancing at Appendix B. Complex grouping is generally unnecessary, however, in ordinary manuscripts, so you needn't worry about it. Just don't forget to finish each group that you've started, because a lost '}' might cause trouble.

Here's an example of two groups, one nested inside the other:

```
\centerline{This information should be {\it centered}.}
```

As you might expect, TeX will produce a centered line that also contains italics:

This information should be centered.

But let's look at the example more closely: '\centerline' appears outside the curly braces, while '\it' appears inside. Why are the two cases different? And how can a beginner learn to remember which is which? Answer: \centerline is a control sequence that applies only to the very next thing that follows, so you want to put braces around the text that is to be centered (unless that text consists of a single symbol or control sequence). For example, to center the TeX logo on a line, it would suffice to type '\centerline\TeX', but to center the phrase 'TeX has groups' you need braces: '\centerline{\TeX\ has groups}'. On the other hand, \it is a control sequence that simply means "change the current font"; it acts without looking ahead, so it affects *everything* that follows, at least potentially. The braces surround \it in order to confine the font change to a local region.

In other words, the two sets of braces in this example actually have different functions: One serves to treat several words of the text as if they were a single object, while the other provides local block structure.

▶ **EXERCISE 5.3**
What do you think happens if you type the following:

```
\centerline{This information should be {centered}.}
\centerline So should this.
```

▶ **EXERCISE 5.4**
And how about this one?

```
\centerline{This information should be \it centered.}
```

▶ **EXERCISE 5.5**
Define a control sequence \ital so that a user could type '\ital{text}' instead of '{\it text\/}'. Discuss the pros and cons of \ital versus \it.

Subsequent chapters describe many primitive operations of TEX for which the locality of grouping is important. For example, if one of TEX's internal parameters is changed within a group, the previous contents of that parameter will be restored when the group ends. Sometimes, however, it's desirable to make a definition that transcends its current group. This effect can be obtained by prefixing '\global' to the definition. For example, TEX keeps the current page number in a register called \count0, and the routine that outputs a page wants to increase the page number. Output routines are always protected by enclosing them in groups, so that they do not inadvertently mess up the rest of TEX; but the change to \count0 would disappear if it were kept local to the output group. The command

> \global\advance\count0 by 1

solves the problem; it increases \count0 and makes this value stick around at the end of the output routine. In general, \global makes the immediately following definition pertain to all existing groups, not just to the innermost one.

▶ **EXERCISE 5.6**
If you think you understand local and global definitions, here's a little test to make sure: Suppose \c stands for '\count1=', \g stands for '\global\count1=', and \s stands for '\showthe\count1'. What values will be shown?

> {\c1\s\g2{\s\c3\s\g4\s\c5\s}\s\c6\s}\s

Another way to obtain block structure with TEX is to use the primitives \begingroup and \endgroup. These control sequences make it easy to begin a group within one control sequence and end it within another. The text that TEX actually executes, after control sequences have been expanded, must have properly nested groups, i.e., groups that don't overlap. For example,

> { \begingroup } \endgroup

is not legitimate.

▶ **EXERCISE 5.7**
Define control sequences \beginthe⟨block name⟩ and \endthe⟨block name⟩ that provide a "named" block structure. In other words,

> \beginthe{beguine}\beginthe{waltz}\endthe{waltz}\endthe{beguine}

should be permissible, but not

> \beginthe{beguine}\beginthe{waltz}\endthe{beguine}\endthe{waltz}.

I have had recourse to varieties of type,
and to braces.
— JAMES MUIRHEAD, *The Institutes of Gaius* (1880)

An encounter group is a gathering, for a few hours or a few days,
of twelve or eighteen personable, responsible, certifiably normal
and temporarily smelly people.
— JANE HOWARD, *Please Touch* (1970)

6
Running TEX

The best way to learn how to use TEX is to use it. Thus, it's high time for you to sit down at a computer terminal and interact with the TEX system, trying things out to see what happens. Here are some small but complete examples suggested for your first encounter.

Caution: This chapter is rather a long one. Why don't you stop reading now, and come back fresh tomorrow?

OK, let's suppose that you're rested and excited about having a trial run of TEX. Step-by-step instructions for using it appear in this chapter. First do this: Go to the lab where the graphic output device is, since you will be wanting to see the output that you get—it won't really be satisfactory to run TEX from a remote location, where you can't hold the generated documents in your own hands. Then log in; and start TEX. (You may have to ask somebody how to do this on your local computer. Usually the operating system prompts you for a command and you type 'TeX' or 'run tex' or something like that.)

When you're successful, TEX will welcome you with a message such as

```
This is TeX, Version 3.0 (preloaded format=plain 89.7.15)
**
```

The '**' is TEX's way of asking you for an input file name.

Now type '\relax' (including the backslash), and ⟨return⟩ (or whatever is used to mean "end-of-line" on your terminal). TEX is all geared up for action, ready to read a long manuscript; but you're saying that it's all right to take things easy, since this is going to be a real simple run. In fact, \relax is a control sequence that means "do nothing."

The machine will type another asterisk at you. This time type something like 'Hello?' and wait for another asterisk. Finally type '\end', and stand back to see what happens.

TEX should respond with '[1]' (meaning that it has finished page 1 of your output); then the program will halt, probably with some indication that it has created a file called 'texput.dvi'. (TEX uses the name texput for its output when you haven't specified any better name in your first line of input; and dvi stands for "device independent," since texput.dvi is capable of being printed on almost any kind of typographic output device.)

Now you're going to need some help again from your friendly local computer hackers. They will tell you how to produce hardcopy from texput.dvi. And when you see the hardcopy—Oh, glorious day!—you will see a magnificent 'Hello?' and the page number '1' at the bottom. Congratulations on your first masterpiece of fine printing.

The point is, you understand now how to get something through the whole cycle. It only remains to do the same thing with a somewhat longer document. So our next experiment will be to work from a file instead of typing the input online.

Use your favorite text editor to create a file called `story.tex` that contains the following 18 lines of text (no more, no less):

```
 1  \hrule
 2  \vskip 1in
 3  \centerline{\bf A SHORT STORY}
 4  \vskip 6pt
 5  \centerline{\sl by A. U. Thor}
 6  \vskip .5cm
 7  Once upon a time, in a distant
 8    galaxy called \"O\"o\c c,
 9  there lived a computer
10  named R.~J. Drofnats.
11
12  Mr.~Drofnats---or ``R. J.,'' as
13  he preferred to be called---
14  was happiest when he was at work
15  typesetting beautiful documents.
16  \vskip 1in
17  \hrule
18  \vfill\eject
```

(Don't type the numbers at the left of these lines, of course; they are present only for reference.) This example is a bit long, and more than a bit silly; but it's no trick for a good typist like you and it will give you some worthwhile experience, so do it. For your own good. And think about what you're typing, as you go; the example introduces a few important features of TₑX that you can learn as you're making the file.

Here is a brief explanation of what you have just typed: Lines 1 and 17 put a horizontal rule (a thin line) across the page. Lines 2 and 16 skip past one inch of space; '`\vskip`' means "vertical skip," and this extra space will separate the horizontal rules from the rest of the copy. Lines 3 and 5 produce the title and the author name, centered, in boldface and in slanted type. Lines 4 and 6 put extra white space between those lines and their successors. (We shall discuss units of measure like '`6pt`' and '`.5cm`' in Chapter 10.)

The main bulk of the story appears on lines 7–15, and it consists of two paragraphs. The fact that line 11 is blank informs TₑX that line 10 is the end of the first paragraph; and the '`\vskip`' on line 16 implies that the second paragraph ends on line 15, because vertical skips don't appear in paragraphs. Incidentally, this example seems to be quite full of TₑX commands; but it is atypical in that respect, because it is so short and because it is supposed to be teaching things. Messy constructions like `\vskip` and `\centerline` can be expected at the very beginning of a manuscript, unless you're using a canned format, but they don't last long; most of the time you will find yourself typing straight text, with relatively few control sequences.

And now comes the good news, if you haven't used computer typesetting before: You don't have to worry about where to break lines in a paragraph (i.e., where to stop at the right margin and to begin a new line), because TEX will do that for you. Your manuscript file can contain long lines or short lines, or both; it doesn't matter. This is especially helpful when you make changes, since you don't have to retype anything except the words that changed. *Every time you begin a new line in your manuscript file it is essentially the same as typing a space.* When TEX has read an entire paragraph—in this case lines 7 to 11—it will try to break up the text so that each line of output, except the last, contains about the same amount of copy; and it will hyphenate words if necessary to keep the spacing consistent, but only as a last resort.

Line 8 contains the strange concoction

```
\"O\"o\c c
```

and you already know that \" stands for an umlaut accent. The \c stands for a "cedilla," so you will get 'Ööç' as the name of that distant galaxy.

The remaining text is simply a review of the conventions that we discussed long ago for dashes and quotation marks, except that the '~' signs in lines 10 and 12 are a new wrinkle. These are called *ties*, because they tie words together; i.e., TEX is supposed to treat '~' as a normal space but not to break between lines there. A good typist will use ties within names, as shown in our example; further discussion of ties appears in Chapter 14.

Finally, line 18 tells TEX to '\vfill', i.e., to fill the rest of the page with white space; and to '\eject' the page, i.e., to send it to the output file.

Now you're ready for Experiment 2: Get TEX going again. This time when the machine says '**' you should answer 'story', since that is the name of the file where your input resides. (The file could also be called by its full name 'story.tex', but TEX automatically supplies the suffix '.tex' if no suffix has been specified.)

You might wonder why the first prompt was '**', while the subsequent ones are '*'; the reason is simply that the first thing you type to TEX is slightly different from the rest: If the first character of your response to '**' is not a backslash, TEX automatically inserts '\input'. Thus you can usually run TEX by merely naming your input file. (Previous TEX systems required you to start by typing '\input story' instead of 'story', and you can still do that; but most TEX users prefer to put all of their commands into a file instead of typing them online, so TEX now spares them the nuisance of starting out with \input each time.) Recall that in Experiment 1 you typed '\relax'; that started with a backslash, so \input was not implied.

There's actually another difference between '**' and '*': If the first character after ** is an ampersand ('&'), TEX will replace its memory with a precomputed format file before proceeding. Thus, for example, you can type '&plain \input story' or even '&plain story' in response to '**', if you are running some version of TEX that might not have the plain format preloaded.

Incidentally, many systems allow you to invoke TEX by typing a one-liner like '`tex story`' instead of waiting for the '`**`'; similarly, '`tex \relax`' works for Experiment 1, and '`tex &plain story`' loads the plain format before inputting the `story` file. You might want to try this, to see if it works on your computer, or you might ask somebody if there's a similar shortcut.

As TEX begins to read your story file, it types '`(story.tex`', possibly with a version number for more precise identification, depending on your local operating system. Then it types '`[1]`', meaning that page 1 is done; and '`)`', meaning that the file has been entirely input.

TEX will now prompt you with '`*`', because the file did not contain '`\end`'. Enter `\end` into the computer now, and you should get a file `story.dvi` containing a typeset version of Thor's story. As in Experiment 1, you can proceed to convert `story.dvi` into hardcopy; go ahead and do that now. The typeset output won't be shown here, but you can see the results by doing the experiment personally. Please do so before reading on.

▶ **EXERCISE 6.1**
Statistics show that only 7.43 of 10 people who read this manual actually type the `story.tex` file as recommended, but that those people learn TEX best. So why don't you join them?

▶ **EXERCISE 6.2**
Look closely at the output of Experiment 2, and compare it to `story.tex`: If you followed the instructions carefully, you will notice a typographical error. What is it, and why did it sneak in?

With Experiment 2 under your belt, you know how to make a document from a file. The remaining experiments in this chapter are intended to help you cope with the inevitable anomalies that you will run into later; we will intentionally do things that will cause TEX to "squeak."

But before going on, it's best to fix the error revealed by the previous output (see exercise 6.2): Line 13 of the `story.tex` file should be changed to

```
he preferred to be called---% error has been fixed!
```

The '`%`' sign here is a feature of plain TEX that we haven't discussed before: It effectively terminates a line of your input file, without introducing the blank space that TEX ordinarily inserts when moving to the next line of input. Furthermore, TEX ignores everything that you type following a `%`, up to the end of that line in the file; you can therefore put comments into your manuscript, knowing that the comments are for your eyes only.

Experiment 3 will be to make TEX work harder, by asking it to set the story in narrower and narrower columns. Here's how: After starting the program, type

```
\hsize=4in \input story
```

in response to the '**'. This means, "Set the story in a 4-inch column." More precisely, \hsize is a primitive of TₑX that specifies the horizontal size, i.e., the width of each normal line in the output when a paragraph is being typeset; and \input is a primitive that causes TₑX to read the specified file. Thus, you are instructing the machine to change the normal setting of \hsize that was defined by plain TₑX, and then to process story.tex under this modification.

TₑX should respond by typing something like '(story.tex [1])' as before, followed by '*'. Now you should type

```
\hsize=3in \input story
```

and, after TₑX says '(story.tex [2])' asking for more, type three more lines

```
\hsize=2.5in \input story
\hsize=2in \input story
\end
```

to complete this four-page experiment.

Don't be alarmed when TₑX screams 'Overfull \hbox' several times as it works at the 2-inch size; that's what was supposed to go wrong during Experiment 3. There simply is no good way to break the given paragraphs into lines that are exactly two inches wide, without making the spaces between words come out too large or too small. Plain TₑX has been set up to ensure rather strict tolerances on all of the lines it produces:

you don't get spaces between words narrower than this, and
you don't get spaces between words wider than this.

If there's no way to meet these restrictions, you get an overfull box. And with the overfull box you also get (1) a warning message, printed on your terminal, and (2) a big black bar inserted at the right of the offending box, in your output. (Look at page 4 of the output from Experiment 3; the overfull boxes should stick out like sore thumbs. On the other hand, pages 1–3 should be perfect.)

Of course you don't want overfull boxes in your output, so TₑX provides several ways to remove them; that will be the subject of our Experiment 4. But first let's look more closely at the results of Experiment 3, since TₑX reported some potentially valuable information when it was forced to make those boxes too full; you should learn how to read this data:

```
Overfull \hbox (0.98807pt too wide) in paragraph at lines 7--11
\tenrm tant galaxy called []O^^?o^^Xc, there lived|
Overfull \hbox (0.4325pt too wide) in paragraph at lines 7--11
\tenrm a com-puter named R. J. Drof-nats. |
Overfull \hbox (5.32132pt too wide) in paragraph at lines 12--16
\tenrm he pre-ferred to be called---was hap-|
```

Each overfull box is correlated with its location in your input file (e.g., the first two were generated when processing the paragraph on lines 7 11 of story.tex), and you also learn by how much the copy sticks out (e.g., 0.98807 points).

Notice that TeX also shows the contents of the overfull boxes in abbreviated form. For example, the last one has the words 'he preferred to be called—was hap-', set in font `\tenrm` (10-point roman type); the first one has a somewhat curious rendering of 'Ööç', because the accents appear in strange places within that font. In general, when you see '[]' in one of these messages, it stands either for the paragraph indentation or for some sort of complex construction; in this particular case it stands for an umlaut that has been raised up to cover an 'O'.

▶ **EXERCISE 6.3**
Can you explain the '|' that appears after '`lived`' in that message?

▶ **EXERCISE 6.4**
Why is there a space before the '|' in '`Drof-nats. |`'?

You don't have to take out pencil and paper in order to write down the overfull box messages that you get before they disappear from view, since TeX always writes a "transcript" or "log file" that records what happened during each session. For example, you should now have a file called `story.log` containing the transcript of Experiment 3, as well as a file called `texput.log` containing the transcript of Experiment 1. (The transcript of Experiment 2 was probably overwritten when you did number 3.) Take a look at `story.log` now; you will see that the overfull box messages are accompanied not only by the abbreviated box contents, but also by some strange-looking data about hboxes and glue and kerns and such things. This data gives a precise description of what's in that overfull box; TeX wizards will find such listings important, if they are called upon to diagnose some mysterious error, and you too may want to understand TeX's internal code some day.

The abbreviated forms of overfull boxes show the hyphenations that TeX tried before it resorted to overfilling. The hyphenation algorithm, which is described in Appendix H, is excellent but not perfect; for example, you can see from the messages in `story.log` that TeX finds the hyphen in 'pre-ferred', and it can even hyphenate 'Drof-nats'. Yet it discovers no hyphen in 'galaxy', and every once in a while an overfull box problem can be cured simply by giving TeX a hint about how to hyphenate some word more completely. (We will see later that there are two ways to do this, either by inserting discretionary hyphens each time as in '`gal\-axy`', or by saying '`\hyphenation{gal-axy}`' once at the beginning of your manuscript.)

In the present example, hyphenation is not a problem, since TeX found and tried all the hyphens that could possibly have helped. The only way to get rid of the overfull boxes is to change the tolerance, i.e., to allow wider spaces between words. Indeed, the tolerance that plain TeX uses for wide lines is completely inappropriate for 2-inch columns; such narrow columns simply can't be achieved without loosening the constraints, unless you rewrite the copy to fit.

TeX assigns a numerical value called "badness" to each line that it sets, in order to assess the quality of the spacing. The exact rules for badness are different for different fonts, and they will be discussed in Chapter 14; but here is the way badness works for the roman font of plain TEX:

The badness of this line is 100.	(very tight)
The badness of this line is 12.	(somewhat tight)
The badness of this line is 0.	(perfect)
The badness of this line is 12.	(somewhat loose)
The badness of this line is 200.	(loose)
The badness of this line is 1000.	(bad)
The badness of this line is 5000.	(awful)

Plain TEX normally stipulates that no line's badness should exceed 200; but in our case, the task would be impossible since

'tant galaxy called Ööç, there'	has badness 1521;
'he preferred to be called—was'	has badness 568.

So we turn now to Experiment 4, in which spacing variations that are more appropriate to narrow columns will be used.

Run TEX again, and begin this time by saying

`\hsize=2in \tolerance=1600 \input story`

so that lines with badness up to 1600 will be tolerated. Hurray! There are no overfull boxes this time. (But you do get a message about an *underfull* box, since TEX reports all boxes whose badness exceeds a certain threshold called `\hbadness`; plain TEX sets `\hbadness=1000`.) Now make TEX work still harder by trying

`\hsize=1.5in \input story`

(thus leaving the tolerance at 1600 but making the column width still skimpier). Alas, overfull boxes return; so try typing

`\tolerance=10000 \input story`

in order to see what happens. TEX treats 10000 as if it were "infinite" tolerance, allowing arbitrarily wide space; thus, a tolerance of 10000 will *never* produce an overfull box, unless something strange occurs like an unhyphenatable word that is wider than the column itself.

The underfull box that TEX produces in the 1.5-inch case is really bad; with such narrow limits, an occasional wide space is unavoidable. But try

`\raggedright \input story`

for a change. (This tells TEX not to worry about keeping the right margin straight, and to keep the spacing uniform within each line.) Finally, type

`\hsize=.75in \input story`

followed by '`\end`', to complete Experiment 4. This makes the columns almost impossibly narrow.

The output from this experiment will give you some feeling for the problem of breaking a paragraph into approximately equal lines. When the lines are relatively wide, TeX will almost always find a good solution. But otherwise you will have to figure out some compromise, and several options are possible. Suppose you want to ensure that no lines have badness exceeding 500. Then you could set \tolerance to some high number, and \hbadness=500; TeX would not produce overfull boxes, but it would warn you about the underfull ones. Or you could set \tolerance=500; then TeX might produce overfull boxes. If you really want to take corrective action, the second alternative is better, because you can look at an overfull box to see how much sticks out; it becomes graphically clear what remedies are possible. On the other hand, if you don't have time to fix bad spacing—if you just want to know how bad it is—then the first alternative is better, although it may require more computer time.

▶ **EXERCISE 6.5**
When \raggedright has been specified, badness reflects the amount of space at the right margin, instead of the spacing between words. Devise an experiment by which you can easily determine what badness TeX assigns to each line, when the **story** is set ragged-right in 1.5-inch columns.

A parameter called \hfuzz allows you to ignore boxes that are only slightly overfull. For example, if you say \hfuzz=1pt, a box must stick out more than one point before it is considered erroneous. Plain TeX sets \hfuzz=0.1pt.

▶ **EXERCISE 6.6**
Inspection of the output from Experiment 4, especially page 3, shows that with narrow columns it would be better to allow white space to appear before and after a dash, whenever other spaces in the same line are being stretched. Define a \dash macro that does this.

You were warned that this is a long chapter. But take heart: There's only one more experiment to do, and then you will know enough about TeX to run it fearlessly by yourself forever after. The only thing you are still missing is some information about how to cope with error messages—i.e., not just with warnings about things like overfull boxes, but with cases where TeX actually stops and asks you what to do next.

Error messages can be terrifying when you aren't prepared for them; but they can be fun when you have the right attitude. Just remember that you really haven't hurt the computer's feelings, and that nobody will hold the errors against you. Then you'll find that running TeX might actually be a creative experience instead of something to dread.

The first step in Experiment 5 is to plant two intentional mistakes in the **story.tex** file. Change line 3 to

```
\centerline{\bf A SHORT \ERROR STORY}
```

and change '\vskip' to '\vship' on line 2.

Now run TeX again; but instead of 'story' type 'sorry'. The computer should respond by saying that it can't find file **sorry.tex**, and it will ask you to try again. Just hit ⟨return⟩ this time; you'll see that you had better give the name of a real file. So type 'story' and wait for T_EX to find one of the *faux pas* in that file.

Ah yes, the machine will soon stop,* after typing something like this:

```
! Undefined control sequence.
l.2 \vship
              1in
?
```

T_EX begins its error messages with '!', and it shows what it was reading at the time of the error by displaying two lines of context. The top line of the pair (in this case '\vship') shows what T_EX has looked at so far, and where it came from ('l.2', i.e., line number 2); the bottom line (in this case '1in') shows what T_EX has yet to read.

The '?' that appears after the context display means that T_EX wants advice about what to do next. If you've never seen an error message before, or if you've forgotten what sort of response is expected, you can type '?' now (go ahead and try it!); T_EX will respond as follows:

```
Type <return> to proceed, S to scroll future error messages,
R to run without stopping, Q to run quietly,
I to insert something, E to edit your file,
1 or ... or 9 to ignore the next 1 to 9 tokens of input,
H for help, X to quit.
```

This is your menu of options. You may choose to continue in various ways:

1. Simply type ⟨return⟩. T_EX will resume its processing, after attempting to recover from the error as best it can.

2. Type 'S'. T_EX will proceed without pausing for instructions if further errors arise. Subsequent error messages will flash by on your terminal, possibly faster than you can read them, and they will appear in your log file where you can scrutinize them at your leisure. Thus, 'S' is sort of like typing ⟨return⟩ to every message.

3. Type 'R'. This is like 'S' but even stronger, since it tells T_EX not to stop for any reason, not even if a file name can't be found.

4. Type 'Q'. This is like 'R' but even more so, since it tells T_EX not only to proceed without stopping but also to suppress all further output to your terminal. It is a fast, but somewhat reckless, way to proceed (intended for running T_EX with no operator in attendance).

5. Type 'I', followed by some text that you want to insert. T_EX will read this line of text before encountering what it would ordinarily see next. Lines inserted in this way are not assumed to end with a blank space.

---

* Some installations of T_EX do not allow interaction. In such cases all you can do is look at the error messages in your log file, where they will appear together with the "help" information.

6. Type a small number (less than 100). TEX will delete this many characters and control sequences from whatever it is about to read next, and it will pause again to give you another chance to look things over.

7. Type 'H'. This is what you should do now and whenever you are faced with an error message that you haven't seen for a while. TEX has two messages built in for each perceived error: a formal one and an informal one. The formal message is printed first (e.g., '! Undefined control sequence.'); the informal one is printed if you request more help by typing 'H', and it also appears in your log file if you are scrolling error messages. The informal message tries to complement the formal one by explaining what TEX thinks the trouble is, and often by suggesting a strategy for recouping your losses.

8. Type 'X'. This stands for "exit." It causes TEX to stop working on your job, after putting the finishing touches on your log file and on any pages that have already been output to your dvi file. The current (incomplete) page will not be output.

9. Type 'E'. This is like 'X', but it also prepares the computer to edit the file that TEX is currently reading, at the current position, so that you can conveniently make a change before trying again.

After you type 'H' (or 'h', which also works), you'll get a message that tries to explain that the control sequence just read by TEX (i.e., \vship) has never been assigned a meaning, and that you should either insert the correct control sequence or you should go on as if the offending one had not appeared.

In this case, therefore, your best bet is to type

    I\vskip

(and ⟨return⟩), with no space after the 'I'; this effectively replaces \vship by \vskip. (Do it.)

If you had simply typed ⟨return⟩ instead of inserting anything, TEX would have gone ahead and read '1in', which it would have regarded as part of a paragraph to be typeset. Alternatively, you could have typed '3'; that would have deleted '1in' from TEX's input. Or you could have typed 'X' or 'E' in order to correct the spelling error in your file. But it's usually best to try to detect as many errors as you can, each time you run TEX, since that increases your productivity while decreasing your computer bills. Chapter 27 explains more about the art of steering TEX through troubled text.

▶**EXERCISE 6.7**
What would have happened if you had typed '5' after the \vship error?

You can control the level of interaction by giving commands in your file as well as online: The TEX primitives \scrollmode, \nonstopmode, and \batchmode correspond respectively to typing 'S', 'R', or 'Q' in response to an error message, and \errorstopmode puts you back into the normal level of interaction. (Such changes are global, whether or not they appear inside a group.) Furthermore, many installations have implemented a way to interrupt T_EX while it is running; such an interruption causes the program to revert to \errorstopmode, after which it pauses and waits for further instructions.

What happens next in Experiment 5? T_EX will hiccup on the other bug that we planted in the file. This time, however, the error message is more elaborate, since the context appears on six lines instead of two:

```
! Undefined control sequence.
<argument> \bf A SHORT \ERROR
                                STORY
\centerline #1->\line {\hss #1
                               \hss }
1.3 \centerline{\bf A SHORT \ERROR STORY}

?
```

You get multiline error messages like this when the error is detected while T_EX is processing some higher-level commands—in this case, while it is trying to carry out \centerline, which is not a primitive operation (it is defined in plain T_EX). At first, such error messages will appear to be complete nonsense to you, because much of what you see is low-level T_EX code that you never wrote. But you can overcome this hangup by getting a feeling for the way T_EX operates.

First notice that the context information always appears in pairs of lines. As before, the top line shows what T_EX has just read ('\bf A SHORT \ERROR'), then comes what it is about to read ('STORY'). The next pair of lines shows the context of the first two; it indicates what T_EX was doing just before it began to read the others. In this case, we see that T_EX has just read '#1', which is a special code that tells the machine to "read the first argument that is governed by the current control sequence"; i.e., "now read the stuff that \centerline is supposed to center on a line." The definition in Appendix B says that \centerline, when applied to some text, is supposed to be carried out by sticking that text in place of the '#1' in '\line{\hss#1\hss}'. So T_EX is in the midst of this expansion of \centerline, as well as being in the midst of the text that is to be centered.

The bottom line shows how far T_EX has gotten until now in the story file. (Actually the bottom line is blank in this example; what appears to be the bottom line is really the first of two lines of context, and it indicates that T_EX has read everything including the '}' in line 3 of the file.) Thus, the context in this error message gives us a glimpse of how T_EX went about its business. First, it saw \centerline at the beginning of line 3. Then it looked at the definition of \centerline and noticed that \centerline takes an "argument," i.e., that \centerline applies to the next character or control sequence or group that follows. So T_EX read on, and filed '\bf A SHORT \ERROR STORY' away as the argument to \centerline. Then it began to read the expansion, as defined in Appendix B. When it reached the #1, it began to read the argument it had saved. And when it reached \ERROR, it complained about an undefined control sequence.

▶ **EXERCISE 6.8**
Why didn't TEX complain about \ERROR being undefined when \ERROR was first encountered, i.e., before reading 'STORY}' on line 3?

When you get a multiline error message like this, the best clues about the source of the trouble are usually on the bottom line (since that is what you typed) and on the top line (since that is what triggered the error message). Somewhere in there you can usually spot the problem.

Where should you go from here? If you type 'H' now, you'll just get the same help message about undefined control sequences that you saw before. If you respond by typing ⟨return⟩, TEX will go on and finish the run, producing output virtually identical to that in Experiment 2. In other words, the conventional responses won't teach you anything new. So type 'E' now; this terminates the run and prepares the way for you to fix the erroneous file. (On some systems, TEX will actually start up the standard text editor, and you'll be positioned at the right place to delete '\ERROR'. On other systems, TEX will simply tell you to edit line 3 of file story.tex.)

When you edit story.tex again, you'll notice that line 2 still contains \vship; the fact that you told TEX to insert \vskip doesn't mean that your file has changed in any way. In general, you should correct all errors in the input file that were spotted by TEX during a run; the log file provides a handy way to remember what those errors were.

Well, this has indeed been a long chapter, so let's summarize what has been accomplished. By doing the five experiments you have learned at first hand (1) how to get a job printed via TEX; (2) how to make a file that contains a complete TEX manuscript; (3) how to change the plain TEX format to achieve columns with different widths; and (4) how to avoid panic when TEX issues stern warnings.

So you could now stop reading this book and go on to print a bunch of documents. It is better, however, to continue bearing with the author (after perhaps taking another rest), since you're just at the threshold of being able to do a lot more. And you ought to read Chapter 7 at least, because it warns you about certain symbols that you must not type unless you want TEX to do something special. While reading the remaining chapters it will, of course, be best for you to continue making trial runs, using experiments of your own design.

If you use TEX format packages designed by others, your error messages may involve many inscrutable two-line levels of macro context. By setting \errorcontextlines=0 at the beginning of your file, you can reduce the amount of information that is reported; TEX will show only the top and bottom pairs of context lines together with up to \errorcontextlines additional two-line items. (If anything has thereby been omitted, you'll also see '...'.) Chances are good that you can spot the source of an error even when most of a large context has been suppressed; if not, you can say 'I\errorcontextlines=100\oops' and try again. (That will usually give you an undefined control sequence error and plenty of context.) Plain TEX sets \errorcontextlines=5.

What we have to learn to do we learn by doing.
— ARISTOTLE, *Ethica Nicomachea* II (c. 325 B.C.)

He may run who reads.
— HABAKKUK 2 : 2 (c. 600 B.C.)
He that runs may read.
— WILLIAM COWPER, *Tirocinium* (1785)

7

How TEX Reads What You Type

We observed in the previous chapter that an input manuscript is expressed in terms of "lines," but that these lines of input are essentially independent of the lines of output that will appear on the finished pages. Thus you can stop typing a line of input at any place that's convenient for you, as you prepare or edit a file. A few other related rules have also been mentioned:

- A ⟨return⟩ is like a space.
- Two spaces in a row count as one space.
- A blank line denotes the end of a paragraph.

Strictly speaking, these rules are contradictory: A blank line is obtained by typing ⟨return⟩ twice in a row, and this is different from typing two spaces in a row. Some day you might want to know the *real* rules. In this chapter and the next, we shall study the very first stage in the transition from input to output.

In the first place, it's wise to have a precise idea of what your keyboard sends to the machine. There are 256 characters that TₑX might encounter at each step, in a file or in a line of text typed directly on your terminal. These 256 characters are classified into 16 categories numbered 0 to 15:

Category	Meaning	
0	Escape character	(\ in this manual)
1	Beginning of group	({ in this manual)
2	End of group	(} in this manual)
3	Math shift	($ in this manual)
4	Alignment tab	(& in this manual)
5	End of line	(⟨return⟩ in this manual)
6	Parameter	(# in this manual)
7	Superscript	(^ in this manual)
8	Subscript	(_ in this manual)
9	Ignored character	(⟨null⟩ in this manual)
10	Space	(␣ in this manual)
11	Letter	(A, ..., Z and a, ..., z)
12	Other character	(none of the above or below)
13	Active character	(~ in this manual)
14	Comment character	(% in this manual)
15	Invalid character	(⟨delete⟩ in this manual)

It's not necessary for you to learn these code numbers; the point is only that TₑX responds to 16 different types of characters. At first this manual led you to believe that there were just two types—the escape character and the others— and then you were told about two more types, the grouping symbols { and }. In Chapter 6 you learned two more: ~ and %. Now you know that there are really 16. This is the whole truth of the matter; no more types remain to be revealed. The category code for any character can be changed at any time, but it is usually wise to stick to a particular scheme.

The main thing to bear in mind is that each TEX format reserves certain characters for its own special purposes. For example, when you are using plain TEX format (Appendix B), you need to know that the ten characters

$$\backslash \quad \{ \quad \} \quad \$ \quad \& \quad \# \quad \char`^ \quad \_ \quad \% \quad \char`~$$

cannot be used in the ordinary way when you are typing; each of them will cause TEX to do something special, as explained elsewhere in this book. If you really need these symbols as part of your manuscript, plain TEX makes it possible for you to type

$\backslash\$$ for \$, $\backslash\%$ for %, $\backslash\&$ for &, $\backslash\#$ for #, $\backslash\_$ for _;

the $\backslash\_$ symbol is useful for *compound_identifiers* in computer programs. In mathematics formulas you can use $\backslash\{$ and $\backslash\}$ for { and }, while `\backslash` produces a reverse slash; for example,

'$\$\backslash\{a \backslash backslash b\backslash\}\$$' yields '${a\backslash b}$'.

Furthermore $\backslash\char`^$ produces a circumflex accent (e.g., '$\backslash\char`^$e' yields 'ê'); and $\backslash\char`~$ yields a tilde accent (e.g., '$\backslash\char`~$n' yields 'ñ').

▸ **EXERCISE 7.1**
What horrible errors appear in the following sentence?

```
Procter & Gamble's stock climbed to $2, a 10% gain.
```

▸ **EXERCISE 7.2**
Can you imagine why the designer of plain TEX decided not to make '$\backslash\backslash$' the control sequence for reverse slashes?

When TEX reads a line of text from a file, or a line of text that you entered directly on your terminal, it converts that text into a list of "tokens." A token is either (a) a single character with an attached category code, or (b) a control sequence. For example, if the normal conventions of plain TEX are in force, the text '{\hskip 36 pt}' is converted into a list of eight tokens:

$$\{_1 \quad \boxed{\text{hskip}} \quad 3_{12} \quad 6_{12} \quad \sqcup_{10} \quad p_{11} \quad t_{11} \quad \}_2$$

The subscripts here are the category codes, as listed earlier: 1 for "beginning of group," 12 for "other character," and so on. The $\boxed{\text{hskip}}$ doesn't get a subscript, because it represents a control sequence token instead of a character token. Notice that the space after `\hskip` does not get into the token list, because it follows a control word.

It is important to understand the idea of token lists, if you want to gain a thorough understanding of TEX, and it is convenient to learn the concept by thinking of TEX as if it were a living organism. The individual lines of input in your files are seen only by TEX's "eyes" and "mouth"; but after that text has been gobbled up, it is sent to TEX's "stomach" in the form of a token list, and the digestive processes that do the actual typesetting are based entirely on tokens. As far as the stomach is concerned, the input flows in as a stream of tokens, somewhat as if your TEX manuscript had been typed all on one extremely long line.

You should remember two chief things about TₑX's tokens: (1) A control sequence is considered to be a single object that is no longer composed of a sequence of symbols. Therefore long control sequence names are no harder for TₑX to deal with than short ones, after they have been replaced by tokens. Furthermore, spaces are not ignored after control sequences inside a token list; the ignore-space rule applies only in an input file, during the time that strings of characters are being tokenized. (2) Once a category code has been attached to a character token, the attachment is permanent. For example, if character '{' were suddenly declared to be of category 12 instead of category 1, the characters '{₁' already inside token lists of TₑX would still remain of category 1; only newly made lists would contain '{₁₂' tokens. In other words, individual characters receive a fixed interpretation as soon as they have been read from a file, based on the category they have at the time of reading. Control sequences are different, since they can change their interpretation at any time. TₑX's digestive processes always know exactly what a character token signifies, because the category code appears in the token itself; but when the digestive processes encounter a control sequence token, they must look up the current definition of that control sequence in order to figure out what it means.

▶ **EXERCISE 7.3**
Some of the category codes 0 to 15 will never appear as subscripts in character tokens, because they disappear in TₑX's mouth. For example, characters of category 0 (escapes) never get to be tokens. Which categories can actually reach TₑX's stomach?

There's a program called **INITEX** that is used to install TₑX, starting from scratch; **INITEX** is like TₑX except that it can do even more things. It can compress hyphenation patterns into special tables that facilitate rapid hyphenation, and it can produce format files like '`plain.fmt`' from '`plain.tex`'. But **INITEX** needs extra space to carry out such tasks, so it generally has less memory available for typesetting than you would expect to find in a production version of TₑX.

When **INITEX** begins, it knows nothing but TₑX's primitives. All 256 characters are initially of category 12, except that ⟨return⟩ has category 5, ⟨space⟩ has category 10, ⟨null⟩ has category 9, ⟨delete⟩ has category 15, the 52 letters **A**...**Z** and **a**...**z** have category 11, **%** and **** have the respective categories 14 and 0. It follows that **INITEX** is initially incapable of carrying out some of TₑX's primitives that depend on grouping; you can't use **\def** or **\hbox** until there are characters of categories 1 and 2. The format in Appendix B begins with **\catcode** commands to provide characters of the necessary categories; e.g.,

> **\catcode`\\{=1**

assigns category 1 to the { symbol. The **\catcode** operation is like many other primitives of TₑX that we shall study later; by modifying internal quantities like the category codes, you can adapt TₑX to a wide variety of applications.

▶ **EXERCISE 7.4**
Suppose that the commands

> **\catcode`\\<=1 \catcode`\\>=2**

appear near the beginning of a group that begins with '{'; these specifications instruct TₑX to treat < and > as group delimiters. According to TₑX's rules of locality, the characters < and > will revert to their previous categories when the group ends. But should the group end with } or with >?

Although control sequences are treated as single objects, TEX does provide a way to break them into lists of character tokens: If you write \string\cs, where \cs is any control sequence, you get the list of characters for that control sequence's name. For example, \string\TeX produces four tokens: $\backslash_{12}$, T_{12}, e_{12}, X_{12}. Each character in this token list automatically gets category code 12 ("other"), including the backslash that \string inserts to represent an escape character. However, category 10 will be assigned to the character '␣' (blank space) if a space character somehow sneaks into the name of a control sequence.

Conversely, you can go from a list of character tokens to a control sequence by saying '\csname⟨tokens⟩\endcsname'. The tokens that appear in this construction between \csname and \endcsname may include other control sequences, as long as those control sequences ultimately expand into characters instead of TEX primitives; the final characters can be of any category, not necessarily letters. For example, '\csname TeX\endcsname' is essentially the same as '\TeX'; but '\csname\TeX\endcsname' is illegal, because \TeX expands into tokens containing the \kern primitive. Furthermore, '\csname\string\TeX\endcsname' will produce the unusual control sequence '\\TeX', i.e., the token $\boxed{\texttt{\textbackslash TeX}}$, which you can't ordinarily write.

▶ **EXERCISE 7.5**
Experiment with TEX to see what \string does when it is followed by an active character like ˜. (Active characters behave like control sequences, but they are not prefixed by an escape.) What is an easy way to conduct such experiments online? What control sequence could you put after \string to obtain the single character token $\backslash_{12}$?

▶ **EXERCISE 7.6**
What tokens does '\expandafter\string\csname a\string\ b\endcsname' produce? (There are three spaces before the b. Chapter 20 explains \expandafter.)

▶ **EXERCISE 7.7**
When \csname is used to define a control sequence for the first time, that control sequence is made equivalent to \relax until it is redefined. Use this fact to design a macro \ifundefined#1 such that, for example,

   \ifundefined{TeX}⟨true text⟩\else⟨false text⟩\fi

expands to the ⟨true text⟩ if \TeX hasn't previously been defined, or if \TeX has been \let equal to \relax; it should expand to the ⟨false text⟩ otherwise.

In the examples so far, \string has converted control sequences into lists of tokens that begin with $\backslash_{12}$. But this backslash token isn't really hardwired into TEX; there's a parameter called \escapechar that specifies what character should be used when control sequences are output as text. The value of \escapechar is normally TEX's internal code for backslash, but it can be changed if another convention is desired.

TEX has two other token-producing operations similar to the \string command. If you write \number⟨number⟩, you get the decimal equivalent of the ⟨number⟩; and if you write \romannumeral⟨number⟩, you get the number expressed in lowercase roman numerals. For example, '\romannumeral24' produces 'xxiv', a list of four tokens each having category 12. The \number operation is redundant when it is applied to an explicit constant (e.g., '\number24' produces '24'); but it does suppress leading zeros, and it can also be used with numbers that are in TEX's internal registers or parameters. For example, '\number-0015' produces '-15'; and if register \count5 holds the value 316, then '\number\count5' produces '316'.

The twin operations \uppercase{⟨token list⟩} and \lowercase{⟨token list⟩} go through a given token list and convert all of the character tokens to their "uppercase" or "lowercase" equivalents. Here's how: Each of the 256 possible characters has two associated values called the \uccode and the \lccode; these values are changeable just as a \catcode is. Conversion to uppercase means that a character is replaced by its \uccode value, unless the \uccode value is zero (when no change is made). Conversion to lowercase is similar, using the \lccode. The category codes aren't changed. When INITEX begins, all \uccode and \lccode values are zero except that the letters a to z and A to Z have \uccode values A to Z and \lccode values a to z.

TEX performs the \uppercase and \lowercase transformations in its stomach, but the \string and \number and \romannumeral and \csname operations are carried out en route to the stomach (like macro expansion), as explained in Chapter 20.

▶ **EXERCISE 7.8**
What token list results from '\uppercase{a\lowercase{bC}}'?

▶ **EXERCISE 7.9**
TEX has an internal integer parameter called \year that is set equal to the current year number at the beginning of every job. Explain how to use \year, together with \romannumeral and \uppercase, to print a copyright notice like '© MCMLXXXVI' for all jobs run in 1986.

▶ **EXERCISE 7.10**
Define a control sequence \appendroman with three parameters such that \appendroman#1#2#3 defines control sequence #1 to expand to a control sequence whose name is the name of control sequence #2 followed by the value of the positive integer #3 expressed in roman numerals. For example, suppose \count20 equals 30; then '\appendroman\a\TeX{\count20}' should have the same effect as '\def\a{\TeXxxx}'.

Some bookes are to bee tasted,
others to bee swallowed,
and some few to bee chewed and disgested.
— FRANCIS BACON, *Essayes* (1597)

'Tis the good reader that makes the good book.
— RALPH WALDO EMERSON, *Society & Solitude* (1870)

8

The Characters You Type

A lot of different keyboards are used with TEX, but few keyboards can produce 256 different symbols. Furthermore, as we have seen, some of the characters that you *can* type on your keyboard are reserved for special purposes like escaping and grouping. Yet when we studied fonts it was pointed out that there are 256 characters per font. So how can you refer to the characters that aren't on your keyboard, or that have been pre-empted for formatting?

One answer is to use control sequences. For example, the plain format of Appendix B, which defines % to be a special kind of symbol so that you can use it for comments, defines the control sequence \% to mean a percent sign.

To get access to any character whatsoever, you can type

> \char⟨number⟩

where ⟨number⟩ is any number from 0 to 255 (optionally followed by a space); you will get the corresponding character from the current font. That's how Appendix B handles \%; it defines '\%' to be an abbreviation for '\char37', since 37 is the character code for a percent sign.

The codes that TEX uses internally to represent characters are based on "ASCII," the American Standard Code for Information Interchange. Appendix C gives full details of this code, which assigns numbers to certain control functions as well as to ordinary letters and punctuation marks. For example, ⟨space⟩ = 32 and ⟨return⟩ = 13. There are 94 standard visible symbols, and they have been assigned code numbers from 33 to 126, inclusive.

It turns out that 'b' is character number 98 in ASCII. So you can typeset the word bubble in a strange way by putting

> \char98 u\char98\char98 le

into your manuscript, if the b-key on your typewriter is broken. (An optional space is ignored after constants like '98'. Of course you need the \, c, h, a, and r keys to type '\char', so let's hope that they are always working.)

⚐　TEX always uses the internal character code of Appendix C for the standard ASCII characters, regardless of what external coding scheme actually appears in the files being read. Thus, b is 98 inside of TEX even when your computer normally deals with EBCDIC or some other non-ASCII scheme; the TEX software has been set up to convert text files to internal code, and to convert back to the external code when writing text files. Device-independent (dvi) output files use TEX's internal code. In this way, TEX is able to give identical results on all computers.

⚐　Character code tables like those in Appendix C often give the code numbers in *octal notation,* i.e., the radix-8 number system, in which the digits are *0, 1, 2, 3, 4, 5, 6,* and *7.** Sometimes *hexadecimal notation* is also used, in which case the digits are 0, 1, 2, 3, 4, 5, 6, 7, 8, 9, A, B, C, D, E, and F. For example, the octal code for 'b' is

---

* The author of this manual likes to use italic digits for octal numbers, and typewriter type for hexadecimal numbers, in order to provide a typographic clue to the underlying radix whenever possible.

142, and its hexadecimal code is 62. A ⟨number⟩ in TEX's language can begin with a ',
in which case it is regarded as octal, or with a ", when it is regarded as hexadecimal.
Thus, \char'142 and \char"62 are equivalent to \char98. The legitimate character
codes in octal notation run from *'0* to *'377*; in hexadecimal, they run from "0 to "FF.

 But TEX actually provides another kind of ⟨number⟩ that makes it unnecessary
for you to know ASCII at all! The token '₁₂ (left quote), when followed by
any character token or by any control sequence token whose name is a single character,
stands for TEX's internal code for the character in question. For example, \char'b and
\char'\b are also equivalent to \char98. If you look in Appendix B to see how \% is
defined, you'll notice that the definition is

> \def\%{\char'\%}

instead of \char37 as claimed above.

▶ **EXERCISE 8.1**
What would be wrong with \def\%{\char'%}?

The preface to this manual points out that the author tells little white lies
from time to time. Well, if you actually check Appendix B you'll find that

> \chardef\%='\%

is the true definition of \%. Since format designers often want to associate a special character with a special control sequence name, TEX provides the construction
'\chardef⟨control sequence⟩=⟨number⟩' for numbers between 0 and 255, as an efficient
alternative to '\def⟨control sequence⟩{\char⟨number⟩}'.

Although you can use \char to access any character in the current font,
you can't use it in the middle of a control sequence. For example, if you type

> \\char98

TEX reads this as the control sequence \\ followed by c, h, a, etc., not as the
control sequence \b.

You will hardly ever need to use \char when typing a manuscript, since
the characters you want will probably be available as predefined control sequences; \char is primarily intended for the designers of book formats like those
in the appendices. But some day you may require a special symbol, and you
may have to hunt through a font catalog until you find it. Once you find it,
you can use it by simply selecting the appropriate font and then specifying the
character number with \char. For example, the "dangerous bend" sign used in
this manual appears as character number 127 of font manfnt, and that font is
selected by the control sequence \manual. The macros in Appendix E therefore
display dangerous bends by saying '{\manual\char127}'.

We have observed that the ASCII character set includes only 94 printable
symbols; but TEX works internally with 256 different character codes, from 0
to 255, each of which is assigned to one of the sixteen categories described in
Chapter 7. If your keyboard has additional symbols, or if it doesn't have the
standard 94, the people who installed your local TEX system can tell you the

correspondence between what you type and the character number that TEX receives. Some people are fortunate enough to have keys marked '≠' and '≤' and '≥'; it is possible to install TEX so that it will recognize these handy symbols and make the typing of mathematics more pleasant. But if you do not have such keys, you can get by with the control sequences \ne, \le, and \ge.

TEX has a standard way to refer to the invisible characters of ASCII: Code 0 can be typed as the sequence of three characters ^^@, code 1 can be typed ^^A, and so on up to code 31, which is ^^_ (see Appendix C). If the character following ^^ has an internal code between 64 and 127, TEX subtracts 64 from the code; if the code is between 0 and 63, TEX adds 64. Hence code 127 can be typed ^^?, and the dangerous bend sign can be obtained by saying {\manual^^?}. However, you must change the category code of character 127 before using it, since this character ordinarily has category 15 (invalid); say, e.g., \catcode'\^^?=12. The ^^ notation is different from \char, because ^^ combinations are like single characters; for example, it would not be permissible to say \catcode'\char127, but ^^ symbols can even be used as letters within control words.

One of the overfull box messages in Chapter 6 illustrates the fact that TEX sometimes uses the funny ^^ convention in its output: The umlaut character in that example appears as ^^?, and the cedilla appears as ^^X, because '¨' and '¸' occur in positions '177 and '30 of the \tenrm font.

There's also a special convention in which ^^ is followed by *two* "lowercase hexadecimal digits," 0–9 or a–f. With this convention, all 256 characters are obtainable in a uniform way, from ^^00 to ^^ff. Character 127 is ^^7f.

Most of the ^^ codes are unimportant except in unusual applications. But ^^M is particularly noteworthy because it is code 13, the ASCII ⟨return⟩ that TEX normally places at the right end of every line of your input file. By changing the category of ^^M you can obtain useful special effects, as we shall see later.

The control code ^^I is also of potential interest, since it's the ASCII ⟨tab⟩. Plain TEX makes ⟨tab⟩ act like a blank space.

People who install TEX systems for use with non-American alphabets can make TEX conform to any desired standard. For example, suppose you have a Norwegian keyboard containing the letter æ, which comes in as code 241 (say). Your local format package should define \catcode'æ=11; then you could have control sequences like \særtrykk. Your TEX input files could be made readable by American installations of TEX that don't have your keyboard, by substituting ^^f1 for character 241. (For example, the stated control sequence would appear as \s^^f1rtrykk in the file; your American friends should also be provided with the format that you used, with its \catcode'^^f1=11.) Of course you should also arrange your fonts so that TEX's character 241 will print as æ; and you should change TEX's hyphenation algorithm so that it will do correct Norwegian hyphenation. The main point is that such changes are not extremely difficult; nothing in the design of TEX limits it to the American alphabet. Fine printing is obtained by fine tuning to the language or languages being used.

European languages can also be accommodated effectively with only a limited character set. For example, let's consider Norwegian again, but suppose that you want to use a keyboard without an æ character. You can arrange the font metric file so that TEX will interpret ae, o/, aa, AE, O/, and AA as ligatures that produce æ, ø, å, Æ, Ø, and Å, respectively; and you could put the characters å and Å into positions 128 and 129 of the font. By setting `\catcode'/=11` you would be able to use the ligature o/ in control sequences like '`\ho/yre`'. TEX's hyphenation method is not confused by ligatures; so you could use this scheme to operate essentially as suggested before, but with two keystrokes occasionally replacing one. (Your typists would have to watch out for the occasional times when the adjacent characters aa, oe, and o/ should not be treated as ligatures; also, '`\/`' would be a control word, not a control symbol.)

The rest of this chapter is devoted to TEX's reading rules, which define the conversion from text to tokens. For example, the fact that TEX ignores spaces after control words is a consequence of the rules below, which imply among other things that spaces after control words never become space tokens. The rules are intended to work the way you would expect them to, so you may not wish to bother reading them; but when you are communicating with a computer, it is nice to understand what the machine thinks it is doing, and here's your chance.

The input to TEX is a sequence of "lines." Whenever TEX is reading a line of text from a file, or a line of text that you entered directly on your terminal, the computer's reading apparatus is in one of three so-called states:

> State N Beginning a new line;
> State M Middle of a line;
> State S Skipping blanks.

At the beginning of every line it's in state N; but most of the time it's in state M, and after a control word or a space it's in state S. Incidentally, "states" are different from the "modes" that we will be studying later; the current *state* refers to TEX's eyes and mouth as they take in characters of new text, but the current *mode* refers to the condition of TEX's gastro-intestinal tract. Most of the things that TEX does when it converts characters to tokens are independent of the current state, but there are differences when spaces or end-of-line characters are detected (categories 10 and 5).

TEX deletes any ⟨space⟩ characters (number 32) that occur at the right end of an input line. Then it inserts a ⟨return⟩ character (number 13) at the right end of the line, except that it places nothing additional at the end of a line that you inserted with '`I`' during error recovery. Note that ⟨return⟩ is considered to be an actual character that is part of the line; you can obtain special effects by changing its catcode.

If TEX sees an escape character (category 0) in any state, it scans the entire control sequence name as follows. (a) If there are no more characters in the line, the name is empty (like `\csname\endcsname`). Otherwise (b) if the next character is not of category 11 (letter), the name consists of that single symbol. Otherwise (c) the name consists of all letters beginning with the current one and ending just before the first nonletter, or at the end of the line. This name becomes a control sequence token. TEX goes into state S in case (c), or in case (b) with respect to a character of category 10 (space); otherwise TEX goes into state M.

If TEX sees a superscript character (category 7) in any state, and if that character is followed by another identical character, and if those two equal characters are followed by a character of code $c < 128$, then they are deleted and 64 is added to or subtracted from the code c. (Thus, `^^A` is replaced by a single character whose code is 1, etc., as explained earlier.) However, if the two superscript characters are immediately followed by two of the lowercase hexadecimal digits `0123456789abcdef`, the four-character sequence is replaced by a single character having the specified hexadecimal code. The replacement is carried out also if such a trio or quartet of characters is encountered during steps (b) or (c) of the control-sequence-name scanning procedure described above. After the replacement is made, TEX begins again as if the new character had been present all the time. If a superscript character is not the first of such a trio or quartet, it is handled by the following rule.

If TEX sees a character of categories 1, 2, 3, 4, 6, 8, 11, 12, or 13, or a character of category 7 that is not the first of a special sequence as just described, it converts the character to a token by attaching the category code, and goes into state M. This is the normal case; almost every nonblank character is handled by this rule.

If TEX sees an end-of-line character (category 5), it throws away any other information that might remain on the current line. Then if TEX is in state N (new line), the end-of-line character is converted to the control sequence token '$\boxed{\text{par}}$' (end of paragraph); if TEX is in state M (mid-line), the end-of-line character is converted to a token for character 32 ('␣') of category 10 (space); and if TEX is in state S (skipping blanks), the end-of-line character is simply dropped.

If TEX sees a character to be ignored (category 9), it simply bypasses that character as if it weren't there, and remains in the same state.

If TEX sees a character of category 10 (space), the action depends on the current state. If TEX is in state N or S, the character is simply passed by, and TEX remains in the same state. Otherwise TEX is in state M; the character is converted to a token of category 10 whose character code is 32, and TEX enters state S. The character code in a space token is always 32.

If TEX sees a comment character (category 14), it throws away that character and any other information that might remain on the current line.

Finally, if TEX sees an invalid character (category 15), it bypasses that character, prints an error message, and remains in the same state.

If TEX has nothing more to read on the current line, it goes to the next line and enters state N. However, if `\endinput` has been specified for a file being `\input`, or if an `\input` file has ended, TEX returns to whatever it was reading when the `\input` command was originally given. (Further details of `\input` and `\endinput` are discussed in Chapter 20.)

▶ **EXERCISE 8.2**
Test your understanding of TEX's reading rules by answering the following quickie questions: (a) What is the difference between categories 5 and 14? (b) What is the difference between categories 3 and 4? (c) What is the difference between categories 11 and 12? (d) Are spaces ignored after active characters? (e) When a line ends with a comment character like %, are spaces ignored at the beginning of the next line? (f) Can an ignored character appear in the midst of a control sequence name?

▶ **EXERCISE 8.3**
Look again at the error message that appears on page 31. When TeX reported that \vship was an undefined control sequence, it printed two lines of context, showing that it was in the midst of reading line 2 of the story file. At the time of that error message, what state was TeX in? What character was it about to read next?

▶ **EXERCISE 8.4**
Given the category codes of plain TeX format, what tokens are produced from the input line ' x^2~   \TeX   ^^62^^6'?

▶ **EXERCISE 8.5**
Consider an input file that contains exactly three lines; the first line says 'Hi!', while the other two lines are completely blank. What tokens are produced when TeX reads this file, using the category codes of plain TeX format?

▶ **EXERCISE 8.6**
Assume that the category codes of plain TeX are in force, except that the characters ^^A, ^^B, ^^C, ^^M belong respectively to categories 0, 7, 10, and 11. What tokens are produced from the (rather ridiculous) input line '^^B^^BM^^A^^B^^C^^M^^@\M␣'? (Remember that this line is followed by ⟨return⟩, which is ^^M; and recall that ^^@ denotes the ⟨null⟩ character, which has category 9 when INITEX begins.)

The special character inserted at the end of each line needn't be ⟨return⟩; TeX actually inserts the current value of an integer parameter called \endlinechar, which normally equals 13 but it can be changed like any other parameter. If the value of \endlinechar is negative or greater than 255, no character is appended, and the effect is as if every line ends with % (i.e., with a comment character).

Since it is possible to change the category codes, TeX might actually use several different categories for the same character on a single line. For example, Appendices D and E contain several ways to coerce TeX to process text "verbatim," so that the author could prepare this manual without great difficulty. (Try to imagine typesetting a TeX manual; backslashes and other special characters need to switch back and forth between their normal categories and category 12!) Some care is needed to get the timing right, but you can make TeX behave in a variety of different ways by judiciously changing the categories. On the other hand, it is best not to play with the category codes very often, because you must remember that characters never change their categories once they have become tokens. For example, when the arguments to a macro are first scanned, they are placed into a token list, so their categories are fixed once and for all at that time. The author has intentionally kept the category codes numeric instead of mnemonic, in order to discourage people from making extensive use of \catcode changes except in unusual circumstances.

▶ **EXERCISE 8.7**
Appendix B defines \lq and \rq to be abbreviations for ' and ' (single left and right quotes, respectively). Explain why the definitions

    \chardef\lq=96   \chardef\rq=39

would not be as good.

▶ **EXERCISE 8.7**
Appendix B defines `\lq` and `\rq` to be abbreviations for ' and ' (single left and right quotes, respectively). Explain why the definitions

> `\chardef\lq=96`   `\chardef\rq=39`

would not be as good.

> *for life's not a paragraph*
>
> *And death i think is no parenthesis.*
> — e. e. cummings, *since feeling is first* (1926)
>
> *This coded character set is to facilitate
> the general interchange of information
> among information processing systems,
> communication systems, and
> associated equipment.
> ... An 8-bit set was considered
> but the need for more than 128 codes
> in general applications was not yet evident.*
> — ASA SUBCOMMITTEE X3.2, *American Standard
> Code for Information Interchange* (1963)

9

TEX's Roman Fonts

When you're typing a manuscript for TₑX, you need to know what symbols are available. The plain TₑX format of Appendix B is based on the Computer Modern fonts, which provide the characters needed to typeset a wide variety of documents. It's time now to discuss what a person can do with plain TₑX when typing straight text. We've already touched on some of the slightly subtle things—for example, dashes and quotation marks were considered in Chapter 2, and certain kinds of accents appeared in the examples of Chapters 3 and 6. The purpose of this chapter is to give a more systematic summary of the possibilities, by putting all the facts together.

Let's begin with the rules for the normal roman font (`\rm` or `\tenrm`); plain TₑX will use this font for everything unless you specify otherwise. Most of the ordinary symbols that you need are readily available and you can type them in the ordinary way: There's nothing special about

the letters A to Z and a to z
the digits 0 to 9
common punctuation marks : ; ! ? ( ) [ ] ' ' - * / . , @

except that TₑX recognizes certain combinations as ligatures:

`ff` yields ff;	`ffi` yields ffi;	`' '` yields ";	`!'` yields ¡;
`fi` yields fi;	`ffl` yields ffl;	`' '` yields ";	`?'` yields ¿.
`fl` yields fl;	`--` yields –;	`---` yields —;	

You can also type + and =, to get the corresponding symbols + and =; but it's much better to use such characters only in math mode, i.e., enclosed between two $ signs, since that tells TₑX to insert the proper spacing for mathematics. Math mode is explained later; for now, it's just a good idea to remember that formulas and text should be segregated. A non-mathematical hyphen and a non-mathematical slash should be specified by typing '-' and '/' outside of mathematics mode, but subtraction and division should be specified by typing '-' and '/' between $ signs.

The previous paragraph covers 80 of the 94 visible characters of standard ASCII; so your keyboard probably contains at least 14 more symbols, and you should learn to watch out for the remaining ones, since they are special. Four of these are preëmpted by plain TₑX; if your manuscript requires the symbols

$ #   %   &

you should remember to type them as

\$ \#   \%   \&

respectively. Plain TₑX also reserves the six symbols

\   {   }   ^   _   ~

but you probably don't mind losing these, since they don't appear in normal copy. Braces and backslashes are available via control sequences in math mode.

There are four remaining special characters in the standard ASCII set:

     " | <   >

Again, you don't really want them when you're typesetting text. (Double-quote marks should be replaced either by `` or by ''; vertical lines and relation signs are needed only in math mode.)

Scholarly publications in English often refer to other languages, so plain TₑX makes it possible to typeset the most commonly used accents:

Type	*to get*	
\`o	ò	(grave accent)
\'o	ó	(acute accent)
\^o	ô	(circumflex or "hat")
\"o	ö	(umlaut or dieresis)
\~o	õ	(tilde or "squiggle")
\=o	ō	(macron or "bar")
\.o	ȯ	(dot accent)
\u o	ŏ	(breve accent)
\v o	ǒ	(háček or "check")
\H o	ő	(long Hungarian umlaut)
\t oo	o͡o	(tie-after accent)

Within the font, such accents are designed to appear at the right height for the letter 'o'; but you can use them over any letter, and TₑX will raise an accent that is supposed to be taller. Notice that spaces are needed in the last four cases, to separate the control sequences from the letters that follow. You could, however, type '\H{o}' in order to avoid putting a space in the midst of a word.

Plain TₑX also provides three accents that go underneath:

Type	*to get*	
\c o	ǫ	(cedilla accent)
\d o	ọ	(dot-under accent)
\b o	o̲	(bar-under accent)

And there are a few special letters:

Type	*to get*	
\oe,\OE	œ, Œ	(French ligature OE)
\ae,\AE	æ, Æ	(Latin and Scandinavian ligature AE)
\aa,\AA	å, Å	(Scandinavian A-with-circle)
\o,\O	ø, Ø	(Scandinavian O-with-slash)
\l,\L	ł, Ł	(Polish suppressed-L)
\ss	ß	(German "es-zet" or sharp S)

The \rm font contains also the dotless letters 'ı' and 'ȷ', which you can obtain by typing '\i' and '\j'. These are needed because 'i' and 'j' should lose their dots when they gain an accent. For example, the right way to obtain 'mīnŭs' is to type 'm\=\i n\u us' or 'm\={\i}n\u{u}s'.

This completes our summary of the \rm font. Exactly the same conventions apply to \bf, \sl, and \it, so you don't have to do things differently when you're using a different typeface. For example, \bf\"o yields ö and \it\& yields &. Isn't that nice?

 However, \tt is slightly different. You will be glad to know that ff, fi, and so on are not treated as ligatures when you're using typewriter type; nor do you get ligatures from dashes and quote marks. That's fine, because ordinary dashes and ordinary double-quotes are appropriate when you're trying to imitate a typewriter. Most of the accents are available too. But \H, \., \l, and \L cannot be used—the typewriter font contains other symbols in their place. Indeed, you are suddenly allowed to type ", |, <, and >; see Appendix F. All of the letters, spaces, and other symbols in \tt have the same width.

▸**EXERCISE 9.1**
What's the non-naive way to type 'naïve'?

▸**EXERCISE 9.2**
List some English words that contain accented letters.

▸**EXERCISE 9.3**
How would you type 'Æsop's Œuvres en français'?

▸**EXERCISE 9.4**
Explain what to type in order to get this sentence: *Commentarii Academiæ scientiarum imperialis petropolitanæ* is now *Akademiiă Nauk SSSR, Doklady.*

▸**EXERCISE 9.5**
And how would you specify the names Ernesto Cesàro, Pál Erdős, Øystein Ore, Stanisław Świerczkowski, Sergeĭ Ĭur'ev, Muḥammad ibn Mûsâ al-Khwârizmî?

 ▸**EXERCISE 9.6**
Devise a way to typeset Pál Erdős in typewriter type.

The following symbols come out looking exactly the same whether you are using \rm, \sl, \bf, \it, or \tt:

Type	*to get*	
\dag	†	(dagger or obelisk)
\ddag	‡	(double dagger or diesis)
\S	§	(section number sign)
\P	¶	(paragraph sign or pilcrow)

(They appear in just one style because plain T_EX gets them from the math symbols font. Lots of other symbols are needed for mathematics; we shall study them later. See Appendix B for a few more non-math symbols.)

▶**EXERCISE 9.7**

In plain TEX's italic font, the '$' sign comes out as '£'. This gives you a way to refer to pounds sterling, but you might want an italic dollar sign. Can you think of a way to typeset a reference to the book *Europe on $15.00 a day*?

Appendix B shows that plain TEX handles most of the accents by using TEX's \accent primitive. For example, \'#1 is equivalent to {\accent19 #1}, where #1 is the argument being accented. The general rule is that \accent⟨number⟩ puts an accent over the next character; the ⟨number⟩ tells where that accent appears in the current font. The accent is assumed to be properly positioned for a character whose height equals the x-height of the current font; taller or shorter characters cause the accent to be raised or lowered, taking due account of the slantedness of the fonts of accenter and accentee. The width of the final construction is the width of the character being accented, regardless of the width of the accent. Mode-independent commands like font changes may appear between the accent number and the character to be accented, but grouping operations must not intervene. If it turns out that no suitable character is present, the accent will appear by itself as if you had said \char⟨number⟩ instead of \accent⟨number⟩. For example, \'{} produces ´.

▶**EXERCISE 9.8**

Why do you think plain TEX defines \'#1 to be '{\accent19 #1}' instead of simply letting \' be an abbreviation for '\accent19 '? (Why the extra braces, and why the argument #1?)

It's important to remember that these conventions we have discussed for accents and special letters are not built into TEX itself; they belong only to the plain TEX format, which uses the Computer Modern fonts. Quite different conventions will be appropriate when other fonts are involved; format designers should provide rules for how to obtain accents and special characters in their particular systems. Plain TEX works well enough when accents are infrequent, but the conventions of this chapter are by no means recommended for large-scale applications of TEX to other languages. For example, a well-designed TEX font for French might well treat accents as ligatures, so that one could `e'crire de cette manie're nai"ve en franc/ais` without backslashes. (See the remarks about Norwegian in Chapter 8.)

Let's doo't after the high Roman fashion.
— WILLIAM SHAKESPEARE, *The Tragedie of Anthony and Cleopatra* (1606)

English is a straightforward, frank, honest, open-hearted, no-nonsense language,
which has little truck with such devilish devious devices as accents;
indeed U.S. editors and printers are often thrown into a dither
when a foreign word insinuates itself into the language.
However there is one word on which Americans seem to have closed ranks,
printing it confidently, courageously, and almost invariably
complete with accent—the cheese presented to us as Münster.

Unfortunately, Munster doesn't take an accent.
— WAVERLEY ROOT, in the *International Herald Tribune* (1982)

10
Dimensions

Sometimes you want to tell TEX how big to make a space, or how wide to make a line. For example, the short story of Chapter 6 used the instruction '\vskip .5cm' to skip vertically by half a centimeter, and we also said '\hsize=4in' to specify a horizontal size of 4 inches. It's time now to consider the various ways such dimensions can be communicated to TEX.

"Points" and "picas" are the traditional units of measure for printers and compositors in English-speaking countries, so TEX understands points and picas. TEX also understands inches and metric units, as well as the continental European versions of points and picas. Each unit of measure is given a two-letter abbreviation, as follows:

pt point (baselines in this manual are 12 pt apart)
pc pica (1 pc = 12 pt)
in inch (1 in = 72.27 pt)
bp big point (72 bp = 1 in)
cm centimeter (2.54 cm = 1 in)
mm millimeter (10 mm = 1 cm)
dd didot point (1157 dd = 1238 pt)
cc cicero (1 cc = 12 dd)
sp scaled point (65536 sp = 1 pt)

The output of TEX is firmly grounded in the metric system, using the conversion factors shown here as exact ratios.

▶ **EXERCISE 10.1**
How many points are there in 254 centimeters?

When you want to express some physical dimension to TEX, type it as

⟨optional sign⟩⟨number⟩⟨unit of measure⟩

or

⟨optional sign⟩⟨digit string⟩.⟨digit string⟩⟨unit of measure⟩

where an ⟨optional sign⟩ is either a '+' or a '−' or nothing at all, and where a ⟨digit string⟩ consists of zero or more consecutive decimal digits. The '.' can also be a ','. For example, here are six typical dimensions:

```
3 in              29 pc
-.013837in        + 42,1 dd
0.mm              123456789sp
```

A plus sign is redundant, but some people occasionally like extra redundancy once in a while. Blank spaces are optional before the signs and the numbers and the units of measure, and you can also put an optional space after the dimension; but you should not put spaces within the digits of a number or between the letters of the unit of measure.

▶ **EXERCISE 10.2**
Arrange those six "typical dimensions" into order, from smallest to largest.

▶**EXERCISE 10.3**
Two of the following three dimensions are legitimate according to TEX's rules. Which two are they? What do they mean? Why is the other one incorrect?

```
'.77pt
"Ccc
-,sp
```

The following "rulers" have been typeset by TEX so that you can get some idea of how different units compare to each other. If no distortion has been introduced during the camera work and printing processes that have taken place after TEX did its work, these rulers are highly accurate.

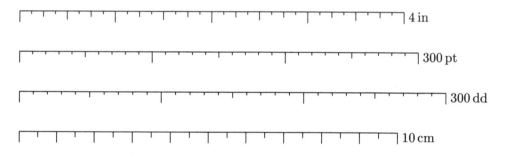

▶**EXERCISE 10.4**
(To be worked after you know about boxes and glue and have read Chapter 21.) Explain how to typeset such a 10 cm ruler, using TEX.

TEX represents all dimensions internally as an integer multiple of the tiny units called sp. Since the wavelength of visible light is approximately 100 sp, rounding errors of a few sp make no difference to the eye. However, TEX does all of its arithmetic very carefully so that identical results will be obtained on different computers. Different implementations of TEX will produce the same line breaks and the same page breaks when presented with the same document, because the integer arithmetic will be the same.

The units have been defined here so that precise conversion to sp is efficient on a wide variety of machines. In order to achieve this, TEX's "pt" has been made slightly larger than the official printer's point, which was defined to equal exactly .013837 in by the American Typefounders Association in 1886 [cf. National Bureau of Standards Circular 570 (1956)]. In fact, one classical point is exactly .99999999 pt, so the "error" is essentially one part in 10^8. This is more than two orders of magnitude less than the amount by which the inch itself changed during 1959, when it shrank to 2.54 cm from its former value of (1/0.3937) cm; so there is no point in worrying about the difference. The new definition 72.27 pt = 1 in is not only better for calculation, it is also easier to remember.

TEX will not deal with dimensions whose absolute value is 2^{30} sp or more. In other words, the maximum legal dimension is slightly less than 16384 pt. This is a distance of about 18.892 feet (5.7583 meters), so it won't cramp your style.

In a language manual like this it is convenient to use "angle brackets" in abbreviations for various constructions like ⟨number⟩ and ⟨optional sign⟩ and ⟨digit string⟩. Henceforth we shall use the term ⟨dimen⟩ to stand for a legitimate TeX dimension. For example,

\hsize=⟨dimen⟩

will be the general way to define the column width that TeX is supposed to use. The idea is that ⟨dimen⟩ can be replaced by any quantity like '4in' that satisfies TeX's grammatical rules for dimensions; abbreviations in angle brackets make it easy to state such laws of grammar.

When a dimension is zero, you have to specify a unit of measure even though the unit is irrelevant. Don't just say '0'; say '0pt' or '0in' or something.

The 10-point size of type that you are now reading is normal in textbooks, but you probably will often find yourself wanting a larger font. Plain TeX makes it easy to do this by providing **magnified output**. If you say

\magnification=1200

at the beginning of your manuscript, everything will be enlarged by 20%; i.e., it will come out at 1.2 times the normal size. Similarly, '\magnification=2000' doubles everything; this actually quadruples the area of each letter, since heights and widths are both doubled. To magnify a document by the factor f, you say \magnification=⟨number⟩, where the ⟨number⟩ is 1000 times f. This instruction must be given before the first page of output has been completed. You cannot apply two different magnifications to the same document.

Magnification has obvious advantages: You'll have less eyestrain when you're proofreading; you can easily make transparencies for lectures; and you can photo-reduce magnified output, in order to minimize the deficiencies of a low-resolution printer. Conversely, you might even want '\magnification=500' in order to create a pocket-size version of some book. But there's a slight catch: You can't use magnification unless your printing device happens to have the fonts that you need at the magnification you desire. In other words, you need to find out what sizes are available before you can magnify. Most installations of TeX make it possible to print all the fonts of plain TeX if you magnify by \magstep0, 1, 2, 3, and perhaps 4 or even 5 (see Chapter 4); but the use of large fonts can be expensive because a lot of system memory space is often required to store the shapes.

▶ **EXERCISE 10.5**
Try printing the short story of Chapter 6 at 1.2, 1.44, and 1.728 times the normal size. What should you type to get TeX to do this?

When you say \magnification=2000, an operation like '\vskip.5cm' will actually skip 1.0 cm of space in the final document. If you want to specify a dimension in terms of the final size, TeX allows you to say 'true' just before pt, pc, in, bp, cm, mm, dd, cc, and sp. This unmagnifies the units, so that the subsequent magnification will cancel out. For example, '\vskip.5truecm' is equivalent to '\vskip.25cm' if you have previously said '\magnification=2000'. Plain TEX uses this feature in the \magnification command itself: Appendix B includes the instruction

> \hsize = 6.5 true in

just after a new magnification has taken effect. This adjusts the line width so that the material on each page will be $6\frac{1}{2}$ inches wide when it is finally printed, regardless of the magnification factor. There will be an inch of margin at both left and right, assuming that the paper is $8\frac{1}{2}$ inches wide.

If you use no 'true' dimensions, TEX's internal computations are not affected by the presence or absence of magnification; line breaks and page breaks will be the same, and the dvi file will change in only two places. TEX simply tells the printing routine that you want a certain magnification, and the printing routine will do the actual enlargement when it reads the dvi file.

▶ **EXERCISE 10.6**
Chapter 4 mentions that fonts of different magnifications can be used in the same job, by loading them 'at' different sizes. Explain what fonts will be used when you give the commands

> \magnification=\magstep1
> \font\first=cmr10 scaled\magstep1
> \font\second=cmr10 at 12truept

Magnification is actually governed by TEX's \mag primitive, which is an integer parameter that should be positive and at most 32768. The value of \mag is examined in three cases: (1) just before the first page is shipped to the dvi file; (2) when computing a true dimension; (3) when the dvi file is being closed. Alternatively, some implementations of TEX produce non-dvi output; they examine \mag in case (2) and also when shipping out each page. Since each document has only one magnification, the value of \mag must not change after it has first been examined.

TEX also recognizes two units of measure that are relative rather than absolute; i.e., they depend on the current context:

> em is the width of a "quad" in the current font;
> ex is the "x-height" of the current font.

Each font defines its own em and ex values. In olden days, an "em" was the width of an 'M', but this is no longer true; ems are simply arbitrary units that come with a font, and so are exes. The Computer Modern fonts have the property that an em-dash is one em wide, each of the digits 0 to 9 is half an em wide, and lowercase 'x' is one ex high; but these are not hard-and-fast rules for all fonts. The \rm font (cmr10) of plain TEX has $1\,\mathrm{em} = 10\,\mathrm{pt}$ and $1\,\mathrm{ex} \approx 4.3\,\mathrm{pt}$; the \bf font (cmbx10) has $1\,\mathrm{em} = 11.5\,\mathrm{pt}$ and $1\,\mathrm{ex} \approx 4.44\,\mathrm{pt}$; and the \tt font (cmtt10) has $1\,\mathrm{em} = 10.5\,\mathrm{pt}$ and $1\,\mathrm{ex} \approx 4.3\,\mathrm{pt}$. All of these are "10-point" fonts, yet they have different em and ex values. It is generally best to use em for horizontal measurements and ex for vertical measurements that depend on the current font.

⟳   A ⟨dimen⟩ can also refer to TEX's internal registers or parameters. We shall discuss registers later, and a complete definition of everything that a ⟨dimen⟩ can be will be given in Chapter 24. For now it will suffice to give some hints about what is to come: '\hsize' stands for the current horizontal line size, and '.5\hsize' is half that amount; '2\wd3' denotes twice the width of register \box3; '-\dimen100' is the negative of register \dimen100.

⟳⟳   Notice that the unit names in dimensions are not preceded by backslashes. The same is true of other so-called keywords of the TEX language. Keywords can be given in uppercase letters or in a mixture of upper and lower case; e.g., 'Pt' is equivalent to 'pt'. The category codes of these letters are irrelevant; you may, for example, be using a p of category 12 (other) that was generated by expanding '\the\hsize' as explained in Chapter 20. TEX gives a special interpretation to keywords only when they appear in certain very restricted contexts. For example, 'pt' is a keyword only when it appears after a number in a ⟨dimen⟩; 'at' is a keyword only when it appears after the external name of a font in a \font declaration. Here is a complete list of TEX's keywords, in case you are wondering about the full set: at, bp, by, cc, cm, dd, depth, em, ex, fil, height, in, l, minus, mm, mu, pc, plus, pt, scaled, sp, spread, to, true, width. (See Appendix I for references to the contexts in which each of these is recognized as a keyword.)

11

Boxes

TEX makes complicated pages by starting with simple individual characters and putting them together in larger units, and putting these together in still larger units, and so on. Conceptually, it's a big paste-up job. The TEXnical terms used to describe such page construction are *boxes* and *glue*.

Boxes in TEX are two-dimensional things with a rectangular shape, having three associated measurements called *height*, *width*, and *depth*. Here is a picture of a typical box, showing its so-called reference point and baseline:

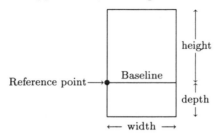

From TEX's viewpoint, a single character from a font is a box; it's one of the simplest kinds of boxes. The font designer has decided what the height, width, and depth of the character are, and what the symbol will look like when it is in the box; TEX uses these dimensions to paste boxes together, and ultimately to determine the locations of the reference points for all characters on a page. In plain TEX's \rm font (cmr10), for example, the letter 'h' has a height of 6.9444 points, a width of 5.5555 points, and a depth of zero; the letter 'g' has a height of 4.3055 points, a width of 5 points, and a depth of 1.9444 points. Only certain special characters like parentheses have height plus depth actually equal to 10 points, although cmr10 is said to be a "10-point" font. You needn't bother to learn these measurements yourself, but it's good to be aware of the fact that TEX deals with such information; then you can better understand what the computer does to your manuscript.

The character shape need not fit inside the boundaries of its box. For example, some characters that are used to build up larger math symbols like matrix brackets intentionally protrude a little bit, so that they overlap properly with the rest of the symbol. Slanted letters frequently extend a little to the right of the box, as if the box were skewed right at the top and left at the bottom, keeping its baseline fixed. For example, compare the letter 'g' in the cmr10 and cmsl10 fonts (\rm and \sl):

In both cases TEX thinks that the box is 5 points wide, so both letters get exactly the same treatment. TEX doesn't have any idea where the ink will go—only the output device knows this. But the slanted letters will be spaced properly in spite of TEX's lack of knowledge, because the baselines will match up.

Actually the font designer also tells TeX one other thing, the so-called *italic correction*: A number is specified for each character, telling roughly how far that character extends to the right of its box boundary, plus a little to spare. For example, the italic correction for 'g' in `cmr10` is 0.1389 pt, while in `cmsl10` it is 0.8565 pt. Chapter 4 points out that this correction is added to the normal width if you type '\/' just after the character. You should remember to use \/ when shifting from a slanted font to an unslanted one, especially in cases like

```
the so-called {\sl italic correction\/}:
```

since no space intervenes here to compensate for the loss of slant.

TeX also deals with another simple kind of box, which might be called a "black box," namely, a rectangle like '▮' that is to be entirely filled with ink at printing time. You can specify any height, width, and depth you like for such boxes—but they had better not have too much area, or the printer might get upset. (Printers generally prefer white space to black space.)

Usually these black boxes are made very skinny, so that they appear as horizontal lines or vertical lines. Printers traditionally call such lines "horizontal rules" and "vertical rules," so the terms TeX uses to stand for black boxes are `\hrule` and `\vrule`. Even when the box is square, as in '■', you must call it either an `\hrule` or a `\vrule`. We shall discuss the use of rule boxes in greater detail later. (See Chapter 21.)

Everything on a page that has been typeset by TeX is made up of simple character boxes or rule boxes, pasted together in combination. TeX pastes boxes together in two ways, either *horizontally* or *vertically*. When TeX builds a horizontal list of boxes, it lines them up so that their reference points appear in the same horizontal row; therefore the baselines of adjacent characters will match up as they should. Similarly, when TeX builds a vertical list of boxes, it lines them up so that their reference points appear in the same vertical column.

Let's take a look at what TeX does behind the scenes, by comparing the computer's methods with what you would do if you were setting metal type by hand. In the time-tested traditional method, you choose the letters that you need out of a type case—the uppercase letters are in the upper case—and you put them into a "composing stick." When a line is complete, you adjust the spacing and transfer the result to the "chase," where it joins the other rows of type. Eventually you lock the type up tightly by adjusting external wedges called "quoins." This isn't much different from what TeX does, except that different words are used; when TeX locks up a line, it creates what is called an "hbox" (horizontal box), because the components of the line are pieced together horizontally. You can give an instruction like

```
\hbox{A line of type.}
```

in a TeX manuscript; this tells the computer to take boxes for the appropriate letters in the current font and to lock them up in an hbox. As far as TeX is concerned, the letter 'A' is a box '□' and the letter 'p' is a box '◻'. So the given instruction causes TeX to form the hbox

representing 'A line of type.' The hboxes for individual lines of type are eventually joined together by putting them into a "vbox" (vertical box). For example, you can say

        \vbox{\hbox{Two lines}\hbox{of type.}}

and TeX will convert this into

        i.e.,   Two lines
                of type.

The principal difference between TeX's method and the old way is that metal types are generally cast so that each character has the same height and depth; this makes it easy to line them up by hand. TeX's types have variable height and depth, because the computer has no trouble lining characters up by their baselines, and because the extra information about height and depth helps in the positioning of accents and mathematical symbols.

Another important difference between TeX setting and hand setting is, of course, that TeX will choose line divisions automatically; you don't have to insert \hbox and \vbox instructions unless you want to retain complete control over where each letter goes. On the other hand, if you do use \hbox and \vbox, you can make TeX do almost everything that Ben Franklin could do in his printer's shop. You're only giving up the ability to make the letters come out charmingly crooked or badly inked; for such effects you need to make a new font. (And of course you lose the tactile and olfactory sensations, and the thrill of doing everything by yourself. TeX will never completely replace the good old ways.)

A page of text like the one you're reading is itself a box, in TeX's view: It is a largish box made from a vertical list of smaller boxes representing the lines of text. Each line of text, in turn, is a box made from a horizontal list of boxes representing the individual characters. In more complicated situations, involving mathematical formulas and/or complex tables, you can have boxes within boxes within boxes ... to any level. But even these complicated situations arise from horizontal or vertical lists of boxes pasted together in a simple way; all that you and TeX have to worry about is one list of boxes at a time. In fact, when you're typing straight text, you don't have to think about boxes at all, since TeX will automatically take responsibility for assembling the character boxes into words and the words into lines and the lines into pages. You need to be aware of the box concept only when you want to do something out of the ordinary, e.g., when you want to center a heading.

From the standpoint of TeX's digestive processes, a manuscript comes in as a sequence of tokens, and the tokens are to be transformed into a sequence of boxes. Each token of input is essentially an instruction or a piece of an instruction; for example, the token 'A$_{11}$' normally means, "put a character box for the letter A at the end of the current hbox, using the current font"; the token '$\boxed{\texttt{vskip}}$' normally means, "skip vertically in the current vbox by the ⟨dimen⟩ specified in the following tokens."

The height, width, or depth of a box might be negative, in which case it is a "shadow box" that is somewhat hard to draw. TEX doesn't balk at negative dimensions; it just does arithmetic as usual. For example, the combined width of two adjacent boxes is the sum of their widths, whether or not the widths are positive. A font designer can declare a character's width to be negative, in which case the character acts like a backspace. (Languages that read from right to left could be handled in this way, but only to a limited extent, since TEX's line-breaking algorithm is based on the assumption that words don't have negative widths.)

TEX can raise or lower the individual boxes in a horizontal list; such adjustments take care of mathematical subscripts and superscripts, as well as the heights of accents and a few other things. For example, here is a way to make a box that contains the TEX logo, putting it into TEX's internal register \box0:

```
\setbox0=\hbox{T\kern-.1667em\lower.5ex\hbox{E}\kern-.125em X}
```

Here '\kern-.1667em' means to insert blank space of −.1667 ems in the current font, i.e., to back up a bit; and '\lower.5ex' means that the box \hbox{E} is to be lowered by half of the current x-height, thus offsetting that box with respect to the others. Instead of '\lower.5ex' one could also say '\raise-.5ex'. Chapters 12 and 21 discuss the details of how to construct boxes for special effects; our goal in the present chapter is merely to get a taste of the possibilities.

TEX will exhibit the contents of any box register, if you ask it to. For example, if you type '\showbox0' after setting \box0 to the TEX logo as above, your log file will contain the following mumbo jumbo:

```
\hbox(6.83331+2.15277)x18.6108
.\tenrm T
.\kern -1.66702
.\hbox(6.83331+0.0)x6.80557, shifted 2.15277
..\tenrm E
.\kern -1.25
.\tenrm X
```

The first line means that \box0 is an hbox whose height, depth, and width are respectively 6.83331 pt, 2.15277 pt, and 18.6108 pt. Subsequent lines beginning with '.' indicate that they are *inside* of a box. The first thing in this particular box is the letter T in font \tenrm; then comes a kern. The next item is an hbox that contains only the letter E; this box has the height, depth, and width of an E, and it has been shifted downward by 2.15277 pt (thereby accounting for the depth of the larger box).

▶ **EXERCISE 11.1**
Why are there two dots in the '..\tenrm E' line here?

Such displays of box contents will be discussed further in Chapters 12 and 17. They are used primarily for diagnostic purposes, when you are trying to figure out exactly what TEX thinks it's doing. The main reason for bringing them up in the present chapter is simply to provide a glimpse of how TEX represents boxes in its guts. A computer program doesn't really move boxes around; it fiddles with lists of representations of boxes.

▶ **EXERCISE 11.2**
By running TEX, figure out how it actually handles italic corrections to characters: How are the corrections represented inside a box?

▶ **EXERCISE 11.3**
The "opposite" of TEX's logo—namely, T E X—is produced by

`\setbox1=\hbox{T\kern+.1667em\raise.5ex\hbox{E}\kern+.125em X}`

What would `\showbox1` show now? (Try to guess, without running the machine.)

▶ **EXERCISE 11.4**
Why do you think the author of TEX didn't make boxes more symmetrical between horizontal and vertical, by allowing reference points to be inside the boundary instead of insisting that the reference point must appear at the left edge of each box?

▶ **EXERCISE 11.5**
Construct a `\demobox` macro for use in writing manuals like this, so that an author can write '`\demobox{Tough exercise.}`' in order to typeset '▮▭▭▯▮ ▭▭▭▭▭▮'.

▶ **EXERCISE 11.6**
Construct a `\frac` macro such that '`\frac1/2`' yields '$1/2$'.

I have several boxes in my memory
in which I will keep them all very safe,
there shall not a one of them be lost.
— IZAAK WALTON, *The Compleat Angler* (1653)

How very little does the amateur, dwelling at home at ease,
comprehend the labours and perils of the author.
— R. L. STEVENSON and L. OSBOURNE, *The Wrong Box* (1889)

12
Glue

But there's more to the story than just boxes: There's also some magic mortar called *glue* that TEX uses to paste boxes together. For example, there is a little space between the lines of text in this manual; it has been calculated so that the baselines of consecutive lines within a paragraph are exactly 12 points apart. And there is space between words too; such space is not an "empty" box, it is part of the glue between boxes. This glue can stretch or shrink so that the right-hand margin of each page comes out looking straight.

When TEX makes a large box from a horizontal or vertical list of smaller boxes, there often is glue between the smaller boxes. Glue has three attributes, namely its natural *space*, its ability to *stretch*, and its ability to *shrink*.

In order to understand how this works, consider the following example of four boxes in a horizontal list separated by three globs of glue:

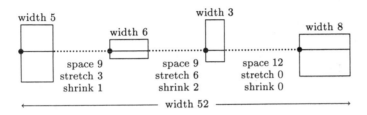

The first glue element has 9 units of space, 3 of stretch, and 1 of shrink; the next one also has 9 units of space, but 6 units of stretch and 2 of shrink; the last one has 12 units of space, but it is unable to stretch or to shrink, so it will remain 12 units of space no matter what.

The total width of boxes and glue in this example, considering only the space components of the glue, is $5 + 9 + 6 + 9 + 3 + 12 + 8 = 52$ units. This is called the *natural width* of the horizontal list; it's the preferred way to paste the boxes together. Suppose, however, that TEX is told to make the horizontal list into a box that is 58 units wide; then the glue has to stretch by 6 units. Well, there are $3 + 6 + 0 = 9$ units of stretchability present, so TEX multiplies each unit of stretchability by 6/9 in order to obtain the extra 6 units needed. The first glob of glue becomes $9 + (6/9) \times 3 = 11$ units wide, the next becomes $9 + (6/9) \times 6 = 13$ units wide, the last remains 12 units wide, and we obtain the desired box looking like this:

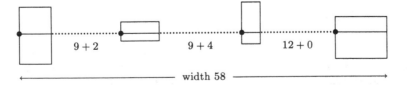

On the other hand, if TEX is supposed to make a box 51 units wide from the given list, it is necessary for the glue to shrink by a total of one unit. There are three units of shrinkability present, so the first glob of glue would shrink by 1/3 and the second by 2/3.

The process of determining glue thickness when a box is being made from a horizontal or vertical list is called *setting the glue*. Once glue has been set, it becomes rigid; it won't stretch or shrink any more, and the resulting box is essentially indecomposable.

Glue will never shrink more than its stated shrinkability. For example, the first glob of glue in our illustration will never be allowed to become narrower than 8 units wide, and TEX will never shrink the given horizontal list to make its total width less than 49 units. But glue is allowed to stretch arbitrarily far, whenever it has a positive stretch component.

▶ **EXERCISE 12.1**
How wide would the glue globs be if the horizontal list in the illustration were to be made 100 units wide?

Once you understand TEX's concept of glue, you may well decide that it was misnamed; real glue doesn't stretch or shrink in such ways, nor does it contribute much space between boxes that it welds together. Another word like "spring" would be much closer to the essential idea, since springs have a natural width, and since different springs compress and expand at different rates under tension. But whenever the author has suggested changing TEX's terminology, numerous people have said that they like the word "glue" in spite of its inappropriateness; so the original name has stuck.

TEX is somewhat reluctant to stretch glue more than the stated stretchability; therefore you can decide how big to make each aspect of the glue by using the following rules: (a) The natural glue space should be the amount of space that looks best. (b) The glue stretch should be the maximum amount of space that can be added to the natural spacing before the layout begins to look bad. (c) The glue shrink should be the maximum amount of space that can be subtracted from the natural spacing before the layout begins to look bad.

In most cases the designer of a book layout will have specified all the kinds of glue that are to be used, so a typist will not need to decide how big any glue attributes should be. For example, users of the plain TEX format of Appendix B can type '\smallskip' when they want a little extra space between paragraphs; a \smallskip turns out to be 3 pt worth of vertical glue that can stretch or shrink by an additional 1 pt. Here is a \smallskip:

Instead of sprinkling various amounts of glue throughout a manuscript, expressing each of them explicitly in terms of points, you will find it much better to explain your intentions more clearly by typing something like '\smallskip' when you want abnormal spacing. The definition of \smallskip can readily be changed later, in case you want such spaces to be smaller or larger. Plain TEX also provides you with '\medskip', which is worth two smallskips, and '\bigskip', which is worth two medskips.

A plain TEX \medskip appears before and after each "dangerous bend" section of this manual, so you have already seen numerous examples of such spacing before you knew what it was called. Vertical glue is created by writing '\vskip⟨glue⟩', where ⟨glue⟩ is any glue specification. The usual way to specify ⟨glue⟩ to TEX is

⟨dimen⟩ plus⟨dimen⟩ minus⟨dimen⟩

where the 'plus⟨dimen⟩' and 'minus⟨dimen⟩' are optional and assumed to be zero if not present; 'plus' introduces the amount of stretchability, 'minus' introduces the amount of shrinkability. For example, Appendix B defines \medskip to be an abbreviation for '\vskip6pt plus2pt minus2pt'. The normal-space component of glue must always be given as an explicit ⟨dimen⟩, even when it is zero.

Horizontal glue is created in the same way, but with \hskip instead of \vskip. For example, plain TEX defines \enskip as an abbreviation for the command '\hskip.5em\relax'; this skips horizontally by one "en," i.e., by exactly half of an em in the current font. There is no stretching or shrinking in an \enskip. The control sequence \relax after '.5em' prevents TEX from thinking that a keyword is present, in case the text following \enskip just happens to begin with 'plus' or 'minus'.

One of the interesting things that happens when glue stretches and shrinks at different rates is that there might be glue with *infinite* stretchability. For example, consider again the four boxes we had at the beginning of this chapter, with the same glue as before except that the glue in the middle can stretch infinitely far. Now the total stretchability is infinite; and when the line has to grow, all of the additional space is put into the middle glue. If, for example, a box of width 58 is desired, the middle glue expands from 9 to 15 units, and the other spacing remains unchanged.

If such infinitely stretchable glue is placed at the left of a row of boxes, the effect is to place them "flush right," i.e., to move them over to the rightmost boundary of the constructed box. And if you take *two* globs of infinitely stretchable glue, putting one at the left and one at the right, the effect is to *center* the list of boxes within a larger box. This in fact is how the \centerline instruction works in plain TEX: It places infinite glue at both ends, then makes a box whose width is the current value of \hsize.

The short story example of Chapter 6 used infinite glue not only for centering, but also in the \vfill instruction at the end; '\vfill' essentially means "skip vertically by zero, but with infinite stretchability." In other words, \vfill fills up the rest of the current page with blank space.

TEX actually recognizes several kinds of infinity, some of which are "more infinite" than others. You can say both \vfil and \vfill; the second is stronger than the first. In other words, if no other infinite stretchability is present, \vfil will expand to fill the remaining space; but if both \vfil and \vfill are present simultaneously, the \vfill effectively prevents \vfil from stretching. You can think of it as if \vfil has one mile of stretchability, while \vfill has a trillion miles.

Besides \vfil and \vfill, TEX has \hfil and \hfill, for stretching indefinitely in the horizontal direction. You can also say \hss or \vss, in order to get glue that is infinitely shrinkable as well as infinitely stretchable. (The name '\hss' stands for "horizontal stretch or shrink"; '\vss' is its vertical counterpart.) Finally, the primitives \hfilneg and \vfilneg will cancel the stretchability of \hfil and \vfil; we shall discuss applications of these curious glues later.

Here are some examples of \hfil, using the \line macro of plain TeX, which creates an hbox whose width is the current \hsize:

```
\line{This text will be flush left.\hfil}
\line{\hfil This text will be flush right.}
\line{\hfil This text will be centered.\hfil}
\line{Some text flush left\hfil and some flush right.}
\line{Alpha\hfil centered between Alpha and Omega\hfil Omega}
\line{Five\hfil words\hfil equally\hfil spaced\hfil out.}
```

▶ **EXERCISE 12.2**
Describe the result of

```
\line{\hfil\hfil What happens now?\hfil}
\line{\hfill\hfil and now?\hfil}
```

▶ **EXERCISE 12.3**
How do the following three macros behave differently?

```
\def\centerlinea#1{\line{\hfil#1\hfil}}
\def\centerlineb#1{\line{\hfill#1\hfill}}
\def\centerlinec#1{\line{\hss#1\hss}}
```

In order to specify such infinities, you are allowed to use the special units 'fil', 'fill', and 'filll' in the ⟨dimen⟩ parts of a stretchability or shrinkability component. For example, \vfil, \vfill, \vss, and \vfilneg are essentially equivalent to the glue specifications

```
\vskip 0pt plus 1fil
\vskip 0pt plus 1fill
\vskip 0pt plus 1fil minus 1fil
\vskip 0pt plus -1fil
```

respectively. It's usually best to stick to the first order infinity (fil) as much as you can, resorting to second order (fill) only when you really need something extremely infinite. Then the ultimate order (filll) is always available as a last resort in emergencies. (TeX does not provide a '\vfilll' primitive, since the use of this highest infinity is not encouraged.)   You can use fractional multiples of infinity like '3.25fil', as long as you stick to fewer than 16384 fil units. TeX actually does its calculations with integer multiples of 2^{-16} fil (or fill or filll); so 0.000007filll turns out to be indistinguishable from 0pt, but 0.00001filll is infinitely greater than 16383.99999fill.

Now here's something important for all TeXnical typists to know: Plain TeX puts extra space at the end of a sentence; furthermore, it automatically increases the stretchability (and decreases the shrinkability) after punctuation marks. The reason is that it's usually better to put more space after punctuation than between two ordinary words, when spreading a line out to reach the desired margins. Consider, for example, the following sentences from a classic kindergarten pre-primer:

```
``Oh, oh!'' cried Baby Sally. Dick and Jane laughed.
```

If TEX sets this at its natural width, all the spaces will be the same, except after the quote and after 'Baby Sally.':

> "Oh, oh!" cried Baby Sally. Dick and Jane laughed.

But if the line needs to be expanded by 5 points, 10 points, 15 points, or more, TEX will set it as

> "Oh, oh!" cried Baby Sally. Dick and Jane laughed.
> "Oh, oh!" cried Baby Sally. Dick and Jane laughed.
> "Oh, oh!" cried Baby Sally. Dick and Jane laughed.
> "Oh, oh!" cried Baby Sally. Dick and Jane laughed.

The glue after the comma stretches at 1.25 times the rate of the glue between adjacent words; the glue after the period and after the ! '' stretches at 3 times the rate. There is no glue between adjacent letters, so individual words will always look the same. If TEX had to shrink this line to its minimum width, the result would be

> "Oh, oh!" cried Baby Sally. Dick and Jane laughed.

The glue after a comma shrinks only 80 percent as much as ordinary inter-word glue, and after a period or exclamation point or question mark it shrinks by only one third as much.

This all makes for nice-looking output, but it unfortunately adds a bit of a burden to your job as a typist, because TEX's rule for determining the end of a sentence *doesn't always work*. The problem is that a period sometimes comes in the middle of a sentence ... like when it is used (as here) to make an "ellipsis" of three dots.

Moreover, if you try to specify '...' by typing three periods in a row, you get '...'—the dots are too close together. One way to handle this is to go into *mathematics* mode, using the \ldots control sequence defined in plain TEX format. For example, if you type

> `Hmmm $\ldots$ I wonder why?`

the result is 'Hmmm ... I wonder why?'. This works because math formulas are exempt from the normal text spacing rules. Chapter 18 has more to say about \ldots and related topics.

Abbreviations present problems too. For example, the short story in Chapter 6 referred to 'Mr. Drofnats'; TEX must be told somehow that the period after 'Mr.' or 'Mrs.' or 'Ms.' or 'Prof.' or 'Dr.' or 'Rt. Hon.', etc., doesn't count as a sentence-ending full stop.

We avoided that embarrassment in Chapter 6 by typing 'Mr.~Drofnats'; the "tie" mark ~ tells plain TEX to insert a normal space, and to refrain from breaking between lines at that space. Another way to get TEX to put out a normal space is to type '\␣' (control space); e.g., 'Mr.\ Drofnats' would be almost the same as 'Mr.~Drofnats', except that a line might end after the 'Mr.'.

The tie mark is best for abbreviations within a name, and after several other common abbreviations like 'Fig.' and 'cf.' and 'vs.' and 'resp.'; you will find that it's easy to train yourself to type 'cf.~Fig.~5'. In fact, it's usually wise to type ~ (instead of a space) just after a common abbreviation that occurs in the middle of a sentence. Manuals of style will tell you that the abbreviations 'e.g.' and 'i.e.' should always be followed by commas, never by spaces, so those particular cases shouldn't need any special treatment.

The only remaining abbreviations that arise with significant frequency occur in bibliographic references; control spaces are appropriate here. If, for example, you are typing a manuscript that refers to 'Proc. Amer. Math. Soc.', you should say

```
Proc.\ Amer.\ Math.\ Soc.
```

Granted that this input looks a bit ugly, it makes the output look right. It's one of the things we occasionally must do when dealing with a computer that tries to be smart.

▸**EXERCISE 12.4**
Explain how to type the following sentence: "Mr. & Mrs. User were married by Rev. Drofnats, who preached on Matt. 19:3–9."

▸**EXERCISE 12.5**
Put the following bibliographic reference into plain TEX language: Donald E. Knuth, "Mathematical typography," *Bull. Amer. Math. Soc.* **1** (1979), 337–372.

On the other hand, if you don't care about such refinements of spacing you can tell plain TEX to make all spaces the same, regardless of punctuation marks, by simply typing '\frenchspacing' at the beginning of your manuscript. French spacing looks like this:

"Oh, oh!" cried Baby Sally. Dick and Jane laughed.

You can also shift back and forth between the two styles, either by saying '\nonfrenchspacing' to establish sophisticated spacing, or by making your use of \frenchspacing local to some group. For example, you might want to use French spacing only when typing the bibliography of some document.

TEX doesn't consider a period or question mark or exclamation point to be the end of a sentence if the preceding character is an uppercase letter, since TEX assumes that such uppercase letters are most likely somebody's initials. Thus, for example, the '\' is unnecessary after the 'I.' in 'Dr.~Livingstone~I.\ Presume'; that particular period is not assumed to be a full stop.

▸**EXERCISE 12.6**
What can you do to make TEX recognize the ends of sentences that do end with uppercase letters (e.g., '... launched by NASA.' or 'Did I?' or '... see Appendix A.')?

You can see the glue that TeX puts between words by looking at the contents of hboxes in the internal diagnostic format that we discussed briefly in Chapter 11. For example, Baby Sally's exclamation begins as follows, after TeX has digested it and put it into a box, assuming \nonfrenchspacing:

```
.\tenrm \ (ligature '')
.\tenrm O
.\tenrm h
.\tenrm ,
.\glue 3.33333 plus 2.08331 minus 0.88889
.\tenrm o
.\tenrm h
.\tenrm !
.\tenrm " (ligature '')
.\glue 4.44444 plus 4.99997 minus 0.37036
.\tenrm c
.\tenrm r
.\tenrm i
.\tenrm e
.\tenrm d
.\glue 3.33333 plus 1.66666 minus 1.11111
.\tenrm B
.\tenrm a
.\tenrm b
.\kern-0.27779
.\tenrm y
.\glue 3.33333 plus 1.66666 minus 1.11111
.\tenrm S
.\tenrm a
.\tenrm l
.\tenrm l
.\tenrm y
.\kern-0.83334
.\tenrm .
.\glue 4.44444 plus 4.99997 minus 0.37036
```

The normal interword glue in font \tenrm is 3.33333 pt, plus 1.66666 pt of stretchability, minus 1.11111 pt of shrinkability. Notice that the interword \glue in this list stretches more, and shrinks less, after the punctuation marks; and the natural space is in fact larger at the end of each sentence. This example also shows several other things that TeX does while it processes the sample line of text: It converts '' and '' into single characters, i.e., ligatures; and it inserts small kerns in two places to improve the spacing. A \kern is similar to glue, but it is not the same, because kerns cannot stretch or shrink; furthermore, TeX will never break a line at a kern, unless that kern is immediately followed by glue.

You may be wondering what TeX's rules for interword glue really are, exactly. For example, how did TeX remember the effect of Baby Sally's exclamation point, when quotation marks intervened before the next space? The details are slightly tricky, but not incomprehensible. When TEX is processing a horizontal list of boxes and glue, it keeps track of a positive integer called the current "space factor." The space factor is normally 1000, which means that the interword glue should not be modified. If the space factor f is different from 1000, the interword glue is computed as follows: Take the normal space glue for the current font, and add the extra space if $f \geq 2000$. (Each font specifies a normal space, normal stretch, normal shrink, and extra space; for example, these quantities are 3.33333 pt, 1.66666 pt, 1.11111 pt, and 1.11111 pt, respectively, in cmr10. We'll discuss such font parameters in greater detail later.) Then the stretch component is multiplied by $f/1000$, while the shrink component is multiplied by $1000/f$.

However, TEX has two parameters \spaceskip and \xspaceskip that allow you to override the normal spacing of the current font. If $f \geq 2000$ and if \xspaceskip is nonzero, the \xspaceskip glue is used for an interword space. Otherwise if \spaceskip is nonzero, the \spaceskip glue is used, with stretch and shrink components multiplied by $f/1000$ and $1000/f$. For example, the \raggedright macro of plain TEX uses \spaceskip and \xspaceskip to suppress all stretching and shrinking of interword spaces.

The space factor f is 1000 at the beginning of a horizontal list, and it is set to 1000 just after a non-character box or a math formula has been put onto the current horizontal list. You can say '\spacefactor=⟨number⟩' to assign any particular value to the space factor; but ordinarily, f gets set to a number other than 1000 only when a simple character box goes on the list. Each character has a space factor code, and when a character whose space factor code is g enters the current list the normal procedure is simply to assign g as the new space factor. However, if g is zero, f is not changed; and if $f < 1000 < g$, the space factor is set to 1000. (In other words, f doesn't jump from a value less than 1000 to a value greater than 1000 in a single step.) The maximum space factor is 32767 (which is much higher than anybody would ever want to use).

When INITEX creates a brand new TEX, all characters have a space factor code of 1000, except that the uppercase letters 'A' through 'Z' have code 999. (This slight difference is what makes punctuation act differently after an uppercase letter; do you see why?) Plain TEX redefines a few of these codes using the \sfcode primitive, which is similar to \catcode (see Appendix B); for example, the instructions

    \sfcode'(=0   \sfcode'.=3000

make right parentheses "transparent" to the space factor, while tripling the stretchability after periods. The \frenchspacing operation resets \sfcode'. to 1000.

When ligatures are formed, or when a special character is specified via \char, the space factor code is computed from the individual characters that generated the ligature. For example, plain TEX sets the space factor code for single-right-quote to zero, so that the effects of punctuation will be propagated. Two adjacent characters '' combine to form a ligature that is in character position '042; but the space factor code of this double-right-quote ligature is never examined by TEX, so plain TEX does not assign any value to \sfcode'042.

▶ **EXERCISE 12.7**
What are the space factors after each token of the Dick-and-Jane example?

Here's the way TeX goes about setting the glue when an hbox is being wrapped up: The natural width, x, of the box contents is determined by adding up the widths of the boxes and kerns inside, together with the natural widths of all the glue inside. Furthermore the total amount of glue stretchability and shrinkability in the box is computed; let's say that there's a total of $y_0 + y_1$ fil $+ y_2$ fill $+ y_3$ filll available for stretching and $z_0 + z_1$ fil $+ z_2$ fill $+ z_3$ filll available for shrinking. Now the natural width x is compared to the desired width w. If $x = w$, all glue gets its natural width. Otherwise the glue will be modified, by computing a "glue set ratio" r and a "glue set order" i in the following way: (a) If $x < w$, TeX attempts to stretch the contents of the box; the glue order is the highest subscript i such that y_i is nonzero, and the glue ratio is $r = (w - x)/y_i$. (If $y_0 = y_1 = y_2 = y_3 = 0$, there's no stretchability; both i and r are set to zero.) (b) If $x > w$, TeX attempts to shrink the contents of the box in a similar way; the glue order is the highest subscript i such that $z_i \neq 0$, and the glue ratio is normally $r = (x - w)/z_i$. However, r is set to 1.0 in the case $i = 0$ and $x - w > z_0$, because the maximum shrinkability must not be exceeded. (c) Finally, every glob of glue in the horizontal list being boxed is modified. Suppose the glue has natural width u, stretchability y, and shrinkability z, where y is a jth order infinity and z is a kth order infinity. Then if $x < w$ (stretching), this glue takes the new width $u + ry$ if $j = i$; it keeps its natural width u if $j \neq i$. If $x > w$ (shrinking), this glue takes the new width $u - rz$ if $k = i$; it keeps its natural width u if $k \neq i$. Notice that stretching or shrinking occurs only when the glue has the highest order of infinity that doesn't cancel out.

TeX will construct an hbox that has a given width w if you issue the command '\hbox to ⟨dimen⟩{⟨contents of box⟩}', where w is the value of the ⟨dimen⟩. For example, the \line macro discussed earlier in this chapter is simply an abbreviation for '\hbox to\hsize'. TeX also allows you to specify the exact amount of stretching or shrinking; the command '\hbox spread⟨dimen⟩{⟨contents of box⟩}' creates a box whose width w is a given amount more than the natural width of the contents. For example, one of the boxes displayed earlier in this chapter was generated by

```
\hbox spread 5pt{``Oh, oh!'' ... laughed.}
```

In the simplest case, when you just want a box to have its natural width, you don't have to write '\hbox spread 0pt'; you can simply say '\hbox{⟨contents of box⟩}'.

The baseline of a constructed hbox is the common baseline of the boxes inside. (More precisely, it's the common baseline that they would share if they weren't raised or lowered.) The height and depth of a constructed hbox are determined by the maximum distances by which the interior boxes reach above and below the baseline, respectively. The result of \hbox never has negative height or negative depth, but the width can be negative.

▸ **EXERCISE 12.8**
Assume that \box1 is 1 pt high, 1 pt deep, and 1 pt wide; \box2 is 2 pt high, 2 pt deep, and 2 pt wide. A third box is formed by saying

```
\setbox3=\hbox to3pt{\hfil\lower3pt\box1\hskip-3pt plus3fil\box2}
```

What are the height, depth, and width of \box3? Describe the position of the reference points of boxes 1 and 2 with respect to the reference point of box 3.

The process of setting glue for vboxes is similar to that for hboxes; but before we study the \vbox operation, we need to discuss how TeX stacks boxes up vertically so that their baselines tend to be a fixed distance apart. The boxes in a horizontal list often touch each other, but it's usually wrong to do this in a vertical list; imagine how awful a page would look if its lines of type were brought closer together whenever they didn't contain tall letters, or whenever they didn't contain any letters that descended below the baseline.

TeX's solution to this problem involves three primitives called \baselineskip, \lineskip, and \lineskiplimit. A format designer chooses values of these three quantities by writing

\baselineskip=⟨glue⟩
\lineskip=⟨glue⟩
\lineskiplimit=⟨dimen⟩

and the interpretation is essentially this: Whenever a box is added to a vertical list, TeX inserts "interline glue" intended to make the distance between the baseline of the new box and the baseline of the previous box exactly equal to the value of \baselineskip. But if the interline glue calculated by this rule would cause the top edge of the new box to be closer than \lineskiplimit to the bottom edge of the previous box, then \lineskip is used as the interline glue. In other words, the distance between adjacent baselines will be the \baselineskip setting, unless that would bring the boxes too close together; the \lineskip glue will separate adjacent boxes in the latter case.

The rules for interline glue in the previous paragraph are carried out without regard to other kinds of glue that might be present; all vertical spacing due to explicit appearances of \vskip and \kern acts independently of the interline glue. Thus, for example, a \smallskip between two lines always makes their baselines further apart than usual, by the amount of a \smallskip; it does not affect the decision about whether \lineskip glue is used between those lines.

For example, let's suppose that \baselineskip=12pt plus 2pt, \lineskip= 3pt minus 1pt, and \lineskiplimit=2pt. (These values aren't particularly useful; they have simply been chosen to illustrate the rules.) Suppose further that a box whose depth is 3 pt was most recently added to the current vertical list; we are about to add a new box whose height is h. If $h = 5$ pt, the interline glue will be 4 pt plus 2 pt, since this will make the baselines 12 pt plus 2 pt apart when we add h and the previous depth to the interline glue. But if $h = 8$ pt, the interline glue will be 3 pt minus 1 pt, since \lineskip will be chosen in order to keep from violating the given \lineskiplimit when stretching and shrinking are ignored.

When you are typesetting a document that spans several pages, it's generally best to define the \baselineskip so that it cannot stretch or shrink, because this will give more uniformity to the pages. A small variation in the distance between baselines—say only half a point—can make a substantial difference in the appearance of the type, since it significantly affects the proportion of white to black. On the other hand, if you are preparing a one-page document, you might want to give the baselineskip some stretchability, so that TeX will help you fit the copy on the page.

▶ **EXERCISE 12.9**
What settings of \baselineskip, \lineskip, and \lineskiplimit will cause

the interline glue to be a "continuous" function of the next box height (i.e., the interline glue will never change a lot when the box height changes only a little)?

A study of TeX's internal box-and-glue representation should help to firm up some of these ideas. Here is an excerpt from the vertical list that TeX constructed when it was typesetting this very paragraph:

```
\glue 6.0 plus 2.0 minus 2.0
\glue(\parskip) 0.0 plus 1.0
\glue(\baselineskip) 1.25
\hbox(7.5+1.93748)x312.0, glue set 0.80154, shifted 36.0 []
\penalty 10000
\glue(\baselineskip) 2.81252
\hbox(6.25+1.93748)x312.0, glue set 0.5816, shifted 36.0 []
\penalty 50
\glue(\baselineskip) 2.81252
\hbox(6.25+1.75)x348.0, glue set 116.70227fil []
\penalty 10000
\glue(\abovedisplayskip) 6.0 plus 3.0 minus 1.0
\glue(\lineskip) 1.0
\hbox(149.25+0.74998)x348.0 []
```

The first `\glue` in this example is the `\medskip` that precedes each dangerous-bend paragraph. Then comes the `\parskip` glue, which is automatically supplied before the first line of a new paragraph. Then comes some interline glue of 1.25 pt; it was calculated to make a total of 11 pt when the height of the next box (7.5 pt) and the depth of the previous box were added. (The previous box is not shown—it's the bottom line of exercise 12.9—but we can deduce that its depth was 2.25 pt.) The `\hbox` that follows is the first line of this paragraph; it has been shifted right 36 pt because of hanging indentation. The glue set ratio for this hbox is 0.80154; i.e., the glue inside is stretched by 80.154% of its stretchability. (In the case of shrinking, the ratio following '`glue set`' would have been preceded by '- '; hence we know that stretching is involved here.) TeX has put '`[]`' at the end of each hbox line to indicate that there's something in the box that isn't shown. (The box contents would have been displayed completely, if `\showboxdepth` had been set higher.) The `\penalty` indications are used to discourage bad breaks between pages, as we will see later. The third hbox has a glue ratio of 116.70227, which applies to first-order-infinite stretching (i.e., fil); this results from an `\hfil` that was implicitly inserted just before the displayed material, to fill up the third line of the paragraph. Finally the big hbox whose height is 149.25 pt causes `\lineskip` to be the interline glue. This large box contains the individual lines of typewriter type that are displayed; they have been packaged into a single box so that they cannot be split between pages. Careful study of this example will teach you a lot about TeX's inner workings.

Exception: No interline glue is inserted before or after a rule box. You can also inhibit interline glue by saying `\nointerlineskip` between boxes.

TeX's implementation of interline glue involves another primitive quantity called `\prevdepth`, which usually contains the depth of the most recent box on the current vertical list. However, `\prevdepth` is set to the sentinel value −1000 pt at the beginning of a vertical list, or just after a rule box; this serves to suppress the next interline glue. The user can change the value of \prevdepth at any time when building a vertical list; thus, for example, the \nointerlineskip macro of Appendix B simply expands to '\prevdepth=-1000pt'.

Here are the exact rules by which TeX calculates the interline glue between boxes: Assume that a new box of height h (not a rule box) is about to be appended to the bottom of the current vertical list, and let \prevdepth $= p$, \lineskiplimit $= l$, \baselineskip $= (b$ plus y minus $z)$. If $p \leq -1000$ pt, no interline glue is added. Otherwise if $b - p - h \geq l$, the interline glue '$(b - p - h)$ plus y minus z' will be appended just above the new box. Otherwise the \lineskip glue will be appended. Finally, \prevdepth is set to the depth of the new box.

▶ **EXERCISE 12.10**
Mr. B. L. User had an application in which he wanted to put a number of boxes together in a vertical list, with no space between them. He didn't want to say \nointerlineskip after each box; so he decided to set \baselineskip, \lineskip, and \lineskiplimit all equal to 0pt. Did this work?

The vertical analog of \hbox is \vbox, and TeX will obey the commands '\vbox to⟨dimen⟩' and '\vbox spread⟨dimen⟩' in about the way you would expect, by analogy with the horizontal case. However, there's a slight complication because boxes have both height and depth in the vertical direction, while they have only width in the horizontal direction. The dimension in a \vbox command refers to the final height of the vbox, so that, for example, '\vbox to 50pt{...}' produces a box that is 50 pt high; this is appropriate because everything that can stretch or shrink inside a vbox appears in the part that contributes to the height, while the depth is unaffected by glue setting.

The depth of a constructed \vbox is best thought of as the depth of the bottom box inside. Thus, a vbox is conceptually built by taking a bunch of boxes and arranging them so that their reference points are lined up vertically; then the reference point of the lowest box is taken as the reference point of the whole, and the glue is set so that the final height has some desired value.

However, this description of vboxes glosses over some technicalities that come up when you consider unusual cases. For example, TeX allows you to shift boxes in a vertical list to the right or to the left by saying '\moveright⟨dimen⟩⟨box⟩' or '\moveleft⟨dimen⟩⟨box⟩'; this is like the ability to \raise or \lower boxes in a horizontal list, and it implies that the reference points inside a vbox need not always lie in a vertical line. Furthermore, it is necessary to guard against boxes that have too much depth, lest they extend too far into the bottom margin of a page; and later chapters will point out that vertical lists can contain other things like penalties and marks, in addition to boxes and glue.

Therefore, the actual rules for the depth of a constructed vbox are somewhat TeXnical. Here they are: Given a vertical list that is being wrapped up via \vbox, the problem is to determine its natural depth. (1) If the vertical list contains no boxes, the depth is zero. (2) If there's at least one box, but if the final box is followed by kerning or glue, possibly with intervening penalties or other things, the depth is zero. (3) If there's at least one box, and if the final box is not followed by kerning or glue, the depth is the depth of that box. (4) However, if the depth computed by rules (1), (2), or (3) exceeds \boxmaxdepth, the depth will be the current value of \boxmaxdepth. (Plain TeX sets \boxmaxdepth to the largest possible dimension; therefore rule (4) won't apply unless you specify a smaller value. When rule (4) does decrease the depth, TeX adds the excess depth to the box's natural height, essentially moving the reference point down until the depth has been reduced to the stated maximum.)

The glue is set in a vbox just as in an hbox, by determining a glue set ratio and a glue set order, based on the difference between the natural height x and the desired height w, and based on the amounts of stretchability and shrinkability that happen to be present.

The width of a computed \vbox is the maximum distance by which an enclosed box extends to the right of the reference point, taking possible shifting into account. This width is always nonnegative.

▶ **EXERCISE 12.11**
Assume that \box1 is 1 pt high, 1 pt deep, and 1 pt wide; \box2 is 2 pt high, 2 pt deep, and 2 pt wide; the baselineskip, lineskip, and lineskiplimit are all zero; and the \boxmaxdepth is very large. A third box is formed by saying

```
\setbox3=\vbox to3pt{\moveright3pt\box1\vskip-3pt plus3fil\box2}
```

What are the height, depth, and width of \box3? Describe the position of the reference points of boxes 1 and 2 with respect to the reference point of box 3.

▶ **EXERCISE 12.12**
Under the assumptions of the previous exercise, but with \baselineskip=9pt minus3fil, describe \box4 after

```
\setbox4=\vbox to4pt{\vss\box1\moveleft4pt\box2\vss}
```

▶ **EXERCISE 12.13**
Solve the previous problem but with \boxmaxdepth=-4pt.

We have observed that \vbox combines a bunch of boxes into a larger box that has the same baseline as the bottom box inside. TeX has another operation called \vtop, which gives you a box like \vbox but with the same baseline as the top box inside. For example,

```
\hbox{Here are \vtop{\hbox{two lines}\hbox{of text.}}}
```

produces

> Here are two lines
>   of text.

You can say '\vtop to⟨dimen⟩' and '\vtop spread⟨dimen⟩' just as with \vbox, but you should realize what such a construction means. TeX implements \vtop as follows: (1) First a vertical box is formed as if \vtop had been \vbox, using all of the rules for \vbox as given above. (2) The final height x is defined to be zero unless the very first item inside the new vbox is a box; in the latter case, x is the height of that box. (3) Let h and d be the height and depth of the vbox in step (1). TeX completes the \vtop by moving the reference point up or down, if necessary, so that the box has height x and depth $h + d - x$.

▷ **EXERCISE 12.14**
Describe the empty boxes that you get from '\vbox to⟨dimen⟩{}' and '\vtop to⟨dimen⟩{}'. What are their heights, depths, and widths?

▷ **EXERCISE 12.15**
Define a macro \nullbox#1#2#3 that produces a box whose height, depth, and width are given by the three parameters. The box should contain nothing that will show up in print.

The \vbox operation tends to produce boxes with large height and small depth, while \vtop tends to produce small height and large depth. If you're trying to make a vertical list out of big vboxes, however, you may not be satisfied with either \vbox or \vtop; you might well wish that a box had two reference points simultaneously, one for the top and one for the bottom. If such a dual-reference-point scheme were in use, one could define interline glue based on the distance between the lower reference point of one box and the upper reference point of its successor in a vertical list. But alas, TEX gives you only one reference point per box.

There's a way out of this dilemma, using an important idea called a "strut." Plain TEX defines \strut to be an invisible box of width zero that extends just enough above and below the baseline so that you would need no interline glue at all if every line contained a strut.   (Baselines are 12 pt apart in plain TEX; it turns out that \strut is a vertical rule, 8.5 pt high and 3.5 pt deep and 0 pt wide.)   If you contrive to put a strut on the top line and another on the bottom line, inside your large vboxes, then it's possible to obtain the correct spacing in a larger assembly by simply letting the boxes butt together. For example, the \footnote macro in Appendix B puts struts at the beginning and end of every footnote, so that the spacing will be right when several footnotes occur together at the bottom of some page.

If you understand boxes and glue, you're ready to learn the \rlap and \llap macros of plain TEX; these names are abbreviations for "right overlap" and "left overlap." Saying '\rlap{⟨something⟩}' is like typesetting ⟨something⟩ and then backing up as if you hadn't typeset anything. More precisely, '\rlap{⟨something⟩}' creates a box of width zero, with '⟨something⟩' appearing just at the right of that box (but not taking up any space). The \llap macro is similar, but it does the backspacing first; in other words, '\llap{⟨something⟩}' creates a box of width zero, with '⟨something⟩' extending just to the left of that box. Using typewriter type, for example, you can typeset '≠' by saying either '\rlap/=' or '/\llap='. It's possible to put text into the left margin using \llap, or into the right margin using \rlap, because TEX does not insist that the contents of a box must be strictly confined within that box's boundaries.

The interesting thing about \rlap and \llap is that they can be done so simply with infinite glue. One way to define \rlap would be

```
\def\rlap#1{{\setbox0=\hbox{#1}\copy0\kern-\wd0}}
```

but there's no need to do such a lengthy computation. The actual definition in Appendix B is much more elegant, namely,

```
\def\rlap#1{\hbox to 0pt{#1\hss}}
```

and it's worth pondering why this works. Suppose, for example, that you're doing `\rlap{g}` where the letter 'g' is 5 pt wide. Since `\rlap` makes an hbox of width 0 pt, the glue represented by `\hss` must shrink by 5 pt. Well, that glue has 0 pt as its natural width, but it has infinite shrinkability, so it can easily shrink to −5 pt; and '`\hskip-5pt`' is exactly what `\rlap` wants in this case.

 ▶ **EXERCISE 12.16**
Guess the definition of `\llap`, without peeking at Appendices A or B.

 ▶ **EXERCISE 12.17**
(This is a sequel to exercise 12.2, but it's trickier.) Describe the result of

`\line{\hfil A puzzle.\hfilneg}`

There was things which he stretched,
but mainly he told the truth.
— MARK TWAIN, *Huckleberry Finn* (1884)

Every shape exists only because of the space around it.
... Hence there is a 'right' position for every shape in every situation.
If we succeed in finding that position, we have done our job.
— JAN TSCHICHOLD, *Typographische Gestaltung* (1935)

13

Modes

Just as people get into different moods, TeX gets into different "modes." (Except that TeX is more predictable than people.) There are six modes:

- Vertical mode. [Building the main vertical list, from which the pages of output are derived.]
- Internal vertical mode. [Building a vertical list for a vbox.]
- Horizontal mode. [Building a horizontal list for a paragraph.]
- Restricted horizontal mode. [Building a horizontal list for an hbox.]
- Math mode. [Building a mathematical formula to be placed in a horizontal list.]
- Display math mode. [Building a mathematical formula to be placed on a line by itself, temporarily interrupting the current paragraph.]

In simple situations, you don't need to be aware of what mode TeX is in, because the computer just does the right thing. But when you get an error message that says '! You can't do such-and-such in restricted horizontal mode', a knowledge of modes helps to explain why TeX thinks you goofed.

Basically TeX is in one of the vertical modes when it is preparing a list of boxes and glue that will be placed vertically above and below one another on the page; it's in one of the horizontal modes when it is preparing a list of boxes and glue that will be strung out horizontally next to each other with baselines aligned; and it's in one of the math modes when it is reading a formula.

A play-by-play account of a typical TeX job should make the mode idea clear: At the beginning, TeX is in vertical mode, ready to construct pages. If you specify glue or a box when TeX is in vertical mode, the glue or the box gets placed on the current page below what has already been specified. For example, the \vskip instructions in the sample run we discussed in Chapter 6 contributed vertical glue to the page; and the \hrule instructions contributed horizontal rules at the top and bottom of the story. The \centerline commands also produced boxes that were included in the main vertical list; but those boxes required a bit more work than the rule boxes: TeX was in vertical mode when it encountered '\centerline{\bf A SHORT STORY}', and it went temporarily into restricted horizontal mode while processing the words 'A SHORT STORY'; then the digestive process returned to vertical mode, after setting the glue in the \centerline box.

Continuing with the example of Chapter 6, TeX switched into horizontal mode as soon as it read the 'O' of 'Once upon a time'. Horizontal mode is the mode for making paragraphs. The entire paragraph (lines 7 to 11 of the story file) was input in horizontal mode; then the text was divided into output lines of the appropriate width, those lines were put in boxes and appended to the page (with appropriate interline glue between them), and TeX was back in vertical mode. The 'M' on line 12 started up horizontal mode again.

When TeX is in vertical mode or internal vertical mode, the first token of a new paragraph changes the mode to horizontal for the duration of a paragraph.

In other words, things that do not have a vertical orientation cause the mode to switch automatically from vertical to horizontal. This occurs when you type any character, or \char or \accent or \hskip or \␣ or \vrule or math shift ($); TeX inserts the current paragraph indentation and rereads the horizontal token as if it had occurred in horizontal mode.

You can also tell TeX explicitly to go into horizontal mode, instead of relying on such implicit mode-switching, by saying '\indent' or '\noindent'. For example, if line 7 of the **story** file in Chapter 6 had begun

```
\indent Once upon a time, ...
```

the same output would have been obtained, because '\indent' would have instructed TeX to begin the paragraph. And if that line had begun with

```
\noindent Once upon a time, ...
```

the first paragraph of the story would not have been indented. The \noindent command simply tells TeX to enter horizontal mode if the current mode is vertical or internal vertical; \indent is similar, but it also creates an empty box whose width is the current value of \parindent, and it puts this empty box into the current horizontal list. Plain TeX sets \parindent=20pt. If you say \indent\indent, you get double indentation; if you say \noindent\noindent, the second \noindent does nothing.

▶ **EXERCISE 13.1**
If you say '\hbox{...}' in horizontal mode, TeX will construct the specified box and it will contribute the result to the current paragraph. Similarly, if you say '\hbox{...}' in vertical mode, TeX will construct a box and contribute it to the current page. What can you do if you want to begin a paragraph with an \hbox?

When handling simple manuscripts, TeX spends almost all of its time in horizontal mode (making paragraphs), with brief excursions into vertical mode (between paragraphs). A paragraph is completed when you type \par or when your manuscript has a blank line, since a blank line is converted to \par by the reading rules of Chapter 8. A paragraph also ends when you type certain things that are incompatible with horizontal mode. For example, the command '\vskip 1in' on line 16 of Chapter 6's **story** file was enough to terminate the paragraph about '...beautiful documents.'; no \par was necessary, since \vskip introduced vertical glue that couldn't belong to the paragraph.

If a begin-math token ($) appears in horizontal mode, TeX plunges into math mode and processes the formula up until the closing '$', then appends the text of this formula to the current paragraph and returns to horizontal mode. Thus, in the "I wonder why?" example of Chapter 12, TeX went into math mode temporarily while processing \ldots, treating the dots as a formula.

However, if two consecutive begin-math tokens appear in a paragraph ($$), TeX interrupts the paragraph where it is, contributes the paragraph-so-far to the enclosing vertical list, then processes a math formula in display math mode, then contributes this formula to the enclosing list, then returns to horizontal mode for more of the paragraph. (The formula to be displayed should end with '$$'.) For example, suppose you type

```
the number $$\pi \approx 3.1415926536$$ is important.
```

TEX goes into display math mode between the $$'s, and the output you get
states that the number

$$\pi \approx 3.1415926536$$

is important.

TEX ignores blank spaces and blank lines (or \par commands) when it's
in vertical or internal vertical mode, so you need not worry that such things
might change the mode or affect a printed document. A control space (\␣) will,
however, be regarded as the beginning of a paragraph; the paragraph will start
with a blank space after the indentation.

At the end of a TEX manuscript it's usually best to finish everything
off by typing '\bye', which is plain TEX's abbreviation for '\vfill\eject\end'.
The '\vfill' gets TEX into vertical mode and inserts enough space to fill up the
last page; '\eject' outputs that last page; and '\end' sends the computer into
its endgame routine.

⊘ TEX gets into internal vertical mode when you ask it to construct something
from a vertical list of boxes (using \vbox or \vtop or \vcenter or \valign
or \vadjust or \insert). It gets into restricted horizontal mode when you ask it to
construct something from a horizontal list of boxes (using \hbox or \halign). Box
construction is discussed in Chapters 12 and 21. We will see later that there is very
little difference between internal vertical mode and ordinary vertical mode, and very
little difference between restricted horizontal mode and ordinary horizontal mode; but
they aren't quite identical, because they have different goals.

⊘ Whenever TEX looks at a token of input to decide what should be done next,
the current mode has a potential influence on what that token means. For
example, \kern specifies vertical spacing in vertical mode, but it specifies horizontal
spacing in horizontal mode; a math shift character like '$' causes entry to math mode
from horizontal mode, but it causes exit from math mode when it occurs in math mode;
two consecutive math shifts ($$) appearing in horizontal mode will initiate display math
mode, but in restricted horizontal mode they simply denote an empty math formula.
TEX uses the fact that some operations are inappropriate in certain modes to help you
recover from errors that might have crept into your manuscript. Chapters 24 to 26
explain exactly what happens to every possible token in every possible mode.

⊘ TEX often interrupts its work in one mode to do some task in another mode,
after which the original mode is resumed again. For example, you can say
'\hbox{' in any mode; when TEX digests this, it suspends whatever else it was doing
and enters restricted horizontal mode. The matching '}' will eventually cause the hbox
to be completed, whereupon the postponed task will be taken up anew. In this sense
TEX can be in many modes simultaneously, but only the innermost mode influences the
calculations at any time; the other modes have been pushed out of TEX's consciousness.

One way to become familiar with TeX's modes is to consider the following curious test file called `modes.tex`, which exercises all the modes at once:

```
1 \tracingcommands=1
2 \hbox{
3 $
4 \vbox{
5 \noindent$$
6 x\showlists
7 $$}$}\bye
```

The first line of `modes.tex` tells TeX to log every command it receives; TeX will produce diagnostic data whenever \tracingcommands is positive. Indeed, if you run TeX on `modes.tex` you will get a `modes.log` file that includes the following information:

```
{vertical mode: \hbox}
{restricted horizontal mode: blank space}
{math shift character $}
{math mode: blank space}
{\vbox}
{internal vertical mode: blank space}
{\noindent}
{horizontal mode: math shift character $}
{display math mode: blank space}
{the letter x}
```

The meaning is that TeX first saw an \hbox token in vertical mode; this caused it to go ahead and read the '{' behind the scenes. Then TeX entered restricted horizontal mode, and saw the blank space token that resulted from the end of line 2 in the file. Then it saw a math shift character token (still in restricted horizontal mode), which caused a shift to math mode; another blank space came through. Then \vbox inaugurated internal vertical mode, and \noindent instituted horizontal mode within that; two subsequent $ signs led to display math mode. (Only the first $ was shown by \tracingcommands, because that one caused TeX to look ahead for another.)

The next thing in `modes.log` after the output above is '{\showlists}'. This is another handy diagnostic command that you can use to find out things that TeX ordinarily keeps to itself; it causes TeX to display the lists that are being worked on, in the current mode and in all enclosing modes where the work has been suspended:

```
### display math mode entered at line 5
\mathord
.\fam1 x
### internal vertical mode entered at line 4
prevdepth ignored
### math mode entered at line 3
### restricted horizontal mode entered at line 2
\glue 3.33333 plus 1.66666 minus 1.11111
spacefactor 1000
### vertical mode entered at line 0
prevdepth ignored
```

In this case the lists represent five levels of activity, all present at the end of line 6 of
`modes.tex`. The current mode is shown first, namely, display math mode, which began
on line 5. The current math list contains one "mathord" object, consisting of the
letter x in family 1. (Have patience and you will understand what that means, when
you learn about TeX's math formulas.) Outside of display math mode comes internal
vertical mode, to which TeX will return when the paragraph containing the displayed
formula is complete. The vertical list on that level is empty; 'prevdepth ignored'
means that `\prevdepth` has a value ≤ -1000 pt, so that the next interline glue will be
omitted (cf. Chapter 12). The math mode outside of this internal vertical mode has
an empty list, likewise, but the restricted horizontal mode enclosing the math mode
contains some glue. Finally, we see the main vertical mode that encloses everything;
this mode was 'entered at line 0', i.e., before the file `modes.tex` was input; nothing
has been contributed so far to the vertical list on this outermost level.

▶ **EXERCISE 13.2**
Why is there glue in one of these lists but not in the others?

▶ **EXERCISE 13.3**
After this output of `\showlists`, the `modes.log` file contains further output
from `\tracingcommands`. In fact, the next two lines of that file are

    {math shift character $}
    {horizontal mode: end-group character }}

because the '$$' on line 7 finishes the displayed formula, and this resumes horizontal
mode for the paragraph that was interrupted. What do you think are the next three
lines of `modes.log`?

▶ **EXERCISE 13.4**
Suppose TeX has generated a document without ever leaving vertical mode.
What can you say about that document?

▶ **EXERCISE 13.5**
Some of TeX's modes cannot immediately enclose other modes; for example,
display math mode is never directly enclosed by horizontal mode, even though displays
occur within paragraphs, because an interrupted paragraph-so-far of horizontal mode is
always completed and removed from TeX's memory before the processing of a displayed
formula begins. Give a complete characterization of all pairs of consecutive modes that
can occur in the output of `\showlists`.

Every mode of life has its conveniences.
— SAMUEL JOHNSON, *The Idler* (1758)

[Hindu musicians] have eighty-four modes,
of which thirty-six are in general use,
and each of which, it appears, has a peculiar expression,
and the power of moving some particular sentiment or affection.
— MOUNTSTUART ELPHINSTONE, *History of India* (1841)

14

How TeX Breaks Paragraphs into Lines

One of a typesetting system's chief duties is to take a long sequence of words and to break it up into individual lines of the appropriate size. For example, every paragraph of this manual has been broken into lines that are 29 picas wide, but the author didn't have to worry about such details when he composed the manuscript. TₑX chooses breakpoints in an interesting way that considers each paragraph in its entirety; the closing words of a paragraph can actually influence the appearance of the first line. As a result, the spacing between words is as uniform as possible, and the computer is able to reduce the number of times that words must be hyphenated or formulas must be split between lines.

The experiments of Chapter 6 have already illustrated the general ideas: We discussed the notion of "badness," and we ran into "overfull" and "underfull" boxes in difficult situations. We also observed that different settings of TₑX's `\tolerance` parameter will produce different effects; a higher tolerance means that wider spaces are acceptable.

TₑX will find the absolutely best way to typeset any given paragraph, according to its ideas of minimum badness. But such "badness" doesn't account for everything, and if you rely entirely on an automatic scheme you will occasionally encounter line breaks that are not really the best on psychological grounds; this is inevitable, because computers don't understand things the way people do (at least not yet). Therefore you'll sometimes want to tell the machine that certain places are not good breakpoints. Conversely, you will sometimes want to force a break at a particular spot. TₑX provides a convenient way to avoid psychologically bad breaks, so that you will be able to obtain results of the finest quality by simply giving a few hints to the machine.

"Ties"—denoted by '~' in plain TₑX—are the key to successful line breaking. Once you learn how to insert them, you will have graduated from the ranks of ordinary TₑXnical typists to the select group of Distinguished TₑXnicians. And it's really not difficult to train yourself to insert occasional ties, almost without thinking, as you type a manuscript.

When you type ~ it's the same as typing a space, except that TₑX won't break a line at this space. Furthermore, you shouldn't leave any blanks next to the ~, since they will count as additional spaces. If you put ~ at the very end of a line in your input file, you'll get a wider space than you want, because the ⟨return⟩ that follows the ~ produces an extra space.

We have already observed in Chapter 12 that it's generally a good idea to type ~ after an abbreviation that does not come at the end of a sentence. Ties also belong in several other places:

- In references to named parts of a document:

```
Chapter~12            Theorem~1.2
Appendix~A            Table~\hbox{B-8}
Figure~3              Lemmas 5 and~6
```

(No ~ appears after 'Lemmas' in the final example, since there's no harm in having '5 and 6' at the beginning of a line. The use of \hbox is explained below.)

- Between a person's forenames and between multiple surnames:

```
Donald~E. Knuth                      Luis~I. Trabb~Pardo
Bartel~Leendert van~der~Waerden      Charles~XII
```

Note that it is sometimes better to hyphenate a name than to break it between words; e.g., 'Don-' and 'ald E. Knuth' is more tolerable than 'Donald' and 'E. Knuth'. The previous rule can be regarded as a special case of this one, since we may think of 'Chapter 12' as a compound name; another example is 'register~X'. Sometimes a name is so long that we dare not tie it all together, lest there be no way to break the line:

```
Charles Louis Xavier~Joseph de~la Vall\'ee~Poussin.
```

- Between math symbols in apposition with nouns:

```
dimension~$d$      width~$w$      function~$f(x)$
string~$s$ of length~$l$
```

However, the last example should be compared with

```
string~$s$ of length $l$~or more.
```

- Between symbols in series:

```
1,~2, or~3
$a$,~$b$, and~$c$.
1,~2, \dots,~$n$.
```

- When a symbol is a tightly bound object of a preposition:

```
of~$x$
from 0 to~1
increase $z$ by~1
in common with~$m$.
```

The rule does not, however, apply to compound objects:

```
of $u$~and~$v$.
```

- When mathematical phrases are rendered in words:

```
equals~$n$      less than~$\epsilon$      (given~$X$)
mod~2           modulo~$p^e$              for all large~$n$
```

Compare 'is~15' with 'is 15~times the height'.

- When cases are being enumerated within a paragraph:

```
(b)~Show that $f(x)$ is (1)~continuous; (2)~bounded.
```

It would be nice to boil all of these rules down to one or two simple principles, and it would be even nicer if the rules could be automated so that keyboarding could be done without them; but subtle semantic considerations seem to be involved. Therefore it's best to use your own judgment with respect to ties. The computer needs your help.

A tie keeps TEX from breaking at a space, but sometimes you want to prevent the machine from breaking at a hyphen or a dash. This can be done by using \hbox, because TEX will not split up the contents of a box; boxes are indecomposable units, once they have been constructed. We have already illustrated this principle in the 'Table~\hbox{B-8}' example considered earlier. Another example occurs when you are typing the page numbers in a bibliographic reference: It doesn't look good to put '22.' on a line by itself, so you can type '\hbox{13--22}.' to prohibit breaking '13–22.' On the other hand, TEX doesn't often choose line breaks at hyphens, so you needn't bother to insert \hbox commands unless you need to correct a bad break that TEX has already made on a previous run.

▶ **EXERCISE 14.1**
Here are some phrases culled from previous chapters of this manual. How do you think the author typed them?

> (cf. Chapter 12).
> Chapters 12 and 21.
> line 16 of Chapter 6's story
> lines 7 to 11
> lines 2, 3, 4, and 5.
> (2) a big black bar
> All 256 characters are initially of category 12,
> letter x in family 1.
> the factor f, where n is 1000 times f.

▶ **EXERCISE 14.2**
How would you type the phrase 'for all n greater than n_0'?

▶ **EXERCISE 14.3**
And how would you type 'exercise 4.3.2–15'?

▶ **EXERCISE 14.4**
Why is it better to type 'Chapter~12' than to type '\hbox{Chapter 12}'?

▶ **EXERCISE 14.5**
TEX will sometimes break a math formula after an equals sign. How can you stop the computer from breaking the formula '$x = 0$'?

▶ **EXERCISE 14.6**
Explain how you could instruct TEX not to make any breaks after explicit hyphens and dashes. (This is useful in lengthy bibliographies.)

Sometimes you want to permit a line break after a '/' just as if it were a hyphen. For this purpose plain TEX allows you to say '\slash'; for example, 'input\slash output' produces 'input/output' with an optional break.

If you want to force TEX to break between lines at a certain point in the middle of a paragraph, just say '\break'. However, that might cause the line to be   really   spaced   out. If you want TEX to fill up the right-hand part of a line with blank space just before a forced line break, without indenting the next line, say '\hfil\break'.

You may have several consecutive lines of input for which you want the output to appear line-for-line in the same way. One solution is to type '\par' at the end of each input line; but that's somewhat of a nuisance, so plain TEX provides the abbreviation '\obeylines', which causes each end-of-line in the input to be like \par. After you say \obeylines you will get one line of output per line of input, unless an input line ends with '%' or unless it is so long that it must be broken. For example, you probably want to use \obeylines if you are typesetting a poem. Be sure to enclose \obeylines in a group, unless you want this "poetry mode" to continue to the end of your document.

```
{\obeylines\smallskip
Roses are red,
\quad Violets are blue;
Rhymes can be typeset
\quad With boxes and glue.
\smallskip}
```

▶ **EXERCISE 14.7**
Explain the uses of \quad in this poem. What would have happened if '\quad' had been replaced by '\indent' in both places?

Roughly speaking, TEX breaks paragraphs into lines in the following way: Breakpoints are inserted between words or after hyphens so as to produce lines whose badnesses do not exceed the current \tolerance. If there's no way to insert such breakpoints, an overfull box is set. Otherwise the breakpoints are chosen so that the paragraph is mathematically optimal, i.e., best possible, in the sense that it has no more "demerits" than you could obtain by any other sequence of breakpoints. Demerits are based on the badnesses of individual lines and on the existence of such things as consecutive lines that end with hyphens, or tight lines that occur next to loose ones.

But the informal description of line breaking in the previous paragraph is an oversimplification of what really happens. The remainder of this chapter explains the details precisely, for people who want to apply TEX in nonstandard ways. TEX's line-breaking algorithm has proved to be general enough to handle a surprising variety of different applications; this, in fact, is probably the most interesting aspect of the whole TEX system. However, every paragraph from now on until the end of the chapter is prefaced by at least one dangerous bend sign, so you may want to learn the following material in easy stages instead of all at once.

Before the lines have been broken, a paragraph inside of TEX is actually a *horizontal list*, i.e., a sequence of items that TEX has gathered while in hori-zontal mode. We have been saying informally that a horizontal list consists of boxes and glue; the truth is that boxes and glue aren't the whole story. Each item in a horizontal list is one of the following types of things:

- a box (a character or ligature or rule or hbox or vbox);
- a discretionary break (to be explained momentarily);
- a "whatsit" (something special to be explained later);
- vertical material (from \mark or \vadjust or \insert);
- a glob of glue (or \leaders, as we will see later);
- a kern (something like glue that doesn't stretch or shrink);
- a penalty (representing the undesirability of breaking here);
- "math-on" (beginning a formula) or "math-off" (ending a formula).

The last four types (glue, kern, penalty, and math items) are called *discardable*, since they may change or disappear at a line break; the first four types are called non-discardable, since they always remain intact. Many of the things that can appear in horizontal lists have not been touched on yet in this manual, but it isn't necessary to understand them in order to understand line breaking. Sooner or later you'll learn how each of the gismos listed above can infiltrate a horizontal list; and if you want to get a thorough understanding of TEX's internal processes, you can always use \showlists with various features of the language, in order to see exactly what TEX is doing.

 A discretionary break consists of three sequences of characters called the *pre-break*, *post-break*, and *no-break* texts. The idea is that if a line break occurs here, the pre-break text will appear at the end of the current line and the post-break text will occur at the beginning of the next line; but if no break occurs, the no-break text will appear in the current line. Users can specify discretionary breaks in complete generality by writing

\discretionary{⟨pre-break text⟩}{⟨post-break text⟩}{⟨no-break text⟩}

where the three texts consist entirely of characters, boxes, and kerns. For example, TEX can hyphenate the word 'difficult' between the f's, even though this requires breaking the 'ffi' ligature into 'f-' followed by an 'fi' ligature, if the horizontal list contains

di\discretionary{f-}{fi}{ffi}cult.

Fortunately you need not type such a mess yourself; TEX's hyphenation algorithm works behind the scenes, taking ligatures apart and putting them into discretionary breaks when necessary.

 The most common case of a discretionary break is a simple discretionary hyphen

\discretionary{-}{}{}

for which TEX accepts the abbreviation '\-'. The next most common case is

\discretionary{}{}{}

(an "empty discretionary"), which TEX automatically inserts after '-' and after every ligature that ends with '-'. In the case of plain TEX, empty discretionaries are therefore inserted after hyphens and dashes. (Each font has an associated \hyphenchar, which we can assume for simplicity is equal to '-'.)

When TEX hyphenates words, it simply inserts discretionary breaks into the horizontal list. For example, the words '`discretionary hyphens`' are transformed into the equivalent of

`dis\-cre\-tionary hy\-phens`

if hyphenation becomes necessary. But TEX doesn't apply its hyphenation algorithm to any word that already contains a discretionary break; therefore you can use explicit discretionaries to override TEX's automatic method, in an emergency.

▶ **EXERCISE 14.8**
Some compound words in German text change their spelling when they are split between lines. For example, 'backen' becomes 'bak-ken' and 'Bettuch' becomes 'Bett-tuch'. How can you instruct TEX to produce this effect?

In order to save time, TEX tries first to break a paragraph into lines without inserting any discretionary hyphens. This first pass will succeed if a sequence of breakpoints is found for which none of the resulting lines has a badness exceeding the current value of `\pretolerance`. If the first pass fails, the method of Appendix H is used to hyphenate each word of the paragraph by inserting discretionary breaks into the horizontal list, and a second attempt is made using `\tolerance` instead of `\pretolerance`. When the lines are fairly wide, as they are in this manual, experiments show that the first pass succeeds more than 90% of the time, and that fewer than 2 words per paragraph need to be subjected to the hyphenation algorithm, on the average. But when the lines are very narrow the first pass usually fails rather quickly. Plain TEX sets `\pretolerance=100` and `\tolerance=200` as the default values. If you make `\pretolerance=10000`, the first pass will essentially always succeed, so hyphenations will not be tried (and the spacing may be terrible); on the other hand if you make `\pretolerance=-1`, TEX will omit the first pass and will try to hyphenate immediately.

Line breaks can occur only in certain places within a horizontal list. Roughly speaking, they occur between words and after hyphens, but in actuality they are permitted in the following five cases:

a) at glue, provided that this glue is immediately preceded by a non-discardable item, and that it is not part of a math formula (i.e., not between math-on and math-off). A break "at glue" occurs at the left edge of the glue space.

b) at a kern, provided that this kern is immediately followed by glue, and that it is not part of a math formula.

c) at a math-off that is immediately followed by glue.

d) at a penalty (which might have been inserted automatically in a formula).

e) at a discretionary break.

Notice that if two globs of glue occur next to each other, the second one will never be selected as a breakpoint, since it is preceded by glue (which is discardable).

Each potential breakpoint has an associated "penalty," which represents the "aesthetic cost" of breaking at that place. In cases (a), (b), (c), the penalty is zero; in case (d) an explicit penalty has been specified; and in case (e) the penalty is the current value of `\hyphenpenalty` if the pre-break text is nonempty, or the current value of `\exhyphenpenalty` if the pre-break text is empty. Plain TEX sets `\hyphenpenalty=50` and `\exhyphenpenalty=50`.

For example, if you say '\penalty 100' at some point in a paragraph, that position will be a legitimate place to break between lines, but a penalty of 100 will be charged. If you say '\penalty-100' you are telling TₑX that this is a rather good place to break, because a negative penalty is really a "bonus"; a line that ends with a bonus might even have "merits" (negative demerits).

Any penalty that is 10000 or more is considered to be so large that TₑX will never break there. At the other extreme, any penalty that is −10000 or less is considered to be so small that TₑX will always break there. The \nobreak macro of plain TₑX is simply an abbreviation for '\penalty10000', because this prohibits a line break. A tie in plain TₑX is equivalent to '\nobreak\␣'; there will be no break at the glue represented by \␣ in this case, because glue is never a legal breakpoint when it is preceded by a discardable item like a penalty.

▶**EXERCISE 14.9**
Guess how the \break macro is defined in plain TₑX.

▶**EXERCISE 14.10**
What happens if you say \nobreak\break or \break\nobreak?

When a line break actually does occur, TₑX removes all discardable items that follow the break, until coming to something non-discardable, or until coming to another chosen breakpoint. For example, a sequence of glue and penalty items will vanish as a unit, if no boxes intervene, unless the optimum breakpoint sequence includes one or more of the penalties. Math-on and math-off items act essentially as kerns that contribute the spacing specified by \mathsurround; such spacing will disappear into the line break if a formula comes at the very end or the very beginning of a line, because of the way the rules have been formulated above.

The badness of a line is an integer that is approximately 100 times the cube of the ratio by which the glue inside the line must stretch or shrink to make an hbox of the required size. For example, if the line has a total shrinkability of 10 points, and if the glue is being compressed by a total of 9 points, the badness is computed to be 73 (since $100 \times (9/10)^3 = 72.9$); similarly, a line that stretches by twice its total stretchability has a badness of 800. But if the badness obtained by this method turns out to be more than 10000, the value 10000 is used. (See the discussion of "glue set ratio" r and "glue set order" i in Chapter 12; if $i \neq 0$, there is infinite stretchability or shrinkability, so the badness is zero, otherwise the badness is approximately $\min(100r^3, 10000)$.) Overfull boxes are considered to be infinitely bad; they are avoided whenever possible.

A line whose badness is 13 or more has a glue set ratio exceeding 50%. We call such a line *tight* if its glue had to shrink, *loose* if its glue had to stretch, and *very loose* if it had to stretch so much that the badness is 100 or more. But if the badness is 12 or less we say that the line is *decent*. Two adjacent lines are said to be *visually incompatible* if their classifications are not adjacent, i.e., if a tight line is next to a loose or very loose line, or if a decent line is next to a very loose one.

TₑX rates each potential sequence of breakpoints by totalling up *demerits* that are assessed to individual lines. The goal is to choose breakpoints that yield the fewest total demerits. Suppose that a line has badness b, and suppose that the penalty p is associated with the breakpoint at the end of this line. As stated above, TEX will not even consider such a line if $p \geq 10000$, or if b exceeds the current tolerance or pretolerance. Otherwise the demerits of such a line are defined by the formula

$$d = \begin{cases} (l+b)^2 + p^2, & \text{if } 0 \leq p < 10000; \\ (l+b)^2 - p^2, & \text{if } -10000 < p < 0; \\ (l+b)^2, & \text{if } p \leq -10000. \end{cases}$$

Here l is the current value of \linepenalty, a parameter that can be increased if you want TEX to try harder to keep all paragraphs to the minimum number of lines; plain TEX sets \linepenalty=10. For example, a line with badness 20 ending at glue will have $(10 + 20)^2 = 900$ demerits, if $l = 10$, since there's no penalty for a break at glue. Minimizing the total demerits of a paragraph is roughly the same as minimizing the sum of the squares of the badnesses and penalties; this usually means that the maximum badness of any individual line is also minimized, over all sequences of breakpoints.

▷ **EXERCISE 14.11**
The formula for demerits has a strange discontinuity: It seems more reasonable at first to define $d = (l+b)^2 - 10000^2$, in the case $p \leq -10000$. Can you account for this apparent discrepancy?

Additional demerits are assessed based on pairs of adjacent lines. If two consecutive lines are visually incompatible, in the sense explained a minute ago, the current value of \adjdemerits is added to d. If two consecutive lines end with discretionary breaks, the \doublehyphendemerits are added. And if the second-last line of the entire paragraph ends with a discretionary, the \finalhyphendemerits are added. Plain TEX sets up the values \adjdemerits=10000, \doublehyphendemerits=10000, and \finalhyphendemerits=5000. Demerits are in units of "badness squared," so the demerit-oriented parameters need to be rather large if they are to have much effect; but tolerances and penalties are given in the same units as badness.

If you set \tracingparagraphs=1, your log file will contain a summary of TEX's line-breaking calculations, so you can watch the tradeoffs that occur when parameters like \linepenalty and \hyphenpenalty and \adjdemerits are twiddled. The line-break data looks pretty scary at first, but you can learn to read it with a little practice; this, in fact, is the best way to get a solid understanding of line breaking. Here is the trace that results from the second paragraph of the **story** file in Chapter 6, when \hsize=2.5in and \tolerance=1000:

```
[]\tenrm Mr. Drofnats---or ''R. J.,'' as he pre-
@\discretionary via @@0 b=0 p=50 d=2600
@@1: line 1.2- t=2600 -> @@0
ferred to be called---was hap-pi-est when
@ via @@1 b=131 p=0 d=29881
@@2: line 2.0 t=32481 -> @@1
he
@ via @@1 b=25 p=0 d=1225
@@3: line 2.3 t=3825 -> @@1
was at work type-set-ting beau-ti-ful doc-
@\discretionary via @@2 b=1 p=50 d=12621
@\discretionary via @@3 b=291 p=50 d=103101
```

```
@@4: line 3.2- t=45102 -> @@2
u-
@\discretionary via @@3 b=44 p=50 d=15416
@@5: line 3.1- t=19241 -> @@3
ments.
@\par via @@4 b=0 p=-10000 d=5100
@\par via @@5 b=0 p=-10000 d=5100
@@6: line 4.2- t=24341 -> @@5
```

Lines that begin with '@@' represent *feasible breakpoints*, i.e., breakpoints that can be reached without any badness exceeding the tolerance. Feasible breakpoints are numbered consecutively, starting with @@1; the beginning of the paragraph is considered to be feasible too, and it is number @@0. Lines that begin with '@' but not '@@' are candidate ways to reach the feasible breakpoint that follows; TEX will select only the best candidate, when there is a choice. Lines that do not begin with '@' indicate how far TEX has gotten in the paragraph. Thus, for example, we find '@@2: line 2.0 t=32481 -> @@1' after '...hap-pi-est when' and before 'he', so we know that feasible breakpoint @@2 occurs at the space between the words when and he. The notation 'line 2.0' means that this feasible break comes at the end of line 2, and that this line will be very loose. (The suffixes .0, .1, .2, .3 stand respectively for very loose, loose, decent, and tight.) A hyphen is suffixed to the line number if that line ends with a discretionary break, or if it is the final line of the paragraph; for example, 'line 1.2-' is a decent line that was hyphenated. The notation 't=32481' means that the total demerits from the beginning of the paragraph to @@2 are 32481, and '-> @@1' means that the best way to get to @@2 is to come from @@1. On the preceding line of trace data we see the calculations for a typeset line to this point from @@1: the badness is 131, the penalty is 0, hence there are 29881 demerits. Similarly, breakpoint @@3 presents an alternative for the second line of the paragraph, obtained by breaking between 'he' and 'was'; this one makes the second line tight, and it has only 3825 demerits when the demerits of line 1 are added, so it appears that @@3 will work much better than @@2. However, the next feasible breakpoint (@@4) occurs after 'doc-', and the line from @@2 to @@4 has only 12621 demerits, while the line from @@3 to @@4 has a whopping 103101; therefore the best way to get from @@0 to @@4 is via @@2. If we regard demerits as distances, TEX is finding the "shortest paths" from @@0 to each feasible breakpoint (using a variant of a well-known algorithm for shortest paths in an acyclic graph). Finally the end of the paragraph comes at breakpoint @@6, and the shortest path from @@0 to @@6 represents the best sequence of breakpoints. Following the arrows back from @@6, we deduce that the best breaks in this particular paragraph go through @@5, @@3, and @@1.

▶ **EXERCISE 14.12**
Explain why there are 29881 demerits from @@1 to @@2, and 12621 demerits from @@2 to @@4.

If 'b=*' appears in such trace data, it means that an infeasible breakpoint had to be chosen because there was no feasible way to keep total demerits small.

We still haven't discussed the special trick that allows the final line of a paragraph to be shorter than the others. Just before TEX begins to choose breakpoints, it does two important things: (1) If the final item of the current horizontal list is glue, that glue is discarded. (The reason is that a blank space often gets into a token list just before \par or just before \$\$, and this blank space should not be part of the paragraph.) (2) Three more items are put at the end of the current horizontal list: \penalty10000 (which prohibits a line break); \hskip\parfillskip (which adds "finishing glue" to the paragraph); and \penalty-10000 (which forces the final break). Plain TeX sets \parfillskip=0pt plus1fil, so that the last line of each paragraph will be filled with white space if necessary; but other settings of \parfillskip are appropriate in special applications. For example, the present paragraph ends flush with the right margin, because it was typeset with \parfillskip=0pt; the author didn't have to rewrite any of the text in order to make this possible, since a long paragraph generally allows so much flexibility that a line break can be forced at almost any point. You can have some fun playing with paragraphs, because the algorithm for line breaking occasionally appears to be clairvoyant. Just write paragraphs that are long enough.

▶ **EXERCISE 14.13**
Ben User decided to say '\hfilneg\par' at the end of a paragraph, intending that the negative stretchability of \hfilneg would cancel with the \parfillskip of plain TeX. Why didn't his bright idea work?

▶ **EXERCISE 14.14**
How can you set \parfillskip so that the last line of a paragraph has exactly as much white space at the right as the first line has indentation at the left?

▶ **EXERCISE 14.15**
Since TeX reads an entire paragraph before it makes any decisions about line breaks, the computer's memory capacity might be exceeded if you are typesetting the works of some philosopher or modernistic novelist who writes 200-line paragraphs. Suggest a way to cope with such authors.

TeX has two parameters called \leftskip and \rightskip that specify glue to be inserted at the left and right of every line in a paragraph; this glue is taken into account when badnesses and demerits are computed. Plain TeX normally keeps \leftskip and \rightskip zero, but it has a '\narrower' macro that increases both of their values by the current \parindent. You may want to use \narrower when quoting lengthy passages from a book.

```
{\narrower\smallskip\noindent
This paragraph will have narrower lines than
the surrounding paragraphs do, because it
uses the ``narrower'' feature of plain \TeX.
The former margins will be restored after
this group ends.\smallskip}
```

(Try it.) The second '\smallskip' in this example ends the paragraph. It's important to end the paragraph before ending the group, for otherwise the effect of \narrower will disappear before TeX begins to choose line breaks.

▶ **EXERCISE 14.16**
When an entire paragraph is typeset in italic or slanted type, it sometimes appears to be offset on the page with respect to other paragraphs. Explain how you could use \leftskip and \rightskip to shift all lines of a paragraph left by 1 pt.

▶**EXERCISE 14.17**
The \centerline, \leftline, \rightline, and \line macros of plain TₑX don't take \leftskip and \rightskip into account. How could you make them do so?

If you suspect that \raggedright setting is accomplished by some appropriate manipulation of \rightskip, you are correct. But some care is necessary. For example, a person can set \rightskip=0pt plus1fil, and every line will be filled with space at the right. But this isn't a particularly good way to make ragged-right margins, because the infinite stretchability will assign zero badness to lines that are very short. To do a decent job of ragged-right setting, the trick is to set \rightskip so that it will stretch enough to make line breaks possible, yet not too much, because short lines should be considered bad. Furthermore the spaces between words should be fixed so that they do not stretch or shrink. (See the definition of \raggedright in Appendix B.) It would also be possible to allow a little variability in the interword glue, so that the right margin would not be quite so ragged but the paragraphs would still have an informal appearance.

TₑX looks at the parameters that affect line breaking only when it is breaking lines. For example, you shouldn't try to change the \hyphenpenalty in the middle of a paragraph, if you want TₑX to penalize the hyphens in one word more than it does in another word. The relevant values of \hyphenpenalty, \rightskip, \hsize, and so on, are the ones that are current at the end of the paragraph. On the other hand, the width of indentation that you get implicitly at the beginning of a paragraph or when you say '\indent' is determined by the value of \parindent at the time the indentation is contributed to the current horizontal list, not by its value at the end of the paragraph. Similarly, penalties that are inserted into math formulas within a paragraph are based on the values of \binoppenalty and \relpenalty that are current at the end of each particular formula. Appendix D contains an example that shows how to have both ragged-right and ragged-left margins within a single paragraph, without using \leftskip or \rightskip.

It's possible to control the length of lines in a much more general way, if simple changes to \leftskip and \rightskip aren't flexible enough for your purposes. For example, a semicircular hole has been cut out of the present paragraph, in order to make room for a circular illustration that contains some of Galileo's immortal words about circles; all of the line breaks in this paragraph and in the circular quotation were found by TₑX's line-breaking algorithm. You can specify an essentially arbitrary paragraph shape by saying \parshape=⟨number⟩, where the ⟨number⟩ is a positive integer n, followed by $2n$ ⟨dimen⟩ specifications. In general, '\parshape=n i_1 l_1 i_2 l_2 ... i_n l_n' specifies a paragraph whose first n lines will have lengths l_1, l_2, ..., l_n, respectively, and they will be indented from the left margin by the respective amounts i_1, i_2, ..., i_n. If the paragraph has fewer than n lines, the additional specifications will be ignored; if it has more than n lines, the specifications for line n will be repeated ad infinitum. You can cancel the effect of a previously specified \parshape by saying '\parshape=0'.

The area of a circle is a mean proportional between any two regular and similar polygons of which one circumscribes it and the other is isoperimetric with it. In addition, the area of the circle is less than that of any circumscribed polygon and greater than that of any isoperimetric polygon. And further, of these circumscribed polygons, the one that has the greater number of sides has a smaller area than the one that has a lesser number; but, on the other hand, the isoperimetric polygon that has the greater number of sides is the larger. [Galileo, 1638]

▶**EXERCISE 14.18**
Typeset the following Pascalian quotation in the shape of an isosceles triangle:

"I turn, in the following treatises, to various uses of those triangles whose generator is unity. But I leave out many more than I include; it is extraordinary how fertile in properties this triangle is. Everyone can try his hand."

You probably won't need unusual parshapes very often. But there's a special case that occurs rather frequently, so TₑX provides a special abbreviation for it in terms of two parameters called `\hangindent` and `\hangafter`. The command '`\hangindent=⟨dimen⟩`' specifies a so-called hanging indentation, and the command '`\hangafter=⟨number⟩`' specifies the duration of that indentation. Let x and n be the respective values of `\hangindent` and `\hangafter`, and let h be the value of `\hsize`; then if $n \geq 0$, hanging indentation will occur on lines $n+1$, $n+2$, ... of the paragraph, but if $n < 0$ it will occur on lines $1, 2, \ldots, |n|$. Hanging indentation means that lines will be of width $h - |x|$ instead of their normal width h; if $x \geq 0$, the lines will be indented at the left margin, otherwise they will be indented at the right margin. For example, the "dangerous bend" paragraphs of this manual have a hanging indentation of 3 picas that lasts for two lines; they were set with `\hangindent=3pc` and `\hangafter=-2`.

Plain TₑX uses hanging indentation in its '`\item`' macro, which produces a paragraph in which every line has the same indentation as a normal `\indent`. Furthermore, `\item` takes a parameter that is placed into the position of the indentation on the first line. Another macro called '`\itemitem`' does the same thing but with double indentation. For example, suppose you type

```
\item{1.} This is the first of several cases that are being
enumerated, with hanging indentation applied to entire paragraphs.
\itemitem{a)} This is the first subcase.
\itemitem{b)} And this is the second subcase. Notice
that subcases have twice as much hanging indentation.
\item{2.} The second case is similar.
```

Then you get the following output:

1. This is the first of several cases that are being enumerated, with hanging indentation applied to entire paragraphs.
    a) This is the first subcase.
    b) And this is the second subcase. Notice that subcases have twice as much hanging indentation.
2. The second case is similar.

(Indentations in plain TₑX are not actually as dramatic as those displayed here; Appendix B says '`\parindent=20pt`', but this manual has been set with `\parindent=36pt`.) It is customary to put `\medskip` before and after a group of itemized paragraphs, and to say `\noindent` before any closing remarks that apply to all of the cases. Blank lines are not needed before `\item` or `\itemitem`, since those macros begin with `\par`.

▶ **EXERCISE 14.19**
Suppose one of the enumerated cases continues for two or more paragraphs. How can you use `\item` to get hanging indentation on the subsequent paragraphs?

▶ **EXERCISE 14.20**
Explain how to make a "bulleted" item that says '•' instead of '1.'.

▷ **EXERCISE 14.21**
The '\item' macro doesn't alter the right-hand margin. How could you indent at both sides?

▷ **EXERCISE 14.22**
Explain how you could specify a hanging indentation of −2 ems (i.e., the lines should project into the left margin), after the first two lines of a paragraph.

If \parshape and hanging indentation have both been specified, \parshape takes precedence and \hangindent is ignored. You get the normal paragraph shape, in which every line width is \hsize, when \parshape=0, \hangindent=0pt, and \hangafter=1. TℰX automatically restores these normal values at the end of every paragraph, and (by local definitions) whenever it enters internal vertical mode. For example, hanging indentation that might be present outside of a \vbox construction won't occur inside that vbox, unless you ask for it inside.

▷ **EXERCISE 14.23**
Suppose you want to leave room at the right margin for a rectangular illustration that takes up 15 lines, and you expect that three paragraphs will go by before you have typeset enough text to get past that illustration. Suggest a good way to do this without trial and error, given the fact that TℰX resets hanging indentation.

If displayed equations occur in a paragraph that has a nonstandard shape, TℰX always assumes that the display takes up exactly three lines. For example, a paragraph that has four lines of text, then a display, then two more lines of text, is considered to be $4 + 3 + 2 = 9$ lines long; the displayed equation will be indented and centered using the paragraph shape information appropriate to line 6.

TℰX has an internal integer variable called \prevgraf that records the number of lines in the most recent paragraph that has been completed or partially completed. You can use \prevgraf in the context of a ⟨number⟩, and you can set \prevgraf to any desired nonnegative value if you want to make TℰX think that it is in some particular part of the current paragraph shape. For example, let's consider again a paragraph that contains four lines plus a display plus two more lines. When TℰX starts the paragraph, it sets \prevgraf=0; when it starts the display, \prevgraf will be 4; when it finishes the display, \prevgraf will be 7; and when it ends the paragraph, \prevgraf will be 9. If the display is actually one line taller than usual, you could set \prevgraf=8 at the beginning of the two final lines; then TℰX will think that a 10-line paragraph is being made. The value of \prevgraf affects line breaking only when TℰX is dealing with nonstandard \parshape or \hangindent.

▷ **EXERCISE 14.24**
Solve exercise 14.23 using \prevgraf.

You are probably convinced by now that TℰX's line-breaking algorithm has plenty of bells and whistles, perhaps even too many. But there's one more feature, called "looseness"; some day you might find yourself needing it, when you are fine-tuning the pages of a book. If you set \looseness=1, TℰX will try to make the current paragraph one line longer than its optimum length, provided that there is a way to choose such breakpoints without exceeding the tolerance you have specified for the badnesses of individual lines. Similarly, if you set \looseness=2, TℰX will try to

make the paragraph two lines longer; and `\looseness=-1` causes an attempt to make
it shorter. The general idea is that TEX first finds breakpoints as usual; then if the
optimum breakpoints produce n lines, and if the current `\looseness` is l, TEX will
choose the final breakpoints so as to make the final number of lines as close as possible
to $n+l$ without exceeding the current tolerance. Furthermore, the final breakpoints will
have fewest total demerits, considering all ways to achieve the same number of lines.

For example, you can set `\looseness=1` if you want to avoid a lonely "club
line" or "widow line" on some page that does not have sufficiently flexible glue,
or if you want the total number of lines in some two-column document to come out
to be an even number. It's usually best to choose a paragraph that is already pretty
"full," i.e., one whose last line doesn't have much white space, since such paragraphs
can generally be loosened without much harm. You might also want to insert a tie
between the last two words of that paragraph, so that the loosened version will not
end with only one "widow word" on the line; this tie will cover your tracks, so that
people will find it hard to detect the fact that you have tampered with the spacing.
On the other hand, TEX can take almost any sufficiently long paragraph and stretch it
a bit, without substantial harm; the present paragraph is, in fact, one line looser than
its optimum length.

TEX resets the looseness to zero at the same time as it resets `\hangindent`,
`\hangafter`, and `\parshape`.

▶ **EXERCISE 14.25**
Explain what TEX will do if you set `\looseness=-1000`.

Just before switching to horizontal mode to begin scanning a paragraph, TEX
inserts the glue specified by `\parskip` into the vertical list that will contain
the paragraph, unless that vertical list is empty so far. For example, '`\parskip=3pt`'
will cause 3 points of extra space to be placed between paragraphs. Plain TEX sets
`\parskip=0pt plus1pt`; this gives a little stretchability, but no extra space.

After line breaking is complete, TEX appends the lines to the current vertical
list that encloses the current paragraph, inserting interline glue as explained in
Chapter 12; this interline glue will depend on the values of `\baselineskip`, `\lineskip`,
and `\lineskiplimit` that are currently in force. TEX will also insert penalties into the
vertical list, just before each glob of interline glue, in order to help control page breaks
that might have to be made later. For example, a special penalty will be assessed for
breaking a page between the first two lines of a paragraph, or just before the last line,
so that "club" or "widow" lines that are detached from the rest of a paragraph will not
appear all alone on a page unless the alternative is worse.

Here's how interline penalties are calculated: TEX has just chosen the breakpoints for some paragraph, or for some partial paragraph that precedes a
displayed equation; and n lines have been formed. The penalty between lines j and
$j + 1$, given a value of j in the range $1 \leq j < n$, is the value of `\interlinepenalty`
plus additional charges made in special cases: The `\clubpenalty` is added if $j = 1$,
i.e., just after the first line; then the `\displaywidowpenalty` or the `\widowpenalty` is
added if $j = n - 1$, i.e., just before the last line, depending on whether or not the
current lines immediately precede a display; and finally the `\brokenpenalty` is added,
if the jth line ended at a discretionary break. (Plain TEX sets `\clubpenalty=150`,

`\widowpenalty=150`, `\displaywidowpenalty=50`, and `\brokenpenalty=100`; the value of `\interlinepenalty` is normally zero, but it is increased to 100 within footnotes, so that long footnotes will tend not to be broken between pages.)

▶ **EXERCISE 14.26**
Consider a five-line paragraph in which the second and fourth lines end with hyphens. What penalties does plain TₑX put between the lines?

▶ **EXERCISE 14.27**
What penalty goes between the lines of a two-line paragraph?

If you say `\vadjust{⟨vertical list⟩}` within a paragraph, TₑX will insert the specified internal vertical list into the vertical list that encloses the paragraph, immediately after whatever line contained the position of the `\vadjust`. For example, you can say '`\vadjust{\kern1pt}`' to increase the amount of space between lines of a paragraph if those lines would otherwise come out too close together. (The author did it in the previous line, just to illustrate what happens.) Also, if you want to make sure that a page break will occur immediately after a certain line, you can say '`\vadjust{\eject}`' anywhere in that line.

Later chapters discuss `\insert` and `\mark` commands that are relevant to TₑX's page builder. If such commands appear within a paragraph, they are removed from whatever horizontal lines contain them and placed into the enclosing vertical list, together with other vertical material from `\vadjust` commands that might be present. In the final vertical list, each horizontal line of text is an hbox that is immediately preceded by interline glue and immediately followed by vertical material that has "migrated out" from that line (with left to right order preserved, if there are several instances of vertical material); then comes the interline penalty, if it is nonzero. Inserted vertical material does not influence the interline glue.

▶ **EXERCISE 14.28**
Design a `\marginalstar` macro that can be used anywhere in a paragraph. It should use `\vadjust` to place an asterisk in the margin just to the left of the line where `\marginalstar` occurs.

When TₑX enters horizontal mode, it will interrupt its normal scanning to read tokens that were predefined by the command `\everypar={⟨token list⟩}`. For example, suppose you have said '`\everypar={A}`'. If you type 'B' in vertical mode, TₑX will shift to horizontal mode (after contributing `\parskip` glue to the current page), and a horizontal list will be initiated by inserting an empty box of width `\parindent`. Then TₑX will read 'AB', since it reads the `\everypar` tokens before getting back to the 'B' that triggered the new paragraph. Of course, this is not a very useful illustration of `\everypar`; but if you let your imagination run you will think of better applications.

▶ **EXERCISE 14.29**
Use `\everypar` to define an `\insertbullets` macro: All paragraphs in a group of the form '`{\insertbullets ...\par}`' should have a bullet symbol '•' as part of their indentation.

A paragraph of zero lines is formed if you say '`\noindent\par`'. If `\everypar` is null, such a paragraph contributes nothing except `\parskip` glue to the current vertical list.

▷ **EXERCISE 14.30**
Guess what happens if you say '\noindent$$...$$ \par'.

Experience has shown that TEX's line-breaking algorithm can be harnessed to a surprising variety of tasks. Here, for example, is an application that indicates one of the possibilities: Articles that are published in *Mathematical Reviews* are generally signed with the reviewer's name and address, and this information is typeset flush right, i.e., at the right-hand margin. If there is sufficient space to put such a name and address at the right of the final line of the paragraph, the publishers can save space, and at the same time the results look better because there are no strange gaps on the page.

> This is a case where the name and address fit in nicely
> with the review.   *A. Reviewer* (Ann Arbor, Mich.)

> But sometimes an extra line must be added.
>   *N. Bourbaki* (Paris)

Let's suppose that a space of at least two ems should separate the reviewer's name from the text of the review, if they occur on the same line. We would like to design a macro so that the examples shown above could be typed as follows in an input file:

```
... with the review. \signed A. Reviewer (Ann Arbor, Mich.)
... an extra line must be added. \signed N. Bourbaki (Paris)
```

Here is one way to solve the problem:

```
\def\signed #1 (#2){{\unskip\nobreak\hfil\penalty50
   \hskip2em\hbox{}\nobreak\hfil\sl#1\/ \rm(#2)
   \parfillskip=0pt \finalhyphendemerits=0 \par}}
```

If a line break occurs at the \penalty50, the \hskip2em will disappear and the empty \hbox will occur at the beginning of a line, followed by \hfil glue. This yields two lines whose badness is zero; the first of these lines is assessed a penalty of 50. But if no line break occurs at the \penalty50, there will be glue of 2 em plus 2 fil between the review and the name; this yields one line of badness zero. TEX will try both alternatives, to see which leads to the fewest total demerits. The one-line solution will usually be preferred if it is feasible.

▷ **EXERCISE 14.31**
Explain what would happen if '\hbox{}' were left out of the \signed macro.

▷ **EXERCISE 14.32**
Why does the \signed macro say '\finalhyphendemerits=0'?

▷ **EXERCISE 14.33**
In one of the paragraphs earlier in this chapter, the author used \break to force a line break in a specific place; as a result, the third line of that particular paragraph was really   spaced   out.
Explain why all the extra space went into the third line, instead of being distributed impartially among the first three lines.

If you want to avoid overfull boxes at all costs without trying to fix them manually, you might be tempted to set `tolerance=10000`; this allows arbitrarily bad lines to be acceptable in tough situations. But infinite tolerance is a bad idea, because TeX doesn't distinguish between terribly bad and preposterously horrible lines. Indeed, a tolerance of 10000 encourages TeX to concentrate all the badness in one place, making one truly unsightly line instead of two moderately bad ones, because a single "write-off" produces fewest total demerits according to the rules. There's a much better way to get the desired effect: TeX has a parameter called `\emergencystretch` that is added to the assumed stretchability of every line when badness and demerits are computed, in cases where overfull boxes are otherwise unavoidable. If `\emergencystretch` is positive, TeX will make a third pass over a paragraph before choosing the line breaks, when the first passes did not find a way to satisfy the `\pretolerance` and `\tolerance`. The effect of `\emergencystretch` is to scale down the badnesses so that large infinities are distinguishable from smaller ones. By setting `\emergencystretch` high enough (based on `\hsize`) you can be sure that the `\tolerance` is never exceeded; hence overfull boxes will never occur unless the line-breaking task is truly impossible.

▶ **EXERCISE 14.34**
Devise a `\raggedcenter` macro (analogous to `\raggedright`) that partitions the words of a paragraph into as few as possible lines of approximately equal size and centers each individual line. Hyphenation should be avoided if possible.

When the author objects to [a hyphenation]
he should be asked to add or cancel or substitute
a word or words that will prevent the breakage.

Authors who insist on even spacing always,
with sightly divisions always,
do not clearly understand the rigidity of types.
— T. L. DE VINNE, *Correct Composition* (1901)

In reprinting his own works, whenever [William Morris]
found a line that justified awkwardly, he altered the wording
solely for the sake of making it look well in print.

When a proof has been sent me with two or three
lines so widely spaced as to make a grey band across the page,
I have often rewritten the passage so as to fill up the lines better;
but I am sorry to say that my object has generally been so little
understood that the compositor has spoilt all the rest
of the paragraph instead of mending his former bad work.
— GEORGE BERNARD SHAW, in *The Dolphin* (1940)

15

How TEX Makes Lines into Pages

TEX attempts to choose desirable places to divide your document into individual pages, and its technique for doing this usually works pretty well. But the problem of page make-up is considerably more difficult than the problem of line breaking that we considered in the previous chapter, because pages often have much less flexibility than lines do. If the vertical glue on a page has little or no ability to stretch or to shrink, TEX usually has no choice about where to start a new page; conversely, if there is too much variability in the glue, the result will look bad because different pages will be too irregular. Therefore if you are fussy about the appearance of pages, you can expect to do some rewriting of the manuscript until you achieve an appropriate balance, or you might need to fiddle with the \looseness as described in Chapter 14; no automated system will be able to do this as well as you.

Mathematical papers that contain a lot of displayed equations have an advantage in this regard, because the glue that surrounds a display tends to be quite flexible. TEX also gets valuable room to maneuver when you have occasion to use \smallskip or \medskip or \bigskip spacing between certain paragraphs. For example, consider a page that contains a dozen or so exercises, and suppose that there is 3 pt of additional space between exercises, where this space can stretch to 4 pt or shrink to 2 pt. Then there is a chance to squeeze an extra line on the page, or to open up the page by removing one line, in order to avoid splitting an exercise between pages. Similarly, it is possible to use flexible glue in special publications like membership rosters or company telephone directories, so that individual entries need not be split between columns or pages, yet every column appears to be the same height.

For ordinary purposes you will probably find that TEX's automatic method of page breaking is satisfactory. And when it occasionally gives unpleasant results, you can force the machine to break at your favorite place by typing '\eject'. But be careful: \eject will cause TEX to stretch the page out, if necessary, so that the top and bottom baselines agree with those on other pages. If you want to eject a short page, filling it with blank space at the bottom, type '\vfill\eject' instead.

> If you say '\eject' in the middle of a paragraph, the paragraph will end first, as if you typed '\par\eject'. But Chapter 14 mentions that you can say '\vadjust{\eject}' in mid-paragraph, if you want to force a page break after whatever line contains your current position when the full paragraph is eventually broken up into lines; the rest of the paragraph will go on the following page.

> To prevent a page break, you can say '\nobreak' in vertical mode, just as \nobreak in horizontal mode prevents breaks between lines. For example, it is wise to say \nobreak between the title of a subsection and the first line of text in that subsection. But \nobreak does not cancel the effect of other commands like \eject that tell TEX to break; it only inhibits a break at glue that immediately follows. You should become familiar with TEX's rules for line breaks and page breaks if you want to maintain fine control over everything. The remainder of this chapter is devoted to the intimate details of page breaking.

TEX breaks lists of lines into pages by computing badness ratings and penalties, more or less as it does when breaking paragraphs into lines. But pages are made up one at a time and removed from TEX's memory; there is no looking ahead to see how one page break will affect the next one. In other words, TEX uses a special method to find the optimum breakpoints for the lines in an entire paragraph, but it doesn't attempt to find the optimum breakpoints for the pages in an entire document. The computer doesn't have enough high-speed memory capacity to remember the contents of several pages, so TEX simply chooses each page break as best it can, by a process of "local" rather than "global" optimization.

Let's look now at the details of TEX's page-making process. Everything you contribute to the pages of your document is placed on the *main vertical list*, which is the sequence of items that TEX has accumulated while in vertical mode. Each item in a vertical list is one of the following types of things:

- a box (an hbox or vbox or rule);
- a "whatsit" (something special to be explained later);
- a mark (another thing that will be explained later);
- an insertion (yet another thing that we will get to);
- a glob of glue (or \leaders, as we will see later);
- a kern (something like glue that doesn't stretch or shrink);
- a penalty (representing the undesirability of breaking here).

The last three types (glue, kern, and penalty items) are called discardable, for the same reason that we called them discardable in horizontal lists. You might want to compare these specifications with the analogous rules for the horizontal case, found in Chapter 14; it turns out that vertical lists are just like horizontal ones except that character boxes, discretionary breaks, \vadjust items, and math shifts cannot appear in vertical lists. Chapter 12 exhibits a typical vertical list in TEX's internal box-and-glue representation.

Page breaks can occur only at certain places within a vertical list. The permissible breakpoints are exactly the same as in the horizontal case, namely

a) at glue, provided that this glue is immediately preceded by a non-discardable item (i.e., by a box, whatsit, mark, or insertion);

b) at a kern, provided that this kern is immediately followed by glue;

c) at a penalty (which might have been inserted automatically in a paragraph).

Interline glue is usually inserted automatically between the boxes of a vertical list, as explained in Chapter 12, so there is usually a valid breakpoint between boxes.

As in horizontal lists, each potential breakpoint has an associated penalty, which is high for undesirable breakpoints and negative for desirable ones. The penalty is zero at glue and kern breaks, so it is nonzero only at explicit penalty breaks. If you say '\penalty-100' between two paragraphs, you are indicating that TEX should try to break here because the penalty is negative; a bonus of 100 points for breaking at this place will essentially cancel up to 100 units of badness that might be necessary to achieve such a break. A penalty of 10000 or more is so large that it inhibits breaking; a penalty of −10000 or less is so small that it forces breaking.

Plain TₑX provides several control sequences that help to control page breaks. For example, `\smallbreak`, `\medbreak`, and `\bigbreak` specify increasingly desirable places to break, having respective penalties of -50, -100, and -200; furthermore, they will insert a `\smallskip`, `\medskip`, or `\bigskip` of space, respectively, if a break is not taken. However, `\smallbreak`, `\medbreak`, and `\bigbreak` do not increase existing glue unnecessarily; for example, if you say `\smallbreak` just after a displayed equation, you won't get a `\smallskip` of space in addition to the glue that already follows a display. Therefore these commands can conveniently be used before and after the statements of theorems, in a format for mathematical papers. In the present manual the author has used a macro that puts `\medbreak` before and after every dangerous-bend paragraph; `\medbreak\medbreak` is equivalent to a single `\medbreak`, so you don't see two medskips when one such paragraph ends and another one begins.

The `\goodbreak` macro is an abbreviation for '`\par\penalty-500`'. This is a good thing to insert in your manuscript when proofreading, if you are willing to stretch some page a little bit extra in order to improve the following one. Later on if you make another change so that this `\goodbreak` command does not appear near the bottom of a page, it will have no effect; thus it is not as drastic as `\eject`.

The most interesting macro that plain TₑX provides for page make-up is called `\filbreak`. It means, roughly, "Break the page here and fill the bottom with blank space, unless there is room for more copy that is itself followed by `\filbreak`." Thus if you put `\filbreak` at the end of every paragraph, and if your paragraphs aren't too long, every page break will occur between paragraphs, and TₑX will fit as many paragraphs as possible on each page. The precise meaning of `\filbreak` is

`\vfil\penalty-200\vfilneg`

according to Appendix B; and this simple combination of TₑX's primitives produces the desired result: If a break is taken at the `\penalty-200`, the preceding `\vfil` will fill the bottom of the page with blank space, and the `\vfilneg` will be discarded after the break; but if no break is taken at the penalty, the `\vfil` and `\vfilneg` will cancel each other and have no effect.

Plain TₑX also provides a `\raggedbottom` command, which is a vertical analog of `\raggedright`: It tells TₑX to permit a small amount of variability in the bottom margins on different pages, in order to make the other spacing uniform.

We saw in Chapter 14 that breakpoints for paragraphs are chosen by computing "demerits" for each line and summing them over all lines. The situation for pages is simpler because each page is considered separately. TₑX figures the "cost" of a page break by using the following formula:

$$c = \begin{cases} p, & \text{if } b < \infty \text{ and } p \le -10000 \text{ and } q < 10000; \\ b+p+q, & \text{if } b < 10000 \text{ and } -10000 < p < 10000 \text{ and } q < 10000; \\ 100000, & \text{if } b = 10000 \text{ and } -10000 < p < 10000 \text{ and } q < 10000; \\ \infty, & \text{if } (b = \infty \text{ or } q \ge 10000) \text{ and } p < 10000. \end{cases}$$

Here b is the badness of the page that would be formed if a break were chosen here; p is the penalty associated with the current breakpoint; and q is '`\insertpenalties`', the sum of all penalties for split insertions on the page, as explained below. Vertical badness is computed by the same rules as horizontal badness; it is an integer between 0 and 10000, inclusive, except when the box is overfull, when it is ∞ (infinity).

When a page is completed, it is removed from the main vertical list and passed to an "output routine," as we will see later; so its boxes and glue eventually disappear from TeX's memory. The remainder of the main vertical list exists in two parts: First comes the "current page," which contains all the material that TeX has considered so far as a candidate for the next page to be broken off; then there are "recent contributions," i.e., items that will be moved to the current page as soon as TeX finds it convenient to do so. If you say \showlists, TeX will display the contents of the current page and the recent contributions, if any, on your log file. (The example in Chapter 13 doesn't show any such lists because they were both empty in that case. Chapter 24 explains more about TeX's timing.)

Whenever TeX is moving an item from the top of the "recent contributions" to the bottom of the "current page," it discards a discardable item (glue, kern, or penalty) if the current page does not contain any boxes. This is how glue disappears at a page break. Otherwise if a discardable item is a legitimate breakpoint, TeX calculates the cost c of breaking at this point, using the formula that we have just discussed. If the resulting c is less than or equal to the smallest cost seen so far on the current page, TeX remembers the current breakpoint as the best so far. And if $c = \infty$ or if $p \leq -10000$, TeX seizes the initiative and breaks the page at the best remembered breakpoint. Any material on the current page following that best breakpoint is moved back onto the list of recent contributions, where it will be considered again; thus the "current page" typically gets more than one page's worth of material before the breakpoint is chosen.

This procedure may seem mysterious until you see it in action. Fortunately, there is a convenient way to watch it; you can set \tracingpages=1, thereby instructing TeX to put its page-cost calculations into your log file. For example, here is what appeared on the log file when the author used \tracingpages=1 at the beginning of the present chapter:

```
%% goal height=528.0, max depth=2.2
% t=10.0 g=528.0 b=10000 p=150 c=100000#
% t=22.0 g=528.0 b=10000 p=0 c=100000#
% t=34.0 g=528.0 b=10000 p=0 c=100000#
    ⋮   (25 similar lines are being omitted here)
% t=346.0 plus 2.0 g=528.0 b=10000 p=0 c=100000#
% t=358.0 plus 2.0 g=528.0 b=10000 p=150 c=100000#
% t=370.02223 plus 2.0 g=528.0 b=10000 p=-100 c=100000#
% t=398.0 plus 5.0 minus 2.0 g=528.0 b=10000 p=0 c=100000#
% t=409.0 plus 5.0 minus 2.0 g=528.0 b=10000 p=0 c=100000#
% t=420.0 plus 5.0 minus 2.0 g=528.0 b=10000 p=150 c=100000#
% t=431.0 plus 5.0 minus 2.0 g=528.0 b=10000 p=-100 c=100000#
% t=459.0 plus 8.0 minus 4.0 g=528.0 b=10000 p=0 c=100000#
% t=470.0 plus 8.0 minus 4.0 g=528.0 b=10000 p=0 c=100000#
% t=481.0 plus 8.0 minus 4.0 g=528.0 b=10000 p=0 c=100000#
% t=492.0 plus 8.0 minus 4.0 g=528.0 b=10000 p=0 c=100000#
% t=503.0 plus 8.0 minus 4.0 g=528.0 b=3049 p=0 c=3049#
% t=514.0 plus 8.0 minus 4.0 g=528.0 b=533 p=150 c=683#
% t=525.0 plus 8.0 minus 4.0 g=528.0 b=5 p=-100 c=-95#
% t=553.0 plus 11.0 minus 6.0 g=528.0 b=* p=0 c=*
```

This trace output is admittedly not "user-friendly" in appearance, but after all it comes from deep inside TₑX's bowels where things have been reduced to numeric calculations. You can learn to read it with a little practice, but you won't need to do so very often unless you need to plunge into page-breaking for special applications. Here's what it means: The first line, which starts with '%%', is written when the first box or insertion enters the current page list; it shows the "goal height" and the "max depth" that will be used for that page (namely, the current values of \vsize and \maxdepth). In the present manual we have \vsize=44pc and \maxdepth=2.2pt; dimensions in the log file are always displayed in points. The subsequent lines, which start with a single '%', are written whenever a legal breakpoint is being moved from the list of recent contributions to the current page list. Every % line shows t, which is the total height so far if a page break were to occur, and g, which is the goal height; in this example g stays fixed at 528 pt, but g would have decreased if insertions such as footnotes had occurred on the page. The values of t are steadily increasing from 10 to 22 to 34, etc.; baselines are 12 pt apart at the top of the page and 11 pt apart at the bottom (where material is set in nine-point type). We are essentially seeing one % line per hbox of text being placed on the current page. However, the % lines are generated by the penalty or glue items that follow the hboxes, not by the boxes themselves. Each % line shows also the badness b, the penalty p, and the cost c associated with a breakpoint; if this cost is the best so far, it is marked with a '#' sign, meaning that "this breakpoint will be used for the current page if nothing better comes along." Notice that the first 40 or so breaks all have $b = 10000$, since they are so bad that TₑX considers them indistinguishable; in such cases $c = 100000$, so TₑX simply accumulates material until the page is full enough to have $b < 10000$. A penalty of 150 reflects the \clubpenalty or the \widowpenalty that was inserted as described in Chapter 14. The three lines that say p=-100 are the breakpoints between "dangerous bend" paragraphs; these came from \medbreak commands. The notation b=* and c=* on the final line means that b and c are infinite; the total height of 553 pt cannot be reduced to 528 pt by shrinking the available glue. Therefore the page is ejected at the best previous place, which turns out to be a pretty good break: b=5 and p=-100 yield a net cost of -95.

▸ EXERCISE 15.1
Suppose the paragraph at the bottom of the example page had been one line shorter; what page break would have been chosen?

▸ EXERCISE 15.2
The last two "% lines" of this example show the natural height of t jumping by 28 pt, from 525.0 to 553.0. Explain why there was such a big jump.

The \maxdepth parameter tells TₑX to raise the bottom box on the page if that box has too much depth, so that the depth of the constructed page will not exceed a specified value. (See the discussion of \boxmaxdepth in Chapter 12.) In our example \maxdepth=2.2pt, and the influence of this parameter can be seen in the line that says '% t=370.02223'. Ordinarily t would have been 370.0 at that breakpoint; but the hbox preceding it was unusual because it contained the letter j in \tt, and a 10-point typewriter-style j descends 2.22223 pt below the baseline. Therefore TₑX figured badness as if the hbox were .02223 pt higher and only 2.2 pt deep.

Notice that the first "% line" of our example says t=10.0; this is a consequence of another parameter, called \topskip. Glue disappears at a page break, but it is desirable to produce pages whose top and bottom baselines occur in predetermined positions, whenever possible; therefore TEX inserts special glue just before the first box on each page. This special glue is equal to \topskip, except that the natural space has been decreased by the height of the first box, or it has been set to zero in lieu of a negative value. For example, if \topskip=20pt plus2pt, and if the first box on the current page is 13 pt tall, TEX inserts '\vskip7pt plus2pt' just above that box. Furthermore, if the first box is more than 20 pt tall, '\vskip0pt plus2pt' is inserted. But this example is atypical, since the \topskip glue usually has no stretchability or shrinkability; plain TEX sets \topskip=10pt.

▷ **EXERCISE 15.3**
Assume that \vsize=528pt, \maxdepth=2.2pt, \topskip=10pt, and that no \insert commands are being used. TEX will make pages that are 528 pt high, and the following two statements will normally be true: (a) The baseline of the topmost box on the page will be 10 pt from the top, i.e., 518 pt above the baseline of the page itself. (b) The baseline of the bottommost box on the page will coincide with the baseline of the page itself. Explain under what circumstances (a) and (b) will fail.

Since \vsize, \maxdepth, and \topskip are parameters, you can change them at any time; what happens if you do? Well, TEX salts away the values of \vsize and \maxdepth when it prints the "%% line," i.e., when the first box or insertion occurs on the current page; subsequent changes to those two parameters have no effect until the next current page is started. On the other hand, TEX looks at \topskip only when the first box is being contributed to the current page. If insertions occur before the first box, the \topskip glue before that box is considered to be a valid breakpoint; this is the only case in which a completed page might not contain a box.

You can look at the t and g values that are used in page breaking by referring to the ⟨dimen⟩ values '\pagetotal' and '\pagegoal', respectively. You can even change them (but let's hope that you know what you are doing). For example, the command \pagegoal=500pt overrides the previously saved value of \vsize. Besides \pagetotal, which represents the accumulated natural height, TEX maintains the quantities \pagestretch, \pagefilstretch, \pagefillstretch, \pagefilllstretch, \pageshrink, and \pagedepth. When the current page contains no boxes, \pagetotal and its relatives are zero and \pagegoal is 16383.99998 pt (TEX's largest ⟨dimen⟩); changing their values has no effect at such times. The integer q in the formula for page costs is also available for inspection and change; it is called \insertpenalties.

Page breaking differs from line breaking in one small respect that deserves mention here: If you say \eject\eject, the second \eject is ignored, because it is equivalent to \penalty-10000 and penalties are discarded after a page break. But if you say \break\break in a paragraph, the second \break causes an empty line, because penalties are discarded after a break in a paragraph only if they do not belong to the final sequence of breakpoints. This technicality is unimportant in practice, because \break\break isn't a good way to make an empty line; that line will usually be an underfull hbox, since it has only the \leftskip and \rightskip glue in it. Similarly, '\eject\eject' would not be a good way to make an empty page, even if TEX were to change its rules somehow so that an \eject would never be ignored. The best way to eject an empty page is to say '\eject\line{}\vfil\eject', and the best way to create an empty line is '\break\hbox{}\hfil\break'. Both of these avoid underfull boxes.

You are probably wondering how page numbers and such things get attached to pages. The answer is that TEX allows you to do further processing after each page break has been chosen; a special "output routine" goes into action before pages actually receive their final form. Chapter 23 explains how to construct output routines and how to modify the output routine of plain TEX.

Every once in a while, TEX will produce a really awful-looking page and you will wonder what happened. For example, you might get just one paragraph and a lot of white space, when some of the text on the following page would easily fit into the white space. The reason for such apparently anomalous behavior is almost always that no good page break is possible; even the alternative that looks better to you is quite terrible as far as TEX is concerned! TEX does not distinguish between two choices that both have 10000 units of badness or more, even though some bad breaks do look much worse than others. The solution in such cases is to insert \eject or \vfill\eject in some acceptable spot, or to revise the manuscript. If this problem arises frequently, however, you probably are using a format that sets overly strict limitations on page format; try looking at the output of \tracingpages and modifying some of TEX's parameters, until you have better luck.

The remainder of this chapter is about insertions: things like footnotes and illustrations, and how they interact with page breaks. Before we discuss the primitive operations by which TEX deals with insertions, we will take a look at the facilities that plain TEX provides at a higher level.

Illustrations can be inserted in several ways using plain TEX. The simplest of these is called a "floating topinsert"; you say

\topinsert⟨vertical mode material⟩\endinsert

and TEX will attempt to put the vertical mode material at the top of the current page. If there's no room for such an insertion on one page, TEX will insert it at the top of the next page. The ⟨vertical mode material⟩ can contain embedded paragraphs that temporarily interrupt vertical mode in the usual way; for example:

```
\topinsert \vskip 2in
\hsize=3in \raggedright
\noindent{\bf Figure 3.} This is the caption to the
third illustration of my paper. I have left two inches
of space above the caption so that there will be room
to introduce special artwork. \endinsert
```

The caption in this example will be set ragged-right in a 3-inch column at the left of the page. Plain TEX automatically adds a "bigskip" below each topinsert; this will separate the caption from the text. The effects of \hsize=3in and \raggedright do not extend past the \endinsert, since grouping is implied.

▶ **EXERCISE 15.4**
Modify this example so that the caption is moved over next to the right margin, instead of appearing at the left.

Similarly, if you say '\pageinsert ⟨vertical mode material⟩ \endinsert', the vertical mode material will be justified to the size of a full page (without a bigskip below it); the result will appear on the following page.

There's also '`\midinsert` ⟨vertical mode material⟩ `\endinsert`', which tries first to insert the material in place, wherever you happen to be, in the middle of the current page. If there is enough room, you get the effect of

`\bigskip\vbox{`⟨vertical mode material⟩`}\bigbreak`

otherwise the `\midinsert` is effectively converted to a `\topinsert`. There is a slight probability that `\midinsert` will not find the best placement, because TₑX is sometimes processing text ahead of the current page. You may want to say '`\goodbreak`' just before `\midinsert`.

You should use the commands `\topinsert`, `\pageinsert`, `\midinsert` in vertical mode (i.e., between paragraphs), not inside of boxes or other insertions.

If you have two or more `\topinsert` or `\pageinsert` commands in quick succession, TₑX may need to carry them over to several subsequent pages; but they will retain their relative order when they are carried over. For example, suppose you have pages that are nine inches tall, and suppose you have already specified 4 inches of text for some page, say page 25. Then suppose you make seven topinserts in a row, of respective sizes $1, 2, 3, 9, 3, 2, 1$ inches; the 9-inch one is actually a `\pageinsert`. What happens? Well, the first and second will appear at the top of page 25, followed by the 4 inches of copy you have already typed; that copy will immediately be followed by two more inches that you type after the seven inserts. The third topinsert will appear at the top of page 26, followed by six more inches of text; the fourth will fill page 27; and the remaining three will appear at the top of page 28.

▶ **EXERCISE 15.5**
What would happen in the example just discussed if the final 1-inch insertion were a `\midinsert` instead of a `\topinsert`?

At the end of a paper, you probably want to make sure that no insertions are lost; and at the end of a chapter, you probably want to make sure that no insertions float into the following chapter. Plain TₑX will flush out all remaining insertions, with blank space filling the bottom of incomplete pages, if you say '`\vfill\supereject`'.

Besides illustrations that are inserted at the top of a page, plain TₑX will also insert footnotes at the bottom of a page. The `\footnote` macro is provided for use within paragraphs;* for example, the footnote in the present sentence was typed in the following way:

`... paragraphs;\footnote*{Like this.} for example, ...`

There are two parameters to a `\footnote`; first comes the reference mark, which will appear both in the paragraph** and in the footnote itself, and then comes the text of the footnote.[45] The latter text may be several paragraphs long, and it may contain

---

* Like this.

** The author typed '`paragraph\footnote{**}{The author ...}`' here.

[45] And '`footnote.\footnote{$^{45}$}{And ...}`' here. The footnotes in this manual appear in smaller type, and they are set with hanging indentation; furthermore a smallskip occurs between footnotes on the same page. But in plain TₑX, footnotes

displayed equations and such things, but it should not involve other insertions. TEX will ensure that each footnote occurs at the bottom of the same page as its reference.† A long footnote will be split, if necessary, and continued at the bottom of the following page, as you can see in the somewhat contrived example that appears here. Authors who are interested in good exposition should avoid footnotes whenever possible, since footnotes tend to be distracting.‡

The \footnote macro should be used only in paragraphs or hboxes that are contributed to TEX's main vertical list; insertions will be lost if they occur inside of boxes that are inside of boxes. Thus, for example, you should not try to put a \footnote into a subformula of a math formula. But it's OK to use footnotes within \centerline, e.g.,

```
\centerline{A paper by A. U. Thor%
  \footnote*{Supported by NSF.}}
```

or even on the outer level of a table entry inside an \halign.

Topinserts work fine by themselves, and footnotes work fine by themselves, but complications can arise when you try to mix them in devious ways. For example, if a \pageinsert floats to the page that follows a long footnote that had to be broken, both of the held-over insertions may try to force themselves onto the same page, and an overfull vbox may result. Furthermore, insertions cannot appear within insertions, so you can't use \footnote within a \topinsert. If you really need a footnote in some caption, there's a \vfootnote macro that can be used in vertical mode. To use it, you put a reference mark like '*' in the caption, and then you say '\vfootnote*{The footnote}' somewhere on the page where you guess that the caption will finally fall. In such complex circumstances you might want to rethink whether or not you are really using the most appropriate format for the exposition of your ideas.

Chapter 24 explains the exact rules about migration of vertical-mode material (like footnotes) from horizontal lists to the enclosing vertical list. Insertions, marks, and the results of \vadjust all migrate in the same fashion.

Now let's study the primitives of TEX that are used to construct macros like \topinsert and \footnote. We are about to enter behind the scenes into a sublanguage of TEX that permits users to do complex manipulations with boxes and glue. Our discussion will be in two parts: First we shall consider TEX's "registers," with which a user can do arithmetic related to typesetting; and then we shall discuss the insertion items that can appear in horizontal and vertical lists. Our discussion of the first topic (registers) will be marked with single dangerous-bend signs, since registers are of general use in advanced applications of TEX, whether or not they relate to insertions. But the second topic will be marked with double dangerous-bend signs, since insertions are rather esoteric.

---

are typeset with the normal size of type, with \textindent used for the reference mark, and without extra smallskips. The \textindent macro is like \item, but it omits hanging indentation.

† Printers often use the symbols \dag (†), \ddag (‡), \S (§), and \P (¶) as reference marks; sometimes also $\|$ (‖). You can say, e.g., '\footnote\dag{...}'.

‡ Yet Gibbon's *Decline and Fall* would not have been the same without footnotes.

TₑX has 256 registers called \count0 to \count255, each capable of containing integers between -2147483647 and $+2147483647$, inclusive; i.e., the magnitudes should be less than 2^{31}. TₑX also has 256 registers called \dimen0 to \dimen255, each capable of containing a ⟨dimen⟩ (see Chapter 10). There are another 256 registers called \skip0 to \skip255, each containing ⟨glue⟩ (see Chapter 12); and \muskip0 to \muskip255, each containing ⟨muglue⟩ (see Chapter 18). You can assign new values to these registers by saying

```
\count⟨number⟩ = ⟨number⟩
\dimen⟨number⟩ = ⟨dimen⟩
\skip⟨number⟩ = ⟨glue⟩
\muskip⟨number⟩ = ⟨muglue⟩
```

and then you can add or subtract values of the same type by saying

```
\advance\count⟨number⟩ by ⟨number⟩
\advance\dimen⟨number⟩ by ⟨dimen⟩
\advance\skip⟨number⟩ by ⟨glue⟩
\advance\muskip⟨number⟩ by ⟨muglue⟩
```

For example, '\dimen8=\hsize \advance\dimen8 by 1in' sets register \dimen8 to an inch more than the current value of the normal line size.

 If infinite glue components are added, lower order infinities disappear. For example, after the two commands

```
\skip2 = 0pt plus 2fill minus 3fill
\advance\skip2 by 4pt plus 1fil minus 2filll
```

the value of \skip2 will be 4 pt plus 2 fill minus 2 filll.

 Multiplication and division are possible too, but only by integers. For example, '\multiply\dimen4 by 3' triples the value of \dimen4, and '\divide\skip5 by 2' cuts in half all three components of the glue that is currently registered in \skip5. You shouldn't divide by zero, nor should you multiply by numbers that will make the results exceed the register capacities. Division of a positive integer by a positive integer discards the remainder, and the sign of the result changes if you change the sign of either operand. For example, 14 divided by 3 yields 4; -14 divided by 3 yields -4; -14 divided by -3 yields 4. Dimension values are integer multiples of sp (scaled points).

 You can use any \count register in the context of a ⟨number⟩, any \dimen register in the context of a ⟨dimen⟩, any \skip register in the context of ⟨glue⟩, and any \muskip register in the context of ⟨muglue⟩. For example, '\hskip\skip1' puts horizontal glue into a list, using the value of \skip1; and if \count5 is 20, the command '\advance\dimen20 by\dimen\count5' is equivalent to '\multiply\dimen20 by 2'.

 A \dimen register can be used also in the context of a ⟨number⟩, and a \skip register can be used as a ⟨dimen⟩ or a ⟨number⟩. TₑX converts ⟨glue⟩ to ⟨dimen⟩ by omitting the stretch and shrink components, and it converts ⟨dimen⟩ to ⟨number⟩ by assuming units of sp (scaled points). For example, if \skip1 holds the value 1pt plus 2pt, then '\dimen1=\skip1' sets \dimen1 equal to 1pt; and the commands '\count2=\dimen1' or '\count2=\skip1' will set \count2 equal to 65536. These rules also apply to TₑX's internal parameters; for example, '\dimen2=\baselineskip' will set \dimen2 to the natural space component of the current baselineskip glue.

▶ **EXERCISE 15.6**
Test your knowledge of TEX's registers by stating the results of each of the following commands when they are performed in sequence:

```
\count1=50   \dimen2=\count1pt   \divide\count1 by 8
\skip2=-10pt plus\count1fil minus\dimen2
\multiply\skip2 by-\count1   \divide\skip2 by \dimen2   \count6=\skip2
\skip1=.5\dimen2 plus\skip2 minus\count\count1fill
\multiply\skip2 by\skip1   \advance\skip1 by-\skip2
```

▶ **EXERCISE 15.7**
What is in \skip5 after the following three commands have acted?

```
\skip5=0pt plus 1pt
\advance\skip5 by \skip4   \advance\skip5 by -\skip4
```

▶ **EXERCISE 15.8**
(For mathematicians.) Explain how to round \dimen2 to the nearest multiple of \dimen3, assuming that \dimen3 is nonzero.

The registers obey TEX's group structure. For example, changes to \count3 inside {...} will not affect the value of \count3 outside. Therefore TEX effectively has more than 256 registers of each type. If you want the effect of a register command to transcend its group, you must say \global when you change the value.

▶ **EXERCISE 15.9**
What is in \count1 after the following sequence of commands?

```
\count1=5 {\count1=2 \global\advance\count1by\count1
   \advance\count1by\count1}
```

The first ten \count registers, \count0 through \count9, are reserved for a special purpose: TEX displays these ten counts on your terminal whenever outputting a page, and it transmits them to the output file as an identification of that page. The counts are separated by decimal points on your terminal, with trailing '.0' patterns suppressed. Thus, for example, if \count0=5 and \count2=7 when a page is being shipped out to the dvi file, and if the other count registers are zero, TEX will type '[5.0.7]'. Plain TEX uses \count0 for the page number, and it keeps \count1 through \count9 equal to zero; that is why you see just '[1]' when page 1 is being output. In more complex applications the page numbers can have further structure; ten counts are shipped out so that there will be plenty of identification.

It's usually desirable to have symbolic names for registers. TEX provides a \countdef command (similar to \chardef, cf. Chapter 8), which makes it easy to do this: You just say

```
\countdef\chapno=28
```

and \chapno is henceforth an abbreviation for \count28. Similar commands \dimendef, \skipdef, and \muskipdef are available for the other types of numeric registers. After a control sequence has been defined by \countdef, it can be used in TEX commands exactly as if it were an integer parameter like \tolerance. Similarly, \dimendef effectively creates a new dimension parameter, \skipdef effectively creates a new glue parameter, and \muskipdef effectively creates a new muglue parameter.

Besides the numerical registers, TₑX also has 256 box registers called \box0 to \box255. A box register gets a value when you say \setbox⟨number⟩=⟨box⟩; for example, '\setbox3=\hbox{A}' sets \box3 to an hbox that contains the single letter A. Several other examples of \setbox have already appeared in Chapter 12. Chapter 10 points out that '2\wd3' is a ⟨dimen⟩ that represents twice the width of \box3; similarly, \ht⟨number⟩ and \dp⟨number⟩ can be used to refer to the height and depth of a given box register.

Box registers are local to groups just as arithmetic registers are. But there's a big difference between box registers and all the rest: When you use a \box, it loses its value. For example, the construction '\raise2pt\box3' in a horizontal list not only puts the contents of \box3 into the list after raising it by 2 pt, it also makes \box3 void. TₑX does this for efficiency, since it is desirable to avoid copying the contents of potentially large boxes. If you want to use a box register without wiping out its contents, just say '\copy' instead of '\box'; for example, '\raise2pt\copy3'.

Another way to use a box register is to extract the inside of an hbox by saying '\unhbox'. This annihilates the contents of the register, like '\box' does, and it also removes one level of boxing. For example, the commands

```
\setbox3=\hbox{A} \setbox3=\hbox{\box3 B}
\setbox4=\hbox{A} \setbox4=\hbox{\unhbox4 B}
```

put \hbox{\hbox{A}B} into \box3 and \hbox{AB} into \box4. Similarly, \unvbox unwraps a vbox. If you want to construct a large box by accretion (e.g., a table of contents), it is best to use \unhbox or \unvbox as in the \setbox4 example; otherwise you use more of TₑX's memory space, and you might even obtain boxes inside boxes nested to such a deep level that hardware or software limits are exceeded.

The operations \unhcopy and \unvcopy are related to \unhbox and \unvbox as \copy is to \box. (But their names are admittedly peculiar.)

An unboxing operation "unsets" any glue that was set at the box's outer level. For example, consider the sequence of commands

```
\setbox5=\hbox{A \hbox{B C}} \setbox6=\hbox to 1.05\wd5{\unhcopy5}
```

This makes \box6 five percent wider than \box5; the glue between A and \hbox{B C} stretches to make the difference, but the glue inside the inner hbox does not change.

A box register is either "void" or it contains an hbox or a vbox. There is a difference between a void register and one that contains an empty box whose height, width, and depth are zero; for example, if \box3 is void, you can say \unhbox3 or \unvbox3 or \unhcopy3 or \unvcopy3, but if \box3 is equal to \hbox{} you can say only \unhbox3 or \unhcopy3. If you say '\global\setbox3=⟨box⟩', register \box3 will become "globally void" when it is subsequently used or unboxed.

▶ **EXERCISE 15.10**
What is in register \box5 after the following commands?

```
\setbox5=\hbox{A}   \setbox5=\hbox{\copy5\unhbox5\box5\unhcopy5}
```

▶ **EXERCISE 15.11**
And what's in \box3 after '{\global\setbox3=\hbox{A}\setbox3=\hbox{}}'?

If you are unsure about how TₑX operates on its registers, you can experiment online by using certain '\show' commands. For example,

\showthe\count1   \showthe\dimen2   \showthe\skip3

will display the contents of \count1, \dimen2, and \skip3; and '\showbox4' will display the contents of \box4. Box contents will appear only in the log file, unless you say '\tracingonline=1'. Plain TₑX provides a macro '\tracingall' that turns on every possible mode of interaction, including \tracingonline. The author used these features to check the answers to several of the exercises above.

Large applications of TₑX make use of different sets of macros written by different groups of people. Chaos would reign if a register like \count100, say, were being used simultaneously for different purposes in different macros. Therefore plain TₑX provides an allocation facility; cooperation will replace confusion if each macro writer uses these conventions. The idea is to say, e.g., '\newcount' when you want to dedicate a \count register to a special purpose. For example, the author designed a macro called '\exercise' to format the exercises in this manual, and one of the features of \exercise is that it computes the number of the current exercise. The format macros in Appendix E reserve a \count register for this purpose by saying

\newcount\exno

and then the command '\exno=0' is used at the beginning of each chapter. Similarly, '\advance\exno by1' is used whenever a new exercise comes along, and '\the\exno' is used to typeset the current exercise number. The \newcount operation assigns a unique count register to its argument \exno, and it defines \exno with a \countdef command. All of the other format macros are written without the knowledge of exactly which \count register actually corresponds to \exno.

Besides \newcount, plain TₑX provides \newdimen, \newskip, \newmuskip, and \newbox; there also are \newtoks, \newread, \newwrite, \newfam, and \newinsert, for features we haven't discussed yet. Appendices B and E contain several examples of the proper use of allocation. In the cases of \newbox, \newread, etc., the allocated number is defined by \chardef. For example, if the command '\newbox\abstract' is used to define a box register that will contain an abstract, and if the \newbox operation decides to allocate \box45 for this purpose, then it defines the meaning of \abstract by saying '\chardef\abstract=45'. TₑX allows \chardef'd quantities to be used as integers, so that you can say \box\abstract and \copy\abstract, etc. (There is no \boxdef command.)

▸ **EXERCISE 15.12**
Design a \note macro that produces footnotes numbered sequentially. For example,[1] it should produce the footnotes here[2] if you type

... example,\note{First note.} it should produce
the footnotes here\note{Second note.} if ...

(Use \newcount to allocate a \count register for the footnotes.)

---

[1] First note.

[2] Second note.

Sometimes, however, you want to use a register just for temporary storage, and you know that it won't conflict with anybody else's macros. Registers \count255, \dimen255, \skip255, and \muskip255 are traditionally kept available for such purposes. Furthermore, plain TEX reserves \dimen0 to \dimen9, \skip0 to \skip9, \muskip0 to \muskip9, and \box0 to \box9 for "scratchwork"; these registers are never allocated by the \new... operations. We have seen that \count0 through \count9 are special, and \box255 also turns out to be special; so those registers should be avoided unless you know what you are doing.

Of course any register can be used for short-term purposes inside a group (including \count0 to \count9 and \box255, and including registers that have been allocated for other purposes), since register changes are local to groups. However, you should be sure that TEX will not output any pages before the group has ended, because output routines might otherwise be invoked at unfortunate times. TEX is liable to invoke an output routine whenever it tries to move something from the list of recent contributions to the current page, because it might discover a page break with $c = \infty$ then. Here is a list of the times when that can happen: (a) At the beginning or end of a paragraph, provided that this paragraph is being contributed to the main vertical list. (b) At the beginning or end of a displayed equation within such a paragraph. (c) After completing an \halign in vertical mode. (d) After contributing a box or penalty or insertion to the main vertical list. (e) After an \output routine has ended.

Now that we are armed with the knowledge of TEX's flexible registers, we can plunge into the details of insertions. There are 255 classes of insertions, \insert0 to \insert254, and they are tied to other registers of the same number. For example, \insert100 is connected with \count100, \dimen100, \skip100, and \box100. Therefore plain TEX provides an allocation function for insertions as it does for registers; Appendix B includes the command

> \newinsert\footins

which defines \footins as the number for footnote insertions. Other commands that deal with footnotes refer to \count\footins, \dimen\footins, and so on. The macros for floating topinserts are similarly prefaced by '\newinsert\topins', which defines \topins as the number of their class. Each class of insertions is independent, but TEX preserves the order of insertions within a class. It turns out that \footins is class 254, and \topins is class 253, but the macros do not use such numbers directly.

For our purposes let's consider a particular class of insertions called class n; we will then be dealing with TEX's primitive command

> \insert n{⟨vertical mode material⟩}

which puts an insertion item into a horizontal or vertical list. For this class of insertions

> \box n is where the material appears when a page is output;
> \count n is the magnification factor for page breaking;
> \dimen n is the maximum insertion size per page;
> \skip n is the extra space to allocate on a page.

For example, material inserted with \insert100 will eventually appear in \box100.

Let the natural height plus depth of \insert n be x; then \count n is 1000 times the factor by which x affects the page goal. For example, plain TₑX sets \count\footins=1000, since there is a one-to-one relationship: A 10-point footnote effectively makes a page 10 pt shorter. But if we have an application where footnotes appear in double columns, a count value of 500 would be appropriate. One of the insertion classes in Appendix E makes marginal notes for proofreading purposes; in that case the count value is zero. No actual magnification is done; \count n is simply a number used for bookkeeping, when estimating the costs of various page breaks.

The first footnote on a page requires extra space, since we want to separate the footnotes from the text, and since we want to output a horizontal rule. Plain TₑX sets '\skip\footins=\bigskipamount'; this means that a bigskip of extra space is assumed to be added by the output routine to any page that contains at least one insertion of class \footins.

Sometimes it is desirable to put a maximum limitation on the size of insertions; for example, people usually don't want an entire page to consist of footnotes. Plain TₑX sets \dimen\footins=8in; this means that \box\footins is not supposed to accumulate more than 8 inches of footnotes for any one page.

You might want to review the page-breaking algorithm explained at the beginning of this chapter, before reading further. On the other hand, maybe you don't really want to read the rest of this chapter at all, ever.

Here now is the algorithm that TₑX performs when an \insert n is moved from the "recent contributions" to the "current page." (Remember that such a move does not mean that the insertion will actually take place; the current page will be backed up later, to the breakpoint of least cost, and only the insertions preceding that breakpoint will actually be performed.) Let g and t be the current \pagegoal and \pagetotal; let q be the \insertpenalties accumulated for the current page; and let d and z be the current \pagedepth and \pageshrink. (The value of d is at most \maxdepth; this value has not yet been incorporated into t.) Finally, let x be the natural height plus depth of the \insert n that we are moving to the current page; and let f be the corresponding magnification factor, i.e., \count n divided by 1000.

Step 1. If there is no previous \insert n on the current page, decrease g by $hf + w$, where h is the current height plus depth of \box n, and where w is the natural space component of \skip n; also include the stretch and shrink components of \skip n in the totals for the current page (in particular, this affects z).

Step 2. If a previous \insert n on the current page has been split, add the parameter called \floatingpenalty to q, and omit Steps 3 and 4.

Step 3. Test if the current insertion will fit on the page without splitting. This means that it will not make the height plus depth of \box n surpass \dimen n, when it is added to \box n together with all previous \insert n amounts on the current page; furthermore, it means that either $xf \leq 0$ or $t + d + xf - z \leq g$. If both tests are passed, subtract xf from g and omit Step 4.

Step 4. (The current insertion will be split, at least tentatively; but the split will not actually take place if the least-cost page turns out to have occurred earlier than the present insertion.) First compute the largest amount v such that a height plus depth of v will not make the total insertions into \box n bigger than \dimen n, and such that $t + d + vf \leq g$. (Notice that z is omitted from the latter formula, but the available shrinkability was considered in Step 3 when we tried to avoid splitting.) Then find the least-cost way to split the beginning of the vertical list of the insertion so as to obtain a box of height v. (Use an algorithm just like page-breaking, but without the complexity of insertion; an additional '\penalty-10000' item is assumed to be present at the end of the vertical list, to ensure that a legal breakpoint exists.) Let u be the natural height plus depth of that least-cost box, and let r be the penalty associated with the optimum breakpoint. Decrease g by uf, and increase q by r. (If \tracingpages=1, the log file should now get a cryptic message that says '% split n to v,u p=r'. For example,

% split254 to 180.2,175.3 p=100

means that the algorithm has tried to split an \insert254 to 180.2 pt; the best split is actually 175.3 pt tall, and the penalty for breaking there is 100.)

This algorithm is admittedly complicated, but no simpler mechanism seems to do nearly as much. Notice that penalties of -10000 inside insertions will make certain splits very attractive in Step 4, so the user can provide hints about where to break, in difficult situations. The algorithm provides a variety of different behaviors: Floating insertions can be accommodated as a special case of split insertions, by making each floating topinsert start with a small penalty, and by having zero as the associated \floatingpenalty; non-floating insertions like footnotes are accommodated by associating larger penalties with split insertions (see Appendix B).

The splitting operation mentioned in Step 4 is also available as a primitive: '\vsplit⟨number⟩ to⟨dimen⟩' produces a vbox obtained by splitting off a specified amount of material from a box register. For example,

\setbox200=\vsplit100 to 50pt

sets \box200 to a vbox whose height is 50 pt; it goes through the vertical list inside \box100 (which should be a vbox) and finds the least-cost break assuming a goal height of 50 pt, considering badnesses and penalties just as in the case of page-breaking (but with $q = 0$). The algorithm uses \splitmaxdepth instead of \maxdepth to govern the maximum depth of boxes. Then it prunes the top of \box100 by removing everything up to and including any discardable items that immediately follow the optimum breakpoint; and it uses \splittopskip to insert new glue before the first box inside \box100, just as \topskip glue appears at the top of a page. However, if the optimum breakpoint occurs at the end of the vertical list inside \box100—a '\penalty-10000' item is assumed to be present there—or if all items after the optimum breakpoint are discarded, \box100 will be void after the \vsplit. And if \box100 was void before the \vsplit, both \box100 and \box200 will be void afterwards.

You'd better not change \box n, \count n, \dimen n, or \skip n while T_EX is contributing insertions to the current page, since T_EX's algorithm assumes that those quantities are static. But you can change \floatingpenalty, \splittopskip, and \splitmaxdepth; T_EX will use the values that were current just inside the closing right brace of '\insert n\{...\}' when it splits and floats insertions. For example, Appendix B uses \floatingpenalty=20000 in footnote insertions, to discourage footnotes that split before others can start, but \floatingpenalty=0 in floating topinserts. Appendix B also uses special values of \splittopskip and \splitmaxdepth, together with struts, so that split footnotes will be typeset with the same spacing as unsplit ones.

The \footnote macro puts an \insert into the horizontal list of a paragraph. After the paragraph has been broken into lines, this insertion will move out into the vertical list just after the line that contained it (see Chapter 14). Since there is no legal breakpoint between that box (i.e., that line) and the insertion, TₑX will put the insertion onto the page that contains the line that contains the insertion.

▶ **EXERCISE 15.13**
Study the page-breaking algorithm carefully. Is it possible that a footnote might not appear on the same page as its reference?

When the best page break is finally chosen, TₑX removes everything after the chosen breakpoint from the bottom of the "current page," and puts it all back at the top of the "recent contributions." The chosen breakpoint itself is placed at the very top of the recent contributions. If it is a penalty item, the value of the penalty is recorded in \outputpenalty and the penalty in the contribution list is changed to 10000; otherwise \outputpenalty is set to 10000. The insertions that remain on the current page are of three kinds: For each class n there are unsplit insertions, followed possibly by a single split insertion, followed possibly by others. If \holdinginserts > 0, all insertions remain in place (so that they might be contributed again); otherwise they are all removed from the current page list as follows: The unsplit insertions are appended to \box n, with no interline glue between them. (Struts should be used, as in the \vfootnote macro of Appendix B.) If a split insertion is present, it is effectively \vsplit to the size that was computed previously in Step 4; the top part is treated as an unsplit insertion, and the remainder (if any) is converted to an insertion as if it had not been split. This remainder, followed by any other floating insertions of the same class, is held over in a separate place. (They will show up on the "current page" if \showlists is used while an \output routine is active; the total number of such insertions appears in \insertpenalties during an \output routine.) Finally, the remaining items before the best break on the current page are put together in a \vbox of height g, where g was the \pagegoal at the time of the break, using the saved value of \maxdepth; this box becomes \box255. Now the user's \output routine enters TₑX's scanner (see Chapter 23); its duty is to assemble the final pages based on the contents of \box255 and any insertion boxes that it knows about. The output routine will probably unbox those boxes, so that their glue can be reset; the glue in insertion boxes usually cooperates nicely with the glue on the rest of the page, when it is given a chance. After the \output routine is finished, held-over insertion items are placed first on the list of recent contributions, followed by the vertical list constructed by \output, followed by the recent contributions beginning with the page break. (Deep breath.) You got that?

Since it is impossible to foresee how [footnotes] will happen to come out in the make-up, it is impracticable to number them from 1 up on each page. The best way is to number them consecutively throughout an article or by chapters in a book.
— UNIVERSITY OF CHICAGO PRESS, *Manual of Style* (1910)

Don't use footnotes in your books, Don.
— JILL KNUTH (1962)

16
Typing
Math Formulas

TEX is designed to handle complex mathematical expressions in such a way that most of them are easy to input. The basic idea is that a complicated formula is composed of less complicated formulas put together in a simple way; the less complicated formulas are, in turn, made up of simple combinations of formulas that are even less complicated; and so on. Stating this another way, if you know how to type simple formulas and how to combine formulas into larger ones, you will be able to handle virtually any formula at all. So let's start with simple ones and work our way up.

The simplest formula is a single letter, like 'x', or a single number, like '2'. In order to put these into a TEX text, you type 'x' and '2', respectively. Notice that all mathematical formulas are enclosed in special math brackets; we are using $ as the math bracket in this manual, in accord with the plain TEX format defined in Appendix B, because mathematics is supposedly expensive.

When you type 'x' the 'x' comes out in italics, but when you type '2' the '2' comes out in roman type. In general, all characters on your keyboard have a special interpretation in math formulas, according to the normal conventions of mathematics printing: Letters now denote italic letters, while digits and punctuation denote roman digits and punctuation; a hyphen (-) now denotes a minus sign ($-$), which is almost the same as an em-dash but not quite (see Chapter 2). The first $ that you type puts you into "math mode" and the second takes you out (see Chapter 13). So if you forget one $ or type one $ too many, TEX will probably become thoroughly confused and you will probably get some sort of error message.

Formulas that have been typeset by a printer who is unaccustomed to mathematics usually look quite strange to a mathematician, because a novice printer usually gets the spacing all wrong. In order to alleviate this problem, TEX does most of its own spacing in math formulas; and it *ignores* any spaces that you yourself put between $'s. For example, if you type '$ x$' and '$ 2 $', they will mean the same thing as 'x' and '2'. You can type '$(x + y)/(x - y)$' or '$(x+y) / (x-y)$', but both will result in '$(x+y)/(x-y)$', a formula in which there is a bit of extra space surrounding the + and $-$ signs but none around the / sign. Thus, you do not have to memorize the complicated rules of math spacing, and you are free to use blank spaces in any way you like. Of course, spaces are still used in the normal way to mark the end of control sequences, as explained in Chapter 3. In most circumstances TEX's spacing will be what a mathematician is accustomed to; but we will see in Chapter 18 that there are control sequences by which you can override TEX's spacing rules if you want to.

One of the things mathematicians like to do is make their formulas look like Greek to the uninitiated. In plain TEX language you can type '$$\alpha, \beta, \gamma, \delta;$$' and you will get the first four Greek letters

$$\alpha, \beta, \gamma, \delta;$$

furthermore there are uppercase Greek letters like 'Γ', which you can get by typing 'Γ'. Don't feel intimidated if you aren't already familiar with

Greek letters; they will be easy to learn if you need them. The only difficulty is that some symbols that look nearly the same must be carefully distinguished. For example, the Greek letters \nu (ν) and \kappa (κ) should not be confused with the italic letters v and x; the Greek \phi (ϕ) is different from the slashed zero called \emptyset ($\emptyset$). A lowercase epsilon (ϵ) is quite different from the symbol used to denote membership in a set ($\in$); type 'ϵ' for ϵ and '$\in$' for $\in$. Some of the lowercase Greek letters have variant forms in plain TEX's math italic fonts: '$(\phi,\theta,\epsilon,\rho)$' yields '$(\phi, \theta, \epsilon, \rho)$' while '$(\varphi,\vartheta,\varepsilon,\varrho)$' yields '$(\varphi, \vartheta, \varepsilon, \varrho)$'.

Besides Greek letters, there are a lot of funny symbols like '$\approx$' (which you get by typing '$\approx$') and '$\mapsto$' (which you get by typing '$\mapsto$'). A complete list of these control sequences and the characters they correspond to appears in Appendix F. Such control sequences are allowed only in math mode, i.e., between $'s, because the corresponding symbols appear in the math fonts.

▸ **EXERCISE 16.1**
What should you type to get the formula '$\gamma + \nu \in \Gamma$'?

▸ **EXERCISE 16.2**
Look at Appendix F to discover the control sequences for '$\leq$', '$\geq$', and '$\neq$'. (These are probably the three most commonly used math symbols that are not present on your keyboard.) What does plain TEX call them?

Now let's see how the more complex formulas get built up from simple ones. In the first place, you can get superscripts $^{(up\ high)}$ and subscripts $_{(down\ low)}$ by using '^' and '_', as shown in the following examples:

Input	*Output*
x^2	x^2
x_2	x_2
2^x	2^x
x^2y^2	x^2y^2
$x ^ 2y ^ 2$	x^2y^2
x_2y_2	x_2y_2
$_2F_3$	$_2F_3$

Notice that ^ and _ apply only to the next single character. If you want several things to be superscripted or subscripted, just enclose them in braces:

x^{2y}	x^{2y}
2^{2^x}	2^{2^x}
$2^{2^{2^x}}$	$2^{2^{2^x}}$
y_{x_2}	y_{x_2}
y_{x^2}	y_{x^2}

The braces in these examples have been used to specify "subformulas," i.e., simpler parts of a larger formula. TₑX makes a box for each subformula, and treats that box as if it were a single symbol. Braces also serve their usual purpose of grouping, as discussed in Chapter 5.

It is illegal to type 'x^y^z' or 'x_y_z'; TₑX will complain of a "double superscript" or "double subscript." You must type 'x^{y^z}' or 'x^{yz}' or 'x_{y_z}' or 'x_{yz}' in order to make your intention clear.

A superscript or subscript following a character applies to that character only; but when following a subformula it applies to that whole subformula, and it will be raised or lowered accordingly. For example,

$((x^2)^3)^4$ $((x^2)^3)^4$

${({(x^2)}^3)}^4$ $\left((x^2)^3\right)^4$

In the first formula the '^3' and '^4' are superscripts on the right parentheses, i.e., on the ')' characters that immediately precede them, but in the second formula they are superscripts on the subformulas that are enclosed in braces. The first alternative is preferable, because it is much easier to type and it is just as easy to read.

 A subscript or superscript following nothing (as in the '_2F_3' example on the preceding page, where the '_2' follows nothing) is taken to mean a subscript or superscript of an empty subformula. Such notations are (fortunately) rare in mathematics; but if you do encounter them it is better to make your intention clear by showing the empty subformula explicitly with braces. In other words, the best way to get '$_2F_3$' in a formula is to type '{}_2F_3' or '{_2}F_3' or '{_2F_3}'.

 ▶ **EXERCISE 16.3**
What difference, if any, is there between the output of '\$x + _2F_3\$' and the output of '\$x + {}_2F_3\$'?

 ▶ **EXERCISE 16.4**
Describe the differences between the outputs of '\${x^y}^z\$' and '\$x^{y^z}\$'.

You can have simultaneous subscripts and superscripts, and you can specify them in any order:

x^2_3 x_3^2

x_3^2 x_3^2

$x^{31415}_{92}+\pi$ $x^{31415}_{92}+\pi$

$x_{y^a_b}^{z_c^d}$ $x_{y_b^a}^{z_c^d}$

Notice that simultaneous su$^{per}_{b}$scripts are positioned over each other. However, a subscript will be "tucked in" slightly when it follows certain letters; for example, 'P_2^2' produces 'P_2^2'. If for some reason you want the left edges of both subscript and superscript to be aligned, you can fool TₑX by inserting a null subformula: '$P{}_2^2$' produces '$P{}_2^2$'.

The control sequence \prime stands for the symbol '$\prime$', which is used mostly in superscripts. In fact, '$\prime$' is so big as it stands that you would never want to use it except in a subscript or superscript, where it occurs in a smaller size. Here are some typical examples:

Input	*Output*
`$y_1^\prime$`	y_1'
`$y_2^{\prime\prime}$`	y_2''
`$y_3^{\prime\prime\prime}$`	y_3'''

Since single and double primes occur rather frequently, plain TeX provides a convenient abbreviation: You can simply type ' instead of ^\prime, and '' instead of ^{\prime\prime}, and so on.

`$f'[g(x)]g'(x)$`	$f'[g(x)]g'(x)$
`$y_1'+y_2''$`	$y_1' + y_2''$
`$y'_1+y''_2$`	$y_1' + y_2''$
`$y'''_3+g'^2$`	$y_3''' + g'^2$

▶ **EXERCISE 16.5**
Why do you think TeX treats \prime as a large symbol that appears only in superscripts, instead of making it a smaller symbol that has already been shifted up into the superscript position?

▶ **EXERCISE 16.6**
Mathematicians sometimes use "tensor notation" in which subscripts and superscripts are staggered, as in '$R_i{}^{jk}{}_l$'. Explain how to achieve such an effect.

Another way to get complex formulas from simple ones is to use the control sequences \sqrt, \underline, or \overline. Like ^ and _, these operations apply to the character or subformula that follows them:

`$\sqrt2$`	$\sqrt{2}$
`$\sqrt{x+2}$`	$\sqrt{x+2}$
`$\underline4$`	$\underline{4}$
`$\overline{x+y}$`	$\overline{x+y}$
`$\overline x+\overline y$`	$\overline{x} + \overline{y}$
`$x^{\underline n}$`	$x^{\underline{n}}$
`$x^{\overline{m+n}}$`	$x^{\overline{m+n}}$
`$\sqrt{x^3+\sqrt\alpha}$`	$\sqrt{x^3 + \sqrt{\alpha}}$

You can also get cube roots '$\sqrt[3]{\ }$' and similar things by using \root:

`$\root 3 \of 2$`	$\sqrt[3]{2}$
`$\root n \of {x^n+y^n}$`	$\sqrt[n]{x^n + y^n}$
`$\root n+1 \of a$`	$\sqrt[n+1]{a}$

The \sqrt and \underline and \overline operations are able to place lines above or below subformulas of any size or shape; the bar lines change their size and position, so that they are long enough to cover the subformula, and high enough or low enough not to bump into it. For example, consider '\overline l' ($\overline{l}$) versus '\overline m' ($\overline{m}$): the first has a shorter bar line, and this line has been raised higher than the bar in the second. Similarly, the bar in '\underline y' ($\underline{y}$) is lower than the bar in '\underline x' ($\underline{x}$); and square root signs appear in a variety of positions based on the height and depth of what is being \sqrt'd: $\sqrt{a} + \sqrt{d} + \sqrt{y}$. TEX knows the height, depth, and width of every letter and every subformula, because it considers them to be boxes, as explained in Chapter 11. If you have a formula in which there is only one \sqrt, or only one \overline or \underline, the normal positioning rules work fine; but sometimes you want to have uniformity between different members of a complex formula. For example, you might want to typeset '$\sqrt{a} + \sqrt{d} + \sqrt{y}$', putting all square roots in the same vertical position. There's an easy way to do this, using the control sequence \mathstrut as follows:

$$\$\sqrt{\mathstrut a}+\sqrt{\mathstrut d}+\sqrt{\mathstrut y}\$.$$

A \mathstrut is an invisible box whose width is zero; its height and depth are the height and depth of a parenthesis '('. Therefore subformulas that contain \mathstrut will always have the same height and depth, unless they involve more complicated constructions like subscripts and superscripts. Chapter 18 discusses more powerful operations called \smash and \phantom by which you can obtain complete control over the positioning of roots and similar signs.

▶ **EXERCISE 16.7**
Test your understanding of what you have read so far in this chapter by explaining what should be typed to get the following formulas. (Be sure to check your answer with Appendix A to confirm that you're right.)

$$10^{10} \quad 2^{n+1} \quad (n+1)^2 \quad \sqrt{1-x^2} \quad \overline{w+\overline{z}} \quad p_1^{e_1} \quad a_{b_{c_{d_e}}} \quad \sqrt[3]{h_n''(\alpha x)}$$

▶ **EXERCISE 16.8**
What mistake did B. C. Dull discover after he typed the following?

If\$ x = y\$, then \$x\$ is equal to \$y.\$

▶ **EXERCISE 16.9**
Explain how to type the following sentence:

Deleting an element from an n-tuple leaves an $(n-1)$-tuple.

▶ **EXERCISE 16.10**
List all the italic letters that descend below the baseline. (These are the letters for which \underline will lower its bar line.)

We have discussed the fact that the characters you type have special meanings in math mode, but the examples so far are incomplete; they don't reveal all the power that is at your fingertips just after you press the '\$' key. It's time now to go back to basics: Let us make a systematic survey of what each character does, when it is used in a formula.

The 52 letters (A to Z and a to z) denote italic symbols (A to Z and a to z), which a mathematician would call "variables." TEX just calls them "ordinary symbols," because they make up the bulk of math formulas. There are two variants of lowercase L in plain TEX, namely 'l' (which you get by simply typing 'l') and 'ℓ' (which you get by typing '\ell'). Although mathematicians commonly write something that looks like 'ℓ' in their manuscripts, they do so only to distinguish it from the numeral '1'. This distinguishability problem is not present in printed mathematics, since an italic 'l' is quite different from a '1'; therefore it is traditional to use 'l' unless 'ℓ' has been specifically requested.

Plain TEX also treats the 18 characters

$$0\ \ 1\ \ 2\ \ 3\ \ 4\ \ 5\ \ 6\ \ 7\ \ 8\ \ 9\ \ !\ \ ?\ \ .\ \ |\ \ /\ \ `\ \ @\ \ "$$

as ordinary symbols; i.e., it doesn't insert any extra space when these symbols occur next to each other or next to letters. Unlike the letters, these 18 characters remain in roman type when they appear in formulas. There's nothing special for you to remember about them, except that the vertical line '|' has special uses that we shall discuss later. Furthermore, you should be careful to distinguish between 'oh' and 'zero': The italic letter O is almost never used in formulas unless it appears just before a left parenthesis, as in '$O(n)$'; and the numeral 0 is almost never used just before a left parenthesis unless it is preceded by another digit, as in '$10(n-1)$'. Watch for left parentheses and you'll be $0K$. (Lowercase o's also tend to appear only before left parentheses; type 'x_0' instead of 'x_o', since the formula 'x_0' is generally more correct than 'x_o'.)

The three characters +, -, and * are called "binary operations," because they operate on two parts of a formula. For example, + is a plus sign, which is used for the sum of two numbers; - is a minus sign. The asterisk (*) is rarer in mathematics, but it also behaves as a binary operation. Here are some examples of how TEX typesets binary operations when they appear next to ordinary symbols:

Input	*Output*
$x+y-z$	$x + y - z$
$x+y*z$	$x + y * z$
$x*y/z$	$x * y / z$

Notice that - and * produce quite different math symbols from what you get in normal text: The hyphen (-) becomes a minus sign ($-$), and the raised asterisk (*) drops down to a lower level ($*$).

TEX does not treat / as a binary operation, even though a slash stands for division (which qualifies as a binary operation on mathematical grounds). The reason is that printers traditionally put extra space around the symbols +, $-$, and $*$, but not around /. If TEX were to typeset / as a binary operation, the formula '$1/2$' would come out '$1 / 2$', which is wrong; so TEX considers / to be an ordinary symbol.

Appendix F lists many more binary operations, for which you type control
sequences instead of single characters. Here are some examples:

`$x\times y\cdot z$`	$x \times y \cdot z$
`$x\circ y\bullet z$`	$x \circ y \bullet z$
`$x\cup y\cap z$`	$x \cup y \cap z$
`$x\sqcup y\sqcap z$`	$x \sqcup y \sqcap z$
`$x\vee y\wedge z$`	$x \vee y \wedge z$
`$x\pm y\mp z$`	$x \pm y \mp z$

It is important to distinguish $\times$ (`\times`) from X (`X`) and from x (`x`); to distinguish $\cup$
(`\cup`) from U (`U`) and from u (`u`); to distinguish $\vee$ (`\vee`) from V (`V`) and from v (`v`);
to distinguish $\circ$ (`\circ`) from O (`O`) and from o (`o`). The symbols '$\vee$' and '$\wedge$' can also
be called `\lor` and `\land`, since they frequently stand for binary operations that are
called "logical or" and "logical and."

Incidentally, binary operations are treated as ordinary symbols if they don't
occur between two quantities that they can operate on. For example, no extra
space is inserted next to the $+$, $-$, and $*$ in cases like the following:

`$x=+1$`	$x = +1$
`$3.142-$`	$3.142-$
`$(D*)$`	$(D*)$

Consider also the following examples, which show that binary operations can be used
as ordinary symbols in superscripts and subscripts:

`$K_n^+,K_n^-$`	K_n^+, K_n^-
`$z^*_{ij}$`	z^*_{ij}
`$g^\circ \mapsto g^\bullet$`	$g^\circ \mapsto g^\bullet$
`$f^*(x) \cap f_*(y)$`	$f^*(x) \cap f_*(y)$

▶ **EXERCISE 16.11**
How would you obtain the formulas 'z^{*2}' and '$h'_*(z)$'?

Plain TeX treats the four characters $=$, $<$, $>$, and $:$ as "relations" because
they express a relationship between two quantities. For example, '$x < y$' means
that x is less than y. Such relationships have a rather different meaning from
binary operations like $+$, and the symbols are typeset somewhat differently:

`$x=y>z$`	$x = y > z$
`$x:=y$`	$x := y$
`$x\le y\ne z$`	$x \le y \ne z$
`$x\sim y\simeq z$`	$x \sim y \simeq z$
`$x\equiv y\not\equiv z$`	$x \equiv y \not\equiv z$
`$x\subset y\subseteq z$`	$x \subset y \subseteq z$

(The last several examples show some of the many other relational symbols that
plain TeX makes available via control sequences; see Appendix F.)

The two characters ',' (comma) and ';' (semicolon) are treated as punctuation marks in formulas; this means that TEX puts a little extra space after them, but not before them.

$f(x,y;z)$ $f(x, y; z)$

It isn't customary to put extra space after a '.' (period) in math formulas, so TEX treats a period as an ordinary symbol. If you want the ':' character to be treated as a punctuation mark instead of as a relation, just call it \colon:

$f:A\to B$ $f : A \to B$

$f\colon A\to B$ $f: A \to B$

If you want to use a comma as an ordinary symbol (e.g., when it appears in a large number), just put it in braces; TEX treats anything in braces as an ordinary symbol. For instance,

$12,345x$ $12, 345x$ (wrong)

$12{,}345x$ $12,345x$ (right)

▶ **EXERCISE 16.12**
    What's an easy way to get a raised dot in a decimal constant (e.g., '3·1416')?

So far we have considered letters, other ordinary symbols, binary operations, relations, and punctuation marks; hence we have covered almost every key on the typewriter. There are just a few more: The characters '(' and '[' are called "openings," while ')' and ']' are called "closings"; these act pretty much like ordinary symbols, but they help TEX to decide when a binary operation is not really being used in a binary way. Then there is the character ', which we know is used as an abbreviation for \prime superscripts. Finally, we know that plain TEX reserves the other ten characters:

    \ $ % # & ~ { } _ ^

These are not usable for symbols in math mode unless their \catcode values are changed (see Chapter 7). Although { and } specify grouping, the control sequences '\{' and '\}' can be used to get '{' as an opening and '}' as a closing.

All of these math mode interpretations are easily changeable, since each character has a \mathcode, as explained in Chapter 17; none of the conventions are permanently built into TEX. However, most of them are so standard that it is usually unwise to make many changes, except perhaps in the interpretations of ', ", and @.

The special characters ^ and _ that designate superscripts and subscripts should not be used except in formulas. Similarly, the names of math symbols like \alpha and \approx, and the control sequences for math operations like \overline, must not invade ordinary text. TEX uses these facts to detect missing dollar signs in your input, before such mistakes cause too much trouble. For example, suppose you were to type

    The smallest n such that $2^n>1000$ is~10.

TEX doesn't know that you forgot a '\$' after the first 'n', because it doesn't understand English; so it finds a "formula" between the first two \$ signs:

The smallest *nsuchthat*

after which it thinks that '2' is part of the text. But then the ˆ reveals an inconsistency; TEX will automatically insert a \$ before the ˆ, and you will get an error message. In this way the computer has gotten back into synch, and the rest of the document can be typeset as if nothing had happened.

Conversely, a blank line or \par is not permitted in math mode. This gives TEX another way to recover from a missing \$; such errors will be confined to the paragraph in which they occur.

If for some reason you cannot use ˆ and _ for superscripts and subscripts, because you have an unusual keyboard or because you need ˆ for French accents or something, plain TEX lets you type \sp and \sb instead. For example, '\$x\sp2\$' is another way to get 'x^2'. On the other hand, some people are lucky enough to have keyboards that contain additional symbols besides those of standard ASCII. When such symbols are available, TEX can be set up to make math typing a bit more pleasant. For example, at the author's installation there are keys labeled ↑ and ↓ that produce visible symbols (these make superscripts and subscripts look much nicer on the screen); there are keys for the relations ≤, ≥, and ≠ (these save time); and there are about two dozen more keys that occasionally come in handy. (See Appendix C.)

Mathematicians are fond of using accents over letters, because this is often an effective way to indicate relationships between mathematical objects, and because it greatly extends the number of available symbols without increasing the number of necessary fonts. Chapter 9 discusses the use of accents in ordinary text, but mathematical accents are somewhat different, because spacing is not the same; TEX uses special conventions for accents in formulas, so that the two sorts of accents will not be confused with each other. The following math accents are provided by plain TEX:

`$\hat a$`	$\hat a$
`$\check a$`	$\check a$
`$\tilde a$`	$\tilde a$
`$\acute a$`	$\acute a$
`$\grave a$`	$\grave a$
`$\dot a$`	$\dot a$
`$\ddot a$`	$\ddot a$
`$\breve a$`	$\breve a$
`$\bar a$`	$\bar a$
`$\vec a$`	$\vec a$

The first nine of these are called \ˆ, \v, \~, \', \`, \., \", \u, and \=, respectively, when they appear in text; \vec is an accent that appears only in formulas. TEX will complain if you try to use \ˆ or \v, etc., in formulas, or if you try to use \hat or \check, etc., in ordinary text.

It's usually a good idea to define special control sequences for accented letters that you need frequently. For example, you can put

```
\def\Ahat{{\hat A}}
\def\chat{{\hat c}}
\def\scheck{{\check s}}
\def\xtilde{{\tilde x}}
\def\zbar{{\bar z}}
```

at the beginning of a manuscript that uses the symbols $\hat{A}$, $\hat{c}$, $\check{s}$, $\tilde{x}$, and $\bar{z}$ more than, say, five times. This saves you a lot of keystrokes, and it makes the manuscript easier to read. Chapter 20 explains how to define control sequences.

When the letters i and j are accented in math formulas, dotless symbols $\imath$ and $\jmath$ should be used under the accents. These symbols are called \imath and \jmath in plain TeX. Thus, for example, a paper that uses '$\hat{\imath}$' and '$\hat{\jmath}$' ought to begin with the following definitions:

```
\def\ihat{{\hat\imath}}
\def\jhat{{\hat\jmath}}
```

You can put accents on top of accents, making symbols like $\hat{\hat{A}}$ that might cause a mathematician to squeal with ecstasy. However, it takes a bit of finesse to get the upper accent into a position that looks right, because the designer of a font for mathematics usually tells TeX to position math accents in special ways for special letters. Plain TeX provides a control sequence called \skew that makes it fairly easy to shift superaccents into their proper place. For example, '\skew6\hat\Ahat' was used to produce the symbol above. The number '6' in this example was chosen by trial and error; '5' seems to put the upper accent a bit too far left, while '7' makes it a bit too far right, at least in the author's opinion. The idea is to fiddle with the amount of skew until you find what pleases you best.

It's possible, in fact, to put math accents on any subformula, not just on single characters or accented characters. But there's usually not much point in doing so, because TeX just centers the accent over the whole subformula. For example, '$\hat{I+M}$' yields '$\hat{I+M}$'. In particular, a \bar accent always stays the same size; it's not like \overline, which grows with the formula under it. Some people prefer the longer line from \overline even when it applies to only a single letter; for example, '$\bar z+\overline z$' produces '$\bar{z}+\overline{z}$', and you can take your pick when you define \zbar. However, plain TeX does provide two accents that grow; they are called \widehat and \widetilde:

`$\widehat x,\widetilde x$`	$\widehat{x},\widetilde{x}$
`$\widehat{xy},\widetilde{xy}$`	$\widehat{xy},\widetilde{xy}$
`$\widehat{xyz},\widetilde{xyz}$`	$\widehat{xyz},\widetilde{xyz}$

The third example here shows the maximum size available.

▶ **EXERCISE 16.13**

This has been another long chapter; but cheer up, you have learned a lot! Prove it by explaining what to type in order to get the formulas e^{-x^2}, $D \sim p^{\alpha} M + l$, and $\hat{g} \in (H^{\pi_1^{-1}})'$.   (In the last example, assume that a control sequence \ghat has already been defined, so that \ghat produces the accented letter $\hat{g}$.)

Producing Greek letters is as easy as π.
You just type ... `as easy as $\pi$`.
— LESLIE LAMPORT, *The L^{a}T$_E$X Document Preparation System* (1983)

T$_E$X has no regard for the glories of the Greek tongue—
as far as it is concerned, Greek letters are just additional weird symbols,
and they are allowed only in math mode.
In a pinch you can get the output $\tau\epsilon\chi$ by typing `$\tau\epsilon\chi$`,
but if you're actually setting Greek text, you will be using
a different version of T$_E$X, designed for a keyboard with Greek letters on it,
and you shouldn't even be reading this
manual, which is undoubtedly all English to you.
— MICHAEL SPIVAK, *The Joy of T$_E$X* (1982)

17
More about Math

Another thing mathematicians like to do is make fractions—and they like to build symbols up on top of each other in a variety of different ways:

$$\frac{1}{2} \quad \text{and} \quad \frac{n+1}{3} \quad \text{and} \quad \binom{n+1}{3} \quad \text{and} \quad \sum_{n=1}^{3} Z_n^2 \,.$$

You can get these four formulas as displayed equations by typing '`$$1\over2$$`' and '`$$n+1\over3$$`' and '`$$n+1\choose3$$`' and '`$$\sum_{n=1}^3 Z_n^2$$`'; we shall study the simple rules for such constructions in this chapter.

First let's look at fractions, which use the '`\over`' notation. The control sequence `\over` applies to everything in the formula unless you use braces to enclose it in a specific subformula; in the latter case, `\over` applies to everything in that subformula.

Input	Output
`$$x+y^2\over k+1$$`	$\dfrac{x+y^2}{k+1}$
`$${x+y^2\over k}+1$$`	$\dfrac{x+y^2}{k}+1$
`$$x+{y^2\over k}+1$$`	$x+\dfrac{y^2}{k}+1$
`$$x+{y^2\over k+1}$$`	$x+\dfrac{y^2}{k+1}$
`$$x+y^{2\over k+1}$$`	$x+y^{\frac{2}{k+1}}$

You aren't allowed to use `\over` twice in the same subformula; instead of typing something like '`a \over b \over 2`', you must specify what goes over what:

`$${a\over b}\over 2$$`	$\dfrac{\frac{a}{b}}{2}$
`$$a\over{b\over 2}$$`	$\dfrac{a}{\frac{b}{2}}$

Unfortunately, both of these alternatives look pretty awful. Mathematicians tend to "overuse" `\over` when they first begin to typeset their own work on a system like TeX. A good typist or copy editor will convert fractions to a "slashed form," whenever a built-up construction would be too small or too crowded. For example, the last two cases should be treated as follows:

`$$a/b \over 2$$`	$\dfrac{a/b}{2}$
`$$a \over b/2$$`	$\dfrac{a}{b/2}$

Conversion to slashed form takes a little bit of mathematical knowhow, since parentheses sometimes need to be inserted in order to preserve the meaning of the formula. Besides substituting '/' for '\over', the two parts of the fraction should be put in parentheses unless they are single symbols; for example, $\frac{a}{b}$ becomes simply a/b, but $\frac{a+1}{b}$ becomes $(a+1)/b$, and $\frac{a+1}{b+1}$ becomes $(a+1)/(b+1)$. Furthermore, the entire fraction should generally be enclosed in parentheses if it appears next to something else; for example, $\frac{a}{b}x$ becomes $(a/b)x$. If you are a typist without mathematical training, it's best to ask the author of the manuscript for help, in doubtful cases; you might also tactfully suggest that unsightly fractions be avoided altogether in future manuscripts.

▶ **EXERCISE 17.1**
What's a better way to render the formula $x + y^{\frac{2}{k+1}}$?

▶ **EXERCISE 17.2**
Convert '$\frac{a+1}{b+1}x$' to slashed form.

▶ **EXERCISE 17.3**
What surprise did B. L. User get when he typed '`$$x = (y^2\over k+1)$$`'?

▶ **EXERCISE 17.4**
How can you make '$7\frac{1}{2}\cent$'? (Assume that the control sequence `\cents` yields '$\cent$'.)

The examples above show that letters and other symbols sometimes get smaller when they appear in fractions, just as they get smaller when they are used as exponents. It's about time that we studied TeX's method for choosing the sizes of things. TeX actually has eight different styles in which it can treat formulas, namely

display style	(for formulas displayed on lines by themselves)
text style	(for formulas embedded in the text)
script style	(for formulas used as superscripts or subscripts)
scriptscript style	(for second-order superscripts or subscripts)

and four other "cramped" styles that are almost the same except that exponents aren't raised quite so much. For brevity we shall refer to the eight styles as

$$D, \ D', \ T, \ T', \ S, \ S', \ SS, \ SS',$$

where D is display style, D' is cramped display style, T is text style, etc. TeX also uses three different sizes of type for mathematics; they are called text size, script size, and scriptscript size.

The normal way to typeset a formula with TeX is to enclose it in dollar signs `$...$`; this yields the formula in text style (style T). Or you can enclose it in double dollar signs `$$...$$`; this displays the formula in display style (style D). The subformulas of a formula might, of course, be in different styles. Once you know the style, you can determine the size of type that TeX will use:

If a letter is in style	then it will be set in	
D, D', T, T'	text size	(like this)
S, S'	script size	(like this)
SS, SS'	scriptscript size	(like this)

There is no "*SSS*" style or "scriptscriptscript" size; such tiny symbols would be even less readable than the scriptscript ones. Therefore TEX stays with scriptscript size as the minimum:

In a formula of style	the superscript style is	and the subscript style is
D, T	S	S'
D', T'	S'	S'
S, SS	SS	SS'
S', SS'	SS'	SS'

For example, if `x^{a_b}` is to be typeset in style D, then `a_b` will be set in style S, and `b` in style SS'; the result is 'x^{a_b}'.

So far we haven't seen any difference between styles D and T. Actually there is a slight difference in the positioning of exponents, although script size is used in each case: You get x^2 in D style and x^2 in T style and x^2 in D' or T' style—do you see the difference? But there is a big distinction between D style and T style when it comes to fractions:

In a formula α`\over`β of style	the style of the numerator α is	and the style of the denominator β is
D	T	T'
D'	T'	T'
T	S	S'
T'	S'	S'
S, SS	SS	SS'
S', SS'	SS'	SS'

Thus if you type '`1\over2`' (in a text) you get $\frac{1}{2}$, namely style S over style S'; but if you type '`$$1\over2$$`' you get

$$\frac{1}{2}$$

(a displayed formula), which is style T over style T'.

While we're at it, we might as well finish the style rules: `\underline` does not change the style. Math accents, and the operations `\sqrt` and `\overline`, change uncramped styles to their cramped counterparts; for example, D changes to D', but D' stays as it was.

▶ **EXERCISE 17.5**
State the style and size of each part of the formula $\sqrt{p_2^{e'}}$, assuming that the formula itself is in style D.

Suppose you don't like the style that TEX selects by its automatic style rules. Then you can specify the style you want by typing `\displaystyle` or `\textstyle` or `\scriptstyle` or `\scriptscriptstyle`; the style that you select will apply until the end of the formula or subformula, or until you select another style. For example, '`$$n+\scriptstyle n+\scriptscriptstyle n.$$`' produces the display

$$n + {\scriptstyle n+n}.$$

This is a rather silly example, but it does show that the plus signs get smaller too, as the style changes. TEX puts no space around + signs in script styles.

Here's a more useful example of style changes: Sometimes you need to typeset a "continued fraction" made up of many other fractions, all of which are supposed to be in display style:

$$a_0 + \cfrac{1}{a_1 + \cfrac{1}{a_2 + \cfrac{1}{a_3 + \cfrac{1}{a_4}}}}$$

In order to get this effect, the idea is to type

```
$$a_0+{1\over\displaystyle a_1+
      {\strut 1\over\displaystyle a_2+
         {\strut 1\over\displaystyle a_3+
            {\strut 1\over a_4}}}}$$
```

(The control sequence \strut has been used to make the denominators taller; this is a refinement that will be discussed in Chapter 18. Our concern now is with the style commands.) Without the appearances of \strut and \displaystyle in this formula, the result would be completely different:

$$a_0 + \frac{1}{a_1 + \frac{1}{a_2+\frac{1}{a_3+\frac{1}{a_4}}}}$$

⚠ These examples show that the numerator and denominator of a fraction are generally centered with respect to each other. If you prefer to have the numerator or denominator appear flush left, put '\hfill' after it; or if you prefer flush right, put '\hfill' at the left. For example, if the first three appearances of '1\over' in the previous example are replaced by '1\hfill\over', you get the display

$$a_0 + \cfrac{1}{a_1 + \cfrac{1}{a_2 + \cfrac{1}{a_3 + \cfrac{1}{a_4}}}}$$

(a format for continued fractions that many authors prefer). This works because \hfill stretches at a faster rate than the glue that is actually used internally by TEX when it centers the numerators and denominators.

TEX has another operation '\atop', which is like \over except that it leaves out the fraction line:

$$x\atop y+2$$
$$\begin{array}{c} x \\ y+2 \end{array}$$

The plain TEX format in Appendix B also defines '\choose', which is like \atop but it encloses the result in parentheses:

$$n\choose k$$
$$\binom{n}{k}$$

It is called \choose because it's a common notation for the so-called binomial coefficient that tells how many ways there are to choose k things out of n things.

You can't mix \over and \atop and \choose with each other. For example, '$$n \choose k \over 2$$' is illegal; you must use grouping, to get either '$${n\choose k}\over2$$' or '$$n\choose{k\over2}$$', i.e.,

$$\frac{\binom{n}{k}}{2} \quad \text{or} \quad \binom{n}{\frac{k}{2}}.$$

The latter formula, incidentally, would look better as '$$n\choose k/2$$' or '$$n\choose{1\over2}k$$', yielding

$$\binom{n}{k/2} \quad \text{or} \quad \binom{n}{\frac{1}{2}k}.$$

▶ **EXERCISE 17.6**
As alternatives to $\dfrac{\binom{n}{k}}{2}$, discuss how you could obtain the two displays

$$\frac{1}{2}\binom{n}{k} \quad \text{and} \quad \frac{\binom{n}{k}}{2}.$$

▶ **EXERCISE 17.7**
Explain how to specify the displayed formula

$$\binom{p}{2}x^2y^{p-2} - \frac{1}{1-x}\frac{1}{1-x^2}.$$

 TEX has a generalized version of \over and \atop in which you specify the exact thickness of the line rule by typing '\above⟨dimen⟩'. For example,

$$\displaystyle{a\over b}\above1pt\displaystyle{c\over d}$$

will produce a compound fraction with a heavier (1 pt thick) rule as its main bar:

$$\frac{\dfrac{a}{b}}{\dfrac{c}{d}}.$$

This sort of thing occurs primarily in textbooks on elementary mathematics.

Mathematicians often use the sign $\sum$ to stand for "summation" and the sign $\int$ to stand for "integration." If you're a typist but not a mathematician, all you need to remember is that `\sum` stands for $\sum$ and `\int` for $\int$; these abbreviations appear in Appendix F together with all the other symbols, in case you forget. Symbols like $\sum$ and $\int$ (and a few others like $\bigcup$ and $\prod$ and $\oint$ and $\otimes$, all listed in Appendix F) are called *large operators*, and you type them just as you type ordinary symbols or letters. The difference is that TeX will choose a *larger* large operator in display style than it will in text style. For example,

$\verb|$\sum x_n$|$ yields $\sum x_n$ (*T* style)

$\verb|$$\sum x_n$$|$ yields $\displaystyle\sum x_n$ (*D* style).

A displayed `\sum` usually occurs with "limits," i.e., with subformulas that are to appear above and below it. You type limits just as if they were superscripts and subscripts; for example, if you want

$$\sum_{n=1}^{m}$$

you type either '`$$\sum_{n=1}^m$$`' or '`$$\sum^m_{n=1}$$`'. According to the normal conventions of mathematical typesetting, TeX will change this to '$\sum_{n=1}^{m}$' (i.e., without limits) if it occurs in text style rather than in display style.

Integrations are slightly different from summations, in that the superscripts and subscripts are not set as limits even in display style:

$\verb|$\int_{-\infty}^{+\infty}$|$ yields $\int_{-\infty}^{+\infty}$ (*T* style)

$\verb|$$\int_{-\infty}^{+\infty}$$|$ yields $\displaystyle\int_{-\infty}^{+\infty}$ (*D* style).

 Some printers prefer to set limits above and below $\int$ signs; this takes more space on the page, but it gives a better appearance if the subformulas are complex, because it keeps them out of the way of the rest of the formula. Similarly, limits are occasionally desirable in text style or script style; but some printers prefer not to set limits on displayed $\sum$ signs. You can change TeX's convention by simply typing '`\limits`' or '`\nolimits`' immediately after the large operator. For example,

$\verb|$$\int\limits_0^{\pi\over2}$$|$ yields $\displaystyle\int\limits_0^{\frac{\pi}{2}}$

$\verb|$$\sum\nolimits_{n=1}^m$$|$ yields $\displaystyle\sum\nolimits_{n=1}^m$

If you say '`\nolimits\limits`' (presumably because some macro like `\int` specifies `\nolimits`, but you do want them), the last word takes precedence. There's also a command '`\displaylimits`' that can be used to restore TeX's normal conventions; i.e., the limits will be displayed only in styles *D* and *D'*.

Sometimes you need to put two or more rows of limits under a large operator; you can do this with '\atop'. For example, if you want the displayed formula

$$\sum_{\substack{0\le i\le m\\0<j<n}} P(i,j)$$

the correct way to type it is

$$\sum_{\scriptstyle0\le i\le m\atop\scriptstyle0<j<n}P(i,j)$$

(perhaps with a few more spaces to make it look nicer in the manuscript file). The instruction '\scriptstyle' was necessary here, twice—otherwise the lines '$0 \le i \le m$' and '$0 < j < n$' would have been in scriptscript size, which is too small. This is another instance of a rare case where TeX's automatic style rules need to be overruled.

▸ **EXERCISE 17.8**

How would you type the displayed formula $\sum_{i=1}^{p}\sum_{j=1}^{q}\sum_{k=1}^{r} a_{ij}b_{jk}c_{ki}$?

▸ **EXERCISE 17.9**
And how would you handle $\sum_{\substack{1\le i\le p\\1\le j\le q\\1\le k\le r}} a_{ij}b_{jk}c_{ki}$?

Since mathematical formulas can get horribly large, TeX has to have some way to make ever-larger symbols. For example, if you type

```
$$\sqrt{1+\sqrt{1+\sqrt{1+
        \sqrt{1+\sqrt{1+\sqrt{1+\sqrt{1+x}}}}}}}$$
```

the result shows a variety of available square-root signs:

$$\sqrt{1+\sqrt{1+\sqrt{1+\sqrt{1+\sqrt{1+\sqrt{1+\sqrt{1+x}}}}}}}$$

The three largest signs here are all essentially the same, except for a vertical segment ' | ' that gets repeated as often as necessary to reach the desired size; but the smaller signs are distinct characters found in TeX's math fonts.

A similar thing happens with parentheses and other so-called "delimiter" symbols. For example, here are some of the different sizes of parentheses and braces that plain TeX might use in formulas:

$$\Biggl(\biggl(\Bigl(\bigl(((()))\bigr)\Bigr)\biggr)\Biggr)\Biggl\{\biggl\{\Bigl\{\bigl\{\{\{\}\}\}\bigr\}\Bigr\}\biggr\}\Biggr\}$$

The three largest pairs in each case are made with repeatable extensions, so they can become as large as necessary.

Delimiters are important to mathematicians, because they provide good visual clues to the underlying structure of complex expressions; they delimit the boundaries of individual subformulas. Here is a list of the 22 basic delimiters provided by plain TeX:

Input	*Delimiter*
(	left parenthesis: (
)	right parenthesis:)
[or \lbrack	left bracket: [
] or \rbrack	right bracket:]
\{ or \lbrace	left curly brace: {
\} or \rbrace	right curly brace: }
\lfloor	left floor bracket: ⌊
\rfloor	right floor bracket: ⌋
\lceil	left ceiling bracket: ⌈
\rceil	right ceiling bracket: ⌉
\langle	left angle bracket: ⟨
\rangle	right angle bracket: ⟩
/	slash: /
\backslash	reverse slash: \
| or \vert	vertical bar: |
\\| or \Vert	double vertical bar: ‖
\uparrow	upward arrow: ↑
\Uparrow	double upward arrow: ⇑
\downarrow	downward arrow: ↓
\Downarrow	double downward arrow: ⇓
\updownarrow	up-and-down arrow: ↕
\Updownarrow	double up-and-down arrow: ⇕

In some cases, there are two ways to get the same delimiter; for example, you can specify a left bracket by typing either '[' or '\lbrack'. The latter alternative has been provided because the symbol '[' is not readily available on all computer keyboards. Remember, however, that you should never try to specify a left brace or right brace simply by typing '{' or '}'; the { and } symbols are reserved for grouping. The right way is to type '\{' or '\}' or '\lbrace' or '\rbrace'.

In order to get a slightly larger version of any of these symbols, just precede them by '\bigl' (for opening delimiters) or '\bigr' (for closing ones). This makes it easier to read formulas that contain delimiters inside delimiters:

Input	*Output*
`$\bigl(x-s(x)\bigr)\bigl(y-s(y)\bigr)$`	$\bigl(x - s(x)\bigr)\bigl(y - s(y)\bigr)$
`$\bigl[x-s[x]\bigr]\bigl[y-s[y]\bigr]$`	$\bigl[x - s[x]\bigr]\bigl[y - s[y]\bigr]$
`$\bigl| |x|+|y| \bigr|$`	$\bigl\| |x| + |y| \bigr\|$
`$\bigl\lfloor\sqrt A\bigr\rfloor$`	$\bigl\lfloor\sqrt{A}\bigr\rfloor$

The \big delimiters are just enough bigger than ordinary ones so that the difference can be perceived, yet small enough to be used in the text of a paragraph. Here are all 22 of them, in the ordinary size and in the \big size:

$$()[]\{\}\lfloor\rfloor\lceil\rceil\langle\rangle/\backslash|\|\uparrow\Uparrow\downarrow\Downarrow\updownarrow\Updownarrow$$

You can also type \Bigl and \Bigr to get larger symbols suitable for displays:

$$()[]\{\}\lfloor\rfloor\lceil\rceil\langle\rangle/\backslash\|\|\uparrow\Uparrow\downarrow\Downarrow\updownarrow\Updownarrow$$

These are 50% taller than their \big counterparts. Displayed formulas most often use delimiters that are even taller (twice the size of \big); such delimiters are constructed by \biggl and \biggr, and they look like this:

$$\left(\right)\left[\right]\{\}\lfloor\rfloor\lceil\rceil\langle\rangle/\backslash\|\|\uparrow\Uparrow\downarrow\Downarrow\updownarrow\Updownarrow$$

Finally, there are \Biggl and \Biggr versions, 2.5 times as tall as the \bigl and \bigr delimiters:

$$\left(\right)\left[\right]\{\}\lfloor\rfloor\lceil\rceil\langle\rangle/\backslash\|\|\uparrow\Uparrow\downarrow\Downarrow\updownarrow\Updownarrow$$

▶ **EXERCISE 17.10**
Guess how to type the formula $\left(\dfrac{\partial^2}{\partial x^2} + \dfrac{\partial^2}{\partial y^2}\right)\bigl|\varphi(x+iy)\bigr|^2 = 0$, in display style, using \bigg delimiters for the large parentheses. (The symbols ∂ and φ that appear here are called \partial and \varphi.)

▶ **EXERCISE 17.11**
In practice, \big and \bigg delimiters are used much more often than \Big and \Bigg ones. Why do you think this is true?

A \bigl or \Bigl or \biggl or \Biggl delimiter is an opening, like a left parenthesis; a \bigr or \Bigr or \biggr or \Biggr delimiter is a closing, like a right parenthesis. Plain TEX also provides \bigm and \Bigm and \biggm and \Biggm delimiters, for use in the middle of formulas; such a delimiter plays the rôle of a relation, like an equals sign, so TEX puts a bit of space on either side of it.

$\bigl(x\in A(n)\bigm|x\in B(n)\bigr)$ $\bigl(x \in A(n) \mid x \in B(n)\bigr)$

$\bigcup_n X_n\bigm\|\bigcap_n Y_n$ $\bigcup_n X_n \,\|\, \bigcap_n Y_n$

You can also say just \big or \Big or \bigg or \Bigg; this produces a delimiter that acts as an ordinary variable. It is used primarily with slashes and backslashes, as in the following example.

$${a+1\over b}\bigg/{c+1\over d}$$ $\dfrac{a+1}{b} \bigg/ \dfrac{c+1}{d}$

▶ **EXERCISE 17.12**
What's the professional way to type $\bigl(x + f(x)\bigr)\big/\bigl(x - f(x)\bigr)$? (Look closely.)

TeX has a built-in mechanism that figures out how tall a pair of delimiters needs to be, in order to enclose a given subformula; so you can use this method, instead of deciding whether a delimiter should be \big or \bigg or whatever. All you do is say

\left⟨delim₁⟩⟨subformula⟩\right⟨delim₂⟩

and TeX will typeset the subformula, putting the specified delimiters at the left and the right. The size of the delimiters will be just big enough to cover the subformula. For example, in the display

$$1+\left(1\over1-x^2\right)^3$$ $$1+\left(\frac{1}{1-x^2}\right)^3$$

TeX has chosen \biggl(and \biggr), because smaller delimiters would be too small for this particular fraction. A simple formula like '$\left(x\right)$' yields just '(x)'; thus, \left and \right sometimes choose delimiters that are smaller than \bigl and \bigr.

Whenever you use \left and \right they must pair up with each other, just as braces do in groups. You can't have \left in one formula and \right in another, nor are you allowed to type things like '\left(...{...\right)...}' or '\left(...\begingroup...\right)...\endgroup'. This restriction makes sense, because TeX needs to typeset the subformula that appears between \left and \right before it can decide how big to make the delimiters. But it is worth explicit mention here, because you do *not* have to match parentheses and brackets, etc., when you are not using \left and \right: TeX will not complain if you input a formula like '$[0,1)$' or even '$)($' or just '$)$'. (And it's a good thing TeX doesn't, for such unbalanced formulas occur surprisingly often in mathematics papers.) Even when you do use \left and \right, TeX doesn't look closely at the particular delimiters that you happen to choose; thus, you can type strange things like '\left)' and/or '\right(' if you know what you're doing. Or even if you don't.

The \over operation in the example displayed above does not involve the '1+' at the beginning of the formula; this happens because \left and \right have the function of grouping, in addition to their function of delimiter-making. Any definitions that you happen to make between \left and \right will be local, as if braces had appeared around the enclosed subformula.

▶ **EXERCISE 17.13**
Use \left and \right to typeset the following display (with \phi for ϕ):

$$\pi(n) = \sum_{k=2}^{n} \left\lfloor \frac{\phi(k)}{k-1} \right\rfloor.$$

At this point you are probably wondering why you should bother learning about \bigl and \bigr and their relatives, when \left and \right are there to calculate sizes for you automatically. Well, it's true that \left and \right are quite handy, but there are at least three situations in which you

will want to use your own wisdom when selecting the proper delimiter size:
(1) Sometimes `\left` and `\right` choose a smaller delimiter than you want. For
example, we used `\bigl` and `\bigr` to produce $\|x\| + \|y\|$ in one of the previous
illustrations; `\left` and `\right` don't make things any bigger than necessary,
so '`$\left|\left|x\right|+\left|y\right|\right|$`' yields only '$\|x\| + \|y\|$'.
(2) Sometimes `\left` and `\right` choose a larger delimiter than you want. This
happens most frequently when they enclose a large operator in a display; for
example, compare the following two formulas:

$$\text{\$\$\textbackslash left(\textbackslash sum\_\{k=1\}\^{}n A\_k \textbackslash right)\$\$}\qquad \left(\sum_{k=1}^{n} A_k \right)$$

$$\text{\$\$\textbackslash biggl(\textbackslash sum\_\{k=1\}\^{}n A\_k \textbackslash biggr)\$\$}\qquad \biggl(\sum_{k=1}^{n} A_k \biggr)$$

The rules of `\left` and `\right` cause them to enclose the `\sum` together with
its limits, but in special cases like this it looks better to let the limits hang out
a bit; `\bigg` delimiters are better here. (3) Sometimes you need to break a huge
displayed formula into two or more separate lines, and you want to make sure
that its opening and closing delimiters have the same size; but you can't use
`\left` on the first line and `\right` on the last, since `\left` and `\right` must
occur in pairs. The solution is to use `\Biggl` (say) on the first line and `\Biggr`
on the last.

Of course, one of the advantages of `\left` and `\right` is that they can make
arbitrarily large delimiters—much bigger than `\biggggg`! The slashes and
angle brackets do have a maximum size, however; if you ask for really big versions of
those symbols you will get the largest ones available.

▶ **EXERCISE 17.14**
Prove that you have mastered delimiters: Coerce TeX into producing the formula

$$\pi(n) = \sum_{m=2}^{n} \left\lfloor \left(\sum_{k=1}^{m-1} \lfloor (m/k)/\lceil m/k \rceil \rfloor \right)^{-1} \right\rfloor.$$

If you type '`.`' after `\left` or `\right`, instead of specifying one of the basic
delimiters, you get a so-called null delimiter (which is blank). Why on earth
would anybody want that, you may ask. Well, you sometimes need to produce formulas
that contain only one large delimiter. For example, the display

$$|x| = \begin{cases} x, & \text{if } x \geq 0 \\ -x, & \text{if } x < 0 \end{cases}$$

has a '{' but no '}'. It can be produced by a construction of the form

$$\text{\$\$|x|=\textbackslash left\textbackslash\{ ... \textbackslash right.\$\$}$$

Chapter 18 explains how to fill in the '`...`' to finish this construction; let's just notice
for now that the '`\right.`' makes it possible to have an invisible right delimiter to go
with the visible left brace.

A null delimiter isn't completely void; it is an empty box whose width is a TeX parameter called `\nulldelimiterspace`. We will see later that null delimiters are inserted next to fractions. Plain TeX sets `\nulldelimiterspace=1.2pt`.

You can type '<' or '>' as convenient abbreviations for `\langle` and `\rangle`, when TeX is looking for a delimiter. For example, '`\bigl<`' is equivalent to '`\bigl\langle`', and '`\right>`' is equivalent to '`\right\rangle`'. Of course '<' and '>' ordinarily produce the less-than and greater-than relations '$<>$', which are quite different from angle brackets '$\langle\rangle$'.

Plain TeX also makes available a few more delimiters, which were not listed in the basic set of 22 because they are sort of special. The control sequences `\arrowvert`, `\Arrowvert`, and `\bracevert` produce delimiters made from the repeatable parts of the vertical arrows, double vertical arrows, and large braces, respectively, without the arrowheads or the curly parts of the braces. They produce results similar to `\vert` or `\Vert`, but they are surrounded by more white space and they have a different weight. You can also use `\lgroup` and `\rgroup`, which are constructed from braces without the middle parts; and `\lmoustache` and `\rmoustache`, which give you the top and bottom halves of large braces. For example, here are the `\Big` and `\bigg` versions of `\vert`, `\Vert`, and these seven special delimiters:

$$\cdots\Big|\cdots\Big\|\cdots\Big|\cdots\Big\|\cdots\Big|\cdots\Big(\cdots\Big)\cdots\int\cdots\Big\}\cdots;$$

$$\cdots\bigg|\cdots\bigg\|\cdots\bigg|\cdots\bigg\|\cdots\bigg|\cdots\bigg(\cdots\bigg)\cdots\int\cdots\bigg\{\cdots$$

Notice that `\lgroup` and `\rgroup` are rather like bold parentheses, with sharper bends at the corners; this makes them attractive for certain large displays. But you cannot use them exactly like parentheses, because they are available only in large sizes (`\Big` or more).

Question: What happens if a subscript or superscript follows a large delimiter? Answer: That's a good question. After a `\left` delimiter, it is the first subscript or superscript of the enclosed subformula, so it is effectively preceded by {}. After a `\right` delimiter, it is a subscript or superscript of the entire `\left...\right` subformula. And after a `\bigl` or `\bigr` or `\bigm` or `\big` delimiter, it applies only to that particular delimiter. Thus, '`\bigl(_2`' works quite differently from '`\left(_2`'.

If you look closely at the examples of math typesetting in this chapter, you will notice that large parentheses and brackets are symmetric with respect to an invisible horizontal line that runs a little bit above the baseline; when a delimiter gets larger, its height and depth both grow by the same amount. This horizontal line is called the *axis* of the formula; for example, a formula in the text of the present paragraph would have an axis at this level: ——. The bar line in every fraction is centered on the axis, regardless of the size of the numerator or denominator.

Sometimes it is necessary to create a special box that should be centered vertically with respect to the axis. (For example, the '$|x| = \{$...' example above was done with such a box.) TeX provides a simple way to do this: You just say

`\vcenter{⟨vertical mode material⟩}`

and the vertical mode material will be packed into a box just as if \vcenter had been
\vbox. Then the box will be raised or lowered until its top edge is as far above the axis
as the bottom edge is below.

The concept of "axis" is meaningful for TeX only in math formulas, not in
ordinary text; therefore TeX allows you to use \vcenter only in math mode.
If you really need to center something vertically in horizontal mode, the solution is
to say '$\vcenter{...}$'. (Incidentally, the constructions '\vcenter to⟨dimen⟩' and
'\vcenter spread⟨dimen⟩' are legal too, in math mode; vertical glue is always set by
the rules for \vbox in Chapter 12. But \vcenter by itself is usually sufficient.)

Any box can be put into a formula by simply saying \hbox or \vbox or \vtop
or \box or \copy in the normal way, even when you are in math mode. Furthermore you can use \raise or \lower, as if you were in horizontal mode, and you
can insert vertical rules with \vrule. Such constructions, like \vcenter, produce boxes
that can be used like ordinary symbols in math formulas.

Sometimes you need to make up your own symbols, when you run across
something unusual that doesn't occur in the fonts. If the new symbol occurs
only in one place, you can use \hbox or \vcenter or something to insert exactly what
you want; but if you are defining a macro for general use, you may want to use different
constructions in different styles. TeX has a special feature called \mathchoice that
comes to the rescue in such situations: You write

$$\mathchoice\{⟨math⟩\}\{⟨math⟩\}\{⟨math⟩\}\{⟨math⟩\}$$

where each ⟨math⟩ specifies a subformula. TeX will choose the first subformula in style
D or D', the second in style T or T', the third in style S or S', the fourth in style SS
or SS'. (TeX actually typesets all four subformulas, before it chooses the final one,
because the actual style is not always known at the time a \mathchoice is encountered;
for example, when you type '\over' you often change the style of everything that has
occurred earlier in the formula. Therefore \mathchoice is somewhat expensive in terms
of time and space, and you should use it only when you're willing to pay the price.)

▶ **EXERCISE 17.15**
Guess what output is produced by the following commands:

```
\def\puzzle{{\mathchoice{D}{T}{S}{SS}}}
$$\puzzle{\puzzle\over\puzzle^{\puzzle^\puzzle}}$$
```

▶ **EXERCISE 17.16**
Devise a '\square' macro that produces a '□' for use in math formulas. The
box should be symmetrical with respect to the axis, and its inside dimensions should
be 3 pt in display and text styles, 2.1 pt in script styles, and 1.5 pt in scriptscript styles.
The rules should be 0.4 pt thick in display and text styles, 0.3 pt thick otherwise.

Plain TeX has a macro called \mathpalette that is useful for \mathchoice
constructions; '\mathpalette\a{xyz}' expands to the four-pronged array of
choices '\mathchoice {\a \displaystyle {xyz}}...{\a \scriptscriptstyle {xyz}}'.
Thus the first argument to \mathpalette is a control sequence whose first argument is
a style selection. Appendix B contains several examples that show how \mathpalette
can be applied. (See in particular the definitions of \phantom, \root, and \smash; the
congruence sign \cong ($\cong$) is also constructed from = and ∼ using \mathpalette.)

At the beginning of this chapter we discussed the commands \over, \atop, \choose, and \above. These are special cases of TeX's "generalized fraction" feature, which includes also the three primitives

> \overwithdelims⟨delim₁⟩⟨delim₂⟩
> \atopwithdelims⟨delim₁⟩⟨delim₂⟩
> \abovewithdelims⟨delim₁⟩⟨delim₂⟩⟨dimen⟩

The third of these is the most general, as it encompasses all of the other generalized fractions: \overwithdelims uses a fraction bar whose thickness is the default for the current size, and \atopwithdelims uses an invisible fraction bar whose thickness is zero, while \abovewithdelims uses a bar whose thickness is specified explicitly. TeX places the immediately preceding subformula (the numerator) over the immediately following subformula (the denominator), separated by a bar line of the desired thickness; then it puts ⟨delim₁⟩ at the left and ⟨delim₂⟩ at the right. For example, '\choose' is equivalent to '\atopwithdelims()'. If you define \legendre to be '\overwithdelims()', you can typeset the Legendre symbol '$\left(\frac{a}{b}\right)$' by saying '{a\legendre b}'. The size of the surrounding delimiters depends only on the style, not on the size of the fractions; larger delimiters are used in styles D and D' (see Appendix G). The simple commands \over, \atop, and \above are equivalent to the corresponding 'withdelims' commands when the delimiters are null; for example, '\over' is an abbreviation for '\overwithdelims..'.

▶ **EXERCISE 17.17**
Define a control sequence \euler so that the Eulerian number $\left\langle{n\atop k}\right\rangle$ will be produced when you type '{n\euler k}' in a formula.

Appendix G explains exactly how TeX computes the desired size of delimiters for \left and \right. The general idea is that delimiters are vertically centered with respect to the axis; hence, if we want to cover a subformula between \left and \right that extends y_1 units above the axis and y_2 units below, we need to make a delimiter whose height plus depth is at least y units, where $y = 2\max(y_1, y_2)$. It is usually best not to cover the formula completely, however, but just to come close; so TeX allows you to specify two parameters, the \delimiterfactor f (an integer) and the \delimitershortfall δ (a dimension). The minimum delimiter size is taken to be at least $y \cdot f/1000$, and at least $y - \delta$. Appendix B sets $f = 901$ and $\delta = 5\,$pt. Thus, if $y = 30\,$pt, the plain TeX format causes the delimiter to be more than 27 pt tall; if $y = 100\,$pt, the corresponding delimiter will be at least 95 pt tall.

So far we have been discussing the rules for typing math formulas, but we haven't said much about how TeX actually goes about converting its input into lists of boxes and glue. Almost all of the control sequences that have been mentioned in Chapters 16 and 17 are "high level" features of the plain TeX format; they are not built into TeX itself. Appendix B defines those control sequences in terms of more primitive commands that TeX actually deals with. For example, '\choose' is an abbreviation for '\atopwithdelims()'; Appendix B not only introduces \choose, it also tells TeX where to find the delimiters (and) in various sizes. The plain TeX format defines all of the special characters like \alpha and \mapsto, all of the special accents like \tilde and \widehat, all of the large operators like \sum and \int, and all of the delimiters like \lfloor and \vert. Any of these things can be redefined, in order to adapt TeX to other mathematical styles and/or to other fonts.

The remainder of this chapter discusses the low-level commands that TeX actually obeys behind the scenes. Every paragraph on the next few pages is marked with double dangerous bends, so you should skip to Chapter 18 unless you are a glutton for TeXnicalities.

All characters that are typeset in math mode belong to one of sixteen *families of fonts*, numbered internally from 0 to 15. Each of these families consists of three fonts: one for text size, one for script size, and one for scriptscriptsize. The commands \textfont, \scriptfont, and \scriptscriptfont are used to specify the members of each family. For example, family 0 in the plain TeX format is used for roman letters, and Appendix B contains the instructions

```
\textfont0=\tenrm
\scriptfont0=\sevenrm
\scriptscriptfont0=\fiverm
```

to set up this family: The 10-point roman font (\tenrm) is used for normal symbols, 7-point roman (\sevenrm) is used for subscripts, and 5-point roman (\fiverm) is used for sub-subscripts. Since there are up to 256 characters per font, and 3 fonts per family, and 16 families, TeX can access up to 12,288 characters in any one formula (4096 in each of the three sizes). Imagine that.

A definition like \textfont⟨family number⟩=⟨font identifier⟩ is local to the group that contains it, so you can easily change family membership from one set of conventions to another and back again. Furthermore you can put any font into any family; for example, the command

```
\scriptscriptfont0=\scriptfont0
```

makes sub-subscripts in family 0 the same size as the subscripts currently are. TeX doesn't check to see if the families are sensibly organized; it just follows instructions. (However, fonts cannot be used in families 2 and 3 unless they contain a certain number of special parameters, as we shall see later.) Incidentally, TeX uses \nullfont, which contains no characters, for each family member that has not been defined.

During the time that a math formula is being read, TeX remembers each symbol as being "character position so-and-so in family number such-and-such," but it does not take note of what fonts are actually in the families until reaching the end of the formula. Thus, if you have loaded a font called \Helvetica that contains Swiss-style numerals, and if you say something like

```
$\textfont0=\tenrm 9 \textfont0=\Helvetica 9$
```

you will get two 9's in font \Helvetica, assuming that TeX has been set up to take 9's from family 0. The reason is that \textfont0 is \Helvetica at the end of the formula, and that's when it counts. On the other hand, if you say

```
$\textfont0=\tenrm 9 \hbox{$9\textfont0=\Helvetica$}$
```

the first 9 will be from \tenrm and the second from \Helvetica, because the formula in the hbox will be typeset before it is incorporated into the surrounding formula.

▶ **EXERCISE 17.18**
If you say '${\textfont0=\Helvetica 9}$', what font will be used for the 9?

Every math character is given an identifying code number between 0 and 4095, obtained by adding 256 times the family number to the position number. This is easily expressed in hexadecimal notation, using one hexadecimal digit for the family and two for the character; for example, ˝24A stands for character ˝4A in family 2. Each character is also assigned to one of eight classes, numbered 0 to 7, as follows:

Class	Meaning	Example	Class	Meaning	Example
0	Ordinary	/	4	Opening	(
1	Large operator	\sum	5	Closing	)
2	Binary operation	+	6	Punctuation	,
3	Relation	=	7	Variable family	x

Classes 0 to 6 tell what "part of speech" the character belongs to, in math-printing language; class 7 is a special case discussed below. The class number is multiplied by 4096 and added to the character number, and this is the same as making it the leading digit of a four-digit hexadecimal number. For example, Appendix B defines \sum to be the math character ˝1350, meaning that it is a large operator (class 1) found in position ˝50 of family 3.

▶ **EXERCISE 17.19**
The \oplus and \bullet symbols ($\oplus$ and $\bullet$) are binary operations that appear in positions 8 and 15 (decimal) of family 2, when the fonts of plain TeX are being used. Guess what their math character codes are. (This is too easy.)

Class 7 is a special case that allows math symbols to change families. It behaves exactly like class 0, except that the specified family is replaced by the current value of an integer parameter called \fam, provided that \fam is a legal family number (i.e., if it lies between 0 and 15). TeX automatically sets \fam=-1 whenever math mode is entered; therefore class 7 and class 0 are equivalent unless \fam has been given a new value. Plain TeX changes \fam to 0 when the user types '\rm'; this makes it convenient to get roman letters in formulas, as we will see in Chapter 18, since letters belong to class 7. (The control sequence \rm is an abbreviation for '\fam=0 \tenrm'; thus, \rm causes \fam to become zero, and it makes \tenrm the "current font." In horizontal mode, the \fam value is irrelevant and the current font governs the typesetting of letters; but in math mode, the current font is irrelevant and the \fam value governs the letters. The current font affects math mode only if \␣ is used or if dimensions are given in ex or em units; it also has an effect if an \hbox appears inside a formula, since the contents of an hbox are typeset in horizontal mode.)

The interpretation of characters in math mode is defined by a table of 256 "mathcode" values; these table entries can be changed by the \mathcode command, just as the category codes are changed by \catcode (see Chapter 7). Each mathcode specifies class, family, and character position, as described above. For example, Appendix B contains the commands

```
\mathcode'<="313C
\mathcode'*="2203
```

which cause TeX to treat the character '<' in math mode as a relation (class 3) found in position ˝3C of family 1, and to treat an asterisk '*' as a binary operation found in position 3 of family 2. The initial value of \mathcode'b is ˝7162; thus, b is character

"62 in family 1 (italics), and its family will vary with \fam. (INITEX starts out with \mathcode $x = x$ for all characters x that are neither letters nor digits. The ten digits have \mathcode $x = x +$ "7000; the 52 letters have \mathcode $x = x +$ "7100.) TEX looks at the mathcode only when it is typesetting a character whose catcode is 11 (letter) or 12 (other), or when it encounters a character that is given explicitly as \char⟨number⟩.

A \mathcode can also have the special value "8000, which causes the character to behave as if it has catcode 13 (active). Appendix B uses this feature to make ' expand to ^{\prime} in a slightly tricky way. The mathcode of ' does not interfere with the use of ' in octal constants.

The mathcode table allows you to refer indirectly to any character in any family, with the touch of a single key. You can also specify a math character code directly, by typing \mathchar, which is analogous to \char. For example, the command '\mathchar"1ABC' specifies a character of class 1, family 10 ("A), and position "BC. A hundred or so definitions like

> \def\sum{\mathchar"1350 }

would therefore suffice to define the special symbols of plain TEX. But there is a better way: TEX has a primitive command \mathchardef, which relates to \mathchar just as \chardef does to \char. Appendix B has a hundred or so definitions like

> \mathchardef\sum="1350

to define the special symbols. A \mathchar must be between 0 and 32767 ("7FFF).

A character of class 1, i.e., a large operator like \sum, will be vertically centered with respect to the axis when it is typeset. Thus, the large operators can be used with different sizes of type. This vertical adjustment is not made for symbols of the other classes.

TEX associates classes with subformulas as well as with individual characters. Thus, for example, you can treat a complex construction as if it were a binary operation or a relation, etc., if you want to. The commands \mathord, \mathop, \mathbin, \mathrel, \mathopen, \mathclose, and \mathpunct are used for this purpose; each of them is followed either by a single character or by a subformula in braces. For example, \mathopen\mathchar"1234 is equivalent to \mathchar"4234, because \mathopen forces class 4 (opening). In the formula '$G\mathbin:H$', the colon is treated as a binary operation. And Appendix B constructs large opening symbols by defining \bigl#1 to be an abbreviation for

> \mathopen{\hbox{$\left#1 ...\right.$}}

There's also an eighth classification, \mathinner, which is not normally used for individual symbols; fractions and \left...\right constructions are treated as "inner" subformulas, which means that they will be surrounded by additional space in certain circumstances. All other subformulas are generally treated as ordinary symbols, whether they are formed by \overline or \hbox or \vcenter or by simply being enclosed in braces. Thus, \mathord isn't really a necessary part of the TEX language; instead of typing '$1\mathord,234$' you can get the same effect from '$1{,}234$'.

▷ **EXERCISE 17.20**

Commands like `\mathchardef\alpha="010B` are used in Appendix B to define the lowercase Greek letters. Suppose that you want to extend plain TEX by putting boldface math italic letters in family 9, analogous to the normal math italic letters in family 1. (Such fonts aren't available in stripped down versions of TEX, but let's assume that they exist.) Assume that the control sequence `\bmit` has been defined as an abbreviation for '`\fam=9`'; hence '`{\bmit b}`' will give a boldface math italic **b**. What change to the definition of `\alpha` will make `{\bmit\alpha}` produce a boldface alpha?

Delimiters are specified in a similar but more complicated way. Each character has not only a `\catcode` and a `\mathcode` but also a `\delcode`, which is either negative (for characters that should not act as delimiters) or less than `"1000000`. In other words, nonnegative delcodes consist of six hexadecimal digits. The first three digits specify a "small" variant of the delimiter, and the last three specify a "large" variant. For example, the command

> `\delcode'x="123456`

means that if the letter `x` is used as a delimiter, its small variant is found in position `"23` of family 1, and its large variant is found in position `"56` of family 4. If the small or large variant is given as 000, however (position 0 of family 0), that variant is ignored. TEX looks at the delcode when a character follows `\left` or `\right`, or when a character follows one of the `withdelims` commands; a negative delcode leads to an error message, but otherwise TEX finds a suitable delimiter by first trying the small variant and then the large. (Appendix G discusses this process in more detail.) For example, Appendix B contains the commands

> `\delcode'(="028300   \delcode'.=0`

which specify that the small variant of a left parenthesis is found in position `"28` of family 0, and that the large variant is in position 0 of family 3; also, a period has no variants, hence '`\left.`' will produce a null delimiter. There actually are several different left parenthesis symbols in family 3; the smallest is in position 0, and the others are linked together by information that comes with the font. All delcodes are −1 until they are changed by a `\delcode` command.

▷ **EXERCISE 17.21**

Appendix B defines `\delcode'<` so that there is a shorthand notation for angle brackets. Why do you think Appendix B doesn't go further and define `\delcode'{`?

A delimiter can also be given directly, as '`\delimiter⟨number⟩`'. In this case the number can be as high as `"7FFFFFF`, i.e., seven hexadecimal digits; the leading digit specifies a class, from 0 to 7, as in a `\mathchar`. For example, Appendix B contains the definition

> `\def\langle{\delimiter"426830A }`

and this means that `\langle` is an opening (class 4) whose small variant is `"268` and whose large variant is `"30A`. When `\delimiter` appears after `\left` or `\right`, the class digit is ignored; but when `\delimiter` occurs in other contexts, i.e., when TEX isn't looking for a delimiter, the three rightmost digits are dropped and the remaining four digits act as a `\mathchar`. For example, the expression '`$\langle x$`' is treated as if it were '`$\mathchar"4268 x$`'.

▶ **EXERCISE 17.22**
What goes wrong if you type '`\bigl\delimiter"426830A`'?

Granted that these numeric conventions for `\mathchar` and `\delimiter` are not beautiful, they sure do pack a lot of information into a small space. That's why TeX uses them for low-level definitions inside formats. Two other low-level primitives also deserve to be mentioned: `\radical` and `\mathaccent`. Plain TeX makes square root signs and math accents available by giving the commands

```
\def\sqrt{\radical"270370 }
\def\widehat{\mathaccent"362 }
```

and several more like them. The idea is that `\radical` is followed by a delimiter code and `\mathaccent` is followed by a math character code, so that TeX knows the family and character positions for the symbols used in radical and accent constructions. Appendix G gives precise information about the positioning of these characters. By changing the definitions, TeX could easily be extended so that it would typeset a variety of different radical signs and a variety of different accent signs, if such symbols were available in the fonts.

Plain TeX uses family 1 for math italic letters, family 2 for ordinary math symbols, and family 3 for large symbols. TeX insists that the fonts in families 2 and 3 have special `\fontdimen` parameters, which govern mathematical spacing according to the rules in Appendix G; the cmsy and cmex symbol fonts have these parameters, so their assignment to families 2 and 3 is almost mandatory. (There is, however, a way to modify the parameters of any font, using the `\fontdimen` command.) **INITEX** initializes the mathcodes of all letters A to Z and a to z so that they are symbols of class 7 and family 1; that's why it is natural to use family 1 for math italics. Similarly, the digits 0 to 9 are class 7 and family 0. None of the other families is treated in any special way by TeX. Thus, for example, plain TeX puts text italic in family 4, slanted roman in family 5, bold roman in family 6, and typewriter type in family 7, but any of these numbers could be switched around. There is a macro `\newfam`, analogous to `\newbox`, that will assign symbolic names to families that aren't already used.

When TeX is in horizontal mode, it is making a horizontal list; in vertical mode, it is making a vertical list. Therefore it should come as no great surprise that TeX is making a math list when it is in math mode. The contents of horizontal lists were explained in Chapter 14, and the contents of vertical lists were explained in Chapter 15; it's time now to describe what math lists are made of. Each item in a math list is one of the following types of things:

- an atom (to be explained momentarily);
- horizontal material (a rule or discretionary or penalty or "whatsit");
- vertical material (from `\mark` or `\insert` or `\vadjust`);
- a glob of glue (from `\hskip` or `\mskip` or `\nonscript`);
- a kern (from `\kern` or `\mkern`);
- a style change (from `\displaystyle`, `\textstyle`, etc.);
- a generalized fraction (from `\above`, `\over`, etc.);
- a boundary (from `\left` or `\right`);
- a four-way choice (from `\mathchoice`).

The most important items are called *atoms*, and they have three parts: a *nucleus*, a *superscript*, and a *subscript*. For example, if you type

```
(x_i+y)^{\overline{n+1}}
```

in math mode, you get a math list consisting of five atoms: $($, x_i, $+$, y, and $)^{\overline{n+1}}$. The nuclei of these atoms are $($, x, $+$, y, and $)$; the subscripts are empty except for the second atom, which has subscript i; the superscripts are empty except for the last atom, whose superscript is $\overline{n+1}$. This superscript is itself a math list consisting of one atom, whose nucleus is $n+1$; and that nucleus is a math list consisting of three atoms.

There are thirteen kinds of atoms, each of which might act differently in a formula; for example, '$($' is an Open atom because it comes from an opening. Here is a complete list of the different kinds:

Ord   is an ordinary atom like 'x';
Op   is a large operator atom like '$\sum$';
Bin   is a binary operation atom like '$+$';
Rel   is a relation atom like '$=$';
Open   is an opening atom like '$($';
Close is a closing atom like '$)$';
Punct is a punctuation atom like '$,$';
Inner is an inner atom like '$\frac{1}{2}$';
Over   is an overline atom like '$\overline{x}$';
Under is an underline atom like '$\underline{x}$';
Acc   is an accented atom like '$\hat{x}$';
Rad   is a radical atom like '$\sqrt{2}$';
Vcent is a vbox to be centered, produced by \vcenter.

An atom's nucleus, superscript, and subscript are called its *fields*, and there are four possibilities for each of these fields; a field can be

- empty;
- a math symbol (specified by family and position number);
- a box; or
- a math list.

For example, the Close atom $)^{\overline{n+1}}$ considered above has an empty subscript field; its nucleus is the symbol '$)$', which is character "28 of family 0 if the conventions of plain TeX are in force; and its superscript field is the math list $\overline{n+1}$. The latter math list consists of an Over atom whose nucleus is the math list $n+1$; and that math list, in turn, consists of three atoms of types Ord, Bin, Ord.

You can see TeX's view of a math list by typing \showlists in math mode. For example, after '$(x_i+y)^{\overline{n+1}}\showlists$' your log file gets the following curious data:

```
\mathopen
.\fam0 (
\mathord
.\fam1 x
_\fam1 i
```

```
\mathbin
.\fam0 +
\mathord
.\fam1 y
\mathclose
.\fam0 )
^\overline
^.\mathord
^..\fam1 n
^.\mathbin
^..\fam0 +
^.\mathord
^..\fam0 1
```

In our previous experiences with \showlists we observed that there can be boxes within boxes, and that each line in the log file is prefixed by dots to indicate its position in the hierarchy. Math lists have a slightly more complex structure; therefore a dot is used to denote the nucleus of an atom, a '^' is used for the superscript field, and a '_' is used for the subscript field. Empty fields are not shown. Thus, for example, the Ord atom x_i is represented here by three lines '\mathord', '.\fam1 x', and '_\fam1 i'.

Certain kinds of atoms carry additional information besides their nucleus, subscript, and superscript fields: An Op atom will be marked '\limits' or '\nolimits' if the normal \displaylimits convention has been overridden; a Rad atom contains a delimiter field to specify what radical sign is to be used; and an Acc atom contains the family and character codes of the accent symbol.

When you say \hbox{...} in math mode, an Ord atom is placed on the current math list, with the hbox as its nucleus. Similarly, \vcenter{...} produces a Vcent atom whose nucleus is a box. But in most cases the nucleus of an atom will be either a symbol or a math list. You can experiment with \showlists to discover how other things like fractions and mathchoices are represented internally.

Chapter 26 contains complete details of how math lists are constructed. As soon as math mode ends (i.e., when the closing '$' occurs), TeX dismantles the current math list and converts it into a horizontal list. The rules for this conversion are spelled out in Appendix G. You can see "before and after" representations of such math typesetting by ending a formula with '\showlists$\showlists'; the first \showlists will display the math list, and the second will show the (possibly complex) horizontal list that is manufactured from it.

> *The learning time is short. A few minutes gives the general flavor, and typing a page or two of a paper generally uncovers most of the misconceptions.*
> — KERNIGHAN and CHERRY, *A System for Typesetting Mathematics* (1975)

> *Within a few hours (a few days at most) a typist with no math or typesetting experience can be taught to input even the most complex equations.*
> — PETER J. BOEHM, *Software and Hardware Considerations for a Technical Typesetting System* (1976)

18

Fine Points of Mathematics Typing

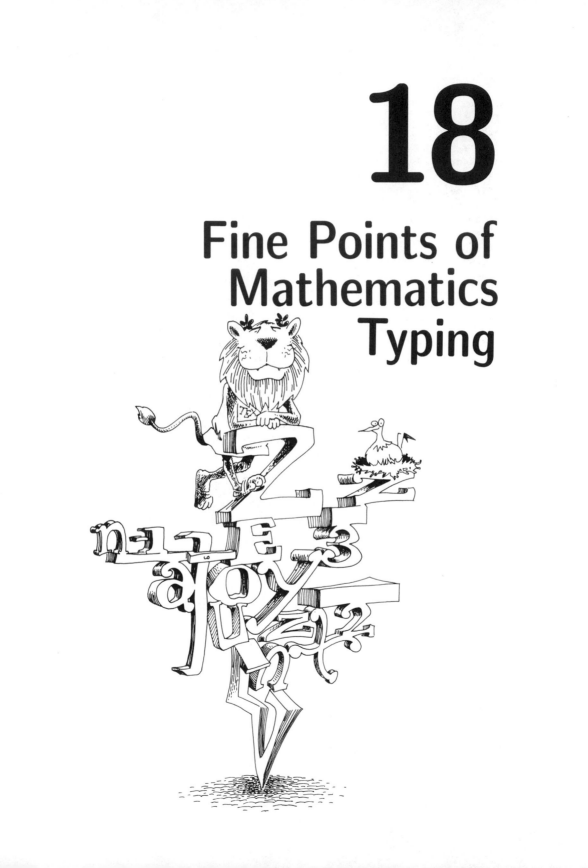

We have discussed most of the facilities needed to construct math formulas, but there are several more things a good mathematical typist will want to watch for. After you have typed a dozen or so formulas using the basic ideas of Chapters 16 and 17, you will find that it's easy to visualize the final appearance of a mathematical expression as you type it. And once you have gotten to that level, there's only a little bit more to learn before you are producing formulas as beautiful as any the world has ever seen; tastefully applied touches of TEXnique will add a professional polish that works wonders for the appearance and readability of the books and papers that you type. This chapter talks about such tricks, and it also fills in a few gaps by mentioning some aspects of math that didn't fit comfortably into Chapters 16 and 17.

1. Punctuation. When a formula is followed by a period, comma, semicolon, colon, question mark, exclamation point, etc., put the punctuation *after* the $, when the formula is in the text; but put the punctuation *before* the $$ when the formula is displayed. For example,

```
If $x<0$, we have shown that $$y=f(x).$$
```

TEX's spacing rules within paragraphs work best when the punctuation marks are not considered to be part of the formulas.

Similarly, don't ever type anything like

```
for $x = a, b$, or $c$.
```

It should be

```
for $x = a$, $b$, or $c$.
```

(Better yet, use a tie: 'or~c'.) The reason is that TEX will typeset expression '$x = a, b$' as a single formula, so it will put a "thin space" between the comma and the *b*. This space will not be the same as the space that TEX puts after the comma *after* the *b*, since spaces between words are always bigger than thin spaces. Such unequal spacing looks bad, but when you type things right the spacing will look good.

Another reason for not typing '$x = a, b$' is that it inhibits the possibilities for breaking lines in a paragraph: TEX will never break at the space between the comma and the b because breaks after commas in formulas are usually wrong. For example, in the equation '$x = f(a, b)$' we certainly don't want to put '$x = f(a,$' on one line and '$b)$' on the next.

Thus, when typing formulas in the text of a paragraph, keep the math properly segregated: Don't take operators like $-$ and $=$ outside of the $'s, and keep commas inside the formula if they are truly part of the formula. But if a comma or period or other punctuation mark belongs linguistically to the sentence rather than to the formula, leave it outside the $'s.

▶ **EXERCISE 18.1**
Type this: $R(n,t) = O(t^{n/2})$, as $t \to 0^+$.

Some mathematical styles insert a bit of extra space around formulas to separate them from the text. For example, when copy is being produced on an ordinary typewriter that doesn't have italic letters, the best technical typists have traditionally put an extra blank space before and after each formula, because this provides a useful visual distinction. You might find it helpful to think of each $ as a symbol that has the potential of adding a little space to the printed output; then the rule about excluding sentence punctuation from formulas may be easier to remember.

TeX does, in fact, insert additional space before and after each formula; the amount of such space is called \mathsurround, which is a ⟨dimen⟩-valued parameter. For example, if you set \mathsurround=1pt, each formula will effectively be 2 points wider (1 pt at each side):

> For $x = a$, b, or c. (\mathsurround=1pt)
> For $x = a$, b, or c. (\mathsurround=0pt)

This extra space will disappear into the left or right margin if the formula occurs at the beginning or end of a line. The value of \mathsurround that is in force when TeX reads the closing $ of a formula is used at both left and right of that formula. Plain TeX takes \mathsurround=0pt, so you won't see any extra space unless you are using some other format, or unless you change \mathsurround yourself.

2. Non-italic letters in formulas. The names of algebraic variables are usually italic or Greek letters, but common mathematical functions like 'log' are always set in roman type. The best way to deal with such constructions is to make use of the following 32 control sequences (all of which are defined in plain TeX format, see Appendix B):

\arccos	\cos	\csc	\exp	\ker	\limsup	\min	\sinh
\arcsin	\cosh	\deg	\gcd	\lg	\ln	\Pr	\sup
\arctan	\cot	\det	\hom	\lim	\log	\sec	\tan
\arg	\coth	\dim	\inf	\liminf	\max	\sin	\tanh

These control sequences lead to roman type with appropriate spacing:

Input	*Output*
`$\sin2\theta=2\sin\theta\cos\theta$`	$\sin 2\theta = 2 \sin\theta \cos\theta$
`$O(n\log n\log\log n)$`	$O(n \log n \log\log n)$
`$\Pr(X>x)=\exp(-x/\mu)$`	$\Pr(X > x) = \exp(-x/\mu)$
`$$\max_{1\le n\le m}\log_2P_n$$`	$\displaystyle \max_{1 \le n \le m} \log_2 P_n$
`$$\lim_{x\to0}{\sin x\over x}=1$$`	$\displaystyle \lim_{x \to 0} \frac{\sin x}{x} = 1$

The last two formulas, which are displays, show that some of the special control sequences are treated by TeX as "large operators" with limits just like $\sum$: The subscript on \max is not treated like the subscript on \log. Subscripts and superscripts will become limits when they are attached to \det, \gcd, \inf, \lim, \liminf, \limsup, \max, \min, \Pr, and \sup, in display style.

▸**EXERCISE 18.2**
Express the following display in plain TEX language, using '\nu' for 'ν':

$$p_1(n) = \lim_{m\to\infty} \sum_{\nu=0}^{\infty} \bigl(1 - \cos^{2m}(\nu!^n \pi/n)\bigr).$$

If you need roman type for some mathematical function or operator that isn't included in plain TEX's list of 32, it is easy to define a new control sequence by mimicking the definitions in Appendix B. Or, if you need roman type just for a "one shot" use, it is even easier to get what you want by switching to \rm type, as follows:

`$\sqrt{{\rm Var}(X)}$`	$\sqrt{\mathrm{Var}(X)}$
`$x_{\rm max}-x_{\rm min}$`	$x_{\mathrm{max}} - x_{\mathrm{min}}$
`${\rm LL}(k)\Rightarrow{\rm LR}(k)$`	$\mathrm{LL}(k) \Rightarrow \mathrm{LR}(k)$
`$\exp(x+{\rm constant})$`	$\exp(x + \mathrm{constant})$
`$x^3+{\rm lower\ order\ terms}$`	$x^3 + \mathrm{lower\ order\ terms}$

Notice the uses of '\␣' in the last case; without them, the result would have been 'x^3 + lowerorderterms', because ordinary blank spaces are ignored in math mode.

You can also use \hbox instead of \rm to get roman letters into formulas. For example, four of the last five formulas can be generated by

`$\sqrt{\hbox{Var}(X)}$`	$\sqrt{\mathrm{Var}(X)}$
`$\hbox{LL}(k)\Rightarrow\hbox{LR}(k)$`	$\mathrm{LL}(k) \Rightarrow \mathrm{LR}(k)$
`$\exp(x+\hbox{constant})$`	$\exp(x \mid \mathrm{constant})$
`$x^3+\hbox{lower order terms}$`	$x^3 + \mathrm{lower\ order\ terms}$

In this case '\␣' isn't necessary, because the material in an \hbox is processed in horizontal mode, when spaces are significant. But such uses of \hbox have two disadvantages: (1) The contents of the box will be typeset in the same size, whether or not the box occurs as a subscript; for example, '$x_{\hbox{max}}$' yields '$x\mathrm{max}$'. (2) The font that's used inside \hbox will be the "current font," so it might not be roman. For example, if you are typesetting the statement of some theorem that is in slanted type, and if that theorem refers to '$\sqrt{\hbox{Var}(X)}$', you will get the unintended result '$\sqrt{\mathit{Var}(X)}$'. In order to make sure that an \hbox uses roman type, you need to specify \rm, e.g., '$\sqrt{\hbox{\rm Var}(X)}$'; and then the \hbox serves no purpose. We will see later, however, that \hbox can be very useful in displayed formulas.

▸**EXERCISE 18.3**
When the displayed formula '`$$\lim_{n\to\infty}x_n {\rm exists} \iff \limsup_{n\to\infty}x_n = \liminf_{n\to\infty}x_n.$$`' is typeset with the standard macros of plain TEX, you get

$$\lim_{n\to\infty} x_n \text{ exists} \iff \limsup_{n\to\infty} x_n = \liminf_{n\to\infty} x_n.$$

But some people prefer a different notation: Explain how you could change the definitions of \limsup and \liminf so that the display would be

$$\lim_{n\to\infty} x_n \text{ exists} \iff \overline{\lim}_{n\to\infty} x_n = \underline{\lim}_{n\to\infty} x_n.$$

The word 'mod' is also generally set in roman type, when it occurs in formulas; but this word needs more care, because it is used in two different ways that require two different treatments. Plain TeX provides two different control sequences, \bmod and \pmod, for the two cases: \bmod is to be used when 'mod' is a binary operation (i.e., when it occurs between two quantities, like a plus sign usually does), and \pmod is to be used when 'mod' occurs parenthetically at the end of a formula. For example,

$\gcd(m,n)=\gcd(n,m\bmod n)$ $\gcd(m, n) = \gcd(n, m \bmod n)$

$x\equiv y+1\pmod{m^2}$ $x \equiv y + 1 \pmod{m^2}$

The 'b' in '\bmod' stands for "binary"; the 'p' in '\pmod' stands for "parenthesized." Notice that \pmod inserts its own parentheses; the quantity that appears after 'mod' in the parentheses should be enclosed in braces, if it isn't a single symbol.

▶ **EXERCISE 18.4**
What did poor B. L. User get when he typed '$x\equiv0 (\pmod y^n)$'?

▶ **EXERCISE 18.5**
Explain how to produce $\binom{n}{k} \equiv \binom{\lfloor n/p \rfloor}{\lfloor k/p \rfloor}\binom{n \bmod p}{k \bmod p} \pmod{p}$.

The same mechanism that works for roman type in formulas can be used to get other styles of type as well. For example, \bf yields boldface:

$\bf a+b=\Phi_m$ $\mathbf{a + b = \Phi_m}$

Notice that whole formula didn't become emboldened in this example; the '+' and '=' stayed the same. Plain TeX sets things up so that commands like \rm and \bf will affect only the uppercase letters A to Z, the lowercase letters a to z, the digits 0 to 9, the uppercase Greek letters \Gamma to \Omega, and math accents like \hat and \tilde. Incidentally, no braces were used in this example, because $'s have the effect of grouping; \bf changes the current font, but the change is local, so it does not affect the font that was current outside the formula.

The bold fonts available in plain TeX are "bold roman," rather than "bold italic," because the latter are rarely needed. However, TeX could readily be set up to make use of bold math italics, if desired (see Exercise 17.20). A more extensive set of math fonts would also include script, Fraktur, and "blackboard bold" styles; plain TeX doesn't have these, but other formats like $\mathcal{AMS}$-TeX do.

Besides \rm and \bf, you can say \cal in formulas to get uppercase letters in a "calligraphic" style. For example, '$\cal A$' produces '$\mathcal{A}$' and '$\cal Z$' produces '$\mathcal{Z}$'. But beware: This works only with the letters A to Z; you'll get weird results if you apply \cal to lowercase or Greek letters.

There's also \mit, which stands for "math italic." This affects uppercase Greek, so that you get $(\Gamma, \Delta, \Theta, \Lambda, \Xi, \Pi, \Sigma, \Upsilon, \Phi, \Psi, \Omega)$ instead of $(\Gamma, \ldots, \Omega)$. When \mit is in effect, the ordinary letters A to Z and a to z are not changed; they are set in italics as usual, because they ordinarily come from the math italic font. Conversely, uppercase Greek letters and math accents are unaffected by \rm, because they ordinarily come from the roman font. Math accents should not be used when the \mit family has been selected, because the math italic font contains no accents.

▶ **EXERCISE 18.6**
Type the formula $\bar{\mathbf{x}}^{\mathrm{T}}\mathbf{M}\mathbf{x} = 0 \iff \mathbf{x} = \mathbf{0}$, using as few keystrokes as possible. (The first '0' is roman, the second is bold. The superscript 'T' is roman.)

▶ **EXERCISE 18.7**
Figure out how to typeset '$S \subseteq \Sigma \iff S \in \mathcal{S}$'.

Plain TeX also allows you to type \it, \sl, or \tt, if you want text italic, slanted, or typewriter letters to occur in a math formula. However, these fonts are available only in text size, so you should not try to use them in subscripts.

If you're paying attention, you probably wonder why both \mit and \it are provided; the answer is that \mit is "math italic" (which is normally best for formulas), and \it is "text italic" (which is normally best for running text).

`$This\ is\ math\ italic.$`	*This is math italic.*
`{\it This is text italic.}`	*This is text italic.*

The math italic letters are a little wider, and the spacing is different; this works better in most formulas, but it fails spectacularly when you try to type certain italic words like '*different*' using math mode ('`$different$`'). A wide '*f*' is usually desirable in formulas, but it is undesirable in text. Therefore wise typists use \it in a math formula that is supposed to contain an actual italic word. Such cases almost never occur in classical mathematics, but they are common when computer programs are being typeset, since programmers often use multi-letter "identifiers":

`$\it last:=first$`	*last := first*
`$\it x\_coord(point\_2)$`	*x_coord(point_2)*

The first of these examples shows that TeX recognizes the ligature '*fi*' when text italic occurs in a math formula; the other example illustrates the use of short underlines to break up identifier names. When the author typeset this manual, he used '`$\it SS$`' to refer to style *SS*, since '`$SS$`' makes the *S*'s too far apart: *SS*.

▶ **EXERCISE 18.8**
What plain TeX commands will produce the following display?

$$available + \sum_{i=1}^{n} \max\bigl(full(i), reserved(i)\bigr) = capacity.$$

▶ **EXERCISE 18.9**
How would you go about typesetting the following computer program, using the macros of plain TeX?

```
for j := 2 step 1 until n do
    begin accum := A[j]; k := j − 1; A[0] := accum;
    while A[k] > accum do
        begin A[k + 1] := A[k]; k := k − 1;
        end;
    A[k + 1] := accum;
    end.
```

3. Spacing between formulas. Displays often contain more than one formula; for example, an equation is frequently accompanied by a side condition:

$$F_n = F_{n-1} + F_{n-2}, \qquad n \ge 2.$$

In such cases you need to tell TeX how much space to put after the comma, because TeX's normal spacing conventions would bunch things together; without special precautions you would get

$$F_n = F_{n-1} + F_{n-2}, n \ge 2.$$

The traditional hot-metal technology for printing has led to some in-grained standards for situations like this, based on what printers call a "quad" of space. Since these standards seem to work well in practice, TeX makes it easy for you to continue the tradition: When you type '\quad' in plain TeX format, you get a printer's quad of space in the horizontal direction. Similarly, '\qquad' gives you a double quad (twice as much); this is the normal spacing for situations like the F_n example above. Thus, the recommended procedure is to type

```
$$ F_n = F_{n-1} + F_{n-2}, \qquad  n \ge 2. $$
```

It is perhaps worth reiterating that TeX ignores all the spaces in math mode (except, of course, the space after '\qquad', which is needed to distinguish between '\qquad n' and '\qquadn'); so the same result would be obtained if you were to leave out all but one space:

```
$$F_n=F_{n-1}+F_{n-2},\qquad n\ge2.$$
```

Whenever you want spacing that differs from the normal conventions, you must specify it explicitly by using control sequences such as \quad and \qquad.

⚠ A quad used to be a square piece of blank type, 1 em wide and 1 em tall— approximately the size of a capital M, as explained in Chapter 10. This tradition has not been fully retained: The control sequence \quad in plain TeX is simply an abbreviation for '\hskip 1em\relax', so TeX's quad has width but no height.

⚠ You can use \quad in text as well as in formulas; for example, Chapter 14 illustrates how \quad applies to poetry. When \quad appears in a formula it stands for one em in the current text font, independent of the current math size or style or family. Thus, for example, \quad is just as wide in a subscript as it is on the main line of a formula.

Sometimes a careless author will put two formulas next to each other in the text of a paragraph. For example, you might find a sentence like this:

The Fibonacci numbers satisfy $F_n = F_{n-1} + F_{n-2}, \; n \ge 2$.

Everybody who teaches proper mathematical style is agreed that formulas ought to be separated by words, not just by commas; the author of that sentence should at least have said 'for $n \ge 2$', not simply '$n \ge 2$'. But alas, such lapses are commonplace, and many prominent mathematicians are hopelessly addicted to clusters of formulas. If we are not allowed to change their writing style, we can at least insert extra space where they neglected to insert an appropriate word. An additional interword space generally works well in such cases; for example, the sentence above was typeset thus:

> `... $F_n=F_{n-1}+F_{n-2}$, \ $n\ge2$.}$$`

The '`\␣`' here gives a visual separation that partly compensates for the bad style.

▶ **EXERCISE 18.10**
Put the following paragraph into TEX form, treating punctuation and spacing carefully; also insert ties to prevent bad line breaks.

> Let H be a Hilbert space, C a closed bounded convex subset of H, T a nonexpansive self map of C. Suppose that as $n \to \infty$, $a_{n,k} \to 0$ for each k, and $\gamma_n = \sum_{k=0}^{\infty}(a_{n,k+1}-a_{n,k})^+ \to 0$. Then for each x in C, $A_n x = \sum_{k=0}^{\infty} a_{n,k}T^k x$ converges weakly to a fixed point of T.

4. Spacing within formulas. Chapter 16 says that TEX does automatic spacing of math formulas so that they look right, and this is almost true. But occasionally you must give TEX some help. The number of possible math formulas is vast, and TEX's spacing rules are rather simple, so it is natural that exceptions should arise. Of course, it is desirable to have fine units of spacing for this purpose, instead of the big chunks that arise from \␣, \quad and \qquad.

The basic elements of space that TEX puts into formulas are called *thin spaces*, *medium spaces*, and *thick spaces*. In order to get a feeling for these units, let's take a look at the F_n example again: Thick spaces occur just before and after the $=$ sign, and also before and after the $\geq$; medium spaces occur just before and after the $+$ sign. Thin spaces are slightly smaller, but noticeable; it's a thin space that makes the difference between 'loglog' and 'log log'. The normal space between words of a paragraph is approximately equal to two thin spaces.

TEX inserts thin spaces, medium spaces, and thick spaces into formulas automatically, but you can add your own spacing whenever you want to, by using the control sequences

> `\,` thin space (normally 1/6 of a quad);
> `\>` medium space (normally 2/9 of a quad);
> `\;` thick space (normally 5/18 of a quad);
> `\!` negative thin space (normally −1/6 of a quad).

In most cases you can rely on TEX's spacing while you are typing a manuscript, and you'll want to insert or delete space with these four control sequences only in rare circumstances after you see what comes out.

We observed a minute ago that \quad spacing does not change with the style of formula, nor does it depend on the math font families that are being used. But thin spaces, medium spaces, and thick spaces do get bigger and smaller as the size of type gets bigger and smaller; this is because they are defined in terms of ⟨muglue⟩, a special brand of glue intended for math spacing. You specify ⟨muglue⟩ just as if it were ordinary glue, except that the units are given in terms of 'mu' (math units) instead of **pt** or **cm** or something else. For example, Appendix B contains the definitions

```
\thinmuskip = 3mu
\medmuskip = 4mu plus 2mu minus 4mu
\thickmuskip = 5mu plus 5mu
```

and this defines the thin, medium, and thick spaces that TEX inserts into formulas. According to these specifications, thin spaces in plain TEX do not stretch or shrink; medium spaces can stretch a little, and they can shrink to zero; thick spaces can stretch a lot, but they never shrink.

There are 18 mu to an em, where the em is taken from family 2 (the math symbols family). In other words, **\textfont** 2 defines the em value for **mu** in display and text styles; **\scriptfont** 2 defines the em for script size material; and **\scriptscriptfont** 2 defines it for scriptscript size.

You can insert math glue into any formula just by giving the command '**\mskip**⟨muglue⟩'. For example, '**\mskip 9mu plus 2mu**' inserts one half em of space, in the current size, together with some stretchability. Appendix B defines '**\,**' to be an abbreviation for '**\mskip\thinmuskip**'. Similarly, you can use the command '**\mkern**' when there is no stretching or shrinking; '**\mkern18mu**' gives one em of horizontal space in the current size. TEX insists that **\mskip** and **\mkern** be used only with **mu**; conversely, **\hskip** and **\kern** (which are also allowed in formulas) must never give units in **mu**.

Formulas involving calculus look best when an extra thin space appears before dx or dy or d whatever; but TEX doesn't do this automatically. Therefore a well-trained typist will remember to insert '**\,**' in examples like the following:

Input	*Output*
`$\int_0^\infty f(x)\,dx$`	$\int_0^\infty f(x)\,dx$
`$y\,dx-x\,dy$`	$y\,dx - x\,dy$
`$dx\,dy=r\,dr\,d\theta$`	$dx\,dy = r\,dr\,d\theta$
`$x\,dy/dx$`	$x\,dy/dx$

Notice that no '**\,**' was desirable after the '/' in the last example. Similarly, there's no need for '**\,**' in cases like

`$$\int_1^x{dt\over t}$$`	$\displaystyle\int_1^x \frac{dt}{t}$

since the dt appears all by itself in the numerator of a fraction; this detaches it visually from the rest of the formula.

▶ **EXERCISE 18.11**
Explain how to handle the display

$$\int_0^\infty \frac{t-ib}{t^2+b^2}e^{iat}\,dt = e^{ab}E_1(ab), \qquad a,b > 0.$$

When physical units appear in a formula, they should be set in roman type and separated from the preceding material by a thin space:

`$55\rm\,mi/hr$`	$55\,\mathrm{mi/hr}$
`$g=9.8\rm\,m/sec^2$`	$g = 9.8\,\mathrm{m/sec}^2$
`$\rm1\,ml=1.000028\,cc$`	$1\,\mathrm{ml} = 1.000028\,\mathrm{cc}$

▶ **EXERCISE 18.12**
Typeset the following display, assuming that '`\hbar`' generates '$\hbar$':

$$\hbar = 1.0545 \times 10^{-27} \text{ erg sec.}$$

Thin spaces should also be inserted after exclamation points (which stand for the "factorial" operation in a formula), if the next character is a letter or a number or an opening delimiter:

`$(2n)!/\bigl(n!\,(n+1)!\bigr)$`	$(2n)!/(n!\,(n+1)!)$
`$${52!\over13!\,13!\,26!}$$`	$\dfrac{52!}{13!\,13!\,26!}$

Besides these cases, you will occasionally encounter formulas in which the symbols are bunched up too tightly, or where too much white space appears, because of certain unlucky combinations of shapes. It's usually impossible to anticipate optical glitches like this until you see the first proofs of what you have typed; then you get to use your judgment about how to add finishing touches that provide extra beauty, clarity, and finesse. A tastefully applied '`\,`' or '`\!`' will open things up or close things together so that the reader won't be distracted from the mathematical significance of the formula. Square root signs and multiple integrals are often candidates for such fine tuning. Here are some examples of situations to look out for:

`$\sqrt2\,x$`	$\sqrt2\,x$
`$\sqrt{\,\log x}$`	$\sqrt{\,\log x}$
`$O\bigl(1/\sqrt n\,\bigr)$`	$O\bigl(1/\sqrt n\,\bigr)$
`$[\,0,1)$`	$[\,0,1)$
`$\log n\,(\log\log n)^2$`	$\log n\,(\log\log n)^2$
`$x^2\!/2$`	$x^2\!/2$
`$n/\!\log n$`	$n/\!\log n$
`$\Gamma_{\!2}+\Delta^{\!2}$`	$\Gamma_{\!2}+\Delta^{\!2}$
`$R_i{}^j{}_{\!kl}$`	$R_i{}^j{}_{\!kl}$
`$\int_0^x\!\int_0^y dF(u,v)$`	$\int_0^x\!\int_0^y dF(u,v)$
`$$\int\!\!\!\int_D dx\,dy$$`	$\iint_D dx\,dy$

In each of these formulas the omission of `\,` or `\!` would lead to somewhat less satisfactory results.

Most of these examples where thin-space corrections are desirable arise because of chance coincidences. For example, the superscript in `$x^2/2$` leaves a hole before the slash $(x^2/2)$; a negative thin space helps to fill that hole. The positive thin space in `$\sqrt{\,\log x}$` compensates for the fact that 'log x' begins with a tall, unslanted letter; and so on. But two of the examples involve corrections that were necessary because TEX doesn't really know a great deal about mathematics: (1) In the formula `$\log n(\log\log n)^2$`, TEX inserts no thin space before the left parenthesis, because there are similar formulas like `$\log n(x)$` where no such space is desired. (2) In the formula `$n/\log n$`, TEX automatically inserts an unwanted thin space before `\log`, since the slash is treated as an ordinary symbol, and since a thin space is usually desirable between an ordinary symbol and an operator like `\log`.

In fact, TEX's rules for spacing in formulas are fairly simple. A formula is converted to a math list as described at the end of Chapter 17, and the math list consists chiefly of "atoms" of eight basic types: Ord (ordinary), Op (large operator), Bin (binary operation), Rel (relation), Open (opening), Close (closing), Punct (punctuation), and Inner (a delimited subformula). Other kinds of atoms, which arise from commands like `\overline` or `\mathaccent` or `\vcenter`, etc., are all treated as type Ord; fractions are treated as type Inner. The following table is used to determine the spacing between pairs of adjacent atoms:

<table>
<tr><td></td><td></td><td colspan="8" align="center">*Right atom*</td></tr>
<tr><td></td><td></td><td>Ord</td><td>Op</td><td>Bin</td><td>Rel</td><td>Open</td><td>Close</td><td>Punct</td><td>Inner</td></tr>
<tr><td></td><td>Ord</td><td>0</td><td>1</td><td>(2)</td><td>(3)</td><td>0</td><td>0</td><td>0</td><td>(1)</td></tr>
<tr><td></td><td>Op</td><td>1</td><td>1</td><td>*</td><td>(3)</td><td>0</td><td>0</td><td>0</td><td>(1)</td></tr>
<tr><td></td><td>Bin</td><td>(2)</td><td>(2)</td><td>*</td><td>*</td><td>(2)</td><td>*</td><td>*</td><td>(2)</td></tr>
<tr><td>*Left*</td><td>Rel</td><td>(3)</td><td>(3)</td><td>*</td><td>0</td><td>(3)</td><td>0</td><td>0</td><td>(3)</td></tr>
<tr><td>*atom*</td><td>Open</td><td>0</td><td>0</td><td>*</td><td>0</td><td>0</td><td>0</td><td>0</td><td>0</td></tr>
<tr><td></td><td>Close</td><td>0</td><td>1</td><td>(2)</td><td>(3)</td><td>0</td><td>0</td><td>0</td><td>(1)</td></tr>
<tr><td></td><td>Punct</td><td>(1)</td><td>(1)</td><td>*</td><td>(1)</td><td>(1)</td><td>(1)</td><td>(1)</td><td>(1)</td></tr>
<tr><td></td><td>Inner</td><td>(1)</td><td>1</td><td>(2)</td><td>(3)</td><td>(1)</td><td>0</td><td>(1)</td><td>(1)</td></tr>
</table>

Here 0, 1, 2, and 3 stand for no space, thin space, medium space, and thick space, respectively; the table entry is parenthesized if the space is to be inserted only in display and text styles, not in script and scriptscript styles. For example, many of the entries in the Rel row and the Rel column are '(3)'; this means that thick spaces are normally inserted before and after relational symbols like '=', but not in subscripts. Some of the entries in the table are '*'; such cases never arise, because Bin atoms must be preceded and followed by atoms compatible with the nature of binary operations. Appendix G contains precise details about how math lists are converted to horizontal lists; this conversion is done whenever TEX is about to leave math mode, and the inter-atomic spacing is inserted at that time.

For example, the displayed formula specification

`$$x+y=\max\{x,y\}+\min\{x,y\}$$`

will be transformed into the sequence of atoms

of respective types Ord, Bin, Ord, Rel, Op, Open, Ord, Punct, Ord, Close, Bin, Op, Open, Ord, Punct, Ord, and Close. Inserting spaces according to the table gives

$$\text{Ord} \> \text{Bin} \> \text{Ord} \; \text{Rel} \; \text{Op Open Ord Punct} \, \text{Ord Close} \>$$
$$\text{Bin} \> \text{Op Open Ord Punct} \, \text{Ord Close}$$

and the resulting formula is

i.e.,

$$x + y = \max\{x, y\} + \min\{x, y\} \quad .$$

This example doesn't involve subscripts or superscripts; but subscripts and superscripts merely get attached to atoms without changing the atomic type.

▶ **EXERCISE 18.13**
Use the table to determine what spacing TeX will insert between the atoms of the formula '`$f(x,y)<x^2+y^2$`'.

The plain TeX macros `\bigl`, `\bigr`, `\bigm`, and `\big` all produce identical delimiters; the only difference between them is that they may lead to different spacing, because they make the delimiter into different types of atoms: `\bigl` produces an Open atom, `\bigr` a Close, `\bigm` a Rel, and `\big` an Ord. On the other hand, when a subformula appears between `\left` and `\right`, it is typeset by itself and placed into an Inner atom. Therefore it is possible that a subformula enclosed by `\left` and `\right` will be surrounded by more space than there would be if that subformula were enclosed by `\bigl` and `\bigr`. For example, Ord followed by Inner (from `\left`) gets a thin space, but Ord followed by Open (from `\bigl`) does not. The rules in Chapter 17 imply that the construction '`\mathinner{\bigl({⟨subformula⟩}}\bigr)}`' within any formula produces a result exactly equivalent to '`\left(⟨subformula⟩\right)`', when the ⟨subformula⟩ doesn't end with Punct, except that the delimiters are forced to be of the `\big` size regardless of the height and depth of the subformula.

TeX's spacing rules sometimes fail when '`|`' and '`\|`' appear in a formula, because | and ‖ are treated as ordinary symbols instead of as delimiters. For example, consider the formulas

`$|-x|=|+x|$`	$\lvert -x \rvert = \lvert + x \rvert$
`$\left|-x\right|=\left|+x\right|$`	$\lvert -x \rvert = \lvert +x \rvert$
`$\lfloor-x\rfloor=-\lceil+x\rceil$`	$\lfloor -x \rfloor = -\lceil +x \rceil$

In the first case the spacing is wrong because TeX thinks that the plus sign is computing the sum of '`|`' and '`x`'. The use of `\left` and `\right` in the second example puts TeX on the right track. The third example shows that no such corrections are needed with other delimiters, because TeX knows whether they are openings or closings.

▶ **EXERCISE 18.14**
Some perverse mathematicians use brackets backwards, to denote "open intervals." Explain how to type the following bizarre formula: $]-\infty, T[\times]-\infty, T[$.

▶ **EXERCISE 18.15**
Study Appendix G and determine what spacing will be used in the formula '`$x++1$`'. Which of the plus signs will be regarded as a binary operation?

5. *Ellipses* ("three dots"). Mathematical copy looks much nicer if you are careful about how groups of three dots are typed in formulas and text. Although it looks fine to type '...' on a typewriter that has fixed spacing, the result looks too crowded when you're using a printer's fonts: '`$x...y$`' results in '$x...y$', and such close spacing is undesirable except in subscripts or superscripts.

An ellipsis can be indicated by two different kinds of dots, one higher than the other; the best mathematical traditions distinguish between these two possibilities. It is generally correct to produce formulas like

$$x_1 + \cdots + x_n \qquad \text{and} \qquad (x_1, \ldots, x_n),$$

but wrong to produce formulas like

$$x_1 + \ldots + x_n \qquad \text{and} \qquad (x_1, \cdots, x_n).$$

The plain TeX format of Appendix B allows you to solve the "three dots" problem very simply, and everyone will be envious of the beautiful formulas that you produce. The idea is simply to type `\ldots` when you want three low dots (...), and `\cdots` when you want three vertically centered dots ($\cdots$).

In general, it is best to use `\cdots` between $+$ and $-$ and $\times$ signs, and also between $=$ signs or $\leq$ signs or $\subset$ signs or other similar relations. Low dots are used between commas, and when things are juxtaposed with no signs between them at all. For example:

`$x_1+\cdots+x_n$`	$x_1 + \cdots + x_n$
`$x_1=\cdots=x_n=0$`	$x_1 = \cdots = x_n = 0$
`$A_1\times\cdots\times A_n$`	$A_1 \times \cdots \times A_n$
`$f(x_1,\ldots,x_n)$`	$f(x_1, \ldots, x_n)$
`$x_1x_2\ldots x_n$`	$x_1 x_2 \ldots x_n$
`$(1-x)(1-x^2)\ldots(1-x^n)$`	$(1 - x)(1 - x^2) \ldots (1 - x^n)$
`$n(n-1)\ldots(1)$`	$n(n - 1) \ldots (1)$

▶ **EXERCISE 18.16**
Type the formulas '$x_1 + x_1 x_2 + \cdots + x_1 x_2 \ldots x_n$' and '$(x_1, \ldots, x_n) \cdot (y_1, \ldots, y_n) = x_1 y_1 + \cdots + x_n y_n$'. [*Hint:* A single raised dot is called '`\cdot`'.]

But there's an important special case in which `\ldots` and `\cdots` don't give the correct spacing, namely when they appear at the very end of a formula, or when they appear just before a closing delimiter like ')'. In such situations an extra thin space is needed. For example, consider sentences like this:

Prove that $(1 - x)^{-1} = 1 + x + x^2 + \cdots$.
Clearly $a_i < b_i$ for $i = 1, 2, \ldots, n$.
The coefficients $c_0, c_1, \ldots, c_n$ are positive.

To get the first sentence, the author typed

    `Prove that $(1-x)^{-1}=1+x+x^2+\cdots\,$.`

Without the '\,' the period would have come too close to the \cdots. Similarly, the second sentence was typed thus:

```
Clearly $a_i<b_i$ for $i=1$,~2, $\ldots\,$,~$n$.
```

Notice the use of ties, which prevent bad line breaks as explained in Chapter 14. Such ellipses are extremely common in some forms of mathematical writing, so plain TEX allows you to say just '\dots' as an abbreviation for '$\ldots\,$' in the text of a paragraph. The third sentence can therefore be typed

```
The coefficients $c_0$,~$c_1$, \dots,~$c_n$ are positive.
```

▶ **EXERCISE 18.17**
B. C. Dull tried to take a shortcut by typing the second example this way:

```
Clearly $a_i<b_i$ for~$i=1, 2, \ldots, n$.
```

What's so bad about that?

▶ **EXERCISE 18.18**
How do you think the author typed the footnote in Chapter 4 of this book?

6. Line breaking. When you have formulas in a paragraph, TEX may have to break them between lines. This is a necessary evil, something like the hyphenation of words; we want to avoid it unless the alternative is worse.

A formula will be broken only after a relation symbol like $=$ or $<$ or $\rightarrow$, or after a binary operation symbol like $+$ or $-$ or $\times$, where the relation or binary operation is on the "outer level" of the formula (i.e., not enclosed in {...} and not part of an '\over' construction). For example, if you type

```
$f(x,y) = x^2-y^2 = (x+y)(x-y)$
```

in mid-paragraph, there's a chance that TEX will break after either of the $=$ signs (it prefers this) or after the $-$ or $+$ or $-$ (in an emergency). But there won't be a break after the comma in any case—commas after which breaks are desirable shouldn't appear between $'s.

If you don't want to permit breaking in this example except after the $=$ signs, you could type

```
$f(x,y) = {x^2-y^2} = {(x+y)(x-y)}$
```

because these additional braces "freeze" the subformulas, putting them into unbreakable boxes in which the glue has been set to its natural width. But it isn't necessary to bother worrying about such things unless TEX actually does break a formula badly, since the chances of this are pretty slim.

A "discretionary multiplication sign" is allowed in formulas: If you type '$(x+y)*(x-y)$', TEX will treat the * something like the way it treats \-; namely, a line break will be allowed at that place, with the hyphenation penalty. However, instead of inserting a hyphen, TEX will insert a $\times$ sign in text size.

If you do want to permit a break at some point in the outer level of a formula, you can say `\allowbreak`. For example, if the formula

```
$(x_1,\ldots,x_m,\allowbreak y_1,\ldots,y_n)$
```

appears in the text of a paragraph, TeX will allow it to be broken into the two pieces '$(x_1,\ldots,x_m,$' and '$y_1,\ldots,y_n)$'.

The penalty for breaking after a Rel atom is called `\relpenalty`, and the penalty for breaking after a Bin atom is called `\binoppenalty`. Plain TeX sets `\relpenalty=500` and `\binoppenalty=700`. You can change the penalty for breaking in any particular case by typing '`\penalty`⟨number⟩' immediately after the atom in question; then the number you have specified will be used instead of the ordinary penalty. For example, you can prohibit breaking in the formula '$x = 0$' by typing '`$x=\nobreak0$`', since `\nobreak` is an abbreviation for '`\penalty10000` '.

▶ **EXERCISE 18.19**
Is there any difference between the results of '`$x=\nobreak0$`' and '`${x=0}$`'?

▶ **EXERCISE 18.20**
How could you prohibit all breaks in formulas, by making only a few changes to the macros of plain TeX?

7. Braces. A variety of different notations have sprung up involving the symbols '{' and '}'; plain TeX includes several control sequences that help you cope with formulas involving such things.

In simple situations, braces are used to indicate a set of objects; for example, '$\{a, b, c\}$' stands for the set of three objects a, b, and c. There's nothing special about typesetting such formulas, except that you must remember to use `\{` and `\}` for the braces:

`$\{a,b,c\}$`	$\{a, b, c\}$
`$\{1,2,\ldots,n\}$`	$\{1, 2, \ldots, n\}$
`$\{\rm red,white,blue\}$`	$\{\text{red}, \text{white}, \text{blue}\}$

A slightly more complex case arises when a set is indicated by giving a generic element followed by a specific condition; for example, '$\{ x \mid x > 5 \}$' stands for the set of all objects x that are greater than 5. In such situations the control sequence `\mid` should be used for the vertical bar, and thin spaces should be inserted inside the braces:

`$\{\,x\mid x>5\,\}$`	$\{ x \mid x > 5 \}$
`$\{\,x:x>5\,\}$`	$\{ x : x > 5 \}$

(Some authors prefer to use a colon instead of '|', as in the second example here.) When the delimiters get larger, as in

$$\big\{ \, (x, f(x)) \mid x \in D \, \big\}$$

they should be called \bigl, \bigm, and \bigr; for example, the formula just given would be typed

$$\bigl\{\,\bigl(x,f(x)\bigr)\bigm|x\in D\,\bigr\}$$

and formulas that involve still larger delimiters would use \Big or \bigg or even \Bigg, as explained in Chapter 17.

▶ **EXERCISE 18.21**
How would you typeset the formula $\{\,x^3 \mid h(x) \in \{-1, 0, +1\}\,\}$?

▶ **EXERCISE 18.22**
Sometimes the condition that defines a set is given as a fairly long English description, not as a formula; for example, consider '$\{\,p \mid p$ and $p + 2$ are prime $\}$'. An hbox would do the job:

$$\$\{\,p\mid\hbox\{\$p\$\ and\ \$p+2\$\ are\ prime\}\,\}\$$$

but a long formula like this is troublesome in a paragraph, since an hbox cannot be broken between lines, and since the glue inside the \hbox does not vary with the interword glue in the line that contains it. Explain how the given formula could be typeset with line breaks allowed. [*Hint:* Go back and forth between math mode and horizontal mode.]

Displayed formulas often involve another sort of brace, to indicate a choice between various alternatives, as in the construction

$$|x| = \begin{cases} x, & \text{if } x \geq 0; \\ -x, & \text{otherwise.} \end{cases}$$

You can typeset it with the control sequence \cases:

```
$$|x|=\cases{x,&if $x\ge0$;\cr
            -x,&otherwise.\cr}$$
```

Look closely at this example and notice that it uses the character **&**, which we said in Chapter 7 was reserved for special purposes. Here for the first time in this manual we have an example of why **&** is so special: Each of the cases has two parts, and the **&** separates those parts. To the left of the **&** is a math formula that is implicitly enclosed in $...$; to the right of the **&** is ordinary text, which is *not* implicitly enclosed in $...$. For example, the '-x,' in the second line will be typeset in math mode, but the 'otherwise' will be typeset in horizontal mode. Blank spaces after the **&** are ignored. There can be any number of cases, but there usually are at least two. Each case should be followed by \cr. Notice that the \cases construction typesets its own '{'; there is no corresponding '}'.

▶ **EXERCISE 18.23**
Typeset the display $\quad f(x) = \begin{cases} 1/3 & \text{if } 0 \leq x \leq 1; \\ 2/3 & \text{if } 3 \leq x \leq 4; \\ 0 & \text{elsewhere.} \end{cases}$

You can insert '`\noalign{⟨vertical mode material⟩}`' just after any `\cr` within `\cases`, as explained in Chapter 22, because `\cases` is an application of the general alignment constructions considered in that chapter. For example, the command '`\noalign{\vskip2pt}`' can be used to put a little extra space between two of the cases.

Horizontal braces will be set over or under parts of a displayed formula if you use the control sequences `\overbrace` or `\underbrace`. Such constructions are considered to be large operators like `\sum`, so you can put limits above them or below them by specifying superscripts or subscripts, as in the following examples:

$$\overbrace{x+\cdots+x}^{k\rm\;times}$$ is typed `$$\overbrace{x+\cdots+x}^{k\rm\;times}$$`

$$\underbrace{x+y+z}_{>\,0}.$$ is typed `$$\underbrace{x+y+z}_{>\,0}.$$`

8. Matrices. Now comes the fun part. Mathematicians in many different disciplines like to construct rectangular arrays of formulas that have been arranged in rows and columns; such an array is called a *matrix*. Plain TEX provides a `\matrix` control sequence that makes it convenient to deal with the most common types of matrices.

For example, suppose that you want to specify the display

$$A = \begin{pmatrix} x-\lambda & 1 & 0 \\ 0 & x-\lambda & 1 \\ 0 & 0 & x-\lambda \end{pmatrix}.$$

All you do is type

```
$$A=\left(\matrix{x-\lambda&1&0\cr
                  0&x-\lambda&1\cr
                  0&0&x-\lambda\cr}\right).$$
```

This is very much like the `\cases` construction we looked at earlier; each row of the matrix is followed by `\cr`, and '&' signs are used between the individual entries of each row. Notice, however, that you are supposed to put your own `\left` and `\right` delimiters around the matrix; this makes `\matrix` different from `\cases`, which inserts a big '{' automatically. The reason is that `\cases` always involves a left brace, but different delimiters are used in different matrix constructions. On the other hand, parentheses are used more often than other delimiters, so you can write `\pmatrix` if you want plain TEX to fill in the parentheses for you; the example above then reduces to

```
$$A=\pmatrix{x-\lambda&...&x-\lambda\cr}.$$
```

▶ **EXERCISE 18.24**
Typeset the display $\begin{pmatrix} a & b & c \\ d & e & f \end{pmatrix} \begin{pmatrix} u & x \\ v & y \\ w & z \end{pmatrix}$, using `\lgroup` and `\rgroup`.

The individual entries of a matrix are normally centered in columns. Each column is made as wide as necessary to accommodate the entries it contains, and there's a quad of space between columns. If you want to put something flush right in its column, precede it by `\hfill`; if you want to put something flush left in its column, follow it by `\hfill`.

Each entry of a matrix is treated separately from the others, and it is typeset as a math formula in text style. Thus, for example, if you say `\rm` in one entry, it does not affect the others. Don't try to say '`{\rm x&y}`'.

Matrices often appear in the form of generic patterns that use ellipses (i.e., dots) to indicate rows or columns that are left out. You can typeset such matrices by putting the ellipses into rows and/or columns of their own. Plain TeX provides `\vdots` (vertical dots) and `\ddots` (diagonal dots) as companions to `\ldots` for constructions like this. For example, the generic matrix

$$A = \begin{pmatrix} a_{11} & a_{12} & \cdots & a_{1n} \\ a_{21} & a_{22} & \cdots & a_{2n} \\ \vdots & \vdots & \ddots & \vdots \\ a_{m1} & a_{m2} & \cdots & a_{mn} \end{pmatrix}$$

is easily specified:

```
$$A=\pmatrix{a_{11}&a_{12}&\ldots&a_{1n}\cr
          a_{21}&a_{22}&\ldots&a_{2n}\cr
          \vdots&\vdots&\ddots&\vdots\cr
          a_{m1}&a_{m2}&\ldots&a_{mn}\cr}$$
```

▸ **EXERCISE 18.25**
How can you get TeX to produce the column vector $\begin{pmatrix} y_1 \\ \vdots \\ y_k \end{pmatrix}$?

Sometimes a matrix is bordered at the top and left by formulas that give labels to the rows and columns. Plain TeX provides a special macro called `\bordermatrix` for this situation. For example, the display

$$M = \begin{matrix} & C & I & C' \\ C \\ I \\ C' \end{matrix}\begin{pmatrix} 1 & 0 & 0 \\ b & 1-b & 0 \\ 0 & a & 1-a \end{pmatrix}$$

is obtained when you type

```
$$M=\bordermatrix{&C&I&C'\cr
          C&1&0&0\cr   I&b&1-b&0\cr   C'&0&a&1-a\cr}$$
```

The first row gives the upper labels, which appear above the big left and right parentheses; the first column gives the left labels, which are typeset flush left, just before the matrix itself. The first column in the first row is normally blank. Notice that `\bordermatrix` inserts its own parentheses, like `\pmatrix` does.

It's usually inadvisable to put matrices into the text of a paragraph, because they are so big that they are better displayed. But occasionally you may want to specify a small matrix like $\left(\begin{smallmatrix} 1 & 1 \\ 0 & 1 \end{smallmatrix}\right)$, which you can typeset for example as '`$1\,1\choose0\,1$`'. Similarly, the small matrix $\left(\begin{smallmatrix} a & b & c \\ l & m & n \end{smallmatrix}\right)$ can be typeset as

> `$\bigl({a\atop l}{b\atop m}{c\atop n}\bigr)$`

The `\matrix` macro does not produce small arrays of this sort.

9. Vertical spacing. If you want to tidy up an unusual formula, you know already how to move things farther apart or closer together, by using positive or negative thin spaces. But such spaces affect only the horizontal dimension; what if you want something to be moved higher or lower? That's an advanced topic.

Appendix B provides a few macros that can be used to fool TEX into thinking that certain formulas are larger or smaller than they really are; such tricks can be used to move other parts of the formula up or down or left or right. For example, we have already discussed the use of `\mathstrut` in Chapter 16 and `\strut` in Chapter 17; these invisible boxes caused TEX to put square root signs and the denominators of continued fractions into different positions than usual.

If you say '`\phantom{`⟨subformula⟩`}`' in any formula, TEX will do all of its spacing as if you had said simply '`{`⟨subformula⟩`}`', but the subformula itself will be invisible. Thus, for example, '`\phantom{0}2`' takes up just as much space as '02' in the current style, but only the 2 will actually appear on the page. If you want to leave blank space for a new symbol that has exactly the same size as $\sum$, but if you are forced to put that symbol in by hand for some reason, '`\mathop{\phantom\sum}`' will leave exactly the right amount of blank space. (The '`\mathop`' here makes this phantom behave like `\sum`, i.e., as a large operator.)

Even more useful than `\phantom` is `\vphantom`, which makes an invisible box whose height and depth are the same as those of the corresponding `\phantom`, but the width is zero. Thus, `\vphantom` makes a vertical strut that can increase a formula's effective height or depth. Plain TEX defines `\mathstrut` to be an abbreviation for '`\vphantom(`'. There's also `\hphantom`, which has the width of a `\phantom`, but its height and depth are zero.

Plain TEX also provides '`\smash{`⟨subformula⟩`}`', a macro that yields the same result as '`{`⟨subformula⟩`}`' but makes the height and depth zero. By using both `\smash` and `\vphantom` you can typeset any subformula and give it any desired nonnegative height and depth. For example,

> `\mathop{\smash\limsup\vphantom\liminf}`

produces a large operator that says 'lim sup', but its height and depth are those of `\liminf` (i.e., the depth is zero).

▶ **EXERCISE 18.26**
If you want to underline some text, you could use a macro like

> `\def\undertext#1{$\underline{\hbox{#1}}$}`

to do the job. But this doesn't always work right. Discuss better alternatives.

You can also use `\raise` and `\lower` to adjust the vertical positions of boxes in formulas. For example, the formula '`$2^{\raise1pt\hbox{$\scriptstyle n$}}$`' will have its superscript n one point higher than usual (2^n instead of 2^n). Note that it was necessary to say `\scriptstyle` in this example, since the contents of an `\hbox` will normally be in text style even when that hbox appears in a superscript, and since `\raise` can be used only in connection with a box. This method of positioning is not used extremely often, but it is sometimes helpful if the `\root` macro doesn't put its argument in a suitable place. For example,

`\root\raise`⟨dimen⟩`\hbox{$\scriptscriptstyle`⟨argument⟩`$}\of...`

will move the argument up by a given amount.

Instead of changing the sizes of subformulas, or using `\raise`, you can also control vertical spacing by changing the parameters that TeX uses when it is converting math lists to horizontal lists. These parameters are described in Appendix G; you need to be careful when changing them, because such changes are global (i.e., not local to groups). Here is an example of how such a change might be made: Suppose that you are designing a format for chemical typesetting, and that you expect to be setting a lot of formulas like '$Fe_2^{+2}Cr_2O_4$'. You may not like the fact that the subscript in Fe_2^{+2} is lower than the subscript in Cr_2; and you don't want to force users to type monstrosities like

`$\rm Fe_2^{+2}Cr_2^{\vphantom{+2}}O_4^{\vphantom{+2}}$`

just to get the formula $Fe_2^{+2}Cr_2O_4$ with all subscripts at the same level. Well, all you need to do is set '`\fontdimen16\tensy=2.7pt`' and '`\fontdimen17\tensy=2.7pt`', assuming that `\tensy` is your main symbol font (`\textfont2`); this lowers all normal subscripts to a position 2.7 pt below the baseline, which is enough to make room for a possible superscript that contains a plus sign. Similarly, you can adjust the positioning of superscripts by changing `\fontdimen14\tensy`. There are parameters for the position of the axis line, the positions of numerator and denominator in a generalized fraction, the spacing above and below limits, the default rule thickness, and so on. Appendix G gives precise details.

10. Special features for math hackers. TeX has a few more primitive operations for math mode that haven't been mentioned yet. They are occasionally useful if you are designing special formats.

If a glue or kern specification is immediately preceded by '`\nonscript`', TeX will not use that glue or kern in script or scriptscript styles. Thus, for example, the sequence '`\nonscript\;`' produces exactly the amount of space specified by '(3)' in the spacing table for mathematics that appeared earlier in this chapter.

Whenever TeX has scanned a `$` and is about to read a math formula that appears in text, it will first read another list of tokens that has been predefined by the command `\everymath={`⟨token list⟩`}`. (This is analogous to `\everypar`, which was described in Chapter 14.) Similarly, you can say `\everydisplay={`⟨token list⟩`}` to predefine a list of tokens for TeX to read just after it has scanned an opening `$$`, i.e., just before reading a formula that is to be displayed. With `\everymath` and `\everydisplay`, you can set up special conventions that you wish to apply to all formulas.

11. Summary. We have discussed more different kinds of formulas in this chapter than you will usually find in any one book of mathematics. If you have faithfully done the exercises so far, you can face almost any formula with confidence.

But here are a few more exercises, to help you review what you have learned. Each of the following "challenge formulas" illustrates one or more of the principles already discussed in this chapter. The author confesses that he is trying to trip you up on several of these. Nevertheless, if you try each one before looking at the answer, and if you're alert for traps, you should find that these formulas provide a good way to consolidate and complete your knowledge.

▶ **EXERCISE 18.27**
Challenge number 1: Explain how to type the phrase 'n^{th} root', where 'n^{th}' is treated as a mathematical formula with a superscript in roman type.

▶ **EXERCISE 18.28**
Challenge number 2: $\mathbf{S}^{-1}\mathbf{TS} = \mathbf{dg}(\omega_1, \ldots, \omega_n) = \mathbf{\Lambda}.$

▶ **EXERCISE 18.29**
Challenge number 3: $\Pr(\, m = n \mid m + n = 3 \,).$

▶ **EXERCISE 18.30**
Challenge number 4: $\sin 18° = \frac{1}{4}(\sqrt{5} - 1).$

▶ **EXERCISE 18.31**
Challenge number 5: $k = 1.38 \times 10^{-16} \text{ erg/°K}.$

▶ **EXERCISE 18.32**
Challenge number 6: $\bar{\bar{\Phi}} \subset NL_1^*/N = \bar{L}_1^* \subseteq \cdots \subseteq NL_n^*/N = \bar{L}_n^*.$

▶ **EXERCISE 18.33**
Challenge number 7: $I(\lambda) = \iint_D g(x, y) e^{i\lambda h(x,y)} \, dx \, dy.$

▶ **EXERCISE 18.34**
Challenge number 8: $\int_0^1 \cdots \int_0^1 f(x_1, \ldots, x_n) \, dx_1 \ldots dx_n.$

▶ **EXERCISE 18.35**
Challenge number 9: Here's a display.

$$x_{2m} \equiv \begin{cases} Q(X_m^2 - P_2 W_m^2) - 2S^2 & (m \text{ odd}) \\ P_2^2(X_m^2 - P_2 W_m^2) - 2S^2 & (m \text{ even}) \end{cases} \pmod{N}.$$

▶ **EXERCISE 18.36**
Challenge number 10: And another.

$$(1 + x_1 z + x_1^2 z^2 + \cdots) \ldots (1 + x_n z + x_n^2 z^2 + \cdots) = \frac{1}{(1 - x_1 z) \ldots (1 - x_n z)}.$$

▶ **EXERCISE 18.37**
Challenge number 11: And another.

$$\prod_{j \geq 0} \left(\sum_{k \geq 0} a_{jk} z^k \right) = \sum_{n \geq 0} z^n \left(\sum_{\substack{k_0, k_1, \ldots \geq 0 \\ k_0 + k_1 + \cdots = n}} a_{0k_0} a_{1k_1} \cdots \right).$$

▸ **EXERCISE 18.38**
Challenge number 12: And,

$$\frac{(n_1 + n_2 + \cdots + n_m)!}{n_1! \, n_2! \ldots n_m!} = \binom{n_1 + n_2}{n_2} \binom{n_1 + n_2 + n_3}{n_3} \ldots \binom{n_1 + n_2 + \cdots + n_m}{n_m}.$$

▸ **EXERCISE 18.39**
Challenge number 13: Yet another display.

$$\Pi_R \begin{bmatrix} a_1, a_2, \ldots, a_M \\ b_1, b_2, \ldots, b_N \end{bmatrix} = \prod_{n=0}^{R} \frac{(1 - q^{a_1+n})(1 - q^{a_2+n}) \ldots (1 - q^{a_M+n})}{(1 - q^{b_1+n})(1 - q^{b_2+n}) \ldots (1 - q^{b_N+n})}.$$

▸ **EXERCISE 18.40**
Challenge number 14: And another.

$$\sum_{p \text{ prime}} f(p) = \int_{t>1} f(t) \, d\pi(t).$$

▸ **EXERCISE 18.41**
Challenge number 15: Still another.

$$\underbrace{\overbrace{\{a, \ldots, a}^{k \ a\text{'s}}, \overbrace{b, \ldots, b}^{l \ b\text{'s}}\}}_{k+l \text{ elements}}.$$

▸ **EXERCISE 18.42**
Challenge number 16: Put a `\smallskip` between the rows of matrices in the compound matrix

$$\begin{pmatrix} \begin{pmatrix} a & b \\ c & d \end{pmatrix} & \begin{pmatrix} e & f \\ g & h \end{pmatrix} \\ 0 & \begin{pmatrix} i & j \\ k & l \end{pmatrix} \end{pmatrix}.$$

▸ **EXERCISE 18.43**
Challenge number 17: Make the columns flush left here.

$$\det \begin{vmatrix} c_0 & c_1 & c_2 & \cdots & c_n \\ c_1 & c_2 & c_3 & \cdots & c_{n+1} \\ c_2 & c_3 & c_4 & \cdots & c_{n+2} \\ \vdots & \vdots & \vdots & & \vdots \\ c_n & c_{n+1} & c_{n+2} & \cdots & c_{2n} \end{vmatrix} > 0.$$

▸ **EXERCISE 18.44**
Challenge number 18: The main problem here is to prime the $\sum$.

$$\sideset{}{'}\sum_{x \in A} f(x) \stackrel{\text{def}}{=} \sum_{\substack{x \in A \\ x \neq 0}} f(x).$$

▶ **EXERCISE 18.45**
Challenge number 19: You may be ready now for this display.

$$2 \uparrow\uparrow k \overset{\text{def}}{=} 2^{2^{2^{\cdot^{\cdot^{\cdot^2}}}}} \Big\} k.$$

▶ **EXERCISE 18.46**
Challenge number 20: And finally, when you have polished off all the other examples, here's the ultimate test. Explain how to obtain the commutative diagram

$$
\begin{array}{ccccccccc}
& & & & & & 0 & & \\
& & & & & & \downarrow & & \\
0 & \longrightarrow & \mathcal{O}_C & \overset{\iota}{\longrightarrow} & \mathcal{E} & \overset{\rho}{\longrightarrow} & \mathcal{L} & \longrightarrow & 0 \\
& & \| & & \downarrow{\scriptstyle\phi} & & \downarrow{\scriptstyle\psi} & & \\
0 & \longrightarrow & \mathcal{O}_C & \longrightarrow & \pi_*\mathcal{O}_D & \overset{\delta}{\longrightarrow} & R^1 f_* \mathcal{O}_V(-D) & \longrightarrow & 0 \\
& & & & & & \downarrow{\scriptstyle\theta_i \otimes \gamma^{-1}} & & \\
& & & & & & R^1 f_*\big(\mathcal{O}_V(-iM)\big) \otimes \gamma^{-1} & & \\
& & & & & & \downarrow & & \\
& & & & & & 0 & &
\end{array}
$$

using `\matrix`. (Many of the entries are blank.)

12. Words of advice. The number of different notations is enormous and still growing, so you will probably continue to find new challenges as you continue to type mathematical papers. It's a good idea to keep a personal notebook in which you record all of the non-obvious formulas that you have handled successfully, showing both the final output and what you typed to get it. Then you'll be able to refer back to those solutions when you discover that you need to do something similar, a few months later.

If you're a mathematician who types your own papers, you have now learned how to get enormously complex formulas into print, and you can do so without going through an intermediary who may somehow distort their meaning. But please, don't get too carried away by your newfound talent; the fact that you are able to typeset your formulas with TeX doesn't necessarily mean that you have found the best notation for communicating with the readers of your work. Some notations will be unfortunate even when they are beautifully formatted.

Mathematicians are like Frenchmen:
whenever you say something to them, they translate it into their own language,
and at once it is something entirely different.

— GOETHE, *Maxims and Reflexions* (1829)

The best notation is no notation;
whenever it is possible to avoid the use of a complicated alphabetic apparatus,
avoid it.
A good attitude to the preparation of written mathematical exposition
is to pretend that it is spoken.
Pretend that you are explaining the subject to a friend
on a long walk in the woods, with no paper available;
fall back on symbolism only when it is really necessary.

— PAUL HALMOS, *How to Write Mathematics* (1970)

19

Displayed Equations

By now you know how to type mathematical formulas so that TEX will handle them with supreme elegance; your knowledge of math typing is nearly complete. But there is one more part to the story, and the purpose of this chapter is to present the happy ending. We have discussed how to deal with individual formulas; but displays often involve a whole bunch of different formulas, or different pieces of a huge formula, and it's a bit of a problem to lay them out so that they line up properly with each other. Fortunately, large displays generally fall into a few simple patterns.

1. One-line displays. Before plunging into the general question of display layout, let's recapitulate what we have already covered. If you type '`$$`⟨formula⟩`$$`', TEX will display the formula in flamboyant display style, centering it on a line by itself. We have also noted in Chapter 18 that it's possible to display two short formulas at once, by typing '`$$`⟨formula$_1$⟩`\qquad`⟨formula$_2$⟩`$$`'; this reduces the two-formula problem to a one-formula problem. You get the two formulas separated by two quads of space, the whole being centered on a line.

Displayed equations often involve ordinary text. Chapter 18 explains how to get roman type into formulas without leaving math mode, but the best way to get text into a display is to put it into an `\hbox`. There needn't even be any math at all; to typeset

Displayed Text

you can simply say '`$$\hbox{Displayed Text}$$`'. But here's a more interesting example:

$$X_n = X_k \qquad \text{if and only if} \qquad Y_n = Y_k \quad \text{and} \quad Z_n = Z_k.$$

Formulas and text were combined in this case by typing

```
$$X_n=X_k \qquad\hbox{if and only if}\qquad
       Y_n=Y_k \quad\hbox{and}\quad Z_n=Z_k.$$
```

Notice that `\qquad` appears around 'if and only if', but a single `\quad` surrounds 'and'; this helps to indicate that the Y and Z parts of the display are related more closely to each other than to the X part.

Consider now the display

$$Y_n = X_n \bmod p \quad \text{and} \quad Z_n = X_n \bmod q \qquad \text{for all } n \ge 0.$$

Can you figure out how to type this? One solution is

```
$$Y_n=X_n\bmod p \quad\hbox{and}\quad Z_n=X_n\bmod q
       \qquad\hbox{for all }n\ge0.$$
```

Notice that a space has been left after 'all' in the hbox here, since spaces disappear when they are out in formula-land. But there's a simpler and more logical way to proceed, once you get used to TEX's idea of modes: You can type

```
...  \qquad\hbox{for all $n\ge0$.}$$
```

Wow—that's math mode inside of horizontal mode inside of display math mode. But in this way your manuscript mirrors what you are trying to accomplish, while the previous solution (with the space after 'all') looks somewhat forced.

▸**EXERCISE 19.1**
Typeset the following four displays (one at a time):

$$\sum_{n=0}^{\infty} a_n z^n \qquad \text{converges if} \qquad |z| < \left(\limsup_{n \to \infty} \sqrt[n]{|a_n|} \right)^{-1}.$$

$$\frac{f(x + \Delta x) - f(x)}{\Delta x} \to f'(x) \qquad \text{as } \Delta x \to 0.$$

$$\|u_i\| = 1, \qquad u_i \cdot u_j = 0 \quad \text{if } i \neq j.$$

$$\textit{The confluent image of} \quad \left\{ \begin{array}{c} \textit{an arc} \\ \textit{a circle} \\ \textit{a fan} \end{array} \right\} \quad \textit{is} \quad \left\{ \begin{array}{c} \textit{an arc} \\ \textit{an arc or a circle} \\ \textit{a fan or an arc} \end{array} \right\}.$$

 ▸**EXERCISE 19.2**
Sometimes display style is too grandiose, when the formula being displayed is

$$y = \frac{1}{2} x$$

or something equally simple. One day B. L. User tried to remedy this by typing it as '`$$y={\scriptstyle1\over\scriptstyle2}x$$`', but the resulting formula

$$y = \frac{1}{2} x$$

wasn't at all what he had in mind. What's the right way to get simply '$y = \frac{1}{2}x$' when you don't want big fractions in displays?

▸**EXERCISE 19.3**
What difference, if any, is there between the result of typing '`$$⟨formula⟩$$`' and the result of typing '`$$\hbox{$⟨formula⟩$}$$`' ?

▸**EXERCISE 19.4**
You may have noticed that most of the displays in this manual are not centered; displayed material is usually aligned at the left with the paragraph indentation, as part of the book design, because this is an unusual book. Explain how you could typeset a formula like

$$1 - \frac{1}{2} + \frac{1}{3} - \frac{1}{4} + \cdots = \ln 2$$

that is off-center in this way.

If you've had previous experience typing mathematical papers, you probably have been thinking, "What about equation numbers? When is this book going to talk about them?" Ah yes, now is the time to discuss those sneaky little labels that appear off to the side of displays. If you type

$$⟨formula⟩\eqno⟨formula⟩$$

TeX will display the first formula and it will also put an equation number (the second formula) at the right-hand margin. For example,

$$\verb|$$x^2-y^2 = (x+y)(x-y).\eqno(15)$$|$$

will produce this:

$$x^2 - y^2 = (x+y)(x-y). \tag{15}$$

You can also get equation numbers at the left-hand margin, with `\leqno`. For example,

$$\verb|$$x^2-y^2 = (x+y)(x-y).\leqno(16)$$|$$

will produce this:

$$\tag{16} x^2 - y^2 = (x+y)(x-y).$$

Notice that you always give the equation number second, even when it is going to appear at the left. Everything from the `\eqno` or `\leqno` command to the `$$` that ends the display is the equation number. Thus, you're not allowed to have two equation numbers in the same display; but there's a way to get around that restriction, as we'll see later.

Nowadays people are using right-hand equation numbers more and more, because a display most often comes at the end of a sentence or clause, and the right-hand convention keeps the number from intruding into the clause. Furthermore, it's often possible to save space when a displayed equation follows a short text line, since less space is needed above the display; such savings are not possible with `\leqno`, because there's no room for overlap. For example, there is less space above display (15) than there is above (16) in our illustrations of `\eqno` and `\leqno`, although the formulas and text are otherwise identical.

If you look closely at (15) and (16) above, you can see that the displayed formulas have been centered without regard to the presence of the equation numbers. But when a formula is large, TeX makes sure that it does not interfere with its number; the equation number may even be placed on a line by itself.

▶ **EXERCISE 19.5**
How would you produce the following display?

$$\prod_{k \geq 0} \frac{1}{(1 - q^k z)} = \sum_{n \geq 0} z^n \left/ \prod_{1 \leq k \leq n} (1 - q^k). \right. \tag{16$'$}$$

▶ **EXERCISE 19.6**
Equation numbers are math formulas, typeset in text style. So how can you get an equation number like '(3–1)' (with an en-dash)?

▶ **EXERCISE 19.7**
B. L. User tried typing '`\eqno(*)`' and '`\eqno(**)`', and he was pleased to discover that this produced the equation numbers '(∗)' and '(∗∗)'. [He had been a bit worried that they would come out '(*)' and '(**)' instead.] But then a few months later he tried '`\eqno(***)`' and got a surprise. What was it?

Somewhere in this manual there ought to be a description of exactly how TeX displays formulas; i.e., how it centers them, how it places the equation numbers, how it inserts extra space above and below, and so on. Well, now is the time for those rules to be stated. They are somewhat complex, because they interact with things like \parshape, and because they involve several parameters that haven't been discussed yet. The purpose of the rules is to explain exactly what sorts of boxes, glue, and penalties are placed onto the current vertical list when a display occurs.

If a display occurs after, say, four lines of a paragraph, TeX's internal register called \prevgraf will be equal to 4 when the display starts. The display will be assumed to take three lines, so \prevgraf will become 7 when the paragraph is resumed at the end of the display (unless you have changed \prevgraf in the meantime). TeX assigns special values to three ⟨dimen⟩ parameters immediately after the opening $$ is sensed: \displaywidth and \displayindent are set to the line width z and the shift amount s for line number \prevgraf$+2$, based on the current paragraph shape or hanging indentation. (Usually \displaywidth is the same as \hsize, and \displayindent is zero, but the paragraph shape can vary as described in Chapter 14.) Furthermore, \predisplaysize is set to the effective width p of the line preceding the display, as follows: If there was no previous line (e.g., if the $$ was preceded by \noindent or by the closing $$ of another display), p is set to -16383.99999 pt (i.e., to the smallest legal dimension, $-$\maxdimen). Otherwise TeX looks inside the hbox that was formed by the previous line, and sets p to the position of the right edge of the rightmost box inside that hbox, plus the indentation by which the enclosing hbox has been moved right, plus two ems in the current font. However, if this value of p depends on the fact that glue in that hbox was stretching or shrinking—for example, if the \parfillskip glue is finite, so that the material preceding it has not been set at its natural width—then p is set to \maxdimen. (This doesn't happen often, but it keeps TeX machine independent, since p never depends on quantities that may be rounded differently on different computers.) Notice that \displaywidth and \displayindent are not affected by \leftskip and \rightskip, but \predisplaysize is. The values of \displaywidth, \displayindent, and \predisplaysize will be used by TeX after the displayed formula has been read, as explained below; your program can examine them and/or change them, if you want the typesetting to be done differently.

After a display has been read, TeX converts it from a math list to a horizontal list h in display style, as explained in Appendix G. An equation number, if present, is processed in text style and put into an hbox a with its natural width. Now the fussy processing begins: Let z, s, and p be the current values of \displaywidth, \displayindent, and \predisplaysize. Let q and e be zero if there is no equation number; otherwise let e be the width of the equation number, and let q be equal to e plus one quad in the symbols font (i.e., in \textfont2). Let w_0 be the natural width of the displayed formula h. If $w_0 + q \leq z$, list h is packaged in an hbox b having its natural width w_0. But if $w_0 + q > z$ (i.e., if the display is too wide to fit at its natural width), TeX performs the following "squeeze routine": If $e \neq 0$ and if there is enough shrinkability in the displayed formula h to reduce its width to $z - q$, then list h is packaged in an hbox b of width $z - q$. Otherwise e is set to zero, and list h is packaged in a (possibly overfull) hbox b of width $\min(w_0, z)$.

(Continuation.) TeX tries now to center the display without regard to the equation number. But if such centering would make it too close to that number (where "too close" means that the space between them is less than the width e), the equation is either centered in the remaining space or placed as far from the equation number as possible. The latter alternative is chosen only if the first item on list h is glue, since TeX assumes that such glue was placed there in order to control the spacing precisely. But let's state the rules more formally: Let w be the width of box b. TeX computes a displacement d, to be used later when positioning box b, by first setting $d = \frac{1}{2}(z - w)$. If $e > 0$ and if $d < 2e$, then d is reset to $\frac{1}{2}(z - w - e)$ or to zero, where zero is chosen if list h begins with a glue item.

◈◈ (Continuation.) TeX is now ready to put things onto the current vertical list, just after the material previously constructed for the paragraph-so-far. First comes a penalty item, whose cost is an integer parameter called \predisplaypenalty. Then comes glue. If $d + s \leq p$, or if there was a left equation number (\leqno), TeX sets g_a and g_b to glue items specified by the parameters \abovedisplayskip and \belowdisplayskip, respectively; otherwise g_a and g_b become glue items corresponding to \abovedisplayshortskip and \belowdisplayshortskip. [Translation: If the predisplaysize is short enough so that it doesn't overlap the displayed formula, the glue above and below the display will be "short" by comparison with the glue that is used when there is an overlap.] If $e = 0$ and if there is an \leqno, the equation number is appended as an hbox by itself, shifted right s and preceded by interline glue as usual; an infinite penalty is also appended, to prevent a page break between this number and the display. Otherwise a glue item g_a is placed on the vertical list.

◈◈ (Continuation.) Now comes the displayed equation itself. If $e \neq 0$, the equation number box a is combined with the formula box b as follows: Let k be a kern of width $z - w - e - d$. In the \eqno case, box b is replaced by an hbox containing (b, k, a); in the \leqno case, box b is replaced by an hbox containing (a, k, b), and d is set to zero. In all cases, box b is then appended to the vertical list, shifted right by $s + d$.

◈◈ (Continuation.) The final task is to append the glue or the equation number that follows the display. If there was an \eqno and if $e = 0$, an infinite penalty is placed on the vertical list, followed by the equation number box a shifted right by $s + z$ minus its width, followed by a penalty item whose cost is the value of \postdisplaypenalty. Otherwise a penalty item for the \postdisplaypenalty is appended first, followed by a glue item for g_b as specified above. TeX now adds 3 to \prevgraf and returns to horizontal mode, ready to resume the paragraph.

◈◈ One consequence of these rules is that you can force an equation number to appear on a line by itself by making its width zero, i.e., by saying either '\eqno\llap{$⟨formula⟩$}' or '\leqno\rlap{$⟨formula⟩$}'. This makes $e = 0$, and the condition $e = 0$ controls TeX's positioning logic, as explained in the rules just given.

◈◈ Plain TeX sets \predisplaypenalty=10000, because fine printers traditionally shun displayed formulas at the very top of a page. You can change \predisplaypenalty and \postdisplaypenalty if you want to encourage or discourage page breaks just before or just after a display. For example, '$$\postdisplaypenalty= -10000⟨formula⟩$$' will force a page break, putting the formula at the bottom line. It is better to force a page break this way than to say \eject right after $$...$$; such an eject (which follows the \belowdisplayskip glue below the display) causes the page to be short, because it leaves unwanted glue at the bottom.

▶ **EXERCISE 19.8**
Read the rules carefully and deduce the final position of '$x = y$' in the formula

$$\quad x=y \hskip10000pt minus 1fil \eqno(5)$$

assuming that there is no hanging indentation. Also consider `\leqno` instead of `\eqno`.

TeX also allows "alignment displays," which are not processed in math mode because they contain no formulas at the outer level. An alignment display is created by commands of the general form

$$\langle\text{assignments}\rangle\text{\texttt{\textbackslash halign}}\{\langle\text{alignment}\rangle\}\langle\text{assignments}\rangle\$$

where the ⟨assignments⟩ are optional things like parameter changes that do not produce any math lists. In such displays, the `\halign` is processed exactly as if it had appeared in vertical mode, and it will construct a vertical list v as usual, except that each row of the alignment will be shifted right by the `\displayindent`. After the alignment and the closing assignments have been processed, TeX will put a `\predisplaypenalty` item and some `\abovedisplayskip` glue on the main vertical list, followed by v, followed by a `\postdisplaypenalty` item and `\belowdisplayskip` glue. Thus, alignment displays are essentially like ordinary alignments, except that they can interrupt paragraphs; furthermore, they are embedded in glue and penalties just like other displays. The `\displaywidth` and `\predisplaysize` do not affect the result, although you could use those parameters in your `\halign`. An entire alignment display is considered to be only three lines long, as far as `\prevgraf` is concerned.

2. Multi-line displays. OK, the use of displayed formulas is very nice. But when you try typing a lot of manuscripts you will run into some displays that don't fit the simple pattern of a one-line formula with or without an equation number. Plain TeX provides special control sequences that will cover most of the remaining cases.

Multi-line displays usually consist of several equations that should be lined up by their '=' signs, as in

$$X_1 + \cdots + X_p = m,$$
$$Y_1 + \cdots + Y_q = n.$$

The recommended procedure for such a display is to use `\eqalign`, which works with special markers `&` and `\cr` that we have already encountered in connection with `\cases` and `\matrix` in Chapter 18. Here's how to type this particular one:

```
$$\eqalign{X_1+\cdots+X_p&=m,\cr
          Y_1+\cdots+Y_q&=n.\cr}$$
```

There can be any number of equations in an `\eqalign`; the general pattern is

```
\eqalign{⟨left-hand side₁⟩&⟨right-hand side₁⟩\cr
         ⟨left-hand side₂⟩&⟨right-hand side₂⟩\cr
              ⋮
         ⟨left-hand sideₙ⟩&⟨right-hand sideₙ⟩\cr}
```

where each ⟨right-hand side⟩ starts with the symbol on which you want alignment to occur. For example, every right-hand side often begins with an = sign. The equations will be typeset in display style.

▶**EXERCISE 19.9**
In practice, the left-hand sides of aligned formulas are often blank, and the alignment is often done with respect to other symbols as well as =. For example, the following display is typical; see if you can guess how the author typed it:

$$T(n) \le T(2^{\lceil \lg n \rceil}) \le c(3^{\lceil \lg n \rceil} - 2^{\lceil \lg n \rceil})$$
$$< 3c \cdot 3^{\lg n}$$
$$= 3c\, n^{\lg 3}.$$

The result of \eqalign is a vertically centered box. This makes it easy to get a formula like

$$\left\{ \begin{aligned} \alpha &= f(z) \\ \beta &= f(z^2) \\ \gamma &= f(z^3) \end{aligned} \right\} \qquad \left\{ \begin{aligned} x &= \alpha^2 - \beta \\ y &= 2\gamma \end{aligned} \right\}.$$

You simply use \eqalign twice in the same line:

```
$$\left\{
\eqalign{\alpha&=f(z)\cr \beta&=f(z^2)\cr \gamma&=f(z^3)\cr}
\right\}\qquad\left\{
\eqalign{x&=\alpha^2-\beta\cr y&=2\gamma\cr}\right\}.$$
```

▶**EXERCISE 19.10**
Try your hand at the numbered two-line display

$$P(x) = a_0 + a_1 x + a_2 x^2 + \cdots + a_n x^n,$$
$$P(-x) = a_0 - a_1 x + a_2 x^2 - \cdots + (-1)^n a_n x^n. \tag{30}$$

[*Hint:* Use the fact that \eqalign produces a vertically centered box; the equation number '(30)' is supposed to appear halfway between the two lines.]

▶**EXERCISE 19.11**
What happens if you forget the & in one equation of an \eqalign?

Multi-line formulas sometimes fit together in odd ways, and you'll find that every once in a while you will want to move certain lines farther apart or closer together. If you type '\noalign{\vskip⟨glue⟩}' after any \cr, TeX will insert the given amount of extra glue just after that particular line. For example,

```
\noalign{\vskip3pt}
```

will put 3 pt of additional space between lines. You can also change the amount of space before the first line, in the same way.

The next level of complexity occurs when you have several aligned equations with several equation numbers. Or perhaps some of the lines are numbered and others are not:

$$\begin{aligned}(x+y)(x-y) &= x^2 - xy + yx - y^2 \\ &= x^2 - y^2; & (4) \\ (x+y)^2 &= x^2 + 2xy + y^2. & (5)\end{aligned}$$

For this situation plain TeX provides `\eqalignno`; you use it like `\eqalign`, but on each line that you want an equation number you add '`&`⟨equation number⟩' just before the `\cr`. The example above was generated by

```
$$\eqalignno{(x+y)(x-y)&=x^2-xy+yx-y^2\cr
      &=x^2-y^2;&(4)\cr
   (x+y)^2&=x^2+2xy+y^2.&(5)\cr}$$
```

Notice that the second `&` is omitted unless there's an equation number.

And there's also `\leqalignno`, which puts equation numbers at the left. In this case it is appropriate to move the '(4)' to the beginning of its equation:

$$(4) \qquad\qquad \begin{aligned}(x+y)(x-y) &= x^2 - xy + yx - y^2 \\ &= x^2 - y^2;\end{aligned}$$
$$(5) \qquad\qquad (x+y)^2 = x^2 + 2xy + y^2.$$

Although the equation numbers appear at the left, you are still supposed to input them at the right, just as you do with `\leqno`; in other words, you should type '`$$\leqalignno{(x+y)(x-y)&...&(4)\cr...}$$`' to get the previous display.

Caution: `\eqalignno` and `\leqalignno` both center the set of equations without regard to the widths of the equation numbers. If the equations or their numbers get too wide, they might overlap, yet no error message will be given.

▶ **EXERCISE 19.12**
Typeset the following display:

$$(9) \qquad\qquad \gcd(u,v) = \gcd(v,u);$$
$$(10) \qquad\qquad \gcd(u,v) = \gcd(-u,v).$$

▶ **EXERCISE 19.13**
And here's another one to try, just to keep in practice:

$$\begin{aligned}\left(\int_{-\infty}^{\infty} e^{-x^2}\,dx\right)^2 &= \int_{-\infty}^{\infty}\int_{-\infty}^{\infty} e^{-(x^2+y^2)}\,dx\,dy \\ &= \int_0^{2\pi}\int_0^{\infty} e^{-r^2} r\,dr\,d\theta \\ &= \int_0^{2\pi}\left(-\frac{e^{-r^2}}{2}\bigg|_{r=0}^{r=\infty}\right)d\theta \\ &= \pi. & (11)\end{aligned}$$

Although \eqalign and \eqalignno look nearly the same, there's really a fundamental distinction between them: \eqalign makes a single, vertically centered box, which is no wider than it needs to be; but \eqalignno generates a set of lines that have the full display width (reaching all the way to both margins). Thus, for example, you can use \eqalign several times in a display, but \eqalignno can appear only once. If you try to use \eqno in conjunction with \eqalign, you get a decent result, but if you try to use \eqno in connection with \eqalignno you'll get some sort of weird error message(s).

The definitions in Appendix B reveal why \eqalign and \eqalignno behave differently: \eqalign is an abbreviation for \vcenter{\halign{...}}, while \eqalignno is an abbreviation for \halign to\displaywidth{...}; thus the \eqalignno macro generates an "alignment display."

This difference between \eqalign and \eqalignno has two interesting consequences. (1) It's impossible to break an \eqalign between pages, but an \eqalignno can be broken. In fact, you can *force* a page break after a particular line if you insert '\noalign{\break}' after the \cr for that line. You can prohibit *all* breaks in an \eqalignno if you set \interdisplaylinepenalty=10000; or you can enclose the whole works in a \vbox:

$$\vbox{\eqalignno{...}}$$

(2) You can also insert a line of text between two equations, without losing the alignment. For example, consider the two displays

$$x = y + z$$

and

$$x^2 = y^2 + z^2.$$

These were actually generated as a single display by typing

```
$$\eqalignno{x&=y+z\cr
  \noalign{\hbox{and}}
  x^2&=y^2+z^2.\cr}$$
```

Therefore the fact that their $=$ signs line up is not just a lucky coincidence. Sometimes you will want to adjust the spacing above or below such a line of inserted text, by putting a \vskip or two inside of the \noalign{...}. Incidentally, this example also shows that it is possible to use \eqalignno without giving any equation numbers.

▶ **EXERCISE 19.14**
What happens if \eqalign is substituted for \eqalignno in this last example?

▶ **EXERCISE 19.15**
Our friend Ben User got into trouble again when he tried to move an equation number up higher than its usual position, by typing this:

```
$$\eqalignno{...&\raise6pt\hbox{(5)}\cr}$$
```

What was his oversight, and what could he have done instead?

For other types of displays, plain TeX provides \displaylines, which lets you display any number of formulas in any way you want, without any alignment. The general form is

$$\displaylines{\langle\text{displayed formula}_1\rangle\cr$$
$$\langle\text{displayed formula}_2\rangle\cr$$
$$\vdots$$
$$\langle\text{displayed formula}_n\rangle\cr}\$\$$

Each formula will be centered, because \displaylines puts \hfil at the left and the right of each line; you can override this centering to get things flush left or flush right by inserting \hfill, which takes precedence over \hfil.

▶ **EXERCISE 19.16**
Use \displaylines to typeset the three-line display

$$x \equiv x; \tag{1}$$
$$\text{if} \quad x \equiv y \quad \text{then} \quad y \equiv x; \tag{2}$$
$$\text{if} \quad x \equiv y \quad \text{and} \quad y \equiv z \quad \text{then} \quad x \equiv z. \tag{3}$$

If you look closely at the multi-line displays in this chapter, you'll see that the baselines are farther apart than they are in normal text; mathematics publishers generally do this in order to make the displays easier to read. In accordance with this tradition, \eqalign and its relatives automatically increase the \baselineskip. If you are making a multi-line display with TeX's primitive \halign command, instead of using one of the plain TeX macros, you might want to make this same baseline adjustment, and you can do it easily by saying '$$\openup1\jot \halign{...}$$'. The \openup macro increases \lineskip and \lineskiplimit as well as \baselineskip. If you say '\openup2\jot', the lines are spread apart 2 extra units, where plain TeX opens things up in units of 3 pt. Since $$...$$ acts as a group, the effect of \openup will disappear when the display is finished. Any ⟨dimen⟩ can follow \openup, but it's customary to express the amount symbolically in terms of a \jot instead of using absolute units; then your manuscript can be used with a variety of different formats.

Plain TeX's \displaylines, \eqalignno, and \leqalignno macros begin with '\openup1\jot'. If you don't want the lines to be opened up, you can cancel this by saying, e.g., '$$\openup-1\jot \eqalignno{...}$$', because \openup has a cumulative effect.

Suppose that you have decided to make a homegrown display having the general form '$$\openup1\jot \halign{...}$$'; and for convenience, let's suppose that the normal conventions of plain TeX are in force, so that \jot=3pt and \baselineskip=12pt. Then the \openup macro changes the baselineskip distance to 15 pt. It follows that the baseline of the text line that immediately precedes the display will be 15 pt above the topmost baseline of the display, plus the \abovedisplayskip. But when the paragraph resumes, its next baseline will be only 12 pt below the bottom baseline of the display, plus the \belowdisplayskip, because the \baselineskip parameter will have reverted to its normal value. The \eqalignno and \displaylines macros say '\noalign{\vskip−d}' before their first lines, where d is the net amount of opening-up, in order to compensate for this difference.

3. Long formulas. Our discussion of mathematics typing is almost complete; we need to deal with just one more problem: What should be done when a formula is so long that it doesn't fit on a single line?

For example, suppose that you encounter the equation

$$\sigma(2^{34}-1, 2^{35}, 1) = -3 + (2^{34}-1)/2^{35} + 2^{35}/(2^{34}-1) + 7/2^{35}(2^{34}-1) - \sigma(2^{35}, 2^{34}-1, 1).$$

You'll have to break it up somehow; TeX has done its best to squeeze everything together by shrinking the spaces next to the $+$ and $-$ signs to zero, but still the line has come out overfull.

Let's try to break that equation just before the '$+7$'. One common way to do this is to type

```
$$\eqalign{\sigma(2^{34}-1,2^{35},1)
 &=-3+(2^{34}-1)/2^{35}+2^{35}\!/(2^{34}-1)\cr
 &\qquad+7/2^{35}(2^{34}-1)-\sigma(2^{35},2^{34}-1,1).\cr}$$
```

which yields

$$\begin{aligned}\sigma(2^{34}-1, 2^{35}, 1) &= -3 + (2^{34}-1)/2^{35} + 2^{35}/(2^{34}-1)\\ &\qquad + 7/2^{35}(2^{34}-1) - \sigma(2^{35}, 2^{34}-1, 1).\end{aligned}$$

The idea is to treat a long one-line formula as a two-line formula, using \qquad on the second line so that the second part of the formula appears well to the right of the $=$ sign on the first line.

▸ **EXERCISE 19.17**
Explain how to deal with the following display.

$$\begin{aligned}x_n u_1 + \cdots + x_{n+t-1} u_t &= x_n u_1 + (a x_n + c) u_2 + \cdots\\ &\quad + \big(a^{t-1} x_n + c(a^{t-2} + \cdots + 1)\big) u_t\\ &= (u_1 + a u_2 + \cdots + a^{t-1} u_t) x_n + h(u_1, \ldots, u_t). \quad (47)\end{aligned}$$

It's quite an art to decide how to break long displayed formulas into several lines; TeX never attempts to break them, because no set of rules is really adequate. The author of a mathematical manuscript is generally the best judge of what to do, since break positions depend on subtle factors of mathematical exposition. For example, it is often desirable to emphasize some of the symmetry or other structure that underlies a formula, and such things require a solid understanding of exactly what is going on in that formula.

Nevertheless, it is possible to state a few rules of thumb about how to deal with long formulas in displays, since there are some principles that the best mathematical typesetters tend to follow:

a) Although formulas within a paragraph always break *after* binary operations and relations, displayed formulas always break *before* binary operations and relations. Thus, we didn't end the first line of our $\sigma(\ldots)$ example with '(2^{34}-1)+'; we ended it with '(2^{34}-1)' and began the second line with '+'.

b) When an equation is broken before a binary operation, the second line should start at least two quads to the right of where the innermost subformula containing that binary operation begins on the first line. For example, if you wish to break

$$\verb|\sum_{0<k<n}\left(|\langle\text{formula}_1\rangle\verb|+|\langle\text{formula}_2\rangle\verb|\right)|$$

at the plus sign between $\langle\text{formula}_1\rangle$ and $\langle\text{formula}_2\rangle$, it is almost mandatory to have the plus sign on the second line appear somewhat to the right of the large left parenthesis that corresponds to '$\verb|\left(|$'.

In the example just considered, special care is needed to break the formula into two lines, because $\verb|\left|$ and $\verb|\right|$ delimiters cannot be used in isolation; you can't have only $\verb|\left|$ in one line of a formula and only $\verb|\right|$ in the second. Furthermore, you'll want the two delimiters to be of the same size, even though they occur in different lines. The best solution is usually to choose the delimiter size yourself; for example, you could type

$$\verb|\eqalign{\sum_{0<k<n}\biggl(&|\langle\text{formula}_1\rangle\verb|\cr|$$
$$\verb|&\qquad{}+|\langle\text{formula}_2\rangle\verb|\biggr)\cr}|$$

if $\verb|\bigg|$ delimiters are best. Notice that the $\verb|&|$ markers don't occur at $=$ signs in this example, they just mark a point of alignment.

There's another way to break long formulas, sometimes called the *two-line* form. The idea is to put the first part of the formula almost flush left, and to put the second part almost flush right, where "almost flush" means "one quad away." Thus, the two-line form of the long $\sigma(\dots)$ equation considered earlier is

$$\sigma(2^{34}-1, 2^{35}, 1) = -3 + (2^{34}-1)/2^{35} + 2^{35}/(2^{34}-1)$$
$$+ 7/2^{35}(2^{34}-1) - \sigma(2^{35}, 2^{34}-1, 1).$$

It isn't difficult to get this two-line effect with $\verb|\displaylines|$:

$$\verb|\displaylines{\quad\sigma(2^{34}-1,2^{35},1)|$$
$$\verb|=-3+(2^{34}-1)/2^{35}+2^{35}\!/(2^{34}-1)\hfill\cr|$$
$$\verb|\hfill{}+7/2^{35}(2^{34}-1)-\sigma(2^{35},2^{34}-1,1).\quad\cr}|$$

An extra '$\verb|{}|$' was typed on the second line here so that TeX would know that the '$+$' is a binary operation. The two-line form is especially recommended for equations that have a long left-hand side; in that case the break generally comes just before the $=$ sign.

▶ **EXERCISE 19.18**
Typeset the following display:

$$\sum_{1 \leq j \leq n} \frac{1}{(x_j - x_1)\dots(x_j - x_{j-1})(x - x_j)(x_j - x_{j+1})\dots(x_j - x_n)}$$
$$= \frac{1}{(x - x_1)\dots(x - x_n)}. \quad (27)$$

▶ **EXERCISE 19.19**
If it is necessary to typeset a huge fraction like

$$\frac{q^{\frac{1}{2}n(n+1)}(ea; q^2)_\infty (eq/a; q^2)_\infty (caq/e; q^2)_\infty (cq^2/ae; q^2)_\infty}{(e; q)_\infty (cq/e; q)_\infty}$$

in a single narrow column, you might have to break up the numerator and resort to

$$\frac{q^{\frac{1}{2}n(n+1)}(ea;q^2)_\infty(eq/a;q^2)_\infty \atop (caq/e;q^2)_\infty(cq^2/ae;q^2)_\infty}{(e;q)_\infty(cq/e;q)_\infty}$$

How would you specify the latter fraction to TEX?

> *When a formula is too long for the page-width*
> *and has to be broken into successive lines*
> *(and we are now, of course, speaking of displayed formulae),*
> *it should be broken, if possible, at the end of a natural 'phrase';*
> *if, for example, it is a much-bracketed formula,*
> *it should be broken at the end of one of the major brackets*
> *and not at an inner symbol.*
> *This natural phrasing (as in music or speech)*
> *makes for intelligibility between writer and reader*
> *and should not be left to the compositor.*
> *An author, when he finds himself writing a longish formula,*
> *should indicate a convenient point of fracture in case of need.*
>
> — CHAUNDY, BARRETT, and BATEY, *The Printing of Mathematics* (1954)

> *Some authors use display with discretion,*
> *some run even extremely long, complicated equations into the text,*
> *while others tend to display every equation in the paper.*
> *The tendency to overdisplay is probably more predominant*
> *than the tendency to underdisplay;*
> *for this reason it is possible for the copy editor to shorten*
> *(and even improve) papers by running displayed material into text. ...*
> *On the other hand, there are occasions when the copy editor needs*
> *to suggest the display of complicated expressions that have been run into text,*
> *particularly when it would involve a bad break at the end of a text line.*
>
> — ELLEN SWANSON, *Mathematics into Type* (1971)

20

Definitions
(also called Macros)

You can often save time typing math formulas by letting control sequences stand for constructions that occur frequently in a particular manuscript. For example, if some document uses the vector '$(x_1, \ldots, x_n)$' a lot, you can type

> `\def\xvec{(x_1,\ldots,x_n)}`

and `\xvec` will henceforth be an abbreviation for '`(x_1,\ldots,x_n)`'. Complex displays like

$$\sum_{(x_1,\ldots,x_n)\neq(0,\ldots,0)} \bigl(f(x_1,\ldots,x_n) + g(x_1,\ldots,x_n)\bigr)$$

can then be typed simply as

> `$$\sum_{\xvec\ne(0,\ldots,0)} \bigl(f\xvec+g\xvec\bigr)$$`

instead of in a tedious long form. By defining a control sequence like `\xvec`, you not only cut down on the number of keystrokes that you need to make, you also reduce your chances of introducing typographical errors and inconsistencies.

Of course, you usually won't be making a definition just to speed up the typing of one isolated formula; that doesn't gain anything, because time goes by when you're deciding whether or not to make a definition, and when you're typing the definition itself. The real payoff comes when some cluster of symbols is used dozens of times throughout a manuscript. A wise typist will look through a document before typing anything, thereby getting a feeling for what sorts of problems will arise and what sorts of definitions will be helpful. For example, Chapter 16 recommends that the control sequence `\Ahat` be defined at the beginning of any manuscript that makes frequent use of the symbol $\hat{A}$.

Abbreviations like `\xvec` turn out to be useful in many applications of computers, and they have come to be known as *macros* because they are so powerful; one little macro can represent an enormous amount of material, so it has a sort of macroscopic effect. System programs like TeX that are designed to deal with macro definitions are said to *expand* the user's macros; for example, `\xvec` expands into `(x_1,\ldots,x_n)`, and `\ldots` in turn is a macro that expands into `\mathinner{\ldotp\ldotp\ldotp}`. Thus, `\xvec` is actually an abbreviation for '`(x_1,\mathinner{\ldotp\ldotp\ldotp},x_n)`'. (The expansion stops here, because `\mathinner` is a primitive control sequence of TeX, and because `\ldotp` has been defined with `\mathchardef`; thus `\mathinner` and `\ldotp` are not macros.)

TeX users generally build up their own personal library of macros for things that they want to do in different documents. For example, it is common to have a file called `macros.tex` that contains definitions of your favorite special control sequences, perhaps together with commands that load your favorite special fonts, etc. If you begin a document with the command

> `\input macros`

then TeX will read all those definitions, saving you all the trouble of retyping them. Of course, TeX's memory is limited, and it takes time to read a file, so you shouldn't put thousands of definitions into `macros.tex`. A large collection of macro definitions (e.g., the set of definitions in Appendix B) is called a *format* (e.g., "plain TeX format"); TeX has a special way to input a format at high speed, assuming that the format doesn't change very often.

The `\xvec` and `\Ahat` examples apply to math formulas, but you can make good use of macro definitions even when you aren't doing any math at all. For example, if you are using TeX for business correspondence, you can have a `\yours` macro that stands for 'Sincerely yours, A. U. Thor'. If you often write form letters you can have macros that generate entire sentences or paragraphs or groups of paragraphs. The Internal Revenue Service could, for example, make use of the following two macros:

```
\def\badcheck{A penalty has been added because your
   check to us was not honored by your bank.\par}
\def\cheater{A penalty of 50\% of the underpaid tax
   has been added for fraud.\par}
```

Simple macro definitions, like these, start with '`\def`'; then comes the control sequence name, e.g., '`\badcheck`'; and then comes the replacement text enclosed in '`{`' and '`}`'. The braces do not represent grouping in this case; they simply show the extent of the replacement text in the definition. You could, of course, define a macro that includes actual braces in its replacement text, as long as those braces match each other properly. For example, '`\def\xbold{{\bf x}}`' makes `\xbold` an abbreviation for '`{\bf x}`'.

▶ **EXERCISE 20.1**
Write a `\punishment` macro that prints 100 lines containing the message 'I must not talk in class.' [*Hint:* First write a macro `\mustnt` that prints the message once; then write a macro `\five` that prints it five times.]

▶ **EXERCISE 20.2**
What is the expansion of `\puzzle`, given the following definitions?

```
\def\a{\b}
\def\b{A\def\a{B\def\a{C\def\a{\b}}}}
\def\puzzle{\a\a\a\a\a}
```

As soon as you get the hang of simple macros like those illustrated above, you will probably begin to think, "Boy, wouldn't it be nice if I could have a macro in which some of the text in the expansion is changeable? I'd like to be able to stick different things into the middle of that text." Well, TeX has good news for you: Control sequences can be defined in terms of *parameters*, and you can supply *arguments* that will be substituted for the parameters.

For example, let's consider `\xvec` again. Suppose that you not only refer to '$(x_1,\ldots,x_n)$', but you also make frequent use of '$(y_1,\ldots,y_n)$' and other similar things. Then you might want to type

```
\def\row#1{(#1_1,\ldots,#1_n)}
```

after which \row x will produce '$(x_1, \ldots, x_n)$' and \row y will produce '$(y_1, \ldots, y_n)$'. The symbol #1 stands for the first parameter to the macro, and when you say '\row x' the x is a so-called argument that will be inserted in place of the #1's in the replacement text. In this case the argument consists of a single letter, x. You can also say \row\alpha, in which case the argument will be the control sequence \alpha, and the result will be '$(\alpha_1, \ldots, \alpha_n)$'. If you want the argument to contain more than one symbol or control sequence, you can simply enclose it in braces; for example, \row{x'} yields $(x'_1, \ldots, x'_n)$. The argument in this case is x' (without the braces). Incidentally, if you say \row{{x'}}, you get $(x'_1, \ldots, x'_n)$; the reason is that only one pair of braces is stripped off when the argument is collected, and $(x'_1, \ldots, x'_n)$ is what you get from ({x'}_1,\ldots,{x'}_n) in math mode, according to the rules of Chapter 16.

▶ **EXERCISE 20.3**
Continuing this example, what is the result of $\row{\bf x}$?

The notation '#1' suggests that there might be an opportunity to have more than one parameter, and indeed there is. You can write, for example,

    \def\row#1#2{(#1_1,\ldots,#1_#2)}

after which '\row xn' would be the proper protocol for '$(x_1, \ldots, x_n)$'. There can be as many as nine parameters, #1 to #9, and when you use them you must number them in order. For example, you can't use #5 in a definition unless the previous parameter in that definition was called #4. (This restriction applies only to the initial statement of parameters, before the replacement text starts; the stated parameters can be used any number of times, in any order, in the replacement text itself.)

A control sequence has only one definition at a time, so the second definition of \row would supersede the first one if both had appeared in the same document. Whenever TeX encounters a macro that it wants to expand, it uses the most recent definition. However, definitions are local to the group that contains them; old definitions will be restored in the usual way when a group ends.

Caution: When you define a macro with simple parameters, as in these examples, you must be careful not to put blank spaces before the '{' that begins the replacement text. For example, '\def\row #1 #2 {...}' will not give the same result as '\def\row#1#2{...}', because the spaces after #1 and #2 tell TeX to look for arguments that are followed by spaces. (Arguments can be "delimited" in a fairly general way, as explained below.) But the space after \row is optional, as usual, because TeX always disregards spaces after control words. After you have said '\def\row#1#2{...}', you are allowed to put spaces between the arguments (e.g., '\row x n'), because TeX doesn't use single spaces as undelimited arguments.

The following exercise is particularly recommended for people who want to learn to write TeX macros. Even if you have gotten into the dangerous habit of skimming other exercises, you should try your hand at this one.

▶ **EXERCISE 20.4**
Extending exercise 20.1, write a "generalized punishment" macro that has two parameters, so that \punishment{run}{the halls} will produce 100 paragraphs that say 'I must not run in the halls.'

TEX also allows you to define macros whose parameters are delimited in quite a general way; you needn't always enclose arguments in braces. For example,

        \def\cs #1. #2\par{...}

defines a control sequence \cs with two parameters, and its two arguments will be determined as follows: #1 will consist of all tokens between \cs and the next subsequent appearance of '.␣' (period and space); #2 will consist of all tokens between that '.␣' and the next \par token. (The \par might be given explicitly, or it might be generated by a blank line as explained in Chapter 8.) For example, when TEX expands

        \cs You owe \$5.00. Pay it.\par

the first argument is 'You owe \$5.00' and the second is 'Pay it.'. The period in '\$5.00' doesn't stop #1, in this example, because TEX keeps going until finding a period that is followed immediately by a space.

 Furthermore, an argument will not stop when its delimiter is enclosed in braces, because that would produce unbalanced braces. For example, in

        \def\cs #1.#2\par{...}

the first argument is now delimited by a single period, so #1 would be 'You owe \$5' and the #2 would be '00. Pay it.' if \cs were invoked as above. But

        \cs You owe {\$5.00}. Pay it.\par

satisfactorily hides the first period, making it part of argument #1, which becomes 'You owe {\$5.00}'.

 If you are designing a format for mathematical papers, you will probably want to include a macro for the statement of theorems, definitions, lemmas, corollaries, and such things. For example, you might want to typeset a statement like

Theorem 1. *TEX has a powerful macro capability.*

from the input

        \proclaim Theorem 1. \TeX\ has a powerful macro capability.\par

In fact, plain TEX includes a \proclaim macro that does just that; its definition is

        \def\proclaim #1. #2\par{\medbreak
          \noindent{\bf#1.\enspace}{\sl#2}\par\medbreak}

so the arguments are delimited exactly as in our first \cs example. The replacement text here uses \medbreak to separate the proclaimed paragraph from what precedes and follows; the title of the proclamation is set in bold face type, while the text itself is set slanted. (The actual definition of \proclaim in Appendix B is not quite the same as this; the final \medbreak has been modified so that a break between pages will be discouraged immediately following the statement of a theorem. Hence a short theorem will tend to appear at the top of a page rather than at the bottom.)

 By making changes to the \proclaim macro, you can change the format of all the proclamations in your paper, without changing the text of the paper itself. For example, you could produce something like

THEOREM 1: *TEX has a powerful macro capability.*

by making simple alterations to the replacement text of \proclaim, assuming that you have a "caps and small caps" font. TEX is intended to support higher-level languages for composition in which all of the control sequences that a user actually types are macros rather than TEX primitives. The ideal is to be able to describe important classes of documents in terms of their components, without mentioning actual fonts or point sizes or details of spacing; a single style-independent document can then be set in many different styles.

Now that we have seen a number of examples, let's look at the precise rules that govern TEX macros. Definitions have the general form

$$\textbf{\textbackslash def}\langle\text{control sequence}\rangle\langle\text{parameter text}\rangle\{\langle\text{replacement text}\rangle\}$$

where the ⟨parameter text⟩ contains no braces, and where all occurrences of { and } in the ⟨replacement text⟩ are properly nested. Furthermore the # symbol has a special significance: In the ⟨parameter text⟩, the first appearance of # must be followed by 1, the next by 2, and so on; up to nine #'s are allowed. In the ⟨replacement text⟩ each # must be followed by a digit that appeared after # in the ⟨parameter text⟩, or else the # should be followed by another #. The latter case stands for a single # token when the macro is expanded; the former case stands for insertion of the corresponding argument.

For example, let's consider a "random" definition that doesn't do anything useful except that it does exhibit TEX's rules. The definition

$$\textbf{\textbackslash def\textbackslash cs AB\#1\#2C\$\#3\textbackslash\$ \{\#3\{ab\#1\}\#1 c\#\#\textbackslash x \#2\}}$$

says that the control sequence \cs is to have a parameter text consisting of nine tokens

$$A_{11},\ B_{11},\ \#1,\ \#2,\ C_{11},\ \$_3,\ \#3,\ \boxed{\$},\ \sqcup 10$$

(assuming the category codes of plain TEX), and a replacement text of twelve tokens

$$\#3,\ \{_1,\ a_{11},\ b_{11},\ \#1,\ \}_2,\ \#1,\ \sqcup 10,\ c_{11},\ \#_6,\ \boxed{x},\ \#2.$$

Henceforth when TEX reads the control sequence \cs it will expect that the next two tokens will be A_{11} and B_{11} (otherwise you will get the error message 'Use of \cs doesn't match its definition'); then comes argument #1, followed by argument #2, then C_{11}, then $\$_3$, then argument #3, then \$, and finally a space token. It is customary to use the word "argument" to mean the string of tokens that gets substituted for a parameter; parameters appear in a definition, and arguments appear when that definition is used. (For the purposes of these rules, we are extending Chapter 7's definition of token: In addition to control sequences and (character code, category code) pairs, TEX also recognizes "parameter tokens," denoted here by #1 to #9. Parameter tokens can appear only in token lists for macros.)

How does TEX determine where an argument stops, you ask. Answer: There are two cases. A *delimited parameter* is followed in the ⟨parameter text⟩ by one or more non-parameter tokens, before reaching the end of the parameter text or the next parameter token; in this case the corresponding argument is the shortest (possibly empty) sequence of tokens with properly nested {...} groups that is followed in the input by this particular list of non-parameter tokens. (Category codes and character codes must both match, and control sequence names must be the same.) An *undelimited parameter* is followed immediately in the ⟨parameter text⟩ by a parameter token, or it occurs at the very end of the parameter text; in this case the corresponding argument is the next nonblank token, unless that token is '{', when the argument will be the entire {...} group that follows. In both cases, if the argument found in this way has the form '{⟨nested tokens⟩}', where ⟨nested tokens⟩ stands for any sequence of tokens that is properly nested with respect to braces, the outermost braces enclosing the argument are removed and the ⟨nested tokens⟩ will remain. For example, let's continue with \cs as defined above and suppose that the subsequent text contains

> \cs AB {\Look}C${And\$ }{look}\$ 5 .

Argument #1 will be the token $\boxed{\text{Look}}$, since #1 is an undelimited parameter (it is followed immediately by #2 in the definition); in this case TEX ignores the blank space after B, and strips the braces off of {\Look}. Argument #2 will be empty, since C$ follows immediately. And argument #3 will be the thirteen tokens corresponding to the text {And\$␣}{look}, because #3 is to be followed by '\$␣', and because the first occurrence of '\$␣' is within braces. Even though argument #3 begins with a left brace and ends with a right brace, the braces are not removed, since that would leave the unnested tokens 'And\$ }{look'. The net effect then, after substituting arguments for parameters in the replacement text, will be that TEX will next read the token list

> {And\$ }{look}{ab\Look}\Look␣c#\x5 .

The space ␣ here will be part of the resulting token list, even though it follows the control word \Look, because spaces are removed after control word tokens only when TEX first converts input lines to token lists as described in Chapter 8.

▶ **EXERCISE 20.5**
The example definition of \cs includes a ## in its replacement text, but the way ## is actually used in that example is rather pointless. Give an example of a definition where ## serves a useful purpose.

A special extension is allowed to these rules: If the very last character of the ⟨parameter text⟩ is #, so that this # is immediately followed by {, TEX will behave as if the { had been inserted at the right end of both the parameter text and the replacement text. For example, if you say '\def\a#1#{\hbox to #1}', the subsequent text '\a3pt{x}' will expand to '\hbox to 3pt{x}', because the argument of \a is delimited by a left brace.

Tokens that precede the first parameter token in the ⟨parameter text⟩ of a definition are required to follow the control sequence; in effect, they become part of the control sequence name. For example, the author might have said

> \def\TeX/{...}

instead of defining \TeX without the slash. Then it would be necessary to type \TeX/ each time the TEX logo is desired, but the new definition would have the advantage that spaces are *not* ignored after '\TeX/'. You can use this idea to define macros that are intended to be used in sentences, so that users don't have to worry about the possible disappearance of spaces.

▶ **EXERCISE 20.6**
Define a control sequence \a such that \a{...} expands to \b{...}, and such that TEX gives an error message if \a is not immediately followed by a left brace.

Complicated macros have a habit of behaving differently from what you expect, when you first define them, even though TeX's rules are not especially complicated. If you have trouble understanding why some `\def` doesn't work the way you think it should, help is available: You can set `\tracingmacros=1`, whereupon TeX will write something in your log file whenever it expands a macro, and whenever it has read a macro argument. For example, if `\tracingmacros` is positive when TeX processes the `\cs` example above, it will put the following four lines into the log:

```
\cs AB#1#2C$#3\$ ->#3{ab#1}#1 c##\x #2
#1<-\Look
#2<-
#3<-{And\$ }{look}
```

In all of the rules stated above, '{' and '}' and '#' stand for any characters whose category codes are respectively 1, 2, and 6 in the token list when TeX reads the macro definition; there's nothing sacred about the particular symbols that plain TeX uses to denote grouping and parameters. You can even make use of several different characters with these category codes, all at the same time.

▶ **EXERCISE 20.7**
Suppose that '[', ']', and '!' have the respective catcodes 1, 2, and 6, as do '{', '}', and '#'. See if you can guess what the following definition means:

```
\def\!!1#2![{!#]#!!2}
```

What token list will result when '\! x{[y]][z}' is expanded?

In practice, we all make mistakes. And one of the most common typographic errors is to forget a '}', or to insert an extra '{', somewhere in an argument to a macro. If TeX were to follow the rules blindly in such a case, it would have to keep absorbing more and more tokens in hopes of finding the end of the argument. But a mistyped argument is unending, like so many arguments in real life (sigh); so TeX would have to go on until the end of the file, or (more likely) until tokens completely fill the computer's memory. In either case, a single typographical error would have ruined the run, and the user would be forced to start over. Therefore TeX has another rule, intended to confine such errors to the paragraph in which they occur: *The token '\par' is not allowed to occur as part of an argument*, unless you explicitly tell TeX that `\par` is OK. Whenever TeX is about to include `\par` as part of an argument, it will abort the current macro expansion and report that a "runaway argument" has been found.

If you actually want a control sequence to allow arguments with `\par` tokens, you can define it to be a "long" macro by saying '`\long`' just before '`\def`'. For example, the `\bold` macro defined by

```
\long\def\bold#1{{\bf#1}}
```

is capable of setting several paragraphs in boldface type. (However, such a macro is not an especially good way to typeset bold text. It would be better to say, e.g.,

```
\def\beginbold{\begingroup\bf}
\def\endbold{\endgroup}
```

because this doesn't fill TeX's memory with a long argument.)

The \par-forbidding mechanism doesn't catch all conceivable missing-brace errors, however; you might forget the } at the end of a \def, and the same problem would arise. In this case it's harder to confine the error, because \par is a useful thing in replacement texts; we wouldn't want to forbid \par there, so TEX has another mechanism: When a macro definition is preceded by '\outer', the corresponding control sequence will not be allowed to appear in any place where tokens are being absorbed at high speed. An \outer macro cannot appear in an argument (not even when \par is allowed), nor can it appear in the parameter text or the replacement text of a definition, nor in the preamble to an alignment, nor in conditional text that is being skipped over. If an \outer macro does show up in such places, TEX stops what it is doing and reports either a "runaway" situation or an "incomplete" conditional. The end of an input file is also considered to be \outer in this sense; for example, a file shouldn't end in the middle of a definition. If you are designing a format for others to use, you can help them detect errors before too much harm is done, by using \outer with all control sequences that should appear only at "quiet times" within a document. For example, Appendix B defines \proclaim to be \outer, since a user shouldn't be stating a theorem as part of a definition or argument or preamble.

We have now seen that \def can be preceded by \long or \outer, and it can also be preceded by \global if the definition is supposed to transcend its group. These three prefixes can be applied to \def in any order, and they can even appear more than once. TEX also has a \gdef primitive that is equivalent to \global\def. Thus, for example,

        \long\outer\global\long\def

means the same thing as '\outer\long\gdef'.

So far in this manual we have encountered several ways to assign a meaning to a control sequence. For example,

        \font\cs=⟨external font name⟩   makes \cs a font identifier;
        \chardef\cs=⟨number⟩   makes \cs a character code;
        \countdef\cs=⟨number⟩   makes \cs a \count register;
        \def\cs...{...}   makes \cs a macro.

It's time now to reveal another important command of this type:

        \let\cs=⟨token⟩   gives \cs the token's current meaning.

If the ⟨token⟩ is another control sequence, \cs will acquire the same significance as that control sequence. For example, if you say '\let\a=\def', you could then say '\a\b...{...}' to define a macro \b, because \a would behave like TEX's primitive \def command. If you say

        \let\a=\b \let\b=\c \let\c=\a

you have interchanged the former meanings of \b and \c. And if you say

        \outer\def\a#1.{#1:}
        \let\b=\a

the effect is exactly the same as '\outer\def\b#1.{#1:} \let\a=\b'.

If the ⟨token⟩ in a \let is a single character—i.e., if it is a (character code, category code) pair—then the control sequence will behave to a certain extent like that character; but there are some differences. For example, after '\let\zero=0' you can't use \zero in a numerical constant, because TeX requires the tokens in a numerical constant to be digits, after macro expansion; \zero is not a macro, so it doesn't expand. However, such uses of \let have their value, as we will see later.

▶ **EXERCISE 20.8**
Is there a significant difference between '\let\a=\b' and '\def\a{\b}'?

▶ **EXERCISE 20.9**
Experiment with TeX to discover the answers to the following questions: (a) If the control sequence \par has been redefined (e.g., '\def\par{\endgroup\par}'), is \par still forbidden to appear in an argument?   (b) If you say \let\xpar=\par, is \xpar also forbidden in an argument?

TeX also allows the construction '\futurelet\cs⟨token₁⟩⟨token₂⟩', which has the effect of '\let\cs = ⟨token₂⟩⟨token₁⟩⟨token₂⟩'. The idea is that you can say, for example, '\futurelet\a\b' at the end of the replacement text of a macro; TeX will set \a to the token that follows the macro, after which \b will be expanded. The control sequence \b can continue the processing, and it can examine \a to see what's coming up next.

The next thing a person wants, after getting used to macros with parameters, is the ability to write macros that change their behavior depending on current conditions. TeX provides a variety of primitive commands for this purpose. The general form of such "conditional text" is

\if⟨condition⟩⟨true text⟩\else⟨false text⟩\fi

where the ⟨true text⟩ is skipped unless the ⟨condition⟩ is true, and the ⟨false text⟩ is skipped unless the ⟨condition⟩ is false. If the ⟨false text⟩ is empty, you can omit the \else. The '\if⟨condition⟩' part of this construction begins with a control sequence whose first two letters are 'if'; for example,

\ifodd\count0 \rightpage \else\leftpage \fi

specifies a condition that is true when TeX's integer register \count0 is odd. Since TeX generally keeps the current page number in \count0, the macro \rightpage will be expanded in this example if the page number is odd, while \leftpage will be expanded if the page number is even. Conditional commands always end with a final '\fi'.

Conditionals are primarily intended for experienced TeX users, who want to define high-level macros; therefore the remaining paragraphs in this chapter are headed by "double dangerous bends." Do not feel guilty about skipping right to Chapter 21; in other words, imagine that the manual says '\ifexperienced' right here, and that there is a matching '\fi' at the end of the present chapter.

Before we discuss TeX's repertoire of \if... commands, let's look at another example, so that the general ideas will be clear. Suppose that the \count register \balance holds an amount that somebody has paid in excess of his or her income tax; this amount is given in pennies, and it might be positive, negative, or zero.

Our immediate goal will be to write a TEX macro that generates a suitable statement for the Internal Revenue Service to include as part of a letter to that person, based on the amount of the balance. The statement will be quite different for positive balances than for negative ones, so we can exploit TEX's ability to act conditionally:

```
\def\statement{\ifnum\balance=0 \fullypaid
   \else\ifnum\balance>0 \overpaid
        \else\underpaid
        \fi
   \fi}
```

Here \ifnum is a conditional command that compares two numbers; the \statement macro reduces to \fullypaid if the balance is zero, and so on.

It is vastly important to notice the spaces after the 0's in this construction. If the example had said

```
...=0\fullypaid...
```

then TEX would have begun to expand '\fullypaid' before it knew the value of the constant 0, because \fullypaid might start with a 1 or something that would change the number. (After all, '01' is a perfectly acceptable ⟨number⟩, in TEX's eyes.) In this particular case the program would still have worked, because we will see in a moment that \fullypaid begins with the letter Y; thus, the only problem caused by the missing space would be that TEX would go slower, since it would have to skip over the whole expansion of \fullypaid instead of just skipping \fullypaid as a single, unexpanded token. But in other situations a missing space like this might cause TEX to expand macros when you don't want any expansion, and such anomalies can cause subtle and confusing errors. For best results, *always put a blank space after a numeric constant*; this blank space tells TEX that the constant is complete, and such a space will never "get through" to the output. In fact, when you don't have a blank space after a constant, TEX actually has to do more work, because each constant continues until a non-digit has been read; if this non-digit is not a space, TEX takes the token you did have and backs it up, ready to be read again. (On the other hand, the author often omits the space when a constant is immediately followed by some other character, because extra spaces do look funny in the file; aesthetics are more important than efficiency.)

▶ **EXERCISE 20.10**
Continuing the IRS example, assume that \fullypaid and \underpaid are defined as follows:

```
\def\fullypaid{Your taxes are fully paid---thank you.}
\def\underpaid{{\count0=-\balance
  \ifnum\count0<100
     You owe \dollaramount, but you need not pay it, because
     our policy is to disregard amounts less than \$1.00.
  \else Please remit \dollaramount\ within ten days,
     or additional interest charges will be due.\fi}}
```

Write a macro \overpaid to go with these, assuming that \dollaramount is a macro that generates the contents of \count0 in dollars and cents. Your macro should say that a check will be mailed under separate cover, unless the amount is less than $1.00, in which case the person must specifically request a check.

▷ **EXERCISE 20.11**
Write a `\dollaramount` macro, to complete the Internal Revenue `\statement`.

Now let's make a complete survey of TeX's conditional commands. Some of them involve features that have not yet been introduced in this manual.

- `\ifnum`⟨number₁⟩⟨relation⟩⟨number₂⟩   (compare two integers)

The ⟨relation⟩ must be either '<₁₂' or '=₁₂' or '>₁₂'. The two integer numbers are compared to each other in the usual way, and the result is true or false accordingly.

- `\ifdim`⟨dimen₁⟩⟨relation⟩⟨dimen₂⟩   (compare two dimensions)

This is like `\ifnum`, but it compares two ⟨dimen⟩ values. For example, to test whether the value of `\hsize` exceeds 100 pt, you can say '`\ifdim\hsize>100pt`'.

- `\ifodd`⟨number⟩   (test for odd integer)

The condition is true if the ⟨number⟩ is odd, false if it is even.

- `\ifvmode`   (test for vertical mode)

True if TeX is in vertical mode or internal vertical mode (see Chapter 13).

- `\ifhmode`   (test for horizontal mode)

True if TeX is in horizontal mode or restricted horizontal mode (see Chapter 13).

- `\ifmmode`   (test for math mode)

True if TeX is in math mode or display math mode (see Chapter 13).

- `\ifinner`   (test for an internal mode)

True if TeX is in internal vertical mode, or restricted horizontal mode, or (nondisplay) math mode (see Chapter 13).

- `\if`⟨token₁⟩⟨token₂⟩   (test if character codes agree)

TeX will expand macros following `\if` until two unexpandable tokens are found. If either token is a control sequence, TeX considers it to have character code 256 and category code 16, unless the current equivalent of that control sequence has been `\let` equal to a non-active character token. In this way, each token specifies a (character code, category code) pair. The condition is true if the character codes are equal, independent of the category codes. For example, after `\def\a{*}` and `\let\b=*` and `\def\c{/}`, the tests '`\if*\a`' and '`\if\a\b`' will be true, but '`\if\a\c`' will be false. Also '`\if\a\par`' will be false, but '`\if\par\let`' will be true.

- `\ifcat`⟨token₁⟩⟨token₂⟩   (test if category codes agree)

This is just like `\if`, but it tests the category codes, not the character codes. Active characters have category 13, but you have to say '`\noexpand`⟨active character⟩' in order to suppress expansion when you are looking at such characters with `\if` or `\ifcat`. For example, after

      `\catcode'[=13 \catcode']=13 \def[{*}`

the tests '`\ifcat\noexpand[\noexpand]`' and '`\ifcat[*`' will be true, but the test '`\ifcat\noexpand[*`' will be false.

- \ifx⟨token₁⟩⟨token₂⟩　(test if tokens agree)

In this case, TeX does *not* expand control sequences when it looks at the two tokens. The condition is true if (a) the two tokens are not macros, and they both represent the same (character code, category code) pair or the same TeX primitive or the same \font or \chardef or \countdef, etc.; or if (b) the two tokens are macros, and they both have the same status with respect to \long and \outer, and they both have the same parameters and "top level" expansion. For example, after '\def\a{\c} \def\b{\d} \def\c{\e} \def\d{\e} \def\e{A}', an \ifx test will find \c and \d equal, but not \a and \b, nor \d and \e, nor any other combinations of \a, \b, \c, \d, \e.

- \ifvoid⟨number⟩, \ifhbox⟨number⟩, \ifvbox⟨number⟩　(test a box register)

The ⟨number⟩ should be between 0 and 255. The condition is true if that \box is void or contains an hbox or a vbox, respectively (see Chapter 15).

- \ifeof⟨number⟩　(test for end of file)

The ⟨number⟩ should be between 0 and 15. The condition is true unless the corresponding input stream is open and not fully read. (See the command \openin below.)

- \iftrue, \iffalse　(always true or always false)

These conditions have a predetermined outcome. But they turn out to be useful in spite of this, as explained below.

Finally, there's one more conditional construction, which is somewhat different from the rest because it is capable of making a many-way branch:

- \ifcase⟨number⟩⟨text for case 0⟩\or⟨text for case 1⟩\or ⋯
  \or⟨text for case *n*⟩\else⟨text for all other cases⟩\fi

Here there are $n + 1$ cases separated by n \or's, where n can be any nonnegative number. The ⟨number⟩ selects the text that will be used. Once again the \else part is optional, if you don't want to specify any text for cases when the ⟨number⟩ is negative or greater than n.

▶ EXERCISE 20.12
Design a \category macro that prints a character's current category code symbolically, given a one-character control sequence for that character. For example, if the category codes of plain TeX are in force, '\category\\' should expand to 'escape', and '\category\a' should expand to 'letter'.

▶ EXERCISE 20.13
Test yourself on the following questions to see if you understand certain borderline situations: After the definitions '\def\a{} \def\b{**} \def\c{True}', which of the following are true? (a) '\if\a\b'; (b) '\ifcat\a\b'; (c) '\ifx\a\b'; (d) '\if\c'; (e) '\ifcat\c'; (f) '\ifx\ifx\ifx'. (g) '\if\ifx\a\b\c\else\if\a\b\c\fi\fi'.

Notice that all of the control sequences for conditionals begin with \if..., and they all have a matching \fi. This convention—that \if... pairs up with \fi—makes it easier to see the nesting of conditionals within your program. The nesting of \if...\fi is independent of the nesting of {...}; thus, you can begin or end a group in the middle of a conditional, and you can begin or end a conditional in the middle of a group. Extensive experience with macros has shown that such independence is important in applications; but it can also lead to confusion if you aren't careful.

It's sometimes desirable to pass information from one macro to another, and there are several ways to do this: by passing it as an argument, by putting it into a register, or by defining a control sequence that contains the information. For example, the macros \hphantom, \vphantom, and \phantom in Appendix B are quite similar, so the author wanted to do most of the work in another macro \phant that would be common to all three. Somehow \phant was to be told what kind of phantom was desired. The first approach was to define control sequences \hph and \vph something like this:

```
\def\hphantom{\ph YN} \def\vphantom{\ph NY} \def\phantom{\ph YY}
\def\ph#1#2{\def\hph{#1}\def\vph{#2}\phant}
```

after which \phant could test '\if Y\hph' and '\if Y\vph'. This worked, but there were various ways to make it more efficient; for example, '\def\hph{#1}' could be replaced by '\let\hph=#1', avoiding macro expansion. An even better idea then suggested itself:

```
\def\yes{\if00} \def\no{\if01}
\def\hphantom{\ph\yes\no}...\def\phantom{\ph\yes\yes}
\def\ph#1#2{\let\ifhph=#1\let\ifvph=#2\phant}
```

after which \phant could test '\ifhph' and '\ifvph'. (This construction was tried before \iftrue and \iffalse were part of the TeX language.) The idea worked fine, so the author started to use \yes and \no in a variety of other situations. But then one day a complex conditional failed, because it contained an \ifhph-like test inside another conditional:

```
\if...  \ifhph...\fi  ... \else  ...  \fi
```

Do you see the problem that developed? When the ⟨true text⟩ of the outermost conditional was executed, everything worked fine, because \ifhph was either \yes or \no and it expanded into either \if00 or \if01. But when the ⟨true text⟩ was skipped, the \ifhph was not expanded, so the first \fi was mistakenly paired with the first \if; everything soon went haywire. That's when \iftrue and \iffalse were put into the language, in place of \yes and \no; now \ifhph is either \iftrue or \iffalse, so TeX will match it properly with a closing \fi, whether or not it is being skipped over.

To facilitate \if... constructions, plain TeX has a \newif macro, such that after you say '\newif\ifabc' three control sequences will be defined: \ifabc (for testing the switch), \abctrue (for making the switch true), and \abcfalse (for making it false). The \phantom problem is now solved in Appendix B by writing

```
\newif\ifhph \newif\ifvph
\def\hphantom{\hphtrue\vphfalse\phant}
```

and with similar definitions of \vphantom and \phantom. There is no longer any need for a \ph macro; again \phant tests \ifhph and \ifvph. Appendix E contains other examples of conditionals created by \newif. New conditionals are initially false.

Caution: Don't say anything like '\let\ifabc=\iftrue' in conditional text. If TeX skips over this command, it will think that both \ifabc and \iftrue require a matching \fi, since the \let is not being executed! Keep such commands buried inside macros, so that TeX will see the '\if...' only when it is not skipping over the text that it is reading.

TEX has 256 "token list registers" called \toks0 through \toks255, so that token lists can easily be shuffled around without passing them through TEX's reading apparatus. There's also a \toksdef instruction so that, e.g.,

> \toksdef\catch=22

makes \catch equivalent to \toks22. Plain TEX provides a \newtoks macro that allocates a new token list register; it is analogous to \newcount. Token list registers behave like the token list parameters \everypar, \everyhbox, \output, \errhelp, etc. To assign a new value to a token list parameter or register, you say either

> ⟨token variable⟩={⟨replacement text⟩}
> or ⟨token variable⟩=⟨token variable⟩

where ⟨token variable⟩ means either a token list parameter or a control sequence defined by \toksdef or \newtoks, or an explicit register designation '\toks⟨number⟩'.

Everyone who makes extensive use of a powerful macro facility encounters situations when the macros do surprising things. We have already mentioned the possibility of setting \tracingmacros=1, in order to see when TEX expands macros and what arguments it finds. There's also another helpful way to watch what TEX is doing: If you set \tracingcommands=1, TEX will show every command that it executes, as we saw in Chapter 13. Furthermore, if you set \tracingcommands=2, TEX will show all conditional commands and their outcomes, as well as the unconditional commands that are actually performed or expanded. This diagnostic information goes into your log file. You can also see it on your terminal, if you say \tracingonline=1. (Incidentally, if you make \tracingcommands greater than 2, you get the same information as when it equals 2.) Similarly, \tracingmacros=2 will trace \output, \everypar, etc.

One way to understand the occasional strangeness of macro operation is to use the tracing features just described, so that you can watch what TEX does in slow motion. Another way is to learn the rules for how macros are expanded; we shall now discuss those rules.

TEX's mastication process converts your input to a long token list, as explained in Chapter 8; and its digestive processes work strictly on this token list. When TEX encounters a control sequence in the token list, it looks up the current meaning, and in certain cases it will expand that token into a sequence of other tokens before continuing to read. The expansion process applies to macros and to certain other special primitives like \number and \if that we shall consider momentarily. Sometimes, however, the expansion is not carried out; for example, when TEX is taking care of a \def, the ⟨control sequence⟩, the ⟨parameter text⟩, and the ⟨replacement text⟩ of that \def are not subject to expansion. Similarly, the two tokens after \ifx are never expanded. A complete list of occasions when tokens are not expanded appears later in this chapter; you can use it for reference in an emergency.

Now let's consider the control sequences that are expanded whenever expansion has not been inhibited. Such control sequences fall into several classes:

■ Macros. When a macro is expanded, TEX first determines its arguments (if any), as explained earlier in this chapter. Each argument is a token list; the tokens are not expanded when they are being accepted as arguments. Then TEX replaces the macro and its arguments by the replacement text.

■ Conditionals. When an \if... is expanded, TEX reads ahead as far as necessary to determine whether the condition is true or false; and if false, it skips ahead (keeping track of \if...\fi nesting) until finding the \else, \or, or \fi that ends the skipped text. Similarly, when \else, \or, or \fi is expanded, TEX reads to the end of any text that ought to be skipped. The "expansion" of a conditional is empty. (Conditionals always reduce the number of tokens that are seen by later stages of the digestive process, while macros usually increase the number of tokens.)

■ \number⟨number⟩. When TEX expands \number, it reads the ⟨number⟩ that follows (expanding tokens as it goes); the final expansion consists of the decimal representation of that number, preceded by '-' if negative.

■ \romannumeral⟨number⟩. This is like \number, but the expansion consists of lowercase roman numerals. For example, '\romannumeral 1984' produces 'mcmlxxxiv'. The expansion is empty if the number is zero or negative.

■ \string⟨token⟩. TEX first reads the ⟨token⟩ without expansion. If a control sequence token appears, its \string expansion consists of the control sequence name (including \escapechar as an escape character, if the control sequence isn't simply an active character). Otherwise the ⟨token⟩ is a character token, and its character code is retained as the expanded result.

■ \jobname. The expansion is the name that TEX has chosen for this job. For example, if TEX is putting its output on files **paper.dvi** and **paper.log**, then \jobname expands to 'paper'.

■ \fontname⟨font⟩. The expansion is the external file name corresponding to the given font; e.g., '\fontname\tenrm' might expand to 'cmr10' (five tokens). If the font is not being used at its design size, the "at size" also appears in the expansion. A ⟨font⟩ is either an identifier defined by \font; or \textfont⟨number⟩, \scriptfont⟨number⟩, or \scriptscriptfont⟨number⟩; or \font, which denotes the current font.

■ \meaning⟨token⟩. TEX expands this to the sequence of characters that would be displayed on your terminal by the commands '\let\test=⟨token⟩ \show\test'. For example, '\meaning A' usually expands to 'the letter A'; '\meaning\A' after '\def\A#1B{\C}' expands to 'macro:#1B->\C '.

■ \csname...\endcsname. When TEX expands \csname it reads to the matching \endcsname, expanding tokens as it goes; only character tokens should remain after this expansion has taken place. Then the "expansion" of the entire \csname...\endcsname text will be a single control sequence token, defined to be like \relax if its meaning is currently undefined.

■ \expandafter⟨token⟩. TEX first reads the token that comes immediately after \expandafter, without expanding it; let's call this token *t*. Then TEX reads the token that comes after *t* (and possibly more tokens, if that token has an argument), replacing it by its expansion. Finally TEX puts *t* back in front of that expansion.

■ \noexpand⟨token⟩. The expansion is the token itself; but that token is interpreted as if its meaning were '\relax' if it is a control sequence that would ordinarily be expanded by TEX's expansion rules.

■ \topmark, \firstmark, \botmark, \splitfirstmark, and \splitbotmark. The expansion is the token list in the corresponding "mark" register (see Chapter 23).

■ \input⟨file name⟩. The expansion is null; but TeX prepares to read from the specified file before looking at any more tokens from its current source.

■ \endinput. The expansion is null. The next time TeX gets to the end of an \input line, it will stop reading from the file containing that line.

■ \the⟨internal quantity⟩. The expansion is a list of tokens representing the current value of one of TeX's variables, as explained below. For example, '\the\skip5' might expand into '5.0pt plus 2.0fil' (17 tokens).

The powerful \the operation has many subcases, so we shall discuss them one at a time. A variety of internal numeric quantities can be brought up front:

■ \the⟨parameter⟩, where ⟨parameter⟩ is the name of one of TeX's integer parameters (e.g., \the\widowpenalty), dimension parameters (e.g., \the\parindent), glue parameters (e.g., \the\leftskip), or muglue parameters (e.g., \the\thinmuskip).

■ \the⟨register⟩, where ⟨register⟩ is the name of one of TeX's integer registers (e.g., \the\count 0), dimension registers (e.g., \the\dimen169), glue registers (e.g., \the\skip255), or muglue registers (e.g., \the\muskip\count2).

■ \the⟨codename⟩⟨8-bit number⟩, where ⟨codename⟩ stands for either \catcode, \mathcode, \lccode, \uccode, \sfcode, or \delcode. For example, \the\mathcode'/ produces the current (integer) math code value for a slash.

■ \the⟨special register⟩, where ⟨special register⟩ is one of the integer quantities \prevgraf, \deadcycles, \insertpenalties, \inputlineno, \badness, or \parshape (denoting only the number of lines of \parshape); or one of the dimensions \pagetotal, \pagegoal, \pagestretch, \pagefilstretch, \pagefillstretch, \pagefilllstretch, \pageshrink, \pagedepth. In horizontal modes you can also refer to a special integer, \the\spacefactor; in vertical modes there's a special dimension, \the\prevdepth.

■ \the\fontdimen⟨parameter number⟩⟨font⟩. This produces a dimension; for example, parameter 6 of a font is its "em" value, so '\the\fontdimen6\tenrm' yields '10.0pt' (six tokens).

■ \the\hyphenchar⟨font⟩, \the\skewchar⟨font⟩. These produce the corresponding integer values defined for the specified font.

■ \the\lastpenalty, \the\lastkern, \the\lastskip. These yield the amount of penalty, kerning, glue, or muglue in the final item on the current list, provided that the item is a penalty, kern, or glue, respectively; otherwise they yield '0' or '0.0pt'.

■ \the⟨defined character⟩, where ⟨defined character⟩ is a control sequence that has been given an integer value with \chardef or \mathchardef; the result is that integer value, in decimal notation.

In all of the cases listed so far, \the produces a result that is a sequence of ASCII character tokens. Category code 12 ("other") is assigned to each token, except that character code 32 gets category 10 ("space"). The same rule is used to assign category codes to the tokens produced by \number, \romannumeral, \string, \meaning, \jobname, and \fontname.

There also are cases in which \the produces non-character tokens, either a font identifier like \tenrm, or an arbitrary token list:

■ \the⟨font⟩ produces a font identifier that selects the specified font. For example, '\the\font' is a control sequence corresponding to the current font.

■ \the⟨token variable⟩ produces a copy of the token list that is the current value of the variable. For example, you can expand '\the\everypar' and '\the\toks5'.

TeX's primitive command '\showthe' will display on your terminal exactly what '\the' would produce in an expanded definition; the expansion is preceded by '> ' and followed by a period. For example, '\showthe\parindent' will display

> 20.0pt.

if the plain TeX paragraph indentation is being used.

Here now is the promised list of all cases when expandable tokens are not expanded. Some of the situations involve primitives that haven't been discussed yet, but we'll get to them eventually. Expansion is suppressed at the following times:

■ When tokens are being deleted during error recovery (see Chapter 6).

■ When tokens are being skipped because conditional text is being ignored.

■ When TeX is reading the arguments of a macro.

■ When TeX is reading a control sequence to be defined by \let, \futurelet, \def, \gdef, \edef, \xdef, \chardef, \mathchardef, \countdef, \dimendef, \skipdef, \muskipdef, \toksdef, \read, and \font.

■ When TeX is reading argument tokens for \expandafter, \noexpand, \string, \meaning, \let, \futurelet, \ifx, \show, \afterassignment, \aftergroup.

■ When TeX is absorbing the parameter text of a \def, \gdef, \edef, or \xdef.

■ When TeX is absorbing the replacement text of a \def or \gdef or \read; or the text of a token variable like \everypar or \toks0; or the token list for \uppercase or \lowercase or \write. (The token list for \write will be expanded later, when it is actually output to a file.)

■ When TeX is reading the preamble of an alignment, except after a token for the primitive command \span or when reading the ⟨glue⟩ after \tabskip.

■ Just after a $_3$ token that begins math mode, to see if another $_3$ follows.

■ Just after a '$_{12}$ token that begins an alphabetic constant.

Sometimes you will find yourself wanting to define new macros whose replacement text has been expanded, based on current conditions, instead of simply copying the replacement text verbatim. TeX provides the \edef (expanded definition) command for this purpose, and also \xdef (which is equivalent to \global\edef). The general format is the same as for \def and \gdef, but TeX blindly expands the tokens of the replacement text according to the expansion rules above. For example, consider

```
\def\double#1{#1#1}
\edef\a{\double{xy}} \edef\a{\double\a}
```

Here the first \edef is equivalent to '\def\a{xyxy}' and the second is equivalent to '\def\a{xyxyxyxy}'. All of the other kinds of expansion will take place too, including conditionals; for example,

```
\edef\b#1#2{\ifmmode#1\else#2\fi}
```

gives a result equivalent to '\def\b#1#2{#1}' if TeX is in math mode at the time of the \edef, otherwise the result is equivalent to '\def\b#1#2{#2}'.

Expanded definitions that are made with \edef or \xdef continue to expand tokens until only unexpandable tokens remain, except that token lists produced by '\the' are not expanded further. Furthermore a token following '\noexpand' will not be expanded, since its ability to expand has been nullified. These two operations can be used to control what gets expanded and what doesn't.

Suppose, for example, that you want to define \a to be equal to \b (expanded) followed by \c (not expanded) followed by \d (expanded), assuming that \b and \d are simple macros without parameters. There are two easy ways to do it:

```
\edef\a{\b\noexpand\c\d}
\toks0={\c} \edef\a{\b\the\toks0 \d}
```

And it's even possible to achieve the same effect without using either \noexpand or \the; a reader who wants to learn more about TeX's expansion mechanism is encouraged to try the next three exercises.

▶ **EXERCISE 20.14**
Figure out a way to define \a as in the previous paragraph, without using TeX's primitives '\noexpand' and '\the'.

▶ **EXERCISE 20.15**
Continuing the example of expansion avoidance, suppose that you want to expand \b completely until only unexpandable tokens are left, but you don't want to expand \c at all, and you want to expand \d only one level. For example, after \def\b{\c\c} and \def\c{*} and \def\d{\b\c} the goal would be to get the effect of \def\a{**\c\b\c}. How can such a partial expansion be achieved, using \the?

▶ **EXERCISE 20.16**
Solve the previous exercise without \the or \noexpand. (This is difficult.)

TeX's primitive commands \mark{...}, \message{...}, \errmessage{...}, \special{...}, and \write⟨number⟩{...} all expand the token lists in braces almost exactly as \edef and \xdef do. However, a macro parameter character like # should not be duplicated in such commands; you need to say ## within an \edef, but only # within a \mark. The \write command is somewhat special, because its token list is first read without expansion; expansion occurs later, when the tokens are actually being written to a file.

▶ **EXERCISE 20.17**
Compare the following two definitions:

```
\def\a{\iftrue{\else}\fi}
\edef\b{\iftrue{\else}\fi}
```

Which of them yields an unmatched left brace? (This is tricky.)

TeX has the ability to read individual lines of text from up to 16 files at once, in addition to the files that are being \input. To initiate reading such an auxiliary file, you should say

```
\openin⟨number⟩=⟨file name⟩
```

where the ⟨number⟩ is between 0 and 15. (Plain TeX allocates input stream numbers 0 through 15 with the \newread command, which is analogous to \newbox.) In most

installations of TEX, the extension '`.tex`' will be appended to the file name, as with
\input, if no extension is given explicitly. If the file cannot be found, TEX will give no
error message; it will simply consider that the input stream is not open, and you can
test this condition with \ifeof. When you're done with a file, you can say

> \closein⟨number⟩

and the file associated with that input stream number will be closed, i.e., returned to
its initial condition, if such a file was open. To get input from an open file, you say

> \read⟨number⟩to⟨control sequence⟩

and the control sequence is defined to be a parameterless macro whose replacement
text is the contents of the next line read from the designated file. This line is converted
to a token list, using the procedure of Chapter 8, based on the current category codes.
Additional lines are read, if necessary, until an equal number of left and right braces
has been found. An empty line is implicitly appended to the end of a file that is being
\read. If the ⟨number⟩ is not between 0 and 15, or if no such file is open, or if the
file has ended, input will be from the terminal; TEX will prompt the user unless the
⟨number⟩ is negative. The macro definition will be local unless you say \global\read.

For example, it's easy to have dialogs with the user, by using \read together
with the \message command (which writes an expanded token list on the
terminal and in the log file):

```
\message{Please type your name:}
\read16 to\myname
\message{Hello, \myname!}
```

The \read command in this case will print '\myname=' and it will wait for a response;
the response will be echoed on the log file. The '\myname=' would have been omitted if
'\read16' had been '\read-1'.

▶ **EXERCISE 20.18**
The \myname example just given doesn't work quite right, because the ⟨return⟩
at the end of the line gets translated into a space. Figure out how to fix that glitch.

▶ **EXERCISE 20.19**
Continuing the previous example, define a macro \MYNAME that contains the
letters of \myname all in uppercase letters. For example, if \myname expands to Arthur,
\MYNAME should expand to ARTHUR. Assume that \myname contains only letters and
spaces in its expansion.

Appendices B, D, and E contain numerous examples of how to make macros
do useful things. Let's close this chapter by presenting a few examples that
show how TEX can actually be used as a primitive programming language, if you want
to achieve special effects, and if you don't care very much about computer costs.

Plain TEX contains a \loop...\repeat construction, which works like this:
You say '\loop α \if... β \repeat', where α and β are any sequences of
commands, and where \if... is any conditional test (without a matching \fi). TEX
will first do α; then if the condition is true, TEX will do β and repeat the whole process
again starting with α. If the condition ever turns out to be false, the loop will stop.

For example, here is a program that carries out a little dialog in which TeX waits for the user to type 'Yes' or 'No':

```
\def\yes{Yes } \def\no{No } \newif\ifgarbage
\loop\message{Are you happy? }
  \read-1 to\answer
  \ifx\answer\yes\garbagefalse % the answer is Yes
    \else\ifx\answer\no\garbagefalse % the answer is No
      \else\garbagetrue\fi\fi % the answer is garbage
  \ifgarbage\message{(Please type Yes or No.)}
\repeat
```

▷ **EXERCISE 20.20**
Use the `\loop...\repeat` mechanism to construct a general `\punishment` macro that repeats any given paragraph any given number of times. For example,

```
\punishment{I must not talk in class.}{100}
```

should produce the results desired in exercise 20.1.

The first thirty prime numbers are 2, 3, 5, 7, 11, 13, 17, 19, 23, 29, 31, 37, 41, 43, 47, 53, 59, 61, 67, 71, 73, 79, 83, 89, 97, 101, 103, 107, 109, and 113. You may not find this fact very startling; but you may be surprised to learn that the previous sentence was typeset by saying

```
The first thirty prime numbers are \primes{30}.
```

TeX did all of the calculation by expanding the `\primes` macro, so the author is pretty sure that the list of prime numbers given above is quite free of typographic errors. Here is the set of macros that did it:

```
\newif\ifprime \newif\ifunknown % boolean variables
\newcount\n \newcount\p \newcount\d \newcount\a % integer variables
\def\primes#1{2,~3% assume that #1 is at least 3
  \n=#1 \advance\n by-2 % n more to go
  \p=5 % odd primes starting with p
  \loop\ifnum\n>0 \printifprime\advance\p by2 \repeat}
\def\printp{, % we will invoke \printp if p is prime
  \ifnum\n=1 and~\fi % 'and' precedes the last value
  \number\p \advance\n by -1 }
\def\printifprime{\testprimality \ifprime\printp\fi}
\def\testprimality{{\d=3 \global\primetrue
  \loop\trialdivision \ifunknown\advance\d by2 \repeat}}
\def\trialdivision{\a=\p \divide\a by\d
  \ifnum\a>\d \unknowntrue\else\unknownfalse\fi
  \multiply\a by\d
  \ifnum\a=\p \global\primefalse\unknownfalse\fi}
```

The computation is fairly straightforward, except that it involves a loop inside a loop; therefore `\testprimality` introduces an extra set of braces, to keep the inner loop control from interfering with the outer loop. The braces make it necessary to say '`\global`' when `\ifprime` is being set true or false. TeX spent more time constructing

that sentence than it usually spends on an entire page; the \trialdivision macro was
expanded 132 times.

The \loop macro that does all these wonderful things is actually quite simple.
It puts the code that's supposed to be repeated into a control sequence called
\body, and then another control sequence iterates until the condition is false:

```
\def\loop#1\repeat{\def\body{#1}\iterate}
\def\iterate{\body\let\next=\iterate\else\let\next=\relax\fi\next}
```

The expansion of \iterate ends with the expansion of \next; therefore TEX is able
to remove \iterate from its memory before invoking \next, and the memory does not
fill up during a long loop. Computer scientists call this "tail recursion."

The \hex macro below, which converts count register \n to hexadecimal notation, illustrates a *recursive* control structure in which many copies of \hex
can be active simultaneously. Recursion works better than simple \loop iteration in
this application because the hexadecimal digits are discovered from right to left, while
they must be output from left to right. (The number in \n should be ≥ 0.)

```
\def\hex{{\count0=\n \divide\n by16
  \ifnum\n>0 \hex\fi \count2=\n \multiply\count2 by-16
  \advance\count0 by\count2 \hexdigit}}
\def\hexdigit{\ifnum\count0<10 \number\count0
  \else\advance\count0 by-10 \advance\count0 by`A \char\count0 \fi}
```

Our final example is a macro that computes the number of nonblank tokens
in its argument; for example, '\length{argument}' expands to '8'. This illustrates yet another aspect of macro technique.

```
\def\length#1{{\count0=0 \getlength#1\end \number\count0}}
\def\getlength#1{\ifx#1\end \let\next=\relax
  \else\advance\count0 by1 \let\next=\getlength\fi \next}
```

By this time [37 A.D.] the influence of Macro had become supreme.
— TACITUS, *Annals* (c. 120 A.D.)

I hate definitions.
— BENJAMIN DISRAELI, *Vivian Grey* (1826)

21
Making Boxes

In Chapters 11 and 12 we discussed the principles of boxes and glue, and by now we have seen many applications of those concepts. You can get by in most cases with the boxes that TEX manufactures automatically with its paragraph builder, its page builder, and its math formula processor; but if you want to do nonstandard things, you have the option of making boxes by yourself. For example, Chapter 14 points out that you can keep something from being hyphenated or split between lines if you enclose it in an \hbox; Chapter 19 points out that \hbox allows you to get ordinary text into a displayed equation.

The purpose of the present chapter is to nail down whatever details about boxes haven't been covered yet. Fortunately, there isn't much more to discuss; we have already mentioned most of the rules, so this chapter is fairly short. In fact, the previous chapters have dealt with almost everything except the rules about rules.

To make a rule box (i.e., a solid black rectangle), you type '\hrule' in vertical mode or '\vrule' in horizontal mode, followed by any or all of the specifications 'width⟨dimen⟩', 'height⟨dimen⟩', 'depth⟨dimen⟩', in any order. For example, if

    \vrule height4pt width3pt depth2pt

appears in the middle of a paragraph, TEX will typeset the black box '▮'. If you specify a dimension twice, the second specification overrules the first. If you leave a dimension unspecified, you get the following by default:

	\hrule	\vrule
width	*	0.4 pt
height	0.4 pt	*
depth	0.0 pt	*

Here '*' means that the actual dimension depends on the context; the rule will extend to the boundary of the smallest box or alignment that encloses it.

For example, the author typed '\hrule' just before typing this paragraph, and you can see what happened: A horizontal rule, 0.4 pt thick, was extended across the page, because the vertical box that encloses it turned out to be just that wide. (In fact, the vertical box that encloses it is the page itself.) Another example appears immediately after this paragraph, where you can see the result of

    \hrule width5cm height1pt \vskip1pt \hrule width6cm

TEX does not put interline glue between rule boxes and their neighbors in a vertical list, so these two rules are exactly 1 pt apart.

▶ **EXERCISE 21.1**
B. L. User didn't want one of his horizontal rules to touch the left margin, so he put it in a box and moved it right, like this:

    \moveright 1in \vbox{\hrule width3in}

But he found that this produced more space above and below the rule than when he had simply said '\hrule width 4in' with no \vbox. Why did TEX insert more space, and what should he have done to avoid it?

If you specify all three dimensions of a rule, there's no essential difference between \hrule and \vrule, since both will produce exactly the same black box. But you must call it an \hrule if you want to put it in a vertical list, and you must call it a \vrule if you want to put it in a horizontal list, regardless of whether it actually looks like a horizontal rule or a vertical rule or neither. If you say \vrule in vertical mode, TEX starts a new paragraph; if you say \hrule in horizontal mode, TEX stops the current paragraph and returns to vertical mode.

The dimensions of a rule can be negative; for example, here's a rule whose height is 3 pt and whose depth is −2 pt: '——————————'. However, a rule is invisible unless its height plus depth is positive and its width is positive. A rule whose width is negative cannot be seen, but it acts like a backspace when it appears in a horizontal list.

▶ **EXERCISE 21.2**
Explain how the author probably obtained the rule '——————————' in the previous paragraph. [*Hint:* It's one inch long.]

Now let's summarize all of the ways there are to specify boxes explicitly to TEX. (1) A character by itself makes a character box, in horizontal mode; this character is taken from the current font. (2) The commands \hrule and \vrule make rule boxes, as just explained. (3) Otherwise you can make hboxes and vboxes, which fall under the generic term ⟨box⟩. A ⟨box⟩ has one of the following seven forms:

\hbox⟨box specification⟩{⟨horizontal material⟩}	(see Chapter 12)
\vbox⟨box specification⟩{⟨vertical material⟩}	(see Chapter 12)
\vtop⟨box specification⟩{⟨vertical material⟩}	(see Chapter 12)
\box⟨register number⟩	(see Chapter 15)
\copy⟨register number⟩	(see Chapter 15)
\vsplit⟨register number⟩to⟨dimen⟩	(see Chapter 15)
\lastbox	(see Chapter 21)

Here a ⟨box specification⟩ is either 'to⟨dimen⟩' or 'spread⟨dimen⟩' or empty; this governs the setting of glue in the horizontal or vertical lists inside the box, as explained in Chapter 12. A ⟨register number⟩ is between 0 and 255; after you say \box, that register becomes void, but after \copy the register is unchanged, as explained in Chapter 15. The \vsplit operation is also explained in Chapter 15. In math modes an additional type of box is available: \vcenter⟨box specification⟩{⟨vertical material⟩} (see Chapter 17).

The bottom line of the table above refers to \lastbox, a primitive operation that hasn't been mentioned before. If the last item on the current horizontal list or vertical list is an hbox or vbox, it is removed from the list and it becomes the \lastbox; otherwise \lastbox is void. This operation is allowed in internal vertical mode, horizontal mode, and restricted horizontal mode, but you cannot use it to take a box from the current page in vertical mode. In math modes, \lastbox is always void. At the beginning of a paragraph, '{\setbox0=\lastbox}' removes the indentation box.

The operation \unskip is something like \lastbox, except that it applies to glue instead of to boxes. If the last thing on the current list is a glue item (or leaders, as explained below), it is removed. You can't remove glue from the current

page by using \unskip in vertical mode, but you can say '\vskip-\lastskip', which
has almost the same effect.

Chapters 24 to 26 present summaries of all TEX's operations in all modes,
and when those summaries mention a '⟨box⟩' they mean one of the seven
possibilities just listed. For example, you can say '\setbox⟨register number⟩=⟨box⟩' in
any mode, and you can say '\moveright⟨dimen⟩⟨box⟩' in vertical modes. But you can't
say '\setbox⟨register number⟩=C' or '\moveright⟨dimen⟩\hrule'; if you try either of
these, TEX will complain that a ⟨box⟩ was supposed to be present. Characters and
rules are so special, they aren't regarded as ⟨box⟩es.

▶ **EXERCISE 21.3**
Define a control sequence \boxit so that '\boxit{⟨box⟩}' yields the given box
surrounded by 3 points of space and by ruled lines on all four sides.

> For example, the sentence you are now reading was typeset as part of
> the displayed formula $$\boxit{\boxit{\box4}}$$, where box 4 was
> created by typing '\setbox4=\vbox{\hsize 23pc \noindent \strut
> For example, the sentence you are now reading ... \strut}'.

Let's look also at what can go inside a box. An hbox contains a horizontal
list; a vbox contains a vertical list. Both kinds of lists are made up primarily
of things like boxes, glue, kerns, and penalties, as we have seen in Chapters 14 and 15.
But you can also include some special things that we haven't discussed yet, namely
"leaders" and "whatsits." Our goal in the rest of this chapter will be to study how to
make use of such exotic items.

The dots you see before your eyes here · · · · · · · · · · · · are called *leaders*
because they lead your eyes across the page; such things are often used in
indexes or tables of contents. The general idea is to repeat a box as many times as
necessary to fill up some given space. TEX treats leaders as a special case of glue;
no, wait, it's the other way around: TEX treats glue as a special case of leaders.
Ordinary glue fills space with nothing, while leaders fill space with any desired thing.
In horizontal mode you can say

> \leaders⟨box or rule⟩\hskip⟨glue⟩

and the effect will be the same as if you had said just '\hskip⟨glue⟩', except that the
space will be occupied by copies of the specified ⟨box or rule⟩. The glue stretches or
shrinks in the usual way. For example,

> \def\leaderfill{\leaders\hbox to 1em{\hss.\hss}\hfill}
> \line{Alpha\leaderfill Omega}
> \line{The Beginning\leaderfill The Ending}

will produce the following two lines:

Alpha . . . . Omega
The Beginning . . . . The Ending

Here '\hbox to 1em{\hss.\hss}' specifies a box one em wide, with a period in its
center; the control sequence \leaderfill then causes this box to be replicated when

filling space in the \line box. (Plain TEX's \line macro makes an hbox whose width is the \hsize.)

Notice that the dots in the two example lines appear exactly above each other. This is not a coincidence; it's a consequence of the fact that the \leaders operation acts something like a window that lets you see part of an infinite row of boxes. If the words 'Alpha' and 'Omega' are replaced by longer words, the number of dots might be different but the ones that you see will be in the same places as before. The infinitely replicated boxes are lined up so that they touch each other, and so that, if you could see them all, one of them would have the same reference point as the smallest enclosing box. Thus, \leaders will put a box flush with the left edge of an enclosing box, if you start the leaders there; but you won't get a box flush right unless the width of the enclosing box is exactly divisible by the width of the repeated box. If the repeated box has width w, and if the space to be filled is at least $2w$, then you will always see at least one copy of the box; but if the space is less than $2w$ the box may not appear, because boxes in the infinite row are typeset only when their entire width falls into the available space.

When leaders are isolated from each other, you might not want them to be aligned as just described, so TEX also provides for nonaligned leaders. In this case a box of width w will be copied q times when the space to be filled is at least qw and less than $(q+1)w$; furthermore, the results will be centered in the available space. There are two kinds of nonaligned leaders in TEX, namely \cleaders (centered leaders) and \xleaders (expanded leaders). Centered leaders pack the boxes tightly next to each other leaving equal amounts of blank space at the left and right; expanded leaders distribute the extra space equally between the $q+1$ positions adjacent to the q boxes. For example, let's suppose that a 10 pt-wide box is being used in leaders that are supposed to fill 56 pt of space. Five copies of the box will be used; \cleaders will produce 3 pt of space, then the five boxes, then another 3 pt of space. But \xleaders will produce 1 pt of space, then the first box, then another 1 pt of space, then the second box, ..., then the fifth box, and 1 pt of space.

▶ **EXERCISE 21.4**
Suppose that a 10 pt-wide box is to fill 38 pt of space starting 91 pt from the left of its enclosing box. How many copies of the box will be produced by \leaders, \cleaders, and \xleaders? Where will the boxes be positioned, relative to the left edge of the enclosing box, in each of the three cases?

▶ **EXERCISE 21.5**
Assuming that the '.' in the \leaderfill macro on the previous page is only 0.2 em wide, there is 0.4 em of blank space at both sides of the one-em box. Therefore the \leaders construction will leave between 0.4 em and 1.4 em of blank space between the periods and the text at either end. Redefine \leaderfill so that the amount of blank space at either end will be between 0.1 em and 1.1 em, but the leaders on adjacent lines will still be aligned with each other.

Instead of giving a ⟨box⟩ in the leaders construction, you can give a ⟨rule⟩, which means either \hrule or \vrule, followed by optional height, width, and depth specifications as usual. The rule will then be made as wide as the corresponding ⟨glue⟩. This is a case where \hrule makes sense in horizontal mode, because it gives a horizontal rule in text. For example, if the \leaderfill macro in our earlier illustration is changed to

    \def\leaderfill{ \leaders\hrule\hfill\ }

then the results look like this:

Alpha —————————————————————————— Omega
The Beginning ——————————————————————— The Ending

When a rule is used instead of a box, it fills the space completely, so there's no difference between \leaders, \cleaders, and \xleaders.

▶ **EXERCISE 21.6**
What does \leaders\vrule\hfill produce?

Leaders work in vertical mode as well as in horizontal mode. In this case vertical glue (e.g., \vskip⟨glue⟩ or \vfill) is used instead of horizontal glue, and \leaders produces boxes that are aligned so that the top of each repeated box has the same vertical position as the top of the smallest enclosing box, plus a multiple of the height-plus-depth of the repeated box. No interlineskip glue is placed between boxes in vertical leaders; the boxes are just stacked right on top of each other.

If you specify horizontal leaders with a box whose width isn't positive, or if you specify vertical leaders with a box whose height-plus-depth isn't positive, TeX silently ignores the leaders and produces ordinary glue instead.

▶ **EXERCISE 21.7**
Explain how you can end a paragraph with a rule that is at least 10 pt long and extends all the way to the right margin, like this: ———————————— ————

Horizontal leaders differ slightly from horizontal glue, because they have height and depth when TeX calculates the size of the enclosing box (even though the number of replications might be zero). Similarly, vertical leaders have width.

▶ **EXERCISE 21.8**
Demonstrate how to produce the following 'TeXture'

$$\text{TeXTeXTeXTeXTeXTeXTeXTeXTeXTeX}$$

by using vertical leaders inside of horizontal leaders. (The TeX logo has been put into a rectangular box, and copies of this box have been packed together tightly.)

▶ **EXERCISE 21.9**
Use vertical leaders to solve exercise 20.1.

The \overbrace and \underbrace macros of plain TeX are constructed by combining characters with rules. Font cmex10 contains four symbols ⌣⌢⌣⌢, each of which has depth zero and height equal to the thickness of a rule that joins them properly. Therefore it's easy to define \upbracefill and \downbracefill macros so that you can obtain, e.g.,

by saying '\hbox to 100pt{\downbracefill}\hbox to 50pt{\upbracefill}' in vertical mode. Details of those macro definitions appear in Appendix B.

The definition of \overrightarrow in Appendix B is more complex than that of \overbrace, because it involves a box instead of a rule. The fonts of plain TeX are designed so that symbols like ← and → can be extended with minus signs; similarly, ⇐ and ⇒ can be extended with equals signs. However, you can't simply put the characters next to each other, because that leaves gaps ('←−−' and '⇐=='); it is necessary to backspace a little between characters. An additional complication arises because the extension line in a long arrow might need to be some non-integer number of minus signs long. To solve this problem, the \rightarrowfill macro in Appendix B uses \cleaders with a repeatable box consisting of the middle 10 units of a minus sign, where one unit is $\frac{1}{18}$ em. The leaders are preceded and followed by − and →; there's enough backspacing to compensate for up to 5 units of extra space, fore and aft, that \cleaders might leave blank. In this way a macro is obtained such that

> \hbox to 100pt{\rightarrowfill}

yields '⟶'.

Now we know all about leaders. What about whatsits? Well, whatsits have been provided as a general mechanism by which important special printing applications can be handled as extensions to TeX. It's possible for system wizards to modify the TeX program, without changing too much of the code, so that new features can be accommodated at high speed instead of encoding them in macros. The author hopes that such extensions will not be made very often, because he doesn't want incompatible pseudo-TeX systems to proliferate; yet he realizes that certain special books deserve a special treatment. Whatsits make it possible to incorporate new things into boxes without bending the existing conventions too much. But they make applications less portable from one machine to another.

Two kinds of whatsits are defined as part of all TeX implementations. They aren't really extensions to TeX, but they are coded as if they were, so that they provide a model of how other extensions could be made. The first of these is connected with output to text files, and it involves the TeX primitive commands \openout, \closeout, \write, and \immediate. The second is connected with special instructions that can be transmitted to printing devices, via TeX's \special command.

The ability to write text files that can later be input by other programs (including TeX) makes it possible to take care of tables of contents, indexes, and many other things. You can say '\openout⟨number⟩=⟨file name⟩' and '\closeout⟨number⟩' by analogy with the \openin and \closein commands of Chapter 20; the ⟨number⟩ must be between 0 and 15. The filename is usually extended with '.tex' if it has no extension. There is a \write command that writes one line to a file, analogous to the \read command that reads one line; you say

> \write⟨number⟩{⟨token list⟩}

and the material goes out to the file that corresponds to the given stream number. If the ⟨number⟩ is negative or greater than 15, or if the specified stream has no file open for output, the output goes to the user's log file, and to the terminal unless the number is negative. Plain T_EX has a `\newwrite` command that allocates output stream numbers from 0 to 15. Output streams are completely independent of input streams.

⟐⟐ However, the output actually takes place in a delayed fashion; the `\openout`, `\closeout`, and `\write` commands that you give are not performed when T_EX sees them. Instead, T_EX puts these commands into whatsit items, and places them into the current horizontal or vertical or math list that is being built. No actual output will occur until this whatsit is eventually shipped out to the dvi file, as part of a larger box. The reason for this delay is that `\write` is often used to make an index or table of contents, and the exact page on which a particular item will appear is generally unknown when the `\write` instruction occurs in mid-paragraph. T_EX is usually working ahead, reading an entire paragraph before breaking it into lines, and accumulating more than enough lines to fill a page before deciding what goes on the page, as explained in Chapters 14 and 15. Therefore a deferred writing mechanism is the only safe way to ensure the validity of page number references.

⟐⟐ The ⟨token list⟩ of a `\write` command is first stored in a whatsit without performing any macro expansion; the macro expansion takes place later, when T_EX is in the middle of a `\shipout` operation. For example, suppose that some paragraph in your document contains the text

> `... For \write\inx{example: \the\count0}example, suppose ...`

Then the horizontal list for the paragraph will have a whatsit just before the word 'example', and just after the interword space following 'For'. This whatsit item contains the unexpanded token list 'example: \the\count0'. It sits dormant while the paragraph is being broken into lines and put on the current page. Let's suppose that this word 'example' (or some hyphenated initial part of it, like 'ex-') is shipped out on page 256. Then T_EX will write the line

> `example: 256`

on output stream `\inx`, because the '\the\count0' will be expanded at that time. Of course, `\write` commands are usually generated by macros; they are rarely typed explicitly in mid-paragraph.

⟐⟐ T_EX defers `\openout` and `\closeout` commands by putting them into whatsits too; thus, the relative order of output commands will be preserved, unless boxes are shipped out in some other order due to insertions or such things.

⟐⟐ Sometimes you don't want T_EX to defer a `\write` or `\openout` or `\closeout`. You could say, e.g., '`\shipout\hbox{\write...}`', but that would put an unwanted empty page in your dvi file. So T_EX has another feature that gets around this problem: If you type '`\immediate`' just before `\write` or `\openout` or `\closeout`, the operation will be performed immediately, and no whatsit will be made. For example,

> `\immediate\write16{Goodbye}`

prints 'Goodbye' on your terminal. Without the `\immediate`, you wouldn't see the 'Goodbye' until the current list was output. (In fact, you might never see it; or you may see it more than once, if the current list goes into a box that was copied.) An '`\immediate\write16`' differs from `\message` in that `\write` prints the text on a line by itself; the results of several \message commands might appear on the same line, separated by spaces.

The ⟨token list⟩ of a \write ought to be rather short, since it makes one line of output. Some implementations of TEX are unable to write long lines; if you want to write a lot of stuff, just give several \write commands. Alternatively, you can set TEX's \newlinechar parameter to the ASCII code number of some character that you want to stand for "begin a new line"; then TEX will begin a new line whenever it would ordinarily output that character to a file. For example, one way to output two lines to the terminal in a single \write command is to say

```
\newlinechar=`\^^J
\immediate\write16{Two^^Jlines.}
```

Each \write command produces output in the form that TEX always uses to display token lists symbolically: Characters represent themselves (except that you get duplicated characters like ## for macro parameter characters); unexpandable control sequence tokens produce their names, preceded by the \escapechar and followed by a space (unless the name is an active character or a control sequence formed from a single nonletter).

TEX ignores \write, \openout, and \closeout whatsits that appear within boxes governed by leaders. If you are upset about this, you shouldn't be.

Since the ⟨token list⟩ of a deferred \write is expanded at a fairly random time (when \shipout occurs), you should be careful about what control sequences it is allowed to contain. The techniques of Chapter 20 for controlling macro expansion often come in handy with respect to \write.

▶ **EXERCISE 21.10**
Suppose that you want to \write a token list that involves a macro \chapno, containing the current chapter number, as well as '\the\count0' which refers to the current page. You want \chapno to be expanded immediately, because it might change before the token list is written; but you want \the\count0 to be expanded at the time of \shipout. How can you manage this?

Now let's wrap up our study of boxes by considering one more feature. The command '\special{⟨token list⟩}' can be given in any mode. Like \write, it puts its token list into a whatsit; and like \message, it expands the token list immediately. This token list will be output to the **dvi** file with the other typesetting commands that TEX produces. Therefore it is implicitly associated with a particular position on the page, namely the reference point that would have been present if a box of height, depth, and width zero had appeared in place of the whatsit. The ⟨token list⟩ in a \special command should consist of a keyword followed if necessary by a space and appropriate arguments. For example,

```
\special{halftone pic1}
```

might mean that a picture on file **pic1** should be inserted on the current page, with its reference point at the current position. TEX doesn't look at the token list to see if it makes any sense; the list is simply copied to the output. However, you should be careful not to make the list too long, or you might overflow TEX's string memory.

The \special command enables you to make use of special equipment that might be available to you, e.g., for printing books in glorious TEXnicolor.

Software programs that convert dvi files to printed or displayed output should be able to fail gracefully when they don't recognize your special keywords. Thus, \special operations should never do anything that changes the current position. Whenever you use \special, you are taking a chance that your output file will not be printable on all output devices, because all \special functions are extensions to TEX. However, the author anticipates that certain standards for common graphic operations will emerge in the TEX user community, after careful experiments have been made by different groups of people; then there will be a chance for some uniformity in the use of \special extensions.

TEX will report the badness of glue setting in a box if you ask for the numeric quantity \badness after making a box. For example, you might say

```
\setbox0=\line{\trialtexta}
\ifnum\badness>250 \setbox0=\line{\trialtextb}\fi
```

The badness is between 0 and 10000 unless the box is overfull, when \badness=1000000.

If age or weaknes doe prohibyte bloudletting,
you must use boxing.
— PHILIP BARROUGH, *The Methode of Phisicke* (1583)

The only thing that never looks right is a rule.
There is not in existence a page with a rule on it
that cannot be instantly and obviously improved
by taking the rule out.
— GEORGE BERNARD SHAW, in *The Dolphin* (1940)

22

Alignment

Printers charge extra when you ask them to typeset tables, and they do so for good reason: Each table tends to have its own peculiarities, so it's necessary to give some thought to each one, and to fiddle with alternative approaches until finding something that looks good and communicates well. However, you needn't be too frightened of doing tables with TeX, since plain TeX has a "tab" feature that handles simple situations pretty much like you would do them on a typewriter. Furthermore, TeX has a powerful alignment mechanism that makes it possible to cope with extremely complex tabular arrangements. Simple cases of these alignment operations will suffice for the vast majority of applications.

Let's consider tabbing first. If you say '\settabs n \columns', plain TeX makes it easy to produce lines that are divided into n equal-size columns. Each line is specified by typing

> \+⟨text₁⟩&⟨text₂⟩&···\cr

where ⟨text₁⟩ will start flush with the left margin, ⟨text₂⟩ will start at the left of the second column, and so on. Notice that '\+' starts the line. The final column is followed by '\cr', which old-timers will recognize as an abbreviation for the "carriage return" operation on typewriters that had carriages. For example, consider the following specification:

```
\settabs 4 \columns
\+&&Text that starts in the third column\cr
\+&Text that starts in the second column\cr
\+\it Text that starts in the first column, and&&&
    the fourth, and&beyond!\cr
```

After '\settabs4\columns' each \+ line is divided into quarters, so the result is

		Text that starts in the third column	
	Text that starts in the second column		
Text that starts in the first column, and		the fourth, and	beyond!

This example merits careful study because it illustrates several things. (1) The '&' is like the TAB key on many typewriters; it tells TeX to advance to the next tab position, where there's a tab at the right edge of each column. In this example, TeX has set up four tabs, indicated by the dashed lines; a dashed line is also shown at the left margin, although there isn't really a tab there. (2) But '&' isn't exactly like a mechanical typewriter TAB, because it first backs up to the beginning of the current column before advancing to the next. In this way you can always tell what column you're tabbing to, by counting the number of &'s; that's handy, because variable-width type otherwise makes it difficult to know whether you've passed a tab position or not. Thus, on the last line of our example, three &'s were typed in order to get to column 4, even though the text had already extended into column 2 and perhaps into column 3. (3) You can say '\cr' before you have specified a complete set of columns, if the remaining columns are blank. (4) The &'s are different from tabs in another way, too: TEX ignores spaces after '&', hence you can conveniently finish a column by typing '&' at the end of a line in your input file, without worrying that an extra blank space will be introduced there. (The second-last line of the example ends with '&', and there is an implicit blank space following that symbol; if TEX hadn't ignored that space, the words 'the fourth' wouldn't have started exactly at the beginning of the fourth column.) Incidentally, plain TEX also ignores spaces after '\+', so that the first column is treated like the others. (5) The '\it' in the last line of the example causes only the first column to be italicized, even though no braces were used to confine the range of italics, because TEX implicitly inserts braces around each individual entry of an alignment.

Once you have issued a \settabs command, the tabs remain set until you reset them, even though you go ahead and type ordinary paragraphs as usual. But if you enclose \settabs in {...}, the tabs defined inside a group don't affect the tabs outside; '\global\settabs' is not permitted.

Tabbed lines usually are used between paragraphs, in the same places where you would type \line or \centerline to get lines with a special format. But it's also useful to put \+ lines inside a \vbox; this makes it convenient to specify displays that contain aligned material. For example, if you type

```
$$\vbox{\settabs 3 \columns
  \+This is&a strange&example\cr
  \+of displayed&three-column&format.\cr}$$
```

you get the following display:

This is	a strange	example
of displayed	three-column	format.

In this case the first column doesn't appear flush left, because TEX centers a box that is being displayed. Columns that end with \cr in a \+ line are put into a box with their natural width; so the first and second columns here are one-third of the \hsize, but the third column is only as wide as the word 'example'. We have used $$ in this construction even though no mathematics is involved, because $$ does other useful things; for example, it centers the box, and it inserts space above and below.

People don't always want tabs to be equally spaced, so there's another way to set them, by typing '\+⟨sample line⟩\cr' immediately after '\settabs'. In this case tabs are placed at the positions of the &'s in the sample line, and the sample line itself does not appear in the output. For example,

```
\settabs\+\indent&Horizontal lists\quad&\cr % sample line
\+&Horizontal lists&Chapter 14\cr
\+&Vertical lists&Chapter 15\cr
\+&Math lists&Chapter 17\cr
```

causes TEX to typeset the following three lines of material:

Horizontal lists	Chapter 14
Vertical lists	Chapter 15
Math lists	Chapter 17

The \settabs command in this example makes column 1 as wide as a paragraph indentation; and column 2 is as wide as 'Horizontal lists' plus one quad of space. Only two tabs are set in this case, because only two &'s appear in the sample line. (A sample line might as well end with &, because the text following the last tab isn't used for anything.)

The first line of a table can't always be used as a sample line, because it won't necessarily give the correct tab positions. In a large table you have to look ahead and figure out the biggest entry in each column; the sample line is then constructed by typing the widest first column, the widest second column, etc., omitting the last column. Be sure to include some extra space between columns in the sample line, so that the columns won't touch each other.

▶**EXERCISE 22.1**
Explain how to typeset the following table [from Beck, Bertholle, and Child, *Mastering the Art of French Cooking* (New York: Knopf, 1961)]:

Weight	*Servings*	*Approximate Cooking Time**
8 lbs.	6	1 hour and 50 to 55 minutes
9 lbs.	7 to 8	About 2 hours
$9\frac{1}{2}$ lbs.	8 to 9	2 hours and 10 to 15 minutes
$10\frac{1}{2}$ lbs.	9 to 10	2 hours and 15 to 20 minutes

* For a stuffed goose, add 20 to 40 minutes to the times given.

 If you want to put something flush right in its column, just type '\hfill' before it; and be sure to type '&' after it, so that TEX will be sure to move the information all the way until it touches the next tab. Similarly, if you want to center something in its column, type '\hfill' before it and '\hfill&' after it. For example,

```
\settabs 2 \columns
\+\hfill This material is set flush right&
    \hfill This material is centered\hfill&\cr
\+\hfill in the first half of the line.&
    \hfill in the second half of the line.\hfill&\cr
```

produces the following little table:

> This material is set flush right   This material is centered
>   in the first half of the line.   in the second half of the line.

 The \+ macro in Appendix B works by putting the ⟨text⟩ for each column that's followed by & into an hbox as follows:

\hbox to ⟨column width⟩{⟨text⟩\hss}

The \hss means that the text is normally flush left, and that it can extend to the right of its box. Since \hfill is "more infinite" than \hss in its ability to stretch, it has the effect of right-justifying or centering as stated above. Note that \hfill doesn't shrink, but \hss does; if the text doesn't fit in its column, it will stick out at the right. You could cancel the shrinkability of \hss by adding \hfilneg; then an oversize text would produce an overfull box. You could also center some text by putting '\hss' before it and just '**&**' after it; in that case the text would be allowed to extend to the left and right of its column. The last column of a \+ line (i.e., the column entry that is followed by \cr) is treated differently: The ⟨text⟩ is simply put into an hbox with its natural width.

Computer programs present difficulties of a different kind, since some people like to adopt a style in which the tab positions change from line to line. For example, consider the following program fragment:

$$\textbf{if } n < r \textbf{ then } n := n + 1$$
$$\qquad\qquad \textbf{else begin } print\_totals;\ n := 0;$$
$$\qquad\qquad\qquad\textbf{end};$$
$$\quad \textbf{while } p > 0 \textbf{ do}$$
$$\qquad \textbf{begin } q := link(p);\ free\_node(p);\ p := q;$$
$$\qquad \textbf{end};$$

Special tabs have been set up so that '**then**' and '**else**' appear one above the other, and so do '**begin**' and '**end**'. It's possible to achieve this by setting up a new sample line whenever a new tab position is needed; but that's a tedious job, so plain TEX makes it a little simpler. Whenever you type **&** to the right of all existing tabs, the effect is to set a new tab there, in such a way that the column just completed will have its natural width. Furthermore, there's an operation '\cleartabs' that resets all tab positions to the right of the current column. Therefore the computer program above can be TEXified as follows:

```
$$\vbox{\+\bf if $n<r$ \cleartabs&\bf then $n:=n+1$\cr
\+&\bf else &{\bf begin} ${\it print\_totals}$; $n:=0$;\cr
\+&&{\bf end};\cr
```
⟨The remaining part is left as an exercise⟩}$$

▶ **EXERCISE 22.2**
Complete the example computer program by specifying three more \+ lines.

Although \+ lines can be used in vertical boxes, you must never use \+ inside of another \+ line. The \+ macro is intended for simple applications only.

The \+ and \settabs macros of Appendix B keep track of tabs by maintaining register \box\tabs as a box full of empty boxes whose widths are the column widths in reverse order. Thus you can examine the tabs that are currently set, by saying '\showbox\tabs'; this puts the column widths into your log file, from right to left. For example, after '\settabs\+\hskip100pt&\hskip200pt&\cr\showbox\tabs', TEX will show the lines

```
\hbox(0.0+0.0)x300.0
.\hbox(0.0+0.0)x200.0
.\hbox(0.0+0.0)x100.0
```

▶ **EXERCISE 22.3**
Study the \+ macro in Appendix B and figure out how to change it so that tabs work as they do on a mechanical typewriter (i.e., so that '**&**' always moves to the next tab that lies strictly to the right of the current position). Assume that the user doesn't backspace past previous tab positions; for example, if the input is '\+&&\hskip-2em&x\cr', do not bother to put 'x' in the first or second column, just put it at the beginning of the third column. (This exercise is a bit difficult.)

TEX has another important way to make tables, using an operation called \halign ("horizontal alignment"). In this case the table format is based on the notion of a *template*, not on tabbing; the idea is to specify a separate environment for the text in each column. Individual entries are inserted into their templates, and presto, the table is complete.

For example, let's go back to the Horizontal/Vertical/Math list example that appeared earlier in this chapter; we can specify it with \halign instead of with tabs. The new specification is

```
\halign{\indent#\hfil&\quad#\hfil\cr
   Horizontal lists&Chapter 14\cr
   Vertical lists&Chapter 15\cr
   Math lists&Chapter 17\cr}
```

and it produces exactly the same result as the old one. This example deserves careful study, because \halign is really quite simple once you get the hang of it. The first line contains the *preamble* to the alignment, which is something like the sample line used to set tabs for \+. In this case the preamble contains two templates, namely '\indent#\hfil' for the first column and '\quad#\hfil' for the second. Each template contains exactly one appearance of '#', and it means "stick the text of each column entry in this place." Thus, the first column of the line that follows the preamble becomes

```
\indent Horizontal lists\hfil
```

when 'Horizontal lists' is stuffed into its template; and the second column, similarly, becomes '\quad Chapter 14\hfil'. The question is, why \hfil? Ah, now we get to the interesting point of the whole thing: TEX reads an entire \halign{...} specification into its memory before typesetting anything, and it keeps track of the maximum width of each column, assuming that each column is set without stretching or shrinking the glue. Then it goes back and puts every entry into a box, setting the glue so that each box has the maximum column width. That's where the \hfil comes in; it stretches to fill up the extra space in narrower entries.

▸ **EXERCISE 22.4**
What table would have resulted if the template for the first column in this example had been '\indent\hfil#' instead of '\indent#\hfil'?

Before reading further, please make sure that you understand the idea of templates in the example just presented. There are several important differences between \halign and \+: (1) \halign calculates the maximum column widths automatically; you don't have to guess what the longest entries will be, as you do when you set tabs with a sample line. (2) Each \halign does its own calculation of column widths; you have to do something special if you want two different \halign operations to produce identical alignments. By contrast, the \+ operation remembers tab positions until they are specifically reset; any number of paragraphs and even \halign operations can intervene between \+'s, without affecting the tabs. (3) Because \halign reads an entire table in order to determine the maximum column widths, it is unsuitable for huge tables that fill several pages of a book. By contrast, the \+ operation deals with one line at a time, so it places no special demands on TEX's memory. (However, if you have a huge table, you should probably define your own special-purpose macro for each line instead of relying on the general \+ operation.) (4) \halign takes less computer time than \+ does, because \halign is a built-in command of TEX, while \+ is a macro that has been coded in terms of \halign and various other primitive operations. (5) Templates are much more versatile than tabs, and they can save you a lot of typing. For example, the Horizontal/Vertical/Math list table could be specified more briefly by noticing that there's common information in the columns:

```
\halign{\indent# lists\hfil&\quad Chapter #\cr
        Horizontal&14\cr Vertical&15\cr Math&17\cr}
```

You could even save two more keystrokes by noting that the chapter numbers all start with '1'! (Caution: It takes more time to think of optimizations like this than to type things in a straightforward way; do it only if you're bored and need something amusing to keep up your interest.) (6) On the other hand, templates are no substitute for tabs when the tab positions are continually varying, as in the computer program example.

Let's do a more interesting table, to get more experience with \halign. Here is another example based on the Beck/Bertholle/Child book cited earlier:

American Chicken	French Connection	Age (months)	Weight (lbs.)	Cooking Methods
Squab	*Poussin*	2	$\frac{3}{4}$ to 1	Broil, Grill, Roast
Broiler	*Poulet Nouveau*	2 to 3	$1\frac{1}{2}$ to $2\frac{1}{2}$	Broil, Grill, Roast
Fryer	*Poulet Reine*	3 to 5	2 to 3	Fry, Sauté, Roast
Roaster	*Poularde*	$5\frac{1}{2}$ to 9	Over 3	Roast, Poach, Fricassee
Fowl	*Poule de l'Année*	10 to 12	Over 3	Stew, Fricassee
Rooster	*Coq*	Over 12	Over 3	Soup stock, Forcemeat

Note that, except for the title lines, the first column is set right-justified in boldface type; the middle columns are centered; the second column is centered and in italics; the final column is left-justified. We would like to be able to type the rows of the table as simply as possible; hence, for example, it would be nice to be able to specify the bottom row by typing only

```
Rooster&Coq&Over 12&Over 3&Soup stock, Forcemeat\cr
```

without worrying about type styles, centering, and so on. This not only cuts down on keystrokes, it also reduces the chances for making typographical errors. Therefore the template for the first column should be '\hfil\bf#'; for the second column it should be '\hfil\it#\hfil' to get the text centered and italicized; and so on. We also need to allow for space between the columns, say one quad. *Voilà! La typographie est sur la table:*

```
\halign{\hfil\bf#&\quad\hfil\it#\hfil&\quad\hfil#\hfil&
        \quad\hfil#\hfil&\quad#\hfil\cr
    ⟨the title lines⟩
    Squab&Poussin&2&\frac3/4 to 1&Broil, Grill, Roast\cr
    ... Forcemeat\cr}
```

As with the \+ operation, spaces are ignored after &, in the preamble as well as in the individual rows of the table. Thus, it is convenient to end a long row with '&' when the row takes up more than one line in your input file.

▶ **EXERCISE 22.5**
How was the '**Fowl**' line typed? (This is too easy.)

The only remaining problem in this example is to specify the title lines, which have a different format from the others. In this case the style is different only because the typeface is slanted, so there's no special difficulty; we just type

```
\sl American&\sl French&\sl Age&\sl Weight&\sl Cooking\cr
\sl Chicken&\sl Connection&\sl(months)&\sl(lbs.)&\sl Methods\cr
```

It is necessary to say '`\sl`' each time, because each individual entry of a table is implicitly enclosed in braces.

The author used '`\openup2pt`' to increase the distance between baselines in the poultry table; a discriminating reader will notice that there's also a bit of extra space between the title line and the other lines. This extra space was inserted by typing '`\noalign{\smallskip}`' just after the title line. In general, you can say

```
\noalign{⟨vertical mode material⟩}
```

just after any `\cr` in an `\halign`; TeX will simply copy the vertical mode material, without subjecting it to alignment, and it will appear in place when the `\halign` is finished. You can use `\noalign` to insert extra space, as here, or to insert penalties that affect page breaking, or even to insert lines of text (see Chapter 19). Definitions inside the braces of `\noalign{...}` are local to that group.

The `\halign` command also makes it possible for you to adjust the spacing between columns so that a table will fill a specified area. You don't have to decide that the inter-column space is a quad; you can let TeX make the decisions, based on how wide the columns come out, because TeX puts "tabskip glue" between columns. This tabskip glue is usually zero, but you can set it to any value you like by saying '`\tabskip=⟨glue⟩`'. For example, let's do the poultry table again, but with the beginning of the specification changed as follows:

```
\tabskip=1em plus2em minus.5em
\halign to\hsize{\hfil\bf#&\hfil\it#\hfil&\hfil#\hfil&
          \hfil#\hfil&#\hfil\cr
```

The main body of the table is unchanged, but the `\quad` spaces have been removed from the preamble, and a nonzero `\tabskip` has been specified instead. Furthermore '`\halign`' has been changed to '`\halign to\hsize`'; this means that each line of the table will be put into a box whose width is the current value of `\hsize`, i.e., the horizontal line width usually used in paragraphs. The resulting table looks like this:

American Chicken	French Connection	Age (months)	Weight (lbs.)	Cooking Methods
Squab	*Poussin*	2	$3/4$ to 1	Broil, Grill, Roast
Broiler	*Poulet Nouveau*	2 to 3	$1\,1/2$ to $2\,1/2$	Broil, Grill, Roast
Fryer	*Poulet Reine*	3 to 5	2 to 3	Fry, Sauté, Roast
Roaster	*Poularde*	$5\,1/2$ to 9	Over 3	Roast, Poach, Fricassee
Fowl	*Poule de l'Année*	10 to 12	Over 3	Stew, Fricassee
Rooster	*Coq*	Over 12	Over 3	Soup stock, Forcemeat

In general, TeX puts tabskip glue before the first column, after the last column, and between the columns of an alignment. You can specify the final aligned size by saying '\halign to⟨dimen⟩' or '\halign spread⟨dimen⟩', just as you can say '\hbox to⟨dimen⟩' and '\hbox spread⟨dimen⟩'. This specification governs the setting of the tabskip glue; but it does not affect the setting of the glue within column entries. (Those entries have already been packaged into boxes having the maximum natural width for their columns, as described earlier.)

Therefore '\halign to \hsize' will do nothing if the tabskip glue has no stretchability or shrinkability, except that it will cause TeX to report an underfull or overfull box. An overfull box occurs if the tabskip glue can't shrink to meet the given specification; in this case you get a warning on the terminal and in your log file, but there is no "overfull rule" to mark the oversize table on the printed output. The warning message shows a "prototype row" (see Chapter 27).

The poultry example just given used the same tabskip glue everywhere, but you can vary it by resetting \tabskip within the preamble. The tabskip glue that is in force when TeX reads the '{' following \halign will be used before the first column; the tabskip glue that is in force when TeX reads the '&' after the first template will be used between the first and second columns; and so on. The tabskip glue that is in force when TeX reads the \cr after the last template will be used after the last column. For example, in

```
\tabskip=3pt
\halign{\hfil#\tabskip=4pt& #\hfil&
    \hbox to 10em{\hss\tabskip=5pt # \hss}\cr ...}
```

the preamble specifies aligned lines that will consist of the following seven parts:

> tabskip glue 3 pt;
> first column, with template '\hfil#';
> tabskip glue 4 pt;
> second column, with template '#\hfil';
> tabskip glue 4 pt;
> third column, with template '\hbox to 10em{\hss# \hss}';
> tabskip glue 5 pt.

TeX copies the templates without interpreting them except to remove any \tabskip glue specifications. More precisely, the tokens of the preamble are passed directly to the templates without macro expansion; TeX looks only for '\cr' commands, '&', '#', '\span', and '\tabskip'. The ⟨glue⟩ following '\tabskip' is scanned in the usual way (with macro expansion), and the corresponding tokens are not included in the current template. Notice that, in the example above, the space after '5pt' also disappeared. The fact that \tabskip=5pt occurred inside an extra level of braces did not make the definition local, since TeX didn't "see" those braces; similarly, if \tabskip had been preceded by '\global', TeX wouldn't have made a global definition, it would just have put '\global' into the template. All assignments to \tabskip within the preamble are local to the \halign (unless \globaldefs is positive), so the value of \tabskip will be 3 pt again when this particular \halign is completed.

When '\span' appears in a preamble, it causes the next token to be expanded, i.e., "ex-span-ded," before TeX reads on.

▶ **EXERCISE 22.6**
Design a preamble for the following table:

England	P. Philips	1560–1628	*Netherlands*	J. P. Sweelinck		1562–1621
	J. Bull	*c*1563–1628		P. Cornet		*c*1570–1633
Germany	H. L. Hassler	1562–1612	*Italy*	G. Frescobaldi		1583–1643
	M. Prætorius	1571–1621	*Spain*	F. Correa de Arauxo	*c*1576–1654
France	J. Titelouze	1563–1633	*Portugal*	M. R. Coelho		*c*1555–*c*1635

The tabskip glue should be zero at the left and right of each line; it should be 1 em
plus 2 em in the center; and it should be .5 em plus .5 em before the names, 0 em plus
.5 em before the dates. Assume that the lines of the table will be specified by, e.g.,

```
France&J. Titelouze&1563--1633&
    Portugal&M. R. Coelho&\\1555--\\1635\cr
```

where '`\\`' has been predefined by '`\def\\{{\it c\/}}`'.

▶ **EXERCISE 22.7**
Design a preamble so that the table

rydw i = I am	**ydw i** = am I	**roeddwn i** = I was
rwyt ti = thou art	**wyt ti** = art thou	**roeddet ti** = thou wast
mae e = he is	**ydy e** = is he	**roedd e** = he was
mae hi = she is	**ydy hi** = is she	**roedd hi** = she was
rydyn ni = we are	**ydyn ni** = are we	**roedden ni** = we were
rydych chi = you are	**ydych chi** = are you	**roeddech chi** = you were
maen nhw = they are	**ydyn nhw** = are they	**roedden nhw** = they were

can be specified by typing lines like

```
mae hi=she is&ydy hi=is she&roedd hi=she was\cr
```

▶ **EXERCISE 22.8**
The line breaks in the second column of the table at the right were chosen by TEX so that the second column was exactly 16 ems wide. Furthermore, the author specified one of the rows of the table by typing

```
\\393&Plato's {\sl Apology\/};
  Xenophon's
  {\sl Memorabilia\/};
  Aristophanes'
  {\sl Ecclesiazus\ae\/}\cr
```

Can you guess what preamble was used in the alignment? [The data comes from Will Durant's *The Life of Greece* (Simon & Schuster, 1939).]

B.C.
397: War between Syracuse and Carthage
396: Aristippus of Cyrene and Antisthenes of Athens (philosophers)
395: Athens rebuilds the Long Walls
394: Battles of Coronea and Cnidus
*c*393: Plato's *Apology*; Xenophon's *Memorabilia*; Aristophanes' *Ecclesiazusæ*
391–87: Dionysius subjugates south Italy
391: Isocrates opens his school
390: Evagoras Hellenizes Cyprus
387: "King's Peace"; Plato visits Archytas of Taras (mathematician) and Dionysius I
386: Plato founds the Academy
383: Spartans occupy Cadmeia at Thebes
380: Isocrates' *Panegyricus*

Sometimes a template will apply perfectly to all but one or two of the entries in a column. For example, in the exercise just given, the colons in the first column of the alignment were supplied by the template '\hfil#:␣'; but the very first entry in that column, 'B.C.', did not have a colon. TEX allows you to escape from the stated template in the following way: If the very first token of an alignment entry is '\omit' (after macro expansion), then the template of the preamble is omitted; the trivial template '#' is used instead. For example, 'B.C.' was put into the table above by typing '\omit\hfil\sevenrm B.C.' immediately after the preamble. You can use \omit in any column, but it must come first; otherwise TEX will insert the template that was defined in the preamble.

If you think about what TEX has to do when it's processing \halign, you'll realize that the timing of certain actions is critical. Macros are not expanded when the preamble is being read, except as described earlier; but once the \cr at the end of the preamble has been sensed, TEX must look ahead to see if the next token is \noalign or \omit, and macros are expanded until the next non-space token is found. If the token doesn't turn out to be \noalign or \omit, it is put back to be read again, and TEX begins to read the template (still expanding macros). The template has two parts, called the *u* and *v* parts, where *u* precedes the '#' and *v* follows it. When TEX has finished the *u* part, its reading mechanism goes back to the token that was neither \noalign nor \omit, and continues to read the entry until getting to the & or \cr that ends the entry; then the *v* part of the template is read. A special internal operation called \endtemplate is always placed at the end of the *v* part; this causes TEX to put the entry into an "unset box" whose glue will be set later when the final column width is known. Then TEX is ready for another entry; it looks ahead for \omit (and also for \noalign, after \cr) and the process continues in the same way.

One consequence of the process just described is that it may be dangerous to begin an entry of an alignment with \if..., or with any macro that will expand into a replacement text whose first token is \if...; the reason is that the condition will be evaluated before the template has been read. (TEX is still looking to see whether an \omit will occur, when the \if is being expanded.) For example, if \strut has been defined to be an abbreviation for

\ifmmode⟨text for math modes⟩\else⟨text for nonmath modes⟩\fi

and if \strut appears as the first token in some alignment entry, then TEX will expand it into the ⟨text for nonmath modes⟩ even though the template might be '$#$', because TEX will not yet be in math mode when it is looking for a possible \omit. Chaos will probably ensue. Therefore the replacement text for \strut in Appendix B is actually

\relax\ifmmode...

and '\relax' has also been put into all other macros that might suffer from such timing problems. Sometimes you do want TEX to expand a conditional before a template is inserted, but careful macro designers watch out for cases where this could cause trouble.

When you're typesetting numerical tables, it's common practice to line up the decimal points in a column. For example, if two numbers like '0.2010' and '297.1' both appear in the same column, you're supposed to produce '$^{0.2010}_{297.1}$'. This result isn't especially pleasing to the eye, but that's what people do, so you might have to conform to the practice. One way to handle this is to treat the column as two columns, somewhat as \eqalign treats one formula as two formulas; the '.' can be placed at the beginning of the second half-column. But the author usually prefers to use another, less sophisticated method, which takes advantage of the fact that the digits 0, 1, ..., 9 have the same width in most fonts: You can choose a character that's not used elsewhere in the table, say '?', and change it to an active character that produces a blank space exactly equal to the width of a digit. Then it's usually no chore to put such nulls into the table entries so that each column can be regarded as either centered or right-justified or left-justified. For example, '??0.2010' and '297.1???' have the same width, so their decimal points will line up easily. Here is one way to set up '?' for this purpose:

```
\newdimen\digitwidth
\setbox0=\hbox{\rm0}
\digitwidth=\wd0
\catcode'?=\active
\def?{\kern\digitwidth}
```

The last two definitions should be local to some group, e.g., inside a \vbox, so that '?' will resume its normal behavior when the table is finished.

Let's look now at some applications to mathematics. Suppose first that you want to typeset the small table

$$n \ = 0\ 1\ 2\ 3\ 4\ 5\ 6\ 7\quad 8\quad 9\ 10\ 11\ 12\ 13\quad 14\quad 15\quad 16\quad 17\quad 18\quad 19\quad 20\ \dots$$
$$\mathcal{G}(n) = 1\ 2\ 4\ 3\ 6\ 7\ 8\ 16\ 18\ 25\ 32\ 11\ 64\ 31\ 128\ 10\ 256\quad 5\quad 512\ 28\ 1024 \dots$$

as a displayed equation. A brute force approach using \eqalign or \atop is cumbersome because $\mathcal{G}(n)$ and n don't always have the same number of digits. It would be much nicer to type

```
$$\vbox{\halign{⟨preamble⟩\cr
        n\phantom)&0&1&2&3&  ...  &20&\dots\cr
        {\cal G}(n)&1&2&4&3&  ...  &1024&\dots\cr}}$$
```

for some ⟨preamble⟩. On the other hand, the ⟨preamble⟩ is sure to be long, since this table has 23 columns; so it looks as though \settabs and \+ will be easier. TeX has a handy feature that helps a lot in cases like this: Preambles often have a periodic structure, and if you put an extra '&' just before one of the templates, TeX will consider the preamble to be an infinite sequence that begins again at the marked template when the \cr is reached. For example,

$t_1 \& t_2 \& t_3 \&\& t_4 \& t_5 \cr$ is treated like $t_1 \& t_2 \& t_3 \& t_4 \& t_5 \& t_4 \& t_5 \& t_4 \& \cdots$

and

$\& t_1 \& t_2 \& t_3 \& t_4 \& t_5 \cr$ is treated like $t_1 \& t_2 \& t_3 \& t_4 \& t_5 \& t_1 \& t_2 \& t_3 \& \cdots.$

The tabskip glue following each template is copied with that template. The preamble will grow as long as needed, based on the number of columns actually used by the subsequent alignment entries. Therefore all it takes is

```
$\hfil#$ =&&\ \hfil#\hfil\cr
```

to make a suitable ⟨preamble⟩ for the $\mathcal{G}(n)$ problem.

Now suppose that the task is to typeset three pairs of displayed formulas, with all of the = signs lined up:

$$V_i = v_i - q_i v_j, \qquad X_i = x_i - q_i x_j, \qquad U_i = u_i, \qquad \text{for } i \neq j;$$
$$V_j = v_j, \qquad X_j = x_j, \qquad U_j = u_j + \textstyle\sum_{i \neq j} q_i u_i. \tag{23}$$

It's not easy to do this with three \eqalign's, because the $\sum$ with a subscript '$i \neq j$' makes the right-hand pair of formulas bigger than the others; the baselines won't agree unless "phantoms" are put into the other two \eqalign's (see Chapter 19). Instead of using \eqalign, which is defined in Appendix B to be a macro that uses \halign, let's try to use \halign directly. The natural way to approach this display is to type

```
$$\vcenter{\openup1\jot \halign{⟨preamble⟩\cr
   ⟨first line⟩\cr ⟨second line⟩\cr}}\eqno(23)$$
```

because the \vcenter puts the lines into a box that is properly centered with respect to the equation number '(23)'; the \openup macro puts a bit of extra space between the lines, as mentioned in Chapter 19.

OK, now let's figure out how to type the ⟨first line⟩ and ⟨second line⟩. The usual convention is to put '&' before the symbols that we want to line up, so the obvious solution is to type

```
V_i&=v_i-q_iv_j,&X_i&=x_i-q_ix_j,&
  U_i&=u_i,\qquad\hbox{for $i\ne j$};\cr
V_j&=v_j,&X_j&=x_j,&
  U_j&=u_j+\sum_{i\ne j}q_iu_i.\cr
```

Thus the alignment has six columns. We could take common elements into the preamble (e.g., 'V_' and '=v_'), but that would be too error-prone and too tricky.

The remaining problem is to construct a preamble to support those lines. To the left of the = signs we want the column to be filled at the left; to the right of the = signs we want it to be filled at the right. There's a slight complication because we are breaking a math formula into two separate pieces, yet we want the result to have the same spacing as if it were one formula. Since we're putting the '&' just before a relation, the solution is to insert '{}' at the beginning of the right-hand formula; TeX will put the proper space before the equals sign in '${}=...$', but it puts no space before the equals sign in '$=...$'. Therefore the desired ⟨preamble⟩ is

```
$\hfil#$&$\{}#\hfil$&
  \qquad$\hfil#$&$\{}#\hfil$&
  \qquad$\hfil#$&$\{}#\hfil$
```

The third and fourth columns are like the first and second, except for the \qquad that separates the equations; the fifth and sixth columns are like the third and fourth. Once again we can use the handy '&&' shortcut to reduce the preamble to

```
$\hfil#$&&$\{}#\hfil$&\qquad$\hfil#$
```

With a little practice you'll find that it becomes easy to compose preambles as you are typing a manuscript that needs them. However, most manuscripts don't need them, so it may be a while before you acquire even a little practice in this regard.

▶ **EXERCISE 22.9**
Explain how to produce the following display:

$$10w + \quad 3x + 3y + 18z = 1, \qquad\qquad (9)$$
$$6w - 17x \qquad - 5z = 2. \qquad\qquad (10)$$

The next level of complexity occurs when some entries of a table span two or more columns. TₑX provides two ways to handle this. First there's \hidewidth, which plain TₑX defines to be equivalent to

> \hskip-1000pt plus 1fill

In other words, \hidewidth has an extremely negative "natural width," but it will stretch without limit. If you put \hidewidth at the right of some entry in an alignment, the effect is to ignore the width of this entry and to let it stick out to the right of its box. (Think about it; this entry won't be the widest one, when \halign figures the column width.) Similarly, if you put \hidewidth at the left of an entry, it will stick out to the left; and you can put \hidewidth at both left and right, as we'll see later.

The second way to handle table entries that span columns is to use the \span primitive, which can be used instead of '&' in any line of the table. (We've already seen that \span means "expand" in preambles; but outside of preambles its use is completely different.) When '\span' appears in place of '&', the material before and after the \span is processed in the ordinary way, but afterward it is placed into a single box instead of two boxes. The width of this combination box is the sum of the individual column widths plus the width of the tabskip glue between them; therefore the spanning box will line up with non-spanning boxes in other rows.

For example, suppose that there are three columns, with the respective templates u_1 # v_1 & u_2 # v_2 & u_3 # v_3; suppose that the column widths are w_1, w_2, w_3; suppose that g_0, g_1, g_2, g_3 are the tabskip glue widths after the glue has been set; and suppose that the line

> a_1\span a_2\span a_3\cr

has appeared in the alignment. Then the material for '$u_1a_1v_1u_2a_2v_2u_3a_3v_3$' (i.e., the result '$u_1a_1v_1$' of column 1 followed by the results of columns 2 and 3) will be placed into an hbox of width $w_1 + g_1 + w_2 + g_2 + w_3$. That hbox will be preceded by glue of width g_0 and it will be followed by glue of width g_3, in the larger hbox that contains the entire aligned line.

You can use \omit in conjunction with \span. For example, if we continue with the notation of the previous paragraph, the line

> \omit a_1 \span a_2 \span\omit a_3 \cr

would put the material for '$a_1u_2a_2v_2a_3$' into the hbox just considered.

It's fairly common to span several columns and to omit all their templates, so plain TₑX provides a \multispan macro that spans a given number of columns. For example, '\multispan3' expands into '\omit\span\omit\span\omit'. If the number of spanned columns is greater than 9, you must put it in braces, e.g., '\multispan{13}'.

The preceding paragraphs are rather abstract, so let's look at an example that shows what \span actually does. Suppose you type

```
$$\tabskip=3em
\vbox{\halign{&\hrulefill#\hrulefill\cr
    first&second&third\cr
    first-and-second\span\omit&\cr
    &second-and-third\span\omit\cr
    first-second-third\span\omit\span\omit\cr}}$$
```

The preamble specifies arbitrarily many templates equal to '\hrulefill#\hrulefill'; the \hrulefill macro is like \hfill except that the blank space is filled with a horizontal rule. Therefore you can see the filling in the resulting alignment, which shows the spanned columns:

$$\begin{matrix} \text{first} & \text{second} & \text{third} \\ \_\text{first-and-second}\_ & & \rule{2em}{0.4pt} \\ \rule{2em}{0.4pt} & \_\text{second-and-third}\_ & \\ \rule{2em}{0.4pt}\text{first-second-third}\rule{3em}{0.4pt} \end{matrix}$$

The rules stop where the tabskip glue separates columns. You don't see rules in the first line, since the entries in that line were the widest in their columns. However, if the tabskip glue had been 1 em instead of 3 em, the table would have looked like this:

$$\begin{matrix} \text{first} & \_\text{second}\_ & \text{third} \\ \text{first-and-second} & & \rule{2em}{0.4pt} \\ \rule{2em}{0.4pt} & \text{second-and-third} & \\ \rule{2em}{0.4pt}\text{first-second-third}\rule{2em}{0.4pt} \end{matrix}$$

 ▶ **EXERCISE 22.10**
Consider the following table, which is called Walter's worksheet:

```
1 Adjusted gross income..........  $4,000
2 Zero bracket amount for
   a single individual........  $2,300
3 Earned income...........   1,500
4 Subtract line 3 from line 2......    800
5 Add lines 1 and 4. Enter here
   and on Form 1040, line 35......  $4,800
```

Define a preamble so that the following specification will produce Walter's worksheet.

```
\halign{⟨preamble⟩\cr
   1&Adjusted gross income\dotfill\span\omit\span&\$4,000\cr
   2&Zero bracket amount for&\cr
    &a single individual\dotfill\span\omit&\$2,300\cr
   3&Earned income\dotfill\span\omit&\underbar{ 1,500}\cr
   4&Subtract line 3 from line 2\dotfill
       \span\omit\span&\underbar{ 800}\cr
   5&Add lines 1 and 4. Enter here\span\omit\span\cr
    &and on Form 1040, line 35\dotfill\span\omit\span&\$4,800\cr}
```

(The macro \dotfill is like \hrulefill but it fills with dots; the macro \underbar puts its argument into an hbox and underlines it.)

Notice the "early" appearance of \cr in line 2 of the previous exercise. You needn't have the same number of columns in every line of an alignment; '\cr' means that there are no more columns in the current line.

▶ **EXERCISE 22.11**
Explain how to typeset the generic matrix
$$\begin{pmatrix} a_{11} & a_{12} & \cdots & a_{1n} \\ a_{21} & a_{22} & \cdots & a_{2n} \\ \cdots\cdots\cdots\cdots\cdots\cdots \\ a_{m1} & a_{m2} & \cdots & a_{mn} \end{pmatrix}.$$

The presence of spanned columns adds a complication to TeX's rules for calculating column widths; instead of simply choosing the maximum natural width of the column entries, it's also necessary to make sure that the sum of certain widths is big enough to accommodate spanned entries. So here is what TeX actually does: First, if any pair of adjacent columns is always spanned as a unit (i.e., if there's a \span between them whenever either one is used), these two columns are effectively merged into one and the tabskip glue between them is set to zero. This reduces the problem to the case that every tab position actually occurs at a boundary. Let there be n columns remaining after such reductions, and for $1 \le i \le j \le n$ let w_{ij} be the maximum natural width of all entries that span columns i through j, inclusive; if there are no such spanned entries, let $w_{ij} = -\infty$. (The merging of dependent columns guarantees that, for each j, there exists $i \le j$ such that $w_{ij} > -\infty$.) Let t_k be the natural width of the tabskip glue between columns k and $k+1$, for $1 \le k < n$. Now the final width w_j of column j is determined by the formula

$$w_j = \max_{1 \le i \le j} \left(w_{ij} - \sum_{i \le k < j} (w_k + t_k) \right)$$

for $j = 1, 2, \ldots, n$ (in this order). It follows that $w_{ij} \le w_i + t_i + \cdots + t_{j-1} + w_j$, for all $i \le j$, as desired. After the widths w_j are determined, the tabskip amounts may have to stretch or shrink; if they shrink, w_{ij} might turn out to be more than the final width of a box that spans columns i through j, hence the glue in such a box might shrink.

These formulas usually work fine, but sometimes they produce undesirable effects. For example, suppose that $n = 3$, $w_{11} = w_{22} = w_{33} = 10$, $w_{12} = w_{23} = -\infty$, and $w_{13} = 100$; in other words, the columns by themselves are quite narrow, but there's a big wide entry that's supposed to span all three columns. In this case TeX's formula makes $w_1 = w_2 = 10$ but $w_3 = 80 - t_1 - t_2$, so all the excess width is allocated to the third column. If that's not what you want, the remedy is to use \hidewidth, or to increase the natural width of the tabskip glue between columns.

The next level of complexity that occurs in tables is the appearance of horizontal and vertical ruled lines. People who know how to make ruled tables are generally known as TeX Masters. Are you ready?

If you approach vertical rules in the wrong manner, they can be difficult; but there *is* a decent way to get them into tables without shedding too many tears. The first step is to say '\offinterlineskip', which means that there will be no blank space between lines; TeX cannot be allowed to insert interline glue in its normal clever way, because each line is supposed to contain a \vrule that abuts another \vrule in the neighboring lines above and/or below. We will put a strut into every line, by including one in the preamble; then each line will have the proper height and depth, and there will be no need for interline glue. TeX puts every column entry of an alignment into an hbox whose height and depth are set equal to the height and depth of the entire line; therefore \vrule commands will extend to the top and bottom of the lines even when their height and/or depth are not specified.

 A "column" should be allocated to every vertical rule, and such a column can be assigned the template '\vrule#'. Then you obtain a vertical rule by simply leaving the column entries blank, in the normal lines of the alignment; or you can say '\omit' if you want to omit the rule in some line; or you can say 'height 10pt' if you want a nonstandard height; and so on.

 Here is a small table that illustrates the points just made. [The data appeared in an article by A. H. Westing, *BioScience* **31** (1981), 523–524.]

```
\vbox{\offinterlineskip
\hrule
\halign{&\vrule#&
  \strut\quad\hfil#\quad\cr
height2pt&\omit&&\omit&\cr
&Year\hfil&&World Population&\cr
height2pt&\omit&&\omit&\cr
\noalign{\hrule}
height2pt&\omit&&\omit&\cr
&8000\BC&&5,000,000&\cr
&50\AD&&200,000,000&\cr
&1650\AD&&500,000,000&\cr
&1850\AD&&1,000,000,000&\cr
&1945\AD&&2,300,000,000&\cr
&1980\AD&&4,400,000,000&\cr
height2pt&\omit&&\omit&\cr}
\hrule}
```

Year	World Population
8000 B.C.	5,000,000
50 A.D.	200,000,000
1650 A.D.	500,000,000
1850 A.D.	1,000,000,000
1945 A.D.	2,300,000,000
1980 A.D.	4,400,000,000

In this example the first, third, and fifth columns are reserved for vertical rules. Horizontal rules are obtained by saying '\hrule' outside the \halign or '\noalign{\hrule}' inside it, because the \halign appears in a vbox whose width is the full table width. The horizontal rules could also have been specified by saying '\multispan5\hrulefill' inside the \halign, since that would produce a rule that spans all five columns.

 The only other nonobvious thing about this table is the inclusion of several lines that say 'height2pt&\omit&&\omit&\cr'; can you see what they do? The \omit instructions mean that there's no numerical information, and they also suppress the \strut from the line; the 'height2pt' makes the first \vrule 2 pt high, and the other two rules will follow suit. Thus, the effect is to extend the vertical rules by two points, where they touch the horizontal rules. This is a little touch that improves the appearance of boxed tables; look for it as a mark of quality.

 ▶ **EXERCISE 22.12**
Explain why the lines of this table say '&\cr' instead of just '\cr'.

 Another way to get vertical rules into tables is to typeset without them, then back up (using negative glue) and insert them.

Here is another table; this one has become a classic, ever since Michael Lesk published it as one of the first examples in his report on a program to format tables [Bell Laboratories Computing Science Technical Report **49** (1976)]. It illustrates several typical problems that arise in connection with boxed information. In order to demonstrate TEX's ability to adapt a table to different circumstances, tabskip glue is used here to adjust the column widths; the table appears twice, once generated by '\halign to125pt' and once by '\halign to200pt', with nothing else changed.

AT&T Common Stock		
Year	Price	Dividend
1971	41–54	$2.60
2	41–54	2.70
3	46–55	2.87
4	40–53	3.24
5	45–52	3.40
6	51–59	.95*

* (first quarter only)

AT&T Common Stock		
Year	Price	Dividend
1971	41–54	$2.60
2	41–54	2.70
3	46–55	2.87
4	40–53	3.24
5	45–52	3.40
6	51–59	.95*

* (first quarter only)

The following specification did the job:

```
\vbox{\tabskip=0pt \offinterlineskip
\def\tablerule{\noalign{\hrule}}
\halign to⟨dimen⟩{\strut## \vrule#\tabskip=1em plus2em&
  \hfil## \vrule## \hfil#\hfil& \vrule#&
  \hfil## \vrule#\tabskip=0pt\cr\tablerule
&&\multispan5\hfil AT\&T Common Stock\hfil&\cr\tablerule
&&\omit\hidewidth Year\hidewidth&&
  \omit\hidewidth Price\hidewidth&&
  \omit\hidewidth Dividend\hidewidth&\cr\tablerule
&&1971&&41--54&&\$2.60&\cr\tablerule
&&    2&&41--54&&2.70&\cr\tablerule
&&    3&&46--55&&2.87&\cr\tablerule
&&    4&&40--53&&3.24&\cr\tablerule
&&    5&&45--52&&3.40&\cr\tablerule
&&    6&&51--59&&.95\rlap*&\cr\tablerule \noalign{\smallskip}
&\multispan7* (first quarter only)\hfil\cr}}
```

Points of interest are: (1) The first column contains a strut; otherwise it would have been necessary to put a strut on the lines that say 'AT&T' and '(first quarter only)', since those lines omit the templates of all other columns that might have a built-in strut. (2) '\hidewidth' is used in the title line so that the width of columns will be affected only by the width of the numeric data. (3) '\rlap' is used so that the asterisk doesn't affect the alignment of the numbers. (4) If the tabskip specification had been '0em plus3em' instead of '1em plus2em', the alignment wouldn't have come out right, because 'AT&T Common Stock' would have been wider than the natural width of everything it spanned; the excess width would all have gone into the 'Dividend' column.

▶ **EXERCISE 22.13**
Explain how to add 2 pt more space above and below 'AT&T Common Stock'.

▶**EXERCISE 22.14**
Typeset the following chart, making it exactly 36em wide:

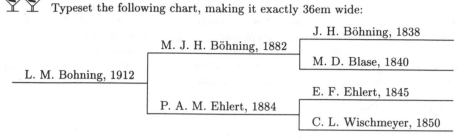

If you're having trouble debugging an alignment, it sometimes helps to put '\ddt' at the beginning and end of the templates in your preamble. This is an undefined control sequence that causes TeX to stop, displaying the rest of the template. When TeX stops, you can use \showlists and other commands to see what the machine thinks it's doing. If TeX doesn't stop, you know that it never reached that part of the template.

It's possible to have alignments within alignments. Therefore when TeX sees a '&' or '\span' or '\cr', it needs some way to decide which alignment is involved. The rule is that an entry ends when '&' or '\span' or '\cr' occurs at the same level of braces that was current when the entry began; i.e., there must be an equal number of left and right braces in every entry. For example, in the line

       \matrix{1&1\cr 0&1\cr}&\matrix{0&1\cr 0&0\cr}\cr

TeX will not resume the template for the first column when it is scanning the argument to \matrix, because the &'s and \cr's in that argument are enclosed in braces. Similarly, &'s and \cr's in the preamble do not denote the end of a template unless the resulting template would have an equal number of left and right braces.

You have to be careful with the use of & and \span and \cr, because these tokens are intercepted by TeX's scanner even when it is not expanding macros. For example, if you say '\let\x=\span' in the midst of an alignment entry, TeX will think that the '\span' ends the entry, so \x will become equal to the first token following the '#' in the template. You can hide this \span by putting it in braces; e.g., '{\global\let\x=\span}'. (And Appendix D explains how to avoid \global here.)

Sometimes people forget the \cr on the last line of an alignment. This can cause mysterious effects, because TeX is not clairvoyant. For example, consider the following apparently simple case:

       \halign{\centerline{#}\cr
         A centered line.\cr
         And another?}

(Notice the missing \cr.)   A curious thing happens here when TeX processes the erroneous line, so please pay attention. The template begins with '\centerline{', so TeX starts to scan the argument to \centerline. Since there's no '\cr' after the question mark, the '}' after the question mark is treated as the end of the argument to \centerline, *not* as the end of the \halign. TeX isn't going to be able to finish the alignment unless the subsequent text has the form '...{...\cr'. Indeed, an entry like '`a}b{c`' is legitimate with respect to the template '`\centerline{#}`', since it yields '`\centerline{a}b{c}`'; TEX is correct when it gives no error message in this case. But the computer's idea of the current situation is different from the user's, so a puzzling error message will probably occur a few lines later.

▷▷ To help avoid such situations, there's a primitive command `\crcr` that acts exactly like `\cr` except that it does nothing when it immediately follows a `\cr` or a `\noalign{...}`. Thus, when you write a macro like `\matrix`, you can safely insert `\crcr` at the end of the user's argument; this will cover up an error if the user forgot the final `\cr`, and it will cause no harm if the final `\cr` was present.

▷▷ Are you tired of typing `\cr`? You can get plain TEX to insert an automatic `\cr` at the end of each input line in the following way:

```
\begingroup \let\par=\cr \obeylines %
\halign{⟨preamble⟩
    ⟨first line of alignment⟩
    ...
    ⟨last line of alignment⟩
    }\endgroup
```

This works because `\obeylines` makes the ASCII ⟨return⟩ into an active character that uses the current meaning of `\par`, and plain TEX puts ⟨return⟩ at the end of an input line (see Chapter 8). If you don't want a `\cr` at the end of a certain line, just type '`%`' and the corresponding `\cr` will be "commented out." (This special mode doesn't work with `\+` lines, since `\+` is a macro whose argument is delimited by the token '`\cr`', not simply by a token that has the same meaning as `\cr`. But you can redefine `\+` to overcome this hurdle, if you want to. For example, define a macro `\alternateplus` that is just like `\+` except that its argument is delimited by the active character `^^M`; then include the command '`\let\+=\alternateplus`' as part of `\obeylines`.)

▷ The control sequence `\valign` is analogous to `\halign`, but rows and columns change rôles. In this case `\cr` marks the bottom of a column, and the aligned columns are vboxes that are put together in horizontal mode. The individual entries of each column are vboxed with depth zero (i.e., as if `\boxmaxdepth` were zero, as explained in Chapter 12); the entry heights for each row of a `\valign` are maximized in the same fashion as the entry widths for each column of an `\halign` are maximized. The `\noalign` operation can now be used to insert horizontal mode material between columns; the `\span` operation now spans rows. People usually work with TEX at least a year before they find their first application for `\valign`; and then it's usually a one-row '`\valign{\vfil#\vfil\cr...}`'. But the general mechanism is there if you need it.

> *If sixteen pennies are arranged in the form of a square*
> *there will be the same number of pennies in every row, every column,*
> *and each of the two long diagonals.*
> *Can you do the same with twenty pennies?*
> — HENRY ERNEST DUDENEY, *The Best Coin Problems* (1909)

> *It was she who controlled the whole of the Fifth Column.*
> — AGATHA CHRISTIE, *N or M?* (1941)

23

Output Routines

We investigated TEX's page-building technique in Chapter 15, where we discussed the basic two-stage strategy that is used: TEX gathers material until it has accumulated more than will fit on a page; then it spews out one page of data, based on what it thinks is the best breakpoint between pages; then it returns to gather material for the next page in the same way. Page numbers, headings, and similar things are attached after each page has been ejected, by a special sequence of TEX commands called the current *output routine*.

Plain TEX has an output routine that takes care of ordinary jobs. It handles the simple things that most manuscripts require, and it also copes with more complicated things like the insertions made with \footnote and \topinsert, as described in the dangerous bends of Chapter 15. We shall begin the present chapter by discussing how to make simple changes to the behavior of plain TEX's output routine; then we shall turn to the details of how to define output routines that do more complex tasks.

If you run TEX without modifying the plain TEX format, you get pages that are numbered at the bottom; and each page will be approximately $8\frac{1}{2}$ inches wide and 11 inches tall, including 1-inch margins at all four sides. This format is suitable for preprints of technical papers, but you might well want to change it, especially if you are not using TEX to make a preprint of a technical paper.

For example, we saw in the experiments of Chapter 6 that the width of the material on a page can be changed by giving a different value to the horizontal line size, \hsize. Plain TEX format says '\hsize=6.5in', in order to obtain 8.5-inch pages with 1-inch margins; you can change \hsize to whatever you want. Similarly, you can control the vertical size of a page by changing \vsize. Plain TEX sets \vsize=8.9in (not 9in, since \vsize doesn't include the space for page numbers at the bottom of each page); if you say '\vsize=4in' you will get shorter pages, with only 4 inches of copy per sheet. It's best not to monkey with \hsize and \vsize except at the very beginning of a job, or after you have ejected all pages from TEX's memory.

If you want your output to be positioned differently when it is ultimately printed, you can offset it by giving nonzero values to \hoffset and \voffset. For example,

```
\hoffset=.5in    \voffset=1.5in
```

will move the output half an inch to the right of its normal position, and 1.5 inches down. You should be careful not to offset the output so much that it falls off the edge of the physical medium on which it is being printed, unless you know that such out-of-bounds activity won't cause trouble.

TEX is often used to typeset announcements, brochures, or other documents for which page numbers are inappropriate. If you say

```
\nopagenumbers
```

at the beginning of your manuscript, plain TEX will refrain from inserting numbers at the bottom of each page.

In fact, \nopagenumbers is a special case of a much more general mechanism by which you can control headings and footings. The plain TeX output routine puts out a special line of text called the *headline* at the top of each page, and another special line of text called the *footline* at the bottom. The headline is normally blank, and the footline is normally a centered page number, but you can specify any headline and footline that you want by redefining the control sequences \headline and \footline. For example,

> \headline={\hrulefill}

will put a horizontal rule at the top of every page. The basic idea is that plain TeX puts '\line{\the\headline}' at the top and '\line{\the\footline}' at the bottom, with blank lines separating these extra lines from the other material. (Recall that \line is an abbreviation for '\hbox to\hsize'; hence the headline and footline are put into boxes as wide as the normal lines on the page itself.) The normal value of \headline is '\hfil', so that no heading is visible. The \nopagenumbers macro described earlier is simply an abbreviation for '\footline={\hfil}'.

The normal value of \footline is '\hss\tenrm\folio\hss'; this centers the page number on a line, using font \tenrm, because \folio is a control sequence that produces the number of the current page in text form.

The page number appears in TeX's internal register \count0, as explained in Chapter 15, and plain TeX makes \pageno an abbreviation for \count0. Thus you can say '\pageno=100' if you want the next page of your output to be number 100. The \folio macro converts negative page numbers to roman numerals; if your manuscript begins with '\pageno=-1', the pages will be numbered i, ii, iii, iv, v, etc. In fact, Appendix B defines \folio to be an abbreviation for

> \ifnum\pageno<0 \romannumeral-\pageno \else\number\pageno \fi

It is important to include the name of each font explicitly whenever you are defining a headline or footline, because an output routine in TeX can come into action at somewhat unpredictable times. For example, suppose that \footline had been set to '\hss\folio\hss', without specifying \tenrm; then the page number would be typeset in whatever font happens to be current when TeX decides to output a page. Mysterious effects can occur in such cases, because TeX is typically in the midst of page 101 when it is outputting page 100.

▶**EXERCISE 23.1**
Explain how to put en-dashes around the page numbers in a plain TeX job. For example, ' – 4 – ' should appear at the bottom of page 4.

Here is an example of a headline in which the page numbers appear at the top. Furthermore, odd-numbered and even-numbered pages are treated differently:

```
\nopagenumbers % suppress footlines
\headline={\ifodd\pageno\rightheadline \else\leftheadline\fi}
\def\rightheadline{\tenrm\hfil RIGHT RUNNING HEAD\hfil\folio}
\def\leftheadline{\tenrm\folio\hfil LEFT RUNNING HEAD\hfil}
\voffset=2\baselineskip
```

English-language books traditionally have odd-numbered pages on the right and even-numbered pages on the left. Text that appears as a headline on several pages is often called a "running head." When you use headlines, it is generally wise to set `\voffset` to the equivalent of two lines of text, as shown in this example, so that there will still be a margin of one inch at the top of your output pages.

▶**EXERCISE 23.2**
Suppose that you're using TEX to typeset your résumé, which is several pages long. Explain how to define `\headline` so that the first page is headed by '**RÉSUMÉ**', centered in boldface type, while each subsequent page has a headline like this:

Résumé of A. U. Thor .... Page 2

If you don't change the `\vsize`, all of the headlines and footlines will occur in the same place regardless of the contents of the page between them. Thus, for example, if you are using `\raggedbottom` as explained in Chapter 15, so that pages do not always contain the same amount of text, the raggedness will occur above the footline; the footline won't move up. If you do change `\vsize`, the footline position will change correspondingly, while the headline will stay put.

The rest of this chapter is intended for people who want an output format that is substantially different from what plain TEX provides. Double dangerous bends are used in all of the subsequent paragraphs, because you should be familiar with the rest of TEX before you plunge into these final mysteries of the language. Chapter 22 taught you how to be a TEX Master, i.e., a person who can produce complicated tables using `\halign` and `\valign`; the following material will take you all the way to the rank of Grandmaster, i.e., a person who can design output routines. When you are ready for this rank, you will be pleased to discover that—like alignments—output routines are not really so mysterious as they may seem at first.

Let's begin by recapping some of the rules at the end of Chapter 15. TEX periodically chooses to output a page of information, by breaking its main vertical list at what it thinks is the best place, and at such times it enters internal vertical mode and begins to read the commands in the current `\output` routine. When the output routine begins, `\box255` contains the page that TEX has completed; the output routine is supposed to do something with this vbox. When the output routine ends, the list of items that it has constructed in internal vertical mode is placed just before the material that follows the page break. In this way TEX's page-break decisions can effectively be changed: Some or all of the material on the broken-off page can be removed and carried forward to the next page.

The current `\output` routine is defined as a token list parameter, just like `\everypar` or `\errhelp`, except that TEX automatically inserts a begin-group symbol '{' at the beginning and an end-group symbol '}' at the end. These grouping characters help to keep the output routine from interfering with what TEX was doing when the page break was chosen; for example, an output routine often changes the `\baselineskip` when it puts a headline or footline on a page, and the extra braces keep this change local. If no `\output` routine has been specified, or if the user has said '`\output={}`', TEX supplies its own routine, which is essentially equivalent to '`\output={\shipout\box255}`'; this outputs the page without any headline or footline, and without changing the page number.

TeX's primitive command \shipout⟨box⟩ is what actually causes output. It sends the contents of the box to the dvi file, which is TeX's main output file; after TeX has finished, the dvi file will contain a compact device-independent encoding of instructions that specify exactly what should be printed. When a box is shipped out, TeX displays the values of \count0 through \count9 on your terminal, as explained in Chapter 15; these ten counters are also recorded in the dvi file, where they can be used to identify the page. All of the \openout, \closeout, and \write commands that appear inside of the ⟨box⟩ are performed in their natural order as that box is being shipped out. Since a \write command expands macros, as explained in Chapter 21, TeX's scanning mechanism might detect syntax errors while a \shipout is in progress. If \tracingoutput is nonzero at the time of a \shipout, the contents of the ⟨box⟩ being shipped are written into your log file in symbolic form. You can say \shipout anywhere, not only in an output routine.

The delayed aspect of \write imposes a noteworthy restriction: It is necessary to be sure that all macros that might appear within the text of a \write are properly defined when a \shipout command is given. For example, the plain TeX format in Appendix B temporarily makes spaces active and says '\global\let␣=\space'; the reason is that \obeyspaces might be in force during a \write command, so a definition for ␣ as an active character should exist during the next \shipout, even though TeX might no longer be making spaces active at that time.

Chapter 15 points out that TeX gives special values to certain internal registers and parameters, in addition to \box255, just before the output routine begins. Insertions are put into their own vboxes, and \insertpenalties is set equal to the total number of heldover insertions; furthermore the \outputpenalty parameter is set to the value of the penalty at the current breakpoint. An output routine can be made to do special things when these quantities have special values. For example, the output routine of plain TeX recognizes a \supereject (which ejects all held-over insertions) by the fact that \supereject causes \outputpenalty to be −20000, and by using \insertpenalties to decide if any insertions are being held over.

The default output routine, '\shipout\box255', illustrates one extreme in which nothing is put into the vertical list that is carried over to the next page. The other extreme is

```
\output={\unvbox255 \penalty\outputpenalty}
```

which ships nothing out and puts *everything* back onto the main vertical list. (The command '\unvbox255' takes the completed page out of its box, and the command '\penalty\outputpenalty' reinserts the penalty at the chosen breakpoint.) This makes a seamless join between the completed page and the subsequent material, because TeX has still not discarded glue and penalties at the breakpoint when it invokes an \output routine; hence TeX will go back and reconsider the page break. If the \vsize hasn't changed, and if all insertions have been held in place, the same page break will be found; but it will be found much faster than before, because the vertical list has already been constructed—the paragraphing doesn't need to be done again. Of course, an output routine like this makes TeX spin its wheels endlessly, so it is of no use except as an example of an extreme case.

To prevent such looping, your output routine should always make progress of some sort whenever it comes into play. If you make a mistake, TEX may be able to help you diagnose the error, because a special loop-detection mechanism has been built in: There is an internal integer variable called \deadcycles, which is cleared to zero after every \shipout and increased by 1 just before every \output. Thus, \deadcycles keeps track of how many times an output routine has been initiated since the most recent \shipout, unless you change the value of \deadcycles yourself. There's also an integer parameter called \maxdeadcycles, which plain TEX sets to 25. If \deadcycles is greater than or equal to \maxdeadcycles when your output routine is about to be started (i.e., when \deadcycles is about to be increased), TEX issues an error message and performs the default output routine instead of yours.

When your output routine is finished, \box255 should be void. In other words, you must do something with the information in that box; it should either be shipped out or put into some other place. Similarly, \box255 should be void when TEX is getting ready to fill it with a new page of material, just before starting an output routine. If \box255 is nonvoid at either of those times, TEX will complain that you are misusing this special register, and the register contents will be destroyed.

But let's not talk forever about borderline cases and special parameters; let's look at some real examples. The output routine of plain TEX, found in Appendix B, is set up by saying '\output={\plainoutput}', where \plainoutput is an abbreviation for

```
\shipout\vbox{\makeheadline
  \pagebody
  \makefootline}
\advancepageno
\ifnum\outputpenalty>-20000 \else\dosupereject\fi
```

Let us consider this "program" one line at a time:

1) The \makeheadline macro constructs a vbox of height and depth zero in such a way that the headline is properly positioned above the rest of the page. Its actual code is

```
\vbox to 0pt{\vskip-22.5pt
  \line{\vbox to8.5pt{}\the\headline}\vss}
\nointerlineskip
```

The magic constant $-22.5\,\mathrm{pt}$ is equal to (topskip − height of strut − 2(baselineskip)), i.e., $10\,\mathrm{pt} - 8.5\,\mathrm{pt} - 24\,\mathrm{pt}$; this places the reference point of the headline exactly 24 pt above the reference point of the top line on the page, unless the headline or the top line are excessively large.

2) The \pagebody macro is an abbreviation for

```
\vbox to\vsize{\boxmaxdepth=\maxdepth \pagecontents}
```

The value of \boxmaxdepth is set to \maxdepth so that the vbox will be constructed under the assumptions that TEX's page builder has used to set up \box255.

3) The \pagecontents macro produces a vertical list for everything that belongs on the main body of the page, namely the contents of \box255 together with illustrations (inserted at the top) and footnotes (inserted at the bottom):

```
\ifvoid\topins \else\unvbox\topins\fi
\dimen0=\dp255 \unvbox255
\ifvoid\footins\else % footnote info is present
  \vskip\skip\footins
  \footnoterule
  \unvbox\footins\fi
\ifraggedbottom \kern-\dimen0 \vfil \fi
```

Here \topins and \footins are the insertion class numbers for the two kinds of insertions used in plain TeX; if more classes of insertions are added, \pagecontents should be changed accordingly. Notice that the boxes are unboxed so that the glue coming from insertions can help out the glue on the main page. The \footnoterule macro in Appendix B places a dividing line between the page and its footnotes; it makes a net contribution of 0 pt to the height of the vertical list. Ragged-bottom setting is achieved by inserting infinite glue, which overpowers the stretchability of \topskip.

4) The \makefootline macro puts \footline into its proper position:

```
\baselineskip=24pt
\line{\the\footline}
```

5) The \advancepageno macro normally advances \pageno by +1; but if \pageno is negative (for roman numerals), the advance is by −1. The new value of \pageno will be appropriate for the next time the output routine is called into action.

```
\ifnum\pageno<0 \global\advance\pageno by-1
\else \global\advance\pageno by 1 \fi
```

6) Finally, the \dosupereject macro is designed to clear out any insertions that have been held over, whether they are illustrations or footnotes or both:

```
\ifnum\insertpenalties>0
  \line{} \kern-\topskip \nobreak
  \vfill\supereject\fi
```

The mysterious negative \kern here cancels out the natural space of the \topskip glue that goes above the empty \line; that empty line box prevents the \vfill from disappearing into a page break. The vertical list that results from \dosupereject is placed on TeX's list of things to put out next, just after the straggling insertions have been reconsidered as explained in Chapter 15. Hence another super-eject will occur, and the process will continue until no insertions remain.

▶ **EXERCISE 23.3**
Explain how to change the output routine of plain TeX so that it will produce twice as many pages. The material that would ordinarily go on pages 1, 2, 3, etc., should go onto pages 1, 3, 5, ...; and the even-numbered pages should be entirely blank except for the headline and footline. (Imagine that photographs will be mounted on those blank pages later.)

Suppose now that double-column format is desired. More precisely, let's attempt to modify plain TeX so that it sets type in columns whose width is `\hsize=3.2in`. Each actual page of output should contain two such columns separated by 0.1 in of space; thus the text area of each page will still be 6.5 inches wide. The headlines and footlines should span both columns, but the columns themselves should contain independent insertions as if they were the facing pages of a book. In other words, each column should contain its own footnotes and its own illustrations; we do not have to change the `\pagebody` macro.

In order to solve this problem, let us first introduce a new dimension register called `\fullhsize` that represents the width of an entire page.

```
\newdimen\fullhsize
\fullhsize=6.5in \hsize=3.2in
\def\fullline{\hbox to\fullhsize}
```

The `\makeheadline` and `\makefootline` macros should be modified so that they use '`\fullline`' instead of '`\line`'.

The new output routine will make use of a control sequence `\lr` that is set to either 'L' or 'R', according as the next column belongs at the left or at the right of the next page. When a left column has been completed, the output routine simply saves it in a box register; when a right column has been completed, the routine outputs both columns and increases the page number.

```
\let\lr=L \newbox\leftcolumn
\output={\if L\lr
    \global\setbox\leftcolumn=\columnbox \global\let\lr=R
  \else \doubleformat \global\let\lr=L\fi
  \ifnum\outputpenalty> 20000 \else\dosupereject\fi}
\def\doubleformat{\shipout\vbox{\makeheadline
    \fullline{\box\leftcolumn\hfil\columnbox}
    \makefootline}
  \advancepageno}
\def\columnbox{\leftline{\pagebody}}
```

The `\columnbox` macro uses `\leftline` in order to ensure that it produces a box whose width is `\hsize`. The width of `\box255` is usually, but not always, equal to `\hsize` at the beginning of an output routine; any other width would louse up the format.

When double-column setting ends, there's a 50-50 chance that the final column has fallen at the left, so it will not yet have been output. The code

```
\supereject
\if R\lr \null\vfill\eject\fi
```

supplies an empty right-hand column in this case, ensuring that all of the accumulated material will be printed. It's possible to do fancier column balancing on the last page, but the details are tricky if footnotes and other insertions need to be accommodated as well. Appendix E includes the macros that were used to balance the columns at the end of the index in Appendix I, and to start two-column format in mid-page.

▶ **EXERCISE 23.4**
How should the example above be modified if you want three-column output?

Since TeX's output routine lags behind its page-construction activity, you can get erroneous results if you change the `\headline` or the `\footline` in an uncontrolled way. For example, suppose that you are typesetting a book, and that the format you are using allows chapters to start in the middle of a page; then it would be a mistake to change the running headline at the moment you begin a new chapter, since the next actual page of output might not yet include anything from the new chapter. Consider also the task of typesetting a dictionary or a membership roster; a well-designed reference book displays the current range of entries at the top of each page or pair of pages, so that it is easy for readers to thumb through the book when they are searching for isolated words or names. But TeX's asynchronous output mechanism makes it difficult, if not impossible, to determine just what range of entries is actually present on a page.

Therefore TeX provides a way to put "marks" into a list; these marks inform the output routine about the range of information on each page. The general idea is that you can say

$$\text{\texttt{\textbackslash mark}\{⟨mark text⟩\}}$$

in the midst of the information you are typesetting, where the ⟨mark text⟩ is a token list that is expanded as in the commands `\edef`, `\message`, etc. TeX puts an internal representation of the mark text into the list it is building; then later on, when a completed page is packed into `\box255`, TeX allows the output routine to refer to the first and last mark texts on that page.

The best way to think of this is probably to imagine that TeX generates an arbitrarily long vertical list of boxes, glue, and other items such as penalties and marks. Somehow that long vertical list gets divided up into pages, and the pages are made available to the output routine, one at a time. Whenever a page is put in `\box255`, TeX sets up the value of three quantities that act essentially like macros:

- `\botmark` is the mark text most recently encountered on the page that was just boxed;
- `\firstmark` is the mark text that was first encountered on the page that was just boxed;
- `\topmark` has the value that `\botmark` had just before the current page was boxed.

Before the first page, all three of these are null, i.e., they expand to nothing. When there is no mark on a page, all three are equal to the previous `\botmark`.

For example, suppose that your manuscript includes exactly four marks, and that the pages are broken in such a way that `\mark{`α`}` happens to fall on page 2, `\mark{`β`}` and `\mark{`γ`}` on page 4, and `\mark{`δ`}` on page 5. Then

On page	`\topmark` is	`\firstmark` is	`\botmark` is
1	null	null	null
2	null	α	α
3	α	α	α
4	α	β	γ
5	γ	δ	δ
6	δ	δ	δ

When you use a \mark command in vertical mode, TEX puts a mark into the main vertical list. When you use a \mark command in horizontal mode, TEX treats it as vertical mode material like \vadjust and \insert; i.e., after the paragraph has been broken into lines, each mark will go into the main vertical list just after the box for the line where that mark originally appeared. If you use \mark in restricted horizontal mode, the mark may migrate out to the enclosing vertical list in the same way that \insert and \vadjust items do (see Chapter 24); but a mark that is locked too deeply inside a box will not migrate, so it will never appear as a \firstmark or \botmark. Similarly, a \mark that occurs in internal vertical mode goes into a vbox, and it is not accessible in the main vertical list.

Chapter 15 discusses the \vsplit command, which allows you to break up vertical lists by yourself. This operation sometimes provides a useful alternative to TEX's ordinary page-building mechanism. For example, if you simply want to typeset some material in two columns of equal height, you can put that material into a vbox, then \vsplit the box into two pieces; no output routine is needed at all. The \vsplit operation sets up the values of two macro-like quantities that were not mentioned in Chapter 15: \splitfirstmark and \splitbotmark expand to the mark texts of the first and last marks that appear in the vertical list that was split off by the most recent \vsplit command. Both quantities are null if there were no such marks. The values of \topmark, \firstmark, \botmark, \splitfirstmark, and \splitbotmark are global; i.e., they are not affected by TEX's grouping mechanism.

Most dictionaries use the equivalent of \firstmark and \botmark to give guide words at the top of each pair of facing pages. For example, if the definition of the word 'type' starts on page 1387 and continues onto page 1388, the guide word on page 1387 (a right-hand page) will be 'type'; but the guide word at the top of page 1388 (a left-hand page) will be the next word in the dictionary (e.g., 'typecast') even though the top of page 1388 is about 'type'.

The dictionary scheme works fine for dictionaries, since a reader should start reading each dictionary entry at its beginning. But a different scheme is appropriate for a technical book like the author's *Art of Computer Programming*, where Section 1.2.8 (for example) starts in the middle of page 78, but the top of page 78 contains exercises 19–24 of Section 1.2.7. The headline at the top of page 78 refers to '1.2.7', because that will help somebody who is searching for exercise 1.2.7–22. Notice that the dictionary convention would put '1.2.8' at the top of page 78, but that would be appropriate only if Section 1.2.8 had begun exactly at the top of that page.

Continuing this example from *The Art of Computer Programming*, let's suppose that the TEX manuscript for Section 1.2.8 begins with a macro call like

```
\beginsection 1.2.8. Fibonacci Numbers.
```

How should \beginsection be defined? Here is one attempt:

```
\def\beginsection #1. #2.
   {\sectionbreak
   \leftline{\sectionfont #1. #2}
   \mark{#1}
   \nobreak\smallskip\noindent}
```

The \sectionbreak macro should encourage TEX either to break the page at the current position, or to leave a goodly amount of blank space; e.g., \sectionbreak might be an abbreviation for '\penalty-200 \vskip18pt plus4pt minus6pt'. The \beginsection macro ends with commands that suppress indentation of the first paragraph in the section. But the thing that concerns us with respect to output routines is the \mark command that follows \leftline. In the example we have been considering, the beginning of Section 1.2.8 would insert '\mark{1.2.8}' into the main vertical list just after the box containing the title of that section.

> Is such a \mark adequate? Unfortunately, no, not even if we assume for simplicity that at most one section begins on each page. The page that contains the beginning of Section 1.2.8 will then have \topmark=1.2.7 and \firstmark=1.2.8, regardless of whether or not the section starts at the very top of the page. What we want in this application is a cross between \topmark and \firstmark: something that will reflect the mark text that represents the state of affairs just after the first line of the page. And TEX doesn't provide that.

> The solution is to emit the \mark just before the \sectionbreak, instead of just after the \leftline. Then \topmark will always reflect the truth about the section that is current at the top line. (Think about it.)

> However, the format for *The Art of Computer Programming* is more complex than this. On left-hand pages, the section number in the headline is supposed to reflect the situation at the top of the page, as we have just discussed, but on right-hand pages it is supposed to refer to the bottom of the page. Our solution to the previous problem made \topmark correct for the top, but it can make \botmark incorrect at the bottom. In order to satisfy both requirements, it is necessary to pack more information into the marks. Here's one way to solve the problem:

```
\def\beginsection #1. #2.
  {\mark{\currentsection \noexpand\else #1}
  \sectionbreak
  \leftline{\sectionfont #1. #2}
  \mark{#1\noexpand\else #1} \def\currentsection{#1}
  \nobreak\smallskip\noindent}
\def\currentsection{} % the current section number
```

The idea is to introduce two marks, one just before the section break and one just after the section has begun. Furthermore each mark has two parts; the mark just before the potential break between Sections 1.2.7 and 1.2.8 is '1.2.7\else 1.2.8', while the one just after that potential break is '1.2.8\else 1.2.8'. It follows that the section number corresponding to the bottom of a page is the left component of \botmark; the section number corresponding to the top of a page is the right component of \topmark. The \rightheadline macro can make use of '\iftrue\botmark\fi' to read the left component, and the \leftheadline macro can say '\expandafter\iffalse\topmark\fi' to read the right component.

> ▶ **EXERCISE 23.5**
> B. C. Dull used a construction very much like the one above, but he put the second \mark just before the \leftline instead of just after it. What went wrong?

▷ **EXERCISE 23.6**
The marks in the previous construction have the form 'α\else$\,\beta$', where α and β are two independent pieces of information. The '\else' makes it possible to select either α or β by means of \iftrue and \iffalse. Generalize this idea: Suppose that you have an application in which marks are supposed to carry five independent pieces of information, and that each mark has the form 'α_0\or$\,\alpha_1$\or$\,\alpha_2$\or$\,\alpha_3$\or$\,\alpha_4$'. Explain how to select any one of the five α's from such a mark.

Let's conclude our discussion of output routines by considering an application to indexes, such as the index to this manual that appears in Appendix I. The most complicated entries in such an index will look something like this:

> Main entry, 4, 6, 8–10, 12, 14–16,
> 18–22, 24–28, 30.
> first subsidiary entry, 1–3, 6, 10–11,
> 15, 21, 24, 28.
> second subsidiary entry, 1, 3, 6–7,
> 10, 15, 21, 25, 28, 31.

Main entries and subsidiary entries are typeset ragged-right, with two ems of hanging indentation after the first line; subsidiary entries are indented one em on the first line. Our goal will be to typeset such material from input that looks like this:

```
\beginindex
...
Main entry, 4, 6, 8--10, 12, 14--16, 18--22, 24--28, 30.
\sub first subsidiary entry, 1--3, 6, 10--11, 15, 21, 24, 28.
\sub second subsidiary entry, 1, 3, 6--7, 10, 15, 21, 25, %
  28, 31.
...
\endindex
```

where '...' stands for other entries. Each line of input normally specifies one main entry or one subsidiary entry; if an entry is so long that it doesn't fit on a single input line, '␣%' is typed at the end of the line so that it merges with the following one.

The interesting thing about this index problem is that it is desirable to set up a system of marks so that the output routine can insert special lines of text when an entry has been broken between columns or pages. For example, if a page break occurs between any of the six lines of typeset output shown above, the output routine should emit the special line

> Main entry (*continued*):

and if a page break occurs within a subsidiary entry, an additional special line

> subsidiary entry (*continued*):

should also appear. The solution below produces marks so that \botmark will be null if a break occurs between main entries; it will be '`Main entry`' if a break occurs after lines 1, 2, or 4 of the six example output lines; it will be '`Main entry\sub first subsidiary entry`' if a break occurs after line 3 (within the first subsidiary entry); and it will be '`Main entry\sub second subsidiary entry`' if a break occurs after line 5.

The reader may wish to try solving this problem before looking at the solution, because it will then be easier to appreciate the subtler issues that are involved. (Go ahead: Try to define a macro \beginindex that does the ragged-right setting and produces the specified marks. Turn back to the previous page to study the problem carefully, before peeking at the answer.)

```
\def\beginindex{\begingroup
  \parindent=1em \maxdepth=\maxdimen
  \def\par{\endgraf \futurelet\next\inxentry}
  \obeylines \everypar={\hangindent 2\parindent}
  \exhyphenpenalty=10000 \raggedright}
\def\inxentry{\ifx\next\sub \let\next=\subentry
  \else\ifx\next\endindex \let\next=\vfill
  \else\let\next=\mainentry \fi\fi \next}
\def\endindex{\mark{}\break\endgroup}
\let\sub=\indent \newtoks\maintoks \newtoks\subtoks
\def\mainentry#1,{\mark{}\noindent
  \maintoks={#1}\mark{\the\maintoks}#1,}
\def\subentry\sub#1,{\mark{\the\maintoks}\indent
  \subtoks={#1}\mark{\the\maintoks\sub\the\subtoks}#1,}
```

Even if you have read this solution, you probably want an explanation of what it does, because it uses "TEXtics" that have not appeared before in this manual.

1) The \beginindex macro uses \begingroup to keep other changes local; thus, it won't be necessary to restore \parindent and \maxdepth, etc., to their former values when the index is finished. The \maxdepth parameter is set to \maxdimen, which is essentially infinite, so that \box255 will have the true depth of the last box that it contains; we will use this fact below. (It is safe to disable \maxdepth in this way, since the entries in an index can be assumed to have reasonably small depth.) Notice that \obeylines is used, so that \par will effectively be inserted at the end of every line of input. The meaning of \par is changed so that it does more than usual: First it does \endgraf, which is TEX's ordinary \par operation; then it sets \next to the first token of the next line, after which the macro \inxentry will be expanded.

2) When \inxentry comes into play it looks at \next to decide what to do. There are three cases: If \next is '\sub', the line will be treated as a subsidiary entry; if \next is '\endindex', the next commands executed will be '\vfill\mark{}\break \endgroup'; otherwise the line will be treated as a main entry.

3) The text of a main entry is put into parameter #1 of \mainentry; this parameter is delimited by a comma. The first thing that \mainentry does is '\mark{}', which clears the mark in case of a break between entries. Then comes '\noindent', which causes TEX to go into horizontal mode and to emit \parskip glue. (The \parskip glue will be a legal breakpoint between lines; it will later be followed by interline glue, when the first line of the main entry has been typeset by TEX's paragraphing routine.) Then another \mark is put into the paragraph itself; this one contains the text of the main entry, and a \toks register called \maintoks is used to inhibit expansion of the mark text. When the paragraph is completed and broken into lines, this particular mark will immediately follow the box for the paragraph's first line, so it will be the \botmark if a page break occurs anywhere within the paragraph.

4) A similar construction is used for `\subentry`, but the mark is more complicated. The `\maintoks` register will still contain the main entry. The text for the
subsidiary entry is added using another token list register, `\subtoks`. Since `\sub` has
been defined to equal `\indent`, it will not be expanded in this `\mark`.

⨳ ⨳ The macros just defined will typeset entries that contain the necessary marks;
now we must construct an output routine that uses these marks in the desired
way, to insert new lines that say '(*continued*)' as mentioned above. Again, the reader
is advised to try solving this problem before looking at the following solution.

```
\output={\dimen0=\dp255 \normaloutput
  \expandafter\inxcheck\botmark\sub\end}
\def\inxcheck#1\sub#2\end{\def\next{#1}%
  \ifx\next\empty % do nothing if \botmark is null
  \else\noindent #1\continued % 'Main entry (continued):'
    \def\next{#2}%
    \ifx\next\empty % nothing more if \botmark has no \sub
    \else\let\sub=\continued \indent #2\fi
    \advance\dimen0 by-\prevdepth \kern\dimen0 \fi}
\def\continued{ ({\it continued}\thinspace):\endgraf}
```

This coding is a bit more subtle than usual. It assumes that `\normaloutput` takes care
of shipping out `\box255` (possibly putting it into multicolumn format) and advancing the page number; then comes new stuff, which is performed by `\inxcheck`. The
`\inxcheck` macro is invoked in an interesting way that allows `\botmark` to be separated
into its components. If `\botmark` is null, argument #1 to `\inxcheck` will be null; hence
`\next` will be found equivalent to `\empty`. (Plain TeX says '`\def\empty{}`' in order to
accommodate situations like this.) If `\botmark` doesn't contain the token `\sub`, argument #1 will be the contents of `\botmark` while #2 will be null. Otherwise, if `\botmark`
has the form α`\sub`β, argument #1 will be α and #2 will be 'β`\sub`'.

⨳ ⨳ If `\botmark` isn't null, the `\inxcheck` macro produces one or more lines of text
that will be contributed to TeX's main vertical list at the position of the page
break. And here's where the most subtle point arises: There will be interline glue at
the page break, computed on the basis of the depth of the box that preceded the break.
That depth is known to the output routine, since it's the depth of `\box255`. (The value
of `\maxdepth` was made infinite for precisely this reason.) Therefore the `\inxcheck`
macro can insert a `\kern` to compensate for the difference in depth between the old
box and the one that will be inserted before the interline glue that has already been
computed. Without this `\kern`, the spacing would be wrong. The reader should study
this example carefully, to understand the reasoning behind the `\kern` command, before
designing an output routine that inserts new boxes between random lines of output.

⨳⨳▸ **EXERCISE 23.7**
Modify this construction so that continuation lines are inserted only in the
left columns of even-numbered pages, assuming two-column format.

⨳⨳▸ **EXERCISE 23.8**
True or false: The `\inxcheck` macro in this example contributes at most two
lines of output to the main vertical list.

⟨⟩⟨⟩ When TeX sees an \end command, it terminates the job only if the main vertical list has been entirely output and if \deadcycles=0. Otherwise it inserts the equivalent of

\line{} \vfill \penalty-'10000000000

into the main vertical list, and prepares to read the '\end' token again. This has the effect of invoking the output routine repeatedly until everything has been shipped out. In particular, the last column of two-column format will not be lost.

⟨⟩⟨⟩ It is possible to devise output routines that always leave a residue on the main vertical list, yet they never allow \deadcycles to increase. In such a case TeX will never come to an end! An output routine can recognize that it is being invoked by TeX's endgame, because of the highly negative \outputpenalty caused by the special \penalty-'10000000000. At such times the output routine should modify its behavior, if necessary, so that a happy ending will ensue.

I think you will like them,
when you shall see them on a beautiful quarto page,
where a neat rivulet of text
shall meander through a meadow of margin.
'Fore Gad they will be the most elegant things of their kind!

— RICHARD BRINSLEY SHERIDAN, *The School for Scandal* (1777)

The influence of technical changes upon outputs
through variation in the general investment level β
is so small that actually it could have been neglected.

— WASSILY W. LEONTIEF, *The Structure of American Economy, 1919–1929* (1941)

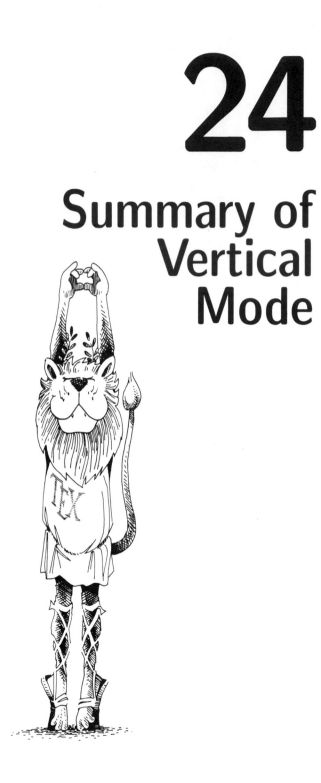

24

Summary of Vertical Mode

The whole TEX language has been presented in the previous chapters; we have finally reached the end of our journey into previously uncharted territory. Hurray! Victory! Now it is time to take a more systematic look at what we have encountered: to consider the facts in an orderly manner, rather than to mix them up with informal examples and applications as we have been doing. A child learns to speak a language before learning formal rules of grammar, but the rules of grammar come in handy later on when the child reaches adulthood. The purpose of this chapter—and of the two chapters that follow—is to present a precise and concise summary of the language that TEX understands, so that mature users will be able to communicate as effectively as possible with the machine.

We will be concerned in these chapters solely with TEX's *primitive* operations, rather than with the higher-level features of plain TEX format that most people deal with. Therefore novice users should put off reading Chapters 24–26 until they feel a need to know what goes on inside the computer. Appendix B contains a summary of plain TEX, together with a ready-reference guide to the things that most people want to know about TEX usage. The best way to get an overview of TEX from a high level is to turn to the opening pages of Appendix B.

Our purpose here, however, is to survey the low-level parts of TEX on which higher-level superstructures have been built, in order to provide a detailed reference for people who do need to know the details. The remainder of this chapter is set in small type, like that of the present paragraph, since it is analogous to material that is marked "doubly dangerous" in other chapters. Instead of using dangerous bend signs repeatedly, let us simply agree that Chapters 24–26 are dangerous by definition.

TEX actually has a few features that didn't seem to be worth mentioning in previous chapters, so they will be introduced here as part of our complete survey. If there is any disagreement between something that was said previously and something that will be said below, the facts in the present chapter and its successors should be regarded as better approximations to the truth.

We shall study TEX's digestive processes, i.e., what TEX does with the lists of tokens that arrive in its "stomach." Chapter 7 has described the process by which input files are converted to lists of tokens in TEX's "mouth," and Chapter 20 explained how expandable tokens are converted to unexpandable ones in TEX's "gullet" by a process similar to regurgitation. When unexpandable tokens finally reach TEX's gastrointestinal tract, the real activity of typesetting begins, and that is what we are going to survey in these summary chapters.

Each token that arrives in TEX's tummy is considered to be a *command* that the computer will obey. For example, the letter 'L' is a command to typeset an 'L' in the current font; '\par' tells TEX to finish a paragraph. TEX is always in one of six modes, as described in Chapter 13, and a command sometimes means different things in different modes. The present chapter is about vertical mode (and internal vertical mode, which is almost the same): We shall discuss TEX's response to every primitive command, when that command occurs in vertical mode. Chapters 25 and 26 characterize horizontal mode and math mode in a similar way, but those chapters are shorter than this one because many commands have the same behavior in all modes; the rules for such commands will not be repeated thrice, they will appear only once.

Some commands have arguments. In other words, one or more of the tokens that follow a command might be used to modify that command's behavior, and those tokens are not considered to be commands themselves. For example, when TeX processes the sequence of tokens that corresponds to '\dimen2=2.5pt', it considers only the first token '\dimen' to be a command; the next tokens are swept up as part of the operation, because TeX needs to know what \dimen register is to be set equal to what ⟨dimen⟩ value.

We shall define TeX's parts of speech by using a modified form of the grammatical notation that was introduced about 1960 by John Backus and Peter Naur for the definition of computer languages. Quantities in angle brackets will either be explained in words or they will be defined by *syntax rules* that show exactly how they are formed from other quantities. For example,

$$\langle\text{unit of measure}\rangle \longrightarrow \langle\text{optional spaces}\rangle\langle\text{internal unit}\rangle$$
$$| \ \langle\text{optional } \textbf{true}\rangle\langle\text{physical unit}\rangle$$

defines a ⟨unit of measure⟩ to be either an occurrence of ⟨optional spaces⟩ followed by an ⟨internal unit⟩, or ⟨optional **true**⟩ followed by ⟨physical unit⟩. The symbol ' ⟶ ' in a syntax rule means "is defined to be," and ' | ' means "or."

Sometimes a syntax rule is recursive, in the sense that the right-hand side of the definition involves the quantity being defined. For example, the rule

$$\langle\text{optional spaces}\rangle \longrightarrow \langle\text{empty}\rangle \ | \ \langle\text{space token}\rangle\langle\text{optional spaces}\rangle$$

defines the grammatical quantity called ⟨optional spaces⟩ to be either ⟨empty⟩, or a ⟨space token⟩ followed by ⟨optional spaces⟩. The quantity ⟨empty⟩ stands for "nothing," i.e., for no tokens at all; hence the syntax rule just given is a formalized way of saying that ⟨optional spaces⟩ stands for a sequence of zero or more spaces.

The alternatives on the right-hand side of a syntax rule need not consist entirely of quantities in angle brackets. Explicit tokens can be used as well. For example, the rule

$$\langle\text{plus or minus}\rangle \longrightarrow {+}_{12} \ | \ {-}_{12}$$

says that ⟨plus or minus⟩ stands for a character token that is either a plus sign or a minus sign, with category code 12.

We shall use a special convention for keywords, since the actual syntax of a keyword is somewhat technical. Letters in typewriter type like ' pt ' will stand for

$$\langle\text{optional spaces}\rangle\langle\text{p or P}\rangle\langle\text{t or T}\rangle,$$

where ⟨p or P⟩ denotes any non-active character token for either p or P (independent of the category code), and where ⟨t or T⟩ is similar.

When a control sequence like '\dimen' is used in the syntax rules below, it stands for any token whose current meaning is the same as the meaning that \dimen had when TeX started up. Other tokens can be given this same meaning, using \let or \futurelet, and the meaning of the control sequence \dimen itself may be redefined by the user, but the syntax rules take no note of this; they just use '\dimen' as a way of referring to a particular primitive command of TeX. (This notation is to be distinguished from ' $\boxed{\text{dimen}}$ ', which stands for the control sequence token whose actual name is dimen; see Chapter 7.)

Control sequences sometimes masquerade as characters, if their meaning has been assigned by \let or \futurelet. For example, Appendix B says

\let\bgroup={   \let\egroup=}

and these commands make \bgroup and \egroup act somewhat like left and right curly braces. Such control sequences are called "implicit characters"; they are interpreted in the same way as characters, when TeX acts on them as commands, but not always when they appear in arguments to commands. For example, the command '\let\plus=+' does not make \plus an acceptable substitute for the character token '$+_{12}$' in the syntax rule for ⟨plus or minus⟩ given above, nor does the command '\let\p=p' make \p acceptable as part of the keyword pt. When TeX's syntax allows both explicit and implicit characters, the rules below will be careful to say so, explicitly.

The quantity ⟨space token⟩, which was used in the syntax of ⟨optional spaces⟩ above, stands for an explicit or implicit space. In other words, it denotes either a character token of category 10, or a control sequence or active character whose current meaning has been made equal to such a token by \let or \futurelet.

It will be convenient to use the symbols '{', '}', and '$' to stand for any explicit or implicit character tokens of the respective categories 1, 2, and 3, whether or not the actual character codes are braces or dollar signs. Thus, for example, plain TeX's \bgroup is an example of a '{', and so are the tokens '$\{_1$' and '$(_1$'; but '$\{_{12}$' is not.

The last few paragraphs can be summarized by saying that the alternatives on the right-hand sides of TeX's formal syntax rules are made from one or more of the following things: (1) syntactic quantities like ⟨optional spaces⟩; (2) explicit character tokens like $+_{12}$; (3) keywords like pt; (4) control sequence names like \dimen; or (5) the special symbols {, }, $.

Let us begin our study of TeX's syntax by discussing the precise meanings of quantities like ⟨number⟩, ⟨dimen⟩, and ⟨glue⟩ that occur frequently as arguments to commands. The most important of these is ⟨number⟩, which specifies an integer value. Here's exactly what a ⟨number⟩ is:

⟨number⟩ ⟶ ⟨optional signs⟩⟨unsigned number⟩
⟨optional signs⟩ ⟶ ⟨optional spaces⟩
    | ⟨optional signs⟩⟨plus or minus⟩⟨optional spaces⟩
⟨unsigned number⟩ ⟶ ⟨normal integer⟩ | ⟨coerced integer⟩
⟨normal integer⟩ ⟶ ⟨internal integer⟩
    | ⟨integer constant⟩⟨one optional space⟩
    | $'_{12}$⟨octal constant⟩⟨one optional space⟩
    | $"_{12}$⟨hexadecimal constant⟩⟨one optional space⟩
    | $`_{12}$⟨character token⟩⟨one optional space⟩
⟨integer constant⟩ ⟶ ⟨digit⟩ | ⟨digit⟩⟨integer constant⟩
⟨octal constant⟩ ⟶ ⟨octal digit⟩ | ⟨octal digit⟩⟨octal constant⟩
⟨hexadecimal constant⟩ ⟶ ⟨hex digit⟩ | ⟨hex digit⟩⟨hexadecimal constant⟩
⟨octal digit⟩ ⟶ 0_{12} | 1_{12} | 2_{12} | 3_{12} | 4_{12} | 5_{12} | 6_{12} | 7_{12}
⟨digit⟩ ⟶ ⟨octal digit⟩ | 8_{12} | 9_{12}
⟨hex digit⟩ ⟶ ⟨digit⟩ | A_{11} | B_{11} | C_{11} | D_{11} | E_{11} | F_{11}
    | A_{12} | B_{12} | C_{12} | D_{12} | E_{12} | F_{12}
⟨one optional space⟩ ⟶ ⟨space token⟩ | ⟨empty⟩
⟨coerced integer⟩ ⟶ ⟨internal dimen⟩ | ⟨internal glue⟩

The value of a ⟨number⟩ is the value of the corresponding ⟨unsigned number⟩, times -1 for every minus sign in the ⟨optional signs⟩. An alphabetic constant denotes the character code in a ⟨character token⟩; TEX does not expand this token, which should either be a (character code, category code) pair, or an active character, or a control sequence whose name consists of a single character. (See Chapter 20 for a complete list of all situations in which TEX does not expand tokens.) An ⟨integer constant⟩ must not be immediately followed by a ⟨digit⟩; in other words, if several digits appear consecutively, they are all considered to be part of the same ⟨integer constant⟩. A similar remark applies to the quantities ⟨octal constant⟩ and ⟨hexadecimal constant⟩. The quantity ⟨one optional space⟩ is ⟨empty⟩ only if it has to be; i.e., TEX looks for ⟨one optional space⟩ by reading a token and backing up if a ⟨space token⟩ wasn't there.

▶ **EXERCISE 24.1**
Can you think of a reason why you might want 'A_{12}' to be a ⟨hex digit⟩ even though the letter A has category 11? (Don't worry if your answer is "no.")

The definition of ⟨number⟩ is now complete except for the three quantities called ⟨internal integer⟩, ⟨internal dimen⟩, and ⟨internal glue⟩, which will be explained later; they represent things like parameters and registers. For example, \count1 and \tolerance and \hyphenchar\tenrm are internal integers; \dimen10 and \hsize and \fontdimen6\tenrm are internal dimensions; \skip100 and \baselineskip and \lastskip are internal glue values. An internal dimension can be "coerced" to be an integer by assuming units of scaled points. For example, if \hsize=100pt and if \hsize is used in the context of a ⟨number⟩, it denotes the integer value 6553600. Similarly, an internal glue value can be coerced to be an integer by first coercing it to be a dimension (omitting the stretchability and shrinkability), then coercing that dimension.

Let's turn now to the syntax for ⟨dimen⟩, and for ⟨mudimen⟩ its cousin:

⟨dimen⟩ $\longrightarrow$ ⟨optional signs⟩⟨unsigned dimen⟩
⟨unsigned dimen⟩ $\longrightarrow$ ⟨normal dimen⟩ | ⟨coerced dimen⟩
⟨coerced dimen⟩ $\longrightarrow$ ⟨internal glue⟩
⟨normal dimen⟩ $\longrightarrow$ ⟨internal dimen⟩ | ⟨factor⟩⟨unit of measure⟩
⟨factor⟩ $\longrightarrow$ ⟨normal integer⟩ | ⟨decimal constant⟩
⟨decimal constant⟩ $\longrightarrow$.$_{12}$ | ,$_{12}$
    | ⟨digit⟩⟨decimal constant⟩
    | ⟨decimal constant⟩⟨digit⟩
⟨unit of measure⟩ $\longrightarrow$ ⟨optional spaces⟩⟨internal unit⟩
    | ⟨optional **true**⟩⟨physical unit⟩⟨one optional space⟩
⟨internal unit⟩ $\longrightarrow$ **em** ⟨one optional space⟩ | **ex** ⟨one optional space⟩
    | ⟨internal integer⟩ | ⟨internal dimen⟩ | ⟨internal glue⟩
⟨optional **true**⟩ $\longrightarrow$ **true** | ⟨empty⟩
⟨physical unit⟩ $\longrightarrow$ **pt** | **pc** | **in** | **bp** | **cm** | **mm** | **dd** | **cc** | **sp**
⟨mudimen⟩ $\longrightarrow$ ⟨optional signs⟩⟨unsigned mudimen⟩
⟨unsigned mudimen⟩ $\longrightarrow$ ⟨normal mudimen⟩ | ⟨coerced mudimen⟩
⟨coerced mudimen⟩ $\longrightarrow$ ⟨internal muglue⟩
⟨normal mudimen⟩ $\longrightarrow$ ⟨factor⟩⟨mu unit⟩
⟨mu unit⟩ $\longrightarrow$ ⟨optional spaces⟩⟨internal muglue⟩ | **mu** ⟨one optional space⟩

When '**true**' is present, the factor is multiplied by 1000 and divided by the \mag parameter. Physical units are defined in Chapter 10; mu is explained in Chapter 18.

Encouraged by our success in mastering the precise syntax of the quantities ⟨number⟩, ⟨dimen⟩, and ⟨mudimen⟩, let's tackle ⟨glue⟩ and ⟨muglue⟩:

⟨glue⟩ ⟶ ⟨optional signs⟩⟨internal glue⟩
    | ⟨dimen⟩⟨stretch⟩⟨shrink⟩
⟨stretch⟩ ⟶ `plus` ⟨dimen⟩ | `plus` ⟨fil dimen⟩ | ⟨optional spaces⟩
⟨shrink⟩ ⟶ `minus` ⟨dimen⟩ | `minus` ⟨fil dimen⟩ | ⟨optional spaces⟩
⟨fil dimen⟩ ⟶ ⟨optional signs⟩⟨factor⟩⟨fil unit⟩⟨optional spaces⟩
⟨fil unit⟩ ⟶ `fil` | ⟨fil unit⟩`l`
⟨muglue⟩ ⟶ ⟨optional signs⟩⟨internal muglue⟩
    | ⟨mudimen⟩⟨mustretch⟩⟨mushrink⟩
⟨mustretch⟩ ⟶ `plus` ⟨mudimen⟩ | `plus` ⟨fil dimen⟩ | ⟨optional spaces⟩
⟨mushrink⟩ ⟶ `minus` ⟨mudimen⟩ | `minus` ⟨fil dimen⟩ | ⟨optional spaces⟩

TeX makes a large number of internal quantities accessible so that a format designer can influence TeX's behavior. Here is a list of all these quantities, except for the parameters (which will be listed later).

⟨internal integer⟩ ⟶ ⟨integer parameter⟩ | ⟨special integer⟩ | `\lastpenalty`
    | ⟨countdef token⟩ | `\count`⟨8-bit number⟩ | ⟨codename⟩⟨8-bit number⟩
    | ⟨chardef token⟩ | ⟨mathchardef token⟩ | `\parshape` | `\inputlineno`
    | `\hyphenchar`⟨font⟩ | `\skewchar`⟨font⟩ | `\badness`
⟨special integer⟩ ⟶ `\spacefactor` | `\prevgraf`
    | `\deadcycles` | `\insertpenalties`
⟨codename⟩ ⟶ `\catcode` | `\mathcode`
    | `\lccode` | `\uccode` | `\sfcode` | `\delcode`
⟨font⟩ ⟶ ⟨fontdef token⟩ | `\font` | ⟨family member⟩
⟨family member⟩ ⟶ ⟨font range⟩⟨4-bit number⟩
⟨font range⟩ ⟶ `\textfont` | `\scriptfont` | `\scriptscriptfont`
⟨internal dimen⟩ ⟶ ⟨dimen parameter⟩ | ⟨special dimen⟩ | `\lastkern`
    | ⟨dimendef token⟩ | `\dimen`⟨8-bit number⟩
    | ⟨box dimension⟩⟨8-bit number⟩ | `\fontdimen`⟨number⟩⟨font⟩
⟨special dimen⟩ ⟶ `\prevdepth` | `\pagegoal` | `\pagetotal`
    | `\pagestretch` | `\pagefilstretch` | `\pagefillstretch`
    | `\pagefilllstretch` | `\pageshrink` | `\pagedepth`
⟨box dimension⟩ ⟶ `\ht` | `\wd` | `\dp`
⟨internal glue⟩ ⟶ ⟨glue parameter⟩ | `\lastskip`
    | ⟨skipdef token⟩ | `\skip`⟨8-bit number⟩
⟨internal muglue⟩ ⟶ ⟨muglue parameter⟩ | `\lastskip`
    | ⟨muskipdef token⟩ | `\muskip`⟨8-bit number⟩

A ⟨countdef token⟩ is a control sequence token in which the control sequence's current meaning has been defined by `\countdef`; the other quantities ⟨dimendef token⟩, etc., are defined similarly. A ⟨fontdef token⟩ refers to a definition by `\font`, or it can be the predefined font identifier called `\nullfont`. When a ⟨countdef token⟩ is used as an internal integer, it denotes the value of the corresponding `\count` register, and similar statements hold for ⟨dimendef token⟩, ⟨skipdef token⟩, ⟨muskipdef token⟩. When a ⟨chardef token⟩ or ⟨mathchardef token⟩ is used as an internal integer, it denotes the value in the `\chardef` or `\mathchardef` itself. An ⟨8-bit number⟩ is a ⟨number⟩ whose value is between 0 and $2^8 - 1 = 255$; a ⟨4-bit number⟩ is similar.

TEX allows `\spacefactor` to be an internal integer only in horizontal modes; `\prevdepth` can be an internal dimension only in vertical modes; `\lastskip` can be ⟨internal muglue⟩ only in math mode when the current math list ends with a muglue item; and `\lastskip` cannot be ⟨internal glue⟩ in such a case. When `\parshape` is used as an internal integer, it denotes only the number of controlled lines, not their sizes or indentations. The seven special dimensions `\pagetotal`, `\pagestretch`, and so on are all zero when the current page contains no boxes, and `\pagegoal` is `\maxdimen` at such times (see Chapter 15).

From the syntax rules just given, it's possible to deduce exactly what happens to spaces when they are in the vicinity of numerical quantities: TEX allows a ⟨number⟩ or ⟨dimen⟩ to be preceded by arbitrarily many spaces, and to be followed by at most one space; however, there is no optional space after a ⟨number⟩ or ⟨dimen⟩ that ends with an unexpandable control sequence. For example, if TEX sees '`\space\space24\space\space`' when it is looking for a ⟨number⟩, it gobbles up the first three spaces, but the fourth one survives; similarly, one space remains when '`24pt\space\space`' and '`\dimen24\space\space`' and '`\pagegoal\space`' are treated as ⟨dimen⟩ values.

▶ **EXERCISE 24.2**
Is '`24\space\space pt`' a legal ⟨dimen⟩?

▶ **EXERCISE 24.3**
Is there any difference between '`+\baselineskip`', '`- -\baselineskip`', and '`1\baselineskip`', when TEX reads them as ⟨glue⟩?

▶ **EXERCISE 24.4**
What ⟨glue⟩ results from `"DD DDPLUS2,5 \spacefactor\space`, assuming the conventions of plain TEX, when `\spacefactor` equals 1000?

Let's turn now to TEX's parameters, which the previous chapters have introduced one at a time; it will be convenient to assemble them all together. An ⟨integer parameter⟩ is one of the following tokens:

`\pretolerance`   (badness tolerance before hyphenation)
`\tolerance`   (badness tolerance after hyphenation)
`\hbadness`   (badness above which bad hboxes will be shown)
`\vbadness`   (badness above which bad vboxes will be shown)
`\linepenalty`   (amount added to badness of every line in a paragraph)
`\hyphenpenalty`   (penalty for line break after discretionary hyphen)
`\exhyphenpenalty`   (penalty for line break after explicit hyphen)
`\binoppenalty`   (penalty for line break after binary operation)
`\relpenalty`   (penalty for line break after math relation)
`\clubpenalty`   (penalty for creating a club line at bottom of page)
`\widowpenalty`   (penalty for creating a widow line at top of page)
`\displaywidowpenalty`   (ditto, before a display)
`\brokenpenalty`   (penalty for page break after a hyphenated line)
`\predisplaypenalty`   (penalty for page break just before a display)
`\postdisplaypenalty`   (penalty for page break just after a display)
`\interlinepenalty`   (additional penalty for page break between lines)
`\floatingpenalty`   (penalty for insertions that are split)

\outputpenalty   (penalty at the current page break)
\doublehyphendemerits   (demerits for consecutive broken lines)
\finalhyphendemerits   (demerits for a penultimate broken line)
\adjdemerits   (demerits for adjacent incompatible lines)
\looseness   (change to the number of lines in a paragraph)
\pausing   (positive if pausing after each line is read from a file)
\holdinginserts   (positive if insertions remain dormant in output box)
\tracingonline   (positive if showing diagnostic info on the terminal)
\tracingmacros   (positive if showing macros as they are expanded)
\tracingstats   (positive if showing statistics about memory usage)
\tracingparagraphs   (positive if showing line-break calculations)
\tracingpages   (positive if showing page-break calculations)
\tracingoutput   (positive if showing boxes that are shipped out)
\tracinglostchars   (positive if showing characters not in the font)
\tracingcommands   (positive if showing commands before they are executed)
\tracingrestores   (positive if showing deassignments when groups end)
\language   (the current set of hyphenation rules)
\uchyph   (positive if hyphenating words beginning with capital letters)
\lefthyphenmin   (smallest fragment at beginning of hyphenated word)
\righthyphenmin   (smallest fragment at end of hyphenated word)
\globaldefs   (nonzero if overriding \global specifications)
\defaulthyphenchar   (\hyphenchar value when a font is loaded)
\defaultskewchar   (\skewchar value when a font is loaded)
\escapechar   (escape character in the output of control sequence tokens)
\endlinechar   (character placed at the right end of an input line)
\newlinechar   (character that starts a new output line)
\maxdeadcycles   (upper bound on \deadcycles)
\hangafter   (hanging indentation changes after this many lines)
\fam   (the current family number)
\mag   (magnification ratio, times 1000)
\delimiterfactor   (ratio for variable delimiters, times 1000)
\time   (current time of day in minutes since midnight)
\day   (current day of the month)
\month   (current month of the year)
\year   (current year of our Lord)
\showboxbreadth   (maximum items per level when boxes are shown)
\showboxdepth   (maximum level when boxes are shown)
\errorcontextlines   (maximum extra context shown when errors occur)

The first few of these parameters have values in units of "badness" and "penalties" that affect line breaking and page breaking. Then come demerit-oriented parameters; demerits are essentially given in units of "badness squared," so those parameters tend to have larger values. By contrast, the next few parameters (\looseness, \pausing, etc.) generally have quite small values (either −1 or 0 or 1 or 2). Miscellaneous parameters complete the set. TEX computes the date and time when it begins a job, if the operating system provides such information; but afterwards the clock does not keep ticking: The user can change \time just like any ordinary parameter. Chapter 10 points out that \mag must not be changed after TEX is committed to a particular magnification.

A ⟨dimen parameter⟩ is one of the following:

> \hfuzz   (maximum overrun before overfull hbox messages occur)
> \vfuzz   (maximum overrun before overfull vbox messages occur)
> \overfullrule   (width of rules appended to overfull boxes)
> \emergencystretch   (reduces badnesses on final pass of line-breaking)
> \hsize   (line width in horizontal mode)
> \vsize   (page height in vertical mode)
> \maxdepth   (maximum depth of boxes on main pages)
> \splitmaxdepth   (maximum depth of boxes on split pages)
> \boxmaxdepth   (maximum depth of boxes on explicit pages)
> \lineskiplimit   (threshold where \baselineskip changes to \lineskip)
> \delimitershortfall   (maximum space not covered by a delimiter)
> \nulldelimiterspace   (width of a null delimiter)
> \scriptspace   (extra space after subscript or superscript)
> \mathsurround   (kerning before and after math in text)
> \predisplaysize   (length of text preceding a display)
> \displaywidth   (length of line for displayed equation)
> \displayindent   (indentation of line for displayed equation)
> \parindent   (width of \indent)
> \hangindent   (amount of hanging indentation)
> \hoffset   (horizontal offset in \shipout)
> \voffset   (vertical offset in \shipout)

And the possibilities for ⟨glue parameter⟩ are:

> \baselineskip   (desired glue between baselines)
> \lineskip   (interline glue if \baselineskip isn't feasible)
> \parskip   (extra glue just above paragraphs)
> \abovedisplayskip   (extra glue just above displays)
> \abovedisplayshortskip   (ditto, following short lines)
> \belowdisplayskip   (extra glue just below displays)
> \belowdisplayshortskip   (ditto, following short lines)
> \leftskip   (glue at left of justified lines)
> \rightskip   (glue at right of justified lines)
> \topskip   (glue at top of main pages)
> \splittopskip   (glue at top of split pages)
> \tabskip   (glue between aligned entries)
> \spaceskip   (glue between words, if nonzero)
> \xspaceskip   (glue between sentences, if nonzero)
> \parfillskip   (additional \rightskip at end of paragraphs)

Finally, there are three permissible ⟨muglue parameter⟩ tokens:

> \thinmuskip   (thin space in math formulas)
> \medmuskip   (medium space in math formulas)
> \thickmuskip   (thick space in math formulas)

All of these quantities are explained in more detail somewhere else in this book, and you can use Appendix I to find out where.

TEX also has parameters that are token lists. Such parameters do not enter into the definitions of ⟨number⟩ and such things, but we might as well list them now so that our tabulation of parameters is complete. A ⟨token parameter⟩ is any of:

\output   (the user's output routine)
\everypar   (tokens to insert when a paragraph begins)
\everymath   (tokens to insert when math in text begins)
\everydisplay   (tokens to insert when display math begins)
\everyhbox   (tokens to insert when an hbox begins)
\everyvbox   (tokens to insert when a vbox begins)
\everyjob   (tokens to insert when the job begins)
\everycr   (tokens to insert after every \cr or nonredundant \crcr)
\errhelp   (tokens that supplement an \errmessage)

That makes a total of 103 parameters of all five kinds.

▷ **EXERCISE 24.5**
Explain how \everyjob can be non-null when a job begins.

It's time now to return to our original goal, namely to study the commands that are obeyed by TEX's digestive organs. Many commands are carried out in the same way regardless of the current mode. The most important commands of this type are called *assignments*, since they assign new values to the meaning of control sequences or to TEX's internal quantities. For example, '\def\a{a}' and '\parshape=1 5pt 100pt' and '\advance\count20 by-1' and '\font\ff = cmff at 20pt' are all assignments, and they all have the same effect in all modes. Assignment commands often include an = sign, but in all cases this sign is optional; you can leave it out if you don't mind the fact that the resulting TEX code might not look quite like an assignment.

⟨assignment⟩ ⟶ ⟨non-macro assignment⟩ | ⟨macro assignment⟩
⟨non-macro assignment⟩ ⟶ ⟨simple assignment⟩
        | \global⟨non-macro assignment⟩
⟨macro assignment⟩ ⟶ ⟨definition⟩ | ⟨prefix⟩⟨macro assignment⟩
⟨prefix⟩ ⟶ \global | \long | \outer
⟨equals⟩ ⟶ ⟨optional spaces⟩ | ⟨optional spaces⟩ =₁₂

This syntax shows that every assignment can be prefixed by \global, but only macro-definition assignments are allowed to be prefixed by \long or \outer. Incidentally, if the \globaldefs parameter is positive at the time of the assignment, a prefix of \global is automatically implied; but if \globaldefs is negative at the time of the assignment, a prefix of \global is ignored. If \globaldefs is zero (which it usually is), the appearance or nonappearance of \global determines whether or not a global assignment is made.

⟨definition⟩ ⟶ ⟨def⟩⟨control sequence⟩⟨definition text⟩
⟨def⟩ ⟶ \def | \gdef | \edef | \xdef
⟨definition text⟩ ⟶ ⟨parameter text⟩⟨left brace⟩⟨balanced text⟩⟨right brace⟩

Here ⟨control sequence⟩ denotes a token that is either a control sequence or an active character; ⟨left brace⟩ and ⟨right brace⟩ are explicit character tokens whose category codes are respectively of types 1 and 2. The ⟨parameter text⟩ contains no ⟨left brace⟩ or ⟨right brace⟩ tokens, and it obeys the rules of Chapter 20. All occurrences of

⟨left brace⟩ and ⟨right brace⟩ tokens within the ⟨balanced text⟩ must be properly nested like parentheses. A \gdef command is equivalent to \global\def, and \xdef is equivalent to \global\edef. TeX reads the ⟨control sequence⟩ and ⟨parameter text⟩ tokens and the opening ⟨left brace⟩ without expanding them; it expands the ⟨balanced text⟩ ⟨right brace⟩ tokens only in the case of \edef and \xdef.

Several commands that we will study below have a syntax somewhat like that of a definition, but the ⟨parameter text⟩ is replaced by an arbitrary sequence of spaces and '\relax' commands, and the ⟨left brace⟩ token can be implicit:

⟨filler⟩ ⟶ ⟨optional spaces⟩ | ⟨filler⟩\relax⟨optional spaces⟩
⟨general text⟩ ⟶ ⟨filler⟩{⟨balanced text⟩⟨right brace⟩

The main purpose of a ⟨general text⟩ is to specify the ⟨balanced text⟩ inside.

Many different kinds of assignments are possible, but they fall into comparatively few patterns, as indicated by the following syntax rules:

⟨simple assignment⟩ ⟶ ⟨variable assignment⟩ | ⟨arithmetic⟩
   | ⟨code assignment⟩ | ⟨let assignment⟩ | ⟨shorthand definition⟩
   | ⟨fontdef token⟩ | ⟨family assignment⟩ | ⟨shape assignment⟩
   | \read⟨number⟩ to ⟨optional spaces⟩⟨control sequence⟩
   | \setbox⟨8-bit number⟩⟨equals⟩⟨filler⟩⟨box⟩
   | \font⟨control sequence⟩⟨equals⟩⟨file name⟩⟨at clause⟩
   | ⟨global assignment⟩
⟨variable assignment⟩ ⟶ ⟨integer variable⟩⟨equals⟩⟨number⟩
   | ⟨dimen variable⟩⟨equals⟩⟨dimen⟩
   | ⟨glue variable⟩⟨equals⟩⟨glue⟩
   | ⟨muglue variable⟩⟨equals⟩⟨muglue⟩
   | ⟨token variable⟩⟨equals⟩⟨general text⟩
   | ⟨token variable⟩⟨equals⟩⟨filler⟩⟨token variable⟩
⟨arithmetic⟩ ⟶ \advance⟨integer variable⟩⟨optional by⟩⟨number⟩
   | \advance⟨dimen variable⟩⟨optional by⟩⟨dimen⟩
   | \advance⟨glue variable⟩⟨optional by⟩⟨glue⟩
   | \advance⟨muglue variable⟩⟨optional by⟩⟨muglue⟩
   | \multiply⟨numeric variable⟩⟨optional by⟩⟨number⟩
   | \divide⟨numeric variable⟩⟨optional by⟩⟨number⟩
⟨optional by⟩ ⟶ by | ⟨optional spaces⟩
⟨integer variable⟩ ⟶ ⟨integer parameter⟩ | ⟨countdef token⟩
   | \count⟨8-bit number⟩
⟨dimen variable⟩ ⟶ ⟨dimen parameter⟩ | ⟨dimendef token⟩
   | \dimen⟨8-bit number⟩
⟨glue variable⟩ ⟶ ⟨glue parameter⟩ | ⟨skipdef token⟩
   | \skip⟨8-bit number⟩
⟨muglue variable⟩ ⟶ ⟨muglue parameter⟩ | ⟨muskipdef token⟩
   | \muskip⟨8-bit number⟩
⟨token variable⟩ ⟶ ⟨token parameter⟩ | ⟨toksdef token⟩
   | \toks⟨8-bit number⟩
⟨numeric variable⟩ ⟶ ⟨integer variable⟩ | ⟨dimen variable⟩
   | ⟨glue variable⟩ | ⟨muglue variable⟩

⟨code assignment⟩ ⟶ ⟨code name⟩⟨8-bit number⟩⟨equals⟩⟨number⟩
⟨let assignment⟩ ⟶ \futurelet⟨control sequence⟩⟨token⟩⟨token⟩
  | \let⟨control sequence⟩⟨equals⟩⟨one optional space⟩⟨token⟩
⟨shorthand definition⟩ ⟶ \chardef⟨control sequence⟩⟨equals⟩⟨8-bit number⟩
  | \mathchardef⟨control sequence⟩⟨equals⟩⟨15-bit number⟩
  | ⟨registerdef⟩⟨control sequence⟩⟨equals⟩⟨8-bit number⟩
⟨registerdef⟩ ⟶ \countdef | \dimendef | \skipdef | \muskipdef | \toksdef
⟨family assignment⟩ ⟶ ⟨family member⟩⟨equals⟩⟨font⟩
⟨shape assignment⟩ ⟶ \parshape⟨equals⟩⟨number⟩⟨shape dimensions⟩

The ⟨number⟩ at the end of a ⟨code assignment⟩ must not be negative, except in the case that a \delcode is being assigned. Furthermore, that ⟨number⟩ should be at most 15 for \catcode, 32768 for \mathcode, 255 for \lccode or \uccode, 32767 for \sfcode, and $2^{24} - 1$ for \delcode. In a ⟨shape assignment⟩ for which the ⟨number⟩ is n, the ⟨shape dimensions⟩ are ⟨empty⟩ if $n \leq 0$, otherwise they consist of $2n$ consecutive occurrences of ⟨dimen⟩. TeX does not expand tokens when it scans the arguments of \let and \futurelet.

▷ **EXERCISE 24.6**
We discussed the distinction between explicit and implicit character tokens earlier in this chapter. Explain how you can make the control sequence \cs into an implicit space, using (a) \futurelet, (b) \let.

All of the assignments mentioned so far will obey TeX's grouping structure; i.e., the changed quantities will be restored to their former values when the current group ends, unless the change was global. The remaining assignments are different, since they affect TeX's global font tables or hyphenation tables, or they affect certain control variables of such an intimate nature that grouping would be inappropriate. In all of the following cases, the presence or absence of \global as a prefix has no effect.

⟨global assignment⟩ ⟶ ⟨font assignment⟩
  | ⟨hyphenation assignment⟩
  | ⟨box size assignment⟩
  | ⟨interaction mode assignment⟩
  | ⟨intimate assignment⟩
⟨font assignment⟩ ⟶ \fontdimen⟨number⟩⟨font⟩⟨equals⟩⟨dimen⟩
  | \hyphenchar⟨font⟩⟨equals⟩⟨number⟩
  | \skewchar⟨font⟩⟨equals⟩⟨number⟩
⟨at clause⟩ ⟶ at ⟨dimen⟩ | scaled ⟨number⟩ | ⟨optional spaces⟩
⟨hyphenation assignment⟩ ⟶ \hyphenation⟨general text⟩
  | \patterns⟨general text⟩
⟨box size assignment⟩ ⟶ ⟨box dimension⟩⟨8-bit number⟩⟨equals⟩⟨dimen⟩
⟨interaction mode assignment⟩ ⟶ \errorstopmode | \scrollmode
  | \nonstopmode | \batchmode
⟨intimate assignment⟩ ⟶ ⟨special integer⟩⟨equals⟩⟨number⟩
  | ⟨special dimen⟩⟨equals⟩⟨dimen⟩

When a \fontdimen value is assigned, the ⟨number⟩ must be positive and not greater than the number of parameters in the font's metric information file, unless that font information has just been loaded into TeX's memory; in the latter case, you are allowed to increase the number of parameters (see Appendix F). The ⟨special integer⟩ and ⟨special dimen⟩ quantities were listed above when we discussed internal integers and dimensions. When \prevgraf is set to a ⟨number⟩, the number must not be negative.

The syntax for ⟨file name⟩ is not standard in TeX, because different operating systems have different conventions. You should ask your local system wizards for details on just how they have decided to implement file names. However, the following principles should hold universally: A ⟨file name⟩ should consist of ⟨optional spaces⟩ followed by explicit character tokens (after expansion). A sequence of six or fewer ordinary letters and/or digits followed by a space should be a file name that works in essentially the same way on all installations of TeX. Uppercase letters are not considered equivalent to their lowercase counterparts in file names; for example, if you refer to fonts cmr10 and CMR10, TeX will not notice any similarity between them, although it might input the same font metric file for both fonts.

TeX takes precautions so that constructions like '\chardef\cs=10\cs' and '\font\cs=name\cs' won't expand the second \cs until the assignments are done.

Our discussion of assignments is complete except that the \setbox assignment involves a quantity called ⟨box⟩ that has not yet been defined. Here is its syntax:

$$\langle\text{box}\rangle \longrightarrow \text{\textbackslash box}\langle\text{8-bit number}\rangle \mid \text{\textbackslash copy}\langle\text{8-bit number}\rangle$$
$$\mid \text{\textbackslash lastbox} \mid \text{\textbackslash vsplit}\langle\text{8-bit number}\rangle \text{ to }\langle\text{dimen}\rangle$$
$$\mid \text{\textbackslash hbox}\langle\text{box specification}\rangle\{\langle\text{horizontal mode material}\rangle\}$$
$$\mid \text{\textbackslash vbox}\langle\text{box specification}\rangle\{\langle\text{vertical mode material}\rangle\}$$
$$\mid \text{\textbackslash vtop}\langle\text{box specification}\rangle\{\langle\text{vertical mode material}\rangle\}$$
$$\langle\text{box specification}\rangle \longrightarrow \text{to }\langle\text{dimen}\rangle\langle\text{filler}\rangle$$
$$\mid \text{spread }\langle\text{dimen}\rangle\langle\text{filler}\rangle \mid \langle\text{filler}\rangle$$

The \lastbox operation is not permitted in math modes, nor is it allowed in vertical mode when the main vertical list has been entirely contributed to the current page. But it is allowed in horizontal modes and in internal vertical mode; in such modes it refers to (and removes) the last item of the current list, provided that the last item is an hbox or vbox.

The three last alternatives for a ⟨box⟩ present us with a new situation: The ⟨horizontal mode material⟩ in an \hbox and the ⟨vertical mode material⟩ in a \vbox can't simply be swallowed up in one command like an ⟨8-bit number⟩ or a ⟨dimen⟩; thousands of commands may have to be executed before that box is constructed and before the \setbox command can be completed.

Here's what really happens: A command like

\setbox⟨number⟩=\hbox to⟨dimen⟩{⟨horizontal mode material⟩}

causes TeX to evaluate the ⟨number⟩ and the ⟨dimen⟩, and to put those values on a "stack" for safe keeping. Then TeX reads the '{' (which stands for an explicit or implicit begin-group character, as explained earlier), and this initiates a new level of grouping. At this point TeX enters restricted horizontal mode and proceeds to execute commands in that mode. An arbitrarily complex box can now be constructed; the fact that this box is eventually destined for a \setbox command has no effect on TeX's behavior while the box is being built. Eventually, when the matching '}' appears, TeX restores values that were changed by assignments in the group just ended; then it packages the hbox (using the size that was saved on the stack), and completes the \setbox command, returning to the mode it was in at the time of the \setbox.

Let us now consider other commands that, like assignments, are obeyed in basically the same way regardless of TEX's current mode.

■ \relax. This is an easy one: TEX does nothing.

■ }. This one is harder, because it depends on the current group. TEX should now be working on a group that began with {; and it knows why it started that group. So it does the appropriate finishing actions, undoes the effects of non-global assignments, and leaves the group. At this point TEX might leave its current mode and return to a mode that was previously in effect.

■ \begingroup. When TEX sees this command, it enters a group that must be terminated by \endgroup, not by }. The mode doesn't change.

■ \endgroup. TEX should currently be processing a group that began with \begingroup. Quantities that were changed by non-global assignments in that group are restored to their former values. TEX leaves the group, but stays in the same mode.

■ \show ⟨token⟩, \showbox ⟨8-bit number⟩, \showlists, \showthe⟨internal quantity⟩. These commands are intended to help you figure out what TEX thinks it is doing. The tokens following \showthe should be anything that can follow \the, as explained in Chapter 20.

▷ **EXERCISE 24.7**
Review the rules for what can follow \the in Chapter 20, and construct a formal syntax that defines ⟨internal quantity⟩ in a way that fits with the other syntax rules we have been discussing.

■ \shipout⟨box⟩. After the ⟨box⟩ is formed—possibly by constructing it explicitly and changing modes during the construction, as explained for \hbox earlier—its contents are sent to the dvi file (see Chapter 23).

■ \ignorespaces ⟨optional spaces⟩. TEX reads (and expands) tokens, doing nothing until reaching one that is not a ⟨space token⟩.

■ \afterassignment⟨token⟩. The ⟨token⟩ is saved in a special place; it will be inserted back into the input just after the next assignment command has been performed. An assignment need not follow immediately; if another \afterassignment is performed before the next assignment, the second one overrides the first. If the next assignment is a \setbox, and if the assigned ⟨box⟩ is \hbox or \vbox or \vtop, the ⟨token⟩ will be inserted just after the { in the box construction, not after the }; it will also come just before any tokens inserted by \everyhbox or \everyvbox.

■ \aftergroup⟨token⟩. The ⟨token⟩ is saved on TEX's stack; it will be inserted back into the input just after the current group has been completed and its local assignments have been undone. If several \aftergroup commands occur in the same group, the corresponding commands will be scanned in the same order; for example, '{\aftergroup\a\aftergroup\b}' yields '\a\b'.

■ \uppercase⟨general text⟩, \lowercase⟨general text⟩. The ⟨balanced text⟩ in the general text is converted to uppercase form or to lowercase form using the \uccode or \lccode table, as explained in Chapter 7; no expansion is done. Then TEX will read that ⟨balanced text⟩ again.

■ \message⟨general text⟩, \errmessage⟨general text⟩. The balanced text (with expansion) is written on the user's terminal, using the format of error messages in the case of `\errmessage`. In the latter case the `\errhelp` tokens will be shown if they are nonempty and if the user asks for help.

- `\openin`⟨4-bit number⟩⟨equals⟩⟨filename⟩, `\closein`⟨4-bit number⟩. These commands open or close the specified input stream, for use in `\read` assignments as explained in Chapter 20.

- `\immediate\openout`⟨4-bit number⟩⟨equals⟩⟨filename⟩, `\immediate\closeout`⟨4-bit number⟩. The specified output stream is opened or closed, for use in `\write` commands, as explained in Chapter 21.

- `\immediate\write`⟨number⟩⟨general text⟩. The balanced text is written on the file that corresponds to the specified stream number, provided that such a file is open. Otherwise it is written on the user's terminal and on the log file. (See Chapter 21; the terminal is omitted if the ⟨number⟩ is negative.)

That completes the list of mode-independent commands, i.e., the commands that do not directly affect the lists that TEX is building. When TEX is in vertical mode or internal vertical mode, it is constructing a vertical list; when TEX is in horizontal mode or restricted horizontal mode, it is constructing a horizontal list; when TEX is in math mode or display math mode, it is constructing—guess what—a math list. In each of these cases we can speak of the "current list"; and there are some commands that operate in essentially the same way, regardless of the mode, except that they deal with different sorts of lists:

- `\openout`⟨4-bit number⟩⟨equals⟩⟨filename⟩, `\closeout`⟨4-bit number⟩, `\write`⟨number⟩⟨general text⟩. These commands are recorded into a "whatsit" item, which is appended to the current list. The command will be performed later, during any `\shipout` that applies to this list, unless the list is part of a box inside leaders.

- `\special`⟨general text⟩. The balanced text is expanded and put into a "whatsit" item, which is appended to the current list. The text will eventually appear in the dvi file as an instruction to subsequent software (see Chapter 21).

- `\penalty`⟨number⟩. A penalty item carrying the specified number is appended to the current list. In vertical mode, TEX also exercises the page builder (see below).

- `\kern`⟨dimen⟩, `\mkern`⟨mudimen⟩. A kern item carrying the specified dimension is appended to the current list. In vertical modes this denotes a vertical space; otherwise it denotes a horizontal space. An `\mkern` is allowed only in math modes.

- `\unpenalty`, `\unkern`, `\unskip`. If the last item on the current list is respectively of type penalty, kern, or glue (possibly including leaders), that item is removed from the list. However, like `\lastbox`, these commands are not permitted in vertical mode if the main vertical list-so-far has been entirely contributed to the current page, since TEX never removes items from the current page.

- `\mark`⟨general text⟩. The balanced text is expanded and put into a mark item, which is appended to the current list. The text may eventually become the replacement text for `\topmark`, `\firstmark`, `\botmark`, `\splitfirstmark`, and/or `\splitbotmark`, if this mark item ever gets into a vertical list. (Mark items can appear in horizontal lists and math lists, but they have no effect until they "migrate" out of their list. The migration process is discussed below and in Chapter 25.)

- `\insert`⟨8-bit number⟩⟨filler⟩{⟨vertical mode material⟩}; the ⟨8-bit number⟩ must not be 255. The '{' causes TEX to enter internal vertical mode and a new level of grouping. When the matching '}' is sensed, the vertical list is put into an insertion item that is appended to the current list using the values of \splittopskip, \splitmaxdepth, and \floatingpenalty that were current in the group just ended. (See Chapter 15.) This insertion item leads ultimately to a page insertion only if it appears in TEX's main vertical list, so it will have to "migrate" there if it starts out in a horizontal list or a math list. TEX also exercises the page builder (see below), after an \insert has been appended in vertical mode.

■ \vadjust⟨filler⟩{⟨vertical mode material⟩}. This is similar to \insert; the constructed vertical list goes into an adjustment item that is appended to the current list. However, \vadjust is not allowed in vertical modes. When an adjustment item migrates from a horizontal list to a vertical list, the vertical list inside the adjustment item is "unwrapped" and put directly into the enclosing list.

*   *   *

Almost everything we have discussed so far in this chapter could equally well have appeared in a chapter entitled "Summary of Horizontal Mode" or a chapter entitled "Summary of Math Mode," because TEX treats all of the commands considered so far in essentially the same way regardless of the current mode. Chapters 25 and 26 are going to be a lot shorter than the present one, since it will be unnecessary to repeat all of the mode-independent rules.

But now we come to commands that are mode-dependent; we shall conclude this chapter by discussing what TEX does with the remaining commands, when in vertical mode or internal vertical mode.

One of the things characteristic of vertical mode is the page-building operation described in Chapter 15. TEX periodically takes material that has been put on the main vertical list and moves it from the "contribution list" to the "current page." At such times the output routine might be invoked. We shall say that TEX *exercises the page builder* whenever it tries to empty the current contribution list. The concept of contribution list exists only in the outermost vertical mode, so nothing happens when TEX exercises the page builder in internal vertical mode.

Another thing characteristic of vertical modes is the interline glue that is inserted before boxes, based on the values of \prevdepth and \baselineskip and \lineskip and \lineskiplimit as explained in Chapter 12. If a command changes \prevdepth, that fact is specifically mentioned below. The \prevdepth is initially set to −1000 pt, a special value that inhibits interline glue, whenever TEX begins to form a vertical list, except in the case of \halign and \noalign when the interline glue conventions of the outer list continue inside the inner one.

■ \vskip⟨glue⟩, \vfil, \vfill, \vss, \vfilneg. A glue item is appended to the current vertical list.

■ ⟨leaders⟩⟨box or rule⟩⟨vertical skip⟩. Here ⟨vertical skip⟩ refers to one of the five glue-appending commands just mentioned. The formal syntax for ⟨leaders⟩ and for ⟨box or rule⟩ is

> ⟨leaders⟩ ⟶ \leaders | \cleaders | \xleaders
> ⟨box or rule⟩ ⟶ ⟨box⟩ | ⟨vertical rule⟩ | ⟨horizontal rule⟩
> ⟨vertical rule⟩ ⟶ \vrule⟨rule specification⟩
> ⟨horizontal rule⟩ ⟶ \hrule⟨rule specification⟩

$$\langle\text{rule specification}\rangle \longrightarrow \langle\text{optional spaces}\rangle \mid \langle\text{rule dimension}\rangle\langle\text{rule specification}\rangle$$
$$\langle\text{rule dimension}\rangle \longrightarrow \texttt{width}\,\langle\text{dimen}\rangle \mid \texttt{height}\,\langle\text{dimen}\rangle \mid \texttt{depth}\,\langle\text{dimen}\rangle$$

A glue item that produces leaders is appended to the current list.

■ ⟨space token⟩. Spaces have no effect in vertical modes.

■ ⟨box⟩. The box is constructed, and if the result is void nothing happens. Otherwise the current vertical list receives (1) interline glue, followed by (2) the new box, followed by (3) vertical material that migrates out of the new box (if the ⟨box⟩ was an \hbox command). Then \prevdepth is set to the new box's depth, and TEX exercises the page builder.

■ \moveleft⟨dimen⟩⟨box⟩, \moveright⟨dimen⟩⟨box⟩. This acts exactly like an ordinary ⟨box⟩ command, but the new box that is appended to the vertical list is also shifted left or right by the specified amount.

■ \unvbox⟨8-bit number⟩, \unvcopy⟨8-bit number⟩. If the specified box register is void, nothing happens. Otherwise that register must contain a vbox. The vertical list inside that box is appended to the current vertical list, without changing it in any way. The value of \prevdepth is not affected. The box register becomes void after \unvbox, but it remains unchanged by \unvcopy.

■ ⟨horizontal rule⟩. The specified rule is appended to the current list. Then \prevdepth is set to −1000 pt; this will prohibit interline glue when the next box is appended to the list.

■ \halign⟨box specification⟩{⟨alignment material⟩}. The ⟨alignment material⟩ consists of a preamble followed by zero or more lines to be aligned; see Chapter 22. TEX enters a new level of grouping, represented by the '{' and '}', within which changes to \tabskip will be confined. The alignment material can also contain optional occurrences of '\noalign⟨filler⟩{⟨vertical mode material⟩}' between lines; this adds another level of grouping. TEX operates in internal vertical mode while it works on the material in \noalign groups and when it appends lines of the alignment; the resulting internal vertical list will be appended to the enclosing vertical list after the alignment is completed, and the page builder will be exercised. The value of \prevdepth at the time of the \halign is used at the beginning of the internal vertical list, and the final value of \prevdepth is carried to the enclosing vertical list when the alignment is completed, so that the interline glue is calculated properly at the beginning and end of the alignment. TEX also enters an additional level of grouping when it works on each individual entry of the alignment, during which time it acts in restricted horizontal mode; the individual entries will be hboxed as part of the final alignment, and their vertical material will migrate to the enclosing vertical list. The commands \noalign, \omit, \span, \cr, \crcr, and & (where & denotes an explicit or implicit character of category 4) are intercepted by the alignment process, enroute to TEX's stomach, so they will not appear as commands in the stomach unless TEX has lost track of what alignment they belong to.

■ \indent. The \parskip glue is appended to the current list, unless TEX is in internal vertical mode and the current list is empty. Then TEX enters unrestricted horizontal mode, starting the horizontal list with an empty hbox whose width is \parindent. The \everypar tokens are inserted into TEX's input. The page builder is exercised. When the paragraph is eventually completed, horizontal mode will come to an end as described in Chapter 25.

■ \noindent. This is exactly like \indent, except that TeX starts out in horizontal mode with an empty list instead of with an indentation.

■ \par. The primitive \par command has no effect when TeX is in vertical mode, except that the page builder is exercised in case something is present on the contribution list, and the paragraph shape parameters are cleared.

■ {. A character token of category 1, or a control sequence like \bgroup that has been \let equal to such a character token, causes TeX to start a new level of grouping. When such a group ends—with '}'—TeX will undo the effects of non-global assignments without leaving whatever mode it is in at that time.

■ Some commands are incompatible with vertical mode because they are intrinsically horizontal. When the following commands appear in vertical modes they cause TeX to begin a new paragraph:

$$\langle\text{horizontal command}\rangle \longrightarrow \langle\text{letter}\rangle \mid \langle\text{otherchar}\rangle \mid \text{\char} \mid \langle\text{chardef token}\rangle$$
$$\mid \text{\noboundary} \mid \text{\unhbox} \mid \text{\unhcopy} \mid \text{\valign} \mid \text{\vrule}$$
$$\mid \text{\hskip} \mid \text{\hfil} \mid \text{\hfill} \mid \text{\hss} \mid \text{\hfilneg}$$
$$\mid \text{\accent} \mid \text{\discretionary} \mid \text{\-} \mid \text{\}_\sqcup \mid \text{\$}$$

Here $\langle\text{letter}\rangle$ and $\langle\text{otherchar}\rangle$ stand for explicit or implicit character tokens of categories 11 and 12. If any of these tokens occurs as a command in vertical mode or internal vertical mode, TeX automatically performs an \indent command as explained above. This leads into horizontal mode with the \everypar tokens in the input, after which TeX will see the $\langle\text{horizontal command}\rangle$ again.

■ \end. This command is not allowed in internal vertical mode. In regular vertical mode it terminates TeX if the main vertical list is empty and \deadcycles=0. Otherwise TeX backs up the \end command so that it can be read again; then it exercises the page builder, after appending a box/glue/penalty combination that will force the output routine to act. (See the end of Chapter 23.)

■ \dump. (Allowed only in INITEX, not in production versions of TeX.) This command is treated exactly like \end, but it must not appear inside a group. It outputs a format file that can be loaded into TeX's memory at comparatively high speed to restore the current status.

■ None of the above: If any other primitive command of TeX occurs in vertical mode, an error message will be given, and TeX will try to recover in a reasonable way. For example, if a superscript or subscript symbol appears, or if any other inherently mathematical command is given, TeX will try to insert a '$' (which will start a paragraph and enter math mode). On the other hand if a totally misplaced token like \endcsname or \omit or \eqno or # appears in vertical mode, TeX will simply ignore it, after reporting the error. You might enjoy trying to type some really stupid input, just to see what happens. (Say '\tracingall' first, as explained in Chapter 27, in order to get maximum information.)

> *The first and most striking feature is the Verticality of composition,*
> *as opposed to the Horizontality of all anterior structural modes.*
> — COCKBURN MUIR, *Pagan or Christian?* (1860)

> *Sometimes when I have finished a book I give a summary of the whole of it.*
> — ROBERT WILLIAM DALE, *Nine Lectures on Preaching* (1878)

25
Summary of Horizontal Mode

Continuing the survey that was begun in Chapter 24, let us investigate exactly what TeX's digestive processes can do, when TeX is building lists in horizontal mode or in restricted horizontal mode.

$$* \qquad * \qquad *$$

Three asterisks, just like those that appear here, can be found near the end of Chapter 24. Everything preceding the three asterisks in that chapter applies to horizontal mode as well as to vertical mode, so we need not repeat all those rules. In particular, Chapter 24 explains assignment commands, and it tells how kerns, penalties, marks, insertions, adjustments, and "whatsits" are put into horizontal lists. Our present goal is to consider the commands that have an intrinsically horizontal flavor, in the sense that they behave differently in horizontal mode than they do in vertical or math modes.

One of the things characteristic of horizontal mode is the "space factor," which modifies the width of spaces as described in Chapter 12. If a command changes the value of \spacefactor, that fact is specifically noted here. The space factor is initially set to 1000, when TeX begins to form a horizontal list, except in the case of \valign and \noalign when the space factor of the outer list continues inside the inner one.

- \hskip⟨glue⟩, \hfil, \hfill, \hss, \hfilneg. A glue item is appended to the current horizontal list.

- ⟨leaders⟩⟨box or rule⟩⟨horizontal skip⟩. Here ⟨horizontal skip⟩ refers to one of the five glue-appending commands just mentioned; the formal syntax for ⟨leaders⟩ and for ⟨box or rule⟩ is given in Chapter 24. A glue item that produces leaders is appended.

- ⟨space token⟩. Spaces append glue to the current list; the exact amount of glue depends on \spacefactor, the current font, and the \spaceskip and \xspaceskip parameters, as described in Chapter 12.

- \⊔. A control-space command appends glue to the current list, using the same amount that a ⟨space token⟩ inserts when the space factor is 1000.

- ⟨box⟩. The box is constructed, and if the result is void nothing happens. Otherwise the new box is appended to the current list, and the space factor is set to 1000.

- \raise⟨dimen⟩⟨box⟩, \lower⟨dimen⟩⟨box⟩. This acts exactly like an ordinary ⟨box⟩ command, but the new box that is appended to the horizontal list is also shifted up or down by the specified amount.

- \unhbox⟨8-bit number⟩, \unhcopy⟨8-bit number⟩. If the specified box register is void, nothing happens. Otherwise that register must contain an hbox. The horizontal list inside that box is appended to the current horizontal list, without changing it in any way. The value of \spacefactor is not affected. The box register becomes void after \unhbox, but it remains unchanged by \unhcopy.

- ⟨vertical rule⟩. The specified rule is appended to the current list, and the \spacefactor is set to 1000.

- \valign⟨box specification⟩{⟨alignment material⟩}. The ⟨alignment material⟩ consists of a preamble followed by zero or more columns to be aligned; see Chapter 22. TeX enters a new level of grouping, represented by the '{' and '}', within which changes to \tabskip will be confined. The alignment material can also contain optional occurrences of '\noalign⟨filler⟩{⟨horizontal mode material⟩}' between columns; this adds another level of grouping. TeX operates in restricted horizontal mode while it works on the material in \noalign groups and when it appends columns of the

alignment; the resulting internal horizontal list will be appended to the enclosing horizontal list after the alignment is completed. The value of \spacefactor at the time
of the \valign is used at the beginning of the internal horizontal list, and the final
value of \spacefactor is carried to the enclosing horizontal list when the alignment
is completed. The space factor is set to 1000 after each column; hence it affects the
results only in \noalign groups. TeX also enters an additional level of grouping when
it works on each individual entry of the alignment, during which time it acts in internal
vertical mode; the individual entries will be vboxed as part of the final alignment.

■ \indent. An empty box of width \parindent is appended to the current list,
and the space factor is set to 1000.

■ \noindent. This command has no effect in horizontal modes.

■ \par. The primitive \par command, also called \endgraf in plain TeX, does
nothing in restricted horizontal mode. But it terminates horizontal mode: The current
list is finished off by doing \unskip \penalty10000 \hskip\parfillskip, then it is
broken into lines as explained in Chapter 14, and TeX returns to the enclosing vertical or
internal vertical mode. The lines of the paragraph are appended to the enclosing vertical
list, interspersed with interline glue and interline penalties, and with the migration of
vertical material that was in the horizontal list. Then TeX exercises the page builder.

■ {. A character token of category 1, or a control sequence like \bgroup that
has been \let equal to such a character token, causes TeX to start a new level of
grouping. When such a group ends—with '}'—TeX will undo the effects of non-global
assignments without leaving whatever mode it is in at that time.

■ Some commands are incompatible with horizontal mode because they are intrinsically vertical. When the following commands appear in unrestricted horizontal
mode, they cause TeX to conclude the current paragraph:

$$\langle\text{vertical command}\rangle \longrightarrow \texttt{\textbackslash unvbox} \mid \texttt{\textbackslash unvcopy} \mid \texttt{\textbackslash halign} \mid \texttt{\textbackslash hrule}$$
$$\mid \texttt{\textbackslash vskip} \mid \texttt{\textbackslash vfil} \mid \texttt{\textbackslash vfill} \mid \texttt{\textbackslash vss} \mid \texttt{\textbackslash vfilneg} \mid \texttt{\textbackslash end} \mid \texttt{\textbackslash dump}$$

The appearance of a ⟨vertical command⟩ in restricted horizontal mode is forbidden, but
in regular horizontal mode it causes TeX to insert the token [par] into the input; after
reading and expanding this [par] token, TeX will see the ⟨vertical command⟩ token
again. (The current meaning of the control sequence \par will be used; [par] might
no longer stand for TeX's \par primitive.)

■ ⟨letter⟩, ⟨otherchar⟩, \char⟨8-bit number⟩, ⟨chardef token⟩, \noboundary. The
most common commands of all are the character commands that tell TeX to append a
character to the current horizontal list, using the current font. If two or more commands
of this type occur in succession, TeX processes them all as a unit, converting to ligatures
and/or inserting kerns as directed by the font information. (Ligatures and kerns may be
influenced by invisible "boundary" characters at the left and right, unless \noboundary
appears.) Each character command adjusts \spacefactor, using the \sfcode table as
described in Chapter 12. In unrestricted horizontal mode, a '\discretionary{}{}{}'
item is appended after a character whose code is the \hyphenchar of its font, or after
a ligature formed from a sequence that ends with such a character.

■ \accent⟨8-bit number⟩⟨optional assignments⟩. Here ⟨optional assignments⟩
stands for zero or more ⟨assignment⟩ commands. If the assignments are not followed
by a ⟨character⟩, where ⟨character⟩ stands for any of the commands just discussed in

the previous paragraph, TEX treats \accent as if it were \char, except that the space factor is set to 1000. Otherwise the character that follows the assignment is accented by the character that corresponds to the ⟨8-bit number⟩. (The purpose of the intervening assignments is to allow the accenter and accentee to be in different fonts.) If the accent must be moved up or down, it is put into an hbox that is raised or lowered. Then the accent is effectively superposed on the character by means of kerns, in such a way that the width of the accent does not influence the width of the resulting horizontal list. Finally, TEX sets \spacefactor=1000.

■ \/. If the last item on the current list is a character or ligature, an explicit kern for its italic correction is appended.

■ \discretionary⟨general text⟩⟨general text⟩⟨general text⟩. The three general texts are processed in restricted horizontal mode. They should contain only fixed-width things; hence they aren't really very general in this case. More precisely, the horizontal list formed by each discretionary general text must consist only of characters, ligatures, kerns, boxes, and rules; there should be no glue or penalty items, etc. This command appends a discretionary item to the current list; see Chapter 14 for the meaning of a discretionary item. The space factor is not changed.

■ \-. This "discretionary hyphen" command is defined in Appendix H.

■ \setlanguage⟨number⟩. See the conclusion of Appendix H.

■ \$. A "math shift" character causes TEX to enter math mode or display math mode in the following way: TEX looks at the following token without expanding it. If that token is a \$ and if TEX is currently in unrestricted horizontal mode, then TEX breaks the current paragraph into lines as explained above (unless the current list is empty), returns to the enclosing vertical mode or internal vertical mode, calculates values like \prevgraf and \displaywidth and \predisplaysize, enters a new level of grouping, inserts the \everydisplay tokens into the input, exercises the page builder, processes '⟨math mode material⟩\$\$' in display math mode, puts the display into the enclosing vertical list as explained in Chapter 19 (letting vertical material migrate), exercises the page builder again, increases \prevgraf by 3, and resumes horizontal mode again, with an empty list and with the space factor equal to 1000. (You got that?) Otherwise TEX puts the looked-at token back into the input, enters a new level of grouping, inserts the \everymath tokens, and processes '⟨math mode material⟩\$'; the math mode material is converted to a horizontal list and appended to the current list, surrounded by "math-on" and "math-off" items, and the space factor is set to 1000. One consequence of these rules is that '\$\$' in restricted horizontal mode simply yields an empty math formula.

■ None of the above: If any other primitive command of TEX occurs in horizontal mode, an error message will be given, and TEX will try to recover in a reasonable way. For example, if a superscript or subscript symbol appears, or if any other inherently mathematical command is given, TEX will try to insert a '\$' just before the offending token; this will enter math mode.

> Otherwise. *You may reduce all* Verticals *into* Horizontals.
> — JOSEPH MOXON, *A Tutor to Astronomie and Geographie* (1659)

> ! You can't use '\moveleft' in horizontal mode.
> — TEX (1982)

26

Summary of
Math Mode

To conclude the survey that was begun in Chapter 24, let us investigate exactly what TEX's digestive processes can do when TEX is building lists in math mode or in display math mode.

*   *   *

Three asterisks, just like those that appear here, can be found near the end of Chapter 24. Everything preceding the three asterisks in that chapter applies to math mode as well as to vertical mode, so we need not repeat all those rules. In particular, Chapter 24 explains assignment commands, and it tells how kerns, penalties, marks, insertions, adjustments, and "whatsits" are put into math lists. Our present goal is to consider the commands that have an intrinsically mathematical flavor, in the sense that they behave differently in math mode than they do in vertical or horizontal modes.

Math lists are somewhat different from TEX's other lists because they contain three-pronged "atoms" (see Chapter 17). Atoms come in thirteen flavors: Ord, Op, Bin, Rel, Open, Close, Punct, Inner, Over, Under, Acc, Rad, and Vcent. Each atom contains three "fields" called its nucleus, superscript, and subscript; and each field is either empty or is filled with a math symbol, a box, or a subsidiary math list. Math symbols, in turn, have two components: a family number and a position number.

It's convenient to introduce a few more rules of syntax, in order to specify what goes into a math list:

> ⟨character⟩ ⟶ ⟨letter⟩ | ⟨otherchar⟩ | \char⟨8-bit number⟩ | ⟨chardef token⟩
> ⟨math character⟩ ⟶ \mathchar⟨15-bit number⟩ | ⟨mathchardef token⟩
> | \delimiter⟨27-bit number⟩
> ⟨math symbol⟩ ⟶ ⟨character⟩ | ⟨math character⟩
> ⟨math field⟩ ⟶ ⟨math symbol⟩ | ⟨filler⟩{⟨math mode material⟩}
> ⟨delim⟩ ⟶ ⟨filler⟩\delimiter⟨27-bit number⟩
> | ⟨filler⟩⟨letter⟩ | ⟨filler⟩⟨otherchar⟩

We have already seen the concept of ⟨character⟩ in Chapter 25. Indeed, characters are TEX's staple food: The vast majority of all commands that reach TEX's digestive processes in horizontal mode are instances of the ⟨character⟩ command, which specifies a number between 0 and 255 that causes TEX to typeset the corresponding character in the current font. When TEX is in math mode or display math mode, a ⟨character⟩ command takes on added significance: It specifies a number between 0 and $32767 = 2^{15} - 1$. This is done by replacing the character number by its \mathcode value. If the \mathcode value turns out to be $32768 = "8000$, however, the ⟨character⟩ is replaced by an active character token having the original character code (0 to 255); TEX forgets the original ⟨character⟩ and expands this active character according to the rules of Chapter 20.

A ⟨math character⟩ defines a 15-bit number either by specifying it directly with \mathchar or in a previous \mathchardef, or by specifying a 27-bit \delimiter value; in the latter case, the least significant 12 bits are discarded.

It follows that every ⟨math symbol⟩, as defined by the syntax above, specifies a 15-bit number, i.e., a number between 0 and 32767. Such a number can be represented in the form $4096c + 256f + a$, where $0 \le c < 8$, $0 \le f < 16$, and $0 \le a < 256$. If $c = 7$, TEX changes c to 0; and in this case if the current value of \fam is between 0 and 15, TEX also replaces f by \fam. This procedure yields, in all cases, a class number c between 0 and 6, a family number f between 0 and 15, and a position number a between 0 and 255. (TEX initializes the value of \fam by implicitly putting the assignment '\fam=-1' at the very beginning of \everymath and \everydisplay. Thus, the substitution of \fam for f will occur only if the user has explicitly changed \fam within the formula.)

A ⟨math field⟩ is used to specify the nucleus, superscript, or subscript of an atom. When a ⟨math field⟩ is a ⟨math symbol⟩, the f and a numbers of that symbol go into the atomic field. Otherwise the ⟨math field⟩ begins with a '{', which causes TEX to enter a new level of grouping and to begin a new math list; the ensuing ⟨math mode material⟩ is terminated by a '}', at which point the group ends and the resulting math list goes into the atomic field. If the math list turns out to be simply a single Ord atom without subscripts or superscripts, or an Acc whose nucleus is an Ord, the enclosing braces are effectively removed.

A ⟨delim⟩ is used to define both a "small character" a in family f and a "large character" b in family g, where $0 \le a, b \le 255$ and $0 \le f, g \le 15$; these character codes are used to construct variable-size delimiters, as explained in Appendix G. If the ⟨delim⟩ is given explicitly in terms of a 27-bit number, the desired codes are obtained by interpreting that number as $c \cdot 2^{24} + f \cdot 2^{20} + a \cdot 2^{12} + g \cdot 2^8 + b$, ignoring the value of c. Otherwise the delimiter is specified as a ⟨letter⟩ or ⟨otherchar⟩ token, and the 24-bit \delcode value of that character is interpreted as $f \cdot 2^{20} + a \cdot 2^{12} + g \cdot 2^8 + b$.

Now let's study the individual commands as TEX obeys them in math mode, considering first the ones that have analogs in vertical and/or horizontal mode:

- \hskip⟨glue⟩, \hfil, \hfill, \hss, \hfilneg, \mskip⟨muglue⟩. A glue item is appended to the current math list.

- ⟨leaders⟩⟨box or rule⟩⟨mathematical skip⟩. Here ⟨mathematical skip⟩ refers to one of the six glue-appending commands just mentioned; the formal syntax for ⟨leaders⟩ and for ⟨box or rule⟩ is given in Chapter 24. A glue item that produces leaders is appended to the current list.

- \nonscript. A special glue item of width zero is appended; it will have the effect of cancelling the following item on the list, if that item is glue and if the \nonscript is eventually typeset in "script style" or in "scriptscript style."

- \noboundary. This command is redundant and therefore has no effect; boundary ligatures are automatically disabled in math modes.

- ⟨space token⟩. Spaces have no effect in math modes.

- \␣. A control-space command appends glue to the current list, using the same amount that a ⟨space token⟩ inserts in horizontal mode when the space factor is 1000.

- ⟨box⟩. The box is constructed, and if the result is void nothing happens. Otherwise a new Ord atom is appended to the current math list, and the box becomes its nucleus.

- \raise⟨dimen⟩⟨box⟩, \lower⟨dimen⟩⟨box⟩. This acts exactly like an ordinary ⟨box⟩ command, but the new box that is put into the nucleus is also shifted up or down by the specified amount.

- \vcenter⟨box specification⟩{⟨vertical mode material⟩}. A vbox is formed as if '\vcenter' had been '\vbox'. Then a new Vcent atom is appended to the current math list, and the box becomes its nucleus.

■ ⟨vertical rule⟩. A rule is appended to the current list (not as an atom).

■ `\halign`⟨box specification⟩{⟨alignment material⟩}. This command is allowed only in display math mode, and only when the current math list is empty. The alignment is carried out exactly as if it were done in the enclosing vertical mode (see Chapter 24), except that the lines are shifted right by the `\displayindent`. The closing '}' may be followed by optional ⟨assignment⟩ commands, after which '$$' must conclude the display. TEX will insert the `\abovedisplayskip` and `\belowdisplayskip` glue before and after the result of the alignment.

■ `\indent`. An empty box of width `\parindent` is appended to the current list, as the nucleus of a new Ord atom.

■ `\noindent`. This command has no effect in math modes.

■ {⟨math mode material⟩}. A character token of category 1, or a control sequence like `\bgroup` that has been `\let` equal to such a character token, causes TEX to start a new level of grouping and also to begin work on a new math list. When such a group ends—with '}'—TEX uses the resulting math list as the nucleus of a new Ord atom that is appended to the current list. If the resulting math list is a single Acc atom, however (i.e., an accented quantity), that atom itself is appended.

■ ⟨math symbol⟩. (This is the most common command in math mode; see the syntax near the beginning of this chapter.) A math symbol determines three values, c, f, and a, as explained earlier. TEX appends an atom to the current list, where the atom is of type Ord, Op, Bin, Rel, Open, Close, or Punct, according as the value of c is 0, 1, 2, 3, 4, 5, or 6. The nucleus of this atom is the math symbol defined by f and a.

■ ⟨math atom⟩⟨math field⟩. A ⟨math atom⟩ command is any of the following:

`\mathord` | `\mathop` | `\mathbin` | `\mathrel` | `\mathopen`
| `\mathclose` | `\mathpunct` | `\mathinner` | `\underline` | `\overline`

TEX processes the ⟨math field⟩, then appends a new atom of the specified type to the current list; the nucleus of this atom contains the specified field.

■ `\mathaccent`⟨15-bit number⟩⟨math field⟩. TEX converts the ⟨15-bit number⟩ into c, f, and a as it does with any `\mathchar`. Then it processes the ⟨math field⟩ and appends a new Acc atom to the current list. The nucleus of this atom contains the specified field; the accent character in this atom contains (a, f).

■ `\radical`⟨27-bit number⟩⟨math field⟩. TEX converts the ⟨27-bit number⟩ into a, f, b, and g as it does with any `\delimiter`. Then it processes the ⟨math field⟩ and appends a new Rad atom to the current list. The nucleus of this atom contains the specified field; the delimiter field in this atom contains (a, f) and (b, g).

■ ⟨superscript⟩⟨math field⟩. A ⟨superscript⟩ command is an explicit or implicit character token of category 7. If the current list does not end with an atom, a new Ord atom with all fields empty is appended; thus the current list will end with an atom, in all cases. The superscript field of this atom should be empty; it is made nonempty by changing it to the result of the specified ⟨math field⟩.

■ ⟨subscript⟩⟨math field⟩. A ⟨subscript⟩ command is an explicit or implicit character token of category 8. It acts just like a ⟨superscript⟩ command, except, of course, that it affects the subscript field instead of the superscript field.

■ \displaylimits, \limits, \nolimits. These commands are allowed only if the current list ends with an Op atom. They modify a special field in that Op atom, specifying what conventions should be used with respect to limits. The normal value of that field is \displaylimits.

■ \/. A kern of width zero is appended to the current list. (This will have the effect of adding the italic correction to the previous character, if the italic correction wouldn't normally have been added.)

■ \discretionary⟨general text⟩⟨general text⟩⟨general text⟩. This command is treated just as in horizontal mode (see Chapter 25), but the third ⟨general text⟩ must produce an empty list.

■ \-. This command is usually equivalent to '\discretionary{-}{}{}'; the '-' is therefore interpreted as a hyphen, not as a minus sign. (See Appendix H.)

■ \mathchoice⟨general text⟩⟨general text⟩⟨general text⟩⟨general text⟩. The four general texts are each treated as subformulas (i.e., like the second alternative in the definition of ⟨math field⟩). The four math lists defined in this way are recorded in a "choice item" that is appended to the current list.

■ \displaystyle, \textstyle, \scriptstyle, \scriptscriptstyle. A style-change item that corresponds to the specified style is appended to the current list.

■ \left⟨delim⟩⟨math mode material⟩\right⟨delim⟩. TeX begins a new group, and processes the ⟨math mode material⟩ by starting out with a new math list that begins with a left boundary item containing the first delimiter. This group must be terminated by '\right', at which time the internal math list is completed with a right boundary item containing the second delimiter. Then TeX appends an Inner atom to the current list; the nucleus of this atom contains the internal math list.

■ ⟨generalized fraction command⟩. This command takes one of six forms:

> \over | \atop | \above⟨dimen⟩
> | \overwithdelims⟨delim⟩⟨delim⟩
> | \atopwithdelims⟨delim⟩⟨delim⟩
> | \abovewithdelims⟨delim⟩⟨delim⟩⟨dimen⟩

(See Chapter 17.) When TeX sees a ⟨generalized fraction command⟩ it takes the entire current list and puts it into the numerator field of a generalized fraction item. The denominator field of this new item is temporarily empty; the left and right delimiter fields are set equal to the specified delimiter codes. TeX saves this generalized fraction item in a special place associated with the current level of math mode processing. (There should be no other generalized fraction item in that special place, because constructions like 'a\over b\over c' are illegal.) Then TeX makes the current list empty and continues to process commands in math mode. Later on, when the current level of math mode is completed (either by coming to a '$' or a '}' or a \right, depending on the nature of the current group), the current list will be moved into the denominator field of the generalized fraction item that was saved; then that item, all by itself, will take the place of the entire list. However, in the special case that the current list began with \left and will end with \right, the boundary items will be extracted from the numerator and denominator of the generalized fraction, and the final list will consist of three items: left boundary, generalized fraction, right boundary. (If you want to watch the process by which math lists are built, you might find it helpful to type '\showlists' while TEX is processing the denominator of a generalized fraction.)

■ ⟨eqno⟩⟨math mode material⟩$. Here ⟨eqno⟩ stands for either \eqno or \leqno; these commands are allowed only in display math mode. Upon reading ⟨eqno⟩, TEX enters a new level of grouping, inserts the \everymath tokens, and enters non-display math mode to put the ⟨math mode material⟩ into a math list. When that math list is completed, TEX converts it to a horizontal list and puts the result into a box that will be used as the equation number of the current display. The closing $ token will be put back into the input, where it will terminate the display.

■ $. If TEX is in display math mode, it reads one more token, which must also be $. In either case, the math-shift command terminates the current level of math mode processing and ends the current group, which should have begun with either $ or ⟨eqno⟩. Once the math list is finished, it is converted into a horizontal list as explained in Appendix G.

■ None of the above: If any other primitive command of TEX occurs in math mode, an error message will be given, and TEX will try to recover in a reasonable way. For example, if a \par command appears, or if any other inherently non-mathematical command is given, TEX will try to insert a '$' just before the offending token; this will lead out of math mode. On the other hand if a totally misplaced token like \endcsname or \omit or # appears in math mode, TEX will simply ignore it, after reporting the error. You might enjoy trying to type some really stupid input, just to see what happens. (Say '\tracingall' first, as explained in Chapter 27, in order to get maximum information.)

▶ **EXERCISE 26.1**
Powers of ten: The whole TEX language has now been summarized completely. To demonstrate how much you know, name all of the ways you can think of in which the numbers 10, 100, 1000, 10000, and 100000 have special significance to TEX.

▶ **EXERCISE 26.2**
Powers of two: Name all of the ways you can think of in which the numbers 8, 16, 32, 64, 128, 256, ... have special significance to TEX.

> *Mathematics is known in the trade as difficult, or penalty, copy*
> *because it is slower, more difficult, and more expensive to set in type*
> *than any other kind of copy normally occurring in books and journals.*
> — UNIVERSITY OF CHICAGO PRESS, *A Manual of Style* (1969)

> *The tale of Math is a complex one,*
> *and it resists both a simple plot summary*
> *and a concise statement of its meaning.*
> — PATRICK K. FORD, *The Mabinogi* (1977)

27

Recovery from Errors

OK, everything you need to know about TEX has been explained—unless you happen to be fallible. If you don't plan to make any errors, don't bother to read this chapter. Otherwise you might find it helpful to make use of some of the ways that TEX tries to pinpoint bugs in your manuscript.

In the trial runs you did when reading Chapter 6, you learned the general form of error messages, and you also learned the various ways in which you can respond to TEX's complaints. With practice, you will be able to correct most errors "online," as soon as TEX has detected them, by inserting and deleting a few things. The right way to go about this is to be in a mellow mood when you approach TEX, and to regard the error messages that you get as amusing puzzles—"Why did the machine do that?"—rather than as personal insults.

TEX knows how to issue more than a hundred different sorts of error messages, and you probably never will encounter all of them, because some types of mistakes are very hard to make. We discussed the "undefined control sequence" error in Chapter 6; let's take a look at a few of the others now.

If you misspell the name of some unit of measure—for example, if you type '\hsize=4im' instead of '\hsize=4in'—you'll get an error message that looks something like this:

```
! Illegal unit of measure (pt inserted).
<to be read again>
                     i
<to be read again>
                     m
<*> \hsize=4im
             \input story
?
```

TEX needs to see a legal unit before it can proceed; so in this case it has implicitly inserted 'pt' at the current place in the input, and it has set \hsize=4pt.

What's the best way to recover from such an error? Well, you should always type 'H' or 'h' to see the help message, if you aren't sure what the error message means. Then you can look at the lines of context and see that TEX will read 'i' and then 'm' and then ' \input story ' if you simply hit ⟨return⟩ and carry on. Unfortunately, this easy solution isn't very good, because the 'i' and 'm' will be typeset as part of the text of a new paragraph. A much more graceful recovery is possible in this case, by first typing '2'. This tells TEX to discard the next two tokens that it reads; and after TEX has done so, it will stop again in order to give you a chance to look over the new situation. Here is what you will see:

```
<recently read> m

<*> \hsize=4im
             \input story
?
```

Good; the 'i' and 'm' are read and gone. But if you hit ⟨return⟩ now, TEX will '\input story' and try to typeset the story.tex file with \hsize=4pt; that won't be an especially exciting experiment, because it will simply produce dozens of overfull boxes, one for every syllable of the story. Once again there's a better way: You can insert the command that you had originally intended, by typing

    I\hsize=4in

now. This instructs TEX to change \hsize to the correct value, after which it will \input story and you'll be on your way.

▶**EXERCISE 27.1**
Ben User typed '8', not '2', in response to the error message just considered; his idea was to delete 'i', 'm', '\input', and the five letters of 'story'. But TEX's response was

    <*> \hsize=4im \input stor
                                y

Explain what happened.

TEX usually tries to recover from errors either by ignoring a command that it doesn't understand, or by inserting something that will keep it happy. For example, we saw in Chapter 6 that TEX ignores an undefined control sequence; and we just observed that TEX inserts 'pt' when it needs a physical unit of measure. Here's another example where TEX puts something in:

    ! Missing $ inserted.
    <inserted text>
                      $
    <to be read again>
                        ^
    l.11 the fact that 32768=2^
                                {15} wasn't interesting
    ? H
    I've inserted a begin-math/end-math symbol since I think
    you left one out. Proceed, with fingers crossed.

(The user has forgotten to enclose a formula in $ signs, and TEX has tried to recover by inserting one.) In this case the ⟨inserted text⟩ is explicitly shown, and it has not yet been read; by contrast, our previous example illustrated a case where TEX had already internalized the 'pt' that it had inserted. Thus the user has a chance here to remove the inserted '$' before TEX really sees it.

What should be done? The error in this example occurred before TEX noticed anything wrong; the characters '32768=2' have already been typeset in horizontal mode. There's no way to go back and cancel the past, so the lack of proper spacing around the '=' cannot be fixed. Our goal of error recovery in this case is therefore not to produce perfect output; we want rather to proceed in some way so that TeX will pass by the present error and detect subsequent ones. If we were simply to hit ⟨return⟩ now, our aim would not be achieved, because TeX would typeset the ensuing text as a math formula: '$^{15}wasn'tinteresting\ldots$'; another error would be detected when the paragraph is found to end before any closing '$' has appeared. On the other hand, there's a more elaborate way to recover, namely to type '6' and then 'I^{15}'; this deletes '$^{15}' and inserts a correct partial formula. But that's more complicated than necessary. The best solution in this case is to type just '2' and then go on; TeX will typeset the incorrect equation '32768=215', but the important thing is that you will be able to check out the rest of the document as if this error hadn't occurred.

▶ **EXERCISE 27.2**
Here's a case in which a backslash was inadvertently omitted:
```
! Missing control sequence inserted.
<inserted text>
                \inaccessible
<to be read again>
                m
l.10 \def m
          acro{replacement}
```
TeX needs to see a control sequence after '\def', so it has inserted one that will allow the processing to continue. (This control sequence is shown as '\inaccessible', but it has no relation to any control sequence that you can actually specify in an error-free manuscript.) If you simply hit ⟨return⟩ at this point, TeX will define the inaccessible control sequence, but that won't do you much good; later references to \macro will be undefined. Explain how to recover from this error so that the effect will be the same as if line 10 of the input file had said '\def\macro{replacement}'.

▶ **EXERCISE 27.3**
When you use the 'I' option to respond to an error message, the rules of Chapter 8 imply that TeX removes all spaces from the right-hand end of the line. Explain how you can use the 'I' option to insert a space, in spite of this fact.

Some of the toughest errors to deal with are those in which you make a mistake on line 20 (say), but TeX cannot tell that anything is amiss until it reaches line 25 or so. For example, if you forget a '}' that completes the argument to some macro, TeX won't notice any problem until reaching the end of the next paragraph. In such cases you probably have lost the whole paragraph; but TeX will usually be able to get straightened out in time to do the subsequent paragraphs as if nothing had happened. A "runaway argument" will be displayed, and by looking at the beginning of that text you should be able to figure out where the missing '}' belongs.

It's wise to remember that the first error in your document may well spawn spurious "errors" later on, because anomalous commands can inflict serious injury on TeX's ability to cope with the subsequent material. But most of the time you will find that a single run through the machine will locate all of the places in which your input conflicts with TeX's rules.

When your error is due to misunderstanding rather than mistyping, the situation is even more serious: TEX's error messages will probably not be very helpful, even if you ask TEX for help. If you have unknowingly redefined an important control sequence—for example, if you have said '\def\box{...}'—all sorts of strange disasters might occur. Computers aren't clairvoyant, and TEX can only explain what looks wrong from its own viewpoint; such an explanation is bound to be mysterious unless you can understand the machine's attitude. The solution to this problem is, of course, to seek human counsel and advice; or, as a last resort, to read the instructions in Chapters 2, 3, ..., 26.

▶ **EXERCISE 27.4**
J. H. Quick (a student) once defined the following set of macros:

```
\newcount\serialnumber
\def\firstnumber{\serialnumber=0 }
\def\nextnumber{\advance \serialnumber by 1
   \number\serialnumber)\nobreak\hskip.2em }
```

Thus he could type, for example,

```
\firstnumber
\nextnumber xx, \nextnumber yy, and \nextnumber zz
```

and TEX would typeset '1) xx, 2) yy, and 3) zz'. Well, this worked fine, and he showed the macros to his buddies. But several months later he received a frantic phone call; one of his friends had just encountered a really weird error message:

```
! Missing number, treated as zero.
<to be read again>
                     c
l.107 \nextnumber minusc
                        ule chances of error
?
```

Explain what happened, and advise Quick what to do.

Sooner or later—hopefully sooner—you'll get TEX to process your whole file without stopping once to complain. But maybe the output still won't be right; the mere fact that TEX didn't stop doesn't mean that you can avoid proofreading. At this stage it's usually easy to see how to fix typographic errors by correcting the input. Errors of layout can be overcome by using methods we have discussed before: Overfull boxes can be cured as described in Chapter 6; bad breaks can be avoided by using ties or \hbox commands as discussed in Chapter 14; math formulas can be improved by applying the principles of Chapters 16–19.

But your output may contain seemingly inexplicable errors. For example, if you have specified a font at some magnification that is not supported by your printing software, TEX will not know that there is any problem, but the program that converts your dvi file to hardcopy might not tell you that it has substituted an "approximate" font for the real one; the resultant spacing may look quite horrible.

If you can't find out what went wrong, try the old trick of simplifying your program: Remove all the things that do work, until you obtain the shortest possible input file that fails in the same way as the original. The shorter the file, the easier it will be for you or somebody else to pinpoint the problem.

Perhaps you'll wonder why TEX didn't put a blank space in some position where you think you typed a space. Remember that TEX ignores spaces that follow control words, when it reads your file. (TEX also ignores a space after a ⟨number⟩ or a ⟨unit of measure⟩ that appears as an argument to a primitive command; but if you are using properly designed macros, such rules will not concern you, because you will probably not be using primitive commands directly.)

⚠⚠ On the other hand, if you are designing macros, the task of troubleshooting can be a lot more complicated. For example, you may discover that TEX has emitted three blank spaces when it processed some long sequence of complicated code, consisting of several dozen commands. How can you find out where those spaces crept in? The answer is to set '`\tracingcommands=1`', as mentioned in Chapter 13. This tells TEX to put an entry in your log file whenever it begins to execute a primitive command; you'll be able to see when the command is '`blank space`'.

⚠ Most implementations of TEX allow you to interrupt the program in some way. This makes it possible to diagnose the causes of infinite loops. TEX switches to `\errorstopmode` when interrupted; hence you have a chance to insert commands into the input: You can abort the run, or you can `\show` or change the current contents of control sequences, registers, etc. You can also get a feeling for where TEX is spending most of its time, if you happen to be using an inefficient macro, since random interrupts will tend to occur in whatever place TEX visits most often.

⚠ Sometimes an error is so bad that TEX is forced to quit prematurely. For example, if you are running in `\batchmode` or `\nonstopmode`, TEX makes an "emergency stop" if it needs input from the terminal; this happens when a necessary file cannot be opened, or when no `\end` command was found in the input document. Here are some of the messages you might get just before TEX gives up the ghost:

`Fatal format file error; I'm stymied.`

This means that the preloaded format you have specified cannot be used, because it was prepared for a different version of TEX.

`That makes 100 errors; please try again.`

TEX has scrolled past 100 errors since the last paragraph ended, so it's probably in an endless loop.

`Interwoven alignment preambles are not allowed.`

If you have been so devious as to get this message, you will understand it, and you will deserve no sympathy.

`I can't go on meeting you like this.`

A previous error has gotten TEX out of whack. Fix it and try again.

`This can't happen.`

Something is wrong with the TEX you are using. Complain fiercely.

There's also a dreadful message that TeX issues only with great reluctance. But it can happen:

```
TeX capacity exceeded, sorry.
```

This, alas, means that you have tried to stretch TeX too far. The message will tell you what part of TeX's memory has become overloaded; one of the following fourteen things will be mentioned:

> `number of strings`   (names of control sequences and files)
> `pool size`   (the characters in such names)
> `main memory size`   (boxes, glue, breakpoints, token lists, characters, etc.)
> `hash size`   (control sequence names)
> `font memory`   (font metric data)
> `exception dictionary`   (hyphenation exceptions)
> `input stack size`   (simultaneous input sources)
> `semantic nest size`   (unfinished lists being constructed)
> `parameter stack size`   (macro parameters)
> `buffer size`   (characters in lines being read from files)
> `save size`   (values to restore at group ends)
> `text input levels`   (\input files and error insertions)
> `grouping levels`   (unfinished groups)
> `pattern memory`   (hyphenation pattern data)

The current amount of memory available will also be shown.

If you have a job that doesn't overflow TeX's capacity, yet you want to see just how closely you have approached the limits, just set \tracingstats to a positive value before the end of your job. The log file will then conclude with a report on your actual usage of the first eleven things named above (i.e., the number of strings, . . . , the save size), in that order. Furthermore, if you set \tracingstats equal to 2 or more, TeX will show its current memory usage whenever it does a \shipout command. Such statistics are broken into two parts; '490&5950' means, for example, that 490 words are being used for "large" things like boxes, glue, and breakpoints, while 5950 words are being used for "small" things like tokens and characters.

What can be done if TeX's capacity is exceeded? All of the above-listed components of the capacity can be increased, provided that your computer is large enough; in fact, the space necessary to increase one component can usually be obtained by decreasing some other component, without increasing the total size of TeX. If you have an especially important application, you may be able to convince your local system people to provide you with a special TeX whose capacities have been hand-tailored to your needs. But before taking such a drastic step, be sure that you are using TeX properly. If you have specified a gigantic paragraph or a gigantic alignment that spans more than one page, you should change your approach, because TeX has to read all the way to the end before it can complete the line-breaking or the alignment calculations; this consumes huge amounts of memory space. If you have built up an enormous macro library, you should remember that TeX has to remember all of the replacement texts that you define; therefore if memory space is in short supply, you should load only the macros that you need. (See Appendices B and D, for ideas on how to make macros more compact.)

Some erroneous TeX programs will overflow any finite memory capacity. For example, after '`\def\recurse{(\recurse)}`', the use of `\recurse` will immediately bomb out:

```
! TeX capacity exceeded, sorry [input stack size=80].
\recurse ->(\recurse
                     )
\recurse ->(\recurse
                     )
   ...
```

The same sort of error will obviously occur no matter how much you increase TeX's input stack size.

The special case of "`save size`" capacity exceeded is one of the most troublesome errors to correct, especially if you run into the error only on long jobs. TeX generally uses up two words of save size whenever it performs a non-global assignment to some quantity whose previous value was not assigned at the same level of grouping. When macros are written properly, there will rarely be a need for more than 100 or so things on the "save stack"; but it's possible to make save stack usage grow without limit if you make both local and global assignments to the same variable. You can figure out what TeX puts on the save stack by setting `\tracingrestores=1`; then your log file will record information about whatever is removed from the stack at the end of a group. For example, let `\a` stand for the command '`\advance\day by 1`'; let `\g` stand for '`\global\advance\day by 1`'; and consider the following commands:

> `\day=1 {\a\g\a\g\a}`

The first `\a` sets `\day=2` and remembers the old value `\day=1` by putting it on the save stack. The first `\g` sets `\day=3`, globally; nothing needs to go on the save stack at the time of a global assignment. The next `\a` sets `\day=4` and remembers the old value `\day=3` on the save stack. Then `\g` sets `\day=5`; then `\a` sets `\day=6` and remembers `\day=5`. Finally the '`}`' causes TeX to go back through the save stack; if `\tracingrestores=1` at this point, the log file will get the following data:

```
{restoring \day=5}
{retaining \day=5}
{retaining \day=5}
```

Explanation: The `\day` parameter is first restored to its global value 5. Since this value is global, it will be retained, so the other saved values (`\day=3` and `\day=1`) are essentially ignored. Moral: If you find TeX retaining a lot of values, you have a set of macros that could cause the save stack to overflow in large enough jobs. To prevent this, it's usually wise to be consistent in your assignments to each variable that you use; the assignments should either be global always or local always.

TeX provides several other kinds of tracing in addition to `\tracingstats` and `\tracingrestores`: We have already discussed `\tracingcommands` in Chapters 13 and 20, `\tracingparagraphs` in Chapter 14, `\tracingpages` in Chapter 15, and `\tracingmacros` in Chapter 20. There is also `\tracinglostchars`, which (if positive) causes TeX to record each time a character has been dropped because it does not appear in the current font; and `\tracingoutput`, which (if positive) causes TeX to display in symbolic form the contents of every box that is being shipped out to the dvi file. The latter allows you to see if things have been typeset properly, if you're trying to decide whether some anomaly was caused by TEX or by some other software that acts on TEX's output.

When TEX displays a box as part of diagnostic output, the amount of data is controlled by two parameters called \showboxbreadth and \showboxdepth. The first of these, which plain TEX sets equal to 5, tells the maximum number of items shown per level; the second, which plain TEX sets to 3, tells the deepest level. For example, a small box whose full contents are

```
\hbox(4.30554+1.94444)x21.0, glue set 0.5
.\hbox(4.30554+1.94444)x5.0
..\tenrm g
.\glue 5.0 plus 2.0
.\tenrm | (ligature ---)
```

will be abbreviated as follows when \showboxbreadth=1 and \showboxdepth=1:

```
\hbox(4.30554+1.94444)x21.0, glue set 0.5
.\hbox(4.30554+1.94444)x5.0 []
.etc.
```

And if you set \showboxdepth=0, you get only the top level:

```
\hbox(4.30554+1.94444)x21.0, glue set 0.5 []
```

(Notice how '[]' and 'etc.' indicate that the data has been truncated.)

A nonempty hbox is considered "overfull" if its glue cannot shrink to achieve the specified size, provided that \hbadness is less than 100 or that the excess width (after shrinking by the maximum amount) is more than \hfuzz. It is "tight" if its glue shrinks and the badness exceeds \hbadness; it is "loose" if its glue stretches and the badness exceeds \hbadness but is not greater than 100; it is "underfull" if its glue stretches and the badness is greater than \hbadness and greater than 100. Similar remarks apply to nonempty vboxes. TEX prints a warning message and displays the offending box, whenever such anomalies are discovered. Empty boxes are never considered to be anomalous.

When an alignment is "overfull" or "tight" or "loose" or "underfull," you don't get a warning message for every aligned line; you get only one message, and TEX displays a *prototype row* (or, with \valign, a *prototype column*). For example, suppose you say '\tabskip=0pt plus10pt \halign to200pt{&#\hfil\cr...\cr}', and suppose that the aligned material turns out to make two columns of widths 50 pt and 60 pt, respectively. Then you get the following message:

```
Underfull \hbox (badness 2698) in alignment at lines 11--18
 [] []
\hbox(0.0+0.0)x200.0, glue set 3.0
.\glue(\tabskip) 0.0 plus 10.0
.\unsetbox(0.0+0.0)x50.0
.\glue(\tabskip) 0.0 plus 10.0
.\unsetbox(0.0+0.0)x60.0
.\glue(\tabskip) 0.0 plus 10.0
```

The "unset boxes" in a prototype row show the individual column widths. In this case the tabskip glue has to stretch 3.0 times its stretchability, in order to reach the 200 pt goal, so the box is underfull. (According to the formula in Chapter 14, the badness of this situation is 2700; TEX actually uses a similar but more efficient formula, so it computes a badness of 2698.) Every line of the alignment will be underfull, but only the prototype row will be displayed in a warning message. "Overfull rules" are never appended to the lines of overfull alignments.

The \tracing... commands put all of their output into your log file, unless the \tracingonline parameter is positive; in the latter case, all diagnostic information goes to the terminal as well as to the log file. Plain TEX has a \tracingall macro that turns on the maximum amount of tracing of all kinds. It not only sets up \tracingcommands, \tracingrestores, \tracingparagraphs, and so on, it also sets \tracingonline=1, and it sets \showboxbreadth and \showboxdepth to extremely high values, so that the entire contents of all boxes will be displayed.

Some production versions of TEX have been streamlined for speed. These implementations don't look at the values of the parameters \tracingparagraphs, \tracingpages, \tracingstats, and \tracingrestores, because TEX runs faster when it doesn't have to maintain statistics or keep tabs on whether tracing is required. If you want all of TEX's diagnostic tools, you should be sure to use the right version.

If you set \pausing=1, TEX will give you a chance to edit each line of input as it is read from the file. In this way you can make temporary patches (e.g., you can insert \show... commands) while you're troubleshooting, without changing the actual contents of the file, and you can keep TEX running at human speed.

Final hint: When working on a long manuscript, it's best to prepare only a few pages at a time. Set up a "galley" file and a "book" file, and enter your text on the galley file. (Put control information that sets up your basic format at the beginning of this file; an example of galley.tex appears in Appendix E.) After the galleys come out looking right, you can append them to the book file; then you can run the book file through TEX occasionally, in order to see how the pages really fit together. For example, when the author prepared this manual, he did one chapter at a time, and the longer chapters were split into subchapters.

▶ **EXERCISE 27.5**
Final exercise: Find all of the lies in this manual, and all of the jokes.

Final exhortation: GO FORTH now and create *masterpieces of the publishing art!*

Who can understand his errors?
— *Psalm 19 : 12* (c. 1000 B.C.)

It is one thing, to shew a Man that he is in an Error,
and another, to put him in possession of Truth.
— JOHN LOCKE, *An Essay Concerning Humane Understanding* (1690)

A

Answers to All the Exercises

The preface to this manual points out the wisdom of trying to figure out each exercise before you look up the answer here. But these answers are intended to be read, since they occasionally provide additional information that you are best equipped to understand when you have just worked on a problem.

1.1. A TEXnician (underpaid); sometimes also called a TEXacker.

2.1. `Alice said, ''I always use an en-dash instead of a hyphen when specifying page numbers like '480--491' in a bibliography.''` (The wrong answer to this question ends with `'480-491' in a bibliography."`)

2.2. You get em-dash and hyphen (—-), which looks awful.

2.3. fluffier firefly fisticuffs, flagstaff fireproofing, chiffchaff and riffraff.

2.4. `''\thinspace'`; and either `'{}''` or `{'}''` or something similar. Reason: There's usually less space *preceding* a single left quote than there is preceding a double left quote. (Left and right are opposites.)

2.5. Eliminating `\thinspace` would mean that a user need not learn the term; but it is not advisable to minimize terminology by "overloading" math mode with tricky constructions. For example, a user who wishes to take advantage of TEX's `\mathsurround` feature would be thwarted by non-mathematical uses of dollar signs. (Incidentally, neither `\thinspace` nor `\,` are built into TEX; both are defined in terms of more primitive features, in Appendix B.)

3.1. `\I`, `\exercise`, and `\\`. (The last of these is of type 2, i.e., a control symbol, since the second backslash is not a letter; the first backslash keeps the second one from starting its own control sequence.)

3.2. `math\'ematique` and `centim\`etre`.

3.3. According to the index, `\␣` is primitive but `\⟨return⟩` isn't. The command `'\def\^^M{\ }'` in Appendix B is what actually defines `\⟨return⟩`, since a return is representable as `^^M`. Asking TEX to `\show\^^M` produces the response `'> \^^M=macro:->\␣.'`.

3.4. There are 256 of length 2; most of these are undefined when TEX begins. (TEX allows any character to be an escape, but it does not distinguish between control sequences that start with different escape characters.) If we assume that there are 52 letters, there are exactly 52^2 possible control sequences of length 3 (one for each pair of letters, from `AA` to `zz`). But Chapter 7 explains how to use `\catcode` to change any character into a "letter"; therefore it's possible to use any of 256^2 potential control sequences of length 3.

4.1. `Ulrich Dieter, {\sl Journal f\"ur die reine und angewandte`
`        Mathematik\/ \bf201} (1959), 37--70.`
It's convenient to use a single group for both `\sl` and `\bf` here. The `'\/'` is a refinement that you might not understand until you read the rest of Chapter 4.

4.2. `{\it Explain ... typeset a\/ {\rm roman} word ... sentence.}` Note the position of the italic correction in this case.

4.3. `\def\ic#1{\setbox0=\hbox{#1\/}\dimen0=\wd0`
`        \setbox0=\hbox{#1}\advance\dimen0 by -\wd0}`.

4.4. Control word names are made of letters, not digits.

4.5. Say `\def\sl{\it}` at the beginning, and delete other definitions of `\sl` that might be present in your format file (e.g., there might be one inside a `\tenpoint` macro).

4.6. `\font\squinttenrm=cmr10 at 5pt`
`\font\squinttenrm=cmr10 scaled 500`

5.1. `{shelf}ful` or `shelf{}ful`, etc.; or even `shelf\/ful`, which yields a shelfful instead of a shelfful. In fact, the latter idea—to insert an italic correction—is preferable because TeX will reinsert the ff ligature by itself after hyphenating `shelf{}ful`. (Appendix H points out that ligatures are put into a hyphenated word that contains no "explicit kerns," and an italic correction is an explicit kern.) But the italic correction may be too much (especially in an italic font); `shelf{\kern0pt}ful` is often best.

5.2. '␣{␣}␣' or '␣{}␣{}␣', etc. Plain TeX also has a `\space` macro, so you can type `\space\space\space`. (These aren't strictly equivalent to '␣␣␣', since they adjust the spaces by the current "space factor," as explained later.)

5.3. In the first case, you get the same result as if the innermost braces had not appeared at all, because you haven't used the grouping to change fonts or to control spacing or anything. TeX doesn't mind if you want to waste your time making groups for no particular reason. But in the second case, the necessary braces were forgotten. You get the letter 'S' centered on a line by itself, followed by a paragraph that begins with 'o should this.' on the next line.

5.4. You get the same result as if another pair of braces were present around '`\it centered`', except that the period is typeset from the italic font. (Both periods look about the same.)   The `\it` font will not remain in force after the `\centerline`, but this is something of a coincidence: TeX uses the braces to determine what text is to be centered, but then it removes the braces. The `\centerline` operation, as defined in Appendix B, puts the resulting braceless text inside *another* group; and that's why `\it` disappears after `\centerline`. (If you don't understand this, just don't risk leaving out braces in tricky situations, and you'll be OK.)

5.5. `\def\ital#1{{\it#1\/}}`. Pro: Users might find this easier to learn, because it works more like `\centerline` and they don't have to remember to make the italic correction.   Con: To avoid the italic correction just before a *comma* or *period*, users should probably be taught another control sequence; for example, with

    \def\nocorr{\kern0pt }

a user could type '`\ital{comma} or \ital{period\nocorr},`'. The alternative of putting a period or comma in italics, to avoid the italic correction, doesn't look as good. A long sequence of italics would be inefficient for TeX, since the entire text for the argument to `\ital` must be read into memory only to be scanned again.

5.6. `{1 {2 3 4 5} 4 6} 4.`

5.7. `\def\beginthe#1{\begingroup\def\blockname{#1}}`
`    \def\endthe#1{\def\test{#1}%`
`      \ifx\test\blockname\endgroup`
`      \else\errmessage{You should have said`
`        \string\endthe{\blockname}}\fi}`

6.1. Laziness and/or obstinacy.

6.2. There's an unwanted space after 'called—', because (as the book says) TEX treats the end of a line as if it were a blank space. That blank space is usually what you want, except when a line ends with a hyphen or a dash; so you should WATCH OUT for lines that end with hyphens or dashes.

6.3. It represents the heavy bar that shows up in your output. (This bar wouldn't be present if \overfullrule had been set to 0pt, nor is it present in an underfull box.)

6.4. This is the \parfillskip space that ends the paragraph. In plain TEX the parfillskip is zero when the last line of the paragraph is full; hence no space actually appears before the rule in the output of Experiment 3. But all hskips show up as spaces in an overfull box message, even if they're zero.

6.5. Run TEX with \hsize=1.5in \tolerance=10000 \raggedright \hbadness=-1 and then \input story. TEX will report the badness of all lines (except the final lines of paragraphs, where fill glue makes the badness zero).

6.6. \def\extraspace{\nobreak \hskip 0pt plus .15em\relax}
        \def\dash{\unskip\extraspace---\extraspace}
(If you try this with the story at 2-inch and 1.5-inch sizes, you will notice a substantial improvement. The \unskip allows people to leave a space before typing \dash. TEX will try to hyphenate before \dash, but not before '---'; cf. Appendix H. The \relax at the end of \extraspace is a precaution in case the next word is 'minus'.)

6.7. TEX would have deleted five tokens: 1, i, n, ␣, \centerline. (The space was at the end of line 2, the \centerline at the beginning of line 3.)

6.8. A control sequence like \centerline might well define a control sequence like \ERROR before telling TEX to look at #1. Therefore TEX doesn't interpret control sequences when it scans an argument.

7.1. Three forbidden characters were used. One should type

        Procter \& Gamble's ... \$2, a 10\% gain.

(Also the facts are wrong.)

7.2. Reverse slashes (backslashes) are fairly uncommon in formulas or text, and \\ is very easy to type; it was therefore felt best not to reserve \\ for such limited use. Typists can define \\ to be whatever they want (including \backslash).

7.3. 1, 2, 3, 4, 6, 7, 8, 10, 11, 12, 13. Active characters (type 13) are somewhat special; they behave like control sequences in most cases (e.g., when you say '\let\x=~' or '\ifx\x~'), but they behave like character tokens when they appear in the token list of \uppercase or \lowercase, and when unexpanded after \if or \ifcat.

7.4. It ends with either > or } or any character of category 2; then the effects of all \catcode definitions within the group are wiped out, except those that were \global. TEX doesn't have any built-in knowledge about how to pair up particular kinds of grouping characters. New category codes take effect as soon as a \catcode assignment has been digested. For example,

        {\catcode'\>=2 >

is a complete group. But without the space after '2' it would not be complete, since TEX would have read the '>' and converted it to a token before knowing what category code was being specified; TEX always reads the token following a constant before evaluating that constant.

7.5. If you type '\message{\string~}' and '\message{\string\~}', TEX responds with '~' and '\~', respectively. To get \$_{12}$ from \string you therefore need to make backslash an active character. One way to do this is

$$\{\catcode`/=0 \ \catcode`\\=13 \ /message\{/string\\\}\}$$

(The "null control sequence" that you get when there are no tokens between \csname and \endcsname is not a solution to this exercise, because \string converts it to '\csname\endcsname'. There is, however, another solution: If TEX's \escapechar parameter—which will be explained in one of the next dangerous bends—is negative or greater than 255, then '\string\\' works.)

7.6. \$_{12}$ a$_{12}$ \$_{12}$ ⊔$_{10}$ b$_{12}$.

7.7. \def\ifundefined#1{\expandafter\ifx\csname#1\endcsname\relax}
Note that a control sequence like this must be used with care; it cannot be included in conditional text, because the \ifx will not be seen when \ifundefined isn't expanded.

7.8. First \uppercase produces 'A\lowercase{BC}'; then you get 'Abc'.

7.9. '\copyright\ \uppercase\expandafter{\romannumeral\year}'.   (This is admittedly tricky; the '\expandafter' expands the token after the '{', not the token after the group.)

7.10. (We assume that parameter #2 is not simply an active character, and that \escapechar is between 0 and 255.)

```
\def\gobble#1{} % remove one token
\def\appendroman#1#2#3{\edef#1{\csname
    \expandafter\gobble\string#2\romannumeral#3\endcsname}}
```

8.1. The % would be treated as a comment character, because its category code is 14; thus, no % token or } token would get through to the gullet of TEX where numbers are treated. When a character is of category 0, 5, 9, 14, or 15, the extra \ must be used; and the \ doesn't hurt, so you can always use it to be safe.

8.2. (a) Both characters terminate the current line; but a character of category 5 might be converted into ⊔$_{10}$ or a $\boxed{\text{par}}$ token, while a character of category 14 never produces a token. (b) They produce character tokens stamped with different category numbers. For example, \$$_3$ is not the same token as \$$_4$, so TEX's digestive processes will treat them differently. (c) Same as (b), plus the fact that control sequence names treat letters differently. (d) No. (e) Yes; characters of category 10 are ignored at the beginning of every line, since every line starts in state N. (f) No.

8.3. TEX had just read the control sequence \vship, so it was in state S, and it was just ready to read the space before '1in'. Afterwards it ignored that space, since it was in state S; but if you had typed I\obeyspaces in response to that error message, you would have seen the space. Incidentally, when TEX prints the context of an error message, the bottom pair of lines comes from a text file, but the other pairs of lines are portions of token lists that TEX is reading (unless they begin with '`<*>`', when they represent text inserted during error recovery).

8.4. $\$_3$ x_{11} $\hat{}_7$ 2_{12} $\$_3$ $\tilde{}_{13}$ $\sqcup_{10}$ $\boxed{\text{TeX}}$ b_{12} v_{12} $\sqcup_{10}$. The final space comes from the ⟨return⟩ placed at the end of the line. Code `^^6` yields v only when not followed by 0–9 or a–f. The initial space is ignored, because state N governs the beginning of the line.

8.5. H_{11} i_{11} $!_{12}$ $\sqcup_{10}$ $\boxed{\text{par}}$ $\boxed{\text{par}}$. The '$\sqcup$' comes from the ⟨return⟩ at the end of the first line; the second and third lines each contribute a $\boxed{\text{par}}$.

8.6. The two `^^B`'s are not recognized as consecutive superscript characters, since the first `^^B` is converted to code 2 which doesn't equal the following character `^`. Hence the result is seven tokens: $\hat{}\hat{}B_7$ $\hat{}\hat{}B_7$ M_{11} $\boxed{\text{^^B}}$ $\sqcup_{10}$ $\hat{}\hat{}M_{11}$ $\boxed{\text{M^^M}}$. The last of these is a control word whose name has two letters. The ⟨space⟩ after \M is deleted before TEX inserts the ⟨return⟩ token.

8.7. Both alternatives work fine in text; in particular, they combine as in `\lq\lq` to form ligatures. But the definition in Appendix B works also in connection with constants; e.g., `\char\lq\%` and `\char\rq140` are valid. (Incidentally, the construction `\let\lq=‘` would not work with constants, since the quotes in a ⟨number⟩ must come from character tokens of category 12; after `\let\lq=‘` the control sequence token `\lq` will not expand into a character token, nor *is* it a character token!)

9.1. `na\"\i ve` or `na{\"\i}ve` or `na\"{\i}ve`.

9.2. Belovèd protégé; rôle coördinator; soufflés, crêpes, pâtés, etc.

9.3. `\AE sop's \OE uvres en fran\c cais`.

9.4. `{\sl Commentarii Academi\ae\ scientiarum imperialis petropolitan\ae\/} is now {\sl Akademi\t\i a Nauk SSSR, Doklady}`.

9.5. `Ernesto Ces\'aro, P\'al Erd\H os, \O ystein Ore, Stanis\l aw \'Swier%
czkowski, Serge\u\i\ \t Iur'ev, Mu\d hammad ibn M\^us\^a al-Khw\^arizm\^\i`.

9.6. The proper umlaut is \H, which isn't available in \tt, so it's necessary to borrow the accent from another font. For example, `{\tt P\'al Erd{\bf\H{\tt o}}s}` uses a bold accent, which is suitably dark.

9.7. `{\it Europe on {\sl\$}15.00 a day\/}`

9.8. The extra braces keep font changes local. An argument makes the use of \' more consistent with the use of other accents like \d, which are manufactured from other characters without using the **\accent** primitive.

10.1. Exactly 7227 pt.

10.2. $-.013837$ in, $0.$ mm, $+42.1$ dd, 3 in, 29 pc, 123456789 sp. (The lines of text in this manual are 29 picas wide.)

10.3. The first is not allowed, since octal notation cannot be used with a decimal point. The second is, however, legal, since a ⟨number⟩ can be hexadecimal according to the rule mentioned in Chapter 8; it means 12 cc, which is 144 dd $\approx$ 154.08124 pt. The third is also accepted, since a ⟨digit string⟩ can be empty; it is a complicated way to say 0 sp.

10.4. `\def\tick#1{\vrule height 0pt depth #1pt}`
`\def\\{\hbox to 1cm{\hfil\tick4\hfil\tick8}}`
`\vbox{\hrule\hbox{\tick8\\\\\\\\\\\\\\\\\\\\\\\\}}`

(You might also try putting ticks at every millimeter, in order to see how good your system is; some output devices can't handle 101 rules all at once.)

10.5. For example, say '`\magnification=\magstep1 \input story \end`' to get magnification 1200; `\magstep2` and `\magstep3` are 1440 and 1728. Three separate runs are needed, since there can be at most one magnification per job. The output may look funny if the fonts don't exist at the stated magnifications.

10.6. Magnification is by a factor of 1.2. Since font `\first` is cmr10 at 12 pt, it will be cmr10 at 14.4 pt after magnification; font `\second` will be cmr10 at 12 pt. (TeX changes '12truept' into '10pt', and the final output magnifies it back to 12 pt.)

11.1. This E is inside a box that's inside a box.

11.2. The idea is to construct a box and to look inside. For example,

`\setbox0=\hbox{\sl g\/} \showbox0`

reveals that `\/` is implemented by placing a kern after the character. Further experiment shows that this kern is inserted even when the italic correction is zero.

11.3. The height, depth, and width of the enclosing box should be just large enough to enclose all of the contents, so the result is:

```
\hbox(8.98608+0.0)x24.44484
.\tenrm T
.\kern 1.66702
.\hbox(6.83331+0.0)x6.80557, shifted -2.15277
..\tenrm E
.\kern 1.25
.\tenrm X
```

(You probably predicted a height of 8.9861; TeX's internal calculations are in sp, not pt/100000, so the rounding in the fifth decimal place is not readily predictable.)

11.4. No applications of such symmetrical boxes to English-language printing were apparent; it seemed pointless to carry extra generality as useless baggage that would rarely if ever be used, merely for the sake of symmetry. In other words, the author wore a computer science cap instead of a mathematician's mantle on the day that TeX's boxes were born. Time will tell whether or not this was a fundamental error!

11.5. The following solution is based on a general `\makeblankbox` macro that prints the edges of a box using rules of given thickness outside and inside that box; the box dimensions are those of `\box0`.

```
\def\dolist{\afterassignment\dodolist\let\next= }
\def\dodolist{\ifx\next\endlist \let\next\relax
  \else \\\let\next\dolist \fi
  \next}
\def\endlist{\endlist}
```

```
\def\hidehrule#1#2{\kern-#1%
  \hrule height#1 depth#2 \kern-#2 }
\def\hidevrule#1#2{\kern-#1{\dimen0=#1
    \advance\dimen0 by#2\vrule width\dimen0}\kern-#2 }
\def\makeblankbox#1#2{\hbox{\lower\dp0\vbox{\hidehrule{#1}{#2}%
    \kern-#1 % overlap the rules at the corners
    \hbox to \wd0{\hidevrule{#1}{#2}%
      \raise\ht0\vbox to #1{}% set the vrule height
      \lower\dp0\vtop to #1{}% set the vrule depth
      \hfil\hidevrule{#2}{#1}}%
    \kern-#1\hidehrule{#2}{#1}}}}
\def\maketypebox{\makeblankbox{0pt}{1pt}}
\def\makelightbox{\makeblankbox{.2pt}{.2pt}}
\def\\{\expandafter\if\space\next\
  \else \setbox0=\hbox{\next}\maketypebox\fi}
\def\demobox#1{\setbox0=\hbox{\dolist#1\endlist}%
  \copy0\kern-\wd0\makelightbox}
```

11.6.
```
\def\frac#1/#2{\leavevmode\kern.1em
  \raise.5ex\hbox{\the\scriptfont0 #1}\kern-.1em
  /\kern-.15em\lower.25ex\hbox{\the\scriptfont0 #2}}
```

12.1. $9 + 16$ units, $9 + 32$ units, $12 + 0$ units. (But TeX would consider so much stretching to be "infinitely bad.")

12.2. 'What happens now?' is placed in a line of width \hsize, with twice as much space at the left as at the right; 'and now?' is put flush right on the following line.

12.3. The first two give an "overfull box" if the argument doesn't fit on a line; the third allows the argument to stick out into the margins instead. (Plain TeX's \centerline is \centerlinec; the stickout effect shows up in the narrow-column experiment of Chapter 6.) If the argument contains no infinite glue, \centerlinea and \centerlineb produce the same effect; but \centerlineb will center an argument that contains 'fil' glue.

12.4. `Mr.~\& Mrs.~User were married by Rev.~Drofnats, who preached on Matt.~19\thinspace:\thinspace3--9.` (Such thin spaces are traditional for Biblical references to chapter and verse, but you weren't really expected to know that. Plain TeX defines \thinspace to be a kern, not glue; hence no break between lines will occur at a thinspace.)

12.5. `Donald~E.\ Knuth, ``Mathematical typography,'' {\sl Bull.\ Amer.\ Math.\ Soc.\ \bf1} (1979), 337--372.` (But the '\' after 'E.' isn't necessary, because of a rule you will learn if you venture around the next dangerous bend.)

12.6. There are several ways; perhaps the easiest are to type '\hbox{NASA}.' or 'NASA\null.' (The \null macro is an abbreviation for '\hbox{}'.)

12.7. 1000, except: 999 after B, S, D, and J; 1250 after the comma; 3000 after the exclamation point, the double-right-quote, and the periods. If a period had come right after the B (i.e., if the text had said 'B. Sally'), the space factor after that period would have been 1000, not 3000.

12.8. \box3 is 2 pt high, 4 pt deep, 3 pt wide. Starting at the reference point of \box3, go right .75 pt and down 3 pt to reach the reference point of \box1; or go right 1 pt to reach the reference point of \box2.

12.9. The stretch and shrink components of \baselineskip and \lineskip should be equal, and the \lineskiplimit should equal the normal \lineskip spacing, to guarantee continuity.

12.10. Yes it did, but only because none of his boxes had a negative height or depth. He would have been safer if he had set \baselineskip=-1000pt, \lineskip=0pt, and \lineskiplimit=16383pt. (Plain TEX's \offinterlineskip macro does this.)

12.11. The interline glue will be zero, and the natural height is $1 + 1 - 3 + 2 = 1$ pt (because the depth of \box2 isn't included in the natural height); so the glue will ultimately become \vskip-1pt when it's set. Thus, \box3 is 3 pt high, 2 pt deep, 4 pt wide. Its reference point coincides with that of \box2; to get to the reference point of \box1 you go up 2 pt and right 3 pt.

12.12. The interline glue will be 6 pt minus 3 fil; the final depth will be zero, since \box2 is followed by glue; the natural height is 12 pt; and the shrinkability is 5 fil. So \box4 will be 4 pt high, 0 pt deep, 1 pt wide, and it will contain five items: \vskip -1.6pt, \box1, \vskip1.2pt, \moveleft4pt\box2, \vskip-1.6pt. Starting at the reference point of \box4, you get to the reference point of \box1 by going up 4.6 pt, or to the reference point of \box2 by going up .4 pt and left 4 pt. (For example, you go up 4 pt to get to the upper left corner of \box4; then down −1.6 pt, i.e., up 1.6 pt, to get to the upper left corner of \box1; then down 1 pt to reach its reference point. This problem is clearly academic, since it's rather ridiculous to include infinite shrinkability in the baselineskip.)

12.13. Now \box4 will be 4 pt high, −4 pt deep, 1 pt wide, and it will contain \vskip -2.4pt, \box1, \vskip-1.2pt, \moveleft4pt\box2, \vskip-2.4pt. From the baseline of \box4, go up exactly 5.4 pt to reach the baseline of \box1, or exactly 3.6 pt to reach the baseline of \box2.

12.14. \vbox to x{} produces height x; \vtop to x{} produces depth x; the other dimensions are zero. (This holds even when x is negative.)

12.15. There are several possibilities:

```
\def\nullbox#1#2#3{\vbox to#1{\vss\hrule height-#2depth#2width#3}}
```

works because the rule will be of zero thickness. Less tricky is

```
\def\nullbox#1#2#3{\vbox to#1{\vss\vtop to#2{\vss\hbox to#3{}}}}
```

Both of these are valid with negative height and/or depth, but they do not produce negative width. If the width might be negative, but not the height or depth, you can use, e.g., \def\nullbox#1#2#3{\hbox to#3{\hss\raise#1\null\lower#2\null}}. It's impossible for \hbox to construct a box whose height or depth is negative; it's impossible for \vbox or \vtop to construct a box whose width is negative.

However, there's actually a trivial solution to the general problem, based on features that will be discussed later:

```
\def\nullbox#1#2#3{\setbox0=\null
  \ht0=#1 \dp0=#2 \wd0=#3 \box0 }
```

12.16. `\def\llap#1{\hbox to 0pt{\hss#1}}`

12.17. You get 'A' at the extreme left and 'puzzle.' at the extreme right, because the space between words has the only stretchability that is finite; the infinite stretchability cancels out. (In this case, TEX's rule about infinite glue differs from what you would get in the limit if the value of 1 fil were finite but getting larger and larger. The true limiting behavior would stretch the text 'A puzzle.' in the same way, but it would also move that text infinitely far away beyond the right edge of the page.)

13.1. Simply saying `\hbox{...}` won't work, since that box will just continue the previous vertical list without switching modes. You need to start the paragraph explicitly, and the straightforward way to do that is to say `\indent\hbox{...}`. But suppose you want to define a macro that expands to an hbox, where this macro is to be used in the midst of a paragraph as well as at the beginning; then you don't want to force users to type `\indent` before calling your macro at the beginning of a paragraph, nor do you want to say `\indent` in the macro itself (since that might insert unwanted indentations). One solution to this more general problem is to say '`\␣\unskip\hbox{...}`', since `\␣` makes the mode horizontal while `\unskip` removes the unwanted space. Plain TEX provides a `\leavevmode` macro, which solves this problem in what is probably the most efficient way: `\leavevmode` is an abbreviation for '`\unhbox\voidbox`', where `\voidbox` is a permanently empty box register.

13.2. The output of `\tracingcommands` shows that four blank space tokens were digested; these originated at the ends of lines 2, 3, 4, and 5. Only the first had any effect, since blank spaces are ignored in math formulas and in vertical modes.

13.3. The `end-group character` finishes the paragraph and the `\vbox`, and `\bye` stands for '`\vfill...`', so the next three commands are

```
{math mode: math shift character $}
{restricted horizontal mode: end-group character }}
{vertical mode: \vfill}
```

13.4. It contains only mixtures of vertical glue and horizontal rules whose reference points appear at the left of the page; there's no text.

13.5. Vertical mode can occur only as the outermost mode; horizontal mode and display math mode can occur only when immediately enclosed by vertical or internal vertical mode; ordinary math mode cannot be immediately enclosed by vertical or internal vertical mode; all other cases are possible.

14.1. `(cf.~Chapter~12).`
`Chapters 12 and~21.`
`line~16 of Chapter~6's {\tt story}`
`lines 7 to~11`
`lines 2,~3, 4, and~5.`
`(2)~a big black bar`
`All 256~characters are initially of category~12,`
`letter~{\tt x} in family~1.`
`the factor~$f$, where $n$~is 1000~times~$f$.`

14.2. '`for all $n$~greater than~$n_0$`' avoids distracting breaks.

14.3. 'exercise \hbox{4.3.2--15}' guarantees that there is no break after the en-dash. But this precaution is rarely necessary, so 'exercise 4.3.2--15' is an acceptable answer. No ~ is needed; '4.3.2–15' is so long that it causes no offense at the beginning of a line.

14.4. The space you get from ~ will stretch or shrink with the other spaces in the same line, but the space inside an hbox has a fixed width since that glue has already been set once and for all. Furthermore the first alternative permits the word Chapter to be hyphenated.

14.5. '\hbox{$x=0$}' is unbreakable, and we will see later that '${x=0}$' cannot be broken. Both of these solutions set the glue surrounding the equals sign to some fixed value, but such glue normally wants to stretch; furthermore the \hbox solution might include undesirable blank space at the beginning or end of a line, if \mathsurround is nonzero. A third solution '$x=\nobreak0$' avoids both defects.

14.6. \exhyphenpenalty=10000 prohibits all such breaks, according to the rules found later in this chapter. Similarly, \hyphenpenalty=10000 prevents breaks after implicit (discretionary) hyphens.

14.7. The second and fourth lines are indented by an additional "quad" of space, i.e., by one extra em in the current type style. (The control sequence \quad does an \hskip; when TeX is in vertical mode, \hskip begins a new paragraph and puts glue after the indentation.) If \indent had been used instead, those lines wouldn't have been indented any more than the first and third, because \indent is implicit at the beginning of every paragraph. Double indentation on the second and fourth lines could have been achieved by '\indent\indent'.

14.8. ba\ck en and Be\ttt uch, where the macros \ck and \ttt are defined by

```
\def\ck{\discretionary{k-}{k}{ck}}
\def\ttt{tt\discretionary{-}{t}{}}
```

The English word 'eighteen' might deserve similar treatment. TeX's hyphenation algorithm will not make such spelling changes automatically.

14.9. \def\break{\penalty-10000 }

14.10. You get a forced break as if \nobreak were not present, because \break cannot be cancelled by another penalty. In general if you have two penalties in a row, their combined effect is the same as a single penalty whose value is the minimum of the two original values, unless both of those values force breaks. (You get two breaks from \break\break; the second one creates an empty line.)

14.11. Breaks are forced when $p \leq -10000$, so there's no point in subtracting a large constant whose effect on the total demerits is known *a priori*, especially when that might cause arithmetic overflow.

14.12. $(10 + 131)^2 + 0^2 + 10000 = 29881$ and $(10 + 1)^2 + 50^2 + 10000 = 12621$. In both cases the \adjdemerits were added because the lines were visually incompatible (decent, then very loose, then decent); plain TeX's values for \linepenalty and \adjdemerits were used.

14.13. Because TEX discards a glue item that occurs just before \par. Ben should have said, e.g., '\hfilneg\ \par'.

14.14. Just say \parfillskip=\parindent. Of course, TEX will not be able to find appropriate line breaks unless each paragraph is sufficiently long or sufficiently lucky; but with an appropriate text, your output will be immaculately symmetrical.

14.15. Assuming that the author is deceased and/or set in his or her ways, the remedy is to insert '{\parfillskip=0pt\par\parskip=0pt\noindent}' in random places, after each 50 lines or so of text. (Every space between words is usually a feasible breakpoint, when you get sufficiently far from the beginning of a paragraph.)

14.16. {\leftskip=-1pt \rightskip=1pt ⟨text⟩ \par}

(This applies to a full paragraph; if you want to correct only isolated lines, you have to do it by hand.)

14.17. '\def\line#1{\hbox to\hsize{\hskip\leftskip#1\hskip\rightskip}}' is the only change needed. (Incidentally, displayed equations don't take account of \leftskip and \rightskip either; it's more difficult to change that, because so many variations are possible.)

14.18. The author's best solution is based on a variable \dimen register \x:

```
\setbox1=\hbox{I}
\setbox0=\vbox{\parshape=11 -0\x0\x -1\x2\x -2\x4\x -3\x6\x
   -4\x8\x -5\x10\x -6\x12\x -7\x14\x -8\x16\x -9\x18\x -10\x20\x
   \ifdim \x>2em \rightskip=-\wd1
   \else \frenchspacing \rightskip=-\wd1 plus1pt minus1pt
    \leftskip=0pt plus 1pt minus1pt \fi
   \parfillskip=0pt \tolerance=1000 \noindent I turn, ... hand.}
\centerline{\hbox to \wd1{\box0\hss}}
```

Satisfactory results are obtained with font cmr10 when \x is set to 8.9 pt, 13.4 pt, 18.1 pt, 22.6 pt, 32.6 pt, and 47.2 pt, yielding triangles that are respectively 11, 9, 8, 7, 6, and 5 lines tall.

14.19. \item{} at the beginning of each paragraph that wants hanging indentation.

14.20. \item{$\bullet$}

14.21. Either change \hsize or \rightskip. The trick is to change it back again at the end of a paragraph. Here's one way, without grouping:

```
\let\endgraf=\par \edef\restorehsize{\hsize=\the\hsize}
\def\par{\endgraf \restorehsize \let\par=\endgraf}
\advance\hsize by-\parindent
```

14.22. \dimen0=\hsize \advance\dimen0 by 2em
   \parshape=3 0pt\hsize 0pt\hsize -2em\dimen0

14.23. The three paragraphs can be combined into a single paragraph, if you use '\hfil\vadjust{\vskip\parskip}\break\indent' instead of '\par' after the first two. Then of course you say, e.g., \hangindent=-50pt \hangafter=-15. (The same idea can be applied in connection with \looseness, if you want TEX to make one of three paragraphs looser but if you don't want to choose which one it will be. However, long paragraphs fill TEX's memory; please use restraint.) See also the next exercise.

14.24. Use `\hangcarryover` between paragraphs, defined as follows:

```
\def\hangcarryover{\edef\next{\hangafter=\the\hangafter
    \hangindent=\the\hangindent}
\par\next
\edef\next{\prevgraf=\the\prevgraf}
\indent\next}
```

14.25. It will set the current paragraph in the minimum number of lines that can be achieved without violating the tolerance; and, given that number of lines, it will break them optimally. (However, nonzero looseness makes TEX work harder, so this is not recommended if you don't want to pay for the extra computation. You can achieve almost the same result much more efficiently by setting `\linepenalty=100`, say.)

14.26. 150, 100, 0, 250. (When the total penalty is zero, as between lines 3 and 4 in this case, no penalty is actually inserted.)

14.27. `\interlinepenalty` plus `\clubpenalty` plus `\widowpenalty` (and also plus `\brokenpenalty`, if the first line ends with a discretionary break).

14.28. The tricky part is to avoid "opening up" the paragraph by adding anything to its height; yet this star is to be contributed after a line having an unknown depth, because the depth of the line depends on details of line breaking that aren't known until afterwards. The following solution uses `\strut`, and assumes that the line containing the marginal star does not have depth exceeding `\dp\strutbox`, the depth of a `\strut`.

```
\def\strutdepth{\dp\strutbox}
\def\marginalstar{\strut\vadjust{\kern-\strutdepth\specialstar}}
```

Here `\specialstar` is a box of height zero and depth `\strutdepth`, and it puts an asterisk in the left margin:

```
\def\specialstar{\vtop to \strutdepth{
    \baselineskip\strutdepth
    \vss\llap{* }\null}}
```

14.29. `\def\insertbullets{\everypar={\llap{$\bullet$\enspace}}}`

(A similar device can be used to insert hanging indentation, and/or to number the paragraphs automatically.)

14.30. First comes `\parskip` glue (but you might not see it on the current page if you say `\showlists`, since glue disappears at the top of each page). Then comes the result of `\everypar`, but let's assume that `\everypar` doesn't add anything to the horizontal list, so that you get an empty horizontal list; then there's no partial paragraph before the display. The displayed equation follows the normal rules (it occupies lines 1–3 of the paragraph, and uses the indentation and length of line 2, if there's a nonstandard shape). Nothing follows the display, since a blank space is ignored after a closing '`$$`'.

Incidentally, the behavior is different if you start a paragraph with '`$$`' instead of with `\noindent$$`, since TEX inserts a paragraph indentation that will appear on a line by itself (with `\leftskip` and `\parfillskip` and `\rightskip` glue).

14.31. A break at \penalty50 would cancel \hskip2em\nobreak\hfil, so the next line would be forced to start with the reviewer's name flush left. (But \vadjust{} would actually be better than \hbox{}; it uses TeX more efficiently.)

14.32. Otherwise the line-breaking algorithm might prefer two final lines to one final line, simply in order to move a hyphen from the second-last line up to the third-last line where it doesn't cause demerits. This in fact caused some surprises when the \signed macro was being tested; \tracingparagraphs=1 was used to diagnose the problem.

14.33. Distributing the extra space evenly would lead to three lines of the maximum badness (10000). It's better to have just one bad line instead of three, since TeX doesn't distinguish degrees of badness when lines are really awful. In this particular case the \tolerance was 200, so TeX didn't try any line breaks that would stretch the first two lines; but even if the tolerance had been raised to 10000, the optimum setting would have had only one underfull line. If you really want to spread the space evenly you can do so by using \spaceskip to increase the amount of stretchability between words.

14.34. \def\raggedcenter{\leftskip=0pt plus4em \rightskip=\leftskip
\parfillskip=0pt \spaceskip=.3333em \xspaceskip=.5em
\pretolerance=9999 \tolerance=9999 \parindent=0pt
\hyphenpenalty=9999 \exhyphenpenalty=9999 }

15.1. The last three page-break calculations would have been

```
% t=503.0 plus 8.0 minus 4.0 g=528.0 b=3049 p=150 c=3199#
% t=514.0 plus 8.0 minus 4.0 g=528.0 b=533 p=-100 c=433#
% t=542.0 plus 11.0 minus 6.0 g=528.0 b=* p=0 c=*
```

so the break would have occurred at the same place. The badness would have been 533, but the page would still have looked tolerable. (On the other hand if that paragraph had been two lines shorter instead of one, the first two lines of the next "dangerous bend" paragraph would have appeared on that page; the natural height $t = 531\,\mathrm{pt}$ would have been able to shrink to $g = 528\,\mathrm{pt}$ because the three "medskips" on the page would have had a total shrinkability of 6 pt. This would certainly have been preferable to a stretched-out page whose badness was 3049; but the author might have seen it and written another sentence or two, so that the paragraph would not have been broken up. After all, this manual is supposed to be an example of good practice.)

15.2. The next legal break after the beginning of a dangerous bend paragraph occurs 28 pt later, because there is 6 pt additional space for a \medskip, followed by two lines of 11 pt each. TeX does not allow breaking between those two lines; the \clubpenalty is set briefly to 10000 in Appendix E, since the dangerous bend symbol is two lines tall.

15.3. A page always contains at least one box, if there are no insertions, since the legal breakpoints are discarded otherwise. Statement (a) fails if the height of the topmost box exceeds 10 pt. Statement (b) fails if the depth of the bottommost box exceeds 2.2 pt, or if some glue or kern comes between the bottommost box and the page break (unless that glue or kern exactly cancels the depth of the box).

15.4. \topinsert\vskip2in\rightline{\vbox{\hsize ... artwork.}}\endinsert does the job. But it's slightly more efficient to avoid \rightline by changing \leftskip as follows: '\leftskip=\hsize \advance\leftskip by-3in'. Then TeX doesn't have to read the text of the caption twice.

15.5. It would appear on page 25, since it does fit there. A \midinsert will jump ahead of other insertions only if it is not carried over to another page; for example, if the second 3-inch insertion were a \midinsert, it would not appear on page 26, because it is converted to a \topinsert as soon as the \midinsert macro notices that the insertion is too big for page 25.

15.6. Set \count1 to 50, then \dimen2 to 50 pt, then \count1 to 6, then \skip2 to −10 pt plus 6 fil minus 50 pt, then \skip2 to 60 pt plus −36 fil minus −300 pt, then \skip2 to 1 sp minus −6 sp, then \count6 to 1, then \skip1 to 25 pt plus 1 sp minus 1 fill, then \skip2 to 25 pt minus −150 pt, then \skip1 to 0 pt plus 1 sp minus 1 fill.

15.7. If \skip4 has infinite stretchability, \skip5 will be zero; otherwise it will be 0 pt plus 1 pt.

15.8. \advance\dimen2 by0.5\dimen3 \divide\dimen2 by\dimen3
     \multiply\dimen2 by\dimen3

15.9. \count1 takes the values 5, then 2 (the old 5 is saved), then 4 (which is made global), then 8 (and 4 is saved); finally the value 4 is restored, and that is the answer. (For further remarks, see the discussion of \tracingrestores in Chapter 27.)

15.10. \hbox{\hbox{A}A}. After '\unhbox5', \box5 is void; \unhcopy5 yields nothing.

15.11. \hbox{A}. But after '{\global\setbox3=\hbox{A}\setbox3=\box3}', \box3 will be void.

15.12. \newcount\notenumber
     \def\clearnotenumber{\notenumber=0\relax}
     \def\note{\advance\notenumber by 1
       \footnote{$^{\the\notenumber}$}}

15.13. Yes, in severe circumstances. (1) If there is no other legal breakpoint, TeX will take a break whose cost is ∞. (2) If \vadjust{\eject} occurs on the same line as a footnote, before that footnote, the reference will be forcibly detached. (3) Other \vadjust commands on that line could also interpose breakpoints before the insertion.

16.1. $\gamma+\nu\in\Gamma$.

16.2. \le, \ge, and \ne. (These are short for "less-or-equal," "greater-or-equal," and "not-equal.") You can also use the names \leq, \geq, and \neq. (The fourth most common symbol is, perhaps, '∞', which stands for "infinity" and is called '\infty'.)

16.3. In the former, the '_2' applies to the plus sign ($x +_2 F_3$); but in the latter, it applies to an empty subformula ($x + {}_2F_3$).

16.4. The results are 'x^{y^z}' and 'x^{y^z}'; the z in the first alternative is the same size as the y, but in the second it is smaller. Furthermore, the y and z in the first case aren't quite at the same height. (Good typists never even think of the first construction, because mathematicians never want it.)

16.5. The second alternative doesn't work properly when there's a subscript at the same time as a prime. Furthermore, some mathematicians use \prime also in the subscript position; they write, for example, $F'(w, z) = \partial F(w, z)/\partial z$ and $F_{\prime}(w, z) = \partial F(w, z)/\partial w$.

16.6. `$R_i{}^{jk}{}_l$`.

16.7. `10^{10}`; `2^{n+1}`; `(n+1)^2`; `\sqrt{1-x^2}`; `\overline{w+\overline z}`; `p_1^{e_1}`; `a_{b_{c_{d_e}}}`; `\root3\of{h''_n(\alpha x)}`. (Of course, you should enclose these formulas in dollar signs so that TeX will process them in math mode. Superscripts and subscripts can be given in either order; for example, `h''_n` and `h_n''` both work the same. You should not leave out any of the braces shown here; for example, '`$10^10$`' would yield '10^10'. But it doesn't hurt to insert additional braces around letters or numbers, as in '`({n}+{1})^{2}`'. The indicated blank spaces are necessary unless you use extra braces; otherwise TeX will complain about undefined control sequences `\overlinez` and `\alphax`.)

16.8. He got 'If$x = y$...' because he forgot to leave a space after 'If'; spaces disappear between dollar signs. He should also have ended the sentence with '`$y$.`'; punctuation that belongs to a sentence should not be included in a formula, as we will see in Chapter 18. (But you aren't expected to know that yet.)

16.9. `Deleting an element from an $n$-tuple leaves an $(n-1)$-tuple.`

16.10. Q, f, g, j, p, q, y. (The analogous Greek letters are $\beta, \gamma, \zeta, \eta, \mu, \xi, \rho, \phi, \varphi, \chi, \psi$.)

16.11. `$z^{*2}$` and `$h_*'(z)$`.

16.12. `$3{\cdot}1416$`. (One of the earlier examples in this chapter showed that `\cdot` is a binary operation; putting it in braces makes it act like an ordinary symbol.)

If you have lots of constants like this, for example in a table, there's a way to make ordinary periods act like `\cdot` symbols: Just define `\mathcode`. to be "0201, assuming that the fonts of plain TeX are being used. However, this could be dangerous, since ordinary periods are used frequently in displayed equations; the `\mathcode` change should be confined to places where every period is to be a `\cdot`.

16.13. `$e^{-x^2}$`, `$D\sim p^\alpha M+l$`, and `$\ghat\in(H^{\pi_1^{-1}})'$`. (If you are reading the dangerous bend sections, you know that the recommended way to define `\ghat` is '`\def\ghat{{\hat g}}`'.)

17.1. $x + y^{2/(k+1)}$ (`$x+y^{2/(k+1)}$`).

17.2. $((a + 1)/(b + 1))x$ (`$((a+1)/(b+1))x$`).

17.3. He got the displayed formula
$$\frac{x = (y^2}{k + 1)}$$
because he forgot that an unconfined `\over` applies to everything. (He should probably have typed '`$$x=\left(y^2\over k+1\right)$$`', using ideas that will be presented later in this chapter; this not only makes the parentheses larger, it keeps the '$x =$' out of the fraction, because `\left` and `\right` introduce subformulas.)

17.4. '`$7{1\over2}\cents$`' or '`7$1\over2$\cents`'. (Incidentally, the definition used here was `\def\cents{\hbox{\rm\rlap/c}}`.)

17.5. Style D' is used for the subformula $p_2^{e'}$, hence style S' is used for the superscript e' and the subscript 2, and style SS' is used for the supersuperscript prime. The square root sign and the p appear in text size; the 2 and the e appear in script size; and the $'$ is in scriptscript size.

17.6. `$${1\over2}{n\choose k}$$`; `$$\displaystyle{n\choose k}\over2$$`. All of these braces are necessary.

17.7. `$${p \choose 2} x^2 y^{p-2} - {1 \over 1-x}{1 \over 1-x^2}.$$`

17.8. `$$\sum_{i=1}^p\sum_{j=1}^q\sum_{k=1}^ra_{ij}b_{jk}c_{ki}$$`.

17.9. `$$\sum_{{\scriptstyle 1\le i\le p \atop \scriptstyle 1\le j\le q} \atop \scriptstyle 1\le k\le r} a_{ij} b_{jk} c_{ki}$$`.

17.10. `$\displaystyle\biggl({\partial^2\over\partial x^2}+ {\partial^2\over\partial y^2}\biggr)\bigl|\varphi(x+iy)\bigr|^2=0$`.

17.11. Formulas that are more than one line tall are usually two lines tall, not $1\frac{1}{2}$ or $2\frac{1}{2}$ lines tall.

17.12. `$\bigl(x+f(x)\bigr) \big/ \bigl(x-f(x)\bigr)$`. (Notice especially the '\big/'; an ordinary slash would look too small between the \big parentheses.

17.13. `$$\pi(n)=\sum_{k=2}^n\left\lfloor\phi(k)\over k-1\right\rfloor.$$`

17.14. `$$\pi(n)=\sum_{m=2}^n\left\lfloor\biggl(\sum_{k=1}^{m-1}\bigl \lfloor(m/k)\big/\lceil m/k\rceil\bigr\rfloor\biggr)^{-1}\right\rfloor.$$`

17.15. A displayed formula equivalent to `$$D{{T}\over{T}^{{S}^{SS}}}$$`.

17.16. `\def\sqr#1#2{{\vcenter{\vbox{\hrule height.#2pt`
`            \hbox{\vrule width.#2pt height#1pt \kern#1pt`
`                \vrule width.#2pt}`
`            \hrule height.#2pt}}}}`
`\def\square{\mathchoice\sqr34\sqr34\sqr{2.1}3\sqr{1.5}3}`

17.17. `\def\euler{\atopwithdelims<>}`.

17.18. The \textfont0 that was current at the beginning of the formula will be used, because this redefinition is local to the braces. (It would be a different story if '\global\textfont' had appeared instead; that would have changed the meaning of \textfont0 at all levels.)

17.19. "2208 and "220F.

17.20. `\mathchardef\alpha="710B`. Incidentally, {\rm\alpha} will then give a spurious result, because character position "0B of roman fonts does not contain an alpha; you should warn your users about what characters they are allowed to type under the influence of special conventions like \rm.

17.21. If \delcode'{ were set to some nonnegative delimiter code, you would get no error message when you wrote something like '\left{'. This would be bad because strange effects would happen when certain subformulas were given as arguments to macros, or when they appeared in alignments. But it has an even worse defect, because a user who gets away with '\left{' is likely to try also '\bigl{', which fails miserably.

17.22. Since \bigl is defined as a macro with one parameter, it gets just '\delimiter' as the argument. You have to write '\bigl{\delimiter"426830A}' to make this work. On the other hand, \left will balk if the following character is a left brace. Therefore it's best to have control sequence names for all delimiters.

18.1. `$R(n,t)=O(t^{n/2})$`, as `$t\to0^+$`.   (N.B.: '`O`(', not '`0`('.)

18.2. `$$p_1(n)=\lim_{m\to\infty}\sum_{\nu=0}^\infty`
`        \bigl(1-\cos^{2m}(\nu!^n\pi/n)\bigr).$$`

[Mathematicians may enjoy interpreting this formula; cf. G. H. Hardy, *Messenger of Mathematics* **35** (1906), 145–146.]

18.3. `\def\limsup{\mathop{\overline{\rm lim}}}`
`        \def\liminf{\mathop{\underline{\rm lim}}}`

[Notice that the limits '$n \to \infty$' appear at different levels, in both of the displays, because 'sup' and the underbar descend below the baseline. It is possible to unify the limit positions by using phantoms, as explained later in this chapter. For example,

`\def\limsup{\mathop{\vphantom{\underline{}}\overline{\rm lim}}}`

would give lower limits in the same position as `\liminf`.]

18.4. $x \equiv 0(\pmod{y)^n}$. He should have typed '`$x\equiv0\pmod{y^n}$`'.

18.5. `$${n\choose k}\equiv{\lfloor n/p\rfloor\choose`
`        \lfloor k/p\rfloor}{n\bmod p\choose k\bmod p}\pmod p.$$`

18.6. `$\bf\bar x^{\rm T}Mx={\rm0}\iff x=0$`.   (If you typed a space between `\rm` and `0`, you wasted a keystroke; but don't feel guilty about it.)

18.7. `$S\subseteq{\mit\Sigma}\iff S\in{\cal S}$`. In this case the braces are redundant and could be eliminated; but you shouldn't try to do *everything* with fewest keystrokes, or you'll outsmart yourself some day.

18.8. `$${\it available}+\sum_{i=1}^n\max\bigl({\it full}(i),`
`        {\it reserved}(i)\bigr)={\it capacity}.$$`

[If `\it` had been used throughout the formula, the subscript i and superscript n would have caused error messages saying '`\scriptfont 4 is undefined`', since plain TeX makes `\it` available only in text size.]

18.9. `{\obeylines \sfcode`;=3000`
`        {\bf for $j:=2$ step $1$ until $n$ do}`
`        \quad {\bf begin} ${\it accum}:=A[j]$; $k:=j-1$; $A[0]:=\it accum$;`
`        \quad {\bf while $A[k]>\it accum$ do}`
`        \qquad {\bf begin} $A[k+1]:=A[k]$; $k:=k-1$;`
`        \qquad {\bf end};`
`        \quad $A[k+1]:=\it accum$;`
`        \quad {\bf end}.\par}`

[This is something like the "poetry" example in Chapter 14, but much more difficult. Some manuals of style say that punctuation should inherit the font of the preceding character, so that three kinds of semicolons should be typeset; e.g., these experts recommend '$k := j - 1$; $A[0] := accum$; **end**;'. The author heartily disagrees.]

18.10. Let `$H$~`be a Hilbert space, `\ $C$~`a closed bounded convex subset of~`$H$`, `\ $T$~`a nonexpansive self map of~`$C$`. Suppose that as `$n\to\infty$`, `\ $a_{n,k}\to0$` for each~`$k$`, and `$\gamma_n=\sum_{k=0}^\infty(a_{n,k+1}-`

`a_{n,k})^+\to0$`. Then for each `$x~in~$C$`, \ `$A_nx=\sum_{k=0}^\infty a_{n,k}T^kx$` converges weakly to a fixed point of~`$T$`.

[If any mathematicians are reading this, they might either appreciate or resent the following attempt to edit the given paragraph into a more acceptable style: "Let C be a closed, bounded, convex subset of a Hilbert space H, and let T be a nonexpansive self map of C. Suppose that as $n \to \infty$, we have $a_{n,k} \to 0$ for each k, and $\gamma_n = \sum_{k=0}^{\infty}(a_{n,k+1} - a_{n,k})^+ \to 0$. Then for each x in C, the infinite sum $A_n x = \sum_{k=0}^{\infty} a_{n,k}T^k x$ converges weakly to a fixed point of T."]

18.11. `$$\int_0^\infty{t-ib\over t^2+b^2}e^{iat}\,dt=`
`e^{ab}E_1(ab),\qquad a,b>0.$$`

18.12. `$$\hbar=1.0545\times10^{-27}\rm\,erg\,sec.$$`

18.13. There are ten atoms (the first is f and last is y^2); their types, and the interatomic spacing, are respectively

Ord Open Ord Punct \, Ord Close \; Rel \; Ord \> Bin \> Ord.

18.14. `$\left]-\infty,T\right[\times\left]-\infty,T\right[$`. (Or one could say \mathopen and \mathclose instead of \left and \right; then TeX would not choose the size of the delimiters, nor would it consider the subformulas to be of type Inner.) Open intervals are more clearly expressed in print by using parentheses instead of reversed brackets; for example, compare '$(-\infty, T) \times (-\infty, T)$' to the given formula.

18.15. The first + will become a Bin atom, the second an Ord; hence the result is x, medium space, +, medium space, +, no space, 1.

18.16. `$x_1+x_1x_2+\cdots+x_1x_2\ldots x_n$` and
`$(x_1,\ldots,x_n)\cdot(y_1,\ldots,y_n)=x_1y_1+\cdots+x_ny_n$`.

18.17. The commas belong to the sentence, not to the formula; his decision to put them into math mode meant that TeX didn't put large enough spaces after them. Also, his formula '$i = 1, 2, \ldots, n$' allows no breaks between lines, except after the =, so he's risking overfull box problems. But suppose the sentence had been more terse:

Clearly $a_i < b_i$ $(i = 1, 2, \ldots, n)$.

Then his idea would be basically correct:

Clearly `$a_i<b_i$` \ `($i=1,2,\ldots,n$)`.

18.18. `... never\footnote*{Well \dots, hardly ever.} have ...`

18.19. Neither formula will be broken between lines, but the thick spaces in the second formula will be set to their natural width while the thick spaces in the first formula will retain their stretchability.

18.20. Set `\relpenalty=10000` and `\binoppenalty=10000`. And you also need to change the definitions of \bmod and \pmod, which insert their own penalties.

18.21. `$\bigl\{\,x^3\bigm|h(x)\in\{-1,0,+1\}\,\bigr\}$`.

18.22. `$\{\,p\mid p$~and` $p+2$ are prime`$\,\}$`, assuming that `\mathsurround` is zero. The more difficult alternative '`$\{\,p\mid p\ {\rm and}\ p+2\rm\ are\ prime\,\}$`' is not a solution, because line breaks do not occur at `\`␣ (or at glue of any kind) within math formulas. Of course it may be best to display a formula like this, instead of breaking it between lines.

18.23. `$$f(x)=\cases{1/3&if $0\le x\le1$;\cr 2/3&if $3\le x\le4$;\cr 0&elsewhere.\cr}$$`

18.24. `$$\left\lgroup\matrix{a&b&c\cr d&e&f\cr}\right\rgroup \left\lgroup\matrix{u&x\cr v&y\cr w&z\cr}\right\rgroup$$`.

18.25. `\pmatrix{y_1\cr \vdots\cr y_k\cr}`.

18.26. `\def\undertext#1{$\underline{\smash{\hbox{#1}}}$}` will underline the words and cross <u>through</u> the descenders; or you could insert `\vphantom{y}` before the `\hbox`, thereby lowering all of the underlines to a position below all descenders. Neither of these gives exactly what is wanted. (See also `\underbar` in Appendix B.) Underlining is actually not very common in fine typography, since font changes usually work just as well or better, when you want to emphasize something. If you really want underlined text, it's best to have a special font in which all the letters are underlined.

18.27. `$n^{\rm th}$` root. (Incidentally, it is also acceptable to type '`$n$th`', getting '*n*th', in such situations; the fact that the *n* is in italics distinguishes it from the suffix. Typed manuscripts generally render this with a hyphen, but '*n*-th' is frowned on nowadays when an italic *n* is available.)

18.28. `${\bf S^{\rm-1}TS=dg}(\omega_1,\ldots,\omega_n) =\bf\Lambda$`. (Did you notice the difference between `\omega` (ω) and `w` (w)?)

18.29. `$\Pr(\,m=n\mid m+n=3\,)$`. (Analogous to a set.)

18.30. `$\sin18^\circ={1\over4}(\sqrt5-1)$`.

18.31. `$k=1.38\times10^{-16}\rm\,erg/^\circ K$`.

18.32. `$\bar\Phi\subset NL_1^*/N=\bar L_1^*` `\subseteq\cdots\subseteq NL_n^*/N=\bar L_n^*$`.

18.33. `$I(\lambda)=\int\!\!\!\int_Dg(x,y)e^{i\lambda h(x,y)}\,dx\,dy$`. (Although three `\!`'s work out best between consecutive integral signs in displays, the text style seems to want only two.)

18.34. `$\int_0^1\!\cdots\int_0^1f(x_1,\ldots,x_n)\,dx_1\ldots\,dx_n$`.

18.35. `$$x_{2m}\equiv\cases{Q(X_m^2-P_2W_m^2)-2S^2&($m$ odd)\cr \noalign{\vskip2pt} % spread the lines apart a little P_2^2(X_m^2-P_2W_m^2)-2S^2&($m$ even)\cr}\pmod N.$$`

18.36. `$$(1+x_1z+x_1^2z^2+\cdots\,)\ldots(1+x_nz+x_n^2z^2+\cdots\,) ={1\over(1-x_1z)\ldots(1-x_nz)}.$$` (Notice the uses of `\,`.)

18.37. `$$\prod_{j\ge0}\biggl(\sum_{k\ge0}a_{jk}z^k\biggr)`
`=\sum_{n\ge0}z^n\,\Biggl(\sum_`
`{\scriptstyle k_0,k_1,\ldots\ge0\atop`
`\scriptstyle k_0+k_1+\cdots=n}`
`a_{0k_0}a_{1k_1}\ldots\,\Biggr).$$`

Some people would prefer to have the latter parentheses larger; but `\left` and `\right` come out a bit too large in this case. It's not difficult to define `\bigggl` and `\bigggr` macros, analogous to the definitions of `\biggl` and `\biggr` in Appendix B.

18.38. `$${(n_1+n_2+\cdots+n_m)!\over n_1!\,,n_2!\ldots n_m!}`
`={n_1+n_2\choose n_2}{n_1+n_2+n_3\choose n_3}`
`\ldots{n_1+n_2+\cdots+n_m\choose n_m}.$$`

18.39. `$$\def\\#1#2{(1-q^{#1_#2+n})} % to save typing`
`\Pi_R{a_1,a_2,\ldots,a_M\atopwithdelims[]b_1,b_2,\ldots,b_N}`
`=\prod_{n=0}^R{\\a1\\a2\ldots\\aM\over\\b1\\b2\ldots\\bN}.$$`

18.40. `$$\sum_{p\rm\;;prime}f(p)=\int_{t>1}f(t)\,d\pi(t).$$`

18.41. `$$\{\underbrace{\overbrace{\mathstrut a,\ldots,a}`
`^{k\;a\mathchar`'\rm s},`
`\overbrace{\mathstrut b,\ldots,b}`
`^{l\;b\mathchar`'\rm s}}_{k+l\rm\;;elements}\}.$$`

Notice how apostrophes (instead of primes) were obtained.

18.42. `$$\pmatrix{\pmatrix{a&b\cr c&d\cr}&`
`\pmatrix{e&f\cr g&h\cr}\cr`
`\noalign{\smallskip}`
`0&\pmatrix{i&j\cr k&l\cr}\cr}.$$`

18.43. `$$\det\left|\,\matrix{`
`c_0&c_1\hfill&c_2\hfill&\ldots&c_n\hfill\cr`
`c_1&c_2\hfill&c_3\hfill&\ldots&c_{n+1}\hfill\cr`
`c_2&c_3\hfill&c_4\hfill&\ldots&c_{n+2}\hfill\cr`
`\,\vdots\hfill&\,\vdots\hfill&`
`\,\vdots\hfill&&\,\vdots\hfill\cr`
`c_n&c_{n+1}\hfill&c_{n+2}\hfill&\ldots&c_{2n}\hfill\cr`
`}\right|>0.$$`

18.44. `$$\mathop{{\sum}'}_{x\in A}f(x)\mathrel{\mathop=^{\rm def}}`
`\sum_{\scriptstyle x\in A\atop\scriptstyle x\ne0}f(x).$$`

This works because `{\sum}` is type Ord (so its superscript is not set above), but `\mathop{{\sum}'}` is type Op (so its subscript is set below). The limits are centered on $\sum'$, however, not on $\sum$. If you don't like that, the remedy is more difficult; one solution is to use `\sumprime_{x\in A}` where `\sumprime` is defined as follows:

```
\def\sumprime_#1{\setbox0=\hbox{$\scriptstyle{#1}$}
\setbox2=\hbox{$\displaystyle{\sum}$}
\setbox4=\hbox{${}'\mathsurround=0pt$}
\dimen0=.5\wd0 \advance\dimen0 by-.5\wd2
\ifdim\dimen0>0pt
```

```
      \ifdim\dimen0>\wd4 \kern\wd4 \else\kern\dimen0\fi\fi
  \mathop{{\sum}'}_{\kern-\wd4 #1}}
```

18.45. `$$2\uparrow\uparrow k\mathrel{\mathop=^{\rm def}}`
`2^{2^{2^{\cdot^{\cdot^{\cdot^2}}}}}`
`\vbox{\hbox{$\Big\}\scriptstyle k$}\kern0pt}.$$`

18.46. If you have to do a lot of commutative diagrams, you will want to define some macros like those in the first few lines of this solution. The **\matrix** macro resets the baselines to **\normalbaselines**, because other commands like **\openup** might have changed them, so we redefine **\normalbaselines** in this solution. Some of the things shown here haven't been explained yet, but Chapter 22 will reveal all.

```
  $$\def\normalbaselines{\baselineskip20pt
    \lineskip3pt \lineskiplimit3pt }
  \def\mapright#1{\smash{
    \mathop{\longrightarrow}\limits^{#1}}}
  \def\mapdown#1{\Big\downarrow
    \rlap{$\vcenter{\hbox{$\scriptstyle#1$}}$}}
  \matrix{&&&&&0\cr
    &&&&&\mapdown{}\cr
    0&\mapright{}&{\cal O}_C&\mapright\iota&
      \cal E&\mapright\rho&\cal L&\mapright{}&0\cr
    &&\Big\Vert&&\mapdown\phi&&\mapdown\psi\cr
    0&\mapright{}&{\cal O}_C&\mapright{}&
      \pi_*{\cal O}_D&\mapright\delta&
      R^1f_*{\cal O}_V(-D)&\mapright{}&0\cr
    &&&&&\mapdown{\theta_i\otimes\gamma^{-1}}\cr
    &&&&&\hidewidth R^1f_*\bigl({\cal O}
      _V(-iM)\bigr)\otimes\gamma^{-1}\hidewidth\cr
    &&&&&\mapdown{}\cr
    &&&&&0\cr}$$
```

19.1. `$$\sum_{n=0}^\infty a_nz^n\qquad\hbox{converges if}\qquad`
`|z|<\Bigl(\limsup_{n\to\infty}\root n\!\of{|a_n|}\,\Bigr)^{-1}.$$`

`$${f(x+\Delta x)-f(x)\over\Delta x}\to f'(x)`
`\qquad\hbox{as $\Delta x\to0$.}$$`

`$$\|u_i\|=1,\qquad u_i\cdot u_j=0\quad\hbox{if $i\ne j$.}$$`

`$$\it\hbox{The confluent image of}\quad\left\{`
`\matrix{\hbox{an arc}\hfill\cr\hbox{a circle}\hfill\cr`
`\hbox{a fan}\hfill\cr}`
`\right\}\quad\hbox{is}\quad\left\{`
`\matrix{\hbox{an arc}\hfill\cr`
`\hbox{an arc or a circle}\hfill\cr`
`\hbox{a fan or an arc}\hfill\cr}\right\}.$$`

The first example includes \! and \, to give slightly refined spacing; but the point of the problem was to illustrate the hbox, not to fuss over such extra details. The last example can be done much more simply using the ideas of Chapter 22, if you don't mind descending to the level of TEX primitives; for example, the first matrix could be replaced by

```
\,\vcenter{\halign{#\hfil\cr an arc\cr a circle\cr a fan\cr}}\,,
```

and the second is similar.

19.2. `$$\textstyle y={1\over2}x$$`. (Switching to text style is especially common in multiline formulas. For example, you will probably find occasions to use `\textstyle` on both sides of the `&`'s within an `\eqalign`.)

19.3. The latter formula will be in text style, not display style. And even if you do type '`$$\hbox{$\displaystyle{⟨formula⟩}$}$$`', the results are not quite the same, as we will see later: TEX will compress the glue in '`$$⟨formula⟩$$`' if the formula is too wide to fit on a line at its natural width, but the glue inside `\hbox{...}` is frozen at its natural width. The `\hbox` version also invokes `\everymath`.

19.4. One solution is to put the formula in an hbox that occupies a full line:

```
$$\leftline{\indent$\displaystyle
    1-{1\over2}+{1\over3}-{1\over4}+\cdots=\ln2$}$$
```

But this takes a bit of typing. If you make the definitions

```
\def\leftdisplay#1$${\leftline{\indent$\displaystyle{#1}$}$$}
\everydisplay{\leftdisplay}
```

you can type '`$$⟨formula⟩$$`' as usual, and the formatting will be inserted automatically. (This doesn't work with equation numbers; Appendix D illustrates how to handle them as well.)

19.5. `$$\prod_{k\ge0}{1\over(1-q^kz)}=`
`        \sum_{n\ge0}z^n\bigg/\!\!\!\prod_{1\le k\le n}(1-q^k).\eqno(16')$$`

19.6. `\eqno\hbox{(3--1)}`.

19.7. When you type an asterisk in math mode, plain TEX considers ∗ to be a binary operation. In the cases '(∗)' and '(∗∗)', the binary operations are converted to type Ord, because they don't appear in a binary context; but the middle asterisk in '(∗∗∗)' remains of type Bin. So the result was '(∗ ∗ ∗)'. To avoid the extra medium spaces, you can type '`\eqno(*{*}*)`'; or you can change `\mathcode`'∗, if you never use ∗ as a binary operation.

19.8. Assuming that `\hsize` is less than 10000 pt, the natural width of this equation will be too large to fit on a line; also, `\quad` specifies glue at the left. Therefore '$x = y$' will appear exactly 1 em from the left, and '(5)' will appear flush right. (The widths will satisfy $w = z - q$, $d = 0$, $k = q - e = 18\,\mathrm{mu}$.) In the case of `\leqno`, '(5)' will appear flush left, followed by one quad of space in `\textfont2`, followed by one quad of space in the current text font, followed by '$x = y$'.

19.9. (Note in particular that the final '.' comes *before* the final '`\cr`'.)

```
$$\eqalign{T(n)\le T(2^{\lceil\lg n\rceil})
    &\le c(3^{\lceil\lg n\rceil}-2^{\lceil\lg n\rceil})\cr
    &<3c\cdot3^{\lg n}\cr
    &=3c\,,n^{\lg3}.\cr}$$
```

19.10. `$$\eqalign{P(x)&=a_0+a_1x+a_2x^2+\cdots+a_nx^n,\cr`
`          P(-x)&=a_0-a_1x+a_2x^2-\cdots+(-1)^na_nx^n.\cr}\eqno(30)$$`

19.11. Both sides of that equation are considered to be on the left, so you get results that look like this:

$$\left\{ \begin{aligned} \alpha &= f(z) \\ \beta &= f(z^2) \\ \gamma = f(z^3) \end{aligned} \right\}$$

19.12. `$$\leqalignno{\gcd(u,v)&=\gcd(v,u);&(9)\cr`
`            \gcd(u,v)&=\gcd(-u,v).&(10)\cr}$$`

19.13. `$$\eqalignno{\biggl(\int_{-\infty}^\infty e^{-x^2}\,dx\biggr)^2`
`            &=\int_{-\infty}^\infty\int_{-\infty}^\infty`
`            e^{-(x^2+y^2)}\,dx\,dy\cr`
`            &=\int_0^{2\pi}\int_0^\infty e^{-r^2}r\,dr\,d\theta\cr`
`            &=\int_0^{2\pi}\biggl(-{e^{-r^2}\over2}`
`            \biggl|_{r=0}^{r=\infty}\,\biggr)\,d\theta\cr`
`            &=\pi.&(11)\cr}$$`

19.14. You get the displayed box

$$x = y + z$$
$$\text{and}$$
$$x^2 = y^2 + z^2.$$

Reason: The 'and' occurs at the left of the `\eqalign` box, not at the left of the whole display, and the `\eqalign` box is centered as usual.

19.15. By raising the equation number, he increased the line height, so TeX put extra space between that line and the previous line when it calculated the inter-line glue. If he had said '`\smash{\raise...}`', he wouldn't have had that problem.

19.16. `$$\displaylines{\hfill x\equiv x;\hfill\llap{(1)}\cr`
`              \hfill\hbox{if}\quad x\equiv y\quad\hbox{then}\quad`
`              y\equiv x;\hfill\llap{(2)}\cr`
`              \hfill\hbox{if}\quad x\equiv y\quad\hbox{and}\quad`
`              y\equiv z\quad\hbox{then}\quad`
`              x\equiv z.\hfill\llap{(3)}\cr}$$`

There's also a trickier solution, which begins with

`$$\displaylines{x\equiv x;\hfil\llap{(1)}\hfilneg\cr`

19.17. `$$\eqalignno{x_\nu1+\cdots+x_{n+t-1}u_t`
`            &=x_\nu1+(ax_n+c)u_2+\cdots\cr`
`            &\qquad+\bigl(a^{t-1}x_n+c(a^{t-2}+\cdots+1)\bigr)u_t\cr`
`            &=(u_1+au_2+\cdots+a^{t-1}u_t)x_n+h(u_1,\ldots,u_t).`
`            \quad&(47)\cr}$$`

You weren't expected to insert the '`\quad`' on the last line; such refinements usually can't be anticipated until you see the first proofs. But without that `\quad` the '(47)' would occur half a quad closer to the formula.

19.18. `$$\displaylines{\quad\sum_{1\le j\le n}{1\over`
`    (x_j-x_1)\ldots(x_j-x_{j-1})(x-x_j)(x_j-x_{j+1})`
`    \ldots(x_j-x_n)}\hfill\cr`
`\hfill={1\over(x-x_1)\ldots(x-x_n)}.\quad(27)\cr}$$`

19.19. `$$\def\\#1;{(#1;q^2)_\infty} % to save typing`
`\displaystyle{q^{{1\over2}n(n+1)}\\ea;\\eq/a;\qquad\atop`
`    \hfill\\caq/e;\\cq^2\!/ae;}`
`\over(e;q)_\infty(cq/e;q)_\infty$$`

20.1. `\def\mustnt{I must not talk in class.\par}`
`\def\five{\mustnt\mustnt\mustnt\mustnt\mustnt}`
`\def\twenty{\five\five\five\five}`
`\def\punishment{\twenty\twenty\twenty\twenty\twenty}`

Solutions to more complicated problems of this type are discussed later.

20.2. `ABCAB`. (The first `\a` expands into `A\def\a{B...}`; this redefines `\a`, so the second `\a` expands into `B...`, etc.)   At least, that's what happens if `\puzzle` is encountered when TeX is building a list. But if `\puzzle` is expanded in an `\edef` or `\message` or something like that, we will see later that the interior `\def` commands are not performed while the expansion is taking place, and the control sequences following `\def` are expanded; so the result is an infinite string

   `A\def A\def A\def A\def A\def A\def A\def A\def A...`

which causes TeX to abort because the program's input stack is finite. This example points out that a control sequence (e.g., `\b`) need not be defined when it appears in the replacement text of a definition. The example also shows that TeX doesn't expand a macro until it needs to.

20.3. $(x_1, \ldots, x_n)$. Note that the subscripts are bold here, because the expansion (`\bf x_1,\ldots,\bf x_n`) doesn't "turn off" `\bf`. To prevent this, one should write `\row{{\bf x}}`; or (better), `\row\xbold`, in conjunction with `\def\xbold{{\bf x}}`.

20.4. The catch is that the parameters have to percolate down to the `\mustnt` macro, if you extend the previous answer:

   `\def\mustnt#1#2{I must not #1 in #2.\par}`
   `\def\five#1#2{\mustnt{#1}{#2}...\mustnt{#1}{#2}}`
   `\def\twenty#1#2{\five{#1}{#2}...\five{#1}{#2}}`
   `\def\punishment#1#2{\twenty{#1}{#2}...\twenty{#1}{#2}}`

When you pass parameters from one macro to another in this way, you need to enclose them in braces as shown. But actually this particular solution punishes TeX much more than it needs to, because it takes a lot of time to copy the parameters and read them again and again. There's a much more efficient way to do the job, by defining control sequences:

   `\def\mustnt{I must not \doit\ in \thatplace.\par}`
   `\def\punishment#1#2{\def\doit{#1}\def\thatplace{#2}%`
   `  \twenty\twenty\twenty\twenty\twenty}`

and by defining \five and \twenty without parameters as before. You can also delve more deeply into TeXnicalities, constructing solutions that are more efficient yet; TeX works even faster when macros communicate with each other via boxes. For example,

```
\def\mustnt{\copy0 }
\def\punishment#1#2{\setbox0=
  \vbox{\strut I must not #1 in #2.\strut}%
  \twenty\twenty\twenty\twenty\twenty}
```

sets 100 identical paragraphs at high speed, because TeX has to process the paragraph and break it into lines only once. It's much faster to copy a box than to build it up from scratch. (The struts in this example keep the interbaseline distances correct between boxed paragraphs, as explained in Chapter 12. Two struts are used, for if the message takes more than one line there will be a strut at both top and bottom. If it were known that each sentence will occupy only a single line, no struts would be needed, because interline glue is added as usual when a box created by \copy is appended to the current vertical list.)

20.5. The ## feature is indispensable when the replacement text of a definition contains other definitions. For example, consider

```
\def\a#1{\def\b##1{##1#1}}
```

after which '\a!' will expand to '\def\b#1{#1!}'. We will see later that ## is also important for alignments; see, for example, the definition of \matrix in Appendix B.

20.6. \def\a#{\b}.

20.7. Let's go slowly on this one, so that the answer will give enough background to answer all similar questions. The ⟨parameter text⟩ of the definition consists of the three tokens #1, #2, $[_1$; the ⟨replacement text⟩ consists of the six tokens ${_1}$, #$_6$, $]_2$, !$_6$, #2, $[_1$. (When two tokens of category 6 occur in the replacement text, the character code of the second one survives; the character code of a category-6 character is otherwise irrelevant. Thus, '\def\!#1!2#[{##]!!#2}' would produce an essentially identical definition.) When expanding the given token list, argument #1 is x_{11}, since it is undelimited. Argument #2 is delimited by $[_1$, which is different from ${_1}$, so it is set provisionally to {[y]}; but the outer "braces" are stripped off, so #2 reduces to the three tokens $[_1$, y_{11}, $]_2$. The result of the expansion is therefore

$${_1}$ #$_6$ $]_2$!$_6$ $[_1$ y_{11} $]_2$ $[_1$ z_{11} }$_2$.$$

Incidentally, if you display this with \tracingmacros=1, TeX says

```
\!!1#2[->{##]!!#2[
#1<-x
#2<-[y]
```

Category codes are not shown, but a character of category 6 always appears twice in succession. A parameter token in the replacement text uses the character code of the final parameter in the parameter text.

20.8. Yes indeed. In the first case, \a receives the meaning of \b that is current at the time of the \let. In the second case, \a becomes a macro that will expand into the token \b whenever \a is used, so it has the meaning of \b that is current at the time of use. You need \let, if you want to interchange the meanings of \a and \b.

20.9. (a) Yes. (b) No; any other control sequence can appear (except those declared as \outer macros).

20.10.   \def\overpaid{{\count0=\balance
         You have overpaid your tax by \dollaramount.
         \ifnum\count0<100 It is our policy to refund
            such a small amount only if you ask for it.
         \else A check for this amount is being mailed
            under separate cover.\fi}}

20.11.   The tricky part is to get the zero in an amount like '$2.01'.

         \def\dollaramount{\count2=\count0 \divide\count2 by100
         \$\number\count2.%
         \multiply\count2 by-100 \advance\count2 by\count0
         \ifnum \count2<10 0\fi
         \number\count2 }

20.12.   \def\category#1{\ifcase\catcode'#1
         escape\or begingroup\or endgroup\or math\or
         align\or endline\or parameter\or superscript\or
         subscript\or ignored\or space\or letter\or
         otherchar\or active\or comment\or invalid\fi}

20.13.   (a,b) True. (c,d) False. (e,f) True. In case (e), the ⟨true text⟩ starts with 'ue'. (g) The \ifx is false and the inner \if is true; so the outer \if becomes '\if True...', which is false.   (Interestingly, TEX knows that the outer \if is false even before it has looked at the \fi's that close the \ifx and the inner \if.)

20.14.   One idea is to say

         \let\save=\c \let\c=0 \edef\a{\b\c\d} \let\c=\save

because control sequences equivalent to characters are not expandable. However, this doesn't expand occurrences of \c that might be present in the expansions of \b and \d. Another way, which is free of this defect, is

         \edef\next#1#2{\def#1{\b#2\d}} \next\a\c

(and it's worth a close look!).

20.15.   \toks0={\c} \toks2=\expandafter{\d}
         \edef\a{\b\the\toks0 \the\toks2 }

(Notice that \expandafter expands the token after the left brace here.)

20.16.   The following shouldn't be taken too seriously, but it does work:

         {\setbox0=\vbox{\halign{#{\c\span\d}\cr
             \let\next=0\edef\next#1{\gdef\next{\b#1}}\next\cr}}}
         \let\a=\next

20.17.   Neither one, although \a will behave like an unmatched left brace when it is expanded. The definition of \b is *not complete*, because it expands to '\def\b{{}'; TEX will continue to read ahead, looking for another right brace, possibly discovering a runaway definition! It's impossible to define a macro that has unmatched braces. But you *can* say \let\a={; Appendix D discusses several other brace tricks.

20.18. One way is to redefine \catcode`\^^M=9 (ignored) just before the \read, so that the ⟨return⟩ will be ignored. Another solution is to redefine \endlinechar=-1, so that no character is put at the end of the line. Or you could try to be tricky by stripping off the space with macro expansion as follows:

```
\def\stripspace#1 \next{#1}
\edef\myname{\expandafter\stripspace\myname\next}
```

The latter solution doesn't work if the user types '%' at the end of his or her name, or if the name contains control sequences.

20.19. Here are two solutions:

```
\def\next#1\endname{\uppercase{\def\MYNAME{#1}}}
\expandafter\next\myname\endname

\edef\next{\def\noexpand\MYNAME{\myname}}
\uppercase\expandafter{\next}
```

20.20. (Here's a solution that also numbers the lines, so that the number of repetitions is easily verifiable. The only tricky part about this answer is the use of \endgraf, which is a substitute for \par because \loop is not a \long macro.)

```
\newcount\n
\def\punishment#1#2{\n=0
  \loop\ifnum\n<#2 \advance\n by1
    \item{\number\n.}#1\endgraf\repeat}
```

21.1. The interline skip is added for vboxes, but not for rules; he forgot to say \nointerlineskip, before and after the \moveright construction.

21.2. \vrule height3pt depth-2pt width1in. Notice that it was necessary to call it a \vrule since it appeared in horizontal mode.

21.3. \def\boxit#1{\vbox{\hrule\hbox{\vrule\kern3pt
            \vbox{\kern3pt#1\kern3pt}\kern3pt\vrule}\hrule}}

(The resulting box does not have the baseline of the original one; you have to work a little bit harder to get that.)

21.4. \leaders: two boxes starting at 100 pt, 110 pt.
     \cleaders: three boxes starting at 95 pt, 105 pt, 115 pt.
     \xleaders: three boxes starting at 93 pt, 105 pt, 117 pt.

21.5. \def\leaderfill{\kern-0.3em\leaders\hbox to 1em{\hss.\hss}%
            \hskip0.6em plus1fill \kern-0.3em }

21.6. Since no **height** or **depth** specification follows the \vrule, the height and depth are '*'; i.e., the rule extends to the smallest enclosing box. This usually makes a heavy black band, which is too horrible to demonstrate here. However, it does work in the \downbracefill macro of Appendix B; and \leaders\vrule\vfill works fine in vertical mode.

21.7. For example, say

```
\null\nobreak\leaders\hrule\hskip10pt plus1filll\ \par
```

The '\␣' provides extra glue that is wiped out by the implied \unskip at the end of every paragraph (see Chapter 14), and the '\null\nobreak' makes sure that the leaders do not disappear at a line break; 'filll' overtakes the \parfillskip glue.

21.8.
```
$$\hbox to 2.5in{\cleaders
      \vbox to .5in{\cleaders\hbox{\TeX}\vfil}\hfil}$$
```

21.9. We assume that a strut is 12 pt tall, and that 50 lines fit on a page:

```
\setbox0=\hbox{\strut I must not talk in class.}
\null\cleaders\copy0\vskip600pt\vfill\eject % 50 times on page 1;
\null\cleaders\box0\vskip600pt\bye % 50 more on page 2.
```

The \null keeps glue (and leaders) from disappearing at the top of the page.

21.10. {\let\the=0\edef\next{\write\cont{⟨token list⟩}}\next} will expand everything but \the when the \write command is given.

22.1. Notice the uses of '\smallskip' here to separate the table heading and footing from the table itself; such refinements are often worthwhile.

```
\settabs\+\indent&10\frac1/2 lbs.\qquad&\it Servings\qquad&\cr
\+&\negthinspace\it Weight&\it Servings&
  {\it Approximate Cooking Time\/}*\cr
\smallskip
\+&8 lbs.&6&1 hour and 50 to 55 minutes\cr
\+&9 lbs.&7 to 8&About 2 hours\cr
\+&9\frac1/2 lbs.&8 to 9&2 hours and 10 to 15 minutes\cr
\+&10\frac1/2 lbs.&9 to 10&2 hours and 15 to 20 minutes\cr
\smallskip
\+&* For a stuffed goose,
  add 20 to 40 minutes to the times given.\cr
```

The title line specifies '\it' three times, because each entry between tabs is treated as a group by TeX; you would get error messages galore if you tried to say something like '\+&{\it Weight&Servings&...}\cr'. The '\negthinspace' in the title line is a small backspace that compensates for the slant in an italic W; the author inserted this somewhat unusual correction after seeing how the table looked without it, on the first proofs. (You weren't supposed to think of this, but it has to be mentioned.) See exercise 11.6 for the '\frac' macro; it's better to say '$1/2$' than '$\frac{1}{2}$', in a cookbook.

Another way to treat this table would be to display it in a vbox, instead of including a first column whose sole purpose is to specify indentation.

22.2. In such programs it seems best to type \cleartabs just before &, whenever it is desirable to reset the old tabs. Multiletter identifiers look best when set in text italics with \it, as explained in Chapter 18. Thus, the following is recommended:

```
\+\bf while $p>0$ do\cr
  \+\quad\cleartabs&{\bf begin} $q:={\it link}(p)$;
    ${\it free\_node}(p)$; $p:=q$;\cr
  \+&{\bf end};\cr
```

22.3. Here we retain the idea that **&** inserts a new tab, when there are no tabs to the right of the current position. Only one of the macros that are used to process \+ lines needs to be changed; but (unfortunately) it's the most complex one:

```
\def\t@bb@x{\if@cr\egroup % now \box0 holds the column
  \else\hss\egroup \dimen@=0\p@
    \dimen@ii=\wd0 \advance\dimen@ii by1sp
    \loop\ifdim \dimen@<\dimen@ii
      \global\setbox\tabsyet=\hbox{\unhbox\tabsyet
        \global\setbox1=\lastbox}%
      \ifvoid1 \advance\dimen@ii by-\dimen@
        \advance\dimen@ii by-1sp \global\setbox1
          =\hbox to\dimen@ii{}\dimen@ii=-1pt\fi
      \advance\dimen@ by\wd1 \global\setbox\tabsdone
        =\hbox{\box1\unhbox\tabsdone}\repeat
    \setbox0=\hbox to\dimen@{\unhbox0}\fi
  \box0}
```

22.4. Horizontal lists   Chapter 14
     Vertical lists   Chapter 15
      Math lists   Chapter 17   (i.e., the first column would be right-justified)

22.5. `Fowl&Poule de l'Ann\'ee&10 to 12&Over 3&Stew, Fricassee\cr`

22.6. `$$\halign to\hsize{\sl#\hfil\tabskip=.5em plus.5em&`
       `#\hfil\tabskip=0pt plus.5em&`
       `\hfil#\tabskip=1em plus2em&`
    `\sl#\hfil\tabskip=.5em plus.5em&`
    `#\hfil\tabskip=0pt plus.5em&`
    `\hfil#\tabskip=0pt\cr ...}$$`

22.7. The trick is to define a new macro for the preamble:

```
$$\def\welshverb#1={{\bf#1} = }
\halign to\hsize{\welshverb#\hfil\tabskip=1em plus1em&
  \welshverb#\hfil&\welshverb#\hfil\tabskip=0pt\cr ...}$$
```

22.8. `\hfil#: &\vtop{\parindent=0pt\hsize=16em`
        `\hangindent.5em\strut#\strut}\cr`

With such narrow measure and such long words, the \tolerance should probably also have been increased to, say, 1000 inside the \vtop; luckily it turned out that a higher tolerance wasn't needed.

     Note: The stated preamble solves the problem and demonstrates that TeX's line-breaking capability can be used within tables. But this particular table is not really a good example of the use of \halign, because TeX could typeset it directly, using \everypar in an appropriate manner to set up the hanging indentation, and using \par instead of \cr. For example, one could say

```
\hsize20em \parindent0pt \clubpenalty10000 \widowpenalty10000
\def\history#1&{\hangindent4.5em
  \hbox to4em{\hss#1: }\ignorespaces}
\everypar={\history} \def\\{\leavevmode{\it c\/}}
```

which spares TEX all the work of `\halign` but yields essentially the same result.

22.9. The equation is divided into separate parts for terms and plus/minus signs, and tabskip glue is used to center it:

```
$$\openup1\jot \tabskip=0pt plus1fil
\halign to\displaywidth{\tabskip=0pt
  $\hfil#$&$\hfil{}#{}$&
  $\hfil#$&$\hfil{}#{}$&
  $\hfil#$&$\hfil{}#{}$&
  $\hfil#$&${}#\hfil$\tabskip=0pt plus1fil&
  \llap{#}\tabskip=0pt\cr
10w&+&3x&+&3y&+&18z&=1,&(9)\cr
6w&-&17x&&&-&5z&=2.&(10)\cr}$$
```

22.10. `\hfil# &#\hfil&\quad##\ \hfil##\ \hfil#\cr`

22.11. `\pmatrix{a_{11}&a_{12}&\ldots&a_{1n}\cr`
`        a_{21}&a_{22}&\ldots&a_{2n}\cr`
`        \multispan4\dotfill\cr`
`        a_{m1}&a_{m2}&\ldots&a_{mn}\cr}`

22.12. '`\cr`' would have omitted the final column, which is a vertical rule.

22.13. One way is to include two lines just before and after the title line, saying '`\omit&height2pt&\multispan5&\cr`'. Another way is to put `\bigstrut` into some column of the title line, for some appropriate invisible box `\bigstrut` of width zero. Either way makes the table look better.

22.14. The trick is to have "empty" columns at the extreme left and right; then the `\hrulefill`'s are able to span the tabskip glue.

```
$$\vbox{\tabskip=0pt \offinterlineskip
\halign to 36em{\tabskip=0pt plus1em##&
  #\hfil&#&#\hfil&#&#\hfil&#\tabskip=0pt\cr
&&&&&\strut J. H. B\"ohning, 1838&\cr
&&&&\multispan3\hrulefill\cr
&&&\strut M. J. H. B\"ohning, 1882&\vrule\cr
&&\multispan3\hrulefill\cr
&&\vrule&&\vrule&\strut M. D. Blase, 1840&\cr
&&\vrule&&\multispan3\hrulefill\cr
&\strut L. M. Bohning, 1912&\vrule\cr
\multispan3\hrulefill\cr
&&\vrule&&&\strut E. F. Ehlert, 1845&\cr
&&\vrule&&\multispan3\hrulefill\cr
&&\vrule&\strut P. A. M. Ehlert, 1884&\vrule\cr
&&\multispan3\hrulefill\cr
&&&&\vrule&\strut C. L. Wischmeyer, 1850&\cr
&&&&\multispan3\hrulefill\cr}}$$
```

22.∞. (Solution to Dudeney's problem.) Let `\one` and `\two` be macros that produce a vertical list denoting one and two pennies, respectively. The problem can be solved with `\valign` as follows:

```
\valign{\vfil##&\vfil##&\vfil##&\vfil#\cr
   \two&\one&\one&\one\cr
   \one&\one&\two&\one\cr
   \one&\one&\one&\two\cr
   \one&\two&\one&\one\cr}
```

Since `\valign` transposes rows and columns, the result is

23.1. `\footline={\hss\tenrm-- \folio\ --\hss}`

23.2. `\headline={\ifnum\pageno=1 \hss\tenbf R\'ESUM\'E\hss`
`\else\tenrm R\'esum\'e of A. U. Thor \dotfill\ Page \folio\fi}`

(You should also say `\nopagenumbers` and `\voffset=2\baselineskip`.)

23.3. `\output={\plainoutput\blankpageoutput}`
`\def\blankpageoutput{\shipout\vbox{\makeheadline`
`   \vbox to\vsize{}\makefootline}\advancepageno}`

23.4. Set `\hsize=2.1in`, allocate '`\newbox\midcolumn`', and use the following code:

```
\output={\if L\lr
     \global\setbox\leftcolumn=\columnbox \global\let\lr=M
   \else\if M\lr
     \global\setbox\midcolumn=\columnbox \global\let\lr=R
   \else \tripleformat \global\let\lr=L\fi\fi
   \ifnum\outputpenalty>-20000 \else\dosupereject\fi}
\def\tripleformat{\shipout\vbox{\makeheadline
     \fullline{\box\leftcolumn\hfil\box\midcolumn\hfil\columnbox}
     \makefootline}
   \advancepageno}
```

At the end, `\supereject` and say '`\if L\lr \else\null\vfill\eject\fi`' twice.

23.5. He forgot that interline glue is inserted automatically before the `\leftline`; this permits a legal breakpoint between the `\mark` and the `\leftline` box, according to the rules of page breaking in Chapter 15. One cure would be to say `\nobreak` just after the `\mark`; but it's usually best to put marks and insertions just *after* boxes.

23.6. Say, for example, `\ifcase2\expandafter\relax\botmark\fi` to read part α_2 of `\botmark`. Another solution puts the five components into five parameters of a macro, analogous to the method used by `\inxcheck` later in this chapter; but the `\ifcase` approach is usually more efficient, because it lets TEX pass over the unselected components at high speed.

23.7. `\output={\dimen0=\dp255 \normaloutput`
`      \ifodd\pageno\else\if L\lr`
`         \expandafter\inxcheck\botmark\sub\end\fi\fi}`

In this case the `\normaloutput` macro should be the two-column output routine that was described earlier in this chapter, beginning with '`\if L\lr`' and ending with '`\let\lr=L\fi`'. (There is no need to test for `\supereject`.)

23.8. False. If the text of the main and/or subsidiary entry is lengthy, a continuation line may actually become two or more lines. (Incidentally, hanging indentation will then occur, because the \everypar command—which was set up outside the \output routine—is effective inside.) The \vsize must be large enough to accommodate all continuation lines plus at least one more line of index material, or else infinite looping will occur.

24.1. If \cs has been defined by \chardef or \mathchardef, TeX uses hexadecimal notation when it expands \meaning\cs, and it assigns category 12 to each digit of the expansion. You might have an application in which you want the last part of the expansion to be treated as a ⟨number⟩. (This is admittedly an obscure reason.)

24.2. Yes; any number of spaces can precede any keyword.

24.3. The first two have the same meaning; but the third coerces \baselineskip to a ⟨dimen⟩ by suppressing the stretchability and shrinkability that might be present.

24.4. The natural width is 221 dd (which TeX rounds to 15497423 sp and displays as `236.47191pt`). The stretchability is 2500 sp, since an internal integer is coerced to a dimension when it appears as an ⟨internal unit⟩. The shrinkability is zero. Notice that the final \space is swallowed up as part of the optional spaces of the ⟨shrink⟩ part in the syntax for ⟨glue⟩. (If PLUS had been MINUS, the final \space would *not* have been part of this ⟨glue⟩!)

24.5. If it was non-null when a \dump operation occurred. Here's a nontrivial example, which sets up \batchmode and puts \end at the end of the input file:

```
\everyjob={\batchmode\input\jobname\end}
```

24.6. (a) `\def\\#1\\{}\futurelet\cs\\␣\\`. (b) `\def\\{\let\cs= }\\␣`. (There are many other solutions.)

24.7. ⟨internal quantity⟩ ⟶ ⟨internal integer⟩ | ⟨internal dimen⟩
  | ⟨internal glue⟩ | ⟨internal muglue⟩ | ⟨internal nonnumeric⟩
  ⟨internal nonnumeric⟩ ⟶ ⟨token variable⟩ | ⟨font⟩

26.1. Radix 10 notation is used for numeric constants and for the output of numeric data. The first 10 \count registers are displayed at each \shipout, and their values are recorded on the dvi file at such times. A box whose glue has stretched or shrunk to its stated stretchability or shrinkability has badness 100; this badness value separates "loose" boxes from "very loose" or "underfull" ones. TeX will scroll up to 100 errors in a single paragraph before giving up (see Chapter 27). The normal values of \spacefactor and \mag are 1000. A \prevdepth value of −1000 pt suppresses interline glue. The badness rating of a box is at most 10000, except that the \badness of an overfull box is 1000000. INITEX initializes \tolerance to 10000, thereby making all line breaks feasible. Penalties of 10000 or more prohibit breaks; penalties of −10000 or less make breaks mandatory. The cost of a page break is 100000, if the badness is 10000 and if the associated penalties are less than 10000 in magnitude (see Chapter 15).

26.2. TeX allows constants to be expressed in radix 8 (octal) or radix 16 (hexadecimal) notation, and it uses hexadecimal notation to display \char and \mathchar codes. There are 16 families for math fonts, 16 input streams for \read, 16 output streams for \write. A \catcode value must be less than 16. The notation ^^?, ^^@, ^^A specifies characters whose codes differ by 64 from the codes of ?, @, A; this convention applies only to characters with ASCII codes less than 128. There are 256 possible characters, hence 256 entries in each of the \catcode, \mathcode, \lccode, \uccode, \sfcode, and \delcode tables. All \lccode, \uccode, and \char values must be less than 256. A font has at most 256 characters. There are 256 \box registers, 256 \count registers, 256 \dimen registers, 256 \skip registers, 256 \muskip registers, 256 \toks registers, 256 hyphenation tables. The "at size" of a font must be less than 2048 pt, i.e., 2^{11} pt. Math delimiters are encoded by multiplying the math code of the "small character" by 2^{12}. The magnitude of a ⟨dimen⟩ value must be less than 16384 pt, i.e., 2^{14} pt; similarly, the ⟨factor⟩ in a ⟨fil dimen⟩ must be less than 2^{14}. A \mathchar or \spacefactor or \sfcode value must be less than 2^{15}; a \mathcode or \mag value must be less than or equal to 2^{15}, and 2^{15} denotes an "active" math character. There are 2^{16} sp per pt. A \delcode value must be less than 2^{24}; a \delimiter, less than 2^{27}. The \end command sometimes contributes a penalty of -2^{30} to the current page. A ⟨dimen⟩ must be less than 2^{30} sp in absolute value; a ⟨number⟩ must be less than 2^{31} in absolute value.

27.1. He forgot to count the space; TEX deleted 'i', 'm', '␣', '\input', and four letters. (But all is not lost; he can type '1' or '2', then ⟨return⟩, and after being prompted by '*' he can enter a new line of input.)

27.2. First delete the unwanted tokens, then insert what you want: Type '6' and then 'I\macro'. (Incidentally, there's a sneaky way to get at the \inaccessible control sequence by typing

```
I\garbage{}\let\accessible=
```

in response to an error message like this. The author designed TEX in such a way that you can't destroy anything by playing such nasty tricks.)

27.3. 'I␣%' does the trick, if % is a comment character.

27.4. The 'minus' of 'minuscule' was treated as part of the \hskip command in \nextnumber. Quick should put '\relax' at the end of his macro. (The keywords l, plus, minus, width, depth, or height might just happen to occur in text when TEX is reading a glue specification or a rule specification; designers of general-purpose macros should guard against this. If you get a '**Missing number**' error and you can't guess why TEX is looking for a number, plant the instruction '\tracingcommands=1' shortly before the error point; your log file will show what command TEX is working on.)

27.5. If this exercise isn't just a joke, the title of this appendix is a lie.

> *If you can't solve a problem,*
> *you can always look up the answer.*
> *But please, try first to solve it by yourself;*
> *then you'll learn more and you'll learn faster.*
> — DONALD E. KNUTH, *The TEXbook* (1983)

> *How answer you for your selues?*
> — WILLIAM SHAKESPEARE, *Much Adoe About Nothing* (1598)

B

Basic
Control
Sequences

Let's begin this appendix with a chart that summarizes plain TeX's conventions.

Characters that are reserved for special purposes: \ { } \$ & # % ^ _ ~

\rm roman,   {\sl slanted},   {\bf boldface},   {\it italic\/} type
   roman,   *slanted,*   **boldface,**   *italic* type

`` '' -- --- ?` !` \\$ \\# \\& \\% \ae \AE \oe \OE \aa \AA \ss \o \O
" "   – — ¿ ¡ \$ # & % æ Æ œ Œ å Å ß ø Ø

\\`a \\'e \\^o \\"u \\=y \\~n \\.p \u\i \v s \H\j \t\i u \b k \c c \d h
à   é   ô   ü   ȳ   ñ   ṗ   ĭ   š   ĵ   ȋu   ḵ   ç   ḥ

\l \L \dag \ddag \S \P {\it\\$ \&} \copyright \TeX \dots
ł L † ‡ § ¶ *£* *&* © TeX …

Line break controls: \break \nobreak \allowbreak \hbox{unbreakable}
dis\-cre\-tion\-ary hy\-phens   virgule\slash breakpoint

Breakable horizontal spaces:
\\␣ normal interword space
\enskip this much
\quad this much
\qquad this   much
\hskip ⟨arbitrary dimen⟩

Unbreakable horizontal spaces:
~ normal interword space
\enspace   this much
\thinspace   this much
\negthinspace thismuch
\kern ⟨arbitrary dimen⟩

Vertical spaces: \smallskip ═══   \medskip ════   \bigskip _____

Page break controls: \eject \supereject \nobreak \goodbreak \filbreak
Vertical spaces and good breakpoints: \smallbreak \medbreak \bigbreak

---

\settabs 4 \columns
\+Here's an example&of\hfill some &tabbing:&\hrulefill&\cr
Here's an example of   some tabbing: _____
    \hrulefill _____   \dotfill ....
   \leftarrowfill ⟵—————— \rightarrowfill ——————⟶
    \upbracefill ⏝⏝   \downbracefill ⏜⏜

More general alignments use \halign, \valign, \omit, \span, and \multispan.

Examples of the principal conventions for text layout appear on the next page.

```
% This test file generates the output shown on the opposite page.
% It's a bit complex because it tries to illustrate lots of stuff.
% TeX ignores commentary (like this) that follows a '%' sign.

% First the standard output style is changed slightly:
\hsize=29pc % The lines in this book are 29 picas wide.
\vsize=42pc % The page body is 42 picas (not counting footlines).
\footline={\tenrm Footline\quad\dotfill\quad Page \folio}
\pageno=1009 % This is the starting page number (don't ask why).
% See Chapter 23 for the way to make other page format changes via
% \hoffset, \voffset, \nopagenumbers, \headline, or \raggedbottom.

\topglue 1in % This makes an inch of blank space (1in=2.54cm).
\centerline{\bf A Bold, Centered Title}
\smallskip % This puts a little extra space after the title line.
\rightline{\it avec un sous-titre \`a la fran\c caise}
% Now we use \beginsection to introduce part 1 of the document.
\beginsection 1. Plain \TeX nology % The next line must be blank!

The first paragraph of a new section is not indented.
\TeX\ recognizes the end of a paragraph when it comes to a blank
line in your manuscript file. % or to a '\par': see below.

Subsequent paragraphs {\it are\/} indented.\footnote*{The amount
    of indentation can be changed by changing a parameter called
{\tt\char`\\parindent}. Turn the page for a summary of \TeX's most
important parameters.} (See?) The computer breaks a paragraph's
text into lines in an interesting way---see reference~[1]---and h%
        yphenates words automatically     when necessary.

\midinsert % This begins inserted material, e.g., a figure.
\narrower\narrower % This brings the margins in (see Chapter 14).
\noindent \llap{``}If there hadn't been room for this material on
the present page, it would have been inserted on the next one.''
\endinsert % This ends the insertion and the effect of \narrower.

\proclaim Theorem T. The typesetting of $math$ is discussed in
Chapters 16--19, and math symbols are summarized in Appendix~F.

\beginsection 2. Bibliography\par % '\par' acts like a blank line.
\frenchspacing % (Chapter 12 recommends this for bibliographies.)
\item{[1]} D.~E. Knuth and M.~F. Plass, ``Breaking paragraphs
into lines,'' {\sl Softw. pract. exp. \bf11} (1981), 1119--1184.
\bye % This is the way the file ends, not with a \bang but a \bye.
```

A Bold, Centered Title

avec un sous-titre à la française

1. Plain TEXnology

The first paragraph of a new section is not indented. TEX recognizes the end of a paragraph when it comes to a blank line in your manuscript file.

Subsequent paragraphs *are* indented.* (See?) The computer breaks a paragraph's text into lines in an interesting way—see reference [1]—and hyphenates words automatically when necessary.

> "If there hadn't been room for this material on the present page, it would have been inserted on the next one."

Theorem T. *The typesetting of math is discussed in Chapters 16–19, and math symbols are summarized in Appendix F.*

2. Bibliography

[1] D. E. Knuth and M. F. Plass, "Breaking paragraphs into lines," *Softw. pract. exp.* **11** (1981), 1119–1184.

---

* The amount of indentation can be changed by changing a parameter called \parindent. Turn the page for a summary of TEX's most important parameters.

The preceding example illustrates most of the basic things that you can do directly with plain TeX, but it does not provide an exhaustive list. Thus, it uses \centerline and \rightline, but not \leftline or \line; it uses \midinsert, but not \topinsert or \pageinsert; it uses \smallskip, but not \medskip or \bigskip; it uses \llap but not \rlap, \item but not \itemitem, \topglue but not \hglue. It does not illustrate \raggedright setting of paragraphs; it does not use \obeylines or \obeyspaces to shut off TeX's automatic formatting. All such control sequences are explained later in this appendix, and further information can be found by looking them up in the index. The main purpose of the example is to serve as a reminder of the repertoire of possibilities.

Most of the control sequences used in the example are defined by macros of plain TeX format, but three of them are primitive, i.e., built in: '\par' (end of paragraph), '\noindent' (beginning of non-indented paragraph), and '\/' (italic correction). The example also assigns values to two of TeX's primitive parameters, namely \hsize and \vsize. TeX has scores of parameters, all of which are listed in Chapter 24, but only a few of them are of special concern to the majority of TeX users. Here are examples of how you might want to give new values to the most important parameters other than \hsize and \vsize:

\tolerance=500   (TeX will tolerate lines whose badness is rated 500 or less.)
\looseness=1   (The next paragraph will be one line longer than usual.)
\parindent=4mm   (Paragraphs will be indented by four millimeters.)
\hoffset=1.5in   (All output will be shifted right by one and a half inches.)
\voffset=24pt   (All output will be shifted down by 24 points.)
\baselineskip=11pt plus.1pt   (Baselines will be 11 pt apart, or a bit more.)
\parskip=3pt plus1pt minus.5pt   (Extra space will precede each paragraph.)

Plain TeX uses \parindent also to control the amount of indentation provided by \item, \itemitem, and \narrower.

The remainder of this appendix is devoted to the details of the plain TeX format, which is a set of macros that come with normal implementations of TeX. These macros serve three basic purposes: (1) They make TeX usable, because TeX's primitive capabilities operate at a very low level. A "virgin" TeX system that has no macros is like a newborn baby that has an immense amount to learn about the real world; but it is capable of learning fast. (2) The plain TeX macros provide a basis for more elaborate and powerful formats tailored to individual tastes and applications. You can do a lot with plain TeX, but pretty soon you'll want to do even more. (3) The macros also serve to illustrate how additional formats can be designed.

Somewhere in your computer system you should be able to find a file called `plain.tex` that contains exactly what has been preloaded into the running TeX system that you use. Our purpose in the rest of this appendix will be to discuss the contents of `plain.tex`. However, we will not include a verbatim description, because some parts of that file are too boring, and because the actual macros have been "optimized" with respect to memory space and running time. Unoptimized versions of the macros are easier for humans to understand, so we shall deal with those; `plain.tex` contains equivalent constructions that work better on a machine.

So here's the plan for the rest of Appendix B: We shall go through the contents of `plain.tex`, interspersing an edited transcription of that file with comments about noteworthy details. When we come to macros whose usage has not yet been explained—for example, somehow `\vglue` and `\beginsection` never made it into Chapters 1 through 27—we shall consider them from a user's viewpoint; but most of the time we shall be addressing the issues from the standpoint of a macro designer.

1. The code tables. A format's first duty is to establish `\catcode` values. This is necessary because, for example, a `\def` command can't be used until there are characters like { and } of categories 1 and 2. The `INITEX` program (which reads `plain.tex` so that TeX can be initialized) begins without knowing any grouping characters; hence `plain.tex` starts out as follows:

```
% This is the plain TeX format that's described in The TeXbook.
% N.B.: A version number is defined at the very end of this file;
%         please change that number whenever the file is modified!
% And don't modify the file under any circumstances.

\catcode'\{=1 % left brace is begin-group character
\catcode'\}=2 % right brace is end-group character
\catcode'\$=3 % dollar sign is math shift
\catcode'\&=4 % ampersand is alignment tab
\catcode'\#=6 % hash mark is macro parameter character
\catcode'\^=7 \catcode'\^^K=7 % circumflex and uparrow for superscripts
\catcode'\_=8 \catcode'\^^A=8 % underline and downarrow for subscripts
\catcode'\^^I=10 % ASCII tab is treated as a blank space
\chardef\active=13 \catcode'\~=\active % tilde is active
\catcode'\^^L=\active \outer\def^^L{\par} % ASCII form-feed is \outer\par
\message{Preloading the plain format: codes,}
```

These instructions set up the nonstandard characters ^^K and ^^A for superscripts and subscripts, in addition to ^ and _, so that people with extended character sets can use ↑ and ↓ as recommended in Appendix C. Furthermore ^^I (ASCII ⟨tab⟩) is given category 10 (space); and ^^L (ASCII ⟨formfeed⟩) becomes an active character that will detect runaways on files that have been divided into "file pages" by ⟨formfeed⟩ characters. The control sequence `\active` is defined to yield the constant 13; this is the one category code that seems to deserve a symbolic name, in view of its frequent use in constructing special-purpose macros.

When `INITEX` begins, category 12 (other) has been assigned to all 256 possible characters, except that the 52 letters A...Z and a...z are category 11 (letter), and a few other assignments equivalent to the following have been made:

```
\catcode '\\ =0    \catcode'\  =10    \catcode '\% =14
\catcode'\^^@=9     \catcode'\^^M=5    \catcode'\^^?=15
```

Thus '\' is already an escape character, '␣' is a space, and '%' is available for comments on the first line of the file; ASCII ⟨null⟩ is ignored, ASCII ⟨return⟩ is an end-of-line character, and ASCII ⟨delete⟩ is invalid.

The `\message` command shown above prints a progress report on the terminal when `plain.tex` is being input by `INITEX`. Later on comes '`\message{registers,}`' and several other messages, but we won't mention them specifically. The terminal will eventually display something like this when initialization is complete:

```
** plain
(plain.tex Preloading the plain format: codes, registers,
parameters, fonts, more fonts, macros, math definitions,
output routines, hyphenation (hyphen.tex))
* \dump
Beginning to dump on file plain.fmt
```

followed by a variety of statistics about what fonts were loaded, etc. If you want to make a new format `super.tex` that adds more features to `plain.tex`, it's best not to make a new file containing all the plain stuff, or even to `\input plain`; just type '`&plain super`' in response to INITEX's `**` prompt, to input `plain.fmt` at high speed.

After the opening `\message`, `plain.tex` goes on to define a control sequence `\dospecials` that lists all the characters whose catcodes should probably be changed to 12 (other) when copying things verbatim:

```
\def\dospecials{\do\ \do\\\do\{\do\}\do\$\do\&%
  \do\#\do\^\do\^^K\do\_\do\^^A\do\%\do\~}
```

(Appendix E illustrates how to use `\dospecials`.) The ASCII codes for ⟨null⟩, ⟨tab⟩, ⟨linefeed⟩, ⟨formfeed⟩, ⟨return⟩, and ⟨delete⟩ have not been included in the list.

At this point `plain.tex` completes its initialization of category codes by setting `\catcode`'`\@=11`, thereby making the character '`@`' behave temporarily like a letter. The command `\catcode`'`\@=12` will appear later, hence at-sign characters will act just like ordinary punctuation marks when TEX is running. The idea is to make it easy for plain TEX to have private control sequences that cannot be redefined by ordinary users; all such control sequences will have at least one '`@`' in their names.

The next job is to set up the `\mathcode` table:

```
\mathcode'\^^@="2201 \mathcode'\^^A="3223 \mathcode'\^^B="010B
\mathcode'\^^C="010C \mathcode'\^^D="225E \mathcode'\^^E="023A
\mathcode'\^^F="3232 \mathcode'\^^G="0119 \mathcode'\^^H="0115
\mathcode'\^^I="010D \mathcode'\^^J="010E \mathcode'\^^K="3222
\mathcode'\^^L="2206 \mathcode'\^^M="2208 \mathcode'\^^N="0231
\mathcode'\^^O="0140 \mathcode'\^^P="321A \mathcode'\^^Q="321B
\mathcode'\^^R="225C \mathcode'\^^S="225B \mathcode'\^^T="0238
\mathcode'\^^U="0239 \mathcode'\^^V="220A \mathcode'\^^W="3224
\mathcode'\^^X="3220 \mathcode'\^^Y="3221 \mathcode'\^^Z="8000
\mathcode'\^^[="2205 \mathcode'\^^\="3214 \mathcode'\^^]="3215
\mathcode'\^^^="3211 \mathcode'\^^_="225F \mathcode'\^^?="1273
\mathcode'\ ="8000   \mathcode'\!="5021 \mathcode'\'="8000
\mathcode'\(="4028   \mathcode'\)="5029 \mathcode'\*="2203
\mathcode'\+="202B   \mathcode'\,="613B \mathcode'\-="2200
\mathcode'\.="013A   \mathcode'\/="013D \mathcode'\:="303A
\mathcode'\;="603B   \mathcode'\<="313C \mathcode'\=="303D
\mathcode'\>="313E   \mathcode'\?="503F \mathcode'\[="405B
\mathcode'\\="026E   \mathcode'\]="505D \mathcode'\_="8000
\mathcode'\{="4266   \mathcode'\|="026A \mathcode'\}="5267
```

A mathcode is relevant only when the corresponding category code is 11 or 12; therefore many of these codes will rarely be looked at. For example, the math code for `^^M` specifies the character `\oplus`, but it's hard to imagine a user who would want `^^M` (ASCII ⟨return⟩) to produce an $\oplus$ sign in the middle of a math formula, since plain TEX appends `^^M` to the end of every line of input. The math codes have been set up here, however, to be entirely consistent with the extended character set presented in Appendix C and the Computer Modern fonts described in Appendix F. **INITEX** has done the rest of the work, as far as mathcodes are concerned: It has set `\mathcode`$x =$ $x +$ `"7000` for each of the ten digits $x =$ `'0` to `'9`; `\mathcode`$x = x +$ `"7100` for each of the 52 letters; and `\mathcode`$x = x$ for all other values of x.

There's no need to change the `\uccode` and `\lccode` tables. **INITEX** has made `\uccode'X='X`, `\uccode'x='X`, `\lccode'X='x`, `\lccode'x='x`, and it has made similar assignments for all other letters. The codes are zero for all nonletters. These tables are used by TEX's `\uppercase` and `\lowercase` operations, and the hyphenation algorithm also looks at `\lccode` (see Appendix H). Changes should be made only in format packages that set TEX up for languages with more than 26 letters (see Chapter 8).

Next comes the `\sfcode` table, which **INITEX** has initialized entirely to 1000, except that `\sfcode'X=999` for each of the 26 uppercase letters. Some characters are made "transparent" by setting

---

`\sfcode'\)=0 \sfcode'\'=0 \sfcode'\]=0 % won't change the space factor`

---

and the `\nonfrenchspacing` macro will be used later to change the sfcodes of special punctuation marks. (Chapter 12 explains what an `\sfcode` does.)

The last code table is called `\delcode`, and again it's necessary to change only a few values. **INITEX** has made all delimiter codes equal to -1, which means that no characters are recognized as delimiters in formulas. But there's an exception: The value `\delcode'\.=0` has been prespecified, so that '.' stands for a "null delimiter." (See Chapter 17.) Plain format sets up the following nine values, based on the delimiters available in Computer Modern:

`\delcode'\(="028300`	`\delcode'\/="02F30E`	`\delcode'\)="029301`
`\delcode'\[="05B302`	`\delcode'|="26A30C`	`\delcode'\]="05D303`
`\delcode'\<="26830A`	`\delcode'\\="26E30F`	`\delcode'\>="26930B`

It's important to note that `\delcode'\{` and `\delcode'\}` have been left equal to -1. If those codes were set to certain values, a user would be able to type, e.g., '`\big{`' to get a big left brace; but it would be a big mistake. The reason is that braces are used for grouping, when supplying arguments to macros; all sorts of strange things can happen if you try to use them both as math delimiters and group delimiters.

At this point the `plain.tex` file contains several definitions

`\chardef\@ne=1 \chardef\tw@=2 \chardef\thr@@=3 \chardef\sixt@@n=16`
`\chardef\@cclv=255 \mathchardef\@cclvi=256`
`\mathchardef\@m=1000 \mathchardef\@M=10000 \mathchardef\@MM=20000`

---

which allow "private" control sequences `\@ne`, `\tw@`, etc., to be used as abbreviations for commonly used constants 1, 2, ...; this convention makes TEX run a little faster, and it means that the macros will consume slightly less memory space. The usage of these abbreviations will not, however, be shown below unless necessary; we shall pretend that '1␣' appears instead of `\@ne`, '10000␣' instead of `\@M`, and so on, since that makes the programs more readable. (Notice that the long form of \@ne is '1␣' including a space, because TEX looks for and removes a space following a constant.)

2. Allocation of registers. The second major part of the plain.tex file provides a foundation on which systems of independently developed macros can coexist peacefully without interfering in their usage of registers. The idea is that macro writers should abide by the following ground rules: (1) Registers numbered 0 to 9 are always free for temporary "scratch" use, but their values are always assumed to be clobbered whenever any other macro might get into control. (This applies to registers like \dimen0, \toks0, \skip1, \box3, etc.; but TEX has already reserved \count0 through \count9 for page number identification.) (2) The registers \count255, \dimen255, and \skip255 are freely available in the same way. (3) All assignments to the scratch registers whose numbers are 1, 3, 5, 7, and 9 should be \global; all assignments to the other scratch registers (0, 2, 4, 6, 8, 255) should be non-\global. (This prevents the phenomenon of "save stack buildup" discussed in Chapter 27.) (4) Furthermore, it's possible to use any register in a group, if you ensure that TEX's grouping mechanism will restore the register when you're done with the group, and if you are certain that other macros will not make global assignments to that register when you need it. (5) But when a register is used by several macros, or over long spans of time, it should be allocated by \newcount, \newdimen, \newbox, etc. (6) Similar remarks apply to input/output streams used by \read and \write, to math families used by \fam, to sets of hyphenation rules used by \language, and to insertions (which require \box, \count, \dimen, and \skip registers all having the same number).

Some handy abbreviations are introduced at this point so that the macros below will have easy access to scratch registers:

\countdef\count@=255	\toksdef\toks@=0	\skipdef\skip@=0
\dimendef\dimen@=0	\dimendef\dimen@i=1	\dimendef\dimen@ii=2

Here now are the macros that provide allocation for quantities of more permanent value. These macros use registers \count10 through \count20 to hold the numbers that were allocated most recently; for example, if \newdimen has just reserved \dimen15, the value of \count11 will be 15. However, the rest of the world is not supposed to "know" that \count11 has anything to do with \dimen registers. There's a special counter called \allocationnumber that will be equal to the most recently allocated number, after every \newcount, \newdimen, ..., \newinsert operation; macro packages are supposed to refer to \allocationnumber if they want to find out what number was allocated. The inside story of how allocation is actually performed should be irrelevant when the allocation macros are used at a higher level; you mustn't assume that plain.tex really does allocation in any particular way.

```
\count10=22 % this counter allocates \count registers 23, 24, 25, ...
\count11=9  % this counter allocates \dimen registers 10, 11, 12, ...
\count12=9  % this counter allocates \skip registers 10, 11, 12, ...
\count13=9  % this counter allocates \muskip registers 10, 11, 12, ...
\count14=9  % this counter allocates \box registers 10, 11, 12, ...
\count15=9  % this counter allocates \toks registers 10, 11, 12, ...
\count16=-1 % this counter allocates input streams 0, 1, 2, ...
\count17=-1 % this counter allocates output streams 0, 1, 2, ...
\count18=3  % this counter allocates math families 4, 5, 6, ...
```

```
\count19=0  % this counter allocates language codes 1, 2, 3, ...
\count20=255 % this counter allocates insertions 254, 253, 252, ...
\countdef\insc@unt=20 % nickname for the insertion counter
\countdef\allocationnumber=21 % the most recent allocation
\countdef\m@ne=22 \m@ne=-1 % a handy constant
\def\wlog{\immediate\write-1} % this will write on log file (only)

\outer\def\newcount{\alloc@0\count\countdef\insc@unt}
\outer\def\newdimen{\alloc@1\dimen\dimendef\insc@unt}
\outer\def\newskip{\alloc@2\skip\skipdef\insc@unt}
\outer\def\newmuskip{\alloc@3\muskip\muskipdef\@cclvi}
\outer\def\newbox{\alloc@4\box\chardef\insc@unt}
\let\newtoks=\relax % this allows plain.tex to be read in twice
\outer\def\newhelp#1#2{\newtoks#1#1=\expandafter{\csname#2\endcsname}}
\outer\def\newtoks{\alloc@5\toks\toksdef\@cclvi}
\outer\def\newread{\alloc@6\read\chardef\sixt@@n}
\outer\def\newwrite{\alloc@7\write\chardef\sixt@@n}
\outer\def\newfam{\alloc@8\fam\chardef\sixt@@n}
\outer\def\newlanguage{\alloc@9\language\chardef\@cclvi}

\def\alloc@#1#2#3#4#5{\global\advance\count1#1 by 1
  \ch@ck#1#4#2% make sure there's still room
  \allocationnumber=\count1#1   \global#3#5=\allocationnumber
  \wlog{\string#5=\string#2\the\allocationnumber}}

\outer\def\newinsert#1{\global\advance\insc@unt by-1
  \ch@ck0\insc@unt\count \ch@ck1\insc@unt\dimen
  \ch@ck2\insc@unt\skip  \ch@ck4\insc@unt\box
  \allocationnumber=\insc@unt
  \global\chardef#1=\allocationnumber
  \wlog{\string#1=\string\insert\the\allocationnumber}}

\def\ch@ck#1#2#3{\ifnum\count1#1<#2%
  \else\errmessage{No room for a new #3}\fi}
```

The '\alloc@' macro does most of the work of allocation. It puts a message like '\maxdimen=\dimen10' into the log file after \newdimen has allocated a place for the \dimen register that will be called \maxdimen; such information might be useful when difficult macros are being debugged.

A \newhelp macro has been provided to aid in creating home-made help texts: You can say, e.g., \newhelp\helpout{This is a help message.}, and then give the command '\errhelp=\helpout' just before issuing an \errmessage. This method of creating help texts makes efficient use of TeX's memory, because it puts the text into a control sequence name where it doesn't take up space that is needed for tokens.

The plain file now goes ahead and allocates registers for important constants:

```
\newdimen\maxdimen \maxdimen=16383.99999pt
\newskip\hideskip \hideskip=-1000pt plus1fill
\newskip\centering \centering=0pt plus 1000pt minus 1000pt
\newdimen\p@ \p@=1pt % this saves macro space and time
\newdimen\z@ \z@=0pt \newskip\z@skip \z@skip=0pt plus0pt minus0pt
\newbox\voidb@x % permanently void box register
```

The control sequence \maxdimen stands for the largest permissible ⟨dimen⟩. Alignment macros that appear below will make use of special glue values called \hideskip and \centering. *N.B.: These three constants must not be changed under any circumstances*; you should either ignore them completely or just use them and enjoy them. In fact, the next four constant registers (\p@, \z@, \z@skip, and \voidb@x) have been given private names so that they are untouchable. The control sequence \p@ is used several dozen times as an abbreviation for 'pt ', and \z@ is used quite often to stand for either '0pt ' or '0 '; the use of such abbreviations saves almost 10% of the space needed to store the tokens in plain TEX's macros. But we shall stick to the unabbreviated forms below, so that the macros are more readable.

A different sort of allocation comes next:

```
\outer\def\newif#1{\count@=\escapechar \escapechar=-1
  \expandafter\expandafter\expandafter
  \edef\@if#1{true}{\let\noexpand#1=\noexpand\iftrue}%
  \expandafter\expandafter\expandafter
  \edef\@if#1{false}{\let\noexpand#1=\noexpand\iffalse}%
  \@if#1{false}\escapechar=\count@} % the condition starts out false
\def\@if#1#2{\csname\expandafter\if@\string#1#2\endcsname}
{\uccode'1='i \uccode'2='f \uppercase{\gdef\if@12{}}} % 'if' is required
```

For example, the command \newif\ifalpha creates a trio of control sequences called \alphatrue, \alphafalse, and \ifalpha (see Chapter 20).

3. Parameters. INITEX sets almost all of the numeric registers and parameters equal to zero; it makes all of the token registers and parameters empty; and it makes all of the box registers void. But there are a few exceptions: \mag is set initially to 1000, \tolerance to 10000, \maxdeadcycles to 25, \hangafter to 1, \escapechar to '\\, and \endlinechar to '\^^M. Plain TEX assigns new parameter values as follows:

```
\pretolerance=100 \tolerance=200  \hbadness=1000 \vbadness=1000
\linepenalty=10 \hyphenpenalty=50 \exhyphenpenalty=50
\binoppenalty=700 \relpenalty=500
\clubpenalty=150 \widowpenalty=150 \displaywidowpenalty=50
\brokenpenalty=100 \predisplaypenalty=10000
\doublehyphendemerits=10000 \finalhyphendemerits=5000 \adjdemerits=10000
\tracinglostchars=1 \uchyph=1 \delimiterfactor=901
\defaulthyphenchar='\- \defaultskewchar=-1 \newlinechar=-1
\showboxbreadth=5 \showboxdepth=3 \errorcontextlines=5

\hfuzz=0.1pt \vfuzz=0.1pt \overfullrule=5pt
\hsize=6.5in \vsize=8.9in \parindent=20pt
\maxdepth=4pt \splitmaxdepth=\maxdimen \boxmaxdepth=\maxdimen
\delimitershortfall=5pt \nulldelimiterspace=1.2pt \scriptspace=0.5pt

\parskip=0pt plus 1pt
\abovedisplayskip=12pt plus 3pt minus 9pt
\abovedisplayshortskip=0pt plus 3pt
\belowdisplayskip=12pt plus 3pt minus 9pt
\belowdisplayshortskip=7pt plus 3pt minus 4pt
\topskip=10pt \splittopskip=10pt
\parfillskip=0pt plus 1fil
```

```
\thinmuskip=3mu
\medmuskip=4mu plus 2mu minus 4mu
\thickmuskip=5mu plus 5mu
```

(Some parameters are set by TeX itself as it runs, so it is inappropriate to initialize them: `\time`, `\day`, `\month`, and `\year` are established at the beginning of a job; `\outputpenalty` is given a value when an `\output` routine is invoked; `\predisplaysize`, `\displaywidth`, and `\displayindent` get values just before a display is processed; and the values `\looseness=0`, `\hangindent=0pt`, `\hangafter=1`, `\parshape=0` are assigned at the end of a paragraph and when TeX enters internal vertical mode.)

The parameters `\baselineskip`, `\lineskip`, and `\lineskiplimit` have not been initialized here, but a macro called `\normalbaselines` is defined below; this macro sets `\baselineskip=\normalbaselineskip`, `\lineskip=\normallineskip`, and `\lineskiplimit=\normallineskiplimit`. An indirect approach like this has been used so that several different type sizes may be handled, as illustrated in Appendix E. Plain TeX deals exclusively with 10 pt type, but it supports extension to other styles.

Some "pseudo parameters" come next. These quantities behave just like internal parameters of TeX, and users are free to change them in the same way, but they are part of the plain TeX format rather than primitives of the language.

```
\newskip\smallskipamount % the amount of a \smallskip
  \smallskipamount=3pt plus1pt minus1pt
\newskip\medskipamount % the amount of a \medskip
  \medskipamount=6pt plus2pt minus2pt
\newskip\bigskipamount % the amount of a \bigskip
  \bigskipamount=12pt plus4pt minus4pt
\newskip\normalbaselineskip % normal value of \baselineskip
  \normalbaselineskip=12pt
\newskip\normallineskip % normal value of \lineskip
  \normallineskip=1pt
\newdimen\normallineskiplimit % normal value of \lineskiplimit
  \normallineskiplimit=0pt
\newdimen\jot % unit of measure for opening up displays
  \jot=3pt
\newcount\interdisplaylinepenalty % interline penalty in \displaylines
  \interdisplaylinepenalty=100
\newcount\interfootnotelinepenalty % interline penalty in footnotes
  \interfootnotelinepenalty=100
```

4. Font information. Now `plain.tex` brings in the data that TeX needs to know about how to typeset lots of characters in lots of different fonts. First the `\magstep` macros are defined, to support font scaling:

```
\def\magstephalf{1095 }
\def\magstep#1{\ifcase#1 1000\or
  1200\or 1440\or 1728\or 2074\or 2488\fi\relax}
```

(Incidentally, `\magstep` doesn't use `\multiply` to compute values, since it is supposed to expand to a ⟨number⟩ enroute to TeX's "stomach"; `\multiply` wouldn't work, because it is an assignment command, performed only in the stomach.)

One of the main things that distinguishes one format from another is the fact that each format gives TEX the necessary knowledge about a certain family of typefaces. In this case the Computer Modern types described in Appendix F are taken as a basis, although there is a provision for incorporating other styles.

```
\font\tenrm=cmr10          \font\preloaded=cmr9       \font\preloaded=cmr8
\font\sevenrm=cmr7         \font\preloaded=cmr6       \font\fiverm=cmr5

\font\teni=cmmi10          \font\preloaded=cmmi9      \font\preloaded=cmmi8
\font\seveni=cmmi7         \font\preloaded=cmmi6      \font\fivei=cmmi5

\font\tensy=cmsy10         \font\preloaded=cmsy9      \font\preloaded=cmsy8
\font\sevensy=cmsy7        \font\preloaded=cmsy6      \font\fivesy=cmsy5

\font\tenex=cmex10

\font\tenbf=cmbx10         \font\preloaded=cmbx9      \font\preloaded=cmbx8
\font\sevenbf=cmbx7        \font\preloaded=cmbx6      \font\fivebf=cmbx5

\font\tensl=cmsl10         \font\preloaded=cmsl9      \font\preloaded=cmsl8
\font\tentt=cmtt10         \font\preloaded=cmtt9      \font\preloaded=cmtt8
\font\tenit=cmti10         \font\preloaded=cmti9      \font\preloaded=cmti8
\font\preloaded=cmss10     \font\preloaded=cmssq8
\font\preloaded=cmssi10    \font\preloaded=cmssqi8

\font\preloaded=cmr7 scaled \magstep4 % for titles
\font\preloaded=cmtt10 scaled \magstep2
\font\preloaded=cmssbx10 scaled \magstep2

% Additional \preloaded fonts can be specified here.
% (And those that were \preloaded above can be eliminated.)
\let\preloaded=\undefined % preloaded fonts must be declared anew later.
```

Notice that most of the fonts have been called \preloaded; but the control sequence \preloaded is made undefined at the very end, so those fonts cannot be used directly. There are two reasons for this strange approach: First, it is desirable to keep the total number of fonts of plain TEX relatively small, because plain TEX is a sort of standard format; it shouldn't cost much for someone to acquire all the fonts of plain TEX in addition to those he really wants. Second, it is desirable on many computer systems to preload the information for most of the fonts that people will actually be using, since this saves a lot of machine time. The \preloaded font information goes into TEX's memory, where it will come alive instantly if the user defines the corresponding \font again. For example, the book format in Appendix E says '\font\ninerm=cmr9'; after that assignment has been obeyed, the control sequence \ninerm will identify the cmr9 font, whose information does not have to be loaded again.

The exact number and nature of fonts that are preloaded is unimportant; the only important thing needed for standardization between machines is that sixteen basic fonts (cmr10, cmr7, ..., cmti10) should actually be loaded. The plain.tex files used on different machines can be expected to differ widely with respect to preloaded fonts, since the choice of how many fonts to preload and the selection of the most important fonts depends on local conditions. For example, at the author's university it is useful to preload a font that contains the Stanford seal, but that particular font is not very popular at Berkeley.

Most of these fonts have the default values of \hyphenchar and \skewchar, namely '- and -1; but the math italic and math symbol fonts have special \skewchar values, which are defined next:

```
\skewchar\teni='177 \skewchar\seveni='177 \skewchar\fivei='177
\skewchar\tensy='60 \skewchar\sevensy='60 \skewchar\fivesy='60
```

Once the fonts are loaded, they are also grouped into families for use in math setting, and shorthand names like \rm and \it are defined:

```
\textfont0=\tenrm \scriptfont0=\sevenrm \scriptscriptfont0=\fiverm
\def\rm{\fam0 \tenrm}
\textfont1=\teni  \scriptfont1=\seveni  \scriptscriptfont1=\fivei
\def\mit{\fam1 } \def\oldstyle{\fam1 \teni}
\textfont2=\tensy \scriptfont2=\sevensy \scriptscriptfont2=\fivesy
\def\cal{\fam2 }
\textfont3=\tenex \scriptfont3=\tenex   \scriptscriptfont3=\tenex

\newfam\itfam \def\it{\fam\itfam\tenit} \textfont\itfam=\tenit
\newfam\slfam \def\sl{\fam\slfam\tensl} \textfont\slfam=\tensl
\newfam\bffam \def\bf{\fam\bffam\tenbf} \textfont\bffam=\tenbf
  \scriptfont\bffam=\sevenbf   \scriptscriptfont\bffam=\fivebf
\newfam\ttfam \def\tt{\fam\ttfam\tentt} \textfont\ttfam=\tentt
```

5. Macros for text. The fifth part of plain.tex introduces macros that do basic formatting unrelated to mathematics. First come some macros that were promised above:

```
\def\frenchspacing{\sfcode'\.=1000 \sfcode'\?=1000 \sfcode'\!=1000
  \sfcode'\:=1000 \sfcode'\;=1000 \sfcode'\,=1000 }
\def\nonfrenchspacing{\sfcode'\.=3000 \sfcode'\?=3000 \sfcode'\!=3000
  \sfcode'\:=2000 \sfcode'\;=1500 \sfcode'\,=1250 }
\def\normalbaselines{\lineskip=\normallineskip
  \baselineskip=\normalbaselineskip \lineskiplimit=\normallineskiplimit}
```

The next macros are simple but vital. First \⟨tab⟩ and \⟨return⟩ are defined so that they expand to \⟨space⟩; this helps to prevent confusion, since all three cases look identical when displayed on most computer terminals. Then the macros \lq, \rq, \lbrack, and \rbrack are defined, for people who have difficulty typing quotation marks and/or brackets. The control sequences \endgraf and \endline are made equivalent to TEX's primitive \par and \cr operations, since it is often useful to redefine the meanings of \par and \cr themselves. Then come the definitions of \space (a blank space), \empty (a list of no tokens), and \null (an empty hbox). Finally, \bgroup and \egroup are made to provide "implicit" grouping characters that turn out to be especially useful in macro definitions. (See Chapters 24–26 and Appendix D for information about implicit characters.)

```
\def\^^I{\ } \def\^^M{\ }
\def\lq{'} \def\rq{'} \def\lbrack{[} \def\rbrack{]}
\let\endgraf=\par \let\endline=\cr
\def\space{ } \def\empty{} \def\null{\hbox{}}
\let\bgroup={ \let\egroup=}
```

Something a bit tricky comes up now in the definitions of \obeyspaces and \obeylines, since TeX is only "half obedient" while these definitions are half finished:

```
\def\obeyspaces{\catcode`\ =\active}
{\obeyspaces\global\let =\space}
{\catcode`\^^M=\active % these lines must end with '%'
  \gdef\obeylines{\catcode`\^^M=\active \let^^M=\par}%
  \global\let^^M=\par} % this is in case ^^M appears in a \write
```

The \obeylines macro says '\let^^M=\par' instead of '\def^^M{\par}' because the \let technique allows constructions such as '\let\par=\cr \obeylines \halign{...}' in which \cr's need not be given within the alignment.

The \loop...\repeat macro provides for iterative operations as illustrated at the end of Chapter 20. In this macro and several others, the control sequence '\next' is given a temporary value that is not going to be needed later; thus, \next acts like a "scratch control sequence."

```
\def\loop#1\repeat{\def\body{#1}\iterate}
\def\iterate{\body \let\next=\iterate \else\let\next=\relax\fi \next}
\let\repeat=\fi % this makes \loop...\if...\repeat skippable
```

Spacing is the next concern. The macros \enskip, \quad, and \qquad provide spaces that are legitimate breakpoints within a paragraph; \enspace, \thinspace, and \negthinspace produce space that cannot cause a break (although the space will disappear if it occurs just next to certain kinds of breaks). All six of these spaces are relative to the current font. You can get horizontal space that never disappears by saying '\hglue⟨glue⟩'; this space is able to stretch or shrink. Similarly, there's a vertical analog, '\vglue⟨glue⟩'. The \nointerlineskip macro suppresses interline glue that would ordinarily be inserted before the next box in vertical mode; this is a "one shot" macro, but \offinterlineskip is more drastic—it sets things up so that future interline glue will be present, but zero. There also are macros for potentially breakable vertical spaces: \smallskip, \medskip, and \bigskip.

```
\def\enskip{\hskip.5em\relax}     \def\enspace{\kern.5em }
\def\quad{\hskip1em\relax}        \def\qquad{\hskip2em\relax}
\def\thinspace{\kern .16667em }   \def\negthinspace{\kern-.16667em }
\def\hglue{\afterassignment\hgl@\skip@=}
\def\hgl@{\leavevmode \count@=\spacefactor \vrule width0pt
  \nobreak\hskip\skip@ \spacefactor=\count@}
\def\vglue{\afterassignment\vgl@\skip@=}
\def\vgl@{\par \dimen@=\prevdepth \hrule height0pt
  \nobreak\vskip\skip@ \prevdepth=\dimen@}
\def\topglue{\nointerlineskip \vglue-\topskip \vglue} % for top of page
\def\nointerlineskip{\prevdepth=-1000pt }
\def\offinterlineskip{\baselineskip=-1000pt
  \lineskip=0pt \lineskiplimit=\maxdimen}
\def\smallskip{\vskip\smallskipamount}
\def\medskip{\vskip\medskipamount}
\def\bigskip{\vskip\bigskipamount}
```

Speaking of breakpoints, the following macros introduce penalty markers that make breaking less, or more, desirable. The `\break`, `\nobreak`, and `\allowbreak` macros are intended for use in any mode; the ˜ (tie) and `\slash` (hyphen-like '/') macros are intended for horizontal mode. The others are intended only for vertical mode, i.e., between paragraphs, so they begin with `\par`.

```
\def\break{\penalty-10000 } \def\nobreak{\penalty10000 }
\def\allowbreak{\penalty0 }
\def~{\penalty10000\ }
\def\slash{/\penalty\exhyphenpenalty}
\def\filbreak{\par\vfil\penalty-200\vfilneg}
\def\goodbreak{\par\penalty-500 }
\def\eject{\par\penalty-10000 }
\def\supereject{\par\penalty-20000 }
\def\removelastskip{\ifdim\lastskip=0pt \else\vskip-\lastskip\fi}
\def\smallbreak{\par \ifdim\lastskip<\smallskipamount
  \removelastskip \penalty-50 \smallskip \fi}
\def\medbreak{\par \ifdim\lastskip<\medskipamount
  \removelastskip \penalty-100 \medskip \fi}
\def\bigbreak{\par \ifdim\lastskip<\bigskipamount
  \removelastskip \penalty-200 \bigskip \fi}
```

Boxes are next: `\line`, `\leftline`, `\rightline`, and `\centerline` produce boxes of the full line width, while `\llap` and `\rlap` make boxes whose effective width is zero. The `\underbar` macro puts its argument into an hbox with a straight line at a fixed distance under it.

```
\def\line{\hbox to\hsize}
\def\leftline#1{\line{#1\hss}} \def\rightline#1{\line{\hss#1}}
\def\centerline#1{\line{\hss#1\hss}}
\def\llap#1{\hbox to 0pt{\hss#1}} \def\rlap#1{\hbox to 0pt{#1\hss}}
\def\m@th{\mathsurround=0pt }
\def\underbar#1{$\setbox0=\hbox{#1} \dp0=0pt
  \m@th \underline{\box0}$}
```

(Notice that `\underbar` uses math mode to do its job, although the operation is essentially non-mathematical in nature. A few of the other macros below use math mode in similar ways; thus, TEX's mathematical abilities prove to be useful even when no mathematical typesetting is actually being done. A special control sequence `\m@th` is used to "turn off" `\mathsurround` when such constructions are being performed.)

A `\strut` is implemented here as a rule of width zero, since this takes minimum space and time in applications where numerous struts are present.

```
\newbox\strutbox
\setbox\strutbox=\hbox{\vrule height8.5pt depth3.5pt width0pt}
\def\strut{\relax\ifmmode\copy\strutbox\else\unhcopy\strutbox\fi}
```

The '`\relax`' in this macro and in others below is necessary in case `\strut` appears first in an alignment entry, because TEX is in a somewhat unpredictable mode at such times (see Chapter 22).

The \ialign macro provides for alignments when it is necessary to be sure that \tabskip is initially zero. The \hidewidth macro can be used essentially as \hfill in alignment entries that are permitted to "stick out" of their column. There's also \multispan, which permits alignment entries to span one or more columns.

```
\def\ialign{\everycr={}\tabskip=0pt \halign} % initialized \halign
\def\hidewidth{\hskip\hideskip}

\newcount\mscount
\def\multispan#1{\omit \mscount=#1 \loop\ifnum\mscount>1 \sp@n\repeat}
\def\sp@n{\span\omit \advance\mscount by -1 }
```

Now we get to the "tabbing" macros, which are more complicated than anything else in plain TEX. They keep track of the tab positions by maintaining boxes full of empty boxes having the specified widths. (The best way to understand these macros is probably to watch them in action on simple examples, using \tracingall.)

```
\newif\ifus@ \newif\if@cr
\newbox\tabs \newbox\tabsyet \newbox\tabsdone

\def\cleartabs{\global\setbox\tabsyet=\null \setbox\tabs=\null}
\def\settabs{\setbox\tabs=\null \futurelet\next\sett@b}
\let\+=\relax % in case this file is being read in twice
\def\sett@b{\ifx\next\+ \let\next=\relax % turn off \outerness
    \def\next{\afterassignment\s@tt@b\let\next}%
  \else\let\next=\s@tcols\fi\next}
\def\s@tt@b{\let\next=\relax \us@false\m@ketabbox}
\outer\def\+{\tabalign} \def\tabalign{\us@true \m@ketabbox}
\def\s@tcols#1columns{\count@=#1 \dimen@=\hsize
  \loop \ifnum\count@>0 \@nother \repeat}
\def\@nother{\dimen@ii=\dimen@ \divide\dimen@ii by\count@
  \setbox\tabs=\hbox{\hbox to\dimen@ii{}\unhbox\tabs}%
  \advance\dimen@ by-\dimen@ii \advance\count@ by -1 }

\def\m@ketabbox{\begingroup
  \global\setbox\tabsyet=\copy\tabs \global\setbox\tabsdone=\null
  \def\cr{\@crtrue\crcr\egroup\egroup
    \ifus@ \unvbox0 \lastbox\fi \endgroup
    \setbox\tabs=\hbox{\unhbox\tabsyet\unhbox\tabsdone}}%
  \setbox0=\vbox\bgroup\@crfalse \ialign\bgroup&\t@bbox##\t@bb@x\crcr}

\def\t@bbox{\setbox0=\hbox\bgroup}
\def\t@bb@x{\if@cr\egroup % now \box0 holds the column
  \else\hss\egroup \global\setbox\tabsyet=\hbox{\unhbox\tabsyet
      \global\setbox1=\lastbox}% now \box1 holds its size
    \ifvoid1 \global\setbox1=\hbox to\wd0{}%
    \else\setbox0=\hbox to\wd1{\unhbox0}\fi
    \global\setbox\tabsdone=\hbox{\box1\unhbox\tabsdone}\fi
  \box0}
```

The macro \+ has been declared '\outer' here, so that TEX will be better able to detect runaway arguments and definitions (see Chapter 20). A non-\outer version,

called \tabalign, has also been provided in case it is necessary to use \+ in some
"inner" place. You can use \tabalign just like \+, except after \settabs.

• Paragraph shapes of a limited but important kind are provided by \item,
\itemitem, and \narrower. There are also two macros that haven't been mentioned
before: (1) \hang causes hanging indentation by the normal amount of \parindent,
after the first line; thus, the entire paragraph will be indented by the same amount
(unless it began with \noindent). (2) \textindent{stuff} is like \indent, but it puts
the 'stuff' into the indentation, flush right except for an en space; it also removes spaces
that might follow the right brace in '{stuff}'. For example, the present paragraph
was typeset by the commands '\textindent{$\bullet$} Paragraph shapes ...'; the
opening 'P' occurs at the normal position for a paragraph's first letter.

```
\def\hang{\hangindent\parindent}
\def\item{\par\hang\textindent}
\def\itemitem{\par\indent \hangindent2\parindent \textindent}
\def\textindent#1{\indent\llap{#1\enspace}\ignorespaces}
\def\narrower{\advance\leftskip by\parindent
  \advance\rightskip by\parindent}
```

The \beginsection macro is intended to mark the beginning of a new major
subdivision in a document; to use it, you say '\beginsection⟨section title⟩' followed by
a blank line (or \par). The macro first emits glue and penalties, designed to start a new
page if the present page is nearly full; then it makes a \bigskip and puts the section
title flush left on a line by itself, in boldface type. The section title is also displayed on
the terminal. After a \smallskip, with page break prohibited, a \noindent command
is given; this suppresses indentation in the next paragraph, i.e., in the first paragraph
of the new section. (However, the next "paragraph" will be empty if vertical mode
material immediately follows the \beginsection command.)

```
\outer\def\beginsection#1\par{\vskip0pt plus.3\vsize\penalty-250
  \vskip0pt plus-.3\vsize\bigskip\vskip\parskip
  \message{#1}\leftline{\bf#1}\nobreak\smallskip\noindent}
```

Special statements in a mathematical paper are often called theorems, lemmas,
definitions, axioms, postulates, remarks, corollaries, algorithms, facts, conjectures, or
some such things, and they generally are given special typographic treatment. The
\proclaim macro, which was illustrated earlier in this appendix and also in Chapter 20,
puts the title of the proclamation in boldface, then sets the rest of the paragraph in
slanted type. The paragraph is followed by something similar to \medbreak, except
that the amount of penalty is different so that page breaks are discouraged:

```
\outer\def\proclaim #1. #2\par{\medbreak
  \noindent{\bf#1.\enspace}{\sl#2\par}%
  \ifdim\lastskip<\medskipamount \removelastskip\penalty55\medskip\fi}
```

Ragged-right setting is initiated by restricting the spaces between words to
have a fixed width, and by putting variable space at the right of each line. You should
not call \raggedright until your text font has already been specified; it is assumed that
the ragged-right material will not be in a variety of different sizes. (If this assumption
is not valid, a different approach should be used: \fontdimen parameters 3 and 4 of the
fonts you will be using should be set to zero, by saying, e.g., '\fontdimen3\tenrm=0pt'.

These parameters specify the stretchability and shrinkability of interword spaces.) A special macro \ttraggedright should be used for ragged-right setting in typewriter type, since the spaces between words are generally bigger in that style. (Spaces are already unstretchable and unshrinkable in font cmtt.)

```
\def\raggedright{\rightskip=0pt plus2em
  \spaceskip=.3333em \xspaceskip=.5em\relax}
\def\ttraggedright{\tt\rightskip=0pt plus2em\relax}
```

Now we come to special symbols and accents, which depend primarily on the characters available in the Computer Modern fonts. Different constructions will be necessary if other styles of type are used. When a symbol is built up by forming a box, the \leavevmode macro is called first; this starts a new paragraph, if TEX is in vertical mode, but does nothing if TEX is in horizontal mode or math mode.

```
\chardef\%=`\% \chardef\&=`\& \chardef\#=`\# \chardef\$=`\$
\chardef\ss="19
\chardef\ae="1A \chardef\oe="1B \chardef\o="1C
\chardef\AE="1D \chardef\OE="1E \chardef\O="1F
\chardef\i="10 \chardef\j="11 % dotless letters
\def\aa{\accent'27a} \def\l{\char'40l}

\def\leavevmode{\unhbox\voidb@x} % begins a paragraph, if necessary
\def\_{\leavevmode \kern.06em \vbox{\hrule width0.3em}}
\def\L{\leavevmode\setbox0=\hbox{L}\hbox to\wd0{\hss\char'40L}}
\def\AA{\leavevmode\setbox0=\hbox{h}\dimen@=\ht0 \advance\dimen@ by-1ex
  \rlap{\raise.67\dimen@\hbox{\char'27}}A}

\def\mathhexbox#1#2#3{\leavevmode
  \hbox{$\m@th \mathchar"#1#2#3$}}
\def\dag{\mathhexbox279}  \def\ddag{\mathhexbox27A}
\def\S{\mathhexbox278} \def\P{\mathhexbox27B}

\def\oalign#1{\leavevmode\vtop{\baselineskip0pt \lineskip.25ex
  \ialign{##\crcr#1\crcr}}} % put characters over each other
\def\ooalign{\lineskiplimit-\maxdimen \oalign}
\def\d#1{\oalign{#1\crcr\hidewidth.\hidewidth}}
\def\b#1{\oalign{#1\crcr\hidewidth
    \vbox to.2ex{\hbox{\char'26}\vss}\hidewidth}}
\def\c#1{\setbox0=\hbox{#1}\ifdim\ht0=1ex \accent'30 #1%
  \else{\ooalign{\hidewidth\char'30\hidewidth\crcr\unhbox0}}\fi}
\def\copyright{{\ooalign
    {\hfil\raise.07ex\hbox{c}\hfil\crcr\mathhexbox20D}}}

\def\dots{\relax\ifmmode\ldots\else$\m@th \ldots\,$\fi}
\def\TeX{T\kern-.1667em \lower.5ex\hbox{E}\kern-.125em X}

\def\'#1{{\accent"12 #1}} \def\'#1{{\accent"13 #1}}
\def\v#1{{\accent"14 #1}} \def\u#1{{\accent"15 #1}}
\def\=#1{{\accent"16 #1}} \def\^#1{{\accent"5E #1}}
\def\.#1{{\accent"5F #1}} \def\H#1{{\accent"7D #1}}
\def\~#1{{\accent"7E #1}} \def\"#1{{\accent"7F #1}}
\def\t#1{{\edef\next{\the\font}\the\textfont1\accent"7F\next#1}}
```

At this point three alternative control-symbol accents are defined, suitable for keyboards with extended character sets (cf. Appendix C):

```
\let\^^_=\v        \let\^^S=\u        \let\^^D=\^
```

Various ways to fill space with leaders are provided next.

```
\def\hrulefill{\leaders\hrule\hfill}
\def\dotfill{\cleaders\hbox{$\m@th \mkern1.5mu . \mkern1.5mu$}\hfill}
\def\rightarrowfill{$\m@th \mathord- \mkern-6mu
  \cleaders\hbox{$\mkern-2mu \mathord- \mkern-2mu$}\hfill
  \mkern-6mu \mathord\rightarrow$}
\def\leftarrowfill{$\m@th \mathord\leftarrow \mkern-6mu
  \cleaders\hbox{$\mkern-2mu \mathord- \mkern-2mu$}\hfill
  \mkern-6mu \mathord-$}

\mathchardef\braceld="37A \mathchardef\bracerd="37B
\mathchardef\bracelu="37C \mathchardef\braceru="37D
\def\upbracefill{$\m@th
  \bracelu\leaders\vrule\hfill\bracerd
  \braceld\leaders\vrule\hfill\braceru$}
\def\downbracefill{$\m@th
  \braceld\leaders\vrule\hfill\braceru
  \bracelu\leaders\vrule\hfill\bracerd$}
```

The \upbracefill and \downbracefill macros have restricted usage: they must appear *all by themselves* in an hbox or an alignment entry, except for horizontal spacing.

Finally, the fifth section of plain.tex closes by defining \bye:

```
\outer\def\bye{\par\vfill\supereject\end} % the recommended way to stop
```

6. Macros for math. The sixth section of plain.tex is the longest; but it will suffice to give only excerpts here, because most of it is simply a tedious listing of special symbols together with their font locations, and the same information appears in Appendix F.

Some rudimentary things come first: The control sequences \sp and \sb are provided for people who can't easily type ^ and _; there are four control symbols that provide spacing corrections; a "discretionary times sign" * is defined; and then there's an interesting set of macros that convert f''' into f^{\prime\prime\prime}:

```
\let\sp=^ \let\sb=_        {\catcode`\_=\active \global\let_=\_}
\def\,{\mskip\thinmuskip}  \def\!{\mskip-\thinmuskip}
\def\>{\mskip\medmuskip}    \def\;{\mskip\thickmuskip}
\def\*{\discretionary{\thinspace\the\textfont2\char2}{}{}}
{\catcode`\^^Z=\active \gdef^^Z{\not=}} % ^^Z is like \ne in math

{\catcode`\'=\active \gdef'{^\bgroup\prim@s}}
\def\prim@s{\prime\futurelet\next\pr@m@s}
\def\pr@m@s{\ifx'\next\let\nxt\pr@@@s \else\ifx^\next\let\nxt\pr@@@t
  \else\let\nxt\egroup\fi\fi \nxt}
\def\pr@@@s#1{\prim@s} \def\pr@@@t#1#2{#2\egroup}
```

The next job is to define Greek letters and other symbols of type Ord. Uppercase Greek letters are assigned hexadecimal codes of the form "7xxx, so that they will change families when \fam changes. Three dots '···' are used here and below to indicate that additional symbols, having similar definitions, are listed in Appendix F.

```
\mathchardef\alpha="010B    ···    \mathchardef\omega="0121
\mathchardef\Gamma="7000    ···    \mathchardef\Omega="700A
\mathchardef\aleph="0240    ···    \mathchardef\spadesuit="027F
\def\hbar{{\mathchar'26\mkern-9muh}}
\def\surd{{\mathchar"1270}}
\def\angle{{\vbox{\ialign{$\m@th\scriptstyle##$\crcr
    \not\mathrel{\mkern14mu}\crcr \noalign{\nointerlineskip}
    \mkern2.5mu\leaders\hrule height.34pt\hfill\mkern2.5mu\crcr}}}}
```

Large operators are assigned hexadecimal codes of the form "1xxx:

```
\mathchardef\smallint="1273
\mathchardef\sum="1350      ···    \mathchardef\biguplus="1355
\mathchardef\intop="1352    \def\int{\intop\nolimits}
\mathchardef\ointop="1348   \def\oint{\ointop\nolimits}
```

Integral signs get special treatment so that their limits won't be set above and below.

Binary operations are next; nothing exciting here.

```
\mathchardef\pm="2206       ···    \mathchardef\amalg="2271
```

Relations are also fairly straightforward, except for the ones that are constructed from other characters. The \mapstochar is a character '⊦' of width zero that is quite useless by itself, but it combines with right arrows to make \mapsto '↦' and \longmapsto '⟼'. Similarly, \not is a relation character of width zero that puts a slash over the character that follows. When two relations are adjacent in a math formula, TEX puts no space between them.

```
\mathchardef\leq="3214      ···    \mathchardef\perp="323F
\def\joinrel{\mathrel{\mkern-3mu}}
\def\relbar{\mathrel{\smash-}} \def\Relbar{\mathrel=}
\def\longrightarrow{\relbar\joinrel\rightarrow}
\def\Longrightarrow{\Relbar\joinrel\Rightarrow}
\def\longleftarrow{\leftarrow\joinrel\relbar}
\def\Longleftarrow{\Leftarrow\joinrel\Relbar}
\def\longleftrightarrow{\leftarrow\joinrel\rightarrow}
\def\Longleftrightarrow{\Leftarrow\joinrel\Rightarrow}
\mathchardef\mapstochar="322F \def\mapsto{\mapstochar\rightarrow}
\def\longmapsto{\mapstochar\longrightarrow}
\mathchardef\lhook="312C \def\hookrightarrow{\lhook\joinrel\rightarrow}
\mathchardef\rhook="312D \def\hookleftarrow{\leftarrow\joinrel\rhook}

\def\neq{\not=}    \def\models{\mathrel|\joinrel=}
\def\bowtie{\mathrel\triangleright\joinrel\mathrel\triangleleft}
```

After defining characters \ldotp and \cdotp that act as math punctuation, it is easy to define \ldots and \cdots macros that give the proper spacing in most circumstances. Vertical and diagonal dots (`\vdots` and `\ddots`) are also provided here:

```
\mathchardef\ldotp="613A\mathchardef\cdotp="6201\mathchardef\colon="603A
\def\ldots{\mathinner{\ldotp\ldotp\ldotp}}
\def\cdots{\mathinner{\cdotp\cdotp\cdotp}}
\def\vdots{\vbox{\baselineskip=4pt \lineskiplimit=0pt
    \kern6pt \hbox{.}\hbox{.}\hbox{.}}}
\def\ddots{\mathinner{\mkern1mu\raise7pt\vbox{\kern7pt\hbox{.}}\mkern2mu
    \raise4pt\hbox{.}\mkern2mu\raise1pt\hbox{.}\mkern1mu}}
```

Most of the math accents are handled entirely by the `\mathaccent` primitive, but a few of the variable-width ones are constructed the hard way:

```
\def\acute{\mathaccent"7013 }     ···     \def\ddot{\mathaccent"707F }
\def\widetilde{\mathaccent"0365 } \def\widehat{\mathaccent"0362 }
\def\overrightarrow#1{\vbox{\ialign{##\crcr
    \rightarrowfill\crcr\noalign{\kern-1pt\nointerlineskip}
    $\hfil\displaystyle{#1}\hfil$\crcr}}}
\def\overleftarrow#1{\vbox{\ialign{##\crcr
    \leftarrowfill\crcr\noalign{\kern-1pt\nointerlineskip}
    $\hfil\displaystyle{#1}\hfil$\crcr}}}
\def\overbrace#1{\mathop{\vbox{\ialign{##\crcr\noalign{\kern3pt}
    \downbracefill\crcr\noalign{\kern3pt\nointerlineskip}
    $\hfil\displaystyle{#1}\hfil$\crcr}}}\limits}
\def\underbrace#1{\mathop{\vtop{\ialign{##\crcr
    $\hfil\displaystyle{#1}\hfil$\crcr\noalign{\kern3pt\nointerlineskip}
    \upbracefill\crcr\noalign{\kern3pt}}}}\limits}
\def\skew#1#2#3{{#2{#3\mkern#1mu}\mkern-#1mu}{}}
```

Now we come to 24 delimiters that can change their size:

```
\def\langle{\delimiter"426830A }        \def\rangle{\delimiter"526930B }
\def\lbrace{\delimiter"4266308 }        \def\rbrace{\delimiter"5267309 }
\def\lceil{\delimiter"4264306 }         \def\rceil{\delimiter"5265307 }
\def\lfloor{\delimiter"4262304 }        \def\rfloor{\delimiter"5263305 }
\def\lgroup{\delimiter"400033A }        \def\rgroup{\delimiter"500033B }
\def\lmoustache{\delimiter"4000340 }    \def\rmoustache{\delimiter"5000341 }
\def\uparrow{\delimiter"3222378 }       \def\Uparrow{\delimiter"322A37E }
\def\downarrow{\delimiter"3223379 }     \def\Downarrow{\delimiter"322B37F }
\def\updownarrow{\delimiter"326C33F }   \def\arrowvert{\delimiter"033C000 }
\def\Updownarrow{\delimiter"326D377 }   \def\Arrowvert{\delimiter"033D000 }
\def\vert{\delimiter"026A30C }          \def\Vert{\delimiter"026B30D }
\def\backslash{\delimiter"026E30F }     \def\bracevert{\delimiter"033E000 }
```

The '`\big...\Bigg`' macros produce specific sizes:

```
\def\bigl{\mathopen\big} \def\bigm{\mathrel\big} \def\bigr{\mathclose\big}
\def\Bigl{\mathopen\Big} \def\Bigm{\mathrel\Big} \def\Bigr{\mathclose\Big}
\def\biggl{\mathopen\bigg}               \def\Biggl{\mathopen\Bigg}
\def\biggm{\mathrel\bigg}                \def\Biggm{\mathrel\Bigg}
\def\biggr{\mathclose\bigg}              \def\Biggr{\mathclose\Bigg}
```

```
\def\big#1{{\hbox{$\left#1\vbox to 8.5pt{}\right.\n@space$}}}
\def\Big#1{{\hbox{$\left#1\vbox to 11.5pt{}\right.\n@space$}}}
\def\bigg#1{{\hbox{$\left#1\vbox to 14.5pt{}\right.\n@space$}}}
\def\Bigg#1{{\hbox{$\left#1\vbox to 17.5pt{}\right.\n@space$}}}
\def\n@space{\nulldelimiterspace=0pt \m@th}
```

There are a few other simple abbreviations related to delimiters:

```
\def\choose{\atopwithdelims()}
\def\brack{\atopwithdelims[]}
\def\brace{\atopwithdelims\{\}}
\def\sqrt{\radical"270370 }
```

And now we come to something more interesting. The `\mathpalette` operation constructs a formula in all four styles; it is applied here in the implementation of `\phantom`, `\smash`, `\root`, and other operations.

```
\def\mathpalette#1#2{\mathchoice{#1\displaystyle{#2}}
  {#1\textstyle{#2}}{#1\scriptstyle{#2}}{#1\scriptscriptstyle{#2}}}

\newbox\rootbox
\def\root#1\of{\setbox\rootbox=
  \hbox{$\m@th \scriptscriptstyle{#1}$}
  \mathpalette\r@@t}
\def\r@@t#1#2{\setbox0=\hbox{$\m@th #1\sqrt{#2}$}
  \dimen@=\ht0 \advance\dimen@ by-\dp0
  \mkern5mu \raise.6\dimen@\copy\rootbox \mkern-10mu \box0}

\newif\ifv@ \newif\ifh@
\def\vphantom{\v@true\h@false\ph@nt}
\def\hphantom{\v@false\h@true\ph@nt}
\def\phantom{\v@true\h@true\ph@nt}
\def\ph@nt{\ifmmode\def\next{\mathpalette\mathph@nt}%
  \else\let\next=\makeph@nt\fi \next}
\def\makeph@nt#1{\setbox0=\hbox{#1}\finph@nt}
\def\mathph@nt#1#2{\setbox0=\hbox{$\m@th#1{#2}$}\finph@nt}
\def\finph@nt{\setbox2=\null \ifv@ \ht2=\ht0 \dp2=\dp0 \fi
  \ifh@ \wd2=\wd0 \fi \box2 }
\def\mathstrut{\vphantom(}

\def\smash{\relax % \relax, in case this comes first in \halign
  \ifmmode\def\next{\mathpalette\mathsm@sh}\else\let\next\makesm@sh
  \fi \next}
\def\makesm@sh#1{\setbox0=\hbox{#1}\finsm@sh}
\def\mathsm@sh#1#2{\setbox0=\hbox{$\m@th#1{#2}$}\finsm@sh}
\def\finsm@sh{\ht0=0pt \dp0=0pt \box0 }

\def\cong{\mathrel{\mathpalette\@vereq\sim}} % \sim over =
\def\@vereq#1#2{\lower.5pt\vbox{\baselineskip0pt \lineskip-.5pt
    \ialign{$\m@th#1\hfil##\hfil$\crcr#2\crcr=\crcr}}}
\def\notin{\mathrel{\mathpalette\c@ncel\in}}
\def\c@ncel#1#2{\ooalign{$\hfil#1\mkern1mu/\hfil$\crcr$#1#2$}}
\def\rightleftharpoons{\mathrel{\mathpalette\rlh@{}}}
```

```
\def\rlh@#1{\vcenter{\hbox{\ooalign{\raise2pt
        \hbox{$#1\rightharpoonup$}\crcr $#1\leftharpoondown$}}}}
\def\buildrel#1\over#2{\mathrel{\mathop{\kern0pt #2}\limits^{#1}}}
\def\doteq{\buildrel\textstyle.\over=}
```

These definitions illustrate how other built-up symbol combinations could be defined
to work in all four styles.

Alternate names are defined now:

```
\let\ne=\neq          \let\le=\leq      \let\ge=\geq
\let\{=\lbrace        \let\|=\Vert      \let\}=\rbrace
\let\to=\rightarrow \let\gets=\leftarrow \let\owns=\ni
\let\land=\wedge      \let\lor=\vee      \let\lnot=\neg
\def\iff{\;\Longleftrightarrow\;}
```

The 32 common functions whose names generally appear in roman letters are
listed in Chapter 18. Only a few of the definitions need to be shown here:

```
\def\arccos{\mathop{\rm arccos}\nolimits}
                    ···      \def\tanh{\mathop{\rm tanh}\nolimits}
\def\det{\mathop{\rm det}}    ···      \def\sup{\mathop{\rm sup}}
\def\liminf{\mathop{\rm lim\,inf}} \def\limsup{\mathop{\rm lim\,sup}}

\def\bmod{\mskip-\medmuskip \mkern5mu
  \mathbin{\rm mod} \penalty900 \mkern5mu \mskip-\medmuskip}
\def\pmod#1{\allowbreak \mkern18mu ({\rm mod}\,\,#1)}
```

The definition of \matrix goes to some pains to ensure that two *n*-rowed
matrices will have the same height and the same depth, unless at least one of their
rows is unusually big. The definition of \bordermatrix is even more complicated, but
it seems to work reasonably well; it uses a constant \p@renwd that represents the width
of a big extensible left parenthesis.

```
\def\matrix#1{\null\,\vcenter{\normalbaselines\m@th
  \ialign{\hfil$##$\hfil&&\quad\hfil$##$\hfil\crcr
    \mathstrut\crcr\noalign{\kern-\baselineskip}
    #1\crcr\mathstrut\crcr\noalign{\kern-\baselineskip}}}\,}

\newdimen\p@renwd \setbox0=\hbox{\tenex B} \p@renwd=\wd0
\def\bordermatrix#1{\begingroup \m@th
  \setbox0=\vbox{\def\cr{\crcr\noalign{\kern2pt\global\let\cr=\endline}}
    \ialign{$##$\hfil\kern2pt\kern\p@renwd&\thinspace\hfil$##$\hfil
      &&\quad\hfil$##$\hfil\crcr
      \omit\strut\hfil\crcr\noalign{\kern-\baselineskip}
      #1\crcr\omit\strut\cr}}
  \setbox2=\vbox{\unvcopy0 \global\setbox1=\lastbox}
  \setbox2=\hbox{\unhbox1 \unskip \global\setbox1=\lastbox}
  \setbox2=\hbox{$\kern\wd1\kern-\p@renwd \left( \kern-\wd1
    \global\setbox1=\vbox{\box1\kern2pt}
    \vcenter{\kern-\ht1 \unvbox0 \kern-\baselineskip} \,\right)$}
  \null\;\vbox{\kern\ht1\box2}\endgroup}
```

The next macros are much simpler:

```
\def\cases#1{\left\{\,\vcenter{\normalbaselines\m@th
    \ialign{$##\hfil$&\quad##\hfil\crcr#1\crcr}}\right.}
\def\pmatrix#1{\left( \matrix{#1} \right)}
```

Finally there are macros for displayed equations:

```
\def\openup{\afterassignment\@penup\dimen@=}
\def\@penup{\advance\lineskip\dimen@
  \advance\baselineskip\dimen@ \advance\lineskiplimit\dimen@}
\def\eqalign#1{\null\,\vcenter{\openup1\jot \m@th
  \ialign{\strut\hfil$\displaystyle{##}$&$\displaystyle{{}##}$\hfil
    \crcr#1\crcr}}\,}
\newif\ifdt@p
\def\displ@y{\global\dt@ptrue \openup1\jot \m@th
  \everycr{\noalign{\ifdt@p \global\dt@pfalse
    \vskip-\lineskiplimit \vskip\normallineskiplimit
    \else \penalty\interdisplaylinepenalty \fi}}}
\def\@lign{\tabskip=0pt\everycr={}} % restore inside \displ@y
\def\displaylines#1{\displ@y
  \halign{\hbox to\displaywidth{$\hfil\@lign\displaystyle##\hfil$}\crcr
    #1\crcr}}
\def\eqalignno#1{\displ@y \tabskip=\centering
  \halign to\displaywidth{\hfil$\@lign\displaystyle{##}$\tabskip=0pt
    &$\@lign\displaystyle{{}##}$\hfil\tabskip=\centering
    &\llap{$\@lign##$}\tabskip=0pt\crcr
    #1\crcr}}
\def\leqalignno#1{\displ@y \tabskip=\centering
  \halign to\displaywidth{\hfil$\@lign\displaystyle{##}$\tabskip=0pt
    &$\@lign\displaystyle{{}##}$\hfil\tabskip=\centering
    &\kern-\displaywidth\rlap{$\@lign##$}\tabskip=\displaywidth\crcr
    #1\crcr}}
```

The value of `\lineskiplimit` is assumed to be `\normallineskiplimit` plus the accumulated amount of "opening up." Thus, the `\vskip` instructions in `\displ@y` will compensate for the fact that the first baseline of an alignment is separated by an opened-up baselineskip from the last line preceding the display.

7. Macros for output. The `plain.tex` file also contains the output routine described in Chapters 15 and 23. First there are simple facilities related to page numbers, headings, and footings:

```
\countdef\pageno=0 \pageno=1 % first page is number 1
\newtoks\headline \headline={\hfil} % headline is normally blank
\newtoks\footline \footline={\hss\tenrm\folio\hss}
  % footline is normally a centered page number in font \tenrm
\def\folio{\ifnum\pageno<0 \romannumeral-\pageno \else\number\pageno \fi}
\def\nopagenumbers{\footline={\hfil}} % blank out the footline
\def\advancepageno{\ifnum\pageno<0 \global\advance\pageno by -1
  \else\global\advance\pageno by 1 \fi} % increase |pageno|
```

```
\newif\ifr@ggedbottom
\def\raggedbottom{\topskip10pt plus60pt \r@ggedbottomtrue}
\def\normalbottom{\topskip10pt \r@ggedbottomfalse} % undoes \raggedbottom
```

The \footnote macro has a few subtle features that can best be appreciated by someone who reads Chapter 15 very carefully. It also uses some \bgroup and \futurelet and \aftergroup trickery, so that the footnote text does not need to be a parameter to \vfootnote:

```
\newinsert\footins
\def\footnote#1{\let\@sf=\empty % parameter #2 (the text) is read later
  \ifhmode\edef\@sf{\spacefactor=\the\spacefactor}\/\fi
  #1\@sf\vfootnote{#1}}
\def\vfootnote#1{\insert\footins\bgroup
  \interlinepenalty=\interfootnotelinepenalty
  \splittopskip=\ht\strutbox % top baseline for broken footnotes
  \splitmaxdepth=\dp\strutbox \floatingpenalty=20000
  \leftskip=0pt \rightskip=0pt \spaceskip=0pt \xspaceskip=0pt
  \textindent{#1}\footstrut\futurelet\next\fo@t}
\def\fo@t{\ifcat\bgroup\noexpand\next \let\next\f@@t
  \else\let\next\f@t\fi \next}
\def\f@@t{\bgroup\aftergroup\@foot\let\next}
\def\f@t#1{#1\@foot}
\def\@foot{\strut\egroup}
\def\footstrut{\vbox to\splittopskip{}}
\skip\footins=\bigskipamount % space added when footnote is present
\count\footins=1000 % footnote magnification factor (1 to 1)
\dimen\footins=8in % maximum footnotes per page
```

Floating insertions are handled by doing an \insert whose vertical list consists of a penalty item followed by a single box:

```
\newinsert\topins \newif\ifp@ge \newif\if@mid
\def\topinsert{\@midfalse\p@gefalse\@ins}
\def\midinsert{\@midtrue\@ins}
\def\pageinsert{\@midfalse\p@getrue\@ins}
\skip\topins=0pt % no space added when a topinsert is present
\count\topins=1000 % magnification factor (1 to 1)
\dimen\topins=\maxdimen % no limit per page
\def\@ins{\par\begingroup\setbox0=\vbox\bgroup} % start a \vbox
\def\endinsert{\egroup % finish the \vbox
  \if@mid \dimen@=\ht0 \advance\dimen@ by\dp0
    \advance\dimen@ by12\p@ \advance\dimen@ by\pagetotal
    \ifdim\dimen@>\pagegoal \@midfalse\p@gefalse\fi\fi
  \if@mid \bigskip \box0 \bigbreak
  \else\insert\topins{\penalty100 % floating insertion
    \splittopskip=0pt \splitmaxdepth=\maxdimen \floatingpenalty=0
    \ifp@ge \dimen@=\dp0
     \vbox to\vsize{\unvbox0 \kern-\dimen@} % depth is zero
    \else \box0 \nobreak\bigskip\fi}\fi\endgroup}
```

Most of the \output routine appears in Chapter 23; it is given here in full:

```
\output={\plainoutput}
\def\plainoutput{\shipout\vbox{\makeheadline\pagebody\makefootline}%
  \advancepageno
  \ifnum\outputpenalty>-20000 \else\dosupereject\fi}
\def\pagebody{\vbox to\vsize{\boxmaxdepth=\maxdepth \pagecontents}}
\def\makeheadline{\vbox to 0pt{\vskip-22.5pt
    \line{\vbox to8.5pt{}\the\headline}\vss}\nointerlineskip}
\def\makefootline{\baselineskip=24pt \line{\the\footline}}
\def\dosupereject{\ifnum\insertpenalties>0 % something is being held over
  \line{}\kern-\topskip\nobreak\vfill\supereject\fi}

\def\pagecontents{\ifvoid\topins\else\unvbox\topins\fi
  \dimen@=\dp255 \unvbox255
  \ifvoid\footins\else % footnote info is present
    \vskip\skip\footins \footnoterule \unvbox\footins\fi
  \ifr@ggedbottom \kern-\dimen@ \vfil \fi}
\def\footnoterule{\kern-3pt
  \hrule width 2truein \kern 2.6pt} % the \hrule is .4pt high
```

8. Hyphenation and everything else. The last part of plain.tex reads the hyphenation patterns and exceptions found on file **hyphen.tex** (see Appendix H); then it defines a few miscellaneous macros, sets up \rm type, and that's all!

```
\lefthyphenmin=2 \righthyphenmin=3 % disallow x- or -xx breaks
\input hyphen % the hyphenation patterns and exceptions

\def\magnification{\afterassignment\m@g\count@}
\def\m@g{\mag=\count@
  \hsize6.5truein\vsize8.9truein\dimen\footins8truein}

\def\tracingall{\tracingonline=1 \tracingcommands=2 \tracingstats=2
  \tracingpages=1 \tracingoutput=1 \tracinglostchars=1
  \tracingmacros=2 \tracingparagraphs=1 \tracingrestores=1
  \showboxbreadth=\maxdimen \showboxdepth=\maxdimen \errorstopmode}

\def\showhyphens#1{\setbox0=\vbox{\parfillskip0pt \hsize=\maxdimen \tenrm
  \pretolerance=-1 \tolerance=-1 \hbadness=0 \showboxdepth=0 \ #1}}

\normalbaselines\rm % select roman font
\nonfrenchspacing % punctuation affects the spacing
\catcode`@=12 % at signs are no longer letters

\def\fmtname{plain}\def\fmtversion{3.0} % identifies the current format
```

The format name and version number are recorded in control sequences, in order to help the people who might have to explain why something doesn't work. Macro files like plain.tex should not be changed in any way, except with respect to preloaded fonts, unless the changes are authorized by the author of the macros.

The purpose of a programming system is to make a computer easy to use.
To do this, it furnishes languages and various facilities
that are in fact programs invoked and controlled by language features.
But these facilities are bought at a price:
the external description of a programming system is ten to twenty times
as large as the external description of the computer system itself.
The user finds it far easier to specify any particular function,
but there are far more to choose from,
and far more options and formats to remember.

— FREDERICK P. BROOKS, JR., *The Mythical Man Month* (1975)

When someone says, "I want a programming language
in which I need only say what I wish done,"
give him a lollipop.

— ALAN PERLIS, *Epigrams on Programming* (1982)

C
Character Codes

Different computers tend to have different ways of representing the characters in files of text, but TeX gives the same results on all machines, because it converts everything to a standard internal code when it reads a file. TeX also converts back from its internal representation to the appropriate external code, when it writes a file of text; therefore most users need not be aware of the fact that the codes have actually switched back and forth inside the machine.

The purpose of this appendix is to define TeX's internal code, which has the same characteristics on all implementations of TeX. The existence of such a code is important, because it makes TeX constructions "portable." For example, TeX allows alphabetic constants like `‘b` to be used as numbers; the fact that `‘b` always denotes the integer 98 means that we can write machine-independent macros that decide, for instance, whether a given character is a digit between 0 and 9. Furthermore the internal code of TeX also survives in its `dvi` output files, which can be printed by software that knows nothing about where the `dvi` data originated; essentially the same output will be obtained from all implementations of TeX, regardless of the host computer, because the `dvi` data is expressed in a machine-independent code.

TeX's internal code is based on the American Standard Code for Information Interchange, known popularly as "ASCII." There are 128 codes, numbered 0 to 127; we conventionally express the numbers in octal notation, from `'000` to `'177`, or in hexadecimal notation, from `"00` to `"7F`. Thus, the value of `‘b` is normally called `'142` or `"62`, not 98. In the ASCII scheme, codes `'000` through `'040` and code `'177` are assigned to special functions; for example, code `'007` is called **BEL**, and it means "Ring the bell." The other 94 codes are assigned to visible symbols. Here is a chart that shows ASCII codes in such a way that octal and hexadecimal equivalents can easily be read off:

	$'0$	$'1$	$'2$	$'3$	$'4$	$'5$	$'6$	$'7$	
$'00x$	NUL	SOII	STX	ETX	EOT	ENQ	ACK	BEL	$"0x$
$'01x$	BS	HT	LF	VT	FF	CR	SO	SI	
$'02x$	DLE	DC1	DC2	DC3	DC4	NAK	SYN	ETB	$"1x$
$'03x$	CAN	EM	SUB	ESC	FS	GS	RS	US	
$'04x$	SP	!	"	#	\$	%	&	'	$"2x$
$'05x$	(	)	*	+	,	-	.	/	
$'06x$	0	1	2	3	4	5	6	7	$"3x$
$'07x$	8	9	:	;	<	=	>	?	
$'10x$	@	A	B	C	D	E	F	G	$"4x$
$'11x$	H	I	J	K	L	M	N	O	
$'12x$	P	Q	R	S	T	U	V	W	$"5x$
$'13x$	X	Y	Z	[	\	]	^	_	
$'14x$	‘	a	b	c	d	e	f	g	$"6x$
$'15x$	h	i	j	k	l	m	n	o	
$'16x$	p	q	r	s	t	u	v	w	$"7x$
$'17x$	x	y	z	{			}	~	DEL	
	$"8$	$"9$	$"A$	$"B$	$"C$	$"D$	$"E$	$"F$	

Ever since ASCII was established in the early 1960s, people have had different ideas about what to do with positions ´000 – ´037 and ´177, because most of the functions assigned to those codes are appropriate only for special purposes like file transmission, not for applications to printing or to interactive computing. It turned out that manufacturers soon started producing line printers that were capable of generating 128 characters, 33 of which were tailored to the special needs of particular customers; part of the advantage of a standard code was therefore lost. On the other hand, the remaining 95 codes (including ´40 =SP, a blank space) have become widely adopted, and they are now implanted within most of today's computer terminals. When an ASCII keyboard is available, you can specify each of the 128 codes to TeX in terms of the 95 standard characters, as follows:

	´0	´1	´2	´3	´4	´5	´6	´7	
´00x	^^@	^^A	^^B	^^C	^^D	^^E	^^F	^^G	"0x
´01x	^^H	^^I	^^J	^^K	^^L	^^M	^^N	^^O	
´02x	^^P	^^Q	^^R	^^S	^^T	^^U	^^V	^^W	"1x
´03x	^^X	^^Y	^^Z	^^[	^^\	^^]	^^^	^^_	
´04x	␣	!	"	#	$	%	&	'	"2x
´05x	(	)	*	+	,	-	.	/	
´06x	0	1	2	3	4	5	6	7	"3x
´07x	8	9	:	;	<	=	>	?	
´10x	@	A	B	C	D	E	F	G	"4x
´11x	H	I	J	K	L	M	N	O	
´12x	P	Q	R	S	T	U	V	W	"5x
´13x	X	Y	Z	[	\	]	^	_	
´14x	`	a	b	c	d	e	f	g	"6x
´15x	h	i	j	k	l	m	n	o	
´16x	p	q	r	s	t	u	v	w	"7x
´17x	x	y	z	{	|	}	~	^^?	
	"8	"9	"A	"B	"C	"D	"E	"F	

(Here '^^' doesn't necessarily mean two circumflex characters; it means two identical characters whose current \catcode is 7. In such cases TeX simply adds or subtracts ´100 from the internal code of the character that immediately follows. For example, * can also be typed as ^^j; j can also be typed as ^^*.)

An extended ASCII code intended for text editing and interactive computing was developed at several universities about 1965, and for many years there have been terminals in use at Stanford, MIT, Carnegie-Mellon, and elsewhere that have 120 or 121 symbols, not just 95. Aficionados of these keyboards (like the author of this book) are loath to give up their extra characters; it seems that such people make heavy use of about 5 of the extra 25, and occasional use of the other 20, although different people have different groups of five. For example, the author developed TeX on a keyboard that includes the symbols ←, ↓, ≠, ≤, and ≥, and he finds that this makes it much more pleasant to type class notes, technical papers, and computer programs of the kind he likes to write; his logician friends make heavy use of the ∀ and ∃ keys; and so on. It is recommended that TEX implementations on systems with large character sets be consistent with the following codes:

	´0	´1	´2	´3	´4	´5	´6	´7	
´00x	·	↓	α	β	∧	¬	∈	π	"0x
´01x	λ	γ	δ	↑	±	⊕	∞	∂	
´02x	⊂	⊃	∩	∪	∀	∃	⊗	↔	"1x
´03x	←	→	≠	◇	≤	≥	≡	∨	
´04x		!	"	#	$	%	&	´	"2x
´05x	(	)	*	+	,	-	.	/	
´06x	0	1	2	3	4	5	6	7	"3x
´07x	8	9	:	;	<	=	>	?	
´10x	@	A	B	C	D	E	F	G	"4x
´11x	H	I	J	K	L	M	N	O	
´12x	P	Q	R	S	T	U	V	W	"5x
´13x	X	Y	Z	[	\	]	^	_	
´14x	‘	a	b	c	d	e	f	g	"6x
´15x	h	i	j	k	l	m	n	o	
´16x	p	q	r	s	t	u	v	w	"7x
´17x	x	y	z	{	|	}	~	∫	
	"8	"9	"A	"B	"C	"D	"E	"F	

Of course, designers of TEX macro packages that are intended to be widely used should stick to the standard ASCII characters.

Incidentally, the ASCII character ^ that appears in position ´136 is sometimes called a "caret," but dictionaries of English tell us that a caret is a larger symbol, more like character ´004 in the extended set above. The correct name for ^ is "circumflex," but this is quite a mouthful, so a shorter name like "hat" is preferable. It seems desirable to preserve the traditional distinction between caret and hat.

The extended code shown above was developed at MIT; it is similar to, but slightly better than, the code implemented at Stanford. Seven of the codes are conventionally assigned to the standard ASCII control functions NUL (⟨null⟩), HT (⟨tab⟩), LF (⟨linefeed⟩), FF (⟨formfeed⟩), CR (⟨return⟩), ESC (⟨escape⟩), and DEL (⟨delete⟩), and they appear in the standard ASCII positions; hence the corresponding seven characters · γ δ ± ⊕ ◇ ∫ do not actually appear on the keyboard. These seven "hidden" characters show up only on certain output devices.

Modern keyboards allow 256 codes to be input, not just 128; so TEX represents characters internally as numbers in the range 0–255 (i.e., ´000–´377, or "00–"FF). Implementations of TEX differ in which characters they will accept in input files and which they will transmit to output files; these subsets can be specified independently. A completely permissive version of TEX allows full 256-character input and output; other versions might ignore all but the visible characters of ASCII; still other versions might distinguish the tab character (code *'011*) from a space on input, but might output each tab as a sequence of three characters ^^I.

Many people, unfortunately, have the opposite problem: Instead of the 95 standard characters and some others, they have fewer than 95 symbols actually available. What can be done in such cases? Well, it's possible to use TeX with fewer symbols, by invoking more control sequences; for example, plain TeX defines \lq, \rq, \lbrack, \rbrack, \sp, and \sb, so that you need not type ', ', [,], ^, and _, respectively.

A person who implements TeX on computer systems that do not have 95 externally representable symbols should adhere to the following guidelines: (a) Stay as close as possible to the ASCII conventions.   (b) Make sure that codes *'041–'046*, *'060–'071*, *'141–'146*, and *'160–'171* are present and that each unrepresentable internal code < *'200* leads to a representable code when *'100* is added or subtracted; then all 256 codes can be input and output.   (c) Cooperate with everyone else who shares the same constraints, so that you all adopt the same policy. (See Appendix J for information about the TeX Users Group.)

Very few conventions about character codes are hardwired into TeX: Almost everything can be changed by a format package that changes parameters like \escapechar and sets up the \catcode, \mathcode, \uccode, \lccode, \sfcode, and \delcode tables. Thus a TeX manuscript that has been written in Denmark, say, can be run in California, and vice versa, even though quite different conventions might be used in different countries. The only character codes that TeX actually "knows" are these: (1) INITEX initializes the code tables as described in Appendix B; the same initialization is done by all implementations of TeX. (2) TeX uses the character codes ␣+-.,'"<=>0123456789ABCDEF in its syntax rules (Chapters 20, 24, and Appendix H), and it uses most of the uppercase and lowercase letters in its keywords pt, to, plus, etc. These same codes and keywords are used in all implementations of TeX. For example, when TeX is implemented for Cyrillic keyboards, the letter 'п' should be assigned to code *'160* and 'т' to code *'164*, so that 'пт' still means 'pt'; or else control sequences should be defined so that what TeX sees is equivalent to the keywords it needs. (3) The operations \number, \romannumeral, \the, and \meaning can generate letters, digits, spaces, decimal points, minus signs, double quotes, colons, and '>' signs; these same codes are generated in all implementations of TeX. (4) The \hyphenation and \pattern commands described in Appendix H give special interpretation to the ten digits and to the characters '.' and '-'.   (5) The codes for the four characters $. { } are inserted when TeX recovers from certain errors, and braces are inserted around an \output routine; appropriate catcodes are attached to these tokens, so it doesn't matter if these symbols have their plain TeX meanings or not.   (6) There is a special convention for representing characters 0–255 in the hexadecimal forms ^^00– ^^ff, explained in Chapter 8. This convention is always acceptable as input, when ^ is any character of catcode 7. Text output is produced with this convention only when representing characters of code ≥ 128 that a TeX installer has chosen not to output directly.

*Code sets obtained by modifying the standard as shown above
or by other replacements are nonstandard.*

— ASA SUBCOMMITTEE X3.2, *American Standard
Code for Information Interchange* (1963)

*Both the Stanford and DEC uses of the ASCII control characters
are in violation of the USA Standard Code,
but no Federal Marshal is likely to come running out
and arrest people who type control-T to their computers.*

— BRIAN REID, *SCRIBE Introductory User's Manual* (1978)

D

Dirty Tricks

TEX was designed to do the ordinary tasks of typesetting: to make paragraphs and pages. But the underlying mechanisms that facilitate ordinary typesetting— e.g., boxes, glue, penalties, and macros—are extremely versatile; hence people have discovered sneaky ways to coerce TEX into doing tricks quite different from what its author originally had in mind. Such clever constructions are not generally regarded as examples of "high TEX"; but many of them have turned out to be useful and instructive, worthy of being known (at least by a few wizards). The purpose of this appendix is to introduce crafty and/or courageous readers to the nether world of TEXarcana.

Please don't read this material until you've had plenty of experience with plain TEX. After you have read and understood the secrets below, you'll know all sorts of devious combinations of TEX commands, and you will often be tempted to write inscrutable macros. Always remember, however, that there's usually a simpler and better way to do something than the first way that pops into your head. You may not have to resort to any subterfuge at all, since TEX is able to do lots of things in a straightforward way. Try for simple solutions first.

1. Macro madness. If you need to write complicated macros, you'll need to be familiar with the fine points in Chapter 20. TEX's control sequences are divided into two main categories, "expandable" and "unexpandable"; the former category includes all macros and `\if...\fi` tests, as well as special operations like `\the` and `\input`, while the latter category includes the primitive commands listed in Chapter 24. The expansion of expandable tokens takes place in TEX's "mouth," but primitive commands (including assignments) are done in TEX's "stomach." One important consequence of this structure is that it is impossible to redefine a control sequence or to advance a register while TEX is expanding the token list of, say, a `\message` or `\write` command; assignment operations are done only when TEX is building a vertical or horizontal or math list.

For example, it's possible to put `\n` asterisks into a paragraph, by saying simply '`{\loop\ifnum\n>0 *\advance\n-1 \repeat}`'. But it's much more difficult to define a control sequence `\asts` to consist of exactly `\n` consecutive asterisks. If `\n` were known to be at most 5, say, it would be possible to write

```
\edef\asts{\ifcase\n\or*\or**\or***\or****\or*****\else\bad\fi}
```

since TEX handles `\ifcase` in its mouth. But for general `\n` it would be impossible to use a construction like '`\edef\asts{\loop\ifnum\n>0 *\advance\n-1 \repeat}`', since `\n` doesn't change during an `\edef`. A more elaborate program is needed; e.g.,

```
{\xdef\asts{}
  \loop\ifnum\n>0 \xdef\asts{\asts*}\advance\n-1 \repeat}
```

And here's another solution (which is faster, because token list registers can be expanded more quickly than macros, using `\the`):

```
\newcount\m \newtoks\t \m=\n \t={}
\loop \ifnum\m>0 \t=\expandafter{\the\t *} \advance\m-1 \repeat
\edef\asts{\the\t}
```

However, both of these solutions have a running time proportional to the square of \n. There's a much quicker way to do the job:

```
\begingroup\aftergroup\edef\aftergroup\asts\aftergroup{
\loop \ifnum\n>0 \aftergroup*\advance\n-1 \repeat
\aftergroup}\endgroup
```

Get it? The **\aftergroup** commands cause a whole list of other tokens to be saved up for after the group! This method has only one flaw, namely that it takes up \n cells of space on TEX's input stack and \n more on TEX's save stack; hence a special version of TEX may be required when \n is larger than 150 or so.

(Incidentally, there's a completely different way to put \n asterisks into a paragraph, namely to say '\setbox0=\hbox{*}\cleaders\copy0\hskip\n\wd0'. This may seem to be the fastest solution of all; but actually it is not so fast, when all things are considered, since it generates four bytes of dvi output per asterisk, compared to only one byte per asterisk in the other methods. Input/output time takes longer than computation time, both in TEX itself and in the later stages of the printing process.)

The problem just solved may seem like a rather special application; after all, who needs a control sequence that contains a variable number of asterisks? But the same principles apply in other similar cases, e.g., when you want to construct a variable-length **\parshape** specification. Similarly, many of the "toy problems" solved below are meant to illustrate paradigms that can be used in real-life situations.

The precise rules for expansion are explained in Chapter 20; and the best way to get familiar with TEX's expansion mechanism is to watch it in action, looking at the log file when **\tracingmacros=2** and **\tracingcommands=2**. One of the important ways to change the normal order of expansion is to use **\expandafter**; the construction

```
\expandafter\a\b
```

causes \b to be expanded first, then \a. And since **\expandafter** is itself expandable, the construction

```
\expandafter\expandafter\expandafter\a\expandafter\b\c
```

causes \c to be expanded first, then \b, then \a. (The next step,

```
\expandafter\expandafter\expandafter\expandafter
 \expandafter\expandafter\expandafter\a
 \expandafter\expandafter\expandafter\b\expandafter\c\d
```

is probably too lengthy to be of any use.)

It's possible to make good use of **\expandafter\a\b** even when \a isn't expandable. For example, the token list assignment '\t=\expandafter{\the\t *}' in the example on the previous page was able to invade territory where expansion is normally suppressed, by expanding after a left brace. Similarly,

```
\t=\expandafter{\expandafter*\the\t}
```

would have worked; and

```
\uppercase\expandafter{\romannumeral\n}
```

yields the value of register \n in uppercase roman numerals.

Here's a more interesting example: Recall that \fontdimen1 is the amount of "slant per point" of a font; hence, for example, '\the\fontdimen1\tenit' expands to '0.25pt', where the characters 'pt' are of category 12. After the macro definitions

```
{\catcode`p=12 \catcode`t=12 \gdef\\#1pt{#1}}
\let\getfactor=\\
\def\kslant#1{\kern\expandafter\getfactor\the\fontdimen1#1\ht0}
```

one can write, e.g., '\kslant\tenit' and this will expand to '\kern0.25\ht0'. If the boundary of \box0 is considered to be slanted by 0.25 horizontal units per vertical unit, this kern measures the horizontal distance by which the top edge of the box is skewed with respect to an edge at the baseline. All of the computation of \kslant is done in TeX's mouth; thus, the mouth can do some rather complicated things even though it cannot assign new values. (Incidentally, an indirect method was used here to define the control sequence \getfactor when the character t had category 12, since control words normally consist only of letters. The alternative construction

```
{\catcode`p=12 \catcode`t=12
  \csname expandafter\endcsname\gdef
  \csname getfactor\endcsname#1pt{#1}}
```

would also have worked, since \csname and \endcsname don't contain 'p' or 't'!)

The mechanism by which TeX determines the arguments of a macro can be applied in unexpected ways. Suppose, for example, that \t is a token list register that contains some text; we wish to determine if at least one asterisk ($*_{12}$) appears in that text. Here's one way to do it:

```
\newif\ifresult % for the result of a computed test
\def\atest#1{\expandafter\a\the#1*\atest\a}
\long\def\a#1*#2#3\a{\ifx\atest#2\resultfalse\else\resulttrue\fi}
```

Now after '\atest\t', the control sequence \ifresult will be \iftrue or \iffalse, depending on whether or not \t contains an asterisk. (Do you see why?) And here's a slightly more elegant way to do the same thing, using \futurelet to look ahead:

```
\def\btest#1{\expandafter\b\the#1*\bb}
\long\def\b#1*{\futurelet\next\bb}
\long\def\bb#1\bb{\ifx\bb\next\resultfalse\else\resulttrue\fi}
```

In both cases the solution works if \t contains control sequence tokens as well as character tokens, provided that the special control sequences \atest, \a, and \bb don't appear. Notice, however, that an asterisk is "hidden" if it appears within a group {...}; the test is limited to asterisks at nesting level zero. A token list register is always balanced with respect to grouping, so there is no danger of the test leading to error messages concerning missing braces or extra braces.

We can apply the ideas in the preceding paragraph to solve a problem related to generalized math formatting: The goal is to set TeX up so that the respective constructions '$\$\$ \alpha \$\$$', '$\$\$ \alpha$ \eqno $\beta \$\$$', and '$\$\$ \alpha$ \leqno $\beta \$\$$' will cause a macro $\$\$\generaldisplay\$\$$ to be invoked, with \eq defined to be α; furthermore, the test \ifeqno should be true when an equation number β is present, and \ifleqno should be true in the case of \leqno. When β is present, it should be stored in \eqn. Here

α and β are arbitrary balanced token lists that don't contain either `\eqno` or `\leqno` at nesting level zero. The following macros do the required maneuvers:

```
\newif\ifeqno \newif\ifleqno \everydisplay{\displaysetup}
\def\displaysetup#1$${\displaytest#1\eqno\eqno\displaytest}
\def\displaytest#1\eqno#2\eqno#3\displaytest{%
  \if!#3!\ldisplaytest#1\leqno\leqno\ldisplaytest
  \else\eqnotrue\leqnofalse\def\eqn{#2}\def\eq{#1}\fi
  \generaldisplay$$}
\def\ldisplaytest#1\leqno#2\leqno#3\ldisplaytest{\def\eq{#1}%
  \if!#3!\eqnofalse\else\eqnotrue\leqnotrue\def\eqn{#2}\fi}
```

An examination of the three cases `$$`α`$$`, `$$`α`\eqno`β`$$`, `$$`α`\leqno`β`$$` shows that the correct actions will ensue. Parameter #3 in the tests '`\if!#3!`' will be either empty or `\eqno` or `\leqno`; thus, the condition will be false (and the second '`!`' will be skipped) unless #3 is empty.

Returning to the problem of *'s in `\t`, suppose that it's necessary to consider *'s at all levels of nesting. Then a slower routine must be used:

```
\def\ctest#1{\resultfalse\expandafter\c\the#1\ctest}
\def\c{\afterassignment\cc\let\next= }
\def\cc{\ifx\next\ctest \let\next\relax
  \else\ifx\next*\resulttrue\fi\let\next\c\fi \next}
```

Here `\afterassignment` has been used to retain control after a non-future `\let`; the '`= `' ensures that exactly one token is swallowed per use of `\c`. This routine could be modified in an obvious way to count the total number of *'s and/or tokens in `\t`. Notice the '`\let\next`' instructions in `\cc`; it should be clear why the alternative

```
\def\cc{\ifx\next\ctest\else\ifx\next*\resulttrue\fi\c\fi}
```

would not work. (The latter `\c` would always swallow a '`\fi`'.)

Space tokens are sometimes anomalous, so they deserve special care. The following macro `\futurenonspacelet` behaves essentially like `\futurelet` except that it discards any implicit or explicit space tokens that intervene before a nonspace is scanned:

```
\def\futurenonspacelet#1{\def\cs{#1}%
  \afterassignment\stepone\let\nexttoken= }
\def\\{\let\stoken= } \\ % now \stoken is a space token
\def\stepone{\expandafter\futurelet\cs\steptwo}
\def\steptwo{\expandafter\ifx\cs\stoken\let\next=\stepthree
  \else\let\next=\nexttoken\fi \next}
\def\stepthree{\afterassignment\stepone\let\next= }
```

An operation like `\futurenonspacelet` is useful, for example, when implementing macros that have a variable number of arguments.

Notice that '`\def\stepthree#1{\stepone}`' would not work here, because of TeX's rule that a ⊔10 token is bypassed if it would otherwise be treated as an undelimited argument. Because of this rule it is difficult to distinguish explicit space tokens from implicit ones. The situation is surprisingly complex, because it's possible to use \uppercase to create "funny space" tokens like *₁₀; for example, the commands

$$\text{\uccode\` =\`* \uppercase\{\uppercase\{\def\fspace\{ \}\let\ftoken= \} \}}$$

make \fspace a macro that expands to a funny space, and they make \ftoken an implicit funny space. (The tests \if\fspace*, \if\ftoken*, \ifcat\fspace\stoken, and \ifcat\ftoken\stoken will all be true, assuming that * has category 12; but if * has category 10, \if\fspace* will be false, because TₑX normalizes all newly created space tokens to ⌴₁₀, as explained in Chapter 8.) Since the various forms of space tokens are almost identical in behavior, there's no point in dwelling on the details.†

The argument to \write is expanded when a \shipout occurs, but sometimes expansion isn't desired. Here's a macro (suggested by Todd Allen) that suppresses all expansion, by inserting \noexpand before each control sequence or active character. The macro assumes that ~ is an active character, and that the tokens being written do not include implicit spaces or braces. Funny spaces are changed to ordinary ones.

```
\long\def\unexpandedwrite#1#2{\def\finwrite{\write#1}%
  {\aftergroup\finwrite\aftergroup{\sanitize#2\endsanity}}}
\def\sanitize{\futurelet\next\sanswitch}
\def\sanswitch{\ifx\next\endsanity
  \else\ifcat\noexpand\next\stoken\aftergroup\space\let\next=\eat
  \else\ifcat\noexpand\next\bgroup\aftergroup{\let\next=\eat
   \else\ifcat\noexpand\next\egroup\aftergroup}\let\next=\eat
    \else\let\next=\copytoken\fi\fi\fi\fi \next}
\def\eat{\afterassignment\sanitize \let\next= }
\long\def\copytoken#1{\ifcat\noexpand#1\relax\aftergroup\noexpand
  \else\ifcat\noexpand#1\noexpand~\aftergroup\noexpand\fi\fi
  \aftergroup#1\sanitize}
\def\endsanity\endsanity{}
```

As before, the heavy use of \aftergroup in \unexpandedwrite means that parameter #2 should not include more than about 150 tokens.

---

† The following little program is for TₑX exegetes who insist on learning the whole story: Macro \stest decides whether or not the first token of a given token list register is a ⟨space token⟩ as defined in Chapter 24. If so, the macro decides whether or not the token is "funny," i.e., whether or not the character code is different from an ASCII ⟨space⟩; and the macro also decides whether the token is explicit or implicit.

```
\newif\ifspace \newif\iffunny \newif\ifexplicit
\def\stest#1{\expandafter\s\the#1 \stest}
\def\s{\futurelet\next\ss}
\def\ss{\ifcat\noexpand\next\stoken\spacetrue
  \ifx\next\stoken\let\next=\sss\else\let\next=\ssss\fi
  \else\let\next=\sssss\fi \next}
\long\def\sss#1 #2\stest{\funnyfalse
  \def\next{#1}\ifx\next\empty\explicittrue\else\explicitfalse\fi}
\long\def\ssss#1#2\stest{\funnytrue
  \ifcat\noexpand#1\noexpand~\explicitfalse % active funny space
  \else{\escapechar=\if*#1\`?\else\`*\fi
   \if#1\string#1\global\explicittrue\else\global\explicitfalse\fi}\fi}
\long\def\sssss#1\stest{\spacefalse}
```

2. List macros. The next several macros we shall discuss can be used to maintain lists of information in the form

$$\backslash\backslash\{\langle\text{item}_1\rangle\}\backslash\backslash\{\langle\text{item}_2\rangle\} \dots \backslash\backslash\{\langle\text{item}_n\rangle\}$$

where each ⟨item⟩ is a balanced list of tokens. A parameterless control sequence whose replacement text has this form may be called a *list macro*. The empty list macro has $n = 0$ and it is called `\empty`.

It's easy to add new items at either end of a list macro, and to concatenate list macros, for example as follows:

```
\toksdef\ta=0 \toksdef\tb=2 % token list registers for temp use
\long\def\leftappenditem#1\to#2{\ta={\\{#1}}\tb=\expandafter{#2}%
   \edef#2{\the\ta\the\tb}}
\long\def\rightappenditem#1\to#2{\ta={\\{#1}}\tb=\expandafter{#2}%
   \edef#2{\the\tb\the\ta}}
\def\concatenate#1=#2&#3{\ta=\expandafter{#2}\tb=\expandafter{#3}%
   \edef#1{\the\ta\the\tb}}
```

Conversely, the left item of a list can be removed and placed in a control sequence by the `\lop` macro defined in the following curious way:

```
\def\lop#1\to#2{\expandafter\lopoff#1\lopoff#1#2}
\long\def\lopoff\\#1#2\lopoff#3#4{\def#4{#1}\def#3{#2}}
```

For example, if `\l` expands to the list '`\\{a\b}\\{c}\\{{d}}`', the macro invocation `\lop\l\to\z` makes `\l` expand to '`\\{c}\\{{d}}`' and `\z` expand to '`a\b`'. The `\lop` operation should be used only when `\l` is nonempty, otherwise an error will occur; to test if `\l` is empty, one simply says '`\ifx\l\empty`'.

The programming details of the `\lop` macro indicate why individual items have been enclosed in `{...}` groups. A simpler kind of list, in which grouping is omitted and an extra `\\` appears at the end, suffices for many purposes; one could define, for instance,

```
\long\def\lopoff\\#1\\#2\lopoff#3#4{\def#4{#1}\def#3{\\#2}}
```

and the results would be almost the same as before. In this case an empty list macro expands to '`\\`'. However, the new `\lop` resulting from this new `\lopoff` macro also removes a pair of braces, if the leftmost item happens to be a group; extra braces are included in our general scheme to prevent such anomalies.

So far the examples we've considered haven't revealed why the `\\`'s appear in the general scheme; it appears that grouping by itself should be enough. But in fact, the `\\` separators are enormously useful, because we can define `\\` to be any desired one-argument macro, and then we can *execute* the list! For example, here's a way to count the number of items:

```
\def\cardinality#1\to#2{#2=0 \long\def\\##1{\advance#2 by1 }#1}
```

(Parameter `#2` is supposed to be the name of a count register.) And here's a way to take a list macro and center all its items on individual lines within a `\vbox`:

```
\def\centerlist#1{\def\\##1{\relax##1\cr}%
   \vbox{\halign{\hfil##\hfil\cr#1}}}
```

A particular item can be selected by its position number from the left:

```
\def\select#1\of#2\to#3{\def#3{\outofrange}%
  \long\def\\##1{\advance#1-1 \ifnum#1=0 \def#3{##1}\fi}#2}
```

(Here #1 is a count register, #2 is a list macro, and #3 is a control sequence.) And so on; hundreds of other applications can be imagined.†

TeX does all of the preceding operations efficiently, in the sense that the running time will be proportional to the length of the list macro involved. It's natural to ask if the rightmost item can be removed with equal efficiency, since the final item of a list is somewhat hard to isolate. There is apparently no way to delete the nth item of an n-item list in order n steps, maintaining complete generality, unless the \aftergroup trick (by which we created a macro that expands to n asterisks) is used; and the \aftergroup trick is somewhat unattractive in the list application, because the list might be quite long.‡ However, if we restrict list items to unexpandable tokens, it turns out to be possible to remove the rightmost item quite efficiently:

```
\def\deleterightmost#1{\edef#1{\expandafter\xyzzy#1\xyzzy}}
\long\def\xyzzy\\#1#2{\ifx#2\xyzzy\yzzyx
  \else\noexpand\\{#1}\fi\xyzzy#2}
\long\def\yzzyx#1\xyzzy\xyzzy{\fi}
```

Careful study of this example shows that TeX's mouth is capable of doing recursive operations, given sufficiently tricky macros.

The contents of a \count register can easily be converted to decimal and stored in a control sequence; for example, if \n is a register, '\edef\csn{\the\n}' puts its value into \csn. Conversely, a value from \csn can be put back into \n by saying simply '\n=\csn'. There's usually no point in doing this transformation just to minimize the usage of \count registers, since TeX has 256 of them; but a decimal representation like the expansion of \csn can be stored in a list macro, and that might be useful in some applications. Incidentally, there's a neat way to test if such a control-sequence-number is zero: '\if0\csn⟨true text⟩\else⟨false text⟩\fi' works because extra digits of a nonzero number will be ignored with the ⟨true text⟩.

A technique something like list macros can be used to maintain unordered sets of control sequences. In this case it's convenient to leave off the braces; for example,

```
\def\l{\\\alpha\\\beta\\\gamma}
```

defines a "set macro" \l that represents the control sequences { \alpha, \beta, \gamma }. A straightforward construction tests whether a given control sequence is in the set:

```
\def\ismember#1\of#2{\resultfalse\def\given{#1}%
  \def\\##1{\def\next{##1}\ifx\next\given\resulttrue\fi}#2}
```

And an efficient but not-so-straightforward construction removes all occurrences of

---

† The concept of a list macro is strongly related to the concept of a list procedure in a programming language; see *Communications of the ACM* **7** (1964), 280.

‡ The interested reader may enjoy constructing a macro that removes the kth item of an n-item list macro \l in $O(n \log n)$ steps, given k and \l, without using \aftergroup.

control sequences that are \ifx-equivalent to a given control sequence:

```
\def\remequivalent#1\from#2{\let\given=#1%
    \ifx#2\empty\else\edef#2{\expandafter\plugh#2\plugh}\fi}
\def\plugh\\#1#2{\ifx#1\given\else\noexpand\\\noexpand#1\fi
    \ifx#2\plugh\hgulp\fi\plugh#2}
\def\hgulp\fi\plugh\plugh{\fi}
```

3. Verbatim listing. Plain TeX includes a macro called \dospecials that is essentially a set macro, representing the set of all characters that have a special category code. (The control sequence \do plays the rôle of \\ in the discussion above.) Therefore it's easy to change all of the special characters to category 12 (other):

```
\def\uncatcodespecials{\def\do##1{\catcode`##1=12 }\dospecials}
```

This works even when the set of special characters has been changed, provided that \dospecials has been updated to represent the current set.

The operation \uncatcodespecials just defined is important, of course, when TeX's automatic features need to be temporarily disabled. Let's suppose that we want to create a listing of some computer file, reproducing the characters and the spacing exactly as they appear in the file. To make the problem more interesting, let's also print line numbers in front of each line, as in the listing of story.tex on page 24. To make the problem simpler, let's assume that the file contains only standard ASCII printing characters: no tab marks or form feeds or such things. Our goal is to devise a \listing macro such that, e.g., '\listing{story}' will insert a listing of the story.tex file into a manuscript, after which TeX's normal conventions will be restored. The listing should be in \tt type. A macro of the following form meets the desired specifications:

```
\def\listing#1{\par\begingroup\setupverbatim\input#1 \endgroup}
```

Notice that the \endgroup command here will nicely "turn off" all the weird things that \setupverbatim turns on. Notice also that the commands '\input#1 \endgroup' will not be listed verbatim, even though they follow \setupverbatim, since they entered TeX's reading mechanism when the \listing macro was expanded (i.e., before the verbatim business was actually set up).

But what should \setupverbatim do? Well, it ought to include \obeylines, since this automatically inserts a \par at the end of each line that is input; it ought to include \uncatcodespecials, so that special characters print as themselves; and it ought to include \obeyspaces, so that each space counts. But we need to look carefully at each of these things to see exactly what they do: (1) Plain TeX's \obeylines macro changes the \catcode of ^^M to \active, and then it says '\let^^M=\par'. Since ^^M is placed at the end of each line, this effectively ends each line with \par; however, \obeylines doesn't say '\def^^M{\par}', so we must make any desired changes to \par before invoking \obeylines. (2) The \uncatcodespecials operation changes a space to category 12; but the \tt font has the character '␣' in the ⟨space⟩ position, so we don't really want ␣$_{12}$. (3) The \obeyspaces macro in Appendix B merely changes the ⟨space⟩ character to category 13; active character ␣$_{13}$ has been defined to be the same as \space, a macro that expands to ␣$_{10}$. This is usually what is desired; for example, it means that spaces in constructions like '\hbox to 10 pt {...}' won't cause any trouble. But in our application it has an undesirable effect, because it produces spaces that are affected by the space factor. To defeat this feature, it's necessary either to say `\frenchspacing` or to redefine $\sqcup_{13}$ to be the same as `\`$\sqcup$. The latter alternative is better, because the former will discard spaces at the beginning of each line.

The `\setupverbatim` macro should also take care of putting a line number into the position of the paragraph indentation. We can take care of this by introducing a counter variable and using `\everypar`, as follows:

```
\newcount\lineno % the number of file lines listed
\def\setupverbatim{\tt \lineno=0
  \obeylines \uncatcodespecials \obeyspaces
  \everypar{\advance\lineno by1 \llap{\sevenrm\the\lineno\ \ }}}
{\obeyspaces\global\let =\ } % let active space = control space
```

In theory, this seems like it ought to work; but in practice, it fails in two ways. One rather obvious failure—at least, it becomes obvious when the macro is tested—is that all the empty lines of the file are omitted. The reason is that the `\par` command at the end of an empty line doesn't start up a new paragraph, because it occurs in vertical mode. The other failure is not as obvious, because it occurs much less often: The `\tt` fonts contain ligatures for Spanish punctuation, so the sequences `?‘` and `!‘` will be printed as ¿ and ¡ respectively. Both of these defects can be cured by inserting

```
\def\par{\leavevmode\endgraf} \catcode`\‘=\active
```

before `\obeylines` in the `\setupverbatim` macro, and by defining `‘`$_{13}$ as follows:

```
{\catcode`\‘=\active \gdef‘{\relax\lq}}
```

A similar scheme could be used to produce verbatim listings in other fonts; but more characters would have to be made active, in order to break ligatures and to compensate for ASCII characters that aren't present.

Instead of listing a file verbatim, you might want to define a `\verbatim` macro such that '`\verbatim{$this$ is {\it!}}`' yields '`$this$ is {\it!}`'. It's somewhat dangerous to change category codes, because TeX stamps the category on each character when that character is first read from a file. Thus, if `\verbatim` were defined by a construction of the form `\long\def\verbatim#1{⟨something⟩}`, argument #1 would already be converted to a list of tokens when ⟨something⟩ starts; `\catcode` changes would not affect the argument. The alternative is to change category codes before scanning the argument to `\verbatim`:

```
\def\verbatim{\begingroup\tt\uncatcodespecials
  \obeyspaces\doverbatim}
\newcount\balance
{\catcode`\<=1 \catcode`\>=2 \catcode`\{=12 \catcode`\}=12
  \gdef\doverbatim{<\balance=1\verbatimloop>
  \gdef\verbatimloop#1<\def\next<#1\verbatimloop>%
    \if#1{\advance\balance by1
    \else\if#1}\advance\balance by-1
      \ifnum\balance=0\let\next=\endgroup\fi\fi\fi\next>>
```

This works; but it's slow, and it allows verbatim setting only of text that has balanced braces. It would not be suitable for typesetting the examples in a book like *The TeXbook*. (Appendix E contains the verbatim macros that were actually used.) Note also that if this `\verbatim{...}` macro appears in the argument to another macro like

\centerline, it will fail because the category codes can no longer be changed. The \footnote macro in Appendix B is careful to avoid scanning its argument prematurely; it uses \bgroup and \egroup in a somewhat tricky way, so that category code changes are permitted inside plain TEX footnotes.

On the other hand, there is a fairly fast way to convert a token list to an almost-verbatim transcript:

```
\long\def\verbatim#1{\def\next{#1}%
  {\tt\frenchspacing\expandafter\strip\meaning\next}}
\def\strip#1>{}
```

Tokens are stripped off in this construction since, for example, \meaning\next might be 'macro:->$this$ is {\it !}'. Notice that a space will be inserted after the control word \it, but no space might actually have occurred there in the argument to \verbatim; such information has been irretrievably lost.

One of the problems with verbatim mode is that it's hard to stop; if we turn off all of TEX's normal control capabilities, we end up "painting ourselves into a corner" and reaching a point of no return. The \listing macro was able to solve this problem because the end of a file brings an old token list back to life. Another solution would be to specify a certain number of lines, after which verbatim mode should end. Otherwise it's necessary to put some constraint on the text, i.e., to make certain texts unprintable in verbatim mode. For example, here's an approach that typesets everything between \beginverbatim and \endverbatim, assuming only that the control sequence \endverbatim does not need to be set:

```
\def\beginverbatim{\par\begingroup\setupverbatim\doverbatim}
{\catcode`\|=0 \catcode`\\=12 % | is temporary escape character
 |obeylines|gdef|doverbatim^^M#1\endverbatim{#1|endgroup}}
```

This construction assumes that \beginverbatim appears at the end of a line in the manuscript file. Argument #1 will be read entirely into TEX's memory before anything happens, so the total amount of verbatim material had better not be too voluminous. Incidentally, it isn't necessary to say that this macro is \long, because the \par's inserted by \obeylines are really ^^M's.

Another approach is to keep one character untouchable. For example, it's possible to define things so that '\verbatim⟨char⟩⟨text⟩⟨char⟩' will typeset the ⟨text⟩ verbatim, where the ⟨text⟩ is not supposed to contain any occurrences of the repeated delimiter ⟨char⟩:

```
\def\verbatim{\begingroup\setupverbatim\doverbatim}
\def\doverbatim#1{\def\next##1#1{##1\endgroup}\next}
```

4. Selective loading of macros. Some interesting problems arise when a computer system acquires a large library of macro files. For example, suppose that a file macs.tex contains the lines

```
\let\italcorr=\/
\def\/{\unskip\italcorr}
```

because somebody thought it would be nice to allow an optional space before TEX's primitive \/ command. That's fine, except if macs.tex is input twice; for example, two other macro files might both say \input macs. When those lines are processed the second time, \italcorr will be \let equal to a macro that expands to '\unskip\italcorr', and you can guess what will happen: TEX will get into an infinite loop, stoppable only by interrupting the program manually.

Fortunately there's an easy way to prevent this problem, by placing a suitable interlock near the beginning of every macro file that might introduce such anomalies:

```
\ifx\macsisloaded\relax\endinput\else\let\macsisloaded=\relax\fi
```

Then `\macsisloaded` will be undefined at the time of the first `\ifx`, but the file will not be read twice. A different control sequence should, of course, be used for each file.

Another difficulty with large sets of macros is that they take up space. It would be nice to preload every macro that every TEX user has ever dreamed up; but there might not be enough room, because TEX's memory capacity is finite. You might find it necessary to hold back and to load only the macros that are really needed.

How much memory space does a macro require? Well, there are four kinds of memory involved: token memory, name memory, string memory, and character memory. (If any of these becomes too full, it will be necessary to increase what TEX calls the macro memory size, the hash size, the number of strings, and/or the pool size, respectively; see Chapter 27.) The token memory is most important; a macro takes one cell of token memory for each token in its definition, including the '{' and the '}'. For example, the comparatively short definition

```
\def\example#1\two{\four}
```

takes five tokens: #1, two , {$_1$, four , and }$_2$. Each control sequence also takes up one cell of name memory, one cell of string memory, and as many cells of character memory as there are characters in the name (seven in the case of `\example`). Character memory is comparatively cheap; four characters, or in some cases five, will fit in the same number of bits as a single cell of token memory, inside the machine. Therefore you don't save much by choosing short macro names.

TEX will tell you how close you come to exceeding its current memory capacity if you say `\tracingstats=1`. For example, one of the runs that the author made while testing galley proofs of this appendix reported the following statistics:

```
Here is how much of TeX's memory you used:
 209 strings out of 1685
 1659 string characters out of 17636
 27618 words of memory out of 52821
 1172 multiletter control sequences out of 2500
```

Consequently there was plenty of room for more macros: $52821 - 27618 = 25203$ unused cells of main memory, $2500 - 1172 = 1328$ of name memory, $1685 - 209 = 1476$ of string memory, and $17636 - 1659 = 15977$ of character memory. But a fairly large TEX was being used, and only the macros of Appendices B and E were loaded; in other circumstances it might have been necessary to conserve space.

One obvious way to keep from loading too many macros is to keep the macro files short and to `\input` only the ones that you need. But short files can be a nuisance; sometimes there's a better way. For example, let's suppose that a file contains five optional classes of macros called A, B, C, D, E, and that a typical user will probably want only at most two or three of these five; let's design a `\load` macro so that, for example, '`\load{macs}{AC}`' will load file `macs.tex` including options A and C but not

options B, D, or E. The following `\load` macro converts its second argument into a
set macro called `\options`:

```
\def\load#1#2{\let\options=\empty \addoptions#2\end \input#1 }
\def\addoptions#1{\ifx#1\end \let\next=\relax
  \else\let\\=\relax\edef\options{\options\\#1}%
    \let\next=\addoptions \fi \next}
```

Inside the file `macs.tex`, a portion of code that should be loaded only under option B,
say, can be enclosed by '`\ifoption B ... \fi`', where `\ifoption` is defined thus:

```
\def\ifoption#1{\def\\##1{\if##1#1\resulttrue\fi}%
  \resultfalse \options \ifresult}
```

(This is a simple application of ideas presented earlier in this appendix.)

However, the `\ifoption...\fi` scheme isn't very robust, because it requires
all of the macros in the optional part to be well nested with respect to `\if...` and `\fi`;
a macro like `\ifoption` itself couldn't easily be defined in such a place! There's a better
scheme that also runs faster, based on category code changes. This idea (due to Max
Díaz) requires that the leftmost nonblank character on each line be either '`\`' or '`{`';
it's usually easy to arrange this. Furthermore, one other symbol, say ˜, is reserved.
Then the text material that is to be loaded only under option B is preceded by the line
'`\beginoption B`' and followed by a line that says '`˜endoptionalcode`'. The `\catcode`
for ˜ is set to 14 (comment character), hence the `˜endoptionalcode` line will have no
effect if code is not being skipped. The `\beginoption` macro works like this:

```
\def\beginoption#1{\ifoption#1\else\begingroup\swapcategories\fi}
\def\swapcategories{\catcode'\\=14 \catcode'\{=14 \catcode'\˜=0 }
\let\endoptionalcode=\endgroup
\catcode'\˜=14
```

Once the categories have been swapped, all lines will be skipped at high speed until the
control sequence `˜endoptionalcode` is encountered; then everything will be restored
to its former state. Under this scheme, material that should be loaded only under
both options B and D can be prefaced by both '`\beginoption B`' and '`\beginoption D`';
material that should be loaded under either option B or option D (or both) can be
prefaced by

```
\beginoption B
˜oroption D
```

if we define `\oroption#1` to be an abbreviation for '`\ifoption#1\endgroup\fi`'.

Another kind of selective loading is sometimes appropriate, based on whether
or not a particular control sequence is defined. In this scheme, if the control sequence
is undefined, it should remain undefined and it should take up no space whatever in
TeX's memory. There's a slick way to do this, namely to say

```
\ifx\cs\undefined ... \fi
```

(assuming that `\undefined` has never been defined). TeX does not put undefined
control sequences into its internal tables if they follow `\ifx` or if they are encountered
while skipping conditional text. You can use this idea, for example, to prepare a
bibliography for a paper, by reading a suitably arranged bibliography file; only the
entries that correspond to defined control sequences will be loaded.

5. Brace hacks. Several of TEX's operations depend on grouping, and you'll want to know exactly what this means if you try to do certain tricky things. For example, plain TEX's control sequences \bgroup and \egroup are "implicit braces" because they have been defined by

> \let\bgroup={   \let\egroup=}

This means that you can include them in the replacement texts of definitions without worrying about how they nest; for example, the macros

> \def\beginbox{\setbox0=\hbox\bgroup}
> \def\endbox{\egroup\copy0 }

allow you to make a box between \beginbox and \endbox; the behavior is almost the same as

> \def\beginbox#1\endbox{\setbox0=\hbox{#1}\copy0 }

but different in three important ways: (1) The first alternative allows category codes to change inside the box. (2) The first alternative is faster, because it doesn't need to scan the box contents both as an argument and as a sequence of actual commands. (3) The first alternative takes less memory space, because no argument needs to be stored. Thus, the first alternative is usually superior.

For the purposes of this discussion we shall assume that only '{' has category 1 and that only '}' has category 2, although any characters can actually be used as group delimiters. Group nesting is crucial during two of TEX's main activities: (a) when TEX is scanning a ⟨balanced text⟩, e.g., when TEX is forming the replacement text of a macro, a parameter, or a token list variable; (b) when TEX must determine whether the token & or \span or \cr or \crcr is the end of an entry within an alignment.

TEX's mouth has two internal counting mechanisms to deal with nesting: The "master counter" goes up by 1 for each $\{_1$ scanned by TEX, and down by 1 for each $\}_2$; the "balance counter" is similar, but it is affected only by explicit $\{_1$ and $\}_2$ tokens that are actually contributed to a token list that is being formed. The master counter decreases by 1 when TEX evaluates the alphabetic constant '{, and it increases by 1 when TEX evaluates '}, hence the net change is zero when such constants are evaluated. As a consequence of these rules, certain constructions produce the following effects:

	Master counter change		*Balance counter change*	
Input	*expanded*	*unexpanded*	*expanded*	*unexpanded*
{	1	1	1	1
\bgroup	0	0	0	0
\iffalse{\fi	1	1	0	1
\ifnum0='{\fi	0	1	0	1

The last two cases produce no begin-group tokens when expanded, but they do affect the master counter as shown. Thus, for example,

> \def\eegroup{\ifnum0='{\fi}}

makes \eegroup behave rather like \egroup, but the expansion of \eegroup also decreases the master counter.

Alignment processing uses only the master counter, not the balance counter. An alignment entry ends with the first & or \span or \cr or \crcr that appears when the master counter has the value that was present in the counter at the beginning of the entry. Thus, for example, the curious construction

```
\halign{\show\par#\relax\cr
  \global\let\par=\cr
  {\global\let\par=\cr}\cr
  \par}
```

causes TeX to perform three `\show` instructions, in which the respective values of `\par` shown are `\par`, `\relax`, and `\cr`. Similarly, each template in the preamble to an alignment ends with the first `&` or `\cr` or `\crcr` that appears at the master counter level that was in effect at the beginning of the entry; hence `&` and `\cr` and `\crcr` tokens can appear within a template of an alignment, if they are hidden by braces (e.g., if they appear in a definition).

These facts allow us to draw two somewhat surprising conclusions: (1) If an alignment entry has the form 'α `\iffalse{\fi` β `\iffalse}\fi` γ', it's possible for β to include `&` and `\cr` tokens that aren't local to a group.* (2) The construction

```
{\span\iffalse}\fi
```

appearing in a preamble contributes '`{`' to the template without any net change to the master counter; thus, it's very much like `\bgroup`, except that it produces $\{_1$ explicitly. If you understand (1) and (2), you'll agree that the present appendix deserves its name.

6. Box maneuvers. Let's turn now from syntax to semantics, i.e., from TeX's mouth to its gastro-intestinal tract. Sometimes an odd symbol is needed in boldface type, but it's available only in a normal weight. In such cases you can sometimes get by with "poor man's bold," obtained by overprinting the normal weight symbol with slight offsets. The following macro typesets its argument three times in three slightly different places, equidistant from each other; but the result takes up just as much space as if `\pmb` had been simply `\hbox`:

```
\def\pmb#1{\setbox0=\hbox{#1}%
  \kern-.025em\copy0\kern-\wd0
  \kern.05em\copy0\kern-\wd0
  \kern-.025em\raise.0433em\box0 }
```

For example, '`\pmb{$\infty$}`' yields '$\boldsymbol{\infty}$'. The results are somewhat **fuzzy**, and they certainly are no match for the real thing if it's available; but poor man's bold is better than nothing, and once in a while you can get away with it.

When you put something into a box register, you don't need to put the contents of that register into your document. Thus, you can write macros that do experiments behind the scenes, trying different possibilities before making a commitment to a particular decision. For example, suppose you are typesetting a text in two languages, and you would like to choose the column widths so that the same number of lines is obtained in both cases. For example, the following texts balance perfectly when the

---

* The token list α should not be empty, however, because TeX expands the first token of an alignment entry before looking at the template, in order to see if the entry begins with `\noalign` or `\omit`. The master counter value that is considered to be present at the beginning of an entry is the value in the counter just after the "u part" of the template has been entirely read.

first column is 157.1875 pt wide and the second column is 166.8125 pt wide; but the second column would be one line longer than the first if they were both 162 pt wide:

A. The creative part is really more interesting than the deductive part. Instead of concentrating just on finding good answers to questions, it's more important to learn how to find good questions!	A. La parte creativa es mucho mejor que la deductiva. En vez de concentrarse en buscar buenas respuestas a ciertas cuestiones es más importante aprender a proponerse buenas preguntas.
B. You've got something there. I wish our teachers would give us problems like, "Find something interesting about x," instead of "Prove x."	B. Me parece una buena ocurrencia. Me gustaría que los profesores propusieran problemas del estilo de «Encuentren algo interesante sobre x» en vez de «Demuestre que $x \ldots$».
A. Exactly. But teachers are so conservative, they'd be afraid of scaring off the "grind" type of students who obediently and mechanically do all the homework. Besides, they wouldn't like the extra work of grading the answers to nondirected questions.	A. Exactamente. Pero los profesores son tan conservadores que temerían espantar al tipo de estudiante «apisonadora» que hace lo que le proponen para casa, obedientemente y de forma mecánica. Además, no creo que les gustase el trabajo adicional de calificar respuestas a preguntas abiertas.
The traditional way is to put off all creative aspects until the last part of graduate school. For seventeen or more years, a student is taught examsmanship, then suddenly after passing enough exams in graduate school he's told to do something original.	La forma tradicional es dejar la parte creativa para los cursos altos. Durante diecisiete años o más se enseña al estudiante a aprobar, luego de golpe, cerca de la graduación, se le pide que haga algo original.

Some implementations of TEX display the output as you are running, so that you can choose column widths interactively until a suitable balance is obtained. It's fun to play with such systems, but it's also possible to ask TEX to compute the column widths automatically. The following code tries up to ten times to find a solution in which the natural heights of the two columns are different by less than a given value, \delheight. The macros \firstcol and \secondcol are supposed to generate the columns, and the sum of column widths is supposed to be \doublewidth.

```
\newdimen\doublewidth \newdimen\delheight \newif\iffail \newcount\n
\newdimen\trialwidth \newdimen\lowwidth \newdimen\highwidth
\def\balancetwocols{\lowwidth=10em % lower bound on \trialwidth
  \highwidth=\doublewidth \advance\highwidth-10em % upper bound
  {\n=1 \hbadness=10000 \hfuzz=\maxdimen % disable warnings
    \loop \maketrial \testfailure \iffail \preparenewtrial \repeat}
  \maketrial} % now under/overfull boxes will be shown
\def\maketrial{\trialwidth=.5\lowwidth \advance\trialwidth by.5\highwidth
  \setbox0=\vbox{\hsize=\trialwidth \firstcol}
  \setbox2=\vbox{\hsize=\doublewidth\advance\hsize-\trialwidth\secondcol}}
\def\testfailure{\dimen0=\ht0 \advance\dimen0-\ht2
  \ifnum\dimen0<0 \dimen0=-\dimen0 \fi
  \ifdim\dimen0>\delheight \ifnum\n=10 \failfalse\else\failtrue\fi
  \else\failfalse\fi}
\def\preparenewtrial{\ifdim\ht0>\ht2 \global\lowwidth=\trialwidth
  \else\global\highwidth=\trialwidth\fi \advance\n by1 }
```

Neither column will be less than 10 ems wide. This code does a "binary search," assuming that a column will not increase in height when it is made wider. If no solution is found in 10 trials, there probably is no way to obtain the desired balance, because a tiny increase in the width of the taller column will make it shorter than the other one. The values of \hbadness and \hfuzz are made infinite during the trial settings, because warning messages that relate to unused boxes are irrelevant; after a solution is found, it is computed again, so that any relevant warnings will be issued.

When a box has been put into a box register, you can change its height, width, or depth by assigning a new value to the \ht, \wd, or \dp. Such assignments don't change anything inside the box; in particular, they don't affect the setting of the glue.

But changes to a box's dimensions can be confusing if you don't understand exactly how TEX deals with boxes in lists. The rules are stated in Chapter 12, but it may be helpful to restate them here in a different way. Given a box and the location of its reference point, TEX assigns locations to interior boxes as follows: (1) If the box is an hbox, TEX starts at the reference point and walks through the horizontal list inside. When the list contains a box, TEX puts the reference point of the enclosed box at the current position, and moves right by the width of that box. When the list contains glue or kerning, etc., TEX moves right by the appropriate amount. (2) If the box is a vbox, TEX starts at the upper left corner (i.e., TEX first moves up from the reference point, by the height of the box) and walks through the vertical list inside. When the list contains a box, TEX puts the upper left corner of that box at the current position; i.e., TEX moves down by the height of that box, then puts the box's reference point at the current position, then moves down by the depth of the box. When the list contains glue or kerning, etc., TEX moves down by the appropriate amount.

As a consequence of these rules, we can work out what happens when the dimensions of a box are changed. Let \delta be a ⟨dimen⟩ register, and let \h and \hh specify horizontal lists that don't depend on \box0. Consider the following macro:

```
\newdimen\temp \newdimen\delta
\def\twohboxes#1{\setbox1=\hbox{\h \copy0 \hh}
  \temp=#10 \advance\temp by \delta #10=\temp
  \setbox2=\hbox{\h \copy0 \hh}}
```

For example, \twohboxes\wd makes two hboxes, \box1 and \box2, that are identical except that the width of \box0 has been increased by δ in \box2. What difference does this make? There are several cases, depending on whether #1 is \wd, \ht, or \dp, and depending on whether \box0 is an hbox or a vbox. *Case 1*, \twohboxes\wd: The material from \hh is moved right by δ in \box2, compared to its position in \box1. Also \wd2 is δ more than \wd1. *Case 2*, \twohboxes\ht: If \box0 is an hbox, everything remains in the same position; but if \box0 is a vbox, everything in \copy0 moves up by δ. Also \ht2 may differ from \ht1. *Case 3*, \twohboxes\dp: Everything remains in the same position, but \dp2 may differ from \dp1.

Similarly, we can work out the changes when box dimensions are changed for boxes within vertical lists. In this case we shall ignore the influence of interline glue by defining \twovboxes as follows:

```
\def\twovboxes#1{
  \setbox1=\vbox{\v\nointerlineskip\copy0\nointerlineskip\vv}
  \temp=#10 \advance\temp by \delta #10=\temp
  \setbox2=\vbox{\v\nointerlineskip\copy0\nointerlineskip\vv}}
```

What is the difference between \box1 and \box2 now?   *Case 1,* \twovboxes\wd: Everything remains in the same position, but \wd2 may differ from \wd1.   *Case 2,* \twovboxes\ht: If \box0 is an hbox, everything in \v moves up by δ in \box2, compared to the corresponding positions in \box1, if we make the reference points of the two boxes identical; but if \box0 is a vbox, everything in it moves up by δ, together with the material in \v. Also, \ht2 is δ more than \ht1.   *Case 3,* \twovboxes\dp: If \vv is empty, \dp2 is δ more than \dp1, and nothing else changes. Otherwise everything in \v and in \copy0 moves up by δ, and \ht2 is δ more than \ht1.

TeX is designed to put boxes together either horizontally or vertically, not diagonally. But that's not a serious limitation, because the use of negative spacing makes it possible to put things anywhere on a page. For example, the seven points in the diagram at the right of this paragraph were typeset by saying simply

```
\hbox{\unit=\baselineskip
   \point 0 0
   \point 0 8
   \point 0 -8
   \point -1 -2.5
   \point 4 7
   \point 4 2
   \point 1 1.5
   }
```

The \point macro makes a box of width zero; hence the individual \point specifications can be given in any order, and there's no restriction on the coordinates:

```
\newdimen\unit
\def\point#1 #2 {\rlap{\kern#1\unit
   \raise#2\unit\hbox{$
   \scriptstyle\bullet\;(#1,#2)$}}}
```

If the \point specifications are not enclosed in an \hbox—i.e., if they occur in vertical mode—a similar construction can be used. In this case \point should create a box whose height and depth are zero:

```
\def\point#1 #2 {\vbox to0pt{\kern-#2\unit
   \hbox{\kern#1\unit$\scriptstyle\bullet\;(#1,#2)$}\vss}
   \nointerlineskip}
```

(The \nointerlineskip is necessary to prevent interline glue from messing things up.)

If you enjoy fooling around making pictures, instead of typesetting ordinary text, TeX will be a source of endless frustration/amusement for you, because almost anything is possible if you have suitable fonts. For example, suppose you have a font \qc that contains four quarter circles:

$$a = \text{╮} \qquad b = \text{╯} \qquad c = \text{╲} \qquad d = \text{╭}$$

Each of these characters has the same height, the same width, and the same depth; the width and the height-plus-depth are equal to the diameter of the corresponding full circle. Furthermore, the reference point of each character is in a somewhat peculiar place: Each quarter arc has a horizontal endpoint such that the lower edge of the curve is at the baseline, and a vertical endpoint such that the left edge is directly above or below the reference point. This convention makes it possible to guarantee perfect alignment between these characters and rules that meet them at the endpoints; the thickness of such rules should be `\fontdimen8\qc`.

Given those characters, it's possible to devise macros `\path`, `\L`, `\R`, `\S`, and `\T` such that `\path{⟨any string of \L's, \R's, \S's, and \T's⟩}` produces a path that starts traveling East, but it turns left for each `\L`, right for each `\R`, goes straight for each `\S`, and turns backward for each `\T`. Thus, for example, `\path{\L\T\S\T\R\L\T\S\T\R}` yields '⊔⊔', and you can also get the following effects:

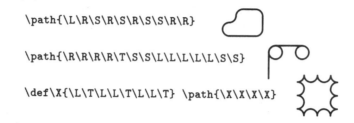

```
\path{\L\R\S\R\S\R\S\S\R\R}

\path{\R\R\R\R\T\S\S\L\L\L\L\L\S\S}

\def\X{\L\T\L\L\T\L\L\T} \path{\X\X\X\X}
```

Furthermore, there are operations `\B` and `\W` that make the path black (visible) and white (invisible), respectively:

```
\path{\R\R\S
 \W\S\S\S\R\R
 \B\R\R\S\R\S\R\S\S\S\R\S\S\S\S\S\R\S\R
 \W\R\R\R\S\L\S
 \B\L\S\S\S\S}
```

(It may be necessary to put kerns before and after the path, since the box produced by `\path` may not be as wide as the actual path itself.)

The `\path` macros work differently from `\point`, since the boxes need not have zero width in this application:

```
\catcode`\ =9 \endlinechar=-1 % ignore all spaces (temporarily)
\newcount\dir \newdimen\y \newdimen\w
\newif\ifvisible \let\B=\visibletrue \let\W=\visiblefalse
\newbox\NE \newbox\NW \newbox\SE \newbox\SW \newbox\NS \newbox\EW
\setbox\SW=\hbox{\qc a} \setbox\NW=\hbox{\qc b}
\setbox\NE=\hbox{\qc c} \setbox\SE=\hbox{\qc d}
\w=\wd\SW \dimen0=\fontdimen8\qc
\setbox\EW=\hbox{\kern-\dp\SW \vrule height\dimen0 width\wd\SW} \wd\EW=\w
\setbox\NS=\hbox{\vrule height\ht\SW depth\dp\SW width\dimen0}  \wd\NS=\w
\def\L{\ifcase\dir \dy+\NW \or\dx-\SW \or\dy-\SE \or\dx+\NE\dd-4\fi \dd+1}
\def\S{\ifcase\dir \dx+\EW \or \dy+\NS \or \dx-\EW \or \dy-\NS \fi}
\def\R{\ifcase\dir \dy-\SW\dd+4 \or\dx+\SE \or\dy+\NE \or\dx-\NW\fi \dd-1}
\def\T{\ifcase\dir\kern-\w\dd+2\or\ey-\dd+2\or\kern\w\dd-2\or\ey+\dd-2\fi}
```

```
\edef\dd#1#2{\global\advance\dir#1#2\space}
\def\dx#1#2{\ifvisible\raise\y\copy#2 \if#1-\kern-2\w\fi\else\kern#1\w\fi}
\def\dy#1#2{\ifvisible\raise\y\copy#2 \kern-\w \fi \global\advance\y#1\w}
\def\ey#1{\global\advance\y#1\w}
\def\path#1{\hbox{\B \dir=0 \y=0pt #1}}
\catcode'\ =10 \endlinechar='\^^M % resume normal spacing conventions

\newcount\n % the current order in the \dragon and \nogard macros
\def\dragon{\ifnum\n>0{\advance\n-1 \dragon\L\nogard}\fi}
\def\nogard{\ifnum\n>0{\advance\n-1 \dragon\R\nogard}\fi}
```

(The last three lines are not part of the \path macros, but they can be used as an interesting test case. To get the famous "dragon curve" of order 9, all you have to say is '\path{\dir=3 \n=9 \dragon}'.)

Let's turn now to another box-oriented problem. The \listing macro discussed earlier in this appendix was restricted to listing files that contain only visible ASCII characters. Sometimes it's desirable to deal with ASCII ⟨tab⟩ marks too, where a ⟨tab⟩ is equivalent to 1 or 2 or ⋯ or 8 spaces (whatever is necessary to make the current line length a multiple of 8). How can this be done?

We shall assume that files can contain a special symbol that TeX will input as character number 9, the ASCII ⟨tab⟩ code; some implementations can't actually do this. If a file contains the three symbols ^^I, plain TeX will normally input them as a single character, number 9; but in a verbatim listing of the file we naturally want such symbols to print as themselves, i.e., as ^^I.

The following construction redefines \setupverbatim so that the previous \listing macro will work with ⟨tab⟩ characters. The idea is to keep the line-so-far in an hbox, which can be "measured" in order to find out how many characters have appeared since the beginning of the line or since the most recent ⟨tab⟩.

```
\def\setupverbatim{\tt \lineno=0
  \def\par{\leavevmode\egroup\box0\endgraf}
  \obeylines \uncatcodespecials \obeyspaces
  \catcode'\`=\active \catcode'\^^I=\active
  \everypar{\advance\lineno by1
    \llap{\sevenrm\the\lineno\ \ }\startbox}}
\newdimen\w \setbox0=\hbox{\tt\space} \w=8\wd0 % tab amount
\def\startbox{\setbox0=\hbox\bgroup}
{\catcode'\^^I=\active
  \gdef^^I{\leavevmode\egroup
    \dimen0=\wd0 % the width so far, or since the previous tab
    \divide\dimen0 by\w
    \multiply\dimen0 by\w % compute previous multiple of \w
    \advance\dimen0 by\w  % advance to next multiple of \w
    \wd0=\dimen0 \box0 \startbox}}
```

(The new things in \setupverbatim are the '\egroup\box0' in the redefinition of \par; the '\catcode'\^^I=\active'; and the '\startbox' in \everypar.) The \settabs and \+ macros of Appendix B provide another example of how tab operations can be simulated by boxing and unboxing.

Chapter 22 explains how to put vertical rules in tables by considering the rules to be separate columns. There's also another way, provided that the rules extend all the way from the top of the table to the bottom. For example,

```
\beginvrulealign
\tabskip=10pt
\halign{&\strut#\hfil\cr
These&     after\cr
vertical&  the\cr
rules&     alignment\cr
were&      was\cr
inserted&  completed!\cr}
\endvrulealign
```

yields

These	after
vertical	the
rules	alignment
were	was
inserted	completed!

The magic macros in this case examine the bottom row of the alignment, which consists of alternating tabskip glue and boxes; each item of tabskip glue in that bottom row will be bisected by a vertical rule. Here's how:

```
\def\beginvrulealign{\setbox0=\vbox\bgroup}
\def\endvrulealign{\egroup % now \box0 holds the entire alignment
  \setbox0=\vbox{\setbox2=\hbox{\vrule height\ht0 depth\dp0 width0pt}
    \unvbox0 \setbox0=\lastbox % now \box0 is the bottom row
    \nointerlineskip \copy0 % put it back
    \global\setbox1=\hbox{} % initialize box that will contain rules
    \setbox4=\hbox{\unhbox0 % now open up the bottom row
      \loop \skip0=\lastskip \unskip % remove tabskip glue
        \advance\skip0 by-.4pt % rules are .4pt wide
        \divide\skip0 by 2
        \global\setbox1=\hbox{\hskip\skip0\vrule\hskip\skip0
          \unhbox2\unhbox1}%
        \setbox2=\lastbox % remove alignment entry
      \ifhbox2 \setbox2=\hbox{\kern\wd2}\repeat}%
  \hbox{\rlap{\box0}\box1}} % superimpose the alignment on the rules
```

This method works with all alignments created by `\halign{...}`. For alignments created by, say, `\halign to100pt{...}`, the method works only if the bottom row of the alignment contains all of the columns, and only if '`\box1`' is replaced by '`\hbox to100pt{\unhbox1}`' at the end of `\endvrulealign`.

7. Paragraph maneuvers. Chapter 14 promised that Appendix D would present an example where ragged right and ragged left setting occur in the same paragraph. The following interesting example was suggested by the "Key Index" in *Mathematical Reviews*, where the entries consist of a possibly long title followed by dot leaders followed by a possibly long list of review numbers. If the title doesn't fit on one line, it should be set ragged right, with hanging indentation on all lines after the first; if the references don't all fit on one line, they should be set ragged left. For example, given the input

```
ACM Symposium on Theory of Computing, Eighth Annual (Hershey, %
  Pa., 1976)\:1879, 4813, 5414, 6918, 6936, 6937, 6946, 6951, %
  6970, 7619, 9605, 10148, 11676, 11687, 11692, 11710, 13869
```

the following three types of output are desired, depending on the column width:

ACM Symposium on
   Theory of Computing,
   Eighth Annual
   (Hershey, Pa., 1976)
    .... 1879, 4813, 5414,
   6918, 6936, 6937, 6946,
   6951, 6970, 7619, 9605,
    10148, 11676, 11687,
    11692, 11710, 13869

ACM Symposium on Theory of
   Computing, Eighth Annual
   (Hershey, Pa., 1976) ....
   1879, 4813, 5414, 6918, 6936, 6937,
   6946, 6951, 6970, 7619, 9605, 10148,
   11676, 11687, 11692, 11710, 13869

ACM Symposium on Theory of Computing, Eighth Annual
   (Hershey, Pa., 1976) ... 1879, 4813, 5414, 6918, 6936, 6937, 6946,
   6951, 6970, 7619, 9605, 10148, 11676, 11687, 11692, 11710, 13869

Notice that the dot leaders are treated in three different ways, depending on which works out best: They may occur at the left of the first line after the title, or they may appear at the end of the last line of the title (in which case they stop well before the right margin), or they may occur in the middle of a line. Furthermore, the ragged-right lines are supposed to end at least 0.5 em from the right margin. Our goal is to achieve all this as a special case of TeX's general paragraphing method. The simple approach of Appendix B won't work, because `\raggedright` is achieved there by adjusting `\rightskip`; TeX uses the same `\rightskip` value in all lines of a paragraph.

    The solution to this problem requires an understanding of the line-breaking algorithm; it depends on how demerits are calculated, and on how items are removed at the breakpoints, so the reader should review Chapter 14 until those concepts are firmly understood. Basically, we need to specify a sequence of box/glue/penalty items for the spaces in the title portion, another sequence for the spaces in the reference portion, and another sequence for the dot leaders. In the title portion of each index entry, interword spaces can be represented by the sequence

```
\penalty10000 \hskip.5em plus3em \penalty0
\hskip-.17em plus-3em minus.11em
```

Thus, there is a stretchability of 3 em if a line break occurs at the `\penalty0`; otherwise the net interword space will be .33 em, shrinkable to .22 em. This gives ragged right margins. The interword spaces in the reference portion are designed to produce ragged left margins and to minimize the number of lines devoted to references:

```
\penalty1000 \hskip.33em plus-3em minus.11em
\vadjust{}\penalty10000 \hskip0pt plus3em
```

The `\vadjust{}` does nothing, but it doesn't disappear at a line break. Thus, if a break occurs at the `\penalty1000`, the following line will begin with stretchability 3 em; but if no break occurs, the net space will be .33 em minus .11 em. Finally, the transition between title and references can be specified by

```
\penalty10000 \hskip.5em plus3em \penalty600
\hskip-.17em plus-3em minus.11em
\vadjust{}\penalty10000
\leaders\copy\dbox\hskip3.3\wd\dbox plus1fil minus.3\wd\dbox
\kern3em \penalty600 \hskip-2.67em plus-3em minus.11em
\vadjust{}\penalty10000 \hskip0pt plus3em
```

(Quite a mouthful.) This long sequence of penalty and glue items begins rather like the interword spaces in the first part, and it ends rather like the interword spaces in the last part. It has two permissible breakpoints, namely at the '\penalty600' items. The first breakpoint causes the leaders to appear at the beginning of a line; the second causes them to appear at the end, but 3 ems away. The leader width will always be at least three times the width of \dbox, so at least two copies of \dbox will always appear. Here is the actual TEX code that can be used to set up the desired behavior:

```
\hyphenpenalty10000 \exhyphenpenalty10000 \pretolerance10000 % no hyphens
\newbox\dbox \setbox\dbox=\hbox to .4em{\hss.\hss} % dot box for leaders
\newskip\rrskipb \rrskipb=.5em plus3em % ragged right space before break
\newskip\rrskipa \rrskipa=-.17em plus-3em minus.11em % ditto, after
\newskip\rlskipa \rlskipa=0pt plus3em % ragged left space after break
\newskip\rlskipb \rlskipb=.33em plus-3em minus .11em % ditto, before
\newskip\lskip \lskip=3.3\wd\dbox plus1fil minus.3\wd\dbox % for leaders
\newskip\lskipa \lskipa=-2.67em plus-3em minus.11em % after leaders
\mathchardef\rlpen=1000 \mathchardef\leadpen=600 % constants used
\def\rrspace{\nobreak\hskip\rrskipb\penalty0\hskip\rrskipa}
\def\rlspace{\penalty\rlpen\hskip\rlskipb\vadjust{}\nobreak\hskip\rlskipa}
\uccode`~=` \uppercase{
  \def\:{\nobreak\hskip\rrskipb \penalty\leadpen \hskip\rrskipa
    \vadjust{}\nobreak\leaders\copy\dbox\hskip\lskip
    \kern3em \penalty\leadpen \hskip\lskipa
    \vadjust{}\nobreak\hskip\rlskipa \let~=\rlspace}
  \everypar{\hangindent=1.5em \hangafter=1 \let~=\rrspace}}
\uccode`~=0 \parindent=0pt \parfillskip=0pt \obeyspaces
```

Putting the interword glue into \skip registers saves a great deal of time and memory space when TEX works with such paragraphs; '\hskip⟨explicit glue⟩' occupies six cells of TEX's box memory, but '\hskip⟨skip register⟩' occupies only two. Notice the tricky use of \uppercase here to convert ~$_{13}$ into ⊔$_{13}$; "random" active characters can be obtained in a similar way.

Let's turn now to a much simpler problem: *hanging punctuation*.

"What is hanging punctuation?" asked Alice, with a puzzled frown. 'Well, y'know, actually,' answered Bill, 'I'd rather demonstrate it than explain it.' "Oh, now I see. Commas, periods, and quotes are allowed to stick out into the margins, if they occur next to a line break." 'Yeah, I guess.' "Really! But why do all your remarks have single quotes, while mine are double?" 'I haven't the foggiest; it's weird. Ask the author of this crazy book.'

Each comma in Alice and Bill's demonstration paragraph was represented inside of TEX by the sequence of three items ',\kern-\commahang\kern\commahang', and there were similar replacements for periods and for closing quotes; opening quotes were represented by the longer sequence

$$\text{\kern\qquotehang\vadjust{}\kern-\qquotehang``\allowhyphens}$$

where \allowhyphens allows the following word to be hyphenated. This construction works because kerns disappear into line breaks in the proper way; the relevant rules from Chapter 14 are: (1) A line break can occur at a kern that is immediately followed by glue. (2) Consecutive glue, kern, and penalty items disappear at a break.

To set TEX up for hanging punctuation, you can say

```
\newdimen\commahang    \setbox0=\hbox{,}    \commahang=\wd0
\newdimen\periodhang   \setbox0=\hbox{.}    \periodhang=\wd0
\newdimen\quotehang    \setbox0=\hbox{'}    \quotehang=\wd0
\newdimen\qquotehang   \setbox0=\hbox{''}   \qquotehang=\wd0
\newskip\zzz \def\allowhyphens{\nobreak\hskip\zzz}
\def\lqq{''} \def\rqq{''} \def\pnt{.}
\def\comma{,\kern-\commahang\kern\commahang}
\def\period{.\kern-\periodhang\kern\periodhang}
\def\rquote{'\kern-\quotehang\kern\quotehang}
\def\lquote{\ifhmode\kern\quotehang\vadjust{}\else\leavevmode\fi
  \kern-\quotehang'\allowhyphens}
\catcode',=\active \let,=\comma \catcode'.=\active \let.=\period
\catcode''=\active \def'{\futurelet\next\rqtest}
\catcode''=\active \def'{\futurelet\next\lqtest}
\def\rqtest{\ifx\next'\let\next=\rquotes\else\let\next=\rquote\fi\next}
\def\lqtest{\ifx\next'\let\next=\lquotes\else\let\next=\lquote\fi\next}
\def\rquotes'{\rqq\kern-\qquotehang\kern\qquotehang}
\def\lquotes'{\ifhmode\kern\qquotehang\vadjust{}\else\leavevmode\fi
  \kern-\qquotehang\lqq\allowhyphens}
```

Notice that the macros need to do their own checking for ligatures, and they also take appropriate actions when a paragraph begins with an opening quote. Since \kern does not affect the space factor, hanging punctuation doesn't affect TEX's spacing conventions within a line. Partially hanging punctuation can be obtained by decreasing the amounts of \commahang, etc. The macros \pnt, \lq, and \rq should be used in constants; for example, a dimension of 6.5in must be written '6\pnt5in' when hanging punctuation is in effect, and '\catcode\lq,=12' makes commas inactive again. A special font with zero-width \hyphenchar should be used for "hanging hyphenation."

And now for our next trick, let's consider an application to short footnotes. The footnotes at the bottom of this page[1,2,3,4,5,6,7,8,9,10] look funny, because most of them are quite short. When a document has lots of footnotes, and when most of them take up only a small part of a line, the output routine ought to reformat them in some more appropriate way.

---

[1] First footnote.

[2] Second footnote. (Every once in a while a long footnote might occur, just to make things difficult.)

[3] Third footnote.

[4] Fourth footnote.

[5] Fifth footnote. (This is incredibly boring, but it's just an example.)

[6] Another.

[7] And another.

[8] Ho hum.

[9] Umpteenth footnote.

[10] Oodles of them.

For example, one approach would be to typeset the footnotes in narrow columns and to put, say, three columns of footnotes at the bottom of each page. The ten example footnotes might then look like this:

[1] First footnote.	[3] Third footnote.	[6] Another.
[2] Second footnote. (Every	[4] Fourth footnote.	[7] And another.
once in a while a long	[5] Fifth footnote. (This is	[8] Ho hum.
footnote might occur,	incredibly boring, but it's	[9] Umpteenth footnote.
just to make things	just an example.)	[10] Oodles of them.
difficult.)		

In this case, the footnotes could be generated by

```
\insert\footins{\eightpoint \hsize=9pc \parindent=1pc
  \leftskip=0pt \raggedright \pretolerance=10000
  \hyphenpenalty=10000 \exhyphenpenalty=10000
  \interlinepenalty=\interfootnotelinepenalty
  \floatingpenalty=20000
  \splittopskip=\ht\strutbox \splitmaxdepth=\dp\strutbox
  \item{$^{\the\footno}$}\strut⟨text of footnote⟩\strut
  \par\allowbreak}
```

and \count\footins would be set to 333 so that each footnote line would be considered to occupy about one third of a line on the page. The output routine would then see a \box\footins that looks like this:

```
\vbox(142.0+2.0)x108.0
.\hbox(7.0+2.0)x108.0, glue set 42.23425fil []
.\penalty 0
.\hbox(7.0+2.0)x108.0, glue set 0.29266 []
.\penalty 250
.\glue(\baselineskip) 1.44444
.\hbox(5.55556+1.55556)x96.0, glue set 0.8693, shifted 12.0 []
.\penalty 100
.\glue(\baselineskip) 1.88889
.\hbox(5.55556+1.55556)x96.0, glue set 0.92438, shifted 12.0 []
      ⋮
.\hbox(7.0+2.0)x108.0, glue set 18.56308fil []
.\penalty 0
.\hbox(7.0+2.0)x108.0, glue set 36.92476fil []
.\penalty 0
```

The individual footnotes each end with '\penalty 0'; footnotes that take up more than one line have larger penalties between the lines, and interline glue appears there too.

How should the output routine break such a box up into three roughly equal pieces? Notice that the contents of the box are completely rigid, i.e, there is no glue that can stretch or shrink. Furthermore, we can assume that the contents of the box are regular, i.e., that the inter-baseline distances are all the same. In such circumstances a fairly simple balancing routine can be used to trisect the box.

Let's consider a more general problem: Suppose that a rigid vbox is given, n lines tall, where adjacent baselines are b units apart. Suppose also that the top baseline is h units from the top of the vbox, where $0 < h < b$.   (In our footnote example, $b = 9\,\mathrm{pt}$ and $h = 7\,\mathrm{pt}$; in the standard settings of plain TeX, $b = 12\,\mathrm{pt}$ and $h = 10\,\mathrm{pt}$. We might as well work the problem for general b and h.)   It follows that the height of the vbox is $H = h + b(n - 1) = bn + h - b$.

If n lines are to be distributed evenly into k columns, the first column should contain $\lceil n/k \rceil$ lines. (This denotes the smallest integer greater than or equal to n/k.) For example, our application to footnotes has $n = 16$ and $k = 3$, hence the first column should contain 6 lines. After forming the first column, we have reduced the problem to $n = 10$ and $k = 2$, so two 5-line columns will complete the operation. (Notice that it is better to divide 16 into $6 + 5 + 5$ instead of $6 + 6 + 4$.)   Once we have found the first column, it's always possible to reduce the k-column problem to a $(k - 1)$-column problem, so we need only concentrate on finding the first column.

Let $m = \lceil n/k \rceil$. The height of the given box is $bn + h - b$, and the height of the first column should be $bm + h - b$; hence we want to do a \vsplit to that height. However, it isn't necessary to calculate $bm + h - b$ exactly, since a bit of arithmetic proves that

$$bm + h - b \;<\; \frac{bn + h - b}{k} + h \;<\; b(m + 1) + h - b.$$

Therefore it suffices to \vsplit to height $H' = H/k + h$; under the assumptions of rigidity, and assuming that a valid break is possible after each line, \vsplit to H' will split after the maximum number of lines that yield a box of height $\leq H'$. (We have observed that m lines produce a box of height $< H'$ while $m + 1$ lines produce a box of height $> H'$.)   The following TeX code does this:

```
\newcount\k \newdimen\h % registers used by the \rigidbalance routine
\def\rigidbalance#1#2 #3 {\setbox0=\box#1 \k=#2 \h=#3
  \line{\splittopskip=\h \vbadness=10000 \hfilneg
    \valign{##\vfil\cr\dosplits}}}
\def\dosplits{\ifnum\k>0 \noalign{\hfil}\splitoff
  \global\advance\k-1\cr\dosplits\fi}
\def\splitoff{\dimen0=\ht0
  \divide\dimen0 by\k \advance\dimen0 by\h
  \vsplit0 to \dimen0 }
```

This code is interesting on a number of counts. First, notice that the calculation does not depend on b, only on h and the height of the given box; hence \rigidbalance has three parameters: a box register number, the number of columns k, and the top baseline height h. The routine splits the given vbox into k nearly equal pieces and justifies the result in a \line. The value of \splittopskip is set to h so that subsequent vboxes will satisfy the ground rules of the original vbox, as the problem is reduced from k to $k - 1$. Each column will be preceded by \hfil, hence \hfilneg is used to cancel the \hfil before the first column. A \valign is used to align all of the columns at the top. Notice that the preamble to this \valign is quite simple; and the body of the \valign is generated by a recursive macro \dosplits that produces the k columns. The value of \vbadness is set to 10000 because each \vsplit operation will produce an underfull vbox whose badness is 10000.

In our application to footnotes, the `\output` routine can reformat the contents of `\box\footins` by saying, for example,

```
\rigidbalance\footins 3 7pt
\setbox\footins=\lastbox
```

since `\lastbox` will be the result of `\rigidbalance`.

This solution to the problem of short footnotes might result in club lines or widow lines, since the balancing routine we have described simply trisects the total number of lines. For example, if the tenth footnote of our example had not been present, the fifteen remaining lines would have been split $5 + 5 + 5$; the second column would have been headed by the lonely word 'difficult.)', and the third column would have started with 'just an example.)'. The rigid balancing procedure could be replaced by one that allows ragged-bottom columns, but there's also another approach: The entire set of footnotes could be combined into a single paragraph, with generous spacing between the individual items. For example, the ten footnotes we have been considering might appear as follows:

[1]First footnote. [2]Second footnote. (Every once in a while a long footnote might occur, just to make things difficult.) [3]Third footnote. [4]Fourth footnote. [5]Fifth footnote. (This is incredibly boring, but it's just an example.) [6]Another. [7]And another. [8]Ho hum. [9]Umpteenth footnote. [10]Oodles of them.

It would be possible to take the contents of `\box\footins` shown previously and to reformat everything into a paragraph, but such an operation would be needlessly complicated. If footnotes are to be paragraphed by the output routine, it's better simply to prepare them in unjustified hboxes. Each of these hboxes will be unboxed later, so we are free to play with their heights, widths, and depths. It's convenient to set the depth to zero and the height to an estimate of how much a particular footnote will contribute to the final paragraph. For example, if a footnote takes up exactly half of the `\hsize`, and if the final footnote is going to be set with `\baselineskip=10pt`, then the height of the footnote hbox should be set to 5 pt. By letting `\count\footins=1000`, we'll have a pretty good estimate of the size of the final footnote paragraph. In other words, the following insertion scheme is suggested:

```
\insert\footins{\floatingpenalty=20000
  \eightpoint \setbox0=\hbox{%
    $^{\the\footno}$⟨text of footnote⟩\penalty-10\hskip\footglue}
  \dp0=0pt \ht0=\fudgefactor\wd0 \box0}
```

The penalty of -10 tends to favor line breaks between footnotes; `\footglue` is the amount of glue between footnotes in the final footnote paragraph; and `\fudgefactor` is the ratio of `\baselineskip` to `\hsize` in that paragraph. The author defined the necessary quantities as follows in his experiments:

```
\eightpoint \newskip\footglue \footglue=1.5em plus.3em minus.3em
\newdimen\footnotebaselineskip \footnotebaselineskip=10pt
\dimen0=\footnotebaselineskip \multiply\dimen0 by 1024
\divide \dimen0 by \hsize \multiply\dimen0 by 64
\xdef\fudgefactor{\expandafter\getfactor\the\dimen0 }
```

(The computation of `\fudgefactor` uses the fact that $1\,\text{pt} = 1024 \times 64\,\text{sp}$, and it assumes that the `\footnotebaselineskip` is less than 16 pt.)

Inside the output routine, `\box\footins` will now be a vbox of hboxes, and the height of this vbox will be an estimate of the height of the final paragraph. For example, our ten footnotes produce

```
\vbox(34.48158+0.0)x386.4221
.\hbox(2.00175+0.0)x70.68285 []
.\hbox(10.94359+0.0)x386.4221 []
.\hbox(2.09749+0.0)x74.06345 []
.\hbox(2.2077+0.0)x77.95517 []
.\hbox(7.6296+0.0)x269.40376 []
.\hbox(1.40851+0.0)x49.73532 []
.\hbox(1.87659+0.0)x66.26334 []
.\hbox(1.38826+0.0)x49.02003 []
.\hbox(2.67213+0.0)x94.35402 []
.\hbox(2.25597+0.0)x79.65926 []
```

and the height of 34.48158 pt corresponds to an estimate of about three and a half lines. (TeX's page builder has also added `\skip\footins` when estimating the total contribution due to footnotes.)

The reformatting of `\box\footins` takes place in three stages. First the vbox of hboxes is changed to an hbox of hboxes, so that we obtain, e.g.,

```
\hbox(10.94359+0.0)x1217.5593
.\hbox(2.00175+0.0)x70.68285 []
     ⋮
.\hbox(2.25597+0.0)x79.65926 []
```

(the same contents as before, but strung in a horizontal row instead of a vertical column). Then the inner hboxes are unboxed, and we obtain

```
\hbox(6.68999+2.0)x1217.5593
.\mathon
.\hbox(3.86665+0.0)x4.16661, shifted -2.82333 []
.\mathoff
.\eightrm F
.etc.
```

Finally the outer hbox is unboxed, and the horizontal list inside it is converted into a paragraph. Here is the actual TeX code:

```
\def\makefootnoteparagraph{\unvbox\footins \makehboxofhboxes
  \setbox0=\hbox{\unhbox0 \removehboxes}
  \baselineskip=\footnotebaselineskip\noindent\unhbox0\par}
\def\makehboxofhboxes{\setbox0=\hbox{}
  \loop\setbox2=\lastbox \ifhbox2 \setbox0=\hbox{\box2\unhbox0}\repeat}
\def\removehboxes{\setbox0=\lastbox
  \ifhbox0{\removehboxes}\unhbox0 \fi}
```

The `\removehboxes` operation is especially noteworthy, because it uses TeX's save stack to hold all of the hboxes before unboxing them. Each level of recursion in this routine uses one cell of input stack space and three cells of save stack space; thus, it is generally safe to do more than 100 footnotes without exceeding TeX's capacity. The \makehboxofhboxes routine is not as efficient; TeX doesn't allow a vbox to be unboxed in horizontal mode, or vice versa, hence the trick of \removehboxes cannot be used. This means that the running time is proportional to n^2, if there are n footnotes, because the time to make or unmake a box is proportional to the number of items in the top-level list inside. However, the constant of proportionality is small, so there is no need to resort to a more complicated scheme that would be asymptotically faster. Indeed, the \lastbox operation itself has a running time approximately equal to $a+mb$, where m is the number of items on the list preceding the box that is removed; hence \removehboxes has a running time of order n^2 as well. But the constant b is so small that for practical purposes it's possible to think of \lastbox as almost instantaneous. Note, however, that it would be a mistake to bypass the \removehboxes operation by saying '\setbox0=\hbox{\unhbox2\unhbox0}' in \makehboxofhboxes; that would make the top-level list inside \box0 too long for efficient unboxing.

8. Communication with output routines. It would be possible to write an entire book about TeX output routines; but the present appendix is already too long, so it will suffice to mention only one or two sneaky tricks that a person might not readily think of. (Appendix E gives some less sneaky examples.)

Sometimes an output routine needs to know why it was invoked, so there's a problem of communicating information from the rest of the program. TeX provides general \mark operations, but marks don't always yield the right sorts of clues. Then there's \outputpenalty, which can be tested to see what penalty occurred at a breakpoint; any penalty of -10000, -10001, -10002, or less, forces the output routine to act, hence different penalty values can be used to pass different messages. (When the output routine puts material back on the list of contributions, it need not restore the penalty at the breakpoint.) If output has been forced by a highly negative value of \outputpenalty, the output routine can use \vbox{\unvcopy255} to discover how full the page-so-far actually is. Underfull and overfull boxes are not reported when \box255 is packaged for use by the output routine, so there's no harm in ejecting a page prematurely if you want to pass a signal. (Set \holdinginserts positive to pass a signal when the contents of \box255 will be sent back through the page builder again, if any insertions are present.)

Perhaps the dirtiest trick of all is to communicate with the output routine via the *depth* of \box255. For example, suppose that you want to know whether or not the current page ends with the last line of a paragraph. If each paragraph ends with '\specialstrut', where \specialstrut is like \strut but 1 sp deeper, then \dp255 will have a recognizable value if a page ends simultaneously with a paragraph. (Of course, \maxdepth must be suitably large; plain TeX takes \maxdepth=4pt, while struts are normally 3.5 pt deep, so there's no problem.) A distance of 1000 sp is invisible to the naked eye, so a variety of messages can be passed in this way.

If the value of \vsize is very small, TeX will construct paragraphs as usual but it will send them to the output routine one line at a time. In this way the output routine could attach marginal notes, etc., based on what occurs in the line. Paragraphs that have been rebuilt in this way can also be sent back from the output routine to the page builder; normal page breaks will then be found, if \vsize has been restored.

An output routine can also write notes on a file, based on what occurs in a manuscript. A two-pass system can be devised where TeX simply gathers information during the first pass; the actual typesetting can be done during the second pass, using \read to recover information that was written during the first.

9. Syntax checking. Suppose you want to run a manuscript through TEX just to check for errors, without getting any output. Is there a way to make TEX run significantly faster while doing this? Yes; here's how: (1) Say '\font\dummy=dummy'; your system should include a file dummy.tfm that defines a font with no characters (but with enough \fontdimen parameters to qualify as a math symbol font). (2) Set all the font identifiers you are using equal to \dummy. For example, \let\tenrm=\dummy, \let\tenbf=\dummy, ..., \textfont0=\dummy, etc. (3) Say '\dummy' to select the dummy font (since plain TEX may have selected the real \tenrm). (4) Set \tracinglostchars=0, so that TEX won't complain when characters aren't present in the dummy font. (5) Set

$$\text{\textbackslash output=\{\textbackslash setbox0=\textbackslash box255\textbackslash deadcycles=0\}}$$

so that nothing will be shipped out, yet TEX will not think that your output routine is flaky. (6) Say \newtoks\output, so that no other output routine will be defined. (7) Say \frenchspacing so that TEX will not have to do space factor calculations. (8) Say \hbadness=10000 so that underfull boxes will not be reported. (9) And if you want to disable \write commands, use the following trick due to Frank Yellin:

$$\text{\textbackslash let\textbackslash immediate=\textbackslash relax \ \textbackslash def\textbackslash write\#1\#\{\{\textbackslash afterassignment\}\textbackslash toks0=\}}$$

These changes usually make TEX run more than four times as fast.

Wolfe, who had moved around the desk and into his chair,
put up a palm at him: "Please, Mr. Hombert.
I think it is always advisable to take a short-cut when it is feasible."
— REX STOUT, *The Rubber Band* (1936)

"My dear Watson, try a little analysis yourself,"
said he, with a touch of impatience.
"You know my methods. Apply them,
and it will be instructive to compare results."
— CONAN DOYLE, *The Sign of the Four* (1890)

E

Example Formats

Although the plain TEX format of Appendix B is oriented to technical reports, it can readily be adapted to quite different applications. Examples of three such adaptations are provided in this appendix: (1) a format for business letters; (2) a format for concert programs; (3) the format used to typeset this book.

Let's consider business letters first. Suppose that you want TEX to format your correspondence, and that you have n letters to send. If your computer system contains a file `letterformat.tex` like the one described later in this appendix, it's easy to do the job by applying TEX to a file that looks like this:

⟨optional magnification⟩
`\input letterformat`
⟨business letter$_1$⟩
   ⋮
⟨business letter$_n$⟩
`\end`

Here each of the n business letters has the form

⟨letterhead⟩
`\address`
⟨one or more lines of address⟩
`\body`
⟨one or more paragraphs of text⟩
`\closing`
⟨one or more lines for salutation and signature⟩
⟨optional annotations⟩
⟨optional postscripts⟩
`\endletter`
`\makelabel` % omit this if you don't want an address label

The ⟨letterhead⟩ at the beginning of this construction is usually a control sequence like `\rjdletterhead` for letters by R. J. D.; each letter writer can have a personalized letterhead that is stored with the `letterformat` macros. The ⟨optional annotations⟩ at the end are any number of one-line notes preceded by '`\annotations`'; the ⟨optional postscripts⟩ are any number of paragraphs preceded by '`\ps`'. When TEX is processing the `\address` and the `\closing` and the optional `\annotations`, it produces output line-for-line just as the lines appear in the input file; but when TEX is processing the `\body` of the letter and the optional `\ps`, it chooses line breaks and justifies lines as it normally does when typesetting paragraphs in books.

A complete example, together with the resulting output, appears on the next two pages. This example starts with '`\magnification=\magstep1`' because the letter is rather short. Magnification is usually omitted if the letters are long-winded; '`\magnification=\magstephalf`' is appropriate when they are medium-size. The same magnification applies to all n letters, so you must run TEX more than once if you want more than one magnification.

```
\magnification=\magstep1
\input letterformat

\rjdletterhead % (see the output on the next page)

\address
Prof.~Brian~K. Reid
Department of Electrical Engineering
Stanford University
Stanford, CA 94305

\body
Dear Prof.~Reid:

I understand that you are having difficulties with
Alka-Seltzer tablets.  Since there are 25~pills
per bottle, while the manufacturer's directions
recommend ''plop,~plop, fizz,~fizz,'' my colleagues
tell me that you have accumulated a substantial
number of bottles in which there is one tablet
left. % (See the 1978 SCRIBE User Manual, page 90.)

At present I am engaged in research on the potential
applications of isolated analgesics. If you would
be so kind as to donate your Alka-Seltzer collection
to our project, I would be more than happy to send
you preprints of any progress reports that we may
publish concerning this critical problem.

\closing
Sincerely,
R. J. Drofnats
Professor

\annotations
RJD/dek
cc: {\sl The \TeX book}

\ps
P. S. \ If you like, I will check into the
possibility that your donation and the meals that
you have been eating might be tax-deductible, in
connection with our research.
\endletter
\makelabel
```

⟨⟨⟨⟩ The University of St. Anford   BOX 1009
HAGA ALTO, CA 94321

R. J. DROFNATS, F.T.U.G.
PROFESSOR OF FARM ECOLOGY
TEX.RJD @ SU-SCORE.ARPA
[415] 497-4975

November 19, 1982

Prof. Brian K. Reid
Department of Electrical Engineering
Stanford University
Stanford, CA 94305

Dear Prof. Reid:

I understand that you are having difficulties with Alka-Seltzer tablets. Since there are 25 pills per bottle, while the manufacturer's directions recommend "plop, plop, fizz, fizz," my colleagues tell me that you have accumulated a substantial number of bottles in which there is one tablet left.

At present I am engaged in research on the potential applications of isolated analgesics. If you would be so kind as to donate your Alka-Seltzer collection to our project, I would be more than happy to send you preprints of any progress reports that we may publish concerning this critical problem.

Sincerely,

R. J. Drofnats
Professor

RJD/dek
cc: *The TEXbook*

P. S. If you like, I will check into the possibility that your donation and the meals that you have been eating might be tax-deductible, in connection with our research.

R. J. Drofnats, Dept. of Farm Ecology
The University of St. Anford
P. O. Box 1009, Haga Alto, CA 94321 USA

ABC
METAFONT
XYZ
USA 20c

Prof. Brian K. Reid
Department of Electrical Engineering
Stanford University
Stanford, CA 94305

If the letter is more than one page long, the addressee, date, and page number will appear at the top of subsequent pages. For example, the previous letter comes out as follows, if additional paragraphs are added to the text:

The macro package `letterformat.tex` that produces this format begins with a simple macro that expands to the current date.

```
\def\today{\ifcase\month\or
  January\or February\or March\or April\or May\or June\or
  July\or August\or September\or October\or November\or December\fi
  \space\number\day, \number\year}
```

Then comes the specification of page layout, which is "ragged" at the bottom. A rather large `\interlinepenalty` is used so that page breaks will tend to occur between paragraphs.

```
\raggedbottom
\interlinepenalty=1000
\hsize=6.25truein
\voffset=24pt
\advance\vsize by-\voffset
\parindent=0pt
\parskip=0pt
\nopagenumbers
\headline={\ifnum\pageno>1
  \tenrm To \addressee\hfil\today\hfil Page \folio
  \else\hfil\fi}
```

The contents of a letter are typeset either in "line mode" (obeying lines) or in "paragraph mode" (producing paragraphs in block style). Control sequences \beginlinemode and \beginparmode are defined to initiate these modes; and another control sequence, \endmode, is defined and redefined so that the current mode will terminate properly:

```
\def\beginlinemode{\endmode
  \begingroup\obeylines\def\endmode{\par\endgroup}}
\def\beginparmode{\endmode
  \begingroup\parskip=\medskipamount \def\endmode{\par\endgroup}}
\let\endmode=\par
\def\endletter{\endmode\vfill\supereject}
```

One of the chief characteristics of this particular business letter format is a parameter called \longindentation, which is used to indent the closing material, the date, and certain aspects of the letterhead. The \address macro creates a box that will be used both in the letter and in the label on the envelope. If individual lines of the address exceed \longindentation, they are broken, and hanging indentation is used for any material that must be carried over.

```
\newdimen\longindentation \longindentation=4truein
\newbox\theaddress
\def\address{\beginlinemode\getaddress}
{\obeylines\gdef\getaddress #1
  #2
  {#1\gdef\addressee{#2}%
    \global\setbox\theaddress=\vbox\bgroup\raggedright%
    \hsize=\longindentation \everypar{\hangindent2em}#2
    \def\endmode{\egroup\endgroup \copy\theaddress \bigskip}}}
```

(Parameter #2 to \getaddress will be the contents of the line following \address, i.e., the name of the addressee.)

The closing macros are careful not to allow a page break anywhere between the end of the \body and the beginning of a \ps.

```
\def\body{\beginparmode}
\def\closing{\beginlinemode\getclosing}
{\obeylines\gdef\getclosing #1
  #2
  {#1\nobreak\bigskip \leftskip=\longindentation #2
    \nobreak\bigskip\bigskip\bigskip % space for signature
    \def
    {\endgraf\nobreak}}}
\def\annotations{\beginlinemode\def\par{\endgraf\nobreak}\obeylines\par}
\def\ps{\beginparmode\nobreak
  \interlinepenalty5000\def\par{\endgraf\penalty5000}}
```

The remaining portion of letterformat.tex deals with letterheads and labels, which of course will be different for different organizations. The following macros were used to generate the examples in this appendix; they can be modified in more-or-less obvious ways to produce suitable letterheads of other kinds. Special fonts are generally needed, and they should be loaded at 'true' sizes so that they are not affected by magnification. One tiny refinement worth noting here is the \up macro, which raises brackets so that they look better in a telephone number.

```
\def\up#1{\leavevmode \raise.16ex\hbox{#1}}
\font\smallheadfont=cmr8 at 8truept
\font\largeheadfont=cmdunh10 at 14.4truept
\font\logofont=manfnt at 14.4truept

\def\rjdletterhead{
  \def\sendingaddress{R. J. DROFNATS, F.T.U.G.\par
    PROFESSOR OF FARM ECOLOGY\par
    TEX.RJD @ SU-SCORE.ARPA\par
    \up[415\up]\thinspace 497-4975\par}
  \def\returnaddress{R. J. Drofnats, Dept.~of Farm Ecology\par
    The University of St.~Anford\par
    P. O. Box 1009, Haga Alto, CA 94321 USA}
  \letterhead}

\def\letterhead{\pageno=1 \def\addressee{} \univletterhead
  {\leftskip=\longindentation
    {\baselineskip9truept\smallheadfont\sendingaddress}
    \bigskip\bigskip\rm\today\bigskip}}

\def\univletterhead{\vglue-\voffset
  \hbox{\hbox to\longindentation{\raise4truemm\hbox{\logofont
        \kern2truept X\kern-1.667truept
        \lower2truept\hbox{X}\kern-1.667truept X}\hfil
      \largeheadfont The University of St.~Anford\hfil}%
    \kern-\longindentation
    \vbox{\smallheadfont\baselineskip9truept
      \leftskip=\longindentation BOX 1009\par HAGA ALTO, CA 94321}}
  \vskip2truept\hrule\vskip4truept }

\def\makelabel{\endletter\hbox{\vrule
    \vbox{\hrule \kern6truept
      \hbox{\kern6truept\vbox to 2truein{\hsize=\longindentation
          \smallheadfont\baselineskip9truept\returnaddress
          \vfill\moveright 2truein\copy\theaddress\vfill}%
        \kern6truept}\kern6truept\hrule}\vrule}
  \pageno=0\vfill\eject}
```

Our second example is a format for concert programs, to be used in connection with orchestra performances, recitals, and the like. We shall assume that the entire program fits on a single page, and that the copy is to be 4 inches wide. Comparatively large type (12 pt) will normally be used, but there is a provision for 10 pt and even 8 pt type in case the program includes pieces with a lot of subparts (e.g., Bach's Mass in B minor, or Beethoven's Diabelli Variations). To select the type size, a user says \bigtype, \medtype, or \smalltype, respectively. These macros for size switching are comparatively simple because concert programs don't require any mathematics; hence the math fonts don't need to be changed. On the other hand, the format does take sharp and flat signs from the "math italic" font, which it calls '\mus':

```
\font\twelverm=cmr12
\font\twelvebf=cmbx12
\font\twelveit=cmti12
\font\twelvesl=cmsl12
\font\twelvemus=cmmi12

\font\eightrm=cmr8
\font\eightbf=cmbx8
\font\eightit=cmti8
\font\eightsl=cmsl8
\font\eightmus=cmmi8
\def\bigtype{\let\rm=\twelverm \let\bf=\twelvebf
  \let\it=\twelveit \let\sl=\twelvesl \let\mus=\twelvemus
  \baselineskip=14pt minus 1pt
  \rm}
\def\medtype{\let\rm=\tenrm \let\bf=\tenbf
  \let\it=\tenit \let\sl=\tensl \let\mus=\teni
  \baselineskip=12pt minus 1pt
  \rm}
\def\smalltype{\let\rm=\eightrm \let\bf=\eightbf
  \let\it=\eightit \let\sl=\eightsl \let\mus=\eightmus
  \baselineskip=9.5pt minus .75pt,
  \rm}
\hsize=4in
\nopagenumbers
\bigtype
```

Notice the shrinkability in the `\baselineskip` settings. This would be undesirable in a book format, because different spacing between lines on different pages would look bad; but in a one-page document it helps squeeze the copy to fit the page, in an emergency. (There's no need for stretchability in the baselineskip here, because a `\vfill` will be used at the bottom of the page.)

Musical programs have a specialized vocabulary, and it is desirable to define a few control sequences for things that plain TeX doesn't make as convenient as they could be for this particular application:

```
\def\(#1){{\rm(}#1\/{\rm)}}
\def\sharp{\raise.4ex\hbox{\mus\char"5D}}
\def\flat{\raise.2ex\hbox{\mus\char"5B}}
\let\,=\thinspace
```

The `\(` macro produces roman parentheses in the midst of italicized text; the `\sharp` and `\flat` macros produce musical signs in the current type size. The `\,` macro makes it easy to specify the thin space that is used in constructions like 'K. 550' and 'Op. 59'. (Plain TeX has already defined `\,` and `\sharp` and `\flat` in a different way; but those definitions apply only to math formulas, so they aren't relevant in this application.)

Before discussing the rest of the music macros, let's take a look at a complete example. The next two pages show the input and output for a typical concert program.

```
\input concert

\tsaologo
\medskip
\centerline{Friday, November 19, 1982, 8:00 p.m.}
\bigskip
\centerline{\bf PROGRAM}
\medskip

\composition{Variations on a Theme by Tchaikovsky}
\composer{Anton S. Arensky (1861--1906)}
\smallskip
{\medtype
\movements{Tema: Moderato\cr
  Var.~I: Un poco pi\`u mosso&Var.~V: Andante\cr
  Var.~II: Allegro non troppo&Var.~VI: Allegro con spirito\cr
  Var.~III: Andantino tranquillo&Var.~VII: Andante con moto\cr
  Var.~IV: Vivace&Coda: Moderato\cr}
}

\bigskip

\composition{Concerto for Horn and Hardart, S.\,27}
\composer{P. D. Q. Bach (1807--1742)?}
\smallskip
\movements{Allegro con brillo\cr
  Tema con variazione \(su una tema differente)\cr
  Menuetto con panna e zucchero\cr}
\medskip
\soloists{Ben Lee User, horn\cr
  Peter Schickele, hardart\cr}

\bigskip
\centerline{INTERMISSION}
\bigskip

\composition{Symphony No.\,3 in E\flat\ Major\cr
  Op.\,55, ``The Eroica''\cr}
\composer{Ludwig van Beethoven (1770--1827)}
\smallskip
\movements{Allegro con brio\cr
  Marcia funebre: Adagio assai\cr
  Scherzo: Allegro vivace\cr
  Finale: Allegro molto\cr}

\bigskip
\smalltype \noindent
Members of the audience are kindly requested to turn off the
alarms on their digital watches, and to cough only between movements.

\bye
```

THE ST. ANFORD ORCHESTRA
R. J. Drofnats, Conductor

Friday, November 19, 1982, 8:00 p.m.

PROGRAM

Variations on a Theme by Tchaikovsky
Anton S. Arensky (1861–1906)

Tema: Moderato
Var. I: Un poco più mosso   *Var. V: Andante*
Var. II: Allegro non troppo   *Var. VI: Allegro con spirito*
Var. III: Andantino tranquillo   *Var. VII: Andante con moto*
Var. IV: Vivace   *Coda: Moderato*

Concerto for Horn and Hardart, S. 27
P. D. Q. Bach (1807–1742)?

Allegro con brillo
Tema con variazione (su una tema differente)
Menuetto con panna e zucchero

Ben Lee User, horn
Peter Schickele, hardart

INTERMISSION

Symphony No. 3 in E♭ Major
Op. 55, "The Eroica"
Ludwig van Beethoven (1770–1827)

Allegro con brio
Marcia funebre: Adagio assai
Scherzo: Allegro vivace
Finale: Allegro molto

Members of the audience are kindly requested to turn off the alarms on their digital watches, and to cough only between movements.

Most of the macros in `concert.tex` have already been defined. Plain TeX takes care of things like `\centerline` and `\bigskip`, so only `\composition`, `\composer`, `\movements`, and `\soloists` remain to be specified:

```
\def\composition#1{\halign{\bf\quad##\hfil\cr
        \kern-1em#1\crcr}} % use \cr's if more than one line
\def\composer#1{\rightline{\bf#1}}
\def\movements#1{\halign{\quad\it##\hfil&&\qquad\it##\hfil\cr#1\crcr}}
\def\soloists#1{\centerline{\bf\vbox{\halign{##\hfil\cr#1\crcr}}}}
```

The `\composition` macro is set up to put the title of the composition on two or more lines, if needed, but a single line usually suffices. Notice that `\crcr` has been used so that the final `\cr` in the argument to `\composition` is not needed. Similarly, `\movements` might be used to produce only a single line, and `\soloists` might be used when there is only one soloist.

There's also a `\tsaologo` macro. It applies only to one particular orchestra, but the definition is somewhat interesting nonetheless:

```
\def\tsaologo{\vbox{\bigtype\bf
        \line{\hrulefill}
        \kern-.5\baselineskip
        \line{\hrulefill\phantom{ THE ST.\,ANFORD ORCHESTRA }\hrulefill}
        \kern-.5\baselineskip
        \line{\hrulefill\hbox{ THE ST.\,ANFORD ORCHESTRA }\hrulefill}
        \kern-.5\baselineskip
        \line{\hrulefill\phantom{ R. J. Drofnats, Conductor }\hrulefill}
        \kern-.5\baselineskip
        \line{\hrulefill\hbox{ R. J. Drofnats, Conductor }\hrulefill}
        }}
```

The author has extended these macros to a more elaborate format that includes special features for listing the members of the orchestra and for program notes, etc.; in this way it becomes fairly easy to typeset little booklets for concert patrons. Such extensions need not be discussed further in this appendix, because they don't illustrate any essentially new ideas.

Notice that the `\composition` and `\movements` and `\soloists` macros do not include any special provision for vertical spacing; the user is supposed to insert `\smallskip`, `\medskip`, and `\bigskip` as desired. This was done deliberately, because different concert programs seem to demand different spacing; no automatic scheme actually works very well in practice, since musical literature is so varied.

Let's turn now to the design of a format for an entire book, using this book itself as an example. How did the author prepare the computer file that generated *The TeXbook*? We have already seen several hundred pages of output produced from that file; our goal in the remainder of this appendix will be to examine the input that was used behind the scenes.

In the first place, the author prepared sample pages and showed them to the publisher's book designer. (The importance of this step cannot be overemphasized. There is a danger that authors—who are now able to typeset their own books with TeX—will attempt to do their own designs, without professional help. Book design is an art that requires considerable creativity, skill, experience, and taste; it is one of the most important services that a publisher traditionally provides to an author.)

Sample pages that are used as the basis of a design should show each of the elements in the book. In this case the elements included chapter titles, illustrations, subchapter headings, footnotes, displayed formulas, typewriter type, dangerous bends, exercises, answers, quotations, tables, numbered lists, bulleted lists, etc.; the author also expressed a desire for generous margins, so that readers could make marginal notes.

The designer, Herb Caswell, faced a difficult problem of bringing all those disparate elements into a consistent framework. He decided to achieve this by using a uniform indentation of 3 picas for normal paragraph openings as well as for dangerous bends; and to establish this element of the design by using it also for all the displayed material, instead of centering the displays.

He decided to put the page numbers in bold type, out in the margins (where there was plenty of room, thanks to the author's request for white space); and he decided to use italic type with caps and lower case for the running headlines, so that the pages would have a somewhat informal flavor.

He chose 10-point type (on a 12-point base) for the main text, and 9-point type (on an 11-point base) for the dangerous bends; the typeface was predetermined. He chose an \hsize of 29 picas and a \vsize of 44 picas. He decided to give subheadings like '▶**EXERCISE 13.8**' in boldface caps before the statement of each exercise. He specified the amount of vertical space before and after such things as exercises, dangerous-bend paragraphs, and displayed equations. He decided to devote an entire left-hand page to each chapter illustration. And so on; each decision influenced the others, so that the final book would appear to be as coherent and attractive as possible under the circumstances. After the main portion of the book was designed, he worked out a format for the front matter (i.e., the pages that precede page 1); he arranged to have the same amount of "sinkage" (white space) at the top of each page there, so that the opening pages of the book would look unified and "open."

The author hasn't actually followed the designer's specifications in every detail. For example, nothing about stretching or shrinking of vertical spaces appeared in the design specs; the author introduced the notion of flexible glue on his own initiative, based on his observations of cut-and-paste operations often used in page makeup. If this book has any beauties, they should be ascribed to Herb Caswell; if it has any blemishes, they should be ascribed to Don Knuth, who wrote the formatting macros that we are now about to discuss.

The computer file `manual.tex` that generated *The TEXbook* begins with a copyright notice, and then it says '\input manmac'. The auxiliary file `manmac.tex` contains the formatting macros, and it begins by loading 9-point, 8-point, and 6-point fonts:

```
\font\ninerm=cmr9    \font\eightrm=cmr8    \font\sixrm=cmr6
\font\ninei=cmmi9    \font\eighti=cmmi8    \font\sixi=cmmi6
\font\ninesy=cmsy9   \font\eightsy=cmsy8   \font\sixsy=cmsy6
\font\ninebf=cmbx9   \font\eightbf=cmbx8   \font\sixbf=cmbx6
\font\ninett=cmtt9   \font\eighttt=cmtt8
\font\nineit=cmti9   \font\eightit=cmti8
\font\ninesl=cmsl9   \font\eightsl=cmsl8
```

(These fonts had been \preloaded in Appendix B; now they're officially loaded.)

The fonts intended for math formulas need to have a nonstandard `\skewchar`. The typewriter fonts are given `\hyphenchar=-1` so that hyphenation is inhibited when control sequence names and keywords appear in the text of a paragraph.

```
\skewchar\ninei='177  \skewchar\eighti='177  \skewchar\sixi='177
\skewchar\ninesy='60  \skewchar\eightsy='60  \skewchar\sixsy='60
\hyphenchar\ninett=-1 \hyphenchar\eighttt=-1 \hyphenchar\tentt=-1
```

A few more fonts are needed for special purposes:

```
\font\tentex=cmtex10               % TeX character set as in Appendix C
\font\inchhigh=cminch              % inch-high caps for chapter openings
\font\titlefont=cmssdc10 at 40pt   % titles in chapter openings
\font\eightss=cmssq8               % quotations in chapter closings
\font\eightssi=cmssqi8             % ditto, slanted
\font\tenu=cmu10                   % unslanted text italic
\font\manual=manfnt                % METAFONT logo and special symbols
\font\magnifiedfiverm=cmr5 at 10pt % to demonstrate magnification
```

Now we come to the size-switching macros, which are much more elaborate than they were in the previous example because mathematics needs to be supported in three different sizes. The format also provides for a pseudo "small caps" (`\sc`); a true caps-and-small-caps font was not really necessary in the few cases that `\sc` was used. A dimension variable `\ttglue` is set equal to the desired spacing for the typewriter-like text that occasionally appears in paragraphs; the `\tt` fonts have fixed spacing, which doesn't mix well with variable spacing, hence the macros below use `\ttglue` between words in appropriate places.

```
\catcode`\@=11 % we will access private macros of plain TeX (carefully)
\newskip\ttglue
\def\tenpoint{\def\rm{\fam0\tenrm}% switch to 10-point type
  \textfont0=\tenrm \scriptfont0=\sevenrm \scriptscriptfont0=\fiverm
  \textfont1=\teni  \scriptfont1=\seveni  \scriptscriptfont1=\fivei
  \textfont2=\tensy \scriptfont2=\sevensy \scriptscriptfont2=\fivesy
  \textfont3=\tenex \scriptfont3=\tenex   \scriptscriptfont3=\tenex
  \textfont\itfam=\tenit  \def\it{\fam\itfam\tenit}%
  \textfont\slfam=\tensl  \def\sl{\fam\slfam\tensl}%
  \textfont\ttfam=\tentt  \def\tt{\fam\ttfam\tentt}%
  \textfont\bffam=\tenbf  \scriptfont\bffam=\sevenbf
   \scriptscriptfont\bffam=\fivebf  \def\bf{\fam\bffam\tenbf}%
  \tt \ttglue=.5em plus.25em minus.15em
  \normalbaselineskip=12pt
  \setbox\strutbox=\hbox{\vrule height8.5pt depth3.5pt width0pt}%
  \let\sc=\eightrm  \let\big=\tenbig  \normalbaselines\rm}
\def\ninepoint{\def\rm{\fam0\ninerm}% switch to 9-point type
  \textfont0=\ninerm \scriptfont0=\sixrm \scriptscriptfont0=\fiverm
  \textfont1=\ninei  \scriptfont1=\sixi  \scriptscriptfont1=\fivei
  \textfont2=\ninesy \scriptfont2=\sixsy \scriptscriptfont2=\fivesy
  \textfont3=\tenex  \scriptfont3=\tenex \scriptscriptfont3=\tenex
  \textfont\itfam=\nineit  \def\it{\fam\itfam\nineit}%
```

mar-
ginal
hacks

```
    \textfont\slfam=\ninesl  \def\sl{\fam\slfam\ninesl}%
    \textfont\ttfam=\ninett  \def\tt{\fam\ttfam\ninett}%
    \textfont\bffam=\ninebf  \scriptfont\bffam=\sixbf
     \scriptscriptfont\bffam=\fivebf  \def\bf{\fam\bffam\ninebf}%
    \tt \ttglue=.5em plus.25em minus.15em
    \normalbaselineskip=11pt
    \setbox\strutbox=\hbox{\vrule height8pt depth3pt width0pt}%
    \let\sc=\sevenrm  \let\big=\ninebig  \normalbaselines\rm}
\def\eightpoint{\def\rm{\fam0\eightrm}% switch to 8-point type
    \textfont0=\eightrm \scriptfont0=\sixrm \scriptscriptfont0=\fiverm
    \textfont1=\eighti  \scriptfont1=\sixi  \scriptscriptfont1=\fivei
    \textfont2=\eightsy \scriptfont2=\sixsy \scriptscriptfont2=\fivesy
    \textfont3=\tenex   \scriptfont3=\tenex \scriptscriptfont3=\tenex
    \textfont\itfam=\eightit  \def\it{\fam\itfam\eightit}%
    \textfont\slfam=\eightsl  \def\sl{\fam\slfam\eightsl}%
    \textfont\ttfam=\eighttt  \def\tt{\fam\ttfam\eighttt}%
    \textfont\bffam=\eightbf  \scriptfont\bffam=\sixbf
     \scriptscriptfont\bffam=\fivebf  \def\bf{\fam\bffam\eightbf}%
    \tt \ttglue=.5em plus.25em minus.15em
    \normalbaselineskip=9pt
    \setbox\strutbox=\hbox{\vrule height7pt depth2pt width0pt}%
    \let\sc=\sixrm  \let\big=\eightbig  \normalbaselines\rm}
\def\tenbig#1{{\hbox{$\left#1\vbox to8.5pt{}\right.\n@space$}}}
\def\ninebig#1{{\hbox{$\textfont0=\tenrm\textfont2=\tensy
    \left#1\vbox to7.25pt{}\right.\n@space$}}}
\def\eightbig#1{{\hbox{$\textfont0=\ninerm\textfont2=\ninesy
    \left#1\vbox to6.5pt{}\right.\n@space$}}}
\def\tenmath{\tenpoint\fam-1 } % for 10-point math in 9-point territory
```

Issues of page layout are dealt with next. First, the basics:

```
\newdimen\pagewidth \newdimen\pageheight \newdimen\ruleht
\hsize=29pc  \vsize=44pc  \maxdepth=2.2pt  \parindent=3pc
\pagewidth=\hsize \pageheight=\vsize \ruleht=.5pt
\abovedisplayskip=6pt plus 3pt minus 1pt
\belowdisplayskip=6pt plus 3pt minus 1pt
\abovedisplayshortskip=0pt plus 3pt
\belowdisplayshortskip=4pt plus 3pt
```

(The curious value of `\maxdepth` was chosen only to provide an example in Chapter 15; there's no deep reason behind it.)

When the author prepared this book, he made notes about what things ought to go into the index from each page. These notes were shown in small type on his proofsheets, like the words 'marginal hacks' in the right margin of this page. The `manmac` format uses an insertion class called `\margin` to handle such notes.

```
\newinsert\margin
\dimen\margin=\maxdimen % no limit on the number of marginal notes
\count\margin=0 \skip\margin=0pt % marginal inserts take up no space
```

The \footnote macro of plain TeX needs to be changed because footnotes are indented and set in 8-point type. Some simplifications have also been made, since footnotes are used so infrequently in this book.

```
\def\footnote#1{\edef\@sf{\spacefactor\the\spacefactor}#1\@sf
      \insert\footins\bgroup\eightpoint
      \interlinepenalty100 \let\par=\endgraf
        \leftskip=0pt \rightskip=0pt
        \splittopskip=10pt plus 1pt minus 1pt \floatingpenalty=20000
        \smallskip\item{#1}\bgroup\strut\aftergroup\@foot\let\next}
\skip\footins=12pt plus 2pt minus 4pt % space added when footnote exists
\dimen\footins=30pc % maximum footnotes per page
```

The text of running headlines will be kept in a control sequence called \rhead. Some pages should not have headlines; the \titlepage macro suppresses the headline on the next page that is output.

```
\newif\iftitle
\def\titlepage{\global\titletrue} % for pages without headlines
\def\rhead{} % \rhead contains the running headline

\def\leftheadline{\hbox to \pagewidth{%
    \vbox to 10pt{}% strut to position the baseline
    \llap{\tenbf\folio\kern1pc}% folio to left of text
    \tenit\rhead\hfil}} % running head flush left
\def\rightheadline{\hbox to \pagewidth{\vbox to 10pt{}%
    \hfil\tenit\rhead\/% running head flush right
    \rlap{\kern1pc\tenbf\folio}}} % folio to right of text
```

Pages are shipped to the output by the \onepageout macro, which attaches headlines, marginal notes, and/or footnotes, as appropriate. Special registration marks are typeset at the top of title pages, so that the pages will line up properly on printing plates that are made photographically from TeX's "camera-ready" output. A small page number is also printed next to the corner markings; such auxiliary information will, of course, be erased before the pages are actually printed.

```
\def\onepageout#1{\shipout\vbox{ % here we define one page of output
    \offinterlineskip % butt the boxes together
    \vbox to 3pc{ % this part goes on top of the 44pc pages
      \iftitle \global\titlefalse \setcornerrules
      \else\ifodd\pageno\rightheadline\else\leftheadline\fi\fi \vfill}
    \vbox to \pageheight{
      \ifvoid\margin\else % marginal info is present
      \rlap{\kern31pc\vbox to0pt{\kern4pt\box\margin \vss}}\fi
      #1 % now insert the main information
      \ifvoid\footins\else % footnote info is present
      \vskip\skip\footins \kern-3pt
      \hrule height\ruleht width\pagewidth \kern-\ruleht \kern3pt
      \unvbox\footins\fi
      \boxmaxdepth=\maxdepth}}
  \advancepageno}
```

```
\def\setcornerrules{\hbox to \pagewidth{% for camera alignment
    \vrule width 1pc height\ruleht \hfil \vrule width 1pc}
  \hbox to \pagewidth{\llap{\sevenrm(page \folio)\kern1pc}%
    \vrule height1pc width\ruleht depth0pt
    \hfil \vrule width\ruleht depth0pt}}
\output{\onepageout{\unvbox255}}
```

A different output routine is needed for Appendix I (the index), because most of that appendix appears in two-column format. Instead of handling double columns with an '\lr' switch, as discussed in Chapter 23, manmac does the job with \vsplit, after collecting more than enough material to fill a page. This approach makes it comparatively easy to balance the columns on the last page of the index. A more difficult approach would be necessary if the index contained insertions (e.g., footnotes); fortunately, it doesn't. Furthermore, there is no need to use \mark as suggested in the index example of Chapter 23, since the entries in Appendix I tend to be quite short. The only real complication that manmac faces is the fact that Appendix I begins and ends with single-column format; partial pages need to be juggled carefully as the format changes back and forth.

```
\newbox\partialpage
\def\begindoublecolumns{\begingroup
  \output={\global\setbox\partialpage=\vbox{\unvbox255\bigskip}}\eject
  \output={\doublecolumnout} \hsize=14pc \vsize=89pc}
\def\enddoublecolumns{\output={\balancecolumns}\eject
  \endgroup \pagegoal=\vsize}
\def\doublecolumnout{\splittopskip=\topskip \splitmaxdepth=\maxdepth
  \dimen@=44pc \advance\dimen@ by-\ht\partialpage
  \setbox0=\vsplit255 to\dimen@ \setbox2=\vsplit255 to\dimen@
  \onepageout\pagesofar \unvbox255 \penalty\outputpenalty}
\def\pagesofar{\unvbox\partialpage
  \wd0=\hsize \wd2=\hsize \hbox to\pagewidth{\box0\hfil\box2}}
\def\balancecolumns{\setbox0=\vbox{\unvbox255} \dimen@=\ht0
  \advance\dimen@ by\topskip \advance\dimen@ by-\baselineskip
  \divide\dimen@ by2 \splittopskip=\topskip
  {\vbadness=10000 \loop \global\setbox3=\copy0
    \global\setbox1=\vsplit3 to\dimen@
    \ifdim\ht3>\dimen@ \global\advance\dimen@ by1pt \repeat}
  \setbox0=\vbox to\dimen@{\unvbox1} \setbox2=\vbox to\dimen@{\unvbox3}
  \pagesofar}
```

The balancing act sets \vbadness infinite while it is searching for a suitable column height, so that underfull vboxes won't be reported unless the actual columns are bad after balancing. The columns in Appendix I have a lot of stretchability, since there's a \parskip of 0pt plus .8pt between adjacent entries, and since there is room for more than 50 lines per column; therefore the manmac balancing routine tries to make both the top and bottom baselines agree at the end of the index. In applications where the glue is not so flexible it would be more appropriate to let the right-hand column be a little short; the best way to do this is probably to replace the command '\unvbox3' by '\dimen2=\dp3 \unvbox3 \kern-\dimen2 \vfil'.

The next macros are concerned with chapter formatting. Each chapter in the manuscript file starts out with the macro `\beginchapter`; it ends with `\endchapter` and two quotations, followed by `\eject`. For example, Chapter 15 was generated by TeX commands that look like this in the file `manual.tex`:

```
\beginchapter Chapter 15. How \TeX\ Makes\\Lines into Pages

\TeX\ attempts to choose desirable places to divide your document into
    ...   (about 1100 lines of the manuscript are omitted here)
break. \ (Deep breath.) \ You got that?

\endchapter

Since it is impossible to foresee how [footnotes] will happen to come out
in the make-up, it is impracticable to number them from 1 up on each page.
The best way is to number them consecutively throughout an article
or by chapters in a book.
\author UNIVERSITY OF CHICAGO PRESS, {\sl Manual of Style\/} (1910)

\bigskip

Don't use footnotes in your books, Don.
\author JILL KNUTH (1962)

\eject
```

The '`\\`' in the title line specifies a line break to be used on the left-hand title page that faces the beginning of the chapter. Most of the `\beginchapter` macro is devoted to preparing that title page; the `\TeX` logo needs somewhat different spacing when it is typeset in `\titlefont`, and the `\inchhigh` digits need to be brought closer together in order to look right in a title.

```
\newcount\exno % for the number of exercises in the current chapter
\newcount\subsecno % for the number of subsections in the current chapter
\outer\def\beginchapter#1 #2#3. #4\par{\def\chapno{#2#3}
  \global\exno=0 \subsecno=0
  \ifodd\pageno
   \errmessage{You had too much text on that last page; I'm backing up}
   \advance\pageno by-1 \fi
  \def\\{ } % \\'s in the title will be treated as spaces
  \message{#1 #2#3:} % show the chapter title on the terminal
  \xdef\rhead{#1 #2#3: #4\unskip} % establish a new running headline
  {\def\TeX{T\kern-.2em\lower.5ex\hbox{E}\kern-.06em X}
   \def\\{#3}
   \ifx\empty\\ \rightline{\inchhigh #2\kern-.04em}
   \else\rightline{\inchhigh #2\kern-.06em#3\kern-.04em}\fi
   \vskip1.75pc \baselineskip=36pt \lineskiplimit=1pt \lineskip=12pt
   \let\\=\cr % now the \\'s are line dividers
   \halign{\line{\titlefont\hfil##}\\#4\unskip\\}
   \titlepage\vfill\eject} % output the chapter title page
 \tenpoint\noindent\ignorespaces} % the first paragraph is not indented
```

An extra page is ejected at the end of a chapter, if necessary, so that the closing quotations will occur on a right-hand page. (The logic for doing this is not perfect, but it doesn't need to be, because it fails only when the chapter has to be shortened or lengthened anyway; book preparation with TeX, as with type, encourages interaction between humans and machines.) The lines of the quotations are set flush right by using `\obeylines` together with a stretchable `\leftskip`:

```
\outer\def\endchapter{\ifodd\pageno \else\vfill\eject\null\fi
  \begingroup\bigskip\vfill % beginning of the quotes
  \def\eject{\endgroup\eject} % ending of the quotes
  \def\par{\ifmmode\/\endgraf\fi}\obeylines
  \def\TeX{T\kern-.2em\lower.5ex\hbox{E}X}
  \eightpoint \let\tt=\ninett \baselineskip=10pt \interlinepenalty=10000
  \leftskip=0pt plus 40pc minus \parindent \parfillskip=0pt
  \let\rm=\eightss \let\sl=\eightssi \everypar{\sl}}
\def\author#1(#2){\smallskip\noindent\rm--- #1\unskip\enspace(#2)}
```

We come now to what goes on inside the chapters themselves. Dangerous and doubly dangerous bends are specified by typing '`\danger`' or '`\ddanger`' just before a paragraph that is supposed to display a warning symbol:

```
\def\dbend{{\manual\char127}} % "dangerous bend" sign
\def\d@nger{\medbreak\begingroup\clubpenalty=10000
  \def\par{\endgraf\endgroup\medbreak} \noindent\hang\hangafter=-2
  \hbox to0pt{\hskip-\hangindent\dbend\hfill}\ninepoint}
\outer\def\danger{\d@nger}
\def\dd@nger{\medbreak\begingroup\clubpenalty=10000
  \def\par{\endgraf\endgroup\medbreak} \noindent\hang\hangafter=-2
  \hbox to0pt{\hskip-\hangindent\dbend\kern1pt\dbend\hfill}\ninepoint}
\outer\def\ddanger{\dd@nger}
\def\enddanger{\endgraf\endgroup} % omits the \medbreak
```

(It's necessary to type '`\enddanger`' at the end of a dangerous bend only in rare cases that a medium space is not desired after the paragraph; e.g., '`\smallskip\item`' might be used to give an itemized list within the scope of the dangerous bend sign.)

A few chapters and appendices of this book (e.g., Chapter 18 and Appendix B) are divided into numbered subsections. Such subsections are specified in the manuscript by typing, for example,

```
\subsection Allocation of registers.
```

Appendix A is subdivided in another way, by paragraphs that have answer numbers:

```
\outer\def\subsection#1. {\medbreak\advance\subsecno by 1
  \noindent{\it \the\subsecno.\enspace#1.\enspace}}
\def\ansno#1.#2:{\medbreak\noindent
  \hbox to\parindent{\bf\hss#1.#2.\enspace}\ignorespaces}
```

We will see below that the manuscript doesn't actually specify an `\ansno` directly; each call of `\ansno` is generated automatically by the `\answer` macro.

Appendix H points out *The TeXbook* calls for three hyphenation exceptions:

```
\hyphenation{man-u-script man-u-scripts ap-pen-dix}
```

A few macros in `manmac` provide special constructions that are occasionally needed in paragraphs: `\MF` for 'METAFONT', `\AmSTeX` for '$\cal A_{\cal M}\cal S$-TeX', `\bull` for '■', `\dn` and `\up` for '↓' and '↑', `\|` and `\]` for '|' and '␣'. To typeset

$$3\,\mathrm{pt} \text{ of } \langle \text{stuff} \rangle,\ '105 = 69,\ ''69 = 105,\ \boxed{\text{wow}}$$

the manuscript says

```
$3\pt$ of \<stuff>, $\oct{105}=69$, $\hex{69}=105$, \cstok{wow}
```

using the macros `\pt`, `\<`, `\oct`, `\hex`, and `\cstok`.

```
\def\MF{{\manual META}\-{\manual FONT}}
\def\AmSTeX{$\cal A\kern-.1667em\lower.5ex\hbox{$\cal M$}\kern-.075em
  S$-\TeX}
\def\bull{\vrule height .9ex width .8ex depth -.1ex } % square bullet
\def\SS{{\it SS}} % scriptscript style
\def\dn{\leavevmode\hbox{\tt\char'14}} % downward arrow
\def\up{\leavevmode\hbox{\tt\char'13}} % upward arrow
\def\|{\leavevmode\hbox{\tt\char'\|}} % vertical line
\def\]{\leavevmode\hbox{\tt\char'\ }} % visible space

\def\pt{\,{\rm pt}} % units of points, in math formulas
\def\<#1>{\leavevmode\hbox{$\langle$#1\/$\rangle$}} % syntactic quantity
\def\oct#1{\hbox{\rm\'{}\kern-.2em\it#1\/\kern.05em}} % octal constant
\def\hex#1{\hbox{\rm\H{}\tt#1}} % hexadecimal constant
\def\cstok#1{\leavevmode\thinspace\hbox{\vrule\vtop{\vbox{\hrule\kern1pt
        \hbox{\vphantom{\tt/}\thinspace{\tt#1}\thinspace}}
    \kern1pt\hrule}\vrule}\thinspace} % control sequence token
```

Displays in this book are usually indented rather than centered, and they usually involve text rather than mathematics. The `manmac` format makes such displays convenient by introducing two macros called `\begindisplay` and `\enddisplay`; there's also a pair of macros `\begintt` and `\endtt` for displays that are entirely in typewriter type. The latter displays are copied verbatim from the manuscript file, without interpreting symbols like `\` or `$` in any special way. For example, part of the paragraph above was typed as follows:

```
... To typeset
\begindisplay
$3\pt$ of \<stuff>, $\oct{105}=69$, $\hex{69}=105$, \cstok{wow}
\enddisplay
the manuscript says
\begintt
$3\pt$ of \<stuff>, $\oct{105}=69$, $\hex{69}=105$, \cstok{wow}
\endtt
using the macros |\pt|, |\<|, |\oct|, |\hex|, and |\cstok|.
```

(The last line of this example illustrates the fact that verbatim typewriter text can be obtained within a paragraph by using vertical lines as brackets.) The `\begindisplay` macro is actually more general than you might expect from this example; it allows multiline displays, with \cr following each line, and it also allows local definitions (which apply only within the display) to be specified immediately after \begindisplay.

```
\outer\def\begindisplay{\obeylines\startdisplay}
{\obeylines\gdef\startdisplay#1
  {\catcode`\^^M=5$$#1\halign\bgroup\indent##\hfil&&\qquad##\hfil\cr}}
\outer\def\enddisplay{\crcr\egroup$$}

\chardef\other=12
\def\ttverbatim{\begingroup \catcode`\\=\other \catcode`\{=\other
  \catcode`\}=\other \catcode`\$=\other \catcode`\&=\other
  \catcode`\#=\other \catcode`\%=\other \catcode`\~=\other
  \catcode`\_=\other \catcode`\^=\other
  \obeyspaces \obeylines \tt}
{\obeyspaces\gdef {\ }} % \obeyspaces now gives \ , not \space

\outer\def\begintt{$$\let\par=\endgraf \ttverbatim \parskip=0pt
  \catcode`\|=0 \rightskip=-5pc \ttfinish}
{\catcode`\|=0 |catcode`|\=\other % | is temporary escape character
  |obeylines % end of line is active
  |gdef|ttfinish#1^^M#2\endtt{#1|vbox{#2}|endgroup$$}}

\catcode`\|=\active
{\obeylines\gdef|{\ttverbatim\spaceskip=\ttglue\let^^M=\ \let|=\endgroup}}
```

These macros are more subtle than the others in this appendix, and they deserve careful study because they illustrate how to disable TEX's normal formatting. The '|' character is normally active (category 13) in **manmac** format, and its appearance causes the \ttverbatim macro to make all of the other unusual characters into normal symbols (category 12). However, within the scope of \begintt...\endtt a vertical line is an escape character (category 0); this permits an escape out of verbatim mode.

The \begintt macro assumes that a comparatively small amount of text will be displayed; the verbatim lines are put into a vbox, so that they cannot be broken between pages. A different approach has been used for most of the typewriter copy in this appendix and in Appendix B: Material that is quoted from a format file is delimited by \beginlines and \endlines, between which it is possible to give commands like '\smallbreak' to help with spacing and page breaking. The \beginlines and \endlines macros also insert rules, fore and aft:

```
\def\beginlines{\par\begingroup\nobreak\medskip\parindent=0pt
  \hrule\kern1pt\nobreak \obeylines \everypar{\strut}}
\def\endlines{\kern1pt\hrule\endgroup\medbreak\noindent}
```

For example, the previous three lines were typeset by the specification

```
\beginlines
|\def\beginlines{\par\begingroup\nobreak\medskip\parindent=0pt|
\nobreak
|  \hrule\kern1pt\nobreak \obeylines \everypar{\strut}}|
|\def\endlines{\kern1pt\hrule\endgroup\medbreak\noindent}|
\endlines
```

A strut is placed in each line so that the rules will be positioned properly. The `manmac` format also has macros `\beginmathdemo...\endmathdemo` that were used to produce examples of mathematics in Chapters 16–19, `\beginsyntax...\endsyntax` for the formal syntax in Chapters 24–26, `\beginchart...\endchart` for the font tables in Appendices C and F, etc.; those macros are comparatively simple and they need not be shown here.

Exercises are specified by an `\exercise` macro; for example, the first exercise in Chapter 1 was generated by the following lines in the manuscript:

```
\exercise After you have mastered the material in this book,
what will you be: A \TeX pert, or a \TeX nician?
\answer A \TeX nician (underpaid); sometimes also called
a \TeX acker.
```

Notice that the `\answer` is given immediately after each exercise; that makes it easy to insert new exercises or to delete old ones, without keeping track of exercise numbers. Exercises that are dangerous or doubly dangerous are introduced by the macros `\dangerexercise` and `\ddangerexercise`.

```
\outer\def\exercise{\medbreak \global\advance\exno by 1
  \noindent\llap{\manual\char'170\rm\kern.15em}% triangle in margin
  {\ninebf EXERCISE \bf\chapno.\the\exno}\par\nobreak\noindent}
\def\dexercise{\global\advance\exno by 1
  \llap{\manual\char'170\rm\kern.15em}% triangle in indented space
  {\eightbf EXERCISE \bf\chapno.\the\exno}\hfil\break}
\outer\def\dangerexercise{\d@nger \dexercise}
\outer\def\ddangerexercise{\dd@nger \dexercise}
```

(The last two lines use `\d@nger` and `\dd@nger`, which are non-`\outer` equivalents of `\danger` and `\ddanger`; such duplication is necessary because control sequences of type `\outer` cannot appear within a `\def`.)

The `\answer` macro copies an answer into a file called `answers.tex`; then Appendix A reads this file by saying '`\immediate\closeout\ans \ninepoint \input answers`'. Each individual answer ends with a blank line; thus, `\par` must be used between the paragraphs of a long answer.

```
\newwrite\ans
\immediate\openout\ans=answers % file for answers to exercises
\outer\def\answer{\par\medbreak
  \immediate\write\ans{}
  \immediate\write\ans{\string\ansno\chapno.\the\exno:}
  \copytoblankline}
\def\copytoblankline{\begingroup\setupcopy\copyans}
\def\setupcopy{\def\do##1{\catcode`##1=\other}\dospecials
  \catcode`\|=\other \obeylines}
{\obeylines \gdef\copyans#1
  {\def\next{#1}%
  \ifx\next\empty\let\next=\endgroup %
  \else\immediate\write\ans{\next} \let\next=\copyans\fi\next}}
```

Notice the use of \dospecials here, to set up the verbatim copying. The \ttverbatim macro could have invoked \dospecials in the same way; but \ttverbatim is used quite frequently, so it was streamlined for speed.

The remaining macros in manmac format are designed to help in producing a good index. When a paragraph contains a word or group of words that deserve to be indexed, the manuscript indicates this by inserting ^{...}; for example, the first sentence of the present paragraph actually ends with 'a good ^{index}'. This caused an appropriate entry to be written onto a file index.tex when TeX was typesetting the page; it also put the word 'index' into the margin of the proofsheets, so that the author could remember what had been marked for indexing without looking into the manuscript file. Indexing with the ^{...} notation doesn't change TeX's behavior in any essential way; thus, the word 'index' appears in the text as well as in the index.

```
\newwrite\inx
\immediate\openout\inx=index % file for index reminders
\def\marginstyle{\sevenrm % marginal notes are in 7-point type
  \vrule height6pt depth2pt width0pt } % a strut for \insert\margin
```

Sometimes it is desirable to index words that don't actually appear on the page; the notation ^^{...} stands for a "silent" index entry, and spaces are ignored after the closing '}' in such a case. For example, Appendix I lists page 1 under 'beauty', even though page 1 contains only the word 'beautiful'; the manuscript achieves this by saying 'beautiful ^^{beauty}'. (The author felt that it was important to index 'beauty' because he had already indexed 'truth'.)

It's not difficult to make ^ into an active character that produces such index entries, while still retaining its use for superscripts in math formulas, because \ifmmode can be used to test whether a control sequence is being used in math mode. However, manmac's use of ^ as an active character means that ^^M cannot be used to refer to a ⟨return⟩ character. Fortunately the ^^M notation isn't needed except when the formatting macros themselves are being defined.

The following macros set things up so that ^ and ^^ are respectively converted to \silentfalse\xref and \silenttrue\xref, outside of math mode:

```
\newif\ifsilent
\def\specialhat{\ifmmode\def\next{^}\else\let\next=\beginxref\fi\next}
\def\beginxref{\futurelet\next\beginxrefswitch}
\def\beginxrefswitch{\ifx\next\specialhat\let\next=\silentxref
  \else\silentfalse\let\next=\xref\fi \next}
\catcode`\^=\active \let ^=\specialhat
\def\silentxref^{\silenttrue\xref}
```

Entries in the index aren't always words in roman type; they might require special typesetting conventions. For example, there are hundreds of items in Appendix I that are preceded by a backslash and set in typewriter type. The manmac format makes it easy to produce such entries by typing, e.g., '^|\immediate|' instead of '^{|\immediate|}'. In this case the backslash is not written onto the index file, because it would interfere with alphabetization of the entries; a code number is written out so that the backslash can be reinstated after the index has been sorted. The code number also is used to put the entry in typewriter type.

The indexing macros of `manmac` produce entries of four kinds, which are assigned to codes 0, 1, 2, and 3. Code 0 applies when the argument is enclosed in braces, e.g., '`^{word}`'; code 1 applies when the argument is enclosed in vertical lines and there's no backslash, e.g., '`^|plus|`'; code 2 is similar but with a backslash, e.g., '`^|\par|`'; code 3 applies when the argument is enclosed in angle brackets, e.g., '`^\<stuff>`'. The four example entries in the previous sentence will be written on file `index.tex` in the form

```
word !0 123.
plus !1 123.
par !2 123.
stuff !3 123.
```

if they appear on page 123 of the book.

```
\chardef\bslash=`\\ % \bslash makes a backslash (in tt fonts)
\def\xref{\futurelet\next\xrefswitch} % branch on the next character
\def\xrefswitch{\begingroup\ifx\next|\aftergroup\vxref
  \else\ifx\next\<\aftergroup\anglexref
    \else\aftergroup\normalxref \fi\fi \endgroup}
\def\vxref|{\catcode`\\=\active \futurelet\next\vxrefswitch}
\def\vxrefswitch#1|{\catcode`\\=0
  \ifx\next\empty\def\xreftype{2}%
    \def\next{{\tt\bslash\text}}% code 2, |\arg|
  \else\def\xreftype{1}\def\next{{\tt\text}}\fi % code 1, |arg|
  \edef\text{#1}\makexref}
{\catcode`\|=0 \catcode`\\=\active |gdef\{}}
\def\anglexref\<#1>{\def\xreftype{3}\def\text{#1}%
  \def\next{\<\text>}\makexref} % code 3, \<arg>
\def\normalxref#1{\def\xreftype{0}\def\text{#1}\let\next=\text\makexref}
```

Indexing is suppressed unless the `proofmode` switch is set to true, since material is gathered for the index only during trial runs—not on the triumphant occasion when the book is finally being printed.

```
\newif\ifproofmode
\proofmodetrue % this should be false when making camera-ready copy
\def\makexref{\ifproofmode\insert\margin{\hbox{\marginstyle\text}}%
  \xdef\writeit{\write\inx{\text\space!\xreftype\space
    \noexpand\number\pageno.}}\writeit
  \else\ifhmode\kern0pt \fi\fi
  \ifsilent\ignorespaces\else\next\fi}
```

(The `\insert` suppresses hyphenation when proofs are being checked; a `\kern0pt` is therefore emitted to provide consistent behavior in the other case.)

The material that accumulates on file `index.tex` gives a good first approximation to an index, but it doesn't contain enough information to do the whole job; a topic often occurs on several pages, but only the first of those pages is typically listed in the file. The author prefers not to generate indexes automatically; he likes to reread his books as he checks the cross-references, thereby having the opportunity to rethink everything and to catch miscellaneous errors before it is too late. As a result, his books tend to be delayed, but the indexes tend to be pretty good. Therefore he designed the indexing scheme of **manmac** to provide only the clues needed to make a real index. On the other hand, it would be possible to extend the macros above and to obtain a comprehensive system that generates an excellent index with no subsequent human intervention; see, for example, "An indexing facility for TEX" by Terry Winograd and Bill Paxton, in *TUGboat* **1** (1980), A1–A12.

The **manmac** macros have now been fully presented; we shall close this appendix by presenting one more example of their use. Chapter 27 mentions the desirability of creating a long book in small parts, by using a "galley" file. The author adopted that strategy for *The TEXbook*, entering each chapter into a small file **galley.tex** that looked like this:

```
\input manmac
\tenpoint
\pageno=800
\def\rhead{Experimental Pages for The \TeX book}
\def\chapno{ X}
{\catcode`\%=12 \immediate\write\ans{% Answers for galley proofs:}}
   ⋮

⟨new text being tested, usually an entire chapter⟩

   ⋮

% that blank line will stop an unfinished \answer
\immediate\closeout\ans
\vfill\eject
\ninepoint \input answers % typeset the new answers, if any
\bye
```

It is much easier to use macros than to define them.

. . .

The use of macro libraries, in fact, mirrors almost exactly the use of subroutine libraries for programming languages. There are the same levels of specialization, from publicly shared subroutines to special subroutines within a single program, and there is the same need for a programmer with particular skills to define the subroutines.

— PETER BROWN, *Macro Processors* (1974)

The epigraph is among the most delightful of scholarly habits. Donald Knuth's work on fundamental algorithms would be just as important if he hadn't begun with a quotation from Betty Crocker, but not so enjoyable. Part of the fun of an epigraph is turning a source to an unexpected use.

— MARY-CLAIRE VAN LEUNEN, *A Handbook for Scholars* (1978)

F

Font Tables

The purpose of this appendix is to summarize the chief characteristics of the Computer Modern typefaces. TeX is able to typeset documents with any fonts, having any arrangement of characters; the fonts and layouts to be described here are the particular ones that correspond to plain TeX format, i.e., to the macros in Appendix B. (Complete information about the Computer Modern family, including the METAFONT programs that draw the characters, can be found in the author's book *Computer Modern Typefaces*.)

The first pages of this appendix show what the fonts contain; the last pages show what the symbols are called when they're used in math formulas. (See Appendix B for the conventions that apply in non-mathematical text.)

There are exactly 128 different characters in each of the Computer Modern fonts, although TeX can work up to 256 characters per font. The text fonts are laid out as shown in the table below, which illustrates font `cmr10` (Computer Modern Roman 10 point). Thus, for example, if you ask for `\char'35` when `cmr10` is the current font, you get the symbol Æ. These text fonts include the ligatures and accents described in Chapter 9; each symbol that happens to be a visible ASCII character appears in its ASCII position. Some of the ASCII symbols (namely " < > \ _ { | }) are not included because they don't occur in normal printer's fonts. If you mistakenly type ", you get "; and < outside of math mode yields ¡! Incidentally, the ten digits all have width `0.5em`.

Figure 1. Text font layout, showing `cmr10` (`\rm`, `\textfont0`).

	ʹ0	ʹ1	ʹ2	ʹ3	ʹ4	ʹ5	ʹ6	ʹ7	
ʹ00x	Γ	Δ	Θ	Λ	Ξ	Π	Σ	Υ	″0x
ʹ01x	Φ	Ψ	Ω	ff	fi	fl	ffi	ffl	
ʹ02x	ı	ȷ	`	´	ˇ	˘	¯	˚	″1x
ʹ03x	¸	ß	æ	œ	ø	Æ	Œ	Ø	
ʹ04x	ˊ	!	"	#	$	%	&	'	″2x
ʹ05x	(	)	*	+	,	-	.	/	
ʹ06x	0	1	2	3	4	5	6	7	″3x
ʹ07x	8	9	:	;	¡	=	¿	?	
ʹ10x	@	A	B	C	D	E	F	G	″4x
ʹ11x	H	I	J	K	L	M	N	O	
ʹ12x	P	Q	R	S	T	U	V	W	″5x
ʹ13x	X	Y	Z	[	"	]	^	˙	
ʹ14x	'	a	b	c	d	e	f	g	″6x
ʹ15x	h	i	j	k	l	m	n	o	
ʹ16x	p	q	r	s	t	u	v	w	″7x
ʹ17x	x	y	z	–	—	˝	~	¨	
	″8	″9	″A	″B	″C	″D	″E	″F	

Plain TEX makes use of sixteen basic fonts:

cmr10	(Computer Modern Roman 10 point)	
cmr7	(Computer Modern Roman 7 point)	
cmr5	(Computer Modern Roman 5 point)	
cmbx10	(Computer Modern Bold Extended 10 point)	text
cmbx7	(Computer Modern Bold Extended 7 point)	
cmbx5	(Computer Modern Bold Extended 5 point)	
cmsl10	(Computer Modern Slanted Roman 10 point)	
cmti10	(Computer Modern Text Italic 10 point)	
cmtt10	(Computer Modern Typewriter Type 10 point)	
cmmi10	(Computer Modern Math Italic 10 point)	
cmmi7	(Computer Modern Math Italic 7 point)	
cmmi5	(Computer Modern Math Italic 5 point)	special
cmsy10	(Computer Modern Math Symbols 10 point)	
cmsy7	(Computer Modern Math Symbols 7 point)	
cmsy5	(Computer Modern Math Symbols 5 point)	
cmex10	(Computer Modern Math Extension 10 point)	

The first eight of these all have essentially the same layout; but cmr5 needs no ligatures, and many of the symbols of cmti10 have different shapes. For example, the ampersand becomes an 'E.T.', and the dollar changes to pound sterling:

Figure 2. Text font layout, showing cmti10 (\it).

	´0	´1	´2	´3	´4	´5	´6	´7	
´00x	Γ	Δ	Θ	Λ	Ξ	Π	Σ	Υ	˝0x
´01x	Φ	Ψ	Ω	ff	fi	fl	ffi	ffl	
´02x	ı	ȷ	`	´	ˇ	˘	¯	˚	˝1x
´03x	¸	ß	æ	œ	ø	Æ	Œ	Ø	
´04x	˝	!	”	#	£	%	&	’	˝2x
´05x	(	)	*	+	,	-	.	/	
´06x	0	1	2	3	4	5	6	7	˝3x
´07x	8	9	:	;	¡	=	¿	?	
´10x	@	A	B	C	D	E	F	G	˝4x
´11x	H	I	J	K	L	M	N	O	
´12x	P	Q	R	S	T	U	V	W	˝5x
´13x	X	Y	Z	[	“	]	^	˙	
´14x	‘	a	b	c	d	e	f	g	˝6x
´15x	h	i	j	k	l	m	n	o	
´16x	p	q	r	s	t	u	v	w	˝7x
´17x	x	y	z	–	—	”	~	¨	
	˝8	˝9	˝A	˝B	˝C	˝D	˝E	˝F	

The typewriter font `cmtt10` is almost like the fonts for ordinary text, but it includes all of the visible ASCII characters, in their correct positions. It also has vertical arrows ↑ and ↓, as well as an undirected single quote mark, '. Fourteen of the 128 positions are changed from the normal text layout conventions, namely codes ´013–´017, ´040, ´042, ´074, ´076, ´134, ´137, and ´173–´175. All of the ligatures are absent, except for the Spanish ¡ and ¿. (The characters for Spanish ligatures appear in different positions, but that makes no difference to the user, because each font tells TEX where to locate its own ligatures.) The Polish ł, the dot accent, and the long Hungarian umlaut have disappeared to make room for new symbols. In a sense, positions ´052 and ´055 also differ from the normal text conventions: The asterisk is not up as high as usual, and the hyphen is just like a minus sign.

Each character in `cmtt10` has the same width, namely 0.5em; the spaces between words also have this width, and they will not stretch or shrink. TEX puts two spaces at the end of each sentence when you are typesetting with a typewriter font. (These spacing conventions can be changed by assigning nonzero values to \spaceskip and \xspaceskip; or you can assign new values to the \fontdimen parameters, which will be described shortly.)

Figure 3. Typewriter text font layout, showing `cmtt10` (\tt).

	´0	´1	´2	´3	´4	´5	´6	´7	
´00x	Γ	Δ	Θ	Λ	Ξ	Π	Σ	Υ	"0x
´01x	Φ	Ψ	Ω	↑	↓	'	¡	¿	
´02x	ı	ȷ	`	´	ˇ	˘	¯	˚	"1x
´03x	¸	ß	æ	œ	ø	Æ	Œ	Ø	
´04x	␣	!	"	#	$	%	&	'	"2x
´05x	(	)	*	+	,	-	.	/	
´06x	0	1	2	3	4	5	6	7	"3x
´07x	8	9	:	;	<	=	>	?	
´10x	@	A	B	C	D	E	F	G	"4x
´11x	H	I	J	K	L	M	N	O	
´12x	P	Q	R	S	T	U	V	W	"5x
´13x	X	Y	Z	[	\	]	^	_	
´14x	`	a	b	c	d	e	f	g	"6x
´15x	h	i	j	k	l	m	n	o	
´16x	p	q	r	s	t	u	v	w	"7x
´17x	x	y	z	{	|	}	~	¨	
	"8	"9	"A	"B	"C	"D	"E	"F	

You can see at a glance that the math italic font, cmmi10, is quite different from text italic. It contains lowercase Greek letters as well as uppercase ones; this, of course, is mathematicians' Greek, not a text font that would be suitable for typesetting classical Greek literature. And if you look closely at the non-Greek italic letters, you will find that their proportions and spacing have been changed from cmti10 to make them work better in TeX's mathematics mode.

Some special unslanted characters appear in positions ´050–´077 and ´133–´137, including "oldstyle numerals": '$\mit1984$' and '$\oldstyle1984$' both yield '1984'. Some of the characters are intended to be combined with others; for example, ´054 forms the first part of the symbol '↪'. (See the definition of \hookrightarrow in Appendix B.) This portion of the font doesn't deserve the name math italic; it's really a resting place for characters that don't fit anywhere else. (The author didn't want to leave any places unfilled, since that would tempt people to create incompatible ways to fill them.)

Plain TeX takes its comma, period, and slash from cmmi10 in math mode, so that appropriate kerning will be computed in certain formulas that would otherwise be spaced poorly. For the correct positioning of math accents with this font, you should set its \skewchar to ´177.

Figure 4. Math italic font layout, showing cmmi10 (\mit, \textfont1).

	´0	´1	´2	´3	´4	´5	´6	´7	
´00x	Γ	Δ	Θ	Λ	Ξ	Π	Σ	Υ	"0x
´01x	Φ	Ψ	Ω	α	β	γ	δ	ϵ	
´02x	ζ	η	θ	ι	κ	λ	μ	ν	"1x
´03x	ξ	π	ρ	σ	τ	υ	ϕ	χ	
´04x	ψ	ω	ε	ϑ	ϖ	ϱ	ς	φ	"2x
´05x	↼	↽	⇀	⇁	‘	’	▷	◁	
´06x	0	1	2	3	4	5	6	7	"3x
´07x	8	9	.	,	<	/	>	$\star$	
´10x	∂	A	B	C	D	E	F	G	"4x
´11x	H	I	J	K	L	M	N	O	
´12x	P	Q	R	S	T	U	V	W	"5x
´13x	X	Y	Z	$\flat$	$\natural$	$\sharp$	$\smile$	$\frown$	
´14x	ℓ	a	b	c	d	e	f	g	"6x
´15x	h	i	j	k	l	m	n	o	
´16x	p	q	r	s	t	u	v	w	"7x
´17x	x	y	z	$\imath$	$\jmath$	$\wp$	⃗	⌢	
	"8	"9	"A	"B	"C	"D	"E	"F	

When TEX typesets mathematics it assumes that family 0 contains normal roman fonts and that families 1, 2, and 3 contain math italic, math symbol, and math extension fonts. The special characters in these fonts are usually given symbolic names by a \mathchardef instruction, which assigns a hexadecimal code to the symbol. This code has four digits, where the first tells what kind of symbol is involved, the second specifies the family, and the other two give the font position. For example,

> \mathchardef\ll="321C

says that \ll is character "1C of the math symbol font (family 2), and that it's a "relation" (class 3). A complete list of the symbolic names provided by the plain TEX format appears later in this appendix.

Font cmsy10 is plain TEX's math symbol font, and it contains 128 symbols laid out as shown below. Its \skewchar should be set to '060 so that math accents will be positioned properly over the calligraphic capital letters.

Figure 5. Math symbol font layout, showing cmsy10 (\cal, \textfont2).

	'0	'1	'2	'3	'4	'5	'6	'7	
'00x	−	·	×	∗	÷	⋄	±	∓	"0x
'01x	⊕	⊖	⊗	⊘	⊙	◯	∘	•	
'02x	≍	≡	⊆	⊇	≤	≥	⪯	⪰	"1x
'03x	∼	≈	⊂	⊃	≪	≫	≺	≻	
'04x	←	→	↑	↓	↔	↗	↘	≃	"2x
'05x	⇐	⇒	⇑	⇓	⇔	↖	↙	∝	
'06x	′	∞	∈	∋	△	▽	/	∣	"3x
'07x	∀	∃	¬	∅	ℜ	ℑ	⊤	⊥	
'10x	ℵ	𝒜	ℬ	𝒞	𝒟	ℰ	ℱ	𝒢	"4x
'11x	ℋ	ℐ	𝒥	𝒦	ℒ	ℳ	𝒩	𝒪	
'12x	𝒫	𝒬	ℛ	𝒮	𝒯	𝒰	𝒱	𝒲	"5x
'13x	𝒳	𝒴	𝒵	∪	∩	⊎	∧	∨	
'14x	⊢	⊣	⌊	⌋	⌈	⌉	{	}	"6x
'15x	⟨	⟩	∣	∥	↕	⇕	\	≀	
'16x	√	⨿	▽	∫	⊔	⊓	⊑	⊒	"7x
'17x	§	†	‡	¶	♣	♢	♡	♠	
	"8	"9	"A	"B	"C	"D	"E	"F	

The final font of plain TeX is `cmex10`, which includes large symbols and pieces that can be used to build even larger ones. For example, arbitrarily large left parentheses can be constructed by putting ´060 at the top and ´100 at the bottom, and by using as many copies of ´102 as necessary in the middle. Large square root signs are made from ´164, ´165, and ´166; large left braces have four component parts: ´070, ´072, ´074, ´076.

Figure 6. Math extension font layout, showing `cmex10` (`\textfont3`).

	´0	´1	´2	´3	´4	´5	´6	´7	
´00x	(	)	[	]	⌊	⌋	⌈	⌉	"0x
´01x	{	}	⟨	⟩	|	‖	/	\	
´02x	(	)	(	)	[	]	⌊	⌋	"1x
´03x	⌈	⌉	{	}	⟨	⟩	/	\	
´04x	(	)	[	]	⌊	⌋	⌈	⌉	"2x
´05x	{	}	⟨	⟩	/	\	/	\	
´06x	(	\	⌈	⌉	⌊	⌋	|	|	"3x
´07x	(	)	⌊	⌋	{	}	.	|	
´10x	\	)	|	|	⟨	⟩	⊔	⊔	"4x
´11x	∮	∮	⊙	⊙	⊕	⊕	⊗	⊗	
´12x	Σ	Π	∫	∪	∩	⊎	∧	∨	"5x
´13x	Σ	Π	∫	∪	∩	⊎	∧	∨	
´14x	⨿	⨿	⌢	⌢	⌢	~	~	~	"6x
´15x	[	]	⌊	⌋	⌈	⌉	{	}	
´16x	√	√	√	√	√	|	⌈	‖	"7x
´17x	↑	↓	⌒	⌒	⌒	⌣	⇑	⇓	
	"8	"9	"A	"B	"C	"D	"E	"F	

When TeX "loads" a font into its memory, it doesn't look at the actual shapes of the characters; it only loads the *font metric* information (e.g., `cmr10.tfm`), which includes the heights, widths, depths, and italic corrections, together with information about ligatures and kerning. Furthermore, the metric information that comes with a font like `cmex10` tells TeX that certain characters form a series; for example, all of the left parentheses are linked together in order of increasing size: $'000$, $'020$, $'022$, and $'040$, followed by the extensible left parenthesis, which is $'060 + ['102]^n + '100$. Similarly, the two summation signs ($'120$, $'130$) and the three `\widehat` accents ($'142$, $'143$, $'144$) are linked together. Appendix G explains how TeX goes about choosing particular sizes for math delimiters, math operators, and math accents.

Each font also has at least seven `\fontdimen` parameters, which have the following significance and typical values (rounded to two decimal places):

#	Meaning	Value in	cmr10	cmbx10	cmsl10	cmti10	cmtt10	cmmi10
1	slant per pt		0.00 pt	0.00 pt	0.17 pt	0.25 pt	0.00 pt	0.25 pt
2	interword space		3.33 pt	3.83 pt	3.33 pt	3.58 pt	5.25 pt	0.00 pt
3	interword stretch		1.67 pt	1.92 pt	1.67 pt	1.53 pt	0.00 pt	0.00 pt
4	interword shrink		1.11 pt	1.28 pt	1.11 pt	1.02 pt	0.00 pt	0.00 pt
5	x-height		4.31 pt	4.44 pt	4.31 pt	4.31 pt	4.31 pt	4.31 pt
6	quad width		10.00 pt	11.50 pt	10.00 pt	10.22 pt	10.50 pt	10.00 pt
7	extra space		1.11 pt	1.28 pt	1.11 pt	1.02 pt	5.25 pt	0.00 pt

The slant parameter is used to position accents; the next three parameters define interword spaces when text is being typeset; the next two define the font-oriented dimensions `1ex` and `1em`; and the last is the additional amount that is added to interword spaces at the end of sentences (i.e., when `\spacefactor` is 2000 or more and `\xspaceskip` is zero). When a font is magnified (using 'at' or 'scaled'), all of the parameters except the slant are subject to magnification at the time the font is loaded into TeX's memory.

Notice that `cmmi10` has zero spacing. This is the mark of a font that is intended only for mathematical typesetting; the rules in Appendix G state that the italic correction is added between adjacent characters from such fonts.

Math symbol fonts (i.e., fonts in family 2) are required to have at least 22 `\fontdimen` parameters instead of the usual seven; similarly, math extension fonts must have at least 13. The significance of these additional parameters is explained in Appendix G. If you want to increase the number of parameters past the number that actually appear in a font's metric information file, you can assign new values immediately after that font has been loaded. For example, if some font `\ff` with seven parameters has just entered TeX's memory, the command `\fontdimen13\ff=5pt` will set parameter number 13 to 5 pt; the intervening parameters, numbers 8–12, will be set to zero. You can even give more than seven parameters to `\nullfont`, provided that you assign the values before any actual fonts have been loaded.

Now that the font layouts have all been displayed, it's time to consider the names of the various mathematical symbols. Plain TeX defines more than 200 control sequences by which you can refer to math symbols without having to find their numerical positions in the layouts. It's generally best to call a symbol by its name, for then you can easily adapt your manuscripts to other fonts, and your manuscript will be much more readable.

The symbols divide naturally into groups based on their mathematical class (Ord, Op, Bin, Rel, Open, Close, or Punct), so we shall follow that order as we discuss them. N.B.: Unless otherwise stated, math symbols are available only in math modes. For example, if you say '\alpha' in horizontal mode, TeX will report an error and try to insert a $ sign.

1. Lowercase Greek letters.

α	\alpha	ι	\iota	ϱ	\varrho
β	\beta	κ	\kappa	σ	\sigma
γ	\gamma	λ	\lambda	ς	\varsigma
δ	\delta	μ	\mu	τ	\tau
ϵ	\epsilon	ν	\nu	υ	\upsilon
ε	\varepsilon	ξ	\xi	ϕ	\phi
ζ	\zeta	o	o	φ	\varphi
η	\eta	π	\pi	χ	\chi
θ	\theta	ϖ	\varpi	ψ	\psi
ϑ	\vartheta	ρ	\rho	ω	\omega

There's no \omicron, because it would look the same as o. Notice that the letter \upsilon (v) is a bit wider than v (v); both of them should be distinguished from \nu (ν). Similarly, \varsigma (ς) should not be confused with \zeta (ζ). It turns out that \varsigma and \upsilon are almost never used in math formulas; they are included in plain TeX primarily because they are sometimes needed in short Greek citations (cf. Appendix J).

2. Uppercase Greek letters.

Γ	\Gamma	Ξ	\Xi	Φ	\Phi
Δ	\Delta	Π	\Pi	Ψ	\Psi
Θ	\Theta	Σ	\Sigma	Ω	\Omega
Λ	\Lambda	Υ	\Upsilon		

The other Greek capitals appear in the roman alphabet (\Alpha $\equiv$ {\rm A}, \Beta $\equiv$ {\rm B}, etc.). It's conventional to use unslanted letters for uppercase Greek, and slanted letters for lowercase Greek; but you can obtain $(\Gamma, \Delta, \ldots, \Omega)$ by typing $({\mit\Gamma}, {\mit\Delta}, \ldots, {\mit\Omega})$.

3. Calligraphic capitals. To get the letters $\mathcal{A}\ldots\mathcal{Z}$ that appear in Figure 5, type ${\cal A}\ldots{\cal Z}$. Several other alphabets are also used with mathematics (notably Fraktur, script, and "blackboard bold"); they don't come with plain TeX, but more elaborate formats like $\mathcal{AMS}$-TeX do provide them.

4. Miscellaneous symbols of type Ord.

ℵ	\aleph	′	\prime	∀	\forall
ℏ	\hbar	∅	\emptyset	∃	\exists
ı	\imath	∇	\nabla	¬	\neg
ȷ	\jmath	√	\surd	♭	\flat
ℓ	\ell	⊤	\top	♮	\natural
℘	\wp	⊥	\bot	♯	\sharp
ℜ	\Re	‖	|	♣	\clubsuit
ℑ	\Im	∠	\angle	◇	\diamondsuit
∂	\partial	△	\triangle	♡	\heartsuit
∞	\infty	\	\backslash	♠	\spadesuit

The dotless letters \imath and \jmath should be used when i and j are accented; for example, $\hat\imath$ yields $\hat\imath$. The \prime symbol is intended for use in subscripts and superscripts, as explained in Chapter 16, so you usually see it in a smaller size. On the other hand, the \angle symbol has been built up from other pieces; it does not get smaller when it appears in a subscript or superscript.

5. Digits. To get italic digits *0123456789*, say {\it0123456789}; to get boldface digits **0123456789**, say {\bf0123456789}; to get oldstyle digits 0123456789, say {\oldstyle0123456789}. These conventions work also outside of math mode.

6. "Large" operators. The following symbols come in two sizes, for text and display styles:

$\sum$	\sum	$\bigcap$	\bigcap	$\bigodot$	\bigodot
$\prod$	\prod	$\bigcup$	\bigcup	$\bigotimes$	\bigotimes
$\coprod$	\coprod	$\bigsqcup$	\bigsqcup	$\bigoplus$	\bigoplus
$\int$	\int	$\bigvee$	\bigvee	$\biguplus$	\biguplus
$\oint$	\oint	$\bigwedge$	\bigwedge		

It is important to distinguish these large Op symbols from the similar but smaller Bin symbols whose names are the same except for a 'big' prefix. Large operators usually occur at the beginning of a formula or subformula, and they usually are subscripted; binary operations usually occur between two symbols or subformulas, and they rarely are subscripted. For example,

$\bigcup_{n=1}^m(x_n\cup y_n)$ yields $\bigcup_{n=1}^{m}(x_n \cup y_n)$

The large operators \sum, \prod, \coprod, and \int should also be distinguished from smaller symbols called \Sigma (Σ), \Pi (Π), \amalg ($\amalg$), and \smallint ($\int$), respectively; the \smallint operator is rarely used.

7. *Binary operations.* Besides + and −, you can type

±	\pm	∩	\cap	∨	\vee
∓	\mp	∪	\cup	∧	\wedge
\	\setminus	⊎	\uplus	⊕	\oplus
·	\cdot	⊓	\sqcap	⊖	\ominus
×	\times	⊔	\sqcup	⊗	\otimes
∗	\ast	◁	\triangleleft	⊘	\oslash
⋆	\star	▷	\triangleright	⊙	\odot
⋄	\diamond	≀	\wr	†	\dagger
∘	\circ	◯	\bigcirc	‡	\ddagger
•	\bullet	△	\bigtriangleup	II	\amalg
÷	\div	▽	\bigtriangledown		

It's customary to say $G\backslash H$ to denote double cosets of G by H ($G\backslash H$), and $p\backslash n$ to mean that p divides n ($p\backslash n$); but $X\setminus Y$ denotes the elements of set X minus those of set Y ($X \setminus Y$). Both operations use the same symbol, but \backslash is type Ord, while \setminus is type Bin (so TEX puts more space around it).

8. *Relations.* Besides <, >, and =, you can type

≤	\leq	≥	\geq	≡	\equiv
≺	\prec	≻	\succ	∼	\sim
⪯	\preceq	⪰	\succeq	≃	\simeq
≪	\ll	≫	\gg	≍	\asymp
⊂	\subset	⊃	\supset	≈	\approx
⊆	\subseteq	⊇	\supseteq	≅	\cong
⊑	\sqsubseteq	⊒	\sqsupseteq	⋈	\bowtie
∈	\in	∋	\ni	∝	\propto
⊢	\vdash	⊣	\dashv	⊨	\models
⌣	\smile	|	\mid	≐	\doteq
⌢	\frown	‖	\parallel	⊥	\perp

The symbols \mid and \parallel define relations that use the same characters as you get from | and \|; TEX puts space around them when they are relations.

9. *Negated relations.* Many of the relations just listed can be negated or "crossed out" by prefixing them with \not, as follows:

≮	\not<	≯	\not>	≠	\not=
≰	\not\leq	≱	\not\geq	≢	\not\equiv
⊀	\not\prec	⊁	\not\succ	≁	\not\sim
⋠	\not\preceq	⋡	\not\succeq	≄	\not\simeq
⊄	\not\subset	⊅	\not\supset	≉	\not\approx
⊈	\not\subseteq	⊉	\not\supseteq	≇	\not\cong
⋢	\not\sqsubseteq	⋣	\not\sqsupseteq	≭	\not\asymp

The symbol \not is a relation character of width zero, so it will overlap a relation that comes immediately after it. The positioning isn't always ideal, because some relation symbols are wider than others; for example, \not\in gives '∉', but it is preferable to have a steeper cancellation, '∉'. The latter symbol is available as a special control sequence called \notin. The definition of \notin in Appendix B indicates how similar symbols can be constructed.

10. Arrows. There's also another big class of relations, namely those that point:

←	\leftarrow	⟵	\longleftarrow	↑	\uparrow
⇐	\Leftarrow	⟸	\Longleftarrow	⇑	\Uparrow
→	\rightarrow	⟶	\longrightarrow	↓	\downarrow
⇒	\Rightarrow	⟹	\Longrightarrow	⇓	\Downarrow
↔	\leftrightarrow	⟷	\longleftrightarrow	↕	\updownarrow
⇔	\Leftrightarrow	⟺	\Longleftrightarrow	⇕	\Updownarrow
↦	\mapsto	⟼	\longmapsto	↗	\nearrow
↩	\hookleftarrow	↪	\hookrightarrow	↘	\searrow
↼	\leftharpoonup	⇀	\rightharpoonup	↙	\swarrow
↽	\leftharpoondown	⇁	\rightharpoondown	↖	\nwarrow
⇌	\rightleftharpoons				

Up and down arrows will grow larger, like delimiters (see Chapter 17). To put symbols over left and right arrows, plain TeX provides a \buildrel macro: You type \buildrel⟨superscript⟩\over⟨relation⟩, and the superscript is placed on top of the relation just as limits are placed over large operators. For example,

$$\xrightarrow{\alpha\beta} \qquad \texttt{\textbackslash buildrel \textbackslash alpha\textbackslash beta \textbackslash over \textbackslash longrightarrow}$$

$$\overset{\text{def}}{=} \qquad \texttt{\textbackslash buildrel \textbackslash rm def \textbackslash over =}$$

(In this context, '\over' does not define a fraction.)

11. Openings. The following left delimiters are available, besides '(':

[	\lbrack	⌊	\lfloor	⌈	\lceil
{	\lbrace	⟨	\langle		

You can also type simply '[' to get \lbrack. All of these will grow if you prefix them by \bigl, \Bigl, \biggl, \Biggl, or \left. Chapter 17 also mentions \lgroup and \lmoustache, which are available in sizes greater than \big. If you need more delimiters, the following combinations work reasonably well in the normal text size:

⟦	\lbrack\!\lbrack	⟪	\langle\!\langle	⦅	(\!(

12. Closings. The corresponding right delimiters are present too:

]	\rbrack	⌋	\rfloor	⌉	\rceil
}	\rbrace	⟩	\rangle		

Everything that works for openings works also for closings, but reversed.

13. Punctuation. TEX puts a thin space after commas and semicolons that appear in mathematical formulas, and it does the same for a colon that is called `\colon`. (Otherwise a colon is considered to be a relation, as in '$x := y$' and '$a : b :: c : d$', which you type by saying '`$x:=y$`' and '`$a:b::c:d$`'.) Examples of `\colon` are

$$f\colon A \rightarrow B \qquad\qquad \text{\$f\textbackslash colon A\textbackslash rightarrow B\$}$$
$$L(a, b; c: x, y; z) \qquad\qquad \text{\$L(a,b;c\textbackslash colon x,y;z)\$}$$

$f\colon A \rightarrow B$	`$f\colon A\rightarrow B$`
$L(a, b; c\colon x, y; z)$	`$L(a,b;c\colon x,y;z)$`

Plain TEX also defines `\ldotp` and `\cdotp` to be '.' and '·' with the spacing of commas and semicolons. These symbols don't occur directly in formulas, but they are useful in the definition of `\ldots` and `\cdots`.

14. Alternate names. If you don't like plain TEX's name for some math symbol—for example, if there's another name that looks better or that you can remember more easily—the remedy is simple: You just say, e.g., '`\let\cupcap=\asymp`'. Then you can type '`f(n)\cupcap n`' instead of '`f(n)\asymp n`'.

Some symbols have alternate names that are so commonly used that plain TEX provides two or more equivalent control sequences:

$\neq$	`\ne` or `\neq`	(same as `\not=`)
$\leq$	`\le`	(same as `\leq`)
$\geq$	`\ge`	(same as `\geq`)
$\{$	`\{`	(same as `\lbrace`)
$\}$	`\}`	(same as `\rbrace`)
$\rightarrow$	`\to`	(same as `\rightarrow`)
$\leftarrow$	`\gets`	(same as `\leftarrow`)
$\ni$	`\owns`	(same as `\ni`)
$\wedge$	`\land`	(same as `\wedge`)
$\vee$	`\lor`	(same as `\vee`)
$\neg$	`\lnot`	(same as `\neg`)
$\vert$	`\vert`	(same as |)
$\Vert$	`\Vert`	(same as `|`)

There's also `\iff` ($\Longleftrightarrow$), which is just like `\Longleftrightarrow` except that it puts an extra thick space at each side.

15. Non-math symbols. Plain TEX makes four special symbols available outside of math mode, although the characters themselves are actually typeset from the math symbols font:

§	`\S`
¶	`\P`
†	`\dag`
‡	`\ddag`

These control sequences do not act like ordinary math symbols; they don't change their size when they appear in subscripts or superscripts, and you must say, e.g.,

`$x^{\P}$` instead of `$x^\P$` when you use them in formulas. However, the `\dag` and `\ddag` symbols are available in math mode under the names `\dagger` and `\ddagger`. It would be easy to define mathematical equivalents of `\S` and `\P`, if these symbols suddenly caught a mathematician's fancy.

Seek not for fresher founts afar,
Just drop your bucket where you are.
— SAM WALTER FOSS, *Back Country Poems* (1892)

No one compositor will have all the signs and symbols available.
The number of special signs and symbols is almost limitless,
with new ones being introduced all the time.
— UNIVERSITY OF CHICAGO PRESS, *Manual of Style* (1969)

G

Generating Boxes from Formulas

People who define new math fonts and/or macros sometimes need to know exactly how TEX manipulates the constituents of formulas. The purpose of this appendix is to explain the precise positioning rules by which TEX converts a math list into a horizontal list. (It is a good idea to review the introduction to math lists in Chapter 17 before reading further; "double dangerous bends" are implied throughout this appendix.)

TEX relies on lots of parameters when it typesets formulas, and you have the option of changing any or all of them. But of course you will want to know what each parameter means, before you change it. Therefore each rule below is numbered, and a table appears at the end to show which rules depend on which parameters.

The most important parameters appear in the symbol fonts (family 2) and the extension fonts (family 3). TEX will not typeset a formula unless `\textfont2`, `\scriptfont2`, and `\scriptscriptfont2` each contain at least 22 `\fontdimen` parameters. For brevity we shall call these parameters σ_1 to σ_{22}, where the parameter is taken from `\textfont2` if the current style is display or text (D or D' or T or T'), from `\scriptfont2` if the current style is S or S', and from `\scriptscriptfont2` otherwise. Similarly, the three fonts in family 3 must each have at least 13 `\fontdimen` parameters, and we will denote them by ξ_1 to ξ_{13}. The notation ξ_9, for example, stands for the ninth parameter of `\scriptfont3`, if TEX is typesetting something in `\scriptstyle`.

A math list is a sequence of items of the various kinds listed in Chapter 17, and TEX typesets a formula by converting a math list to a horizontal list. When such typesetting begins, TEX has two other pieces of information in addition to the math list itself. (a) The starting style tells what style should be used for the math list, unless another style is specified by a style item. For example, the starting style for a displayed formula is D, but for an equation in the text or an equation number it is T; and for a subformula it can be any one of the eight styles defined in Chapter 17. We shall use C to stand for the current style, and we shall say that the math list is being typeset in style C. (b) The typesetting is done either with or without penalties. Formulas in the text of a paragraph are converted to horizontal lists in which additional penalty items are inserted after binary operations and relations, in order to aid in line breaking. Such penalties are not inserted in other cases, because they would serve no useful function.

The eight styles are considered to be $D > D' > T > T' > S > S' > SS > SS'$, in decreasing order. Thus, $C \le S$ means that the current style is S, S', SS, or SS'. Style C' means the current style with a prime added if one isn't there; for example, we have $C' = T'$ if and only if $C = T$ or $C = T'$. Style $C\uparrow$ is the superscript style for C; this means style S if C is D or T, style S' if C is D' or T', style SS if C is S or SS, and style SS' if C is S' or SS'. Finally, style $C\downarrow$ is the subscript style, which is $(C\uparrow)'$.

Chapter 17 stated that the most important components of math lists are called atoms, and that each atom has three fields called its nucleus, subscript, and superscript. We frequently need to execute a subroutine called "Set box x to the so-and-so field in style such-and-such." This means (a) if the specified field is empty, x is set equal to a null box; (b) if the field contains a symbol, x is set to an hbox containing that symbol in the appropriate size, and the italic correction for the character is included in the width of the box; (c) if the field contains a math list or horizontal list, x is set to an hbox containing the result of typesetting that list with the specified starting style. In case (c), the glue is set with no stretching or shrinking, and an additional level of hboxing is omitted if it turns out to be redundant.

Another subroutine sets box x to a specified variable delimiter, having a specified minimum height plus depth. This means that a search is conducted as follows:

The delimiter is defined by two symbols, a "small character" a in family f and a "large character" b in family g. The search looks first at character a in scriptscriptfont f, if $C \leq SS$; then it looks at a in scriptfont f, if $C \leq S$; then it looks at a in textfont f. If nothing suitable is found from a and f, the larger alternative b and g is examined in the same way. Either (a, f) or (b, g) may be $(0, 0)$, which means that the corresponding part of the search is to be bypassed. When looking at a character in a font, the search stops immediately if that character has sufficient height plus depth, or if the character is extensible; furthermore, if the character does not stop the search, but if it has a successor in the font, the successor is looked at next. (See the METAFONT manual or the system documentation of `tfm` files for further information about successors and extensible characters.) If the search runs all the way to completion without finding a suitable character, the one with greatest height plus depth is chosen. If no characters at all were found (either because $a = f = b = g = 0$ or because the characters did not exist in the fonts), x is set to an empty box whose width is `\nulldelimiterspace`. If an extensible character was found, x is set to a vbox containing enough pieces to build up a character of sufficient size; the height of this vbox is the height of the topmost piece, and the width is the width of the repeatable piece. Otherwise x is set to an hbox containing the character that was found; the italic correction of the character is included in the width of this box.

There's also a subroutine that "reboxes" a given box to a given width. If the box doesn't already have the desired width, TEX unpackages it (unless it was a vbox), then adds a kern for an italic correction if one was implied, and inserts `\hss` glue at both left and right; the resulting horizontal list is packaged into an hbox. This process is used, for example, to give a common width to the numerator and denominator of a fraction; it centers whichever is smaller, unless infinite glue is present in addition to the newly added `\hss`.

If x is a box, we shall use the abbreviations $h(x)$, $d(x)$, and $w(x)$ for its height, depth, and width, respectively.

Here now are the rules for typesetting a given math list in starting style C. The process applies from left to right, translating each item in turn. Two passes are made over the list; most of the work is done by the first pass, which compiles individual translations of the math items. We shall consider this part of the task first:

1. If the current item is a rule or discretionary or penalty or "whatsit" or boundary item, simply leave it unchanged and move to the next item.

2. If the current item is glue or a kern, translate it as follows: If it is glue from `\nonscript`, check if the immediately following item is glue or a kern; and if so, remove that item if $C \leq S$. Otherwise, if the current item is from `\mskip` or `\mkern`, convert from `mu` to absolute units by multiplying each finite dimension by $\frac{1}{18}\sigma_6$. Then move on to the next item.

3. If the current item is a style change, set C to the specified style. Delete the current item from the list and move on to the next.

4. If the current item is a four-way choice, it contains four math lists for the four main styles. Replace it by the math list that corresponds to the current style C, then move to the first unprocessed item.

5. If the current item is a Bin atom, and if this was the first atom in the list, or if the most recent previous atom was Bin, Op, Rel, Open, or Punct, change the current Bin to Ord and continue with Rule 14. Otherwise continue with Rule 17.

6. If the current item is a Rel or Close or Punct atom, and if the most recent previous atom was Bin, change that previous Bin to Ord. Continue with Rule 17.

7. If the current item is an Open or Inner atom, go directly to Rule 17.

8. If the current item is a Vcent atom (from `\vcenter`), let its nucleus be a vbox of height-plus-depth v. Change the height to $\frac{1}{2}v + a$ and the depth to $\frac{1}{2}v - a$, where a is the axis height, σ_{22}. Change this atom to type Ord and continue with Rule 17.

9. If the current item is an Over atom (from `\overline`), set box x to the nucleus in style C'. Then replace the nucleus by a vbox containing kern θ, hrule of height θ, kern 3θ, and box x, from top to bottom, where $\theta = \xi_8$ is the default rule thickness. (This puts a rule over the nucleus, with 3θ clearance, and with θ units of extra white space assumed to be present above the rule.) Continue with Rule 16.

10. If the current item is an Under atom (from `\underline`), set box x to the nucleus in style C. Then replace the nucleus by a vtop made from box x, kern 3θ, and hrule of height θ, where $\theta = \xi_8$ is the default rule thickness; and add θ to the depth of the box. (This puts a rule under the nucleus, with 3θ clearance, and with θ units of extra white space assumed to be present below the rule.) Continue with Rule 16.

11. If the current item is a Rad atom (from `\radical`, e.g., `\sqrt`), set box x to the nucleus in style C'. Let $\theta = \xi_8$; and let $\varphi = \sigma_5$ if $C > T$, otherwise $\varphi = \theta$. Set $\psi = \theta + \frac{1}{4}|\varphi|$; this is the minimum clearance that will be allowed between box x and the rule that will go above it. Set box y to a variable delimiter for this radical atom, having height plus depth $h(x) + d(x) + \psi + \theta$ or more. Then set $\theta \leftarrow h(y)$; this is the thickness of the rule to be used in the radical construction. (Note that the font designer specifies the thickness of the rule by making it the height of the radical character; the baseline of the character should be precisely at the bottom of the rule.) If $d(y) > h(x) + d(x) + \psi$, increase ψ by half of the excess; i.e., set $\psi \leftarrow \frac{1}{2}(\psi + d(y) - h(x) - d(x))$. Construct a vbox consisting of kern θ, hrule of height θ, kern ψ, and box x, from top to bottom. The nucleus of the radical atom is now replaced by box y raised by $h(x) + \psi$, followed by the new vbox. Continue with Rule 16.

12. If the current item is an Acc atom (from `\mathaccent`), just go to Rule 16 if the accent character doesn't exist in the current size. Otherwise set box x to the nucleus in style C', and set u to the width of this box. If the nucleus is not a single character, let $s = 0$; otherwise set s to the kern amount for the nucleus followed by the `\skewchar` of its font. If the accent character has a successor in its font whose width is $\leq u$, change it to the successor and repeat this sentence. Now set $\delta \leftarrow \min(h(x), \chi)$, where χ is `\fontdimen5` (the x-height) in the accent font. If the nucleus is a single character, replace box x by a box containing the nucleus together with the superscript and subscript of the Acc atom, in style C, and make the sub/superscripts of the Acc atom empty; also increase δ by the difference between the new and old values of $h(x)$. Put the accent into a new box y, including the italic correction. Let z be a vbox consisting of: box y moved right $s + \frac{1}{2}(u - w(y))$, kern $-\delta$, and box x. If $h(z) < h(x)$, add a kern of $h(x) - h(z)$ above box y and set $h(z) \leftarrow h(x)$. Finally set $w(z) \leftarrow w(x)$, replace the nucleus of the Acc atom by box z, and continue with Rule 16.

13. If the current item is an Op atom, mark this atom as having limits if it has been marked with `\limits`, or if it has been marked with `\displaylimits` and $C > T$. If the nucleus is not a symbol, set $\delta \leftarrow 0$ and go to Rule 13a. Otherwise if $C > T$ and if the nucleus symbol has a successor in its font, move to the successor. (This is where operators like $\sum$ and $\int$ change to a larger size in display styles.) Put the symbol into a new box x, in the current size, and set δ to the italic correction for the character; include δ in the width of box x if and only if limits are to be set or there is no subscript. Shift box x down by $\frac{1}{2}(h(x) - d(x)) - a$, where $a = \sigma_{22}$, so that the operator character is centered vertically on the axis; this shifted box becomes the nucleus of the Op atom.

13a. If limits are not to be typeset for this Op atom, go to Rule 17; otherwise the limits are attached as follows: Set box x to the superscript field in style $C\uparrow$; set box y to the nucleus field in style C; and set box z to the subscript field in style $C\downarrow$. Rebox all three of these boxes to width $\max(w(x), w(y), w(z))$. If the superscript field was not empty, attach box x above box y, separated by a kern of size $\max(\xi_9, \xi_{11} - d(x))$, and shift box x right by $\frac{1}{2}\delta$; also put a kern of size ξ_{13} above box x. If the subscript field was not empty, attach box z below box y, separated by a kern of size $\max(\xi_{10}, \xi_{12} - h(z))$, and shift box z left by $\frac{1}{2}\delta$; also put a kern of size ξ_{13} below box z. The resulting vbox becomes the nucleus of the current Op atom; move to the next item.

14. If the current item is an Ord atom, go to Rule 17 unless all of the following are true: The nucleus is a symbol; the subscript and superscript are both empty; the very next item in the math list is an atom of type Ord, Op, Bin, Rel, Open, Close, or Punct; and the nucleus of the next item is a symbol whose family is the same as the family in the present Ord atom. In such cases the present symbol is marked as a text symbol. If the font information shows a ligature between this symbol and the following one, using the specified family and the current size, then insert the ligature character and continue as specified by the font; two characters may collapse into one, or a new character may appear. Otherwise if the font information shows a kern between the current symbol and the next, insert a kern item after the current Ord atom and move to the next item after that. Otherwise (i.e., if no ligature or kern is specified between the present text symbol and the following character), go to Rule 17.

15. If the current item is a generalized fraction (and it had better be, because that's the only possibility left if Rules 1–14 don't apply), let θ be the thickness of the bar line and let (λ, ρ) be the left and right delimiters. If this fraction was generated by `\over` or `\overwithdelims`, then $\theta = \xi_8$; if it was generated by `\atop` or `\atopwithdelims`, $\theta = 0$; otherwise it was generated by `\above` or `\abovewithdelims`, and a specific value of θ was given at that time. The values of λ and ρ are null unless the fraction is "with delims."

15a. Put the numerator into box x, using style T or T' if C is D or D', otherwise using style $C\uparrow$. Put the denominator into box z, using style T' if $C > T$, otherwise using $C\downarrow$. If $w(x) < w(z)$, rebox x to width $w(z)$; if $w(z) < w(x)$, rebox z to width $w(x)$.

15b. If $C > T$, set $u \leftarrow \sigma_8$ and $v \leftarrow \sigma_{11}$. Otherwise set $u \leftarrow \sigma_9$ or σ_{10}, according as $\theta \neq 0$ or $\theta = 0$, and set $v \leftarrow \sigma_{12}$. (The fraction will be typeset with its numerator shifted up by an amount u with respect to the current baseline, and with the denominator shifted down by v, unless the boxes are unusually large.)

15c. If $\theta = 0$ (`\atop`), the numerator and denominator are combined as follows: Set $\varphi \leftarrow 7\xi_8$ or $3\xi_8$, according as $C > T$ or $C \leq T$; φ is the minimum clearance that will be tolerated between numerator and denominator. Let $\psi = (u - d(x)) - (h(z) - v)$ be the actual clearance that would be obtained with the current values of u and v; if $\psi < \varphi$, add $\frac{1}{2}(\varphi - \psi)$ to both u and v. Then construct a vbox of height $h(x) + u$ and depth $d(z) + v$, consisting of box x followed by an appropriate kern followed by box z.

15d. If $\theta \neq 0$ (\over), the numerator and denominator are combined as follows: Set $\varphi \leftarrow 3\theta$ or θ, according as $C > T$ or $C \leq T$; φ is the minimum clearance that will be tolerated between numerator or denominator and the bar line. Let $a = \sigma_{22}$ be the current axis height; the middle of the bar line will be placed at this height. If $(u - d(x)) - (a + \frac{1}{2}\theta) < \varphi$, increase u by the difference between these quantities; and if $(a - \frac{1}{2}\theta) - (h(z) - v) < \varphi$, increase v by the difference. Finally construct a vbox of height $h(x) + u$ and depth $d(z) + v$, consisting of box x followed by a kern followed by an hrule of height θ followed by another kern followed by box z, where the kerns are figured so that the bottom of the hrule occurs at $a - \frac{1}{2}\theta$ above the baseline.

15e. Enclose the vbox that was constructed in Rule 15c or 15d by delimiters whose height plus depth is at least σ_{20}, if $C > T$, and at least σ_{21} otherwise. Shift the delimiters up or down so that they are vertically centered with respect to the axis. Replace the generalized fraction by an Inner atom whose nucleus is the resulting sequence of three boxes (left delimiter, vbox, right delimiter).

Rules 1–15 account for the preliminary processing of math list items; but we still haven't specified how subscripts and superscripts are to be typeset. Therefore some of those rules lead to the following post-process:

16. Change the current item to an Ord atom, and continue with Rule 17.

17. If the nucleus of the current item is a math list, replace it by a box obtained by typesetting that list in the current style. Then if the nucleus is not simply a symbol, go on to Rule 18. Otherwise we are in the common case that a math symbol is to be translated to its horizontal-list equivalent: Convert the symbol to a character box for the specified family in the current size. If the symbol was not marked by Rule 14 above as a text symbol, or if \fontdimen parameter number 2 of its font is zero, set δ to the italic correction; otherwise set δ to zero. If δ is nonzero and if the subscript field of the current atom is empty, insert a kern of width δ after the character box, and set δ to zero. Continue with Rule 18.

18. (The remaining task for the current atom is to attach a possible subscript and superscript.) If both subscript and superscript fields are empty, move to the next item. Otherwise continue with the following subrules:

18a. If the translation of the nucleus is a character box, possibly followed by a kern, set u and v equal to zero; otherwise set $u \leftarrow h - q$ and $v \leftarrow d + r$, where h and d are the height and depth of the translated nucleus, and where q and r are the values of σ_{18} and σ_{19} in the font corresponding to styles $C\uparrow$ and $C\downarrow$. (The quantities u and v represent minimum amounts by which the superscript and subscript will be shifted up and down; these preliminary values of u and v may be increased later.)

18b. If the superscript field is empty (so that there is a subscript only), set box x to the subscript in style $C\downarrow$, and add \scriptspace to $w(x)$. Append this box to the translation of the current item, shifting it down by $\max(v, \sigma_{16}, h(x) - \frac{4}{5}|\sigma_5|)$, and move to the next item. (The idea is to make sure that the subscript is shifted by at least v and by at least σ_{16}; furthermore, the top of the subscript should not extend above $\frac{4}{5}$ of the current x-height.)

18c. Set box x to the superscript field in style $C\uparrow$, and add \scriptspace to $w(x)$. Then set $u \leftarrow \max(u, p, d(x) + \frac{1}{4}|\sigma_5|)$, where $p = \sigma_{13}$ if $C = D$, $p = \sigma_{15}$ if $C = C'$, and $p = \sigma_{14}$ otherwise; this gives a tentative position for the superscript.

18d. If the subscript field is empty (so that there is a superscript only), append box x to the translation of the current atom, shifting it up by u, and move to the next item. Otherwise (i.e., both subscript and superscript are present), set box y to the subscript in style $C\!\downarrow$, add \scriptspace to $w(y)$, and set $v \leftarrow \max(v, \sigma_{17})$.

18e. (The remaining task is to position a joint subscript/superscript combination.) Let $\theta = \xi_8$ be the default rule thickness. If $(u - d(x)) - (h(y) - v) \geq 4\theta$, go to Rule 18f. (This means that the white space between subscript and superscript is at least 4θ.) Otherwise reset v so that $(u - d(x)) - (h(y) - v) = 4\theta$. Let $\psi = \frac{4}{5}|\sigma_5| - (u - d(x))$. If $\psi > 0$, increase u by ψ and decrease v by ψ. (This means that the bottom of the superscript will be at least as high above the baseline as $\frac{4}{5}$ of the x-height.)

18f. Finally, let δ be zero unless it was set to a nonzero value by Rules 13 or 17. (This is the amount of horizontal displacement between subscript and superscript.) Make a vbox of height $h(x) + u$ and depth $d(y) + v$, consisting of box x shifted right by δ, followed by an appropriate kern, followed by box y. Append this vbox to the translation of the current item and move to the next.

After the entire math list has been processed by Rules 1–18, TeX looks at the last atom (if there was one), and changes its type from Bin to Ord (if it was of type Bin). Then the following rule is performed:

19. If the math list begins and ends with boundary items, compute the maximum height h and depth d of the boxes in the translation of the math list that was made on the first pass, taking into account the fact that some boxes may be raised or lowered. Let $a = \sigma_{22}$ be the axis height, and let $\delta = \max(h - a, d + a)$ be the amount by which the formula extends away from the axis. Replace the boundary items by delimiters whose height plus depth is at least $\max(\lfloor \delta/500 \rfloor f, 2\delta - l)$, where f is the \delimiterfactor and l is the \delimitershortfall. Shift the delimiters up or down so that they are vertically centered with respect to the axis. Change the left boundary item to an Open atom and the right boundary item to a Close atom. (All of the calculations in this step are done with C equal to the starting style of the math list; style items in the middle of the list do not affect the style of the right boundary item.)

20. Rules 1–19 convert the math list into a sequence of items in which the only remaining atoms are of types Ord, Op, Bin, Rel, Open, Close, Punct, and Inner. After that conversion is complete, a second pass is made through the entire list, replacing all of the atoms by the boxes and kerns in their translations. Furthermore, additional inter-element spacing is inserted just before each atom except the first, based on the type of that atom and the preceding one. Inter-element spacing is defined by the three parameters \thinmuskip, \medmuskip, and \thickmuskip; the mu units are converted to absolute units as in Rule 2 above. Chapter 18 has a chart that defines the inter-element spacing, some of which is \nonscript, i.e., it is inserted only in styles $> S$. The list might also contain style items, which are removed during the second pass; they are used to change the current style just as in the the first pass, so that both passes have the same value of C when they work on any particular atom.

21. Besides the inter-element spacing, penalties are placed after the translation of each atom of type Bin or Rel, if the math list was part of a paragraph. The penalty after a Bin is \binoppenalty, and the penalty after a Rel is \relpenalty. However, the penalty is not inserted after the final item in the entire list, or if it has a numeric value ≥ 10000, or if the very next item in the list is already a penalty item, or after a Rel atom that is immediately followed by another Rel atom.

22. After all of the preceding actions have been performed, the math list has been totally converted to a horizontal list. If the result is being inserted into a larger horizontal list, in horizontal mode or restricted horizontal mode, it is enclosed by "math-on" and "math-off" items that each record the current value of \mathsurround. Or if this list is a displayed formula, it is processed further as explained in Chapter 19.

Summary of parameter usage. Here is the promised index that refers to everything affected by the mysterious parameters in the symbol fonts. Careful study of the rules allows you to get the best results by appropriately setting the parameters for new fonts that you may wish to use in mathematical typesetting. Each font parameter has an external name that is used in supporting software packages; for example, σ_{14} is generally referred to as 'sup2' and ξ_8 as 'default_rule_thickness'. These external names are indicated in the table.

Parameter		Used in	Parameter		Used in
σ_2	space	17	σ_{17}	sub2	18d
σ_5	x_height	11, 18b, 18c, 18e	σ_{18}	sup_drop	18a
σ_6	quad	2, 20	σ_{19}	sub_drop	18a
σ_8	num1	15b	σ_{20}	delim1	15e
σ_9	num2	15b	σ_{21}	delim2	15e
σ_{10}	num3	15b	σ_{22}	axis_height	8, 13, 15d, 19
σ_{11}	denom1	15b	ξ_8	default_rule_thickness	9, 10, 11, 15, 15c, 18e
σ_{12}	denom2	15b	ξ_9	big_op_spacing1	13a
σ_{13}	sup1	18c	ξ_{10}	big_op_spacing2	13a
σ_{14}	sup2	18c	ξ_{11}	big_op_spacing3	13a
σ_{15}	sup3	18c	ξ_{12}	big_op_spacing4	13a
σ_{16}	sub1	18b	ξ_{13}	big_op_spacing5	13a

Besides the symbol and extension fonts (families 2 and 3), the rules above also refer to parameters in other families: Rule 17 uses \fontdimen parameter 2 (space) to determine whether to insert an italic correction between adjacent letters, and Rule 12 uses parameter 5 (x_height) to position an accent character. Several non-font parameters also affect mathematical typesetting: dimension parameters \delimitershortfall (Rule 19), \nulldelimiterspace (in the construction of variable delimiters for Rules 11, 15e, 19), \mathsurround (Rule 22), and \scriptspace (Rules 18bcd); integer parameters \delimiterfactor (Rule 19), \binoppenalty (Rule 21), and \relpenalty (Rule 21); muglue parameters \thinmuskip, \medmuskip, and \thickmuskip (Rule 20).

> *Woe to the author who always wants to teach!*
> *The secret of being a bore is to tell everything.*
> — VOLTAIRE, *De la Nature de l'Homme* (1737)

> *Very few Compositors are fond of Algebra,*
> *and rather chuse to be employed upon plain work.*
> — PHILIP LUCKOMBE, *The History and Art of Printing* (1770)

H

Hyphenation

It's better to break a word with a hyphen than to stretch interword spaces too much. Therefore TEX tries to divide words into syllables when there's no good alternative available.

But computers are notoriously bad at hyphenation. When the typesetting of newspapers began to be fully automated, jokes about "the-rapists who pre-ached on wee-knights" soon began to circulate.

It's not hard to understand why machines have behaved poorly at this task, because hyphenation is quite a difficult problem. For example, the word 'record' is supposed to be broken as 'rec-ord' when it is a noun, but 're-cord' when it is a verb. The word 'hyphenation' itself is somewhat exceptional; if 'hy-phen-a-tion' is compared to similar words like 'con-cat-e-na-tion', it's not immediately clear why the 'n' should be attached to the 'e' in one case but not the other. Examples like 'dem-on-stra-tion' vs. 'de-mon-stra-tive' show that the alteration of two letters can actually affect hyphens that are nine positions away.

A good solution to the problem was discovered by Frank M. Liang during 1980–1982, and TEX incorporates the new method. Liang's algorithm works quickly and finds nearly all of the legitimate places to insert hyphens; yet it makes few if any errors, and it takes up comparatively little space in the computer. Moreover, the method is flexible enough to be adapted to any language, and it can also be used to hyphenate words in two languages simultaneously. Liang's Ph.D. thesis, published by Stanford University's Department of Computer Science in 1983, explains how to take a dictionary of hyphenated words and teach it to TEX; i.e., it explains how to compute tables by which TEX will be able to reconstruct most of the hyphens in the given dictionary, without error.

TEX hyphenates a given word by first looking for it in an "exception dictionary," which specifies the hyphen positions for words that deserve special treatment. If the word isn't there, TEX looks for *patterns* in the word, and this is the key idea underlying Liang's method. Here's how it works, using the word 'hyphenation' as an example, when TEX is operating with the English-oriented patterns of plain TEX format: The given word is first extended by special markers at either end; in this case we obtain

```
.hyphenation.
```

if '.' denotes the special marker. The extended word has subwords

```
. h y p h e n a t i o n .
```

of length one,

```
.h hy yp ph he en na at ti io on n.
```

of length two,

```
.hy hyp yph phe hen ena nat ati tio ion on.
```

of length three, and so on. Each subword of length k is a pattern that defines $k + 1$ small integer values relating to the desirability of hyphens in the positions between and adjacent to its letters. We can show these values by attaching them as subscripts; for example, '$_0h_0e_2n_0$' means that the values corresponding to the subword 'hen' are 0, 0, 2, and 0, where the 2 relates to hyphens between the 'e' and the 'n'. The interletter values are entirely zero for all subwords except those that match an entry in TEX's current "pattern dictionary"; and in this case, only the subwords

$$_0h_0y_3p_0h_0 \quad _0h_0e_2n_0 \quad _0h_0e_0n_0a_4$$
$$_0h_0e_0n_5a_0t_0 \quad _1n_0a_0 \quad _0n_2a_0t_0 \quad _1t_0i_0o_0 \quad _2i_0o_0 \quad _0o_2n_0$$

occur as special patterns. TEX now computes the maximum interletter value that occurs at each subword touching each interletter position. For example, between 'e' and 'n' there are four relevant values in this case (2 from $_0h_0e_2n_0$, 0 from $_0h_0e_0n_0a_4$, 0 from $_0h_0e_0n_5a_0t_0$, and 1 from $_1n_0a_0$); the maximum of these is 2. The result of all the maximizations is

$$\cdot _0h_0y_3p_0h_0e_2n_5a_4t_2i_0o_2n_0 \cdot$$

Now comes the final step: A hyphen is considered to be acceptable between two letters if the associated interletter value is *odd*. Thus, two potential breakpoints have been found: 'hy-phen-ation'. Similarly, the word 'concatenation' contains the patterns

$$_0o_2n_0 \quad _0o_0n_1c_0 \quad _1c_0a_0 \quad _1n_0a_0 \quad _0n_2a_0t_0 \quad _1t_0i_0o_0 \quad _2i_0o_0 \quad _0o_2n_0$$

and this yields '$_0c_0o_2n_1c_0a_0t_0e_1n_2a_1t_2i_0o_2n_0$', i.e., 'con-cate-na-tion'.

Let's try a 34-letter word: 'supercalifragilisticexpialidocious' matches the plain TEX patterns

$$u_1pe \quad r_1c \quad _1ca \quad al_1i \quad ag_1i \quad gil_4 \quad il_1i \quad il_4ist \quad is_1ti \quad st_2i$$
$$s_1tic \quad _1exp \quad x_3p \quad pi_3a \quad _2i_1a \quad i_2al \quad _2id \quad _1do \quad _1ci \quad _2io \quad _2us$$

(where subscripts that aren't shown are zero), and this yields

$$\cdot _0s_0u_1p_0e_0r_1c_0a_0l_1i_0f_0r_0a_0g_1i_0l_4i_0s_1t_2i_0c_1e_0x_3p_2i_3a_0l_2i_1d_0o_1c_2i_0o_2u_0s_0 \cdot$$

The resulting hyphens 'su-per-cal-ifrag-ilis-tic-ex-pi-ali-do-cious' agree with Random House's *Unabridged Dictionary* (which also shows a few more: 'su-per-cal-i-frag-i-lis-tic-ex-pi-al-i-do-cious').

Plain TEX loads exactly 4447 patterns into TEX's memory, beginning with '$_0\cdot _0a_0c_0h_4$' and ending with '$_4z_1z_2$' and '$_0z_4z_0y_0$'. The interletter values in these patterns are all between 0 and 5; a large odd value like the 5 in '$_0h_5e_0l_0o_0$' forces desirable hyphen points in words like 'bach-e-lor' and 'ech-e-lon', while a large even value like the 4 in '$_0h_0a_0c_0h_4$' suppresses undesirable hyphens in words like 'tooth-aches'. Liang derived these patterns by preparing a special version of *Webster's Pocket Dictionary* (Merriam, 1966) that contains about 50,000 words including derived forms. Then he checked a preliminary set of patterns obtained from this data against an up-to-date hyphenation dictionary of about 115,000 words obtained from a publisher; errors found in this run led to the addition of about 1000 words like `camp-fire`, `Af-ghan-i-stan`, and `bio-rhythm` to the pocket dictionary list. He weighted a few thousand common words more heavily so that they would be more likely to be hyphenated; as a result, the patterns of plain TEX guarantee complete hyphenation of the 700 or so most common words of English, as well as common technical words like `al-go-rithm`. These patterns find 89.3% of the hyphens in Liang's dictionary as a whole, and they insert no hyphens that are not present.

Patterns derived from the common words of a language tend to work well on uncommon or newly coined words that are not in the original dictionary. For example, Liang's patterns find a correct subset of the hyphens in the word that all of today's unabridged dictionaries agree is the longest in English, namely

> `pneu-monoul-tra-mi-cro-scop-ic-sil-i-co-vol-canoco-nio-sis.`

They even do fairly well on words from other languages that aren't too distant from English; for example, the pseudo-German utterances of Mark Twain's *Connecticut Yankee* come out with only six or seven bad hyphens:

> `Con-stanti-nop-o-li-tanis-cher-`
> `   dudel-sack-spfeifen-mach-ers-ge-sellschafft;`
> `Ni-hilis-ten-dy-na-mitthe-`
> `   aterkaestchensspren-gungsat-ten-taetsver-suchun-gen;`
> `Transvaal-trup-pen-tropen-trans-port-`
> `   tram-pelth-iertreib-er-trau-ungsthrae-nen-tra-goedie;`
> `Mekka-musel-man-nen-massen-menchen-`
> `   mo-er-der-mohren-mut-ter-mar-mor-mon-u-menten-machen.`

But when plain TEX is tried on the name of a famous Welsh city,

> `Llan-fair-p-wll-gwyn-gyll-gogerych-`
> `   wyrn-drob-wl-l-l-lan-tysil-i-o-gogogoch,`

linguistic differences became quite evident, since the correct hyphens are

> `Llan-fair-pwll-gwyn-gyll-go-ger-y-`
> `   chwyrn-dro-bwll-llan-ty-sil-i-o-go-go-goch.`

Appropriate pattern values for other languages can be derived by applying Liang's method to suitable dictionaries of hyphen points.

Dictionaries of English do not always agree on where syllable boundaries occur. For example, the *American Heritage Dictionary* says 'in-de-pend-ent' while *Webster's* says 'in-de-pen-dent'. Plain TEX generally follows Webster except in a few cases where other authorities seem preferable.

[From here to the end of this appendix, TEX will be typesetting with

> `\hyphenpenalty=-1000   \pretolerance=-1   \tolerance=1000`
> `\doublehyphendemerits=-100000   \finalhyphendemerits=-100000`

so that hyphens will be inserted much more often than usual.]

The fact that plain TeX finds only 90% of the permissible hyphen points in a large dictionary is, of course, no cause for alarm. When word frequency is taken into account, the probability rises to well over 95%. Since TeX's line-breaking algorithm often succeeds in finding a way to break a paragraph without needing hyphens at all, and since there's a good chance of finding a different hyphen point near to one that is missed by TeX's patterns, it is clear that manual intervention to correct or insert hyphenations in TeX output is rarely needed, and that such refinements take a negligible amount of time compared to the normal work of keyboarding and proofreading.

But you can always insert words into TeX's exception dictionary, if you find that the patterns aren't quite right for your application. For example, this book was typeset with three exceptional words added: The format in Appendix E includes the command

> `\hyphenation{man-u-script man-u-scripts ap-pen-dix}`

which tells TeX how to hyphenate the words 'manuscript', 'manuscripts', and 'appendix'. Notice that both singular and plural forms of 'manuscript' were entered, since the exception dictionary affects hyphenation only when a word agrees completely with an exceptional entry. (Precise rules for the `\hyphenation` command are discussed below.)

If you want to see all of the hyphens that plain TeX will find in some random text, you can say '`\showhyphens{`⟨random text⟩`}`' and the results will appear on your terminal (and in the log file). For example,

> `*\showhyphens{random manuscript manuscripts appendix}`
>
> `Underfull \hbox (badness 10000) detected at line 0`
> `[] \tenrm ran-dom manuscript manuscripts ap-pendix`

shows the hyphen positions that would have been found in this book without the addition of any `\hyphenation` exceptions. Somehow the word 'manuscript' slips through all of the ordinary patterns; the author added it as an exception for this particular job because he used it 80 times (not counting its appearances in this appendix).

The `\showhyphens` macro creates an hbox that is intentionally underfull, so you should ignore the warning about '`badness 10000`'; this spurious message comes out because TeX displays hyphens in compact form only when it is displaying the contents of anomalous hboxes. (TeX wizards may enjoy studying the way `\showhyphens` is defined in Appendix B.)

If you want to add one or more words to the exception dictionary, just say `\hyphenation{`⟨words⟩`}` where ⟨words⟩ consists of one or more ⟨word⟩ items separated by spaces. A ⟨word⟩ must consist entirely of letters and hyphens; more precisely, a "hyphen" in this context is the token $-_{12}$. A "letter" in this context is a character token whose category code is 11 or 12, or a control sequence defined by `\chardef`, or `\char`⟨8-bit number⟩, such that the corresponding character has a nonzero `\lccode`. TeX uses the `\lccode` to convert each letter to "lowercase" form; a word-to-be-hyphenated will match an entry in the exception dictionary if and only if both words have the same lowercase form after conversion to lowercase.

TeX will henceforth insert discretionary hyphens in the specified positions, whenever it attempts to hyphenate a word that matches an entry in the exception dictionary, except that hyphens are never inserted after the very first letter or before the last or second-last letter of a word. You must insert your own discretionary hyphens if you want to allow them in such positions. A \hyphenation entry might contain no hyphens at all; then TeX will insert no hyphens in the word.

The exception dictionary is global; i.e., exceptions do not disappear at the end of a group. If you specify \hyphenation of the same word more than once, its most recently specified hyphen positions are used.

The exception dictionary is dynamic, but the pattern dictionary is static: To change TeX's current set of hyphenation patterns, you must give an entirely new set, and TeX will spend a little time putting them into a form that makes the hyphenation algorithm efficient. The command format is \patterns{⟨patterns⟩}, where ⟨patterns⟩ is a sequence of ⟨pattern⟩ items separated by spaces. This command is available only in INITEX, not in production versions of TeX, since the process of pattern compression requires extra memory that can be put to better use in a production system. INITEX massages the patterns and outputs a format file that production versions can load at high speed.

A ⟨pattern⟩ in the \patterns list has a more restricted form than a ⟨word⟩ in the \hyphenation list, since patterns are supposed to be prepared by experts who are paid well for their expertise. Each ⟨pattern⟩ consists of one or more occurrences of ⟨value⟩⟨letter⟩, followed by ⟨value⟩. Here ⟨value⟩ is either a digit (0_{12} to 9_{12}) or empty; an empty ⟨value⟩ stands for zero. For example, the pattern '$_0a_1b_0$' can be represented as 0a1b0 or a1b0 or 0a1b or simply a1b. A ⟨letter⟩ is a character token of category 11 or 12 whose \lccode is nonzero. If you want to use a digit as a ⟨letter⟩, you must precede it by a nonempty ⟨value⟩; for example, if for some reason you want the pattern '$_1a_01_2$' you can obtain it by typing '1a012', assuming that \lccode'1 is nonzero. Exception: The character '.' is treated as if it were a ⟨letter⟩ of code 0 when it appears in a pattern. Code 0 (which obviously cannot match a nonzero \lccode) is used by TeX to represent the left or right edge of a word when it is being hyphenated.

Plain TeX inputs a file called hyphen.tex that sets up the pattern dictionary and the initial exception dictionary. The file has the form

```
\patterns{.ach4 .ad4der .af1t .al3t  ⋯  zte4 4z1z2 z4zy}
\hyphenation{as-so-ciate as-so-ciates dec-li-na-tion oblig-a-tory
   phil-an-thropic present presents project projects reci-procity
   re-cog-ni-zance ref-or-ma-tion ret-ri-bu-tion ta-ble}
```

The first thirteen exceptions keep TeX from inserting incorrect hyphens; for example, 'pro-ject' and 'pre-sent' are words like 're-cord', that cannot be hyphenated without knowing the context. The other exception, 'ta-ble', is included just to meet the claim that plain TeX fully hyphenates the 700 or so most common words of English.

But how does TEX decide what sequences of letters are "words" that should be hyphenated? Let's recall that TEX is working on a horizontal list that contains boxes, glue, rules, ligatures, kerns, discretionaries, marks, whatsits, etc., in addition to simple characters; somehow it has to pick out things to hyphenate when it is unable to find suitable breakpoints without hyphenation. The presence of punctuation marks before and/or after a word should not make a word unrecognizable or unhyphenatable; neither should the presence of ligatures and kerns within a word. On the other hand, it is desirable to do hyphenation quickly, not spending too much time trying to handle unusual situations that might be hyphenatable but hard to recognize mechanically.

TEX looks for potentially hyphenatable words by searching ahead from each glue item that is not in a math formula. The search bypasses characters whose \lccode is zero, or ligatures that begin with such characters; it also bypasses whatsits and *implicit kern* items, i.e., kerns that were inserted by TEX itself because of information stored with the font. If the search finds a character with nonzero \lccode, or if it finds a ligature that begins with such a character, that character is called the *starting letter*. But if any other type of item occurs before a suitable starting letter is found, hyphenation is abandoned (until after the next glue item). Thus, a box or rule or mark, or a kern that was explicitly inserted by \kern or \/, must not intervene between glue and a hyphenatable word. If the starting letter is not lowercase (i.e., if it doesn't equal its own \lccode), hyphenation is abandoned unless \uchyph is positive.

If a suitable starting letter is found, let it be in font f. Hyphenation is abandoned unless the \hyphenchar of f is between 0 and 255, and unless a character of that number exists in the font. If this test is passed, TEX continues to scan forward until coming to something that's not one of the following three "admissible items": (1) a character in font f whose \lccode is nonzero; (2) a ligature formed entirely from characters of type (1); (3) an implicit kern. The first inadmissible item terminates this part of the process; the trial word consists of all the letters found in admissible items. Notice that all of these letters are in font f.

If a trial word $l_1 \ldots l_n$ has been found by this process, hyphenation will still be abandoned unless $n \geq \lambda + \rho$, where $\lambda = \max(1, \verb|\lefthyphenmin|)$ and $\rho = \max(1, \verb|\righthyphenmin|)$. (Plain TEX takes $\lambda = 2$ and $\rho = 3$.) Furthermore, the items immediately following the trial word must consist of zero or more characters, ligatures, and implicit kerns, followed immediately by either glue or an explicit kern or a penalty item or a whatsit or an item of vertical mode material from \mark, \insert, or \vadjust. Thus, a box or rule or math formula or discretionary following too closely upon the trial word will inhibit hyphenation. (Since TEX inserts empty discretionaries after explicit hyphens, these rules imply that already-hyphenated compound words will not be further hyphenated by the algorithm.)

Trial words $l_1 \ldots l_n$ that pass all these tests are submitted to the hyphenation algorithm described earlier. Hyphens are not inserted before l_λ or after $l_{n+1-\rho}$. If other hyphenation points are found, one or more discretionary items are inserted in the word; ligatures and implicit kerns are reconstituted at the same time.

Since ligatures and kerns are treated in quite a general manner, it's possible that one hyphenation point might preclude another because the ligatures that occur with hyphenation might overlap the ligatures that occur without hyphenation. This anomaly probably won't occur in real-life situations; therefore TeX's interesting approach to the problem will not be discussed here.

According to the rules above, there's an important distinction between implicit and explicit kerns, because TeX recomputes implicit kerns when it finds at least one hyphen point in a word. You can see the difference between these two types of kerns when TeX displays lists of items in its internal format, if you look closely: '\kern2.0' denotes an implicit kern of 2 pt, and '\kern 2.0' denotes an explicit kern of the same magnitude. The italic correction command \/ inserts an explicit kern.

The control sequence \- is equivalent to \discretionary{\char h}{}{}, where h is the \hyphenchar of the current font, provided that h lies between 0 and 255. Otherwise \- is equivalent to \discretionary{}{}{}.

So far we have assumed that TeX knows only one style of hyphenation at a time; but in fact TeX can remember up to 256 distinct sets of rules, if you have enough memory in your computer. An integer parameter called \language selects the rules actually used; every \hyphenation and \patterns specification appends new rules to those previously given for the current value of \language. (If \language is negative or greater than 255, TeX acts as if \language = 0.) All \patterns for all languages must be given before a paragraph is typeset, if INITEX is used for typesetting.

TeX is able to work with several languages in the same paragraph, because it operates as follows. At the beginning of a paragraph the "current language" is defined to be 0. Whenever a character is added to the current paragraph (i.e., in unrestricted horizontal mode), the current language is compared to \language; if they differ, the current language is reset and a whatsit node specifying the new current language is inserted before the character. Thus, if you say '\def\french{\language1...}' and 'mix {\french franc/ais} with English', TeX will put whatsits before the **f** and the **w**; hence it will use language 1 rules when hyphenating **franc/ais**, after which it will revert to language 0. You can insert the whatsit yourself (even in restricted horizontal mode) by saying \setlanguage⟨number⟩; this changes the current language but it does not change \language. Each whatsit records the current \lefthyphenmin and \righthyphenmin.

If all problems of hyphenation have not been solved,
at least some progress has been made since that night,
when according to legend, an RCA Marketing Manager received
a phone call from a disturbed customer. His 301 had just hyphenated "God."
— PAUL E. JUSTUS, *There's More to Typesetting Than Setting Type* (1972)

The committee skeptically re-
commended more study for a bill
to require warning labels on rec-
ords with subliminal messages re-
corded backward.

— THE PENINSULA TIMES TRIBUNE (April 28, 1982)

Index

The author has tried to provide as complete an index as possible, so that people will be able to find things that are tucked away in obscure corners of this long book. Therefore the index itself is rather long. A short summary of the simpler aspects of TeX appears at the beginning of Appendix B; a summary of special symbols appears at the end of Appendix F; a summary of other special things appears under 'tables' below.

Page numbers are <u>underlined</u> in the index when they represent the definition or the main source of information about whatever is being indexed. (Underlined entries are the most definitive, but not necessarily the easiest for a beginner to understand.) A page number is given in italics (e.g., '*123*') when that page contains an instructive example of how the concept in question might be used. Sometimes both underlining and italics are appropriate. When an index entry refers to a page containing a relevant exercise, the answer to that exercise (in Appendix A) might divulge further information; an answer page is not indexed here unless it refers to a topic that isn't included in the statement of the relevant exercise.

Control sequence names that are preceded by an asterisk (*) in this index are primitives of TeX; i.e., they are built in. It may be dangerous to redefine them.

␣ (visible space), <u>3</u>, 420, 429;
   see also ⟨space⟩, spaces.
*\␣ (control space), *8*, 10, 19, *73*, *74*,
   86–87, 154, *163*, *167*, 283, <u>285</u>,
   290, 323, 351, *381*.
(hash mark), 38, 51, 113, *200–202*, <u>*203*</u>,
   204–205, 228, <u>235</u>, *236–240*.
\# (#), 38, 51, <u>356</u>.
##, 203–205, 228, *359–362*, *378–379*.
###, 88.
#{, 204, *401*.
\$ (dollar sign), 4, 38, 51, 54, 86–88, *92*, 127,
   134–135, *185–186*, <u>269</u>, 283, <u>287</u>, <u>293</u>.
\\$ (\$), 38, 51, *202*, *309*, <u>356</u>.
\$\$, 86–89, <u>185</u>, *186–196*, 232, <u>287</u>, <u>293</u>,
   375–376, *421*.
% (percent sign), *26*, 38, 39, 43, 48, 51, 113,
   124, *249*, *337*, *340*, <u>343</u>.
\% (%), 38, 43–44, 51, <u>356</u>.
%%, 112–113.
& (ampersand), 38, 51, *175–177*, *190–196*,
   231–248, <u>282</u>, *385–386*.
   for preloaded formats, <u>25</u>, 26, 344.
\& (&), 38, 51, 53, <u>356</u>.
&&, 241–242, *361*, *412*.
' (apostrophe or right quote), 3–5, 51, *130*,
   155, 201, *305*, 324, <u>357</u>, 394–395;
   see also octal.
\' (acute accent), *7–9*, 52–53, *305*,
   335, <u>356</u>, *420*.
'' ("), *3–5*, *24*, 394–395.

' (reverse apostrophe or left quote), 3–5, 51,
   132, 134, *305*, 391, 394–395;
   see also alphabetic constant.
\' (grave accent), 8, 52–53, *305*, <u>356</u>.
'' ("), *3–5*, *24*, 394–395.
" (double quote or ditto mark), 52, 53,
   134; *see also* hexadecimal.
\" (dieresis or umlaut accent), *7*, 9, *24*,
   25, 52–53, 55, <u>356</u>.
((left parenthesis), 51, 134, *140*,
   145–150, 345.
\(, 409.
) (right parenthesis), 51, 134, *140*,
   145–150, 345.
[(left bracket), 51, 134, *146–148*,
   171, *408*, *437*.
[], *28*, <u>79</u>, *302*.
[1], 23, <u>119</u>.
] (right bracket), 51, 134, *146–147*,
   171, 345, *408*, *437*.
{ (left brace), *13–14*, *19–21*, 38, 51,
   200–202, <u>*203*</u>–*204*, *205–206*, 216, <u>269</u>,
   275–276, <u>283</u>, <u>286</u>, <u>291</u>, *330*.
\{ ({), 134, *146–147*, *174–175*, <u>361</u>.
{}, *19*, *54*, 82, 95, 114, *129*, 130, 150,
   169, *196*, *242*, 253, 262, *305*, *315*,
   318, 351, 393.
} (right brace), *13–14*, *19–21*, 38, 51,
   200–202, <u>*203*</u>–*204*, *205–206*, <u>269</u>,
   275–276, <u>279</u>, 301, *330*.
\} (}), 134, *146–147*, *174–175*, <u>361</u>.

+ (plus sign), 51, 132, 268.
\+ (begin tabbed line), *231–234*, 249, 339, <u>354</u>.
- (hyphen or minus), *4*, 51, 93, 95, *127*, 132, 268.
*\- (discretionary hyphen), 95, 283, 287, 292, <u>455</u>.
--, ---, *see* en-dash, em-dash.
±, *see* \pm.
∓, *see* \mp.
* (asterisk), 23, 25, 51, 99, 113, 116, *132–133*, 154, *326*.
* (discretionary ×), 173, <u>357</u>.
**, 23, 25, 344.
/ (slash), 51, *132*, *146–147*, *320*, 430.
*\/ (italic correction), *14*, *64*, <u>287</u>, *292*, *306*, 382, 455.
| (vertical line), 52, 53, 132, *146–147*, *171*, *174*, 438.
\| (‖), *146–147*, *171*, <u>361</u>, 435, 438.
\ (backslash), *7*, 38, 39, 40, 51, 146–147, <u>343</u>, *436*.
\\, 38, 378, 418.
< (less than sign), 52, 53, *133*, 150, 154, 209.
≤, 45, 135, 369; *see also* \le.
= (equals sign), 51, *133*, 209, 226, 275, *376*.
\= (macron accent), 52, *53*, <u>356</u>.
^{def}=, 181, *437*.
≠, 45, 135, 369; *see also* \ne.
> (greater than sign), 52, 53, *133*, 150, 209.
\> (medium space), 167, 171, <u>357</u>.
≥, 45, 135, 369; *see also* \ge.
⟨⟩, *see* angle brackets.
, (comma), 51, *72–73*, *134*, *161–162*, *172–174*, *394–395*, 430.
\, (thin space), 5, *167–173*, 305, <u>357</u>, *409–410*.
. (period), 51, *72–73*, 133–134, 149, *161*, <u>345</u>, *394–395*, 430.
space after, *73–75*; <u>76</u>.
\. (dot accent), 52, <u>356</u>.
..., *see* \ldots, ellipses.
⋯, *see* \cdots, ellipses.
⋮, *see* \vdots, ellipses.
; (semicolon), 51, *134*, 161.
\; (thick space), 167, 171, <u>357</u>.
: (colon), 51, *133–134*, *155*, 161, *174*, *438*.
:=, 133.
? (question mark), 31, 51, 73, 161.
¿ (open question), 51.
! (exclamation point), 51, *72*, 73, 75, *169*.
¡ (open exclamation), 51.
\! (negative thin space), *167*, *169*, <u>357</u>.

_ (underscore), 38, 51, *128–130*, 134.
_ (_), 38, *165*, <u>356</u>.
^ (hat), 38, 51, *128–130*, 134, 369, *423*.
\^ (circumflex accent), 52–53, <u>356</u>.
^^, 45, <u>47</u>, *48*, <u>368</u>, 370, 423.
^^M (ASCII ⟨return⟩), 45, 249, 331, <u>343</u>, 345, *348*, 352, 380, *390–391*, *421*, 423.
\^^M, 8, *305*, <u>351</u>.
˜ (tilde), 38, 51, 343, <u>353</u>; *see also* ties.
\˜ (tilde accent), 52, <u>356</u>, 387.
↑↓, 135, 343, 368, 429; *see also* \uparrow, \downarrow.
@ (at sign), 51, 98–99, 132, 134, *344*, *364*, *408*, 414.
@@, 98–99.
\@ne, <u>345</u>.
\aa (å), <u>356</u>.
\AA (Å), <u>356</u>.
abbreviations, *73–74*, *340*; *see also* macros.
*\above (general fraction), *143*, 152, 292, 444–445.
*\abovedisplayshortskip, <u>189</u>, 274, *348*, *415*.
*\abovedisplayskip, <u>189</u>, <u>190</u>, 194, 274, 291, *348*, *415*.
*\abovewithdelims, 152, <u>292</u>, 444–445.
absolute value, *146*, *149*, *171*, *175*.
Acc atom, 158, 289, 443.
*\accent (general accent), 9, 54, 86, 283, <u>286</u>.
accents (´ ` ¨ etc.), 7, *52–53*, *339*, <u>356</u>, 357, 427–429.
as ligatures, 46, 54.
in math, *135–137*, 141, 164–165, <u>359</u>, 435, <u>443</u>.
on top of accents, 136.
table, 52, 135, 339.
\active (category 13), *241*, <u>343</u>, *395*, *421*.
active character, 37, 40, 209, 241, 307, 377, 380–381, 394–395.
active math character, 155, <u>289</u>.
active spaces, 381, 394, 421.
\acute (math accent: ́x), 135, <u>359</u>.
acute accent (´), *see* \', \acute.
\address, *403–404*, <u>407</u>.
*\adjdemerits, <u>98</u>, 273, *314*, *348*.
*\advance, *21*, 118–119, 218, 256, <u>276</u>, 355.
\advancepageno, 256, *257*, <u>362</u>, *416*.
\ae (æ), vii, 17, 45–46, *52–53*, *239*, <u>356</u>.
\AE (Æ), *52–53*, <u>356</u>.
*\afterassignment, 215, <u>279</u>, *352*, *364*, *376*, *401*.
*\aftergroup, 215, <u>279</u>, *363*, *374*, *377*, 379.
'ain, *see* reverse apostrophe.

al-Khwârizmî, abu Ja'far Muhammad
     ibn Mûsâ, 53.
\aleph (ℵ), 9, <u>358</u>, 435.
Alice, 4, 387, 394.
alignment displays, 190, 193, <u>291</u>.
⟨alignment material⟩, 282, 285.
alignments, 231–249, <u>282</u>, 302–303, 385–386,
     392; *see also* tabbing.
Alka-Seltzer, 404–405.
all caps, *see* \uppercase.
Allen, Todd Andrew, 377.
allocation, 121–122, <u>346</u>, <u>347</u>.
\allocationnumber, 346.
\allowbreak, *174*, <u>353</u>, *396*.
\allowhyphens, *394*, <u>395</u>.
\alpha (α), *127*, *201*, <u>358</u>, 434.
\Alpha, 434.
alphabetic constants, *44–46*, 215, <u>269</u>,
     270, 309, <u>367</u>, 385.
alternatives, *see* \cases.
\amalg (II), <u>358</u>, 436.
American Mathematical Society, ii, vii.
ampersand, <u>25</u>, 38, 51, *175–177*, *190–196*,
     231–248, <u>282</u>, 344, 385–386, 428.
𝒜ℳ𝒮-TEX, 164, <u>420</u>, 434.
anatomy of TEX, 38–39, <u>46</u>, 85, <u>267</u>, 349,
     373, 379, 385, 386, <u>456</u>.
\angle (∠), <u>358</u>, 435.
angle brackets (⟨ ⟩), 59, *146–147*, 150, <u>268</u>,
     420, 437; *see also* \langle, \rangle.
angstrom unit, *see* \AA.
\annotations, 403, *404*, <u>407</u>.
answers to the exercises, 305–337.
Antisthenes of Athens, 239.
apostrophe, 3–5, 51, *130*, 155, 201, 324;
     see also octal.
\approx (≈), 128, 436.
Arabic, 66.
\arccos (arccos), 162, <u>361</u>.
Archytas of Taras, 239.
\arcsin (arcsin), 162, 361.
\arctan (arctan), 162, 361.
Arenskiĭ, Anton Stepanovich, 410.
\arg (arg), 162, 361.
arguments, 33, 200–205, *263*, 268, *375–380*.
Aristippus of Cyrene, 239.
Aristophanes, 239.
Aristotle, 35.
arithmetic, 117–119, *see* \advance,
     \multiply, \divide.
⟨arithmetic⟩, <u>276</u>.
arrays, *176–178*, *see* matrices.
arrows, *146–147*, *182*, 226, <u>437</u>.

\arrowvert (|), 150, <u>359</u>.
\Arrowvert (‖), 150, <u>359</u>.
The Art of Computer Programming,
     259–260.
as is, *see* \obeylines, \obeyspaces,
     verbatim.
ASCII, 3, 43–45, 49, 214, 343, <u>367</u>, 371.
⟨assignment⟩, <u>275</u>.
assignments, 275–278, 373.
\ast (*), 436.
asterisk, 23, 25, 51, 99, 113, 116, *132–133*,
     154, *326*.
\asymp (≍), 436.
at, 16–17, 60, 213, 277, *408*, *414*, 433.
⟨at clause⟩, <u>277</u>.
at sign, 51, 98–99, 132, 134, *344*, *364*,
     408, 414.
AT&T, 247.
atoms, 157–159, 170–171, 289–290, 441–447.
     table of atomic types, 158.
*\atop, *143*, *145*, 152, *178*, <u>292</u>, <u>444</u>.
*\atopwithdelims, *152*, <u>292</u>, *324*, *360*, <u>444</u>.
author, typesetting by, 182, 412–413.
auxiliary spaces, *see* ties.
axis line, 150–152, 179, 443–447.

\b (bar-under accent), 52, <u>356</u>.
Bach, Johann Sebastian, 408.
Bach, P. D. Q., 410–411, 481.
backslash, 7, 38, 39, 40, 51, 146–147,
     343, *436*.
\backslash (\ ), *38*, *146–147*, <u>359</u>, 435, *436*.
backspacing, *66*, 82–83, 222, *394–395*, *418*.
Backus, John Warner, 268.
Bacon, Francis, viscount St. Albans, 41.
Bacon, Leonard, 1.
bad breaks, avoiding, 27–30, 91–94,
     173–174, 197.
badness, *28–30*, 97–99, 111–113, 302.
*\badness, 214, *229*, 271.
⟨balanced text⟩, 275, <u>276</u>, 385.
balancing columns, 386–388, *396–397*, *417*.
\bar (math accent: x̄), 135, *136*.
bar accent (¯), *see* \=, \bar.
bar-under accent (ˍ), *see* \b.
Barrett, Percy Reginald, 197.
Barrough, Philip, 229.
baseline, 15, <u>63</u>, 77, 80–81, 150.
*\baselineskip (normal vertical distance
     between baselines), *78–79*, <u>80</u>, 104,
     194, 253, *256*, 274, 281, 342, 349,
     351–352, *409*, *414–415*.
*\batchmode, <u>32</u>, <u>277</u>, 299, *336*.

Batey, Charles, 197.
beauty, 1.
Beck, Simone, 233, 236.
Beethoven, Ludwig van, 408, 410–411.
Beeton, Barbara Ann Neuhaus Friend
    Smith, 483.
\beginchapter, 418.
*\begingroup, 21, *249, 262,* 279, *380,
    407, 419.*
\beginsection, *340–341,* 355.
*\belowdisplayshortskip, 189, 274,
    348, 415.
*\belowdisplayskip, 189, 190, 194, 274,
    291, *348, 415.*
Bemer, Robert William, *see* TEX, ASCII.
bent bars, *see* angle brackets.
Bertholle, Louisette, 233, 236.
\beta (β), *127,* 434.
\Beta, 434.
\bf (use **boldface** type), *13–14, 164–165,
    328,* 351, *409, 414–415.*
\bffam, 351, *414–415.*
\bgroup (implicit {), 269, 351, *363,
    382,* 385, *407, 421.*
Bibby, Duane Robert, i.
Biblical references, 303, *311.*
bibliographies, 4, *74,* 93, *340–341.*
\big (largish delimiter), 147, 171, *320,
    359,* 360, *414–415.*
\Big (between \big and \bigg), 147,
    175, 359, 360.
big-*O* notation, 132, *161–162, 169.*
big point, 57, *see* bp.
\bigbreak, 111, 116, 353, *363.*
\bigcap (large ∩), 147, 435.
\bigcirc (◯), 436.
\bigcup (large ∪), 147, 435.
\bigg (large delimiter), *147,* 175, 196,
    327, *359,* 360.
\Bigg (larger than \bigg), 147, 175,
    359, 360.
\bigggl, \bigggr, 324.
\biggl (\bigg left delimiter), 147,
    149, 359, 437.
\Biggl (\Bigg left delimiter), 147,
    149, 359, 437.
\biggm (\bigg middle delimiter), 147, 359.
\Biggm (\Bigg middle delimiter), 147, 359.
\biggr (\bigg right delimiter), 147,
    149, 359.
\Biggr (\Bigg right delimiter), 147,
    149, 359.

\bigl (\big left delimiter), *146–147,*
    149–150, 155, 171, *175,* 359, 437.
\Bigl (\Big left delimiter), 147, 359, 437.
\bigm (\big middle delimiter), 147,
    359, 171, *175.*
\Bigm (\Big middle delimiter), 147, 359.
\bigodot (large ⊙), 435.
\bigoplus (large ⊕), 435.
\bigotimes (large ⊗), 435.
\bigr (\big right delimiter), *146–147,*
    149–150, 171, *175,* 359.
\Bigr (\Big right delimiter), 147, 359.
\bigskip, 70, 109, 111, 115–116, 352,
    355, 407, 410–412.
\bigskipamount, 123, 349, *352–353, 363.*
\bigsqcup (large ⊔), 435.
\bigtriangledown (▽), 436.
\bigtriangleup (△), 436.
\bigtype, 408–409, 411.
\biguplus (large ⊎), 358, 435.
\bigvee (large ∨), 435.
\bigwedge (large ∧), 435.
Bill, 387, 394.
Bin atom, 158, 170–171, 289, 442–444, 446.
binary operations, *132–133,* 154–155, 164,
    196, 358, 435, 436; *see also* Bin atom.
binary search, 387–388.
binomial coefficient, 143, *see* \choose.
*\binoppenalty, 101, 174, 272, 322, *348,* 446.
black box, 64, 221, 222.
blackboard bold (e.g., ℝ), 164, 434.
blank line in input file, 24, 37, 47,
    340–341, 381.
blank space, *see* spaces.
Blase Böhning, Maria Dorothea, 248.
block structure, *see* grouping.
block style, 405–407.
\bmit (boldface math italic), 156.
\bmod (mod), *164,* 322, 361.
\body, *403–404,* 407.
Boehm, Peter James, 159.
Böhning, Jobst Heinrich, 248.
Böhning, Martin John Henry, 248.
Bohning Knuth, Louise Marie, 248.
boldface, 13, 156, 164–165, 386.
book design, 412.
book preparation, 303, 425.
\bordermatrix, *177,* 361.
\bot (⊥), 435.
*\botmark, 213, 258, 259–260, *262–263,* 280.
boundary item, 157, 442, 446.
Bourbaki, Nicolas, 106.
\bowtie (⋈), 358, 436.

⟨box⟩, 120, 222, <u>278</u>, 282, 285, 290.
*\box (use box register), 120–122, 151, 222, <u>278</u>, 346, *354*, *386*, *387*.
\box255, 125, 253–258.
⟨box dimension⟩, <u>271</u>, 277.
box displays, 66, 75, 79, 158–159, 302, 455.
box memory, 300, 394.
⟨box or rule⟩, <u>281</u>.
⟨box size assignment⟩, <u>277</u>.
⟨box specification⟩, 222, <u>278</u>.
boxed control sequence names, 38.
boxed material, *223*, *420*.
boxes, 63–67, 77–83, 221–229.
*\boxmaxdepth, <u>81</u>, 113, 249, *255*, 274, *348*.
bp (big point), <u>57</u>, 270.
\brace (notation like $\{{n \atop k}\}$), <u>360</u>.
\braceld, \bracelu, \bracerd, \braceru (pieces of horizontal braces), <u>357</u>.
braces, 51, 216, <u>269</u>, 275–276, 279, 283, 286, 289–291, 330, 345, 385–386.
    for arguments to macros, *20*, *200–202*, *203*, <u>204</u>, *205–206*, 385–386.
    for grouping, *13–14*, *19–21*, 232, 248, 253.
    horizontal, *176*, 225–226, *339*.
    implicit, <u>269</u>, *see* \bgroup, \egroup.
    in math formulas, *145–147*, *174–176*.
\bracevert (|), 150, <u>359</u>.
\brack (notation like $[{n \atop k}]$), <u>360</u>.
brackets, 51, 134, *146–148*, 171, *408*, *437*.
\break (force line or page break), 94, 97, 106, 114, 193, <u>353</u>.
breakpoints, <u>96</u>, 97–100, <u>110</u>, 111–114, 394.
    avoiding bad, 27–30, 91–94, 109–111, 173–174, 197.
    discretionary, *95–96*, 173, <u>287</u>, *292*, *357*.
    forcing good, 94, 105, 109–111, 114.
    in displays, 195–197.
    in formulas, 173–174, 446–447.
\breve (math accent: x̆), 135.
breve accent (˘), *see* \u, \breve.
British pound sign, 54.
brochures, 251.
*\brokenpenalty, <u>104</u>, 105, 272, *348*.
Brooks, Frederick Phillips, Jr., 365.
Brown, Peter John, 425.
\buildrel, <u>361</u>, *437*.
built-up (extensible) characters, 442.
built-up fractions, *see* \over.
\bull (▪), <u>420</u>.
Bull, John, 239.
\bullet (•), *133*, 154, *355*, 436.
bulleted lists, 102, 105.
business correspondence, 200, 403–408.

by, *118*, <u>276</u>.
\bye, 87–88, *340*, <u>357</u>.
Byron, George Gordon Noël Byron, baron, vii.
\c (cedilla accent), *24–25*, 52, <u>356</u>.
\cal (calligraphic caps), 164, <u>351</u>, 431, 434.
calculus, 168–169, 180–181.
camera alignment, 416–417.
\cap (∩), 133, 436.
capacity of TₑX, 100, 300–301, 383.
caps and small caps, 203.
captions, 115.
caret, 369.
caron, *see* háček.
carriage return, 231, *see* ⟨return⟩, \cr.
\cases ($\{\vdots$), 175, <u>362</u>.
Caswell, Herbert Ernest, 413.
*\catcode, *39*, 134, 214, <u>271</u>, 305, *343*, *380–382*, *384*, *390–391*, *421*, *424*.
category codes, 37–40, <u>47</u>, 48, 203–205, 209–210, 214, 381.
    table, 37.
cc (cicero), 57, 270.
\cdot (·), *133*, *172*, 319, 436.
\cdotp, 358, <u>359</u>, 438.
\cdots (⋯), *172*, *176*, *180–181*, <u>359</u>, 438.
cedilla accent (¸), 25, 52, 54, *see* \c.
ceiling brackets (⌈ ⌉), 146–147, *see* \lceil, \rceil.
centering, 71, 233, 236.
\centering, <u>347</u>, 348, 362.
\centerline (make a centered line), *20*, *24*, 33, 71, 85, 101, *117*, 232, 311, *340*, <u>353</u>.
\cents (¢), 140, <u>319</u>.
Cesàro, Ernesto, 53.
Chaĭkovskiĭ, Pëtr Il'ich, 410–411.
*\char, *43–46*, 76, 86, 155, 283, <u>286</u>, 289, *340*, *427*, 452.
⟨character⟩, <u>289</u>.
character codes, 43–46, 367–370; *see also* category codes.
⟨character token⟩, <u>270</u>.
*\chardef, 44, 121, 155, 210, 214, 215, 272, <u>277</u>, 336, *343*, *345*, 452.
⟨chardef token⟩, <u>271</u>, 272.
Charles XII of Sweden, 92.
Chaundy, Theodore William, 197.
\check (math accent: x̌), 135.
check accent (ˇ), *see* \v, \check.
chemical typesetting, 179.
Cherry, Lorinda Landgraf, 159.
\chi (χ), 1, 434.

Chicago, University of, Press, 125, 293, 418, 439.
Child, Julia, 233, 236.
Children's Television Workshop, ii.
choice, four-way, 157, <u>292</u>, <u>442</u>.
\choose (notation like $\binom{n}{k}$), 139, 143, 152, 178, <u>360</u>.
Christie Mallowan, Dame Agatha Mary Clarissa (Miller), 249.
cicero, *see* cc.
\circ (∘), *133*, *323*, 436.
circles, *see* \circ, \bigcirc.
circular quotation, 101.
circumflex, 369, *see* hat.
circumflex accent (ˆ), 52, <u>356</u>, *see* \^.
classes of math characters, table, 154.
*\cleaders, <u>224</u>, 225–226, *357*, *374*.
\cleartabs, *234*, <u>354</u>.
Close atom, 158, 170–171, 289, 443–444, 446.
*\closein, 217, 280.
*\closeout, 226–228, 254, <u>280</u>, *422*.
\closing, *403–404*, <u>407</u>.
closings, 134, 147, 154–155, 359, <u>437</u>;
    see also Close atom.
club lines, 104, 272, 398.
*\clubpenalty, 104, 113, 272, 317, *348*, *419*.
\clubsuit (♣), 435.
cm (centimeter), *24*, <u>57</u>, 270.
cmbx fonts, 60, 350, 413, 428, 433.
cmex fonts, 157, 225, 350, 432–433.
cmmi fonts, 350–351, 413–414, 430, 433.
cmr fonts, 16–17, 60, 63–64, 76, 350, 413, 427, 433.
cmsl fonts, 63–64, 350, 413, 428, 433.
cmsy fonts, 157, 350–351, 413–414, 431.
cmti fonts, 350, 413, 428, 433.
cmtt fonts, 60, 350, 413–414, 429, 433.
⟨code assignment⟩, <u>277</u>.
⟨codename⟩, <u>271</u>.
codes for characters, 43–46, 367–370.
Coelho, Manuel Rodrigues, 239.
coerce ⟨dimen⟩ to ⟨number⟩, 270.
coerce ⟨glue⟩ to ⟨dimen⟩, 270.
coerce ⟨number⟩ to ⟨dimen⟩, 336.
⟨coerced dimen⟩, <u>270</u>.
⟨coerced integer⟩, <u>269</u>.
⟨coerced mudimen⟩, <u>270</u>.
collective signs, *see* large operators.
colon, 51, *133–134*, *155*, 161, *174*, *438*.
\colon (:), *134*, <u>359</u>, *438*.
color, 229.
column vector, 177.
column width, 29, 231, *257*, *387*, 417.

\columns, 231, 354.
comma, 51, *72–73*, *134*, *161–162*, *172–174*, *394–395*, 430.
commands, 267–293.
comments, 26, 47, 337, *340*.
communication between macros, 211, 328–329, 375–376, 407–408.
commutative diagram, *182*.
composing stick, 64–65.
compound fraction, *143*.
compound matrix, *181*.
Computer Modern fonts, 16, 350, 427–438.
computer programs, 38, 165, *234*.
concert programs, 408–412.
conditionals, 206–208, <u>209</u>, <u>210</u>, 211, 240, *308*, *384*.
\cong (≅), 151, 360, 436.
constants, <u>269</u>, 270, 308.
continued fractions, *142*.
⟨control sequence⟩, <u>275</u>, 277.
control sequences, 7–11, <u>46</u>, 199, 457.
    misspelled, 31–32.
control space (\␣), *8*, 10, 19, *73*, *74*, 86–87, 154, *163*, *167*, 283, <u>285</u>, <u>290</u>, 351, *381*.
control symbols, 7–8, 46–47.
control words, 7–8, 38, 46–47, 204.
coordinates, 389.
\coprod (large Π), 435.
*\copy (copy a box), 120, 151, <u>222</u>, 278, *329*, *374*, *386*, *407*.
\copyright (©), ii, *308*, 339, <u>356</u>.
Cornet, Peeter, 239.
Correa de Arauxo, Francisco, 239.
correspondence, 200, 403–408.
\cos (cos), 162, 361.
\cosh (cosh), 162, 361.
cost of a page break, 111–113, 124.
\cot (cot), 162, 361.
\coth (coth), 162, 361.
*\count registers, 118–122, 207–208, <u>271</u>, <u>276</u>, *346–347*, *379*.
\count0, <u>119</u>, *207*, 252–254, <u>362</u>.
*\countdef, 119, 121, 210, 215, 271, <u>277</u>, *346–347*.
⟨countdef token⟩, <u>271</u>.
Cowper, William, 35.
*\cr (end of aligned row), *175–177*, *190–197*, *231–238*, <u>245</u>, <u>248</u>, 275, 282, 351, 352, 385–386, *412*, *418*, *421*.
    avoiding, 249.
cramped styles, 140–141, 445.
*\crcr (force \cr), 249, 275, 282, *361–362*, 385, *412*, *421*.

Crocker, Betty, 425.

cross, *see* \dag (†), \times (×).

crotchets, *see* brackets.

\csc (csc), 162, 361.

*\csname, 40–41, 213, *348, 375*.

\csname\endcsname, 46, 308.

cube root, *130–131*.

Cummings, Edward Estlin, 49.

\cup (∪), 133, 436.

curly braces, *see* braces.

current font, 13, 20, 154, 163, 213–214.

current page, 112, 122–125, 278, 280.

cyclic preambles, 241, *242, 246, 361, 412*.

Cyrillic characters, 370.

\d (dot-under accent), 52–53, 356.

\dag (†), 53, 117, 356, 438–439.

\dagger († as binary operator), 436, 439.

Dale, Robert William, 283.

\danger, 419.

dangerous bend, v–vi, 5, 15, 44–45, 70, 419.

Danish characters, 45–46, 52–53, 370.

\dash, 30.

dashes, 4, *26, 30*, 51, 93, 95.

\dashv (⊣), 436.

date, today's, 406.

*\day, 273, 349, *406*.

dd (didot point), 57, 270, 272.

\ddag (‡), 117, 356, 438–439.

\ddagger (‡ as binary operator), 436, 439.

\ddot (math accent: $\ddot{x}$), 135, 359.

\ddots (⋱), 177, 359.

\ddt (debugging aid), 248.

De Vinne, Theodore Low, 107.

*\deadcycles, 214, 255, 264, 271, 283, *401*.

debugging, 205, 248, 298–303, 347.

decent lines, 97, 99.

⟨decimal constant⟩, 270.

decimal points, 57, 134, 240.

⟨def⟩, 275.

*\def, 44, 136, 199–208, 215, 275–276.

default output routine, 253–255.

default rule thickness, 443–447.

default values of parameters, 348–349.

*\defaulthyphenchar, 273, *348*.

*\defaultskewchar, 273, *348*.

defining a control sequence, 199–208.

⟨definition⟩, 275.

⟨definition text⟩, 275.

\deg (deg), 162, 361.

degrees (°), *180*.

*\delcode, 156, 214, 271, 290, 345.

⟨delete⟩ (ASCII code 127), 37, 39, 343, 369.

deleting tokens, 32, 215, *295–297*.

⟨delim⟩, 289–290.

delimited arguments and parameters, 203–205, 249, *263, 375–377, 407*.

*\delimiter, 156, 289–290, *359*.

*\delimiterfactor, 152, 273, *348*, 446.

delimiters, 145–150, 156–157, *171*, 290, 437, 442.

*\delimitershortfall, 152, 274, *348*, 446.

\delta (δ), *127*, 434.

\Delta (Δ), *169, 186*, 434.

demerits, 94, 97–99, 273, *451*.

denominator, 141, 152, 179, 444–445.

depth, 221, 224, 282, 337.

depth of a box, 63–67, 77, 80–82, 225.

Derek, Bo, 293.

descenders, 63, 113, 319, 323.

design size, 16–17, 213.

\det (det), 162, 361.

device-independent output, 23;
    see also .dvi.

Diabelli, Antonio, 408.

diagnostic form of lists, 66, 75, 79, 158–159, 302, 455.

dialogs with the user, 217–218.

\diamond (⋄), 436.

diamond leaders, viii.

\diamondsuit (♢), 435.

Díaz de la Peña, Maximiliano Antonio Temístocles, 384.

Dick and Jane, 72 74, 76.

Dictionaries, 259, 449–453.

Didot, François Ambroise, 57.

didot point, 57, *see* dd.

dieresis (¨), 52, 53, 356, *see* \".

dicsis (‡), *see* \ddag.

Dieter, Ulrich Otto, 14.

⟨digit⟩, 269.

⟨digit string⟩, 57.

digits, 51, 132, 435, 453.
    width of, 60, 241, 427.

\dim (dim), 162, 361.

⟨dimen⟩, 59, 61, 71, 118, 270, 271.

⟨dimen parameter⟩, 271, 274, 276.

*\dimen registers, 118–122, 271, 276, *346–347, 349, 360, 363, 395*.

⟨dimen variable⟩, 276.

*\dimendef, 119, 215, 277, *346–347*.

⟨dimendef token⟩, 271.

dimensions, 57–61.
    as arguments, 204, 362.

Dionysius I of Syracuse, 239.

diphthongs, *see* \ae, \oe.

discardable items, 95, 110–112, 124, *393*.

*\discretionary, 95–96, 283, 286, <u>287</u>, 292.
discretionary hyphens, 28, 95–96, 453, <u>455</u>.
discretionary multiplication signs, 173, <u>357</u>.
display math mode, 85–89, 289–293.
display style, 140–142, 441–447.
*\displayindent, 188, 190, 274, 291, 349.
*\displaylimits, 144, 159, <u>292</u>, 443.
\displaylines, 194, *196*, <u>362</u>.
displays, 87, 103, *139–145, 166–167,*
        185–197, *232, 241,* 315.
    at beginning of paragraph, 316.
    non-centered, 186, 326, 375–376, 420–421.
    positioning of, <u>188–190</u>.
*\displaystyle, 141–142, <u>292</u>, *362*.
*\displaywidowpenalty, 104, 272, *348*.
*\displaywidth, 188, 190, 274, 349.
Disraeli [Beaconsfield], Benjamin, earl, 219.
ditto mark, 53, 441.
\div (÷), 436.
*\divide, *118–119, 218–219,* <u>276</u>, *391,*
        397, 398, 417.
\do, 344, 380, 423.
dollar sign, 4, 38, 51, 54, 86–88, *92,* 127,
        134–135, 185–186, 283, <u>287</u>, <u>293</u>.
Donnelley, Richard Robert, vii.
\dospecials, <u>344</u>, 380, 422–423.
\dosupereject, 256, <u>364</u>.
\dot (math accent: $\dot{x}$), 135.
dot accent (˙), see \., \dot.
dot-under accent (.), see \d.
\doteq ($\doteq$), <u>361</u>, 436.
\dotfill (. . . . .), 244, *334, 335,*
        340–341, <u>357</u>.
dotless letters, 52–53, 136, 435.
\dots (...), 173, <u>356</u>; *see also* ellipses.
double-column format, *257,* 386–388, *417.*
double dagger, *see* \ddag, \ddagger.
double dangerous-bend signs, vi, 419.
double integrals, *169, 180.*
double quote mark, 52, 53, 134;
        see also hexadecimal.
*\doublehyphendemerits, 98, 273, *348, 451.*
\downarrow (↓), *146–147, 182,* <u>359</u>, 437.
\Downarrow (⇓), *146–147,* <u>359</u>, 437.
\downbracefill (︶), 225–226,
        331, <u>357</u>.
Doyle, Sir Arthur Conan, 401.
*\dp, 120, 271, *316,* <u>388–389</u>, *417.*
dragon curve, 391.
Drofnats, Revinu Jitis, 24, 27–28, 73–74,
        404–406, 408, 410–412.
Dudeney, Henry Ernest, 249, 334.
Dull, Brutus Cyclops, 131, 173, 260.

\dummy, 401.
*\dump, <u>283</u>, <u>286</u>, 336, *344.*
Durant, William James, 239.
.dvi, 23, 43, 60, 119, 213, 228, 254, 279,
        280, 302, 367, 374.
Dvořák, Antonín Leopold, 409.
dx, 168.

EBCDIC, 43.
*\edef, *215–216,* 275, *328, 348, 373–374.*
editing, 34, 139, 197.
efficiency, 329, 333, 342, 345, 347, 383,
        384, 394, 400, 423.
\egroup (implicit }), 269, <u>351</u>, *363,*
        382, *385, 407, 421.*
Ehlert, Ernst Fred, 248.
Ehlert Bohning, Pauline Anna Marie, 248.
\eightpoint, <u>415</u>, *416.*
\eject (force page break), *24–25,* 105,
        109, 189, <u>353</u>, *418, 419.*
elbows, *see* angle brackets.
\ell (ℓ), 132, 435.
ellipses (⋯), 73, 172–174, 176–177,
        180–182, 245.
Elphinstone, Mountstuart, 89.
*\else, 207, 210, <u>213</u>.
em, 60, 154, 166, 214, <u>270</u>, *352, 414,* 433.
em-dash (—), 4, 302.
em quad, *see* \quad.
embellished letters, *see* accents.
emergency stops, 299–300.
*\emergencystretch, <u>107</u>, 274.
Emerson, Ralph Waldo, 41.
emphatics, *see* dot-under.
⟨empty⟩, <u>268</u>.
\empty, *263,* <u>351</u>, *378.*
empty discretionary, 95, 286.
empty group, 19, 253, 305.
empty line in input file, 24, 37, <u>47</u>,
        340–341, 381.
    at end of file, 217.
empty line in output, 114, 316.
empty page, 114.
\emptyset (∅), 128, 435.
en-dash (–), 4, 187, 252, 314.
en quad, 71, *see* \enspace.
*\end, 23, 26, *27,* 87, <u>264</u>, *283,* 286,
        299, *336, 403.*
end of an input file, 206, 214, 217.
end of file line, *see* ⟨return⟩, \cr.
end of file page, *see* ⟨formfeed⟩.
end of paragraph, 286, *see* \par.
\endchapter, 418–419.
*\endcsname, 40–41, <u>213</u>, 283, *348, 375.*

endgame, 87, 264, 283.

\endgraf, *262*, 286, *331*, <u>351</u>, *407*, *416*, *419*.

*\endgroup, 21, *249*, *262*, <u>279</u>, *380*, *407*, *419*.

*\endinput, 47, <u>214</u>.

\endinsert, 115–116, <u>363</u>.

\endletter, *403–404*, <u>407</u>.

\endline, <u>351</u>.

*\endlinechar, <u>48</u>, 273, *331*, <u>348</u>, *390–391*.

\endtemplate, 240.

\enskip, 71, <u>352</u>.

\enspace, *202*, <u>352</u>, *419*.

enumerated cases, in formulas, 175.

   in separate paragraphs, *102*, *340*.

   within a paragraph, 92.

enunciations, *see* \proclaim.

epigraphs, 418–419, 425.

\epsilon (ϵ), 1, 128, 434.

\eqalign, *190–191*, 193, 242, 326, <u>362</u>.

\eqalignno, *192–193*, 194, <u>362</u>.

⟨eqno⟩, <u>293</u>.

*\eqno, *186–187*, 189–191, 193, <u>293</u>, 375–376.

⟨equals⟩, <u>275</u>, 276–277.

equals sign, 51, *133*, 209, 226, 275, *376*.

equation numbers, 186–196.

\equiv ($\equiv$), *133*, 436.

Erdős, Pál (= Paul), 53.

*\errhelp, 275, <u>280</u>, *347*.

*\errmessage, 216, <u>279–280</u>, *347*, *418*.

error messages, 30–33, 295–301, 308–309.

error recovery, 31–32, 46, 215, 295–303, 309.

*\errorcontextlines, <u>34</u>, 273, *348*.

*\errorstopmode, <u>32</u>, <u>33</u>, <u>277</u>, 299.

es-zet (ß), *see* \ss.

⟨escape⟩ (ASCII code 27), 369.

escape character, 7, 37, 421.

*\escapechar, 40, 213, <u>228</u>, 273, *308*, <u>348</u>, *377*.

\eta (η), 434.

etc., 302.

Eulerian numbers, 152.

Evagoras of Salamis, 239.

even-numbered pages, 252–253, *416*.

*\everycr, 275, *362*.

*\everydisplay, 179, 275, <u>287</u>, *326*.

*\everyhbox, 275, 279.

*\everyjob, 275.

*\everymath, 179, 275, <u>287</u>, <u>293</u>, 326.

*\everypar, *105*, 215, 253, *262*, 275, <u>282</u>, *283*, *333*, *381*, *407*, *421*.

*\everyvbox, 275, 279.

ex, 60, 154, <u>270</u>, *356*, 433.

exception dictionary, 449, 452–453.

exclamation point, 51, *72*, 73, 75, 161, *169*.

\exercise, 10, <u>422</u>.

exercises, vii, 1–303.

*\exhyphenpenalty, <u>96</u>, *262*, 272, *348*.

\exists ($\exists$), 435.

\exp (exp), 162, 361.

*\expandafter, *40*, <u>213</u>, 215, *260*, *308*, *330*, *348*, *374–380*.

expansion of expandable tokens, 212–216, 238, 267, 373–374.

   avoiding, 216, 262–263, 377.

explicit hyphens, 4, 93, 454.

explicit kerns, 40, 280, 306, 454–455.

exponents, *see* superscripts.

extensible characters, 442.

extension fonts, 157, *351*, 432–433, 441, 447.

extensions to TEX, 226, 228–229.

eyestrain, reducing, 59.

faces, 13, 17, 390.

⟨factor⟩, 270.

factorial, *169*, *181*.

*\fam, 154–159, 273, <u>289–290</u>, 346–347, *351*, 358, *414–415*.

families, 153–159, 289–290, 346, 431, 442.

⟨family assignment⟩, <u>277</u>.

⟨family member⟩, <u>271</u>, 277.

family tree, 248.

family 0 (math roman fonts), 153–157, *351*.

family 1 (math italic fonts), 155–157, *351*.

family 2 (math symbol fonts), 157, *351*, 431, 441, 447.

family 3 (math extension fonts), 157, *351*, 432–433, 441, 447.

Fatal format file error, 299.

feasible breakpoints, 99, 315.

fences, *see* openings, closings, delimiters.

ffl, *see* ligatures.

*\fi, 207, 210, <u>213</u>.

Fibonacci, Leonardo, of Pisa, 166.

fields of atoms, 158–159, 289–291.

fil, 72, 118–119, <u>271</u>, *348*, *394*.

⟨fil dimen⟩, <u>271</u>.

⟨fil unit⟩, <u>271</u>.

\filbreak, 111, <u>353</u>.

⟨file name⟩, 214, 216, 226, 277, <u>278</u>.

file names, 25, 214, 216–217, 226, 278.

file pages, 343.

file types, *see* .dvi, .fmt, .tfm, .tex, log file, terminal.

fill, 72, 118–119, <u>271</u>, *347*.

fill page with blank space, *see* \vfill.

⟨filler⟩, <u>276</u>, 278, 280–282, 289.

filll, 72, 118, <u>271</u>, *332*.

*\finalhyphendemerits, 98, *106*, 273, *348*, *451*.

*\firstmark, 213, <u>258</u>, 259–260, 280.

\fiverm, 153, <u>350</u>, *351*, *414–415*.

\flat (♭), *409*, 435.

floating insertions, 115–116, 125, *363*.

*\floatingpenalty, 123–125, 272, 281, *363*.

floor brackets (⌊⌋), 146–147, *see* \lfloor, \rfloor.

flush left, 72, 142, 177, 181, 196.

flush right, 71–72, 106, 142, 177, 196, 233, 419.

.fmt, 39, 344.

\fmtname and \fmtversion, 364.

\folio (typeset page number), 252–253, <u>362</u>, *406*, *416*.

⟨font⟩, <u>213</u>, 214, 271, 277.

*\font, 16–17, 60, 210, <u>213</u>, 214–215, 271, <u>276</u>.

⟨font assignment⟩, <u>277</u>.

font metric files, 46, 433.

⟨font range⟩, <u>271</u>.

⟨fontdef token⟩, <u>271</u>.

*\fontdimen, 76, 157, *179*, 214, <u>271</u>, <u>277</u>, *355–356*, *375*, *390*, <u>433</u>, 441, 447.

*\fontname, 213, 214.

fonts, 13–17; *see also* Computer Modern fonts.

\footins, 256, <u>363</u>, 396–399, *416*.

\footline, 252, 256, *340–341*, <u>362</u>.

\footnote, 82, 116, 251, 256, 340, <u>363</u>, 382, 416.

\footnoterule, 256, <u>364</u>.

footnotes, 105, *116–117*, 121, 125, *173*, 416–417.

   short, 395–400.

\forall (∀), 435.

forbidden control sequence, 206.

Ford, Patrick Kildea, 293.

foreign languages, 45–46, 52–54, 370, 387, 449, 451.

form letters, 200, 207–209.

format file, 25–26, 39, 283, 344.

format-independent documents, 194, 203.

formats, 11, 39, 200, 403–425, 434.

⟨formfeed⟩ (ASCII code 12), 343, 369.

formulas, 127–199.

Foss, Sam Walter, 439.

fractions, 67, 139–143, 152, 170, 179, 186, 332, 444–445.

   huge, 196.

   slashed form, 67, 139–140, 233, 236.

Fraktur, 164, 434.

Franklin, Benjamin, 65.

French, 54, 340–341, 455.

\frenchspacing, 74, *340*, <u>351</u>, 381, 401.

Frescobaldi, Girolamo, 239.

front matter, 413.

\frown (⌢), 436.

full stop, *see* period.

\fullhsize, 257.

\fullline, 257.

funny space, 377.

*\futurelet, <u>207</u>, 215, *262*, 277, *363*, *375–377*, *423*.

\futurenonspacelet, 376.

Galilei, Galileo, 101.

galley file, 303, 425.

Gamble, James, 38.

\gamma (γ), *127*, 434.

\Gamma (Γ), *127*, *169*, <u>358</u>, 434.

\gcd (gcd), 162, *192*, 361.

*\gdef, <u>206</u>, 215, 275, *352*, *407*.

\ge (≥), 9, 45, *175*, 318, <u>361</u>, 438.

⟨general text⟩, <u>276</u>, 277, 279, 280, 287, 292.

generalized fraction, 152, 157, <u>292</u>, <u>444–445</u>.

generic coding, 194, 203.

generic matrix, 177, 245.

\geq (≥), 318, 436.

German, 52, 96, 451.

German black letters, *see* Fraktur.

\getfactor, <u>375</u>.

\gets (←), <u>361</u>, 438.

\gg (≫), 436.

Gibbon, Edward, 117.

*\global, *21*, 119, 206, *218*, 232, 256, <u>275</u>, 301, 307, 320, 346.

⟨global assignment⟩, 179, <u>277</u>.

*\globaldefs, 238, 273, <u>275</u>.

glue, 63, 69–83, 95, 110, 157, 222–225, 302, 412.

   above and below displays, 189–190, 194.

   at top of page, 113–114, 124, 256.

   between aligned columns, 237–239, 247, 392.

   between lines, *see* interline glue.

   between paragraphs, 79, 104–105, 262, 282, 342, 406, 417.

   between words, 74–76, 356, 393–394, 433.

⟨glue⟩, 71, 118, <u>271</u>.

\glue, 75, 79, 302.

⟨glue parameter⟩, 271, <u>274</u>, 276.

glue set, 79, 302.

glue set order, 77, 79, 81, 97.

glue set ratio, 77, 79, 81, 97.

⟨glue variable⟩, <u>276</u>.

goal height, 112–114, 123–125.
Goethe, Johann Wolfgang von, 183.
\goodbreak, 111, 116, 353.
Grandmaster, 253.
\grave (math accent: $\grave{x}$), 135.
grave accent (` ), *see* \`, \grave.
greater than or equal, *see* \ge.
greater than sign, 52, 53, *133*, 150, 209.
Greek, 127–128, 137, 156, 319, 358, 430, 434.
Green, Walter, 244.
grouping, 13–14, 19–21, 119–120, 122,
    200, 201, 241, 259, 279, 283, 286, 291,
    301, 375, 378, 385, 453.
  characters for, 39–40, *381–382*.
  implicit, 115, 148, 194, 253, 287, 292, 293.
guide words, 259.

\H (long Hungarian umlaut), 52, *53*,
    356, *420*.
H&J, *see* hyphenation, line breaking,
    setting glue.
háček accent (ˇ), *see* \v, \check.
halftones, 228.
*\halign, 117, 190, 193, 194, 235–249,
    282, 286, 291, 302, *326*, 352,
    361–362, *386*, *392*.
  compared to tabbing, 235.
Halmos, Paul Richard, 183.
Hamza, *see* apostrophe.
\hang, 355, *419*.
*\hangafter, 102, 103–104, 273,
    348–349, *419*.
*\hangindent, 102, *262*, 274, 349, *407*.
hanging indentation, 79, 102–103.
hanging punctuation, 394–395.
Hardy, Godfrey Harold, 321.
harpoons, 437.
hash mark, 38, 51, 113, *200–202*, *203*,
    204–205, 228, 235, *236–240*.
Hassler, Hans Leo, 239.
hat, 38, 51, *128–130*, 134, 369, *423*.
\hat (math accent: $\hat{x}$), *135–136*, 164.
hat accent (ˆ), *see* \^, \hat, \widehat.
*\hbadness, 29, 272, 302, *348*, *387–388*, 401.
\hbar ($\hbar$), *169*, 358, 435.
hbox (box with horizontal list inside), 64.
*\hbox, 64–67, 77, 86, 93, 151, 159, 163,
    175, 179, 185–186, 221, 222, 278,
    282, 388–389.
\headline, 252–253, 255, 362, *406*.
\heartsuit ($\heartsuit$), 435.
Hebrew, 66.
height, 221, 224, 282, 337.
height of a box, 63–67, 77, 80–82, 225.

help messages, 32, 280, 295–296.
⟨hex digit⟩, 269.
⟨hexadecimal constant⟩, 269.
hexadecimal notation, 43, *44*, 45, 47–48,
    154, 219, 336, 420.
*\hfil, 71–72, 194, 235–237, 283, 285,
    290, 397.
*\hfill, 71–72, 142, 177, 194, 233,
    283, 285, 290.
*\hfilneg, 72, 100, 233, 283, 285, 290, 397.
*\hfuzz, 30, 274, 302, *348*, *387–388*.
\hglue, 352.
\hideskip, 347, 348, 354.
\hidewidth, 243, 245, 247, 325, 354.
higher-level languages for composition, 203.
Highton, Albert H., 481.
Hilbert, David, 167.
*\hoffset, 251, 274, *342*.
*\holdinginserts, 125, 273, 400.
Holmes, Thomas Sherlock Scott, 401.
\hom (hom), 162, 361.
Hombert, Humbert, 401.
Honeywell Information Systems, 1.
\hookleftarrow (↩), 358, 437.
\hookrightarrow (↪), 358, 430, 437.
hooks, *see* \subset, \supset.
horizontal braces, *176*, 225–226, 339.
⟨horizontal command⟩, 283.
horizontal lists, 64, 94–95.
horizontal mode, 85–89, 105, 285–287.
⟨horizontal mode material⟩, 278.
⟨horizontal rule⟩, 281.
horizontal rules, 24, 64, 221–226, 246, 282.
⟨horizontal skip⟩, 285.
Hornschuch, Hieronymus, 483.
Howard, Jane Temple, 21.
\hphantom, 178, 211, 360.
*\hrule, *24*, 64, 85, 221–225, *246*, 281–282,
    286, 357, *420*, *421*.
\hrulefill (———), *244*, *252*, 357, *412*.
*\hsize, 26–27, *60*, 102, 188, 237, 251,
    257, 274, *340–341*, *348*, *387*, *406*,
    407, 413, 415, *417*.
*\hskip, 71, 86, 168, 283, 285, 290, *314*.
*\hss, 71, *82–83*, 233, 283, 285, 290, 442.
*\ht, 120, 271, 388–389, 417.
Hungarian umlaut (˝), *see* \H.
hyphen, 4, 51, 93, 95, 132, 292.
hyphen.tex, 364, 453.
hyphenation, 28, 39, 96, 306, 314, 394–395,
    414, 424, 449–455.
*\hyphenation, 277, *419*, 452–453, 455.
⟨hyphenation assignment⟩, 277.

*\hyphenchar, 95, 214, <u>271</u>, 273, <u>277</u>, 286, 351, 395, *414*, 454, 455.
*\hyphenpenalty, 96, 101, 272, *348*, *451*.

\i (ı), *52–53*, <u>356</u>.
I can't go on, 299.
\ialign, <u>354</u>.
IBM Corporation, vii.
identifiers in programs, 38, 165, *234*.
*\if, <u>209</u>, 210–211, 307, 377, *379*.
*\ifcase, <u>210</u>, *349*, *373*, *390*, *406*.
*\ifcat, <u>209</u>, 210, 307, *377*.
*\ifdim, <u>209</u>, *353*, *387*, *417*.
*\ifeof, <u>210</u>, 217.
\iff (⟺), 163, <u>361</u>, 438.
*\iffalse, <u>210</u>, 211, *260–261*, *348*, *385–386*.
*\ifhbox, <u>210</u>, *392*, 399.
*\ifhmode, <u>209</u>, *363*.
*\ifinner, <u>209</u>.
*\ifmmode, <u>209</u>, *215*, *240*, *353*, *356*, *360*, *423*.
*\ifnum, *208*, <u>209</u>, *218–219*.
*\ifodd, *207*, <u>209</u>, *416*, *418–419*.
*\iftrue, <u>210</u>, 211, *260–261*, *348*.
\ifundefined, 40.
*\ifvbox, <u>210</u>.
*\ifvmode, <u>209</u>.
*\ifvoid, <u>210</u>, *256*.
*\ifx, <u>210</u>, 215, 307, <u>384</u>, *375–377*, *418*.
ignored characters, 37, 390.
*\ignorespaces, <u>279</u>, *333*, *355*, *424*.
! Illegal unit, 295.
illustrations, 115–116.
   fitting copy around, 101.
\Im (ℑ), 435.
\imath (ı), *136*, 435.
*\immediate, 226–228, <u>280</u>, *422*, *423*.
implicit braces, <u>269</u>, see \bgroup, \egroup.
implicit characters, 269, 277, 309, 351, 376–377.
implicit kerns, 306, <u>454</u>, 455.
in (inch), *24*, <u>57</u>, 270.
\in (∈), *128*, *147*, 436.
\inaccessible, 297.
inch, 57–58.
incomplete conditionals, 206.
*\indent, 86, 94, 101, 263, <u>282</u>, *286*, <u>291</u>, *355*.
indentation, 86, 222, 282.
   hanging, 79, 102–103.
indention, see indentation.
indexes, 261–263, 392–394, 423–425, 481.
indices, see subscripts.
\inf (inf), 162, 361.
inferiors, see subscripts.
infinite badness, 97, 107, 111, 229, 317.

infinite glue, 71–72, 118–119, 256, 313, 332.
infinite loop, 299, 301, 383.
infinite penalty, 97, 111, 254–256, 264, 286, 400.
\infty (∞), 9, 318, 435.
inhibiting expansion, 216, 262–263, 377.
INITEX, 39, 41, 76, 157, 283, 336, 343–345, 453.
Inner atom, 158, 170, 289, 443, 445–446.
*\input, 7, 9, *25–27*, 47, 199, <u>214</u>, 217, *380*, 382–383, *403*, *422*.
input/output commands, see \input, \read, \write, \message, \dump.
input/output streams, 346, see \openin, \openout.
input stack, 300, 374.
*\inputlineno, 214, 271.
*\insert, 95, <u>122–125</u>, 259, 280–281, *363*, 416, 424, 454.
inserting text online, 31.
insertions, 110, 115–117, 122–125, 256, 335.
*\insertpenalties, 111, 114, <u>123–125</u>, 214, 254, *256*, 271.
\int (large ∫), 144, *168–169*, *192*, 358, 435.
⟨integer constant⟩, <u>269–270</u>.
⟨integer parameter⟩, 271, <u>272–273</u>, 276.
⟨integer variable⟩, <u>276</u>.
integral signs, see \int, \smallint.
   multiple, *169*, *180*.
inter-column spacing, 237–239, 247, 392.
interacting with TEX, 31–34, 217–218, 228, 295–299.
⟨interaction mode assignment⟩, <u>277</u>.
\interdisplaylinepenalty, *193*, 349, 362.
\interfootnotelinepenalty, 349, 363.
interline glue, 78–79, <u>80</u>, 104, 105, 221, 245, 263, 281–282, 335, 352, 409.
*\interlinepenalty, <u>104</u>, 272, *363*, *406*, *419*.
internal box-and-glue representation, 66, 75, 79, 158–159, 302, 455.
internal character codes, 43–46, 367–370.
⟨internal dimen⟩, <u>271</u>.
⟨internal glue⟩, <u>271</u>.
⟨internal integer⟩, <u>271</u>.
⟨internal muglue⟩, <u>271</u>.
⟨internal quantity⟩, <u>279</u>.
Internal Revenue Service, 200, 208–209, 244, 404.
⟨internal unit⟩, <u>270</u>.
internal vertical mode, 85, 87–89, 222, 278–283.
interrupts, 33, 299, 383.
interword spacing, <u>74–76</u>, *356*, *393–394*, 433.

Interwoven alignment preambles, 299.
⟨intimate assignment⟩, 277.
invalid characters, 37, 45.
\iota (*ι*), *325*, 434.
Isocrates, 239.
\it (use *italic* type), 13–14, 165, 231–232, *332*, 351, *409*, *414–415*, *419*, 428.
italic corrections, *14*, *64*, 287, *306*, 441, 455.
italic letters with descenders, 319.
italic type, 13–14, 100, 127, 409, 428, 430.
\item, *102–103*, 117, *340–342*, 355, *416*, 419.
\itemitem, *102*, 342, 355.
iteration, *see* \loop.
\itfam, 351, *414–415*.
Îur'ev, Sergeĭ Petrovich, 53.

\j (ɉ), 52, 356.
Jevons, William Stanley, 5.
\jmath (*ȷ*), *136*, 435.
*\jobname, 213, 214, *336*.
Johnson, Samuel, 89.
\joinrel, 358.
jokes, vi, 303, 449.
\jot, *194*, *242*, 349, *362*.
Joyce, James Augustine, 100.
justification, *see* setting glue, line breaking.
Justus, Paul E., 455.

\kappa (*κ*), *128*, 434.
\ker (ker), 162, 361.
*\kern, 10, 40, *66*, 75, 87, 168, *256*, *263*, 280, *306*, *389*, *394–395*, *416*, *424*, 454–455.
Kernighan, Brian Wilson, 159.
kerns, 4, 66, 75, 95–97, 110, 157, 168, 280, 286, 306, 444, 454–455.
Key Index, 392–394.
keyboards, 3, 5, 43–46, 368–370.
keywords, 61, 71, 268, 337, 370.
Knuth, Donald Ervin, i, ii, vii, 74, 92, 211, 259, 337, 340–341, 412–413, 424–425.
Knuth, Nancy Jill Carter, iii, 125, 418.
Köchel, Ludwig, Ritter von, 409.

l after fil, 271, 337.
£, *see* pound sterling.
\l (ł), *52–53*, 356.
\L (Ł), *52–53*, 356.
\lambda (λ), *176*, 434.
\Lambda (Λ), *323*, 434.
Lamport, Leslie B., 137.
\land (∧), 133, 361, 438.
\langle (⟨), *146–147*, 150, 156, 359, 437.
*\language (hyphenation method), 273, 346, 455.
large delimiters, 145–150, 442.

large operators, *144–145*, 154–155, 358, 435; *see also* Op atom.
*\lastbox, 222, 278, *354*, *392*, *398*, *399*.
*\lastkern, 214, 271.
*\lastpenalty, 214, 271.
*\lastskip, 214, *223*, 271, *392*.
LᴬTᴇX, 137.
\lbrace ({), *146–147*, 359, 437.
\lbrack ([ ), *146–147*, 351, 369, 437.
*\lccode, 41, 214, 271, 345, 452–454.
\lceil (⌈), *146–147*, 359, 437.
\ldotp, 358, 359, 438.
\ldots (...), *73*, *172–174*, 177, *180–181*, *199–201*, 359, 438.
\le (≤), 9, 45, *133*, *162*, 318, 361, 438.
leaders, 222, 223–226, 228, 280–282, 285, 290, *357*, *392–394*.
⟨leaders⟩, 281.
*\leaders, 95, 110, 223, 224, 225, *357*, *392–394*.
leading, *see* \baselineskip, \vskip.
\leavevmode, 313, *333*, 356, *408*, *420*.
Lee, Marshall, 17.
*\left, *148–150*, 155–157, *171*, 196, 292, 437.
left brace, *13–14*, *19–21*, 38, 51, *200–202*, 203–204, *205–206*, 216, 269, 275–276, 283, 286, 291, *330*.
⟨left brace⟩, 275.
left bracket, 51, 134, *146–148*, 171, *408*, *437*.
left delimiters, *see* openings.
left-hand pages, 252–253, *416*.
left parenthesis, 51, 134, *140*, *145–150*, 345.
left quote, 3–5, 132, 134, *305*, *394–395*; *see also* alphabetic constant.
\leftarrow (←), 226, 437.
\Leftarrow (⇐), 226, 437.
\leftarrowfill (⟵⟶), 357.
\leftharpoondown (↼), 437.
\leftharpoonup (↼), 437.
*\lefthyphenmin, 273, *364*, 454, 455.
\leftline, 101, *257*, *259–260*, *326*, 353.
\leftrightarrow (↔), 437.
\Leftrightarrow (⇔), 437.
*\leftskip, 100, 274, *317*, *407*, *419*.
Legendre symbol, 152.
Leontief, Wassily Wassily, 265.
\leq (≤), 318, 358, 436.
\leqalignno, 192, 194, 362.
*\leqno, *187*, 189, 293, 375–376.
Lesk, Michael Edward, 247.
less than or equal, *see* \le.
less than sign, 52, 53, *133*, 150, 209.
*\let, 206–207, 215, 277, 307, 309, *352*, *376*.

⟨let assignment⟩, <u>277</u>.

`letterformat.tex`, 403, <u>406–408</u>.

letterheads, 407.

letters, 7–8, <u>37</u>, 41, 45–46, 51, 132, 157, 344, 370.

`\lfloor` (⌊), *146–147*, <u>359</u>, 437.

`\lg` (lg), 162, 361.

`\lgroup`, 150, *176*, <u>359</u>, 437.

`\lhook`, <u>358</u>.

Liang, Franklin Mark, 449.

library of macros, 199, 382–384, 425.

lies, vii, 303.

ligatures, 4, 19, 46, 51, 54, 75, 95, 165, 286, 302, 381, 427, 444, 454.

`\lim` (lim), 162, *163*, 361.

`\liminf` (lim inf), 162, *163*, *178*, <u>361</u>.

*`\limits`, 144, 159, <u>292</u>, *359*, 443.

limits above and below operators, 144–145, 149, 179.

`\limsup` (lim sup), 162, *163*, *178*, <u>361</u>.

Lincoln, Abraham, 11.

`\line`, *72*, 77, 101, 224, 232, 252, *255–257*, <u>353</u>, *412*.

line breaking, 97–100, 173–174, 392–395, 398–400.

line breaks, avoiding bad, 27–30, 91–94, 173–174, 197.

  forcing good, 94, 114.

line rules, *see* `\hrule`, `\vrule`.

⟨linefeed⟩ (ASCII code 10), 369.

*`\linepenalty`, <u>98</u>, 272, 314, *316*, *348*.

lines of input, *24*, 46–48, *340*.

*`\lineskip`, 78–80, 104, 194, 274, 281, 349, *351–352*.

*`\lineskiplimit`, 78–80, 104, 194, 274, 281, 349, *351–352*, *362*.

list macros, 378–380.

`\listing`, 380, 391.

`\ll` (≪), 431, 436.

Llanfair P. G., 451.

`\llap`, 82–83, *189*, *340–341*, <u>353</u>, *355*, *381*, *416–417*, *422*.

`\lmoustache`, 150, <u>359</u>, 437.

`\ln` (ln), 162, *186*, 361.

`\lnot` (¬), <u>361</u>, 438.

local, 19–21, *see* grouping.

Locke, John, 303.

`\log` (log), 162, *169–170*, 361.

log file, 10, 28, 66, 226, 303, 347.

logical operators, *see* `\land`, `\lor`, `\lnot`.

logo, 1, 8, 412, *see* `\TeX`.

*`\long`, 205–206, 210, 275, 331, *375*, *378*, *382*.

long formulas, 195–197.

`\longindentation`, 407.

`\longleftarrow` (⟵), <u>358</u>, 437.

`\Longleftarrow` (⟸), <u>358</u>, 437.

`\longleftrightarrow` (⟷), <u>358</u>, 437.

`\Longleftrightarrow` (⟺), <u>358</u>, 437.

`\longmapsto` (⟼), <u>358</u>, 437.

`\longrightarrow` (⟶), *325*, <u>358</u>, 437.

`\Longrightarrow` (⟹), <u>358</u>, 437.

looking ahead, 207, 376–377.

`\loop`, *217–219*, <u>352</u>, *373–374*, *387*, *417*.

loose lines, 97, 99, 302.

*`\looseness`, 103–104, 109, 273, *342*, 349.

`\lor` (∨), 133, <u>361</u>, 438.

low-resolution printer, 59.

*`\lower`, *66*, 80, 151, 179, <u>285</u>, <u>290</u>.

*`\lowercase`, 41, 215, <u>279</u>, 307, 345.

lowercase letters, 9, 268, 370, 453.

`\lq` ('), 5, 48, <u>351</u>, 369, *395*.

Luckombe, Philip, 447.

lxix, 420.

`\m@ne`, <u>347</u>.

`\m@th`, <u>353</u>.

machine-independence, 58; *see also* `.dvi`.

Macro, Nævius Sertorius, 219.

macro arguments and parameters, 33, 200–205, 249, *263*, *362*, *363*, *375–380*, *407*.

⟨macro assignment⟩, <u>275</u>.

macro conventions, 121, 346, 364.

macron accent (¯), *see* `\=`, `\bar`.

macros, 199–219, 373–401.

  to save typing in math, 136, 199–200, *324*.

*`\mag`, <u>60</u>, 270, 273, 348.

`\magnification`, 17, 59–60, <u>364</u>, *403–404*.

magnified output, 16–17, 59–60, 403, 433.

`\magstep`, 17, 59–60, <u>349</u>, *403–404*.

`\magstephalf`, 17, <u>349</u>, 403.

mail, 403–408.

main vertical list, 85, 110, <u>112</u>, 125, 253–254, 281.

`\maintoks`, 262.

`\makefootline`, 255–257, <u>364</u>.

`\makeheadline`, 255, 257, <u>364</u>.

`\makelabel`, 403, *404–405*, <u>408</u>.

manfnt, 44, 408, 414.

`manmac.tex`, 413–425.

`\manual`, 44, <u>414</u>, *419–420*.

`\mapsto` (↦), 128, <u>358</u>, 437.

`\mapstochar` ('), 358.

`\margin`, 415, 424.

marginal hacks, 82, 105, 400, 415, 424.

margins, *see* `\hsize`, `\narrower`.

*`\mark`, 95, 157, 216, 258–263, <u>280</u>, 417, 454.

marks, 95, 110, 157, 213, <u>258</u>–263.
markup commands, *see* control sequences.
math accents, *135–137*, 141, 164–165,
   <u>359</u>, 435, <u>443</u>.
⟨math atom⟩, <u>291</u>.
⟨math character⟩, <u>289</u>.
math character codes, 154–157.
⟨math field⟩, <u>289</u>.
math fonts, 157, *351*, 430–433, 441, 447.
math formulas, how to type, 127–197.
math italic, 164–165, 409, 430, 433.
math lists, 157–159, 441–446.
math mode, 85–89, 127, 157, <u>289</u>–293.
math spacing table, 170–171.
⟨math symbol⟩, <u>289</u>.
math symbols, 127–128.
   construction of, 151, 178, *358–361*.
   table of, 434–438.
math-off, 95–97, 287, 447.
math-on, 95, 97, 287, 447.
*\mathaccent, 157, 170, <u>291</u>, *359*, <u>443</u>.
*\mathbin, 155, 291, *361*.
*\mathchar, 155, 289.
*\mathchardef, 155, 199, 214, 215, 272,
   277, 289, 336, 394.
⟨mathchardef token⟩, 271.
*\mathchoice, 151, 157, 292.
*\mathclose, 155, 291, *322*, *359*.
*\mathcode, 134, <u>154–155</u>, 214, 271, 289,
   319, 326, *344*.
mathematical expressions, 127–197.
Mathematical Reviews, 106, 392–394.
⟨mathematical skip⟩, 290.
mathematical style, 166–167, 182–183.
\mathhexbox, <u>356</u>.
*\mathinner, 155, 171, 199, 291, *359*.
*\mathop, 155, 178, 291, *324–325*, *361*.
*\mathopen, 155, 291, *322*, *359*.
*\mathord, 88–89, 155, 291.
\mathpalette, 151, *360*.
*\mathpunct, 155, 291.
*\mathrel, 155, 291, *359–361*.
\mathstrut, 131, 178, <u>360</u>.
*\mathsurround, 97, *162*, 274, 305, 314,
   323, *353*, 447.
matrices, 176–178, 181; *see also* alignments.
\matrix, *176–178*, 182, *325*, <u>361</u>.
\max (max), 162–163, *170–171*, 361.
*\maxdeadcycles, <u>255</u>, 273, *348*.
*\maxdepth, *112–114*, 123–125, *255*, *262–263*,
   274, *348*, 400, *415*.
\maxdimen, 58, 188, *262–263*, <u>347</u>, 348.
maximum legal dimension, 58.

maximum legal integer, 118.
*\meaning, <u>213</u>–215, 336, *382*.
measure, *see* \hsize.
\medbreak, 111, 113, <u>353</u>, *355*, *419*, *422*.
*\medmuskip (medium math space),
   167–168, 274, *349*, 446.
\medskip (medium extra vertical space), 70,
   79, 102, 109, 111, <u>352</u>, *410–412*.
\medskipamount, <u>349</u>, *352–353*, 355, *407*.
\medtype, 408–411.
membership, *see* \in, \ni, \notin.
memory space, 100, 300–301, 342, 345,
   347, 383, 384, 394, 400.
*\message, 216, *217–218*, 227–228, <u>279</u>, *308*,
   328, *343–344*, 355, *418*.
METAFONT, 420, 427, 442, 483.
metric units, 57–60.
\mid (|), *174*, 436.
\midinsert, 116, *340–341*, <u>363</u>.
migration, 105, 117, 259, 280–281,
   282, 286, 287.
\min (min), 162–163, *170–171*, 361.
minus, 71, 271, 337.
minus sign, 4, 51, *127*, 132, 226, 268.
! Missing something, 296–297, 337.
\mit (math italic family), 164, <u>351</u>, 430, *434*.
*\mkern, 168, <u>280</u>, *442*.
mm (millimeter), <u>57</u>, 270.
mod, *164*, 322, <u>361</u>.
\models (⊨), <u>358</u>, 436.
modes, 46, 85–89, 175, 267–293.
modes.tex, 88–89.
money, 54, 140, *208–209*.
*\month, 273, 349, *406*.
Morris, William, 107.
moustaches, 150.
mouth, *see* anatomy of TEX.
*\moveleft, 80–81, <u>282</u>, 287.
*\moveright, 80–81, *221*, <u>282</u>.
Moxon, Joseph, 287.
Mozart, Johann Chrysostom Wolfgang Gott-
   lieb (= Theophilus = Amadeus), 409.
\mp (∓), *133*, 436.
*\mskip, 168, <u>290</u>, *442*.
mu (math unit), 168, 270, 442.
\mu (μ), *162*, 434.
⟨mu unit⟩, <u>270</u>.
⟨mudimen⟩, <u>270</u>.
⟨muglue⟩, 118, 167–168, <u>271</u>.
⟨muglue parameter⟩, 271, <u>274</u>, 276.
⟨muglue variable⟩, <u>276</u>.
Muir, Cockburn, 283.
Muirhead, James, 21.

multicolumn format, 257, 396–397, 417.
multiple integrals, *169, 180.*
*\multiply, *118–119, 218,* 276, 349, *391, 398.*
\multispan, 243, 246–247, *334,* 354.
Munster, 55.
⟨mushrink⟩, 271.
music, 408–412.
*\muskip registers, 118, 168, 271, 276.
*\muskipdef, 119, 215, 277.
⟨muskipdef token⟩, 271.
⟨mustretch⟩, 271.

\nabla (∇), 435.
names, 73, 92.
\narrower, 100, *340–341,* 355.
National Science Foundation, vii.
\natural (♮), 435.
natural width, 69.
Naur, Peter, 268.
\ne (≠), 9, 45, *133,* 318, 361, 438.
\nearrow (↗), 437.
\neg (¬), 435.
negated relations, 436–437.
negative dimensions, 66, 222.
\negthinspace, 332, 352.
\neq (≠), 318, 358, 438.
nesting (i.e., groups inside groups),
        20–21, 210, 385.
new symbols, 151, 178, *358–361.*
\newbox, 121, 346, 347, *353, 394, 417.*
\newcount, 121, *218,* 346, 347, *349, 418.*
\newdimen, 121, 346, 347, *349, 415.*
\newfam, 121, 157, 346, 347, *351.*
\newhelp, 346, 347.
\newif, 211, *218,* 348, *354, 375, 416, 423.*
\newinsert, 121, 122, 346, 347, *363, 415.*
\newlanguage, 346, 347.
*\newlinechar, 228, 273, *348.*
\newmuskip, 121, 346, 347.
\newread, 121, 216, 346, 347.
\newskip, 121, 346, 347, *349, 394, 414.*
\newtoks, 121, 212, *262,* 346, 347, *401.*
\newwrite, 121, 227, 346, 347, *422–423.*
\next, 352.
\ni (∋), 436.
\ninepoint, 15, 414, *419.*
\ninerm, 15, 413.
\ninesl, 15, 413.
No room, 347.
*\noalign, 176, 191, *193,* 237, *246,* 249,
        282, 285, 286.
*\noboundary, 283, 286, 290.
\nobreak (inhibit line or page break), 97,
        109, *174, 193,* 335, 353, *394, 407.*

*\noexpand, 209, 213, 215, 216, *348, 377, 424.*
*\noindent, 86, 188, *262–263,* 283, 286,
        291, *340–341, 355, 419.*
\nointerlineskip, 79–80, *255,* 331,
        352, *389.*
*\nolimits, 144, 159, 292, *358, 361.*
⟨non-macro assignment⟩, 275.
nonaligned leaders, 224–226.
\nonfrenchspacing, 74, 351.
*\nonscript, 179, 290, 442, 446.
*\nonstopmode, 32, 277, 299.
\nopagenumbers, 251–252, 362, *406, 409.*
norm symbol, *see* absolute value,
        vertical line.
⟨normal dimen⟩, 270.
⟨normal integer⟩, 269.
⟨normal mudimen⟩, 270.
\normalbaselines, 325, 349, 351, *414–415.*
\normalbaselineskip, 349, *414–415.*
\normalbottom, 363.
\normallineskip, 349, *351.*
\normallineskiplimit, 349, *351, 362.*
Norwegian characters, 45–46, 52–53, 370.
\not (⁄), *133,* 358, *436–437.*
\notin (∉), 360, 437.
*n*th, 323.
\nu (ν), *128, 163,* 434.
nucleus, 158–159, 289–292, 441–446.
\null, 311, *332,* 351.
⟨null⟩ (ASCII code 0), 37, 39, 48, 343, 369.
null control sequence, 46, 308.
null delimiter, 149–150, 152, 156, 345,
        360, 362.
null set, *see* \emptyset.
*\nulldelimiterspace, 150, 274, *348,* 442.
*\nullfont, 14, 153, 271, 433.
⟨number⟩, 44, 118, *269–270,* 272, 309, 349.
*\number, 40–41, 213, 214, *252, 406, 424.*
number sign, *see* hash mark.
numbered footnotes, 121, 125.
numerals, *see* digits, roman numerals.
numerator, 141, 152, 179, 444–445.
⟨numeric variable⟩, 276.
numerical tables, 240–241.
\nwarrow (↖), 437.

O versus 0, 132.
\o (ø), 356.
\O (Ø), 356.
\oalign, 356.
obelisk *or* obelus, 53.
\obeylines, *94, 249, 262,* 342, 352,
        380–382, 407, 419.

\obeyspaces, 254, 308, 342, <u>352</u>, *380–381,*
  394, 421.
oblique, *see* slanted.
⟨octal constant⟩, <u>269</u>.
⟨octal digit⟩, <u>269</u>.
octal notation, <u>43</u>, *44*, 155, 420.
odd-numbered pages, 252–253, *416.*
\odot (⊙), 436.
\oe (œ), 52, <u>356</u>.
\OE (Œ), 52, *53*, <u>356</u>.
Office of Naval Research, vii.
\offinterlineskip, *245–247*, 312, <u>352</u>, *416.*
\oint (large ∮), <u>358</u>, 435.
\oldstyle, <u>351</u>.
oldstyle numerals, 430, 435.
\omega (ω), *323*, <u>358</u>, 434.
\Omega (Ω), <u>358</u>, 434.
\omicron, 434.
\ominus (⊖), 436.
*\omit, 240, 243 244, *246–247*, 282.
one half, 141, 186.
⟨one optional space⟩, <u>269–270</u>.
online interaction, *see* interacting with TEX.
\ooalign, <u>356</u>.
Op atom, 158–159, 170–171, 289, 442–444.
Open atom, 158, 170–171, 289, 442–444, 446.
open intervals, 171.
openface, *see* blackboard bold.
*\openin, <u>216</u>–217, 280.
openings, 134, 147, 154–155, 359, <u>437</u>;
  see also Open atom.
*\openout, 226–228, 254, <u>280</u>, *422, 423.*
\openup, 194, 237, 242, <u>362</u>.
\oplus (⊕), 9, 154, 436.
optimization of macros, 342, 345, 348.
⟨optional assignments⟩, <u>286</u>.
⟨optional by⟩, <u>276</u>.
⟨optional sign⟩, <u>57</u>.
⟨optional signs⟩, <u>269</u>.
⟨optional spaces⟩, <u>268</u>, 269–271.
⟨optional **true**⟩, <u>270</u>.
*\or, 210, <u>213</u>, *406.*
Ord atom, 158, 170–171, 289, 358, 442–446.
ordinary symbols, 132, *see* Ord atom.
Ore, Øystein, 53.
organists, 239.
organs, 38–39, 46, 85, <u>267</u>, 373, <u>456</u>.
orphan, *see* widow word.
Osbourne, Lloyd, 67.
\oslash (⊘), 436.
\other, 421.
other character, 37.
\otimes (⊗), 9, 436.

*\outer, <u>206</u>, 210, 275, *354, 357,*
  418–419, 422.
*\output, 125, <u>253</u>, *254–257*, 275, *364,*
  370, *417.*
output routines, 21, 112, 251–264, 417.
  when invoked, 122, 125, 281.
*\outputpenalty, 125, *254–255*, 273,
  349, 400, *417.*
*\over, *139–141*, *148*, 152, 292, 437, 444–445.
Over atom, 158, 289, 443.
\overbrace, *176*, 225, <u>359</u>.
overfull boxes, 27–30, 94, 229, 238,
  302–303, 307, 400.
  avoiding, 107.
*\overfullrule, 274, 307, *348.*
overlaps, 82–83, 386.
\overleftarrow, <u>359</u>.
*\overline, *130–131*, *136*, 141, 170, 291, 443.
overloading, 54, 243.
\overrightarrow, 226, <u>359</u>.
*\overwithdelims, *152*, 292, 444–445.
\owns (∋), <u>361</u>, 438.

\P (¶), 53, 117, <u>356</u>, 438–439.
\p@, <u>347</u>, 348.
\p@renwd, <u>361</u>.
page breaks, avoiding bad, 109–111,
  189, 193.
  forcing good, 109–111; *see also* \eject.
page builder, 110–114, 122–125, 281.
  when exercised, 122, 280–283, 286–287.
page format, modifying, 251–253.
page make-up, 109, *see* output routines.
page numbers, 21, 23, 119, 207, 251–253.
\pagebody, 255–257, <u>364</u>.
\pagecontents, 256, <u>364</u>.
*\pagedepth, <u>114</u>, 123, 214, 271.
*\pagefilllstretch, <u>114</u>, 214, 271.
*\pagefillstretch, <u>114</u>, 214, 271.
*\pagefilstretch, <u>114</u>, 214, 271.
*\pagegoal, <u>114</u>, 123, 214, 271.
\pageinsert, 115, <u>363</u>.
\pageno, *252*, 256, *340*, <u>362</u>, *406.*
*\pageshrink, <u>114</u>, 123, 214, 271.
*\pagestretch, <u>114</u>, 214, 271.
*\pagetotal, <u>114</u>, 123, 214, 271.
*\par, <u>47</u>, 86–87, 100, 135, 202, 249, 262,
  <u>283</u>, <u>286</u>, *340*, 351, *380–381.*
  forbidden in arguments, 205, 207.
paragraph, implied beginning of, 85–86, <u>283</u>.
  implied end of, *24*, 86, <u>286</u>.
  last line of, 99–100.
  shape parameters reset, 103.
paragraph sign, 53.

\parallel (∥), 436.
⟨parameter text⟩, 203, 275.
parameters, *see* macro arguments and parameters.
parameters, numeric, 119, 342; *see also* \fontdimen.
  default values, 348–349.
  table, 272–274.
parentheses, 51, 129, 134, *140*, *145–150*, 345, 437.
  roman, in italic text, 409–411.
*\parfillskip, 100, 188, 274, <u>286</u>, 307, *315*, 332, *348*, *394*, *419*.
*\parindent, 86, 100, 101–102, 105, *262*, 274, 282, 286, 291, *342*, *348*, *355*, *394*, *406*, *415*.
*\parshape, 101–102, 214, 271, 277, 283, *315*, 349, 374.
*\parskip, 79, 104–105, 262, 274, 282, *342*, *348*, *355*, *406*, *417*.
\partial (∂), *147*, 435.
Pascal, Blaise, 101–102.
\path, 390–391.
*\patterns, 277, <u>453</u>, 455.
patterns for hyphenation, 449–453.
*\pausing, 273, <u>303</u>.
Paxton, William Hamilton, 425.
pc (pica), <u>57</u>, 270, *415*.
penalties, 95–100, 110–114, 189.
  infinite, 97, 111, 286, 400.
  negatively infinite, 97, 111–112, 114, 254–256, 264, 400.
*\penalty, 79, 97, 110–111, 174, <u>280</u>, *353*.
\penalty-'10000000000, 264.
percent sign, 26, 38, 39, 43, 48, 51, 113, 124, *249*, *337*, *340*.
period, 51, *72–73*, 133–134, 149, *161*, 345, *394–395*, 430.
  space after, *73–75*; <u>76</u>.
periodic preambles, 241–242, *244*, *246*, *361*, *412*.
Perlis, Alan J., 365.
\perp (⊥), <u>358</u>, 436.
\phantom, 131, 178, 211, <u>360</u>, *412*.
\phi (φ), *128*, *148*, 434.
\Phi (Φ), *323*, 434.
Philips, Peter, 239.
philosophers, 100, 239.
⟨physical unit⟩, <u>270</u>.
\pi (π), 9, *87*, *137*, *148–149*, 434.
\Pi (Π), 9, *324*, 434, 435.
piano, 17.
pica, 57, 413, *see* pc.

pictures, 228–229.
pieces of symbols, 145, 432, 442.
pilcrow, *see* \P.
plain.tex, 342–364.
plain TeX format, 10–11, <u>343</u>–<u>364</u>.
  summary, 339–342.
\plainoutput, 255, <u>364</u>.
Plass, Michael Frederick, 340–341.
Plato, 1, 239.
plus, 71, 271, 337.
⟨plus or minus⟩, <u>268</u>.
plus sign, 51, 132, 268.
\pm (±), *133*, <u>358</u>, 436.
\pmatrix, 176, *323*, *362*.
\pmod (notation like (mod *p*)), *164*, 322, <u>361</u>.
\pnt, 395.
pocket-size, 59.
poem, 94.
points (printers' units), 15, 57–58.
points with arbitrary coordinates, 389.
Polish characters, 52–53.
Pólya, György (= George), 7.
poor man's bold, 386.
*\postdisplaypenalty, 189–190, 272.
poultry, 236–237.
pound sign, *see* hash mark.
pound sterling, 54, 428.
powers of ten, 293.
powers of two, 293.
\Pr (Pr), 162, *323*, 361.
preambles, 206, 235–249.
\prec (≺), 436.
\preceq (⪯), 436.
*\predisplaypenalty, 189–190, 272, *348*.
*\predisplaysize, 188, 190, 274, 349.
⟨prefix⟩, <u>275</u>.
\preloaded, <u>350</u>, 413.
preloaded formats, 25–26, 39, 283, 344.
Presume, Livingstone Irving, 74.
*\pretolerance, <u>96</u>, 107, 272, *317*, *348*, *364*, *394*, *451*.
pretty-printed programs, 165, 234.
*\prevdepth, 79–80, 89, 271, 281, <u>282</u>.
prevdepth ignored, 88–89.
*\prevgraf, 103, 188, 190, 214, 271.
\prime (′), *130*, 155, 357, 435.
prime numbers, 148–149, 218.
primitive, 9–11, 267, 342, 457.
private control sequences, 344, 364, 414.
\proclaim, 202–203, 206, *340–341*, <u>355</u>.
Procter, William Alexander, 38.
\prod (large Π), *180–181*, 435.
programming with TeX, 217–219, 387–388.

programs, for computers, 38, 165, 234.
  for music, 408–412.
proofreading, 59, 303.
proper names, 73, 92.
\propto (∝), 436.
prototype row, 238, 302 303.
Prætorius [Schultheiss], Michael, 239.
\ps, 403, *404*, <u>407</u>.
pseudo parameters, 119, <u>349</u>.
\psi (ψ), *325*, 434.
\Psi (Ψ), 434.
psychologically bad breaks, *91–93*.
pt (printer's point), *24*, <u>57</u>–<u>58</u>, 268–270.
Punct atom, 158, 170–171, 289,
  442–443, 446.
punctuation, 14, 51, 72–76, 321, 394–395.
  in formulas, 134, 154–155, 161, 358–359,
  438; *see also* Punct atom.

\qquad, *166*, *185*, <u>352</u>.
quad, 60, 166–168, 177, 433.
\quad, *94*, 166–167, *185*, *232–233*, <u>352</u>.
quad left, *see* flush left.
quad middle, *see* \break.
quad right, *see* flush right.
quarter circles, 389–391.
question mark, 51, 73, 161.
Quick, Jonathan Horatio, 298.
quotation marks, *3–5*, *24*, 394–395.
quotations, 100, 418–419, 425.
quotes within quotes, 5.

ℝ, *see* blackboard bold.
Rad atom, 158, 289, 443.
*\radical, 157–159, 291, 443.
ragged bottom margins, 111, 253, 256, 398.
ragged left margins, 392–394.
ragged right margins, 29 30, 101, 261–262,
  355–356, 392–394.
\raggedbottom, 111, 253, <u>363</u>, *406*.
\raggedcenter, 107.
\raggedright, 29–30, 76, 101, 107, *115*,
  262, <u>356</u>, *396*, *407*.
*\raise, *66–67*, 80, 151, 179, *193*, <u>285</u>,
  290, *408*.
\rangle (⟩), *146–147*, 150, <u>359</u>, 437.
Raper, Matthew, 61.
\rbrace (}), *146–147*, <u>359</u>, 437.
\rbrack ( ]), *146–147*, <u>351</u>, 369, 437.
\rceil (⌉), *146–147*, <u>359</u>, 437.
\Re (ℜ), 435.
*\read, 215, 217–218, 276, 346, 401.
recent contributions, 112, 125, 281.
recovery from errors, 30–34, 295–303.

recursion, 219, 268, 301, 379, 391, 397.
  infinite, 299, 301, 383.
reduction, 16.
reference marks, 116–117.
reference point of a box, 63–64, 77,
  80–82, 388–389.
⟨registerdef⟩, <u>277</u>.
registers, 117–122, 212, 214, 346–348.
registration marks, 416.
Reid, Brian Keith, 371, 404–406.
Rel atom, 158, 170–171, 289, 442–444,
  446–447.
⟨relation⟩, <u>209</u>.
relations, *133–134*, 147, 154–155, 358, <u>436</u>,
  <u>437</u>; *see also* Rel atom.
*\relax, 23, 25, 71, 240, 276, <u>279</u>, *307*, *353*.
\relbar (−), <u>358</u>.
\Relbar (=), <u>358</u>.
*\relpenalty, 101, 174, 272, 322, *348*, <u>446</u>.
\removelastskip, <u>353</u>.
\repeat, *217–219*, <u>352</u>.
repeating commands, *see* \loop.
reserved characters, 37–38, 51–52, 134.
reserved words, <u>61</u>, 71, <u>268</u>, 337, 370.
restricted horizontal mode, 85, 87–89,
  <u>285</u>–<u>287</u>.
résumé, 253.
⟨return⟩ (ASCII code 13), 23, 39, 43, 45, 46,
  48, 249, 331, 343, 345, 369, 380.
\⟨return⟩, 8, *305*, <u>351</u>.
reverse apostrophe, *3–5*, 51, 132, 134, 391,
  394–395; *see also* alphabetic constant.
reverse slash, *see* backslash.
Reviewer, Ann Arbor, 106.
\rfloor (⌋), *146–147*, <u>359</u>, 437.
\rgroup, 150, *176*, <u>359</u>, 437.
\rho (ρ), 128, *325*, 434.
\rhook, <u>358</u>.
*\right, *148–150*, 155–157, *171*, 196,
  <u>292</u>, 437.
right brace, *13–14*, *19–21*, 38, 51, *200–202*,
  203–204, *205–206*, <u>269</u>, 275–276,
  <u>279</u>, 301, *330*.
⟨right brace⟩, <u>275</u>.
right bracket, 51, 134, *146–147*, 171,
  345, *408*, *437*.
right delimiters, *see* openings.
right-hand pages, 252–253, *416*.
right justification, 71.
right parenthesis, 51, 134, *140*, *145–150*,
  345.
right quote, *3–5*, 51, *130*, 155, 201, *305*,
  324, 394–395; *see also* octal.

\rightarrow (→), 226, 437.
\Rightarrow (⇒), 226, 437.
\rightarrowfill (——→), 226, *357*.
\rightharpoondown (⇀), 437.
\rightharpoonup (⇁), 437.
*\righthyphenmin, 273, *364*, 454, 455.
\rightleftharpoons (⇌), 360–361, 437.
\rightline, 101, *317, 340–341*, 353.
*\rightskip, 100–101, 274, *317*, 356,
    393, *421*.
\rlap, 82–83, *189, 247, 319*, 353, *389, 416*.
\rm (use roman type), 13–15, 154, *163*, 320,
    351, *364, 409, 414–415, 419*, 427.
\rmoustache, 150, 359.
roman letters in math, 162–164.
roman numerals, 40–41, 252, 256.
    uppercase, 374.
roman parentheses in italic text, 409–411.
roman type, 13–17, 51–55, 127,
    162–165, 427.
*\romannumeral, 40–41, 213, 214, *252*.
Root, Waverley Lewis, 55.
\root, *130–131, 179, 325*, 360.
rounding, 58, 119.
\rq ('), 5, 48, 351, 369, *395*.
rule boxes, 24, 64, 221–225, 281–282,
    285, 291.
⟨rule dimension⟩, 282.
⟨rule specification⟩, 282.
rule thickness, 143, 179, 221, 447.
ruled tables, 245–248, 392.
rulers, 58.
runaways, 205–206, 297.
running headlines, 253, 258–260, 416.
running the program, 23–35.
Russian characters, 370.

\S (§), 53, 117, 356, 438–439.
Sally, Baby, 72–76.
sample line for tabbing, 232–234.
sample pages for book design, 412–413.
save size, 300–301, 374, 399–400.
save stack buildup, 301, 346.
\sb, 135, 357, 369.
\sc (use SMALL CAPS type), 414–415.
scaled, 16–17, 60, 277, *350*, 433.
scaled points, 57–58, 270.
Scandinavian letters, 45–46, 52–53.
Schickele, Prof. Peter, 410–411, 481.
scratch control sequence, 352.
scratch registers, 122, 346.
Scribe, 371, 404.
script letters, 164, 434.
script size, 140, 153, 442.

script style, 140–142, 441–447.
*\scriptfont, 153, 168, 213, 271, 321,
    351, *414–415*, 441–442.
scriptscript size, 140, 145, 153, 442.
scriptscript style, 140–142, 441–447.
*\scriptscriptfont, 153, 168, 213, 271,
    351, *414–415*, 441–442.
*\scriptscriptstyle, 141–142, *179*, 292.
*\scriptspace, 274, 348, 445–446.
*\scriptstyle, 141–142, *145, 179*, 292.
*\scrollmode, 32, 277.
\searrow (↘), 437.
\sec (sec), 162, 361.
section number sign, *see* \S.
Selden, John, 11.
selection, *see* \cases.
semicolon, 51, *134*, 161.
sentences, 72–76.
Sesame Street, 61.
set macro, 379.
set notation, *147, 174–175*.
*\setbox, 66–67, 77, 81, 120, 276, *386–392*.
*\setlanguage, 287, 455.
\setminus (\ ), *436*.
\settabs, 231–234, 354, 355.
setting the glue, 70, 77, 81, 388.
\setupverbatim, 380–381, 391.
\sevenrm, 15, 153, 350, 351, *414–415*.
*\sfcode, 76, 214, 271, 286, *321, 345, 351*.
shadow boxes, 66.
Shakespeare, William, 17, 55, 337.
⟨shape assignment⟩, 277.
⟨shape dimensions⟩, 277.
\sharp (♯), *409*, 435.
sharp S (ß), *see* \ss.
sharp sign, *see* hash mark.
Shaw, George Bernard, 107, 229.
Sheridan, Richard Brinsley Butler, 265.
shifted output, *see* \hoffset, \voffset.
shilling sign, *see* slash.
*\shipout, 227, 253–254, 279, 300, 302.
shortest paths, 99.
⟨shorthand definition⟩, 277.
*\show, *10*, 215, 279, 299.
*\showbox, *66–67*, 121, 234, 279.
*\showboxbreadth, 273, 302, 303, *348*.
*\showboxdepth, 79, 273, 302, 303, *348*.
\showhyphens, *364, 452*.
*\showlists, *88–89*, 95, 112, 125, *158–159*,
    279, 293.
*\showthe, 121, 215, 279.
shriek, *see* exclamation point.
⟨shrink⟩, 271.

shrinkability, 69–71, *75*, 409.
side conditions, *166–167*, *185–186*.
\sigma (σ), *195–196*, 434.
\Sigma (Σ), *165*, 434, 435.
sigma signs, *see* \sum.
\signed, 106.
\sim (∼), *133*, 436.
\simeq (≃), *133*, 436.
⟨simple assignment⟩, 276.
\sin (sin), 162, 361.
\sinh (sinh), 162, 361.
sinkage, 413.
size switching, 15, 408, 414–415.
sizes of type for mathematics, 140, 153.
\skew, *136*, 359.
*\skewchar, 214, 271, 273, 277, *351*,
     414, 430, 431, 443.
*\skip registers, 118–122, 271, 276, *346–347*,
     349, *352*, *363*, *394*.
*\skipdef, 119, 215, 277, *346–347*.
⟨skipdef token⟩, 271.
skipping space, *see* glue.
\sl (use *slanted* type), 13–15, 165, 351,
     409, *414–415*, *419*.
slant of a font, 375, 433.
slanted type, 13, 63–64, 100.
slash, 51, *132*, 146–147, *320*, 430.
\slash (/ with break allowed), *93*, 353.
slashed form of fractions, 139–140.
Slavic háček accent, *see* \v.
\slfam, 351, *414–415*.
slides, 59.
slurs, *see* \smile, \frown.
small caps, 414.
\smallbreak, 111, 353, 421.
\smallint (∫), 358, 435.
\smallskip, 70, 78, *100*, 109, 111, *181*,
     340–341, *352*, 355, *410–412*.
\smallskipamount, 349, *352–353*.
\smalltype, 408–411.
\smash, 131, 178, *327*, 360.
\smile (⌣), 436.
solidus, *see* slash.
sophisticated spacing, 74.
sp (scaled point), 57, 118–119, 270, 398, 400.
\sp (superscript), 135, 357, 369.
⟨space⟩ (ASCII code 32), 39, 43, 46, 343.
\⟨space⟩, *see* \␣ (near the beginning).
\space, 254, 272, *306*, 351, 380, *406*.
space after a constant, 208, 272.
space factor, 76, 285–287, *306*, 380, 395.
⟨space token⟩, 268, 269, 282, 285, 290,
     376–377.

*\spacefactor, 76, 271, 285, *363*, 433.
spaces, 3, 5, 8–9, 19, 37, 40, 47–48, 127, 204,
     232, 272, 297, 299, 319, 336.
   as active characters, 254, 380–381.
*\spaceskip, 76, 274, *317*, *356*, 429.
spacing, *see* glue.
   in formulas, 162, 167–171.
\spadesuit (♠), 358, 435.
*\span, 215, 238, 243, *244*, 245, 248,
     249, 282, *330*, 385.
Spanish ligatures, 51, 381, 427.
spanned columns in tables, 243–245.
spanned rows in tables, 249.
*\special, 216, 226, 228–229, 280.
special characters, 37–38, 43–46, 51–52,
     134, 367–371.
⟨special dimen⟩, 271, 277.
⟨special integer⟩, 271, 277.
special symbols for math, 128, 434–438.
Spivak, Michael David, 137.
% split, 124.
split insertion penalty, 124.
*\splitbotmark, 213, 259, 280.
*\splitfirstmark, 213, 259, 280.
*\splitmaxdepth, 124, 274, 281, *348*,
     363, *417*.
*\splittopskip, 124, 274, 281, *348*,
     363, *397*, *417*.
spread, 77, 222, 238, 278.
springs, 70.
\sqcap (⊓), *133*, 436.
\sqcup (⊔), *133*, 436.
\sqrt, *130–131*, *141*, *145*, 157, *169–170*,
     360, 443.
\sqsubseteq (⊑), 436.
\sqsupseteq (⊒), 436.
\square (□), 151.
square brackets, *see* brackets.
square bullet (■), 420.
square root, *see* \sqrt.
squeeze routine, 188.
squiggle accent (˜), *see* \~, \tilde,
     \widetilde.
squint print, 59.
\ss (ß), 52, 356.
stack positions, 300–301, 374, 399–400.
stacked fractions, *see* \over.
\star (⋆), 436; *cf.* asterisk.
states, 46–48.
sterling, 54, 428.
Stevenson, Robert Louis Balfour, 67.
Stirling numbers, *see* \brace, \brack.
stomach, *see* anatomy of TeX.

stopping TEX, *see* \end.

story.tex, 24, 26, 30–31.

Stout, Rex Todhunter, 401.

⟨stretch⟩, 271.

stretchability, 69–71, *75*, 409.

*\string, 40–41, 213–214, 215, *348*, *377*.

\strut, 82, *142*, 178, 240, *246–247*, *316*, *329*, *333*, 353, *396*, *400*, *421*.

\strutbox, *316*, 353, *396*, *414–415*.

struts, 82, 125, 131, 142, 178, 245–247, 255, 329, 416, 422, 423.

style change items, 157, 442.

style-independent documents, 194, 203.

styles of math formatting, 140–141, 441–447.

styles of math writing, 166–167, 182–183.

subformulas, 129, 171, 173.

⟨subscript⟩, 291.

subscripts, 15, *128–131*, *133*, 150, 158–159, *163*, 179, 289–291, 343.

\subset (⊂), *133*, 436.

\subseteq (⊆), *133*, 436.

\succ (≻), 436.

\succeq (⪰), 436.

\sum (large Σ), *139*, *144–145*, *148–149*, 358, 432–433, 435.

\sum', 181, *324–325*.

summary of plain TEX, 339–342.

summation, *see* \sum.

\sup (sup), 162, 361.

\supereject, 116, 254, 256, 257, 353, *407*.

superiors, *see* superscripts.

⟨superscript⟩, 291.

superscripts, *128–131*, *133*, 150, 158–159, 179, 289–291, 343.

suppressed-L, 52–53.

\supset (⊃), 436.

\supseteq (⊇), 436.

\surd (√), 358, 435.

surd signs, *see* \radical, \sqrt.

Swanson, Ellen Esther, 197.

\swarrow (↙), 437.

Swedish characters, 52–53, 370.

Sweelinck, Jan Pieterszoon, 239.

Świerczkowski, Stanisław Sławomir, 53.

Swift, Jonathan, 5.

symbol fonts, 157, *351*, 431, 433, 441, 447.

symbolic box format, 66, 75, 79, 158–159, 302, 455.

symbols in math, table, 434–438.

syntax rules, 268–269.

System Development Foundation, vii.

Szegő, Gábor, 7.

\t (tie-after accent), 52–53, 356.

⟨tab⟩ (ASCII code 9), 8, 45, 343, 369, 391.

\⟨tab⟩, 8, 351.

\tabalign, 354, 355.

tabbing, 231–234, *339*, 354.

compared to \halign, 235.

tables, *see* alignments, tabbing.

tables of contents, 120, 226.

tables of TEX trivia:

accents (non-math), 52, 339.

atomic types, 158.

category codes, 37.

character codes, 367–369.

default values, 343–345, 348–349.

\fontdimen parameters, 433, 447.

keywords, 61.

math accents, 135.

math classes, 154.

math spacing, 170–171.

math symbols, 434–438.

parameters, 272–275.

units of measure, 57.

\tabs, 234, 354.

*\tabskip, 215, 237–239, *244*, *247*, 274, 282, 285, *354*.

tabskip glue, 237–239, 245, 302–303, 392.

Tacitus, Publius Cornelius, 219.

tags, *see* equation numbers.

tail recursion, 219.

\tan (tan), 162, 361.

\tanh (tanh), 162, 361.

\tau (τ), 1, 434.

Tchaikovsky, *see* Chaĭkovskiĭ.

telephone numbers, 408.

templates, 235–236, 240–243.

\tenex, 350, *351*, *361*, *414–415*.

\tenpoint, 15, 414, *418*.

\tenrm, 15, 27–28, 45, 153, 252, *335*, 350, *351*, *414*.

\tensl, 15, 350, *351*, *414*.

tensor notation, *130*, *169*.

\tensy, *179*, 350, *351*, *414*.

terminal, input from, 217–218.

output to, 217–218, 226–228, 279–280.

TEX, 1.

TEX, bad puns on, 1, 11, 63, 153, 161, 225, 229, 262, 305, *340–341*, 373.

pronunciation of, 1.

TeX, 1.

\TeX (TEX), 8–10, 19, 66–67, 204, 225, *340–341*, 356, *418*, 419.

.tex, 25, 217, 226.

TeX capacity exceeded, 300–301.

TEX Grandmasters, 253.
TEX Users Group, vii, 408, 483.
TEX78, vii.
texput, 23.
text between aligned displays, 193.
text size, 140, 153, 442.
text style, 140–142, 441–447.
*\textfont, 153, 168, 188, 213, 271, 351, *414–415*, 441–442.
\textindent, 117, 355.
*\textstyle, 141–142, *292*, *326*.
.tfm (font metric files), 401, 433, 442.
*\the, *214–215*, *216*, *373*, *375*, *422*.
theorems, 111, 202–203, *340–341*, 355.
\theta (θ), 128, *162*, *325*, 434.
\Theta (Θ), 434.
*\thickmuskip (thick math space), 167–168, 274, *349*, 446.
thin spaces, 161, 167–173, 305, 409.
*\thinmuskip (thin math space), 167–168, 274, *349*, 446.
\thinspace, *5*, 10, 305, *311*, *352*, 409.
This can't happen, 299.
Thor, Arthur Uther, 24, 117, 200, 253.
three-column output, 257, 396–398.
three dots, *see* ellipses.
tie-after accent, *see* \t.
ties, 25, 73–74, *91–93*, 104, *161*, 167, *173*, 353, *404*.
tight lines, 97, 99, 302.
tilde, 38, 51, *91–92*, *see* ties.
\tilde (math accent: $\tilde{x}$), 135, 164.
tilde accent (˜), *see* \~, \tilde, \widetilde.
*\time, 273, 349.
\times (×), *133*, 436.
Times Tribune, Peninsula, 455.
Titelouze, Jehan, 239.
to, 77, 217, 222, 238, *276*, *278*.
\to, *134*, *361*, 438.
\today, *406*.
token list parameters and registers, 212, 215, 275, 373.
token lists, as displayed by TEX, 228, 329, 382.
⟨token parameter⟩, *275*.
⟨token variable⟩, 212, *276*.
tokens, 38–41, 46–48, 203–207.
*\toks, 212, 215, 262, 276.
*\toksdef, 212, 215, 277, *347*, *378*.
⟨toksdef token⟩, *271*.
*\tolerance, *29–30*, 91, 94, *96*, 107, 272, *317*, *333*, *342*, *348*, *364*, *451*.
\top (⊤), 435.

\topglue, *340*, *352*.
\topins, 256, *363*, *364*.
\topinsert, 115–116, 251, *363*.
*\topmark, 213, *258*, 259–260, 280.
*\topskip, *113–114*, 124, 256, 274, *348*.
Trabb Pardo, Luis Isidoro, 92.
\tracingall, 121, 303, *364*.
*\tracingcommands, 88–89, *212*, 273, 299.
*\tracinglostchars, 273, *301*, *348*, *401*.
*\tracingmacros, *205*, *212*, 273, *329*.
*\tracingonline, 121, 212, 273, *303*.
*\tracingoutput, *254*, 273, *301–302*.
*\tracingpages, *112–114*, 124, 273, *303*.
*\tracingparagraphs, *98–99*, 273, *303*.
*\tracingrestores, 273, *301*, *303*.
*\tracingstats, 273, *300*, *303*, *383*.
transcript, *see* log file.
transparencies, 59.
\triangle (△), 435.
\triangleleft (◁), 436.
\triangleright (▷), 436.
triangular quotation, 101–102.
tricky macros, 41, 261–263, 354, 360, 361, 373–401, 421.
true, 59–60, *270*, *407–408*.
truth, vi, 267.
Tschichold, Jan, 83.
\tt (use **typewriter** type), 13, 53, 113, 165, *340–341*, *351*, *380–382*, *414–415*, *429*.
\ttfam, *351*, *414–415*.
\ttglue, 414–415, 421.
\ttraggedright, *356*.
TUGboat, vii, 425, 483.
turtle commands, 390–391.
Twain, Mark (= Clemens, Samuel Langhorne), 83, 451.
two-column format, *257*, 386–388, *417*.
two-line displays, 196.
type size switching, 15, 408, 414–415.
typefaces, 13, 17, 427.
typewriter type, 13, 53, 165, 356, 420–421, 429.

\u (breve accent), 52–53, *356*.
*\uccode, 41, 214, 271, 345, *348*, *377*, *394*.
*\uchyph, 273, *348*, *454*.
umlaut accent (¨), *see* \", \ddot.
unbreakable spaces, *see* ties.
\uncatcodespecials, 380.
\undefined, 384.
undelimited parameters, 203–204, 376–377.
Under atom, 158, 289, 443.
\underbar, *244*, *323*, *353*.
\underbrace, *176*, 225–226, *359*.

underfull box, 29, 94, 238, 302–303, 397, 400, 417, 452.
*\underline, *130–131*, 141, 291, <u>443</u>.
underlined text, 178; *see also* \underbar.
underscore (the character '_'), 38, 51, *128–130*, 134, *165*.
*\unhbox, 120, 283, <u>285</u>, *354*, *356*, *361*, *399*.
*\unhcopy, 120, 283, <u>285</u>, *353*.
⟨unit of measure⟩, 268, <u>270</u>.
units of measure, 57–61, 270.
    in formulas, 169.
    table, 57.
*\unkern, <u>280</u>.
unmatched left brace, 216;
    see also runaways.
*\unpenalty, <u>280</u>.
unset box, 240, 302–303.
⟨unsigned dimen⟩, <u>270</u>.
⟨unsigned mudimen⟩, <u>270</u>.
⟨unsigned number⟩, <u>269</u>.
*\unskip, 222–223, <u>280</u>, 286, *313*, *392*, *418–419*.
*\unvbox, 120, 254, <u>282</u>, 286, *354*, *361*, *363*, *364*, *392*, *399*, *417*.
*\unvcopy, 120, <u>282</u>, 286, *361*.
\up, 408.
\uparrow (↑), *146–147*, *182*, <u>359</u>, 437.
\Uparrow (⇑), *146–147*, <u>359</u>, 437.
\upbracefill (⏞), 225–226, <u>357</u>.
\updownarrow (↕), *146–147*, <u>359</u>, 437.
\Updownarrow (⇕), *146–147*, <u>359</u>, 437.
\uplus (⊎), 436.
*\uppercase, 41, 215, 217, <u>279</u>, 307, 345, *348*, *374*, *377*, *394*.
uppercase letters, 9, 64, 268, 370.
    Greek, 127, 164, 434.
    roman numerals, 374.
\upsilon (υ), 434, 483.
\Upsilon (Υ), 434.
Ursa Major, 389.
User, Ben Lee, 74, 80, 100, 140, 164, 186, 187, 193, 221, 296, 410–411.

\v (check accent), 52, <u>356</u>.
*\vadjust, 95, 105, 109, 110, 117, 259, <u>281</u>, *317*, 393, 454.
*\valign, 249, 283, <u>285–286</u>, 302, *335*, *397*.
Vallée Poussin, Charles Louis Xavier Joseph de la, 92.
van der Waerden, Bartel Leendert, 92.
van Leunen, Mary-Claire, 425.
\varepsilon (ε), 128, 434.
⟨variable assignment⟩, <u>276</u>.
variable family, 154, 289, *358–359*.

variables in formulas, 132, 358, 434–435;
    see also Ord atom.
\varphi (φ), 128, *147*, 434.
\varpi (ϖ), 434.
\varrho (ϱ), 128, 434.
\varsigma (ς), 434, 483.
\vartheta (ϑ), 128, 434.
*\vbadness, 272, *348*, *397*, *417*.
vbox (box with vertical list inside), 65.
*\vbox, 65, 80–82, 103, 151, 193, 222, 278, 388–389.
Vcent atom, 158, 290, 443.
*\vcenter, 150–151, 159, 170, 193, 222, 242, <u>290</u>, *361*, <u>443</u>.
\vdash (⊢), 436.
\vdots (⋮), *177*, <u>359</u>.
\vec (math accent: $\vec{x}$), 135;
    see also \overrightarrow.
vectors, 177, 199–201; *see also* \vec.
\vee (∨), *133*, 436.
verbatim copying, 422–423.
verbatim listing, 48, 380–382, 391, 420–421.
\vert (|), *146–147*, 150, <u>359</u>, 438; *cf.* \mid.
\Vert (‖), 117, *146–147*, 150, <u>359</u>, 186.
⟨vertical command⟩, <u>286</u>.
vertical line (the character '|'), 52, 53, 132, *146–147*, *171*, *174*, 438;
    see also vertical rules.
vertical lists, 64, <u>110</u>.
vertical mode, 85–89, <u>267–283</u>.
⟨vertical mode material⟩, 278.
⟨vertical rule⟩, <u>281</u>.
vertical rules, 64, 151, 221–226, <u>285</u>, <u>291</u>, 392.
⟨vertical skip⟩, <u>281</u>.
very loose lines, 97, 99.
*\vfil, 71, <u>72</u>, 111, 256, 281, 286, 417.
*\vfill, 24, 25, 71, <u>72</u>, 256–257, 281, 286.
\vfilll, 72.
*\vfilneg, <u>72</u>, 111, 281, 286.
\vfootnote, 117, <u>363</u>.
*\vfuzz, 274, *348*.
\vglue, <u>352</u>, *408*.
vinculum, *see* \overline.
virgule, *see* slash, 51.
visible space, <u>3</u>, <u>420</u>, 429.
*\voffset, <u>251</u>, 252–253, 274, *342*, *406*.
void, 120, 210.
\voidb@x, <u>347</u>, 348.
Voltaire, de (= Arouet, François Marie), 447.
\vphantom, *178–179*, 211, *321*, <u>360</u>.

*\vrule, 64, 86, 151, 221–222, 224, *245–247*, <u>281–282</u>, 283, *357, 392, 420*.
*\vsize, 113–114, 251, 253, 255, 274, *340–341, 348*, 400, *406*, 413, *415, 417*.
*\vskip, *24*, 71, 85, 191, <u>281</u>, 286.
*\vsplit, <u>124</u>, 222, 259, 278, *397, 417*.
*\vss, 71, <u>72</u>, *255*, 281, 286.
*\vtop, 81–82, 151, 222, 278, *333*.

Walter's worksheet, 244.
Walton, Izaak, 67.
Watson, John Hamish, M.D., 401.
*\wd, 120, 271, <u>388</u>–<u>389</u>, *391, 417*.
\wedge (∧), *133*, 436.
Weierstrass p, see \wp.
weird error, 298.
Welsh, 239, 451.
Westing, Arthur Herbert, 246.
whatsits, 95, 110, 157, 226–229.
\widehat (math accent: $\widehat{x}$), *136*, <u>359</u>, 433.
\widetilde (math accent: $\widetilde{x}$), *136*, <u>359</u>.
widow lines, 104, 272, 398.
widow words, 104.
*\widowpenalty, 104, 113, 272, *348*.
width, 221, 224, <u>282</u>, 337.
width of a box, 63–67, 77, 80–82, 225.
wiggle, see \sim.
Winograd, Terry Allen, 425.
Wischmeyer Ehlert, Clara Louise, 248.
withdelims, 152, 156.

\wlog, <u>347</u>.
Wolfe [Holmes], Nero, 401.
\wp (℘), 435.
\wr (≀), 436.
wreath product, see \wr.
*\write, 215, 216, 226–228, 254, <u>280</u>, 346, *377, 422, 424*.

×, see \times, *.
x-height, 54, 60, 433, 443, 445–447.
*\xdef, *215–216*, 275, *373, 418, 424*.
Xenophon, 239.
\xi (ξ), 434, 447.
\Xi (Ξ), 434.
*\xleaders, <u>224</u>.
*\xspaceskip, 76, 274, *317*, 356, 429, 433.
\xyzzy, 379.

*\year, 41, 273, 349, *406*.
Yellin, Frank Nathan, 401.

\z@, <u>347</u>, 348.
\z@skip, <u>347</u>, 348.
\zeta (ζ), 434.

1/2, 67, 332.
1/2, in unslashed form, 141, 186.
⟨4-bit number⟩, <u>271</u>.
⟨8-bit number⟩, <u>271</u>, 276–278.
⟨15-bit number⟩, <u>271</u>, 277, 289, 291.
⟨27-bit number⟩, <u>271</u>, 289, 291.

> *Important works such as histories, biographies,*
> *scientific and technical text-books, etc., should contain indexes.*
> *Indeed, such works are scarcely to be considered complete without indexes.*
>
> *An index is almost invariably placed at the end of a volume*
> *and is set in smaller type than the text-matter.*
> *Its subjects should be thoroughly alphabetized.*
>
> *The compiling of an index is interesting work, though*
> *some authors are apt to find it tedious and delegate the work to others.*
> *The proofreader who undertakes it will find that it is splendid mental exercise*
> *and brings out his latent editorial capability.*
>
> — ALBERT H. HIGHTON, *Practical Proofreading* (1926)

> *Important references are given in boldface.*
> *Italicized numbers indicate fleeting references,*
> *whereas numbers in parentheses refer to*
> *mere implications or unwarranted extrapolations.*
> *Asterisks are used to identify particularly distasteful passages.*
>
> — PROF. PETER SCHICKELE, *The Definitive Biography of P. D. Q. Bach* (1976)

J
Joining the T_EX Community

This appendix is about grouping of another kind: TEX users from around the world have banded together to form the TEX Users Group (TUG), in order to exchange information about common problems and solutions.

A newsletter/journal called *TUGboat* has been published since 1980, featuring articles about all aspects of TEX and METAFONT. TUG has a network of "site coordinators" who serve as focal points of communication for people with the same computer configurations. Occasional short courses are given in order to provide concentrated training in special topics; videotapes of these courses are available for rental. Meetings of the entire TUG membership are held at least once a year. You can buy TEX T-shirts at these meetings.

Information about membership in TUG and subscription to *TUGboat* is available from

```
{\obeylines
\TeX\ Users Group
P.O. Box 9506
Providence RI 02940\kern.05em-9506, USA.
}
```

Don't delay, write today! That number again is

TEX Users Group
P.O. Box 9506
Providence RI 02940-9506, USA.

> *[The printer] should refuse to employ wandering men,*
> *foreigners who, after having committed some grievous error,*
> *can easily disappear and return to their own country.*
> — HIERONYMUS HORNSCHUCH, 'Ορθοτυπογραφίας (1608)

> *An author writing an article for publication in TUGboat*
> *is encouraged to create it on a computer file and submit it on magnetic tape.*
> — BARBARA BEETON, \title *How to Prepare a File*\cr
> *For Publication in TUGboat*\cr (1981)